Chester R. Wasson, Ph.D.

MARKETING MANAGEMENT:
The Strategy, Tactics
& Art of Competition

ECR Associates
2441 Hassell Place
Charlotte, NC 28209

Library of Congress Catalog Number 83-090230
ISBN: 0-9600352-6-5

PRINTED IN THE UNITED STATES OF AMERICA

CONTENTS

PREFACE

This book is designed for the advanced course in marketing management. The approach is an applications-oriented one which has proved successful and popular with mature students with some experience in business. The aim is to provide students with a set of basic conceptual tools useful in guiding their thinking about the problems of marketing management, and in developing solutions of their own to unique marketing problems of any kind. It works best with a case and discussion format.

The general approach will be familiar to those acquainted with my **Dynamic Competitive Strategy & Product Life Cycles,** and is intended to be a broadening of that approach to cover a full course in marketing management. Like the previous work, the emphasis is on the offering and the price as the core of strategy, and on the necessity to consider the position in the market life cycle when shaping every aspect of both strategy and tactics. The inescapable competitive character of the marketing process is a major point of emphasis, and the innovation necessary to succeed. Wide acceptance of the previous work in management circles around the world has convinced me of the validity and utility of this approach.

In my own experience with texts in widely varying fields, as a student and as a teacher, I have found that each tends to fall into one of three categories:

- **Basic tools** texts, aimed to furnish students with the intellectual tools with the most general applicability, to help them to an understanding of what **kinds** of reactions to expect as the results of specific **types** of action. The focus is on understanding and application exercises, to develop thinking skills, not "right" answers.
- **How-to** books, providing lists of rules and definitions to be memorized, intended to give students ready-made answers to specific problems. The focus is on memorization of lists and definitions.
- **Literature review** texts, abstracting a wide variety of points of view, usually with a minimum of evaluation and no central theme for the total. The object is to familiarize students with the literature, apparently on the assumption that students will develop their own applications without much practice in the course.

This book belongs completely to the first category. The entire focus is on the handful of basic items of wide general applicability, from our knowledge of human behavior, as they relate to marketing strategy and tactics. The focus is on their application to an understanding of what results can be expected from specific types of strategy and tactics, at the various points in the market life cycle. None of the contents is to be read as a set of formulas to be applied as is to specific marketing problems, without being shaped by the individual. The emphasis is on innovation as

i

the essence of marketing. Although a number of itemized lists are sprinkled throughout the presentation, they are provided as a means of sharpening the presentation, and are not intended for memorization.

The general plan throughout is to present the substance of the material, paralleled with separately inserted items from the news, history, and professional experience to illuminate the points made and get the student to thinking about their meaning. Case histories at the end of each chapter are presented for the purpose labelled: the give students food for thought, and for class discussion. In my own use of these materials, I assign problem cases in addition, a collection of which will be available soon after this appears.

The presentation is organized into five parts:
- Part I presents the basic definition of the central element of marketing, as it will be used throughout the book: an exchange process of any kind conducted in the face of both direct and indirect competition. The full psychological meaning of the offering and the price are developed, as well as all of the dimensions of competition, a central theme of this work.
- Part II presents the handful of basic concepts of human reaction to external stimuli which are necessary to an understanding of what takes place in the transaction process, of why and how markets tend to be segmented, and the various kinds of offering life cycles that result, including fashion and fad.
- Part III is the central core of the book, a discussion of what we know about planning strategy and tactics, and the management of the various functions of marketing operations as they change during the life of an offering.
- Part IV is a single section chapter outlining the management of the information processes essential to planning and executing strategy and tactics.
- Part V has one object: to get students to thinking about the problems inevitably raised when trying to influence other people.

No bibliography is included for three reasons:
- Any students mature enough to understand this complex essential to our society that we call marketing are old enough to find what they feel a need for in the library.
- In the author's quarter of a century experience with marketing students, he has never observed any evidence that students at any level used any of the bibilographies in their books.
- In skimming through the bibilographies presented by others, this author has been impressed by the number of books in which some of the longer ones were found which seemed to have been prepared in blissful ignorance of the contents of some of the works presented in their bibliographies.

Like anyone else, I have built on the contributions of many people, some of them not traceable to a specific originator. The only claim made is that I have brought a new form of organization to the works of scholars in many fields, and to the experience of colleagues and some of my own students. In what follows, I have attempted to develop more fully a logical approach to the understanding of marketing which my students and others facing marketing problems every day tell me they have found useful.

Chester R. Wasson
Charlotte, N.C.

PART I. INTRODUCTION: MARKETING AND THE EXCHANGE PROCESS

Marketing management is the management of a relationship between a seller and a group of buyer segments. The transaction takes place in the context of relatively free choice for buyers, from among differentiated offerings being promoted by other sellers. Both buyer and seller expect mutual benefit and hope for a continuing relationship.

Marketing is thus more than the mere selling of offerings on some market. The difference is in the atmosphere of competition and the long term planning needed to insure the continuity both parties hope for.

Market sales operations have been around since long before recorded history. Managed marketing is a very recent growth, a history reaching back no more than four generations. Its beginnings sprouted from the invention and marketing of labor saving agricultural implements which permitted a surplus over mere subsistence farming, and the parallel building of a national railroad system which could move the implements to farms, and the surplus production to distant markets. The railroads also brought competition to the formerly localized market monopolies, and paved the way for standardized mass production. (It was no accident that the first national marketing system was developed by the inventor of the first workable reaper.) The long lead times and fixed costs of mass production created an inescapable need for forward planning of every aspect of the marketing operation.

Long range plans must have a specific direction—a general overall objective and a general strategy for reaching that objective. The uncertainties of the market ahead dictate the planning of flexible tactics in harmony with that strategy. The certainty of competition requires understanding the needs and probable reactions of buyers, and the art of innovation to keep ahead of the competition.

Successful strategy and tactics are built on an understanding of the unseeable desires which buyers bring to the transaction, on buyers' perceptions of the totality of costs to them in resources of every kind, and their reactions to various means of communicating the benefits offered.

The objective of the marketing operation is to influence consumer behavior toward the seller's offerings. Most of that behavior is habitual. Since the objective is to create or maintain a patronage habit, the task of marketing is the difficult one of influencing or preventing changes in habits.

CHAPTER 1. MARKETS AND MARKETING

What is Marketing?
>   The mutual exchange relationship at the core of market
>   operations
>   Markets vs. marketing

The three aspects of competitive uncertainty
>   The invisible satisfactions sought by buyers
>   Buyers' perceptions of the competition
>>   Potential competition with similar offerings
>   Competition from sellers of different offerings meeting
>   other kinds of needs
>   The total price as perceived by prospects

The participating intermediaries between buyers and sellers

The tripod of successful plans: strategy, tactics, and the art
>   of innovation

Marketing models
>   The four P's management function model
>   The fifth P (promptness) essential for strategy and tactics
>   The (NC)(OPC)T behavioral change model

MARKETS AND MARKETING

1

What Is Marketing?

Marketing is an obvious derivative of the noun, market. But marketing is more than a market operation. Both marketing and market operations involve mutual exchange transactions: the two-way exchange of some kind of offering by an initiating seller, in return for a portion of the resources of another party we designate as the buyer. The choice of the active verb, **marketing,** makes a distinction which goes beyond mere semantics. It recognizes a difference in the approach of both sides to the transaction, an expectation on the part of both of a continuing exchange relationship.

The mutual exchange at the heart of market operations. Most people have a reasonably clear picture of what a market is: a place where goods and services are sold, usually for money, or bartered for other goods and services. Common usage extends this dictionary concept to include almost any kind of interpersonal relationship which involves the persuasion of one person or group of persons by another.

Thus we insist we do not "buy" some politician's promises or explanations, or we may try to "sell" a fellow manager on cooperating with us on some project by showing the advantage of so doing.

Any such sale is a two-way transaction--a type of barter whether the price paid is in cash or in terms of some other goods or return favors. Common usage is quite logical in recognizing that the exchange transaction is no different when the price paid is return favors or other non-monetary considerations which both buyer and receiver perceive are valuable.

But the widespread confusion of any type of single transaction with marketing overlooks a vital difference: the expectation of a continuing relationship implicit in long-term planning and operations.

Marketing vs. markets. Exchange relationships go back beyond recorded history, and may even predate the final evolution of the human species. But the market plazas of ancient and modern times are traditional operations lacking the element of competitive choice of differentiated offerings open to shoppers, rural or urban, in an industrialized country.

The sellers in the stalls of a rural Guatemalan marketplace all offer the same assortment of corn, beans, and textiles, day-in, day-out, year-in, year-out. The cloth and garments for sale follow the identical traditional patterns which local craftsmen have furnished the locality for milleniums. Buyers may haggle over price, but the customer has no real choice of goods, and no feasible access to more distant sellers offering a different choice.

Such localized traditional markets were the universal rule until little more

---

THE HALLS OF IVY DISCOVER MARKETING

To many people, marketing is a somewhat suspect activity associated with profit-making enterprises. And small liberal arts colleges cannot be accused of seeking profits. Neither, however, can they afford losses which follow when admissions fall below a planned level. If the school aims for a high academic reputation, it must also get a substantial excess of applications in order to be selective.

Carleton College, in rural Northfield, Minn., is such an institution, one which faced declining applications when student interest in the 1970's shifted from a liberal arts orientation to more vocational programs.

During the 1960's, Carleton had been able to maintain a target enrollment of 1700 students by admitting only 40% to 50% of the 1600 applications per year. By the mid 1970's officials were having to approve 82% of the applications received to maintain the planned student body size. Carleton's quality reputation was threatened.

Officials decided to investigate the possibility that the same techniques which built customers for breakfast cereals, Budweiser Beer, and Coca-Cola might bring student applications to Carleton: they began to research their market. Questionnaires were sent to all students who showed an interest in Carleton in 1978. Responses revealed some problems. The rural Minnesota location was perceived as cold and isolated. The academic pressure was perceived as too intense to permit socializing. Because the brochure pictured only the front two-story facade of the (four-story) library, some prospects perceived the library as too small.

The literature was revamped. Since the school could do nothing to change Minnesota winters, the attractive side of the climate was stressed. Photographs of cross-country skiing were shown, with the comment that bundling up "makes even the coldest days bearable and most days comfortable." The library was pictured from its rear, four-story facing.

The returns from mailings to high school seniors more than doubled, from 5.9% to over 14%, By the start of 1981, applications had risen to 1850. Further research indicated that prospects in different regions emphasized different interests: Easterners favored academic prestige, Westerners looked for informal atmosphere and outdoor activities, while nearby Minnesotans were concerned about tuition costs. Officials were investigating regionalization of their literature.

(Based on "College Learns to Use the Fine Art of Marketing," **The Wall Street Journal,** February 23, 1981).

than a century past. Marketing, by contrast, is a recent development, one not possible prior to the development of a rapid internal transportation network (starting with the canals and railroads of the mid-19th century), the spread of popular mass periodicals and electrical message systems to facilitate communications beyond the locality, and the rise of standardized mass production.

The transportation networks and national and regional publications opened up the localized market monopolies to competition. The new competition presented customers with choices not previously available, and mass produced items were much less costly than the previous hand crafted goods. The static market was displaced by the kind of fluid, competitive marketing scene we now take for granted—one with all the potential uncertainties that the free play of choice and taste create, and with all of the opportunities for innovation a mass market offers.

The marketing concept was born and has continued to mature. The essence of that concept is that the planning of all marketing strategy and tactics begins with an understanding of consumer needs and reaction patterns, and that the initiating sellers have the responsibility for the performance of their offerings down to and beyond the point and time of sale.

Managed marketing thus differs from the previous forms of market operations by the need to develop a long term strategy, flexible tactics in carrying out the strategy, and insights into opportunities created by changes in consumer choices and tastes, by changes in competitive conditions, and by the fluctuations in volatile economic and political environments. To succeed in all of this requires a careful ear to the ground for early symptoms of changing competitive conditions of all kinds, and signs of changing economic and political environments.

Markets and competition today are truly a single international whole, and the changes possible too numerous to list. Fortunately, drastic, dramatic changes are relatively infrequent. But three key uncertainties of consumer behavior are always with us.

The Three Key Constants of Competitive Uncertainty

On the surface, most individual transactions seem simple: only two visible parties (the seller and the buyer), a price quotation by the seller, and the buyer's purchase for the price agreed upon. What is not visible are the complex realities taking place within the buyer's mind:
  - the bundle of desires which the buyer is hoping to satisfy, and the buyer's perception of the benefits he is expecting to actually receive
  - the totality of active competition perceived by the buyer:
      * competitors with similar offerings
      * sellers with different offerings meeting similar desires

    *   sellers with different offerings meeting competing desires

    -   the total price buyers perceive themselves as having to pay

The bundle of desires.   Customers do not perceive the object or service being purchased as having value in itself. To them, the purchase is simply a necessary element in a use system intended to fulfill a whole set of desires at the top of their current attention. Most of the time, they find that satisfaction as something less than complete, requiring some compromise between desires.

    Competitors with similar offerings.   Some of the benefits which the object or service could, objectively, deliver are perceived by some buyers as having no value for them, or even a negative value. Different buyers are seeking fulfillment of somewhat diverse sets of desires, At the same time, any one benefit will get a different valuation from different buyers of the same offering even within a given market segment.

    The diversity of desire sets and benefit value perceptions is what segments markets and opens up the opportunity for a third group participating indirectly in every transaction: actual and potential sellers capable of delivering similar, but differentiated benefit bundles.

    Competition from other needs.   A fourth group, much less visible, is brought into the picture by the buyer's need to pay a price. Any buyer brings limited resources and nearly unlimited needs to the market. Any resources used for one purchase cannot be paid out for the satisfaction of some other need. Some needs must be left unfulfilled. ("The man who has everything" he desires has not yet been identified.)

    Most transactions involve another set of participants with needs of their own which must be planned for: the distributing intermediaries between the initial seller and the final buyer, discussed below.

The participating intermediaries

    Most transactions directly involve a very visible set of intermediaries in addition to those discussed above: the salespeople and the distributors between the original seller and the final end buyer.

    These intermediaries play a rather anomalous role. They represent the seller to the buyer, but also represent the buyers' side to the seller. Their contractual arrangements with the seller range from the complete independence of the merchant to that of the seller's paid employees, in the case of the seller's own sales people. In actual practice, even the seller's own salesforce exercises a substantial degree of independence in adding satisfaction elements to the total benefit bundle, and in communicating or even shaping the values buyer perceive in the offering. The independent distributors always tend to view themselves as customers of the original sellers.   Final customers tend to perceive them as the responsible sellers.

The Tripod of Successful Market Planning: Strategy, Tactics, And The Art of Innovation

The planning imperative. Marketing management cannot escape the need to plan, despite all of the uncertainties of competition.

Neither the physical nor the personal services of a mass production economy can be ordered, produced, and delivered between the dawn of one day and the sunset of the next. A common cycle of three years is needed to design and bring to market even minor variations of established products built with "off the shelf" components.

Developing new items and components based on a known "state of the art" takes added years. Preparation and organization of a new service operation design also requires substantial lead time. Indeed, even developing what appears to be a simple advertising campaign normally takes months of preparation and effort and the meeting of deadlines weeks or even months ahead of initial publication.

Fortunately, so much of what customers do is governed by well-entrenched habits of thought and action, and thus is to some degree predictable in the short run. If the effort is made to discover these habits of action and perception, rational plans can be laid.

Sound plans also require analysis of competitors, their niches and modes of operation, and trends in market structures and in consumer actions, desires, and tastes. The planner must also be constantly alert to the limitations imposed by the external environment: natural, legal, and political.

Developing strategy and tactics

Rational strategies are not a matter of free choice. The planner must recognize the real strengths, and the very real weaknesses of the seller and his position. Strategy and tactics must be shaped to take advantage of the strengths and minimize the weaknesses. The full extent of actual and potential competition must be pinpointed, and the strategy also fitted to the strengths and weaknesses of that competition.

Plans must start with a clear vision of what objectives are attainable within the resources available. Then objective will be defined in terms of

1. a set of market segments known to be receptive
2. a perceived opportunity to fill needs and desires of those segments which are not presently well met
3. an offering design which can fulfill the opportunity presented

Simply stated, a strategy is a choice of a competitive marketing niche which the seller seems to be able to fill better than any competitor does.

Tactics consist of those specific moves made to achieve as much of the strategic objectives as current conditions permit.

The art of innovation is required to develop the final specifics of tactical moves which can draw customer attention and create interest.

Strategy, tactics and art must all be part of every aspect of the marketing effort, not just of the offering or of some aspect of the promotion. Developing them requires some kind of picture of how the system works--in current parlance, a model of marketing management.

Marketing Models

The "4 P's" is probably the most widely used model of the marketing process. This model has a great deal of value, but lacks some important ingredients. The 4 Ps correspond generally with the internal second level organization of marketing in most organizations: product, pricing, place (distribution), and promotion (sales, advertising, publicity, and sales promotion devices). Consumer orientation is implicit in this model, as are the effects of various environmental influences. Research and control are viewed as internal staff services.

As applied, the model has seemed to take a rather mechanical view of market segmentation and pays only passing attention to the basics of consumer behavior. The most vital inadequacy is the ignoring of the critical factor of timing.

Timing: the critical fifth "P"(promptness). Time, in Roman mythology, was perceived as a messenger with a single forelock of hair. Time could only be grasped as he approached. Failing that, he was gone forever. Hence the adage, "take time by the forelock."

This adage has to be the cardinal rule for marketing strategy, tactics, and everyday operation. To use a space age concept, market opportunities resemble space exploration shots. There exists a certain "window of time," usually quite narrow, during which a design, a new offering, or a new program can be launched and hope to succeed. Once the window closes, the opportunity is gone. Alert competition and the ever-changing tastes of buyers permit few mistakes.

Timing is a critical component of every aspect of marketing operations. Even the simplest program requires careful coordination of the complex structure of production and distributive arrangements through all stages of the sales channels, of advertising agencies, media, sales effort, and inventory placement. There is even a proper timing for market withdrawal, linked to the market life cycle.

The key to the planning of strategy and tactics is knowledge of the appropriate forms at each stage of the market life cycle and a recognition of the type of life cycle and its phase in which a specific offering will be marketed. To ignore this aspect of timing is to court disaster.

Useful as the 4 P's approach has been for understanding the operational functions of marketing, strategic planning needs an approach based on consumer perceptions and the means of influencing consumer behavior through a knowledge of these perceptions.

The Behavioral Change Model, (NC)(OPC)T

The only logical purpose of marketing effort is to influence consumer behavior relative to the offerings of the seller. That behavior is activated by a search for fulfillment of a large number of felt satisfaction needs. The aim of strategy is to identify those needs the seller is in an advantageous position to satisfy, and to get customers to perceive the offerings as filling the needs better than any other available.

Buyers will guide their search on the basis of their own perception of:
- (N) their least satisfied needs
- (C) the competitive offerings which might satisfy the needs
- (O)the relative benefits of the competing offerings, and their value
- (P)the total price of gaining satisfaction from each competing offering
- (C)the meaning and credibility of the communications from possible suppliers

Each of these perceptions will change with time, so all of the terms are modified by T time. The model might then be abbreviated to (NC)(OPT)T.

The (NC) term represents the two perceptions which define the market opportunity: buyers' perceptions of their needs, and their perceptions of the ability of competitors to satisfy them. A workable strategy needs this base information as a foundation.

The (OPC)term includes the perceptions which the seller can hope to shape to the seller's advantage: the offering, the price, and the communications. T emphasizes the timing critical to the planning and execution of all proposed tactics, and also the timing of all aspects of consumer perceptions as they change over the market life cycle.

Distribution is really not a separate element, but part offering design, part price, as will be seen later.

This model centers on perception because perception is the only reality there is for the customer. Any strategy planner must understand the psychology of perception and of the other automatic response patterns by which buyers gain meaning from the offerings, prices, and communications presented to them. The only workable plans are those which start from an understanding of these psychological mechanisms. All other plans are empty fantasies.

SUMMARY

Marketing can be defined as the management of a mutual exchange relationship between a seller and a group of buyer segments in the face of dynamic competition. Both sides enter the exchange transaction in the expectation of a continuing relationship.

All marketing transactions are shaped by 3 perceptions in the minds of the buyers: the perception of the bundle of desires to be satisfied, the perceptions of all types of competitive offerings which might satisfy these desires, and the perceptions of the total prices demanded.

Every transaction therefore involves, besides the buyer and the seller, actual and potential competitors who could furnish similar but somewhat different offerings, and the competition of offerings which could satisfy competing desire sets and thus coopt the resources needed to make payment.

In addition, most transactions involve distributive intermediaries who represent both the buyer and the seller, and have needs of their own.

Successful plans have three legs: a basic strategy, flexible tactics for executing it, and the art of innovation to give them point.

Because all strategy and tactics must be based on an understanding of consumers' habitual perceptions, the most useful marketing model for planning strategy might be abbreviated to (NC)(OPC)T. (NC) denotes consumers' perceptions of their needs and of the various competitive offerings which might satisfy them. (OPC) represents the three variables available to the seller in shaping strategy: the offering, its price, and the communications mix. T emphasizes the critical nature of the timing of every aspect of the effort.

FOOD FOR THOUGHT AND DISCUSSION

The Halls of Ivy Discover Marketing

Is Carleton College using the "fine art of marketing," as the Wall Street Journal asserts? You could get an argument among writers on this. Some insist that it is not marketing unless conducted by business, in the hope of profit. The most they will admit is that Carleton is using some marketing techniques.

Others will assert that the efforts of Carleton College, or any other school, to attract students can be legitimately included under marketing, and so can the efforts of hospitals and other health care agencies to attract patronage, even when no profit is expected. They point out that such efforts can target market segments, design offerings to attract them, and receive compensation for the effort. In addition, some schools and some hospitals are operated for profit, and the operations and methods are not significantly different. But some of these writers would pin a modified label, social marketing or meta marketing, on some other efforts of persuasion, such as campaigns to persuade parents to get their children innoculated for measles, or a city anti-littering campaign. They cannot visualize the existence of an exchange in the situation.

Some will not even agree with any use of the term **marketing** for campaigns to raise endowments for a new art museum of for the symphony. They insist that any satisfaction offered donors is really a self-reward, not something the "seller" provides.

This author takes an even more extreme position, insisting that soliciting donations for the United Way or the symphony are not only susceptible to the art of marketing, but also such interpersonal persuasion as legislative log-rolling and corporate manager interrelations, even ordinary industrial relations between management and labor.

1. Where would you stand, where would you draw the line?   Why?

2. What about symphony campaigns?   Is there nothing such organizations can do to enhance the benefit of giving?   What satisfactions can the donor expect, and how much of this is self-satisfaction?

3. If we exclude donation benefits as mainly self-generated, what about the marketing of cosmetics?   One writer has pointed out that if a lipstick advertising leads a young woman to believe that using it makes her more attractive, then that young woman probably is more attractive because she feels that way (Milton Mayer, **Madison Ave., U.S.A.**). Is there any difference?   Or cigarettes, whose main appeal to men seems to be the connotation of virility?

4. If the exchange of money is the test, then what about panhandling by derelicts?   What about the efforts of volunteers of any kind?

5. What marketing tools other than wages can an employer use to attract the most suitable employees when there is a shortage of those with adequate skills?

CYRUS McCORMICK: MARKETING MANAGEMENT TRAILBLAZER

If there was a Daniel Boone of marketing management, his name was Cyrus McCormick. He is correctly credited with the patent on the first workable grain reaper. For this, he deserves a minor footnote in history—hardly more. At least one other inventor was close behind. His real accomplishment was unique: he invented the first manufacturer's national and international combined marketing and service system, mapping a path for marketing strategy and management which has been little improved on since. Without his genius in analyzing the market and delivering what it needed, the agricultural implement industry would not have developed so rapidly, nor the face of agriculture in America changed so quickly.

McCormick developed his first reaper in 1831 and secured his patent in 1834. But farmers beat no path to his door. He seems to have made only a single token sale before 1840, and turned his interests elsewhere in the interval. The 1837 depression bankrupted the family and most of the side enterprises they had entered. He then turned his attention again to his reaper, which he had apparently improved in the meantime. In 1940, he sold two reapers to farmers in his home state of Virginia, but refused a third order because he knew his reaper would not work in the flood-drenched grain of the third customer.

Keeping in touch with his customers on their experiences, he spent the next year on developing a better machine. Returning to the market in 1842, he sold 7 more machines. And he started to advertise in farm papers, making an unprecedented offer for his day: an unconditional guarantee of satisfactory performance or a full refund of the purchase price. Sales rose to 29 in 1843, and 50 in 1844, all made in the little blacksmith shop on the home farm.

The sources of the 1844 sales surprised McCormick and aroused his curiosity. A number of the orders came from New York, Tennessee, Ohio, Indiana, Illinois, Wisconsin, and Missouri. The principal wheat growing areas of the day were in Western New York, Pennsylvania, and Ohio.

McCormick decided to investigate these surprising new markets. Traveling first to New York, then to Wisconsin, Illinois, Missouri, and back to Ohio, McCormick was amazed by the flat expanses of the midwestern prairies--so unlike the hilly farms of his home Shenandoah Valley and other areas of the East. Letters home noted his conclusion that reapers were a luxury in the East, but a necessity on the plains of the West. Eastern fields were not only hilly and poorly adapted to the machine. Fields were small, wheat production a limited part of a diversified operation with adequate labor to handle the harvesting by hand tools.

Fields in the West were flat, unhindered by fences. Wheat production was the main first crop and the expected source of the cash needed to develop the pioneer prairie farms. Labor was so scarce in the West that a large part of the Illinois 1844 wheat had been left standing in the fields, to be salvaged by turning in stock to feed on it. A machine which could double the output of the available labor would be a boon.

The center of distribution, he perceived, would have to be in a Mississippi Valley state, not in Virginia or any other Eastern point. Writing home from Indiana, he noted that "It seems wrong to pay $20 or $25 freight... when they might be made in the West...considering, too, the greater uncertainty of shipping." [Uncertainty, indeed, with no railroads yet to the West, and most freight moving on waterways or Conestoga wagons!]

Since sales had already grown beyond the capacity of his tiny farm blacksmith shop, McCormick made arrangements to have his reaper produced under license in Brockport, New York (on the Erie Canal in Western New York) by Seymour and Morgan, and by another firm in Cincinnati, and formed a brief partnership with Gray, in Chicago, when he finally moved there in 1847. Meanwhile McCormick started building his sales network (to prove his salvation not many years later). J. B. McCormick, a cousin, was made official traveling representative to develop dealers in the lower Ohio Valley, Tennessee, and Missouri. In 1848, 3 "traveling agents"were hired as territorial supervisors. Their duties were to recruit, appoint, and supervise local agents.

Local sales agents contracted to maintain a sample machine, canvass the wheat district assigned, deliver reapers and instruct buyers in their operation, stock spare parts, be prepared to do repair work and render field service, make reports, collect money due on notes, and distribute advertising. They often made use of country blacksmiths or general stores as sub-agents.

Field service by the manufacturer was a completely new concept at the time, and was no minor assignment, especially in the early days. The McCormick guarantee meant what it said. When the gearing on the 1853 model proved weak, the agents spent the following winter replacing gears at no cost to the purchaser. Not accustomed to machinery maintenance requirements, farmers often left reapers standing in the field over the winter, then made belated calls for service just as the harvest was ready.

Another revolutionary innovation was the granting of consumer credit. McCormick realized that cash working capital was scarce. He has been quoted as saying that a reaper could only be sold by waiting for it to pay for itself. Nominally, the farmer was supposed to pay $35 plus freight from Chicago, with the balance of the $125 price due at 6% interest from July 1st to December 1st. In practice, the down payment could be anywhere from 10% to 25%, and the balance collected whenever possible within the next year and one-half. If crops failed, the firm merely waited until the farmers had some income.

The McCormick sales organization got an early test of its value. The McCormick patent was due to expire in 1848, just one year after the move to Chicago, and McCormick filed for an extension of the patent. His Brockport licensees decided it would be nice to keep the royalties they had been paying, and unfortunately had considerable political influence. Campaigning among fellow licensees and farmers, they argued that the patent was too valuable to be left to one firm's profit, and succeeded in getting Congress to block the extension. Soon, McCormick had 30 competitors. But none had the vision to see the western market, nor to develop a sales network. McCormick continued to sell more than all of his competitors combined.

The McCormick sales force was backed up by extensive advertising and publicity. From the first, he advertised aggressively in local farm papers around the country. He also competed vigorously in well publicized field tests with his first legitimate competitor, Obed Hussey, who had secured an early patent on a different design. The public competitions not only drew local spectators, but attracted newspaper space around the country. As with most advertising of the day, the proprietor wrote his own ads, touting the labor savings of his product in rather vivid language, and prominently featuring his money-back guarantee.

Neither McCormick's vision nor his publicity ended at the water's edge. With an eye to the English market, McCormick designed a special machine for Prince Albert's Royal Agricultural Society in 1849, and took it to the Crystal Palace Exhibition of All Nations Fair in the summer of 1851. Hearing of this, Hussey also also sent a machine, and a contest was held before the jury and some 200 spectators, earning the Council medal, the highest prize at the fair, for McCormick. He then made arrangements for manufacturing the reaper in England.

Formal Research and Development operations were unknown in those days, but McCormick had a useful substitute. In the early years, he kept in close touch with customers after the sale, discussing the machine and its performance with them and other farmers. From them he got leads for improvements, and would try them out. After his move to Chicago, the business became too big for this. He then kept in touch by careful study of agents' reports, analyzing the complaints sent in by his travelers, and used them to improve the designs.

An interesting side note to McCormick's marketing sense: when McCormick made his move to Chicago, Hussey, then based in Cincinnati, moved to Baltimore, then the center of the wheat trade. None of McCormick's early competitors moved to the prairies.

IN MARKETING, LATE CAN BE WORSE THAN NEVER

The local chapter of the American Marketing association was holding its monthly evening meeting, and members were exchanging notes over pre-dinner cocktails. One cluster had drifted into some comments on the recently popular TV shows, one of the "hottest" of which had been a Davy Crockett series. The research director of a large local ad agency remarked, "Does anybody want some Davy Crockett shirts cheap? We ordered them for a client's promotion. Then the craze collapsed before we could use them. We have a warehouse full."

The progress of computer design has moved so fast that the "personal" computers of 1982 had a capacity and speed greater than the earlier mainframe giants. The main reason, of course, has been the ability to cram a multitude of functions on a small silicon chip.

Everyone in the industry knows what the next step should be in capacity: at least a doubling in memory capacity. Achieving that result is no simple task. It usually takes a highly skilled team at least 3 to 4 years to do it.

Competition in engineering is so fierce that the market life of each advance may be no more than a couple of years. Most of the newer personal computer designs of 1981-2 were equipped with at least 64K of RAM (random access memory of about 64,000 characters). The newest ones of 1982 had 128K, using a "16-bit" chip, compared with the 8-bit chip used in the 64K machines.

An industry reporter commenting on the 1982 West coast Computer Faire, noted that "last year there were a number of breathless announcements of Z8000 chip systems. This year, there wasn't a single Z8000 at the show! It looks as if the Z8000 is a chip whose time has passed. It's a pity, because it has good architecture and an excellent instruction set;...it was a victim of too few chips delivered too late, and now I doubt anyone will invest in making a first class system for it."*

*Jerry Pournelle, "Computers for Humanity," BYTE, July, 1982

CHAPTER 2. THE COMPLEXITIES OF THE EXCHANGE PROCESS

The perceived content of the offering
    Product as promise to satisfy a cluster of desires
    Differences in buyer's perceptions of values
    Design compromise value perceptions
The offering and the use system
The purchase and consumption structure
The three dimensions of competition
    Competition between sellers of similar offerings
    Competition between sellers of different offerings satisfying
        the same desires
    Competition of other desire sets for the same consumer resources
Buyer price perceptions
    Price as any perceived resource sacrifice
    The primary role of the design compromise price
The decisive role of habitual responses

THE COMPLEXITIES OF THE EXCHANGE PROCESS 2

On the surface, exchanges appear to be simple two-way transactions. A shopper comes into the supermarket, pushes a cart up one aisle and down another, picking out items, takes them to a checkout counter where the prices are totalled, pays for them and departs. A college junior looks over the course offerings for the next term, makes out a tentative schedule, takes it to the registration desk for approval, pays the fees requested. The purchasing department of an auto manufacturer asks salesmen of two or three approved suppliers for quotations on specified proportions of the estimated tire requirements for the next model year, accepts or rejects them when they come in. The father stops at the drug counter, hands the druggist a prescription which is filled, pays for it and leaves.

All that is visible in any of these is a buyer or his representative, a seller or his representative, a choice of the buyer's offerings, and the payment of some money.

Subconsciously, of course, we know that what we see is only part of the process, on both sides of the transaction. We recognize that most of the choices made by the visible purchaser may have been influenced or even dictated by others not on the scene. We are aware that the clerk at the counter or the salesman in the office are backed by a sales and production organization, itself engaged in a series of transactions to make the offerings available.

From our own experiences as buyers, we can understand that the real object of the purchase was not mere possession of the item chosen, but an expectation that possession and use promised satisfaction of a cluster of desires. Similarly, we would not be surprised to learn that the monetary price paid was perceived as less important than some other "price" required.

We also would expect that the main force behind the choice was not simply price, advertising and salesmanship, but the result of one or more of three kinds of compromises. The most obvious of these was between somewhat similar products offered by different sellers, none of which fit the desire set perfectly: a brand choice compromise. In addition, behind this compromise may have been a choice between this kind of item and a different item satisfying most of the same core desires. The initial decision may well have been between spending the same resources for the satisfaction of different sets of desires. Finally, everyday personal experience tells us that only the smallest fraction of all purchases are the result of concurrent deliberation. Almost all are the result of habitual responses.

The Perceived Content of the Offering

Consider, first, the focal element of the exchange: the offering being bought, and why it was chosen.

The original producer may be prone to perceive the offering as a simple, relatively uniform set of physical or service designs. Buyers, however, see offerings as more or less credible promises: clues or symbols that possession and use can be expected to result in satisfaction of whole sets of related desires. Satisfaction is perceived as following from the employment of the offering in the context of a very specific use system. The use system itself inevitably involves other products and services. The more important use systems are also likely to involve other people in various roles, people whose own desire sets are intimately affected in some manner. Moreover, two different purchasers of the same item may be seeking satisfaction of differing desire sets. Neither producer nor merchant can be sure in advance of sale which desire sets will be most powerful in attracting customers.

Product as Promise to Satisfy a Cluster of Desires. It is a rare offering which is truly perceived by all buyers as fulfilling a single purpose. Generally, customers approach every purchase with a cluster of needs they hope to satisfy simultaneously. Some of the sought-for satisfactions may be perceived as deriving from the physical functioning of the offering in the most obvious use-system. Most buyers of automobiles can be assumed to be expecting a means of flexible transportation as part of their desire sets. If this were all that any buyer expected, however, it would be difficult to explain why some paid as much as $36,000 for mass-produced vehicles and others less than $6,000 in 1982. Such differences are far in excess of the differences in production costs.

Differences in Buyer's Perceptions of Value. The wide differences between prices of top end makes and models and those of low end offerings reflect the much higher perception of value which some customers place on attributes other than the core function of getting from here to there at the owner's option. Any of us could name one such value: the intangible we label "prestige". By prestige we usually mean that the Mercedes-Benz, for example, is often bought as a recognized symbol of wealth and upperclass status. This status element is not built in by the manufacturer (who certainly does whatever is possible to reinforce it). The status perception is part of the current culture of our society. The "excellent engineering" featured in the advertising may be an objective fact motivating fans of perfection to buy. It may be only a rationalization for others seeking prestige. Of course, part of the total offering bundle must be a truly quality mechanical service and strong, well-financed dealers.

THE GREAT OLDSMOBILE ENGINE FLAP: Labels Do Make a Difference!

What's in a name? A great deal of value in the perceptions of many buyers. Consider the great Oldsmobile engine brouhaha of 1977, and what it cost General Motors in adverse publicity as well as dollars.

A key element of GM product policy since 1921 has been to offer a diversity of makes and models matching the variations in buyer tastes and pocketbooks. To do this and still achieve economies of scale, the production policy has been to use as many common components as possible across the whole range of models.

There never was any secret about this. In fact, the policy was spelled out specifically in Sloan's MY YEARS WITH GENERAL MOTORS, published in 1962. The first Pontiac, introduced to fill a price line gap between the Chevrolet and the Oldsmobile, was built on a Chevrolet chassis with an 80% commonality of parts, but with a 6-cylinder engine instead of the Chevrolet's four cylinder plant. The same body shell might cover some models under every GM nameplate, from Chevrolet to Cadillac. Visual differentiation was achieved by different treatments of hood, grill, and fender designs, and perhaps the rear lighting cluster. Although every division tended to have its own engine plant, basic engine designs have always been shared by more than one nameplate. Differences between makes have often been mainly one of cosmetics and refinements. The value difference perceived and paid for by customers has always greatly exceeded production cost variances. The other manufacturers have followed a similar policy.

In 1977, this policy cost GM much embarrassment, however. The demand for certain Oldsmobile models was temporarily greater than the Olds engine foundry could fill. Olds management then procured some engines of the same basic design from Chevrolet to fill the gap. Mechanics familiar with the GM coding system and the differences in engine accessories quickly spotted the substitution. They raised a howl which reached the ears of ambitious state attorneys, the legislatures, and the courts. Buyers claimed that they had "bought an Oldsmobile, not a Chevrolet." State officials were quick to file a series of "class action" suits, which GM finally settled at some cost.

Other market segments might simply admire the cosmetics of the current design (and find it "vulgar" or "outdated" a few years hence), not caring much about what is under the hood. Other segments, in a position to charge off the cost as a business expense, may perceive the purchase as an "excellent investment": a means of owning a quality product and also get a substantial deduction of their income tax to help pay for it.

Among prospects who could well afford top end prices will be segments who consider many of the design or fringe attributes too flamboyant and vulgar, and other segments who consider it unwise to flaunt their wealth.

Others may perceive the refinements not worth the price, for them, and prefer a vehicle with less thirst for fuel and less costly maintenance. Still others may be willing to spend as much, or even far more, but desire an obviously high performance, sporty vehicle, to underline a personal fantasy of kinship with race drivers (but no intention to race).

Such differences in the value perceptions of buyers of the same offering are the rule for purchases of nearly every kind. They form the basis of one kind of competitive opportunity. A related opportunity is opened by the universal need to compromise between design realities and the desire set, faced by all.

ONE MAN'S MEAT IS ANOTHER'S POISON

A product attribute which is perceived by one market segment as especially attractive may be perceived as repellent by other segments. Consider the case of the successful psychiatrist.

The time was around 1959, when the foreign cars had caught the public fancy. As with many gatherings at the time, a family gathering was discussing various foreign models. One in-law participant was a successful psychiatrist on the verge of a car purchase. He had a problem: although quite able to afford a luxury model, and wanting one, he could not "afford to buy a Cadillac." Some of his patients, he felt, would resent his purchase of an obvious status chariot. He finally bought a Rover, an extremely high quality British make with little recognition in the United States, but actually used by British royalty when travelling "incognito".

Consider, also, the case of the wealthy secondary metals broker. When the luncheon conversation turned to cars, he remarked: "You know, I have never owned anything but a Cadillac, since my first car at 17. I don't think I am going to get one the next time. The last time I was at the country club, there wasn't anything else on the drive. I think I will buy a Ford."

Design Compromise Value Perceptions. Nearly all purchases are made in the hope of satisfying a whole cluster of related desires by a single act: to fulfill a desire set. To enlarge on our automobile illustration, almost any driver would like a vehicle with the following specification:
- the maneuverability of a sports car
- the passenger capacity of a bus (occasionally, at least)
- luggage capacity of a good-sized pickup truck
- a total abstainer in respect to fuel
- the power and acceleration to leave everyone else a half block behind at the stoplight
- the comfort of a luxury limousine
- the parkability of a motorcycle

Being realistic, we all know such a combination cannot exist. So we compromise. We look for some design and model which approaches a close fit to those desires which are, at the moment, most deeply felt, including the dominant use system for which the purchase is intended, at a price we are willing and able to pay.

The Offering and the Use System

The real source of the satisfactions which buyers expect from a purchase is the use system. A cake of face soap cleans nothing by itself. It must be used with water in a container or running supply, in a specific set of motions. Even the hypothetical automobile buyer who seeks only a status symbol must follow a use system consisting of a number of component steps. To get the desired recognition, it must be cleaned frequently to maintain an immaculate appearance, kept parked in the full public gaze on the driveway or other spot where it would be associated with the owner. If used for transportation, it must be regularly serviced with fuel and receive regular maintenance service. Driving must be done according to the rules of the road. It must be parked in some permissible place at the destination. The driver must obtain a license from the state and renew it regularly. If prestige remains the central desire, the car must be traded in for the newest model regularly.

Any such use system is a pattern of well-established habits of action and perception which can be represented by a flow diagram. As we shall see later, the acceptance climate for any new offering is determined by the existence of an appropriate use system or the need to learn or change one.

The use system, itself, is only one element in a total system of purchase decision, purchasing operation, and final consumption. The purchase and consumption cycle is determined by a pattern of social roles involving 2 or more people, for all but the simplest and most intimate personal needs.

The Purchase and Consumption Structure

Most purchases tend to be the result of either direct or indirect social decisions. At the least, purchases tend to conform to what is perceived as acceptable in the individual's reference groups. In addition, the person making the actual purchase is quite usually playing a social role circumscribed by the direct influence of others in some well defined system. Every exchange transaction involves four basic roles, some or all of which may be combined in a single person or group in specific situations. These roles are:

- designer-gatekeeper
- financier
- end-product producer
- end-product consumers

THE SURPRISE DISPOSABLE DIAPER MARKET

When Procter & Gamble first introduced disposable diapers, they thought the market target was middle class, who could afford a mild luxury. Post introduction sales analysis turned up a real surprise. Sales were heavy in the poverty stricken Harlem district of New York City. Investigation revealed that buyers were working mothers with babies. Once the disposables became available, all the day care facilities demanded a supply of the disposable diapers accompany the baby each day.

Designer-gatekeepers make the critical choice of product form and brand, within limits set by those putting up the funds and in line with the limits of taste and desires of the end users (who are often in a customer or client relationship to them). For household supplies, this would normally be the housekeeper-shopper. In the factory, this role would be occupied by the design engineer, in the symphony, the music director, in the medical situation, the prescribing physician, in construction, the architect.

The gatekeeper's role is a key one, as the label indicates, but not completely decisive. Any or all of the others can exercise a modifying influence, or even a veto.

Financier: the person(s) who sets the budget and controls the flow of funds. Whoever plays this role inevitably limits what can be spent. Normally, they do not make the specific brand choices.

Producers: those who complete the use system procedures. For the evening supper, this would be the cook; in the factory, the shop foreman and the workers. Producers can and often do modify choices made by the gatekeepers through outright rejection, sabotage, or mere protest and social disapproval.

End product consumers: superficially, these simply receive and dispose of the purchase. Their true role is not quite this passive. Even the family mutt can reject the new advertised food and force a change in brands.

All of the family at the table would be end consumers of the evening meal, including the producer-cook who prepared it, the financier-person(s) who furnished the funds for the food, and Tom and Jennifer who simply gulped down what they liked. The shop foremen and the workers play this role with respect to the raw materials and components purchased by the factory, the clients for the community organization, the patient in the medical situation. As a producer, the factory has its own groups of consumers: the customers who buy the output either to consume in the production of what they have to sell to another factory down the line or to merchants. The merchants, in turn, are themselves true producers, building assortments specifically designed to match the desire sets of their target buyer segments.

For minor items of personal consumption, one person may play all of the roles. For more complex purchases, each role may be played by a different person, or even a group (such as a design team, as a group gatekeeper). The same person carrying out the same objective action of purchasing may be playing different roles under diverse circumstances. Thus the shopper may be the gatekeeper for most of the family's food items, but be simply carrying out the prescriptions of the gatekeeper pediatrician in buying the baby foods.

Gatekeepers are the real key customers who must first be satisfied even when they are not directly involved in the purchase. Their specifications and prescriptions limit or even dictate the specific products and brands to be incorporated in the use system. They must be identified and their tastes and desires planned for, whether or not they have to bear any portion of the cost. The building products producer must keep the tastes and prejudices of zoning authorities and architects in mind, the drug seller the biases of physicians. Textbook writers and publishers must pay close attention to the perceptions and teaching habits of instructors even when they may feel that the final result may not be best for the kind of student targeted.

THE INDUSTRIAL WIPER INCIDENT: He Who Pays The Piper May Not Be Able to Call the Tune

In many kinds of transactions, the final purchase decision may involve many people in quite different roles. At times, those who write the orders and sign the checks may have to bow to others who have no formal purchase authority. If they did not already know this, both Ford Motor Company and Scott Paper learned it when they cooperated on a pre-marketing trial of a new Scott industrial wiper.

Industrial wipers are routinely furnished production workers wherever they are needed to keep grime and grease off the workpieces and the workers' hands. The common wiper for a long time was cotton waste: shredded cotton rags. But cotton waste sheds lint, which may be highly undesirable in the handling of precision parts. Industrial towel leasing services then furnished towels for this purpose, periodically replacing the dirty towels with clean ones, and laundering the dirties.

Seeking new volume markets, Scott Paper laboratories developed a lintless paper wiper. Wishing to give it a thorough test before introducing it to the market, Scott approached Ford for a plant-wide test at Scott expense, and Ford agreed.

As soon as the Scott wipers reached the shop floor, the shop stewards descended on the Ford offices, talking strike. Their men wanted those towels back, not these paper substitutes. Ford compromised: both towels and Scott wipers would be made freely available, at the choice of the workers.

Six months later, Scott ended the test, withdrawing the wiper supply. Again, the Ford offices were beseiged by the shop stewards, talking strike: the men wanted those Scott wipers back!

The tastes and desires of others in the system must also be taken into consideration, because of their veto power. These include the cost limitations imposed by those who must pay. Also, the learning cost perceivable by final consumers must be taken into account: the natural tendency to resist the unfamiliar, or an unfamiliar use-system.

Any established role in any organization implies an established pattern of action and perception. Roles define the status of each individual member of the group. Any downgrading of this role status meets resistance. Instant coffee had a very slow market growth when first introduced on the general consumer market. Research revealed that making coffee was perceived as requiring some skill. The housewife who bought instant coffee was regarded as lazy, shirking her duties. Similarly, the highly skilled typographers actively fought the introduction of computer typesetting because it required little more skill than that of a good typist.

By contrast, introductions fitting easily into established use-system and perception patterns are quickly adopted. Black-and-white television sales rocketed from the beginning because the new product was perceived as familiar movies in a cheaper setting. It required no change in consumer role perceptions or entertainment habits.

Very few purchases are dictated purely by personal whim. Even such apparently personal choices as cigarettes, lipsticks and beer may be shaped by the social influence of peer groups and other reference group perceptions. These influences help define the content of all three dimensions of perceived competition.

The Three Dimensions of Perceived Competition

The textbook economist's model of rival sellers with identical offerings has no visible semblance to modern mass production markets. Competition, as perceived by buyers, is three-dimensional:
- between somewhat similar, but significantly differentiated offerings
- between offerings of quite different forms, but appealing to many of the same core desires
- between use of the same resources to gratify competing desire sets

Competition between Sellers of Similar Offerings. Successful competition is always differentiated in some manner. Even when the physical offering appears to be identical, buyers must be able to perceive substantial differences in benefit levels and types before they will switch from the brand they first became familiar with, tried, and found acceptable. Any switch involves a risk price.

Successful offerings are differentiated in some manner because every purchase is motivated by a complex of desires which no single offering can match completely, and the desire set structure varies from one buyer to the next. They are differentiated because once buyers find a product with a good fit to their desire sets, no other offering will gain their attention unless it offers a very substantial perceived gain in value. Far all of these reasons, the offerings of no two sellers can be perceived as identical, and both succeed. Every department store on Main, Market, or State streets serves a different clientele with substantially different desire sets.

The choice between a Ford and a Chevy is between offerings which are actually, as well as perceptually, different in a number of respects which buyers view as important. The total offerings are differentiated even more. Dealer service networks are far from equal in general, and even more so locally. Furthermore, neither Ford nor Chevy are single offerings, but whole series of significantly different vehicles to take advantage of widely differing desire sets among potential customers. In point of fact, the options are so numerous that Ford executives have stated that they could run one of their assembly plants for a full year without duplicating a single vehicle.

THE PONTIAC INTRODUCTION: A CLASSIC IN SELF-COMPETITION

Although General Motors was formed in 1908, GM had no consistent product policy until Sloan formulated one in 1921. As he analyzed it, the market was segmented into 6 price classes. General Motors then was producing 10 different makes. Several were competing directly against each other, without any clear differentiation. Sloan's proposal, which was adopted, was to have the firm enter one make in each class, at the top of the price range with some refinements over competitor's entries in the same price class. Only 5 of the current GM nameplates seemed viable, and the others were dropped. Of those that remained, the Oakland was a weak sister, without a clear franchise.

At that time, the Chevrolet was scheduled for the lowest of the price lines, but needed redesign to fit its mission. This occupied more than two years. Then Sloan, who was by then the president, turned his attention to gaps in the line. As he saw them in 1924, there were two such gaps. One gap was below the Cadillac. The more dangerous one, however, was between the Olds and the Chevrolet, because it represented a volume demand. As he wrote to the general manager of the Oakland Division, "if General Motors didn't go in there, someone else sooner or later would. If the whole field were left to General Motors I do not know as I would be so anxious about it...". In a report to the Executive Committee at the same time, he noted rumors indicating that one or two of GM's competitors were going to attempt such an entry, and pointed out that "this development [of the Pontiac] will probably take business from both Olds and Chevrolet, [but] it will be better that we take business from our own Divisions than have competitors do so." (Sloan, pp. 156-7)

The Pontiac was duly developed, introduced in the 1927 model year by the Oakland Division, and established a solid market niche. Not long afterward, the Oakland was dropped, and the Oakland Division became the Pontiac Division.

The most often overlooked competition is the invisible potential seller: latent competition from potential new offerings which others may launch if given adequate opportunity. Wise sellers never hesitate to compete with themselves when doing so will close a product line gap and expand market share profitably. Such self-competition is the way of life for even as simple a product as laundry detergent, as scrutiny of any supermarket soap shelf will reveal.

Competition between Different Kinds of Offerings. Perceived competition is not limited to similar offerings. As customers, our desires are not for physical products but for specific results. In recent decades, for example, the major competition of laundry and dry cleaning establishments has been the development of easy-care textiles. In the machine shop, abrasive metal forming competes with cutting tools. Both methods complete in some uses with die-casting processes which produce parts needing no further working. The machine shop itself, and metal working in general, meet increasing competition from molded plastics which do not even require painting and are much lighter.

The couple wishing to parade their affluence at the opera may choose between the latest designer mutation mink stole for the matron and a generous enough donation to the opera endowment to be listed as patrons in the program and on a plaque in the lobby, together with seating preference. A physical offering may even compete with a service or practice. When antibiotic animal feed additives were introduced, most farmers experienced a substantial benefit in feed productivity. Some did not: the stringent sanitation practices they were already following achieved the same result.

Competition of Other Desire Sets for the Same Resources. Rare indeed is the individual whose total desires do not exceed total resources of time and purse. We all seem to have "a champagne appetite and a beer purse," both in what we can afford to spend, and in available time and energy.

Directly or indirectly, all purchase decisions involve all three of these types of competitive choices: between similar offerings, between different offerings promising similar satisfactions, and between allocating our limited resources between competing desire sets. Purchases of minor everyday items such as beverages and face soap probably center on competition between similar brands, all of which are reasonably acceptable. Decisions on major purchases probably involve competing desire sets, and careful forethought of the total prices perceived as required.

Buyer's Price Perceptions

Traditional economics defines price as synonymous with monetary cost (perhaps because this makes a neat fit with the mathematical precision economists seem to prefer to reality). The rest of us use price in a much broader context both in our thinking and in our everyday reactions to transactions of every kind. To us, price means anything we have to give up to get what we wish.

PEPSI-COLA DISCOVERS THE IMPORTANCE OF THE AVAILABILITY PRICE

Popular beverages are excellent examples of convenience goods — offerings for which consumers perceive only minor differences between brands and will seldom spend time and energy to find their favorite choices. In the minds of many sellers, as well as the authors of elementary economics textbooks, this would seem to dictate the use of monetary price as the effective means of competition. As Pepsi-Cola discovered after years of trying, this does not work.

For years, the Pepsi-Cola strategy was pure price, reinforced by price advertising. At a time when Coca-Cola, the market leader, was sold only in 6-once bottles, Pepsi-Cola was delivered in 12-ounce containers and advertised as "twice as much for a nickel, too"(the standard price at the time for any soft drink bottle). This did attract a significant segment of the very young, who were also attracted by the extra sugar in the Pepsi formula. Total market share was not enough to be noticed by Coca-Cola. However, during the sugar shortages of World War II, Pepsi had to reduce the sugar, substituting low calorie sweeteners in part. The less-sweet product had a potential appeal for the older markets, especially the high-usage early adult group. But Pepsi was not getting this group in volume until it decided to revamp its strategy. Part of this strategy was to revamp the advertising approach to appeal to young adults. The most effective move, however, was to review its distribution coverage.

The first step in that review was to ask who the potential buyers are, and when they buy. Who they were was easy to answer: almost anyone with a mouth. The when was a more useful consideration: whenever they were involved in any kind of activity — in effect, whenever they might get thirsty. This could be at home, which meant being in the supermarkets and other retail outlets selling for home consumption. It also meant being at ball parks and stadiums, at filling stations and at vending machines in any location. In short, it meant being available whenever the impulse to buy became active.

Looking at its outlet coverage, Pepsi discovered that it was well represented in the supermarkets, but woefully weak in all other kinds of outlets. A well-organized effort to cover the distribution gaps proved successful, and Pepsi became something more than a mere nuisance to Coca-Cola. It was now a strong second and moving up fast. Coke suddenly discovered it could not take its market for granted. Now Coca-Cola appeared in quart bottles and even larger sizes. Advertising themes were changed, and Coke had to defend itself against a strong competitor who was also at the same point of sale. Coke no longer had an availability price advantage.

Legislators all know that the price for the support needed to pass a bill highly desired by constituents is a return vote on the pet bills of colleagues. The young executive soon learns that the price to be paid to be in line for advancement may be frequent moves plus the mastering of a number of kinds of assignments, some of which he would not choose otherwise. Those seeking the elbow room and the greenery of the affluent suburbs soon become aware that the cost is a high time and effort price of daily commuting. It is obvious that millions of urban workers spurn public transportation for the schedule freedom of the private car at a high monetary cost of car maintenance and use plus the time and energy cost of negotiating jammed freeways.

Any really useful treatment of pricing must be founded on the obvious fact that the monetary sacrifice is only part of the total, and often the lesser part, or even irrelevant at times. Money cost is just one of the trade-offs, and not the first cost element considered in the buying decision.

Design compromise price is the starting point of any transaction decision. Seldom, if ever, does any single offering on the market possess all of the desired ingredients. The prospective buyer must first decide which differentiated offering comes closest to his desire set, then decide whether the satisfaction differences are worth any of the other prices. When buyers set rigid specifications on the intended acquisition, they must expect to pay in shopping energy and time to locate a distribution outlet closest to fitting the desired satisfaction bundle.

By contrast, if most buyers perceive differences between offerings as relatively minor, any seller hoping for a major market share must develop the most extensive and intensive distribution network possible. Dealerships for BMW and Mercedes automobiles can be few and widely scattered even in such metropolises as Chicago and Los Angeles. Chevrolet dealerships must be more numerous and better located than those of any other make.

For new introductions, the most crucial pricing decision is a design factor: the degree of habit change required in the purchase and use system as perceived by prospects.

By habit change we mean every kind of learned automatic response, including the routines of attention and thinking we call attitudes and perceptions, as well as the routines of physical action normally covered by the term habit. Most of them derive from the culture and subculture which predetermine choices of identifiable segments of the market.

All of us routinely allocate our spending according to standards made familiar through our group associations inside and outside the home. Most hesitate to even try the unfamiliar, whether in the home or in the R&D laboratory.

Such habits of perception of what is "good" or "workable" cause consumers to perceive differences in product acceptability not supported on the basis of objective analysis. New England consumers pay more for brown eggs, nearby New Yorkers for white. The home economist can discover no difference in either for any cooking or eating purpose.

A food processor, hoping to enlarge his catsup market share, spent millions in research to eliminate the overcooked, scorched flavor of the standard product and retain the natural tomato flavor. The market rejected the "improved" flavor, and the scorched flavor had to be restored.

An aerosol pack for barbecue sauce was rejected because the bubbles made the product lighter in color, accepted when the color was deepened. Unless butter is colored a deep yellow (by adding concentrated carotene), it does not sell well in the United States. In Iran, long accustomed to a relatively white native butter, naturally yellow Danish butter butter sold at a deep discount when first imported.

Supposedly scientific engineers and financial executives are just as prone to stay in habitual ruts as the everyday supermarket shopper. Years after engineers had learned that oxygen processes were cheaper and more efficient for steel making, the steel industry in the United States was clinging to its outdated air reduction processes, and even building new capacity on the old pattern. The United States automobile industry, habituated to finding its profits in large cars with frequent style changes, ignored the growing demand for smaller, fuel-efficient cars with better quality production being imported even at the high end, until forced to change by the fuel crises of the 1970's.

Any study of business histories reveals the consistent tendency of the later generations of managers of the enterprise to keep to the same specific operational ruts despite dynamic changes in the market, ignoring the innovational character of the original founders. Ruts of any kind, physical or mental, are far more comfortable to follow than to break out of.

Marketing management succeeds only through building on an understanding of what is known about customer learning, habits, changes and diversities, and developing a strategy formulated to take positive advantage of trends in every form of habitual response, and every kind of change. The starting point has to be the target customers and their perceptions of offerings and the competition.

SUMMARY

1. Exchange transactions are more complex than they appear on the surface. The physical object purchased tells us little about what the buyer is seeking. The money price, if any, is only part of the cost perceived by the buyer. The choice made is the result of one or more of 3 kinds of compromises.

2. The buyer making the purchase is hoping to satisfy a whole set of desires with the one act, and different buyers are seeking satisfaction of

different desire sets. Generally, not all of the desires can be equally well satisfied, and some compromise design must be chosen.

3. The object bought can bring the desired satisfactions only as a component of some use system--an habitual pattern of actions and perceptions, involving other items and often other people.

4. Behind any purchase is a total purchase and consumption system, usually involving others besides the visible buyer, in one or more of 4 basic roles: designer-gatekeeper, financier, end product producer, end-product consumer. All play some role in the decision, and any one can be determining in a given situation.

5. The competition for any offering has three perceived dimensions: competition between similar, but differentiated offerings; competition with other forms of offerings appealing to many of the same desires; and competition between desire sets for use of the same resources.

6. The monetary price quoted is almost never the total perceived price, and sometimes only a minor element in the total. Other elements are the design compromise price, time and effort costs related to availability, and the learning requirement price, when the offering does not fit well into established habit patterns.

FOOD FOR THOUGHT AND DISCUSSION

PICKUP TRUCKS: DESIRE SETS AND MULTIPLE SEGMENTS

When automotive market shares are calculated, passenger car shares and truck shares are generally calculated separately, with good reason. Most trucks serve an entirely different market than most passenger cars. But there is substantial overlap in one category: pickup trucks. In recent years, some families have bought pickups as the basic family car, and some of the models sold have been styled to fit in with this trend.

1. How many general groups of market segments are attracted to pickup trucks?
2. What different clusters of desires can you think of which cause buyers to choose pickups? What would the specific component desires be in some of these sets?
3. Some vans are also sold for passenger car usage. What are all of the market segments you think vans appeal to, and what clusters of desires?

THE MUSTANG STORY

The Mustang story apparently started in 1954, when the volume of foreign imports approached 100,000 for the first time. Ford initiated a continuing study of consumer small car demand which first bore fruit in the 1960 introduction of the Falcon. The Falcon, however, did not incorporate all of the research findings. By arbitrary official decision, it was a spartan model with few options--really an updated Model T concept. It sold well, but almost entirely at the expense of Ford's larger and more profitable models. Chevrolet's answer to the foreign invasion, the Corvair, was a more successful bid: it cannibalized very few GM sales, yet did well. The bucket seats of the Monza edition suggested "sports car" to a great many buyers, carved its own niche in the young adult singles market.

Ford decided it needed an answer to the Corvair. To save time, Ford decided to utilize the basic Falcon chassis and power plant. The body, however, would have to be quite different: it would have to suggest "sporty". Analyzing their research, they found that four appearance elements were perceived as "sports car": a long hood, a short rear deck, cut-out fenders, and bucket seats.

When the stylists finished their models, everyone agreed that its looks were right. It was decided to give it the name, "Mustang". Research estimated the initial market penetration at a 2-1/2% market share - quite satisfactory. The base price was set at the low end of the car market. 70 different options were made available, including an optional V-8 engine. It was to become known as a do-it-yourself design.

When released, the Mustang grabbed an immediate 5% market share. Surprised, Ford investigated. It found that the buyers were predominantly the young married. What they were buying was not a sports car, but a compromise of sorts: a "nice small car for a family, with a sporty appearance." Young singles were also buying, adding the more powerful engine and other options which, at times, doubled the price tag.

1. Advance forecasts of new product sales is extremely difficult, partly because it is hard to know what values customers will perceive in the offering, once it is available. Hindsight is always better than foresight. However, in this case, we are dealing with a slightly differentiated model in a market whose dimensions and content are more thoroughly available than in any other market. Why did Ford officials underestimate the demand by so much?

[NOTE: This story has two sequels - a GM sequel, and a Ford sequel.

The GM sequel starts with jealousy: the Corvair, although reasonably successful, never enjoyed the Mustang-size market share. GM decided it must have its own Mustang. The result was the Camaro, which very much resembled the Mustang, except for the Chevrolet nameplate. But Ford was "there" first, and the Camaro, although selling to committed GM buyers in some quantity, never took over Mustang's market.

Ford, however did later lose a substantial part of that market by "walking away from it," making later models larger and more expensive, as Henry Ford II later admitted. (This raises another interesting question: who was probably the gainer of the market Ford sacrificed?)

TIM'S SCHOOLING: A LESSON IN PRICE AND COMPETITION

(About a real boy, whose name is disguised)

Tim first came into view when his parents turned in desperation to a psychological consultant to solve a school problem. The private school he attended insisted that he such an uncooperative, disturbing pupil that they would not let him return the following year, and might not even let him finish the current term.

Investigation of his "problem behavior" raised the question whether the local public school system could cope with it either. The psychologist's tests revealed a visual-motor coordination level far below his chronological age. He had real difficulty coordinating his muscular movements with visual cues. This meant that he would, for example, have difficulty reading a musical score and playing the piano.

As a result, he found such tasks so distasteful that he would use every possible disruptive tactic to avoid carrying them out.

After some search, the psychologist located a summer camp and then a rural academy, both staffed with adequate counselling and staff to handle just such problems, and the parents registered Tim, as suggested.

Two years of camp and school saw Tim well on his way to adequate behavior and achievement, academically, and excelling in athletic accomplishment. It seemed likely that just one more year would permit Tim to fit into a normal school program.

Just then, however, tuition costs responded to inflation, and the family was faced with a 50% increase over the already heavy $8500 per year. The family income was quite comfortable by most standards, but even the previous tuition cost had resulted in some retrenchment in the family standard of living. The psychologist was concerned that the new level would carry the financial burden beyond the breaking point.

Several conferences were held with the family, and the psychologist carefully explored the resources of the local private high school and the large suburban high. Neither, she decided, were adequate for the coming year.

What to do? Finally, Tim's father, an executive in a public relations firm, volunteered that he could do some free lance art work on the side. The mother, who had started a small business, decided that she might be able to pull a couple of thousand dollars out of the business capital. Tim himself volunteered that he could caddy at the local country club during the summer. As an afterthought, the mother also noted that they had been trying to save up for a European trip, and that the cost was about that of the trip.

1. What was the real price of another year at the same school for Tim?
2. What was the competition for Tim's school?
3. Who played what roles in making the decision?

PART II. CUSTOMERS, THEIR REACTION PATTERNS, AND THE EFFECTS ON OFFERING ACCEPTANCE, GROWTH, AND DECLINE

The first prerequisite of any kind of planning in any field is a knowledge of the basic characteristics of the materials being worked with and their responses to the tools available.

In marketing, this translates into understanding people, what moves them to act, how their acts are shaped. It means recognizing how and why different groups of people will react differently to the same influences, and how these different reactions affect the results of marketing plans, including the various forms of offering life cycles.

All transactions originate with a need which is uppermost in the minds of potential buyers. Buyers will respond only to those offerings which are perceived as promising to satisfy those needs. All communications not so perceived will be ignored. Perceptions are automatic forms of mental responses which focus on a few clues in a situation, adding details to create meaning.

The response to offerings is shaped by attitudes, an automatic tendency to react to specific classes of offerings in a specific direction, positive or negative. Positive attitudes cause prospects to impute value to the satisfaction of specific desires, resulting in approach reactions. Negative attitudes are price reactions, resulting in avoidance of the sacrifice of resources required by a purchase. All transactions are thus the result of a mixture of approach and avoidance reactions, of mixed motives. Purchase motives are satisfaction-oriented, not specifically product-oriented. The search for stimulus variation, for novelty, is a universal motive adding value to new introductions, and creating fashion and fad cycles.

Possible buyers vary widely in their salient desires, creating diverse forms of continuous segmentation of the market. Segmentation can result from differences in physical needs, from cultural forces, and from personality differences. Segmentation is what creates the opportunity for new competition.

Buyers' perceived needs and their valuations of the satisfactions promised go through a roughly predictable sequence of changes over the market life cycle of an offering. All offerings pass through some form of life cycle of sales growth, market saturation, and decline. Each phase imposes its own requirements for strategy and tactics, and presents its own kinds of opportunities for the art of innovation. Cycles differ. There are at least four basic types: high learning introductions, low learning introductions, fashion cycles and fads. Fashion cycles follow a predictable pattern, fads a quite different pattern.

CHAPTER 3. UNDERSTANDING CUSTOMERS AND THEIR ACTIONS: BASIC CONCEPTS

UNDERSTANDING CONSUMERS & THEIR ACTIONS: BASIC CONCEPTS

3

Customers: Shapers of the Transaction, Not Puppets

This chapter, and probably this text, would be unnecessary if a popular view of consumer reaction to marketing were valid. However, contrary to an opinion widely held in some so-called intellectual circles, consumers are the true directors of the marketing scene, not sucker puppets whose actions are subject to the strings pulled by heavy advertising, slick salesmen, and designing fashion designers. Customers can be influenced, but only by those who understand their desires, create offerings to satisfy them, and understand how to communicate the benefits they are offering.

Any seller who hopes for continuing patronage must operate with an understanding of how desires become active and how potential customers interpret the benefits of offerings, the various prices asked of them, and the communications intended to arouse their interest and attract that patronage. In brief, sellers must understand the motives which cause people to act, and the forms these reactions take.

Fortunately, the psychological understanding required is contained in a handful of basic concepts, however complex the task of applying them may be:

- The internal origin of all human drives to actions of any sort, including purchase action, and the hierarchy of needs
- The universal effect of selective attention and selective perception in the determination of the stimulus to action
- The roles of other habitual response tendencies such as attitudes and habitual procedures
- Inner motives and their relationship to action

The Consumer Origin of the Purchase Response

The modern "consumer is king" marketing concept is based solidly on the established fact that all human reaction to stimuli of any kind depends on some internal tension or drive in the individual which causes a search for satisfaction. Once some source of satisfaction is found, the drive is extinguished.

The general nature of what will satisfy any given drive is more or less defined by the drive itself, but not rigidly defined. Usually, a wide range of offerings can end the search. Hunger is an obvious case in point. The physical tension of hunger can be appeased by a tremendous range of nutriments, as all history and observation shows. Once a given drive is satiated, it gives way to a different drive.

The Hierarchy of Drives

The human animal possesses an infinity of drives, only a few of which can be satisfied by any one act. Fortunately, they vary in strength at any one moment, and exist in a hierarchy of perceived importance.

Satiation of one drive removes it from the top of the hierarchy to make room for attention to another highly felt need. The existence of a few topmost felt needs at any moment results in a high degree of selectivity of attention and perception.

The Transaction Entry Point: Selective Attention and Selective Perception

A possible transaction gets started only when communications concerning an offering are perceived as promising potential satisfaction of some drive high in the hierarchy.

All customer attention and perception must be highly selective, permitting only a very small fraction of stimuli to be even noticed.

Our environment continuously bombards us with an infinity of stimuli of all kinds, far beyond the capacity of any being to respond: a myriad of shapes, movements, and colors which keep the infant's eyes in constant uncomprehending motion. Even in the much more restricted sphere of daily transactions, all studies have shown that we are besieged by hundreds of advertising messages daily, all seeking our attention. We usually deny that attention to all of them, admitting even one only when it seems to offer a clue to satisfying an active felt want. When we do pay attention, it is not necessarily to the most prominent attempt. It is always one which appeals to some relatively salient drive, one high in our hierarchy of needs.

Even when we do pay attention, it is usually only to a small part of the item—to a few outstanding aspects we perceive as clues that the message promises possible satisfaction of some need. We interpret the meaning of the message in terms of these perceived clues. (This is the reason the choice of headline and illustration is so important in any communication.) The meaning of any message or stimulus is not determined by the originator or by the objective stimulus or object which attracted attention, but by the receiver's perception, based on established patterns of clue translation.

Perception is the first of three basic automatic response patterns which shape the market's reactions to offerings.

Automatic Responses: the Forces Shaping the Response to Any Offering

Customers define the benefits expected, and the value of the benefits to them, in terms of their perceptions, their existing attitudes toward the class of perceived benefits, and the fit of the offering, as perceived, into habitual physical use-procedures. Thus all strategy and tactics must be drawn in terms of three kinds of automatic response patterns, or habits, of the target market segments--the two mental habits of perception and attitudes, and the physical procedures of the expected use-system.

All three forms of automatic responses have negative elements. Inevitably, then, every transaction involves some kind of balance between positive, or approach reactions, and negative, or avoidance reactions.

The Approach/Avoidance Balance

Every transaction of any kind involves an offering design intended to attract the prospect, and some kind of understood price which the prospect perceives as a possible deterrent. If the prospect perceives the values of the benefits as greater than the perceived price, the transaction takes place. If the avoidance characteristics are greater, it "no sale." Since the values are defined by the customer's perception patterns, understanding of the psychology of perception is primary.

Perception: The Patterns by Which We Create Meaning

We all seek to discover some kind of predictable, coherent structure in the buzzing confusion of the world which surrounds us from birth. The mechanism by which we accomplish this is called **perception.**

Perception involves focussing on a few key clues in any given situation, then adding other items habitually associated with those clues to arrive at an interpretation of the meaning of a stimulus--of a sales message, an advertisement, or an offering design, for example. The items chosen may come from past experience, leading to a highly personal interpretation. They may be derived from the culture and subculture in which the individual has been indoctrinated. In any case, the meaning delivered will vary from one market segment to another, often leading to quite opposite interpretations of value by different market segments.

Although perceptions vary widely between market segments and even individuals, all perceptions are formed according to a few basic patterns of stimulus evaluation, labelled as follows:

- The j.n.d. ("just noticeable difference", or discriminal threshold)
- Closure and the related elements of context, proximity, constancy and generalization
- Figure and ground

Discriminal Thresholds: the j..n.d.

Psychologists define the **j.n.d.** as the percentage difference at which the human observer can barely perceive any difference when comparing stimuli of any sort. All experiments show that despite individual differences, the just noticeable difference is a universal attribute of human observation.

Just noticeable differences are by no means insignificant differences. For many stimuli, and for most persons, the size of the j.n.d. is of the order of 10%. The marginal differences in pricing effects which economics writers love to play with do not exist. Perception is a discontinuous process. Very small changes in price and product quality go unnoticed until the accumulated value suddenly becomes noticeable. The relationship between perception and reality is a stepwise one, not a smooth, continuous, one-to-one curve. The implications for pricing strategy and product differentiation are clearly of first importance.

HOW MUCH DIFFERENCE DOES IT TAKE TO MAKE A DIFFERENCE?

This was no academic question for the Florida citrus growers. They used the surpluses of grapefruit and oranges to produce canned juices, including the orange-grapefruit blend. While this blend is nominally half and half, the supplies of fruit to be used do not work out exactly this way, season after season. On the other hand, it is important that consumers perceive the product taste as dependably uniform. So the growers approached the U. S. Dept. of Agriculture with the question: "How much can we vary the blend percentages without changing the taste noticeably?"

Taste tests were run with consumer panels. The result: consumers could not discriminate differences within the range of 40% orange juice to 60% orange juice.

It is possible, of course, to train people to make finer distinctions in any single specific situation. The brewmaster in the brewery can distinguish differences between batches of his own product. But the usual beer drinker cannot identify his own brand without the label.

The finer distinctions which experts can make creates another type of problem. Such experts are likely to place undue emphasis on minor differences in offering or price, see in them competitive advantages which are not viewed as existing by buyers.

If the j.n.d. be defined as ignoring differences which do exist, then closure is the opposite kind of phenomenon. Closure involves reading details into something which are not explicitly there.

Creative Perception: Closure, Context, and Generalization.

These tendencies are so closely related that they are best discussed together. All involve reading something into a situation which is not clearly present. All result, to some degree, in creating more credibility than if the situation were pictured in full reality.

People tend to try to "close up", to tie up any apparent loose ends in any situation attracting attention so as to arrive at some total meaning which makes sense in terms of habitual mental experience and/or training. The resulting meaning is thus their own creation, going beyond the surface details presented.

Figure 1 is a visual example of closure. Objectively, neither the figures nor the letters nearly everyone sees are complete. But, within our own culture, few people have any difficulty naming the first series as representing a circle, a triangle and a rectangle. Nor do they experience difficulty reading the numbers and letters in the second line. Yet none of them are complete. Because the figures and letters are a part of our knowledge, we automatically fill in the details. We do not even think of them as incomplete.

FIGURE 1. CLOSURE: VISUAL EXAMPLES

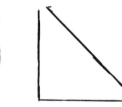

The added details are not random, and will not be added unless the observer has some preexisting mental pattern into which he can fit what is presented. Once a fit is completed, the message gains a credibility it might not have if all of the details had come from some external source.

Some of the patterns come out of experience. Most usually, they are drawn from the habits and values we call our culture.

One important aid is the context in which the detail is missing. Proximity--the juxtaposition of two unrelated elements in the same perceived situation--may cause them to be viewed as part of the same context.

For example, perfumery is widely used to impart a perception of high quality to rather mundane products such as soap and cleansers. Presumably because of its feminine connotations, perfume has been used successfully to get some brands of toilet paper perceived as soft. At least one experiment indicated that bread was more likely to be perceived as fresh when wrapped in cellophane than when wrapped in wax paper (Brown, 1958). A standard laboratory instrument (a $500 potentiometer) was able to command a $100 premium when sold in a well-designed case instead of the standard walnut box.

A classic example of the value of the right context was the history of Steuben high premium hand-blown glassware. When Corning Glass acquired Steuben, sales were rather dismal. At the time, it was sold through 50 outlets throughout the United States, and stock was simply shelved, collecting dust, like cheaper ware. Corning reduced the outlets to four, nationally, all high-end retailers. Each retailer had to use displays of a single piece, in a glass case, on a black velvet background. Total sales increased substantially, and have remained so until the present.

Closure and proximity are widely practiced to build an advertising "image" for products which have relatively little physical physical differentiation, such as beverages and cigarettes. Probably one of the outstanding successes of this kind was the carving of a major market share for Marlboro cigarettes (see appended material at end of the chapter.)

Constancy and generalization are virtual identical twin tendencies very closely related to the closure group. But they differ slightly in one respect: they are based on relatively direct experience.

Constancy and Generalization

Both our visual perceptions and our mental images differ substantially from those of cameras. Although our retina does show the same kind of images that a camera film does, our perception of that image is quite different. On the camera film, a dinner plate shows various profiles, depending on the angle. We always see it as round, however viewed. Whether standing directly in front of a cow, or looking at it from the side at some distance, the head is perceived as the same size relatively to the rest of the animal. To a camera, the close-up front image has a head bigger than the rest of the animal. We perceive things the way we do because of long learning and experience.

Furthermore, we generalize from such experiences. Having learned how round objects appear from different angles, we can interpret correctly the shape of even unfamiliar round objects, however presented.

We generalize on our transaction experiences also. A seller of a well-established brand of any product can introduce some other product of the same general class and achieve a solid market share much easier than can a new and unknown seller. Call it "market acceptance" or "consumer franchise", success breeds success with new introductions.

The way all of these tendencies work differs with different market segments. How they work, and how well, depends on the aspects of offering or communications which draw the attention of the buyers. One factor is the figure and ground phenomenon.

Figure and Ground: the Effect of Point of View

As already indicated, we choose to pay attention to those elements in a situation which touch on our desires at the moment. This affects our perception of the total situation, however much heed we pay to the full context. We select out certain aspects as important to us--as "figure", to use the psychologist's term--and subordinate the other details as mere background ("ground", to use the psychological jargon). Figure 2 uses two well-known visual examples of the effect of figure and ground.

To some extent, what we choose as figure is a matter of personal needs and interest. We vote for the Congressional candidate because he favors a number of issues important to us, overlooking other matters on which the candidate is not in agreement. In the case of the Marlboro campaign, the ladies bought in quantity for a reason quite opposite to the intended message of the campaign. They bought the package, not the implied virility theme.

FIGURE 2. FIGURE AND GROUND: VISUAL EXAMPLES

Which do you see first:

    A bird bath or vase?
         or
    Two silhouetted faces?

Now look again: can you see the other possibilty?

Can you see both at the same time?

Now look at this: What can you see?

Automatic Physical Responses: Habitual Motor Procedures

All automatic response patterns serve a basic survival function. None of us can hope to carry out any task efficiently by carefully considering every possible stimulus in the environment, or even every muscular move in every task. To be able to function at all, we select only a few well-understood clues in the environment for attention. To carry out physical tasks efficiently, we develop habitual sequences of action, and learn to carry them out at some accustomed rhythm, reducing the whole to a thoroughly unconscious level which bypasses the time taken by conscious thought.

Constructing the best procedure and reducing it to a smooth, unconscious procedure, takes substantial time, practice, and effort. If we have to change any element in this procedure in order to gain a greater measure of some benefit, we have to spend at least as much effort to bring the procedure back to the conscious level, and then undergo another learning curve to acquire the new procedure. This is a very high price to pay, and requires a highly credible promise of benefits exceeding the perceived cost.

For this reason, any offering which can be fitted smoothly into an established habit pattern needs to promise a far smaller benefit than one which requires the relearning of any significant detail in established procedures.

The learning requirement price is equally important whether the learning involves a physical habit or the mental habits of perceptions and attitudes.

Attitudes: The Habits Creating Motivation and Value

Attitudes can be defined as general predispositions to evaluate whole classes of offerings, symbols, situations or other stimuli in a specifically favorable or unfavorable light. Attitudes are tendencies, predetermined ahead of any specific situation, to choose to act in one given direction or avoid actions in another direction. "Bias" and "prejudice" are synonyms. All these terms denote a readiness to act in a specific direction. Any attitude is a combination of a set of beliefs in some degree of harmony with a corresponding set of feelings and of resulting action.

Attitudes include such concepts as patronage loyalty, personal taste, personal perceptions of value, perceptions of what is worth paying a price for, and how high that price can be. Much of the task of sellers is to create an attitude favorable to their offerings, or to maintain favorable attitudes in the face of competition.

The Dimensions of Attitudes

Attitudes have dimension as well as direction. We have relatively little depth of commitment to some - such as our choice of gasoline brand - and may change them readily. Some are quite complex and carry a heavy commitment in our total life styles. Such might be a chain smoker's attitudes toward cigarettes.

The degree of commitment or tolerance can be indicated by the ratio of alternative choices deemed acceptable, to those considered unacceptable. The narrower the tolerance, the greater the commitment and the more resistant to change. Convenience goods are those categories toward which few buyers have any great depth of commitment, specialty goods those toward which most customers have such depth of commitment that they admit few or no alternatives.

The depth and type of buyer commitment clearly affects the ability of sellers to gain market share. Such shifts are easiest when the offering is within the range of tolerance, somewhat more difficult, but not impossible, when the object is to shift a brand from the uncommitted range to the acceptable. They are hardly ever worth the effort when the attitude is completely negative, classing the offering in the rejected group. Marketing's history is replete with examples of brands whose reputation had declined so much that a fresh market entry had to be carried out under a different label.

As with the other forms of automatic responses, attitudes are formed because they help maximize some form of satisfaction or avoid some kind of sacrifice. The purposes served have been classified by function (Katz, 1960) into four groups: utilitarian or instrumental, value-expressive, ego-defensive, and knowledge-integrating.

Utilitarian attitudes are adopted primarily to minimize search effort, and probably carry much less emotional commitment than the other three types. Generally, they are based on experience with similar situations. Brand loyalty, patronage loyalty and taste preferences are of this character.

Value-expressive attitudes enable the buyers to give expression to the types of persons they think of themselves as being. Purchases are made to identify themselves with specific groups, a specific social status, or a specific life style. They are intended to say, "This is the kind of person I am."

Teen-agers adopt the hair style and mode, even the brand, of dress currently popular with their peers--primarily to distinguish themselves from earlier teen groups and to assert their growing independence from their families. The social climber works hard to gain the exclusive club membership, buys a prestige make of automobile, moves to the "right" neighborhood--all to proclaim to himself and others, "See, I have arrived."

Those who have not only really arrived, but were there from birth, may engage in anti-status consumption, to demonstrate that their position is so well known they need not display it. A wealthy farmer of the author's acquaintance, who owned half the mortgages in the area, always went to town in a pair of well-worn overalls, driving an ancient, low price car.

Ego-defensive attitudes lead to purchases which help to shield the buyers from unpleasant objective truths about themselves or their life situations. It is the ghetto customer who buys the premium brands of shoes and liquor, rather than the much better off middle class customer. It is the woman who needs a tentmaker for dresses who spends heavily on hair-dos, the man with the tire around the middle who patronizes the custom tailor. All are saying something like, "I am not poor, I am not unattractive."

Knowledge-integrating attitudes attempt to group under some simple label the complex realities of the world and its marketplaces. "Natural" became the approved adjective for the special best in the 1970's and 1980's, superceding any attention to more meaningful measures. "Low calorie" and "light-"whatever became a magic label even for foods and beverages which were more likely to add to the waistline than the reverse. In politics, the simplistic labels of "liberal" and "conservative" have often grouped together a wide range of philosophies.

DO BRAND LOYALTIES DEVELOP MERELY TO ROUTINIZE CHOICES?

An experiment conducted by W. T. Tucker indicated that many buyers can develop brand loyalties even when the offerings are objectively identical in every way, with no inference of any difference.

The researchers secured the cooperation of 42 housewives living in the same section of the city with an experiment on "how women go about purchasing when they moved to a new location and were faced with unfamiliar brands." Each was visited at her home on 12 different occasions and offered her choice of any one of four loaves of bread, presented side-by-side on a tray. All loaves were of the same single type of bread, all were packaged identically, and all four were from the same baking batch.

The brand label was the only perceivable difference – a single capital letter, L, M, P, and H. The position of the loaves was rotated on succesive visits, so that no "brand" was in the same position twice in a row. No suggestion was made or implied as to any possible difference in the loaves offered. The respondent was simply asked to take one, and a notation was made of her choice.

Usually after trying the other brands, 21 of the 42 housewives settled on a single choice 3 times in a row. At that point, her loyalty was tested by taping a penny to the brand she chose least often. If she did not choose the loaf with the premium, an additional penny was taped to that loaf on each succesive visit, up to a maximum possible 7 cents. None switched for one penny. Six switched for amounts varying from 2 cents to 7 cents. Eight respondents never switched, despite the incentive.

Of the 21 housewives who never developed a brand loyalty, 5 developed a position loyalty, always choosing the loaf with the same position on the tray. The loyalties of 3 of these was also tested with the pennies. Two switched for premiums of 1 and 2 cents, respectively. The third switched to another non-premium brand.

Thus, out of the 42 housewives participating, 26 developed some sort of routinizing choice, and some would not switch even with a significant price difference.

(W. T. Tucker,"The development of brand loyalty," **Journal of Marketing Research,** Vol.3, August, 1964, pp. 32-35)

Attitudes really define the person. But, for the most part, they are not part of our original equipment. They are mostly learned, with two possible exceptions discussed below.

The Sources of Our Attitudes

Some part of our attitudes developed through learning. The feelings, beliefs, and accompanying reaction tendencies became fixed by association of actions with need satisfactions. Experiences which occasioned pleasure reinforced an approach attitude. Those which caused pain taught us to avoid them. A major part of the thoughts, beliefs and emotional reactions have come to us in social communications with those we viewed as important people.

Many of the instrumental attitudes certainly grew out of direct experience with a few alternatives. But even in these cases, it is unlikely that all possible alternatives were tried out. Whenever possible, we probably short-circuited the search by seeking suggestions from trusted associates and acquaintances. In any event, the search ceased when we found a reasonably satisfactory source of satisfaction.

In the Tucker bread choice experiment previously cited, one of the housewives stayed with her first choice, and 3 of those who became brand loyal stayed with their final choices before trying all four "brands."

Even many, if not most, of our utilitarian attitudes come out of conditioning in the family and other face-to-face groups, as part of the subculture. Most taste preferences come from this source. There is no question that our allocation of spending arises out of our cultural contacts. Our spending patterns virtually define our class status.

What our group and class culture transmits is essentially a set of attitudes and use-systems. Individuals first employ an item in a specific use pattern to conform to the group and gain social approval. Continued usage creates familiarity. Experiments have shown that, when starting from a neutral position, familiarity is enough to establish a favorable attitude.

Although expressions of a personal feeling, both ego-defensive and value-expressive attitudes gain their entire meaning from the values of those groups to which the holders look for approval. The manufacturers cannot build prestige into the high-end products by merely trying. They gain such images from association with the social group standards.

Learned attitudes comprise by far the greatest part of anyone's personality. They are as many and as diverse as the purchase and other reaction motives to which they give rise. For two special tendencies important to the marketer, however, there is strong evidence for a congenital origin. These tendencies are the individual's basic attitude toward learning situations, and what experiments indicate is a universal drive for stimulus variation.

FAMILIARITY BREEDS LIKING, NOT CONTEMPT

Two classic psychological experiments indicate that familiarity is likely to lead to positive attitudes, even when forced.

Maslow (1937) had 15 students take part in a 10-day series of 2-hour sessions, covering a mix of activities which included viewing a number of paintings by well-known artists and spelling the names of Russian women, in the first few sessions. In the later sessions, the format was changed without warning: they were asked to express their personal preferences. In one session, for example, they were asked to choose between the paintings previously viewed and paired painting by the same artists. There was a marked tendency to prefer the familiar items.

Krugman (1943) assigned two groups of students to listen to a type of music they seldom listened to for 8 weeks. Those who preferred classical music were given swing records, those preferring swing were given classical records. At the end of the 8 weeks, both sets of students had acquired a favorable attitude toward the form of music previously shunned.

Reactions to New Experiences

Promotion of some form of innovation is basic to marketing success. Few customers are overready to accept the new, however--especially any substantially unfamiliar item. Although some cultures are especially resistant to innovation, a wide range of personal differences cuts across all classes and cultural groups, and even varies widely within families. As will be seen later, the degree of resistance varies with the amount of use-system learning involved.

The result, whatever the degree of learning, is a well established curve of adoption and diffusion for any new product.

A well-designed psychological study found that, even at two weeks of age, reactions to new experiences varied from ready acceptance to complete and rigid rejection. The individual patterns proved thoroughly persistent throughout a follow-up period reaching into the teen years of those studied. Members of the same family could be at opposite ends of the same range. There was no relationship to intelligence level or any social factor. (Alexander Thomas, et al,"The Origin of Personality," **Scientific American,** vol.223, no.2, Aug. 1970, p. 102)

When the obvious inborn differences in types of ability and resulting interests are taken into account, it is no wonder that only a small percentage of the market is venturesome.

By contrast, the drive for stimulus variation seems to be a constant across all subjects studied.

The Drive for Stimulus Variation

Psychological research seems to have established that something which can be labelled as a "drive for stimulus variation" is virtually universal. Experiments conducted with people in a stimulus-free environment proved them to be driven to seek some kind of new stimulus.

In any event, clear experience reveals the strong appeal of the element of novelty in the marketing of any new introductions. As will be indicated later, fads catch on quickly because they are pure novelty, requiring no significant learning. Novelty is an obvious element in the fashion cycle. It is also one factor in aiding the introduction of major market innovations of any kind.

Whether of social origin (as the vast majority of attitudes are) or congenital, as a very few tendencies may be, attitudes influence all transaction choices. They vary in their scope, of course. Some concern extremely broad topics, like those toward specific spending categories, world affairs, religion, or racial relations. Others concern trivial details of taste.

Whatever their origin, topic and content, attitudes are important buying influences because they involve some of the more basic emotions as well as complete systems of belief and related actions. Changing them means modifying all three elements: emotional commitments, beliefs, and the actions themselves. The research on this effort carries the label of cognitive balance and cognitive dissonance.

Cognitive Balance, Cognitive Dissonance, and Attitude Change

Balance theory and dissonance theory rest on experimental evidence that people are moved to convince themselves and others that they act rationally, that their beliefs, emotions and actions are in harmony. When any one of these three elements of an attitude are disturbed in any way, the individual tends to adjust the other two to bring all three into a consistent pattern.

If some event or influence causes an individual to change beliefs, he must either adjust feelings and subsequent actions to correspond, or repress conflicting factual evidence to protect the feelings and actions.

Although most advertising and sales communications aim at a change in beliefs, changes in belief are not the only way to change the balance. A change in the emotional associations can bring changes in belief, as can some forced change in the action itself. Heavy smokers, who previously failed all attempts to break their habit, find it possible to quit when faced with a diagnosis of incipient lung cancer, or experience a heart attack.

Even an artificially induced action can modify the attitude balance. Experiments which required subjects to defend a position they opposed tended to shift toward the position they defended (Cohen, A., **Attitude Change and Social Influence**, Basic Books, 1954). The highly questionable sales tactic of "bait and switch" succeeds on the principle of employing a mouth-watering bargain offer to lure the unsuspecting to commit themselves to active purchase consideration. When the offered item is shown to be unsuitable, many prospects are then switched to a much more attractive model at a price they would have originally rejected outright.

In the Tucker bread experiment, those who became brand loyal, under the rather artificial experimental conditions, came to perceive major differences in the really identical loaves. When premium pennies were taped to the rejected brands, they are reported to have remarked, "No wonder you put the special on Brand P--it's the worst one of all!"

The use of some form of sampling for new introductions is one application of the use of an action change to alter brand loyalties by reducing the purchase cost risks and inducing use over a period of time.

CHANGING BELIEFS DOES NOT ALWAYS CHANGE ACTION

Those who are convinced that advertising and publicity alone can swing buying habits should review the experience with nearly two decades of the effort to get our countrymen to stop smoking.

The movement really started in the late 1940's, when a series of articles in consumer magazines published the research evidence of the relationship betwen smoking and cancer of the lung. The early publicity received little attention or credence from even the general public. But the authoritative character of the official Surgeon General's report of 1964, and the backing of the White House, could not be ignored. Not only did non-smokers and pipe smokers accept the conclusions of the report, but even 3 cigarette smokers out of 5 were ready to believe that the link of cigarette smoking to cancer was proved, according to a study conducted in Santa Monica, CAlifornia shortly after the report. (Harold H. kassarjian and Joel B. Cohen, "Cognitive Dissonance and Consumer Behavior," **California Management Review,** vol.8 (Fall, 1965), pp.55-64.)

Nevertheless, only 9 per cent of the Santa Monica smokers had quit smoking, and the national sales drop was of about the same magnitude. Moreover, sales returned to normal within 4 months of the report, and continued to increase thereafter. The evidence was rejected by 3 smokers out of 10. The rest had to dispel the imbalance between their beliefs and action in some other way.

Of the Santa Monica residents who accepted the evidence, about 1 in 5 minimized it: "lots of hazards in life", not much of a threat to me", "can die of many things". Nearly 2 out of 5 simply claimed they could not stop. About 1 in 8 claimed worse alternatives: smoking was better than "taking pills", "becoming a nervous wreck", "excessive drinking". The rest had resolved to "stop soon".

The opposite of cognitive balance--cognitive dissonance or imbalance--is involved in every transaction because all transactions tend to be the result of a conflicting set of motives. At the very least, all purchases require the sacrifice of some resources. Part of the job of advertising and after-purchase service is to reduce this dissonance by reinforcing the perceptions of the positive aspects of the transaction. Studies have shown that new car owners were much more likely to read advertising for the make purchased than were their neighbors who owned older cars.

The Relationship Between Attitudes, Motives, and Action

Attitudes are unquestionably major forces shaping purchase motivation. But neither attitudes nor motives are either product or brand specific, even if we know their exact identity.

Neither attitudes nor motives are subject to precise measurement. They are internal mental patterns which must be inferred from external evidence of some kind. In addition, all significant transactions result from a mixture of motives, and the same item may be bought by one customer for one reason, by another to satisfy a different set of motives or as the end result of a different attitude. One customer may patronize the prestige store because the offerings, prices and quality assortments just match his/her needs. Another may buy there because it is the place "to be seen in." Some go to the opera to be seen, some to enjoy the music.

Generally speaking, the real motives attached to noninstrumental actions are not held at a conscious level. The analysis of such motives depends on the analyst, and two equally skilled analysts may come up with opposite interpretations.

Attitudes alone do not result in purchases: only those attitudes which are connected with a salient felt need at the time. The purchase behavior resulting from any motive depends on at least five conditions:
  - A knowledge of some means for satisfying the motive
  - Absence of any conflicting motive which is stronger or higher in the hierarchy
  - Presence of a significant incentive to purchase. Prospects must be convinced of benefits which they value more than the cost
  - The probability of satisfaction must be credible
  - There must be no significant inhibiting anxiety

Knowledge of How to Satisfy a Motive. The major part of the marketing effort is to increase the knowledge within specific market segments, of how they can satisfy their motives with the sellers' own offerings.

Absence of a Conflicting Stronger Motive. However good the match between needs and offering, only those desires at the top of the hierarchy get attention and purchase consideration.

Importance of an Adequate Incentive. This should be obvious, but the number of me-too introductions indicates that it gets overlooked. There must be some promise of substantially greater satisfaction than is available from some perceived alternate use of the same resources for a similar or different kind of offering. The value offered must be perceived as really promising a unique and valuable benefit.

The Need for Credibility of Benefit Promise. Because the buyer will have to sacrifice some resources to get the benefit, he must perceive the chance of getting satisfaction as very high.

There is no simple way of accomplishing credibility, but it usually takes more than a mere claim. The way in which the claim is presented makes a difference. As the Marlboro story illustrates, it may be necessary to so present the claim that the prospect himself draws a conclusion which might be brushed off if claimed explicitly. It is always better if the claim is put forward by someone other than the seller. A publicity release published in a respected medium will get far more attention and belief than the same presentation in an advertisement. The use of endorsements by outsiders, even in ads, is one attempt to gain greater credibility. Often, only trial of the offering is adequate to gain credibility, and various means of getting sample trials may be the only effective means.

The Inhibiting Effect of Anxiety. Anxiety is the hallmark of any transition period in any person's life. A high degree of anxiety in any situation tends to inhibit the taking of perceived risks, especially purchases which are perceived as deviating from conformity to a reference group's standards. Presentations aimed at those passing through such transition periods need to be made in the context of conformity.

All of the automatic response patterns would seem to make innovation difficult, and they do. They are mental and physical ruts which are easier to follow than to get out of. Fortunately, there are offsetting factors which present opportunities to those who know how to use them to gain market success.

Factors Facilitating Marketing Innovation

Despite the imposing list of market stabilizing factors indicated above, the fast-moving dynamics of the modern marketplace gives clear evidence of countervailing factors which combine to favor both planned and unplanned change. In fact, a constant stream of changes in demand patterns creates the certainty that the only risk greater than that of innovation is the certainty that the seller who avoids innovation will sooner or later lose his market.

Five major factors create competitive opportunities and propel the dynamics of innovation:
- The complexity of the desire set behind every purchase, coupled with the necessity of accepting design compromises
- The changing nature and the increasing diversity of the desire sets as the market passes through the various stages of its life cycle
- The constant turnover of the occupants of any market segment
- The constant changes in the social structure and in the legal, political and economic environments affecting consumption
- The drive for stimulus variation

Complexity of the Desire Set and Resulting Design Compromise

Customers economize their shopping effort by looking for satisfaction of a whole bundle of desires in every purchase. When we enter either the restaurant or our own kitchen, we are looking for more than mere hunger appeasement. Unless really on the edge of pure starvation, we seek flavor, variety, perhaps a social setting and atmosphere ("ambience"), and possibly other factors. The choice made may even override nutritional needs. At some point, cost will dictate some kind of compromise.

The list of desires is usually so broad that some of the attributes desired in the offering sought are inevitably in conflict with attainment of other desired attributes. In addition, the bundle of satisfactions fulfilled which is most attractive to one customer will most certainly fall short of satisfaction for other customers, with different desire sets.

Mass production and distribution, which keep cost down, require a limited set of standardized designs which leave many consumers at the fringes of the various segments less than well satisfied with any of the available choices. This opens opportunities for the insightful competitor who can produce a design fitting the needs of fragments of various fringe segments and carve his own niche in the market.

Changes in Demand Patterns Over the Market Life Cycle

The composition of the desired satisfaction bundles changes and diversifies as the market advances through the various stages of its life cycle. Early customers are seeking mainly the core group of satisfactions, and a single model is adequate. Once these are gained, and the novelty aspect wears off, satiation sets in with respect to the core functions. Increasing familiarity with the possibilities of the offering adds to a growing set of desires, as new segments enter the market with diverse sets of desires.

The broadening and diversifying market opens opportunities for competition unless the original producer anticipates and preempts all of them. For all of Alfred Sloan's organizing and marketing genius, GM might still never have gained dominance if Henry Ford had not held so stubbornly to his Model T design, refusing to recognize the growing importance of styling and the closed body designs (which were far too heavy for the Model T chassis).

Customer Turnover and the Eternal Searchers

Few offerings, if any, enjoy a relatively constant demand over the life of any individual customer. For most customers, the span of the heavy consumption years is very limited, often no more than 5 to 10 years. Thus any offering can expect constant losses of previously good customers. They must be replaced by constant additions of new customers. Being new, these have, as yet, no established buying habits. Their patronage is open to any competitor, new or old, with an offering of a similar design, or with quite different offerings satisfying the same desires.

In addition, every market segment includes a few restless expert customers who constantly search for less design compromise. They have no hesitancy in trying the new which offers any hope of substantial improvement in some desired benefit. It is this group of innovators which creates the initial market for new offering revisions and the really new offerings.

The Drive for Stimulus Variation

As already noted, people tend to seek what might be designated as a frequent change in scenery. Satiation dulls the appeal of some of the fringe aspects of the offerings they buy, and they seek some change in at least the surface, or cosmetic aspects. Thus we can observe a constant cyclical change in tastes of every kind--the fashion cycle. As noted later, these cycles pervade every aspect of our lives, from the "rag trade" of women's clothing to the executive offices and board room organizations of multinational corporations. The same drive is responsible for the much shorter lives of fads, and also adds extra value to new offerings during their initial introduction.

Changes in the Marketing Environment

Fashions and fads involve the values which constitute the emotional components of some of our more important social, economic and political attitudes. These values also are subject to changes over time as the structure of our society and the economy change, creating cognitive dissonances which must be adjusted. Generally, these changes in value mean changes in consumption habits, both for ideas and for purchases.

As the United States passed from a rural economy to an urban one in the middle of this century, the economic roles of women changed drastically, in two phases. In the first phase, women lost the equal economic role which they played as direct producers on the farms, where they had full time tasks in food processing and production. Then, with post World War II inflation, they began to flow into the general urban labor force. The two-income family became the norm, the housewives who stayed home the minority. The result: a growing market for semi-prepared and convenience foods. Where the food stores once needed space only for the basic baking ingredients of flour, shortening, eggs and flavorings, they must now open whole aisles of prepared mixes and ready-to-serve foods and even meals. The electric dishwasher has taken over the cleanup tasks.

Similarly, the industrialization and population concentrations have created pollution problems which began to destroy the recreational uses of streams and countryside, spawning a conservation movement which created markets for new laws, and also a whole set of new consumption systems ("natural foods") and other new products. Whole new industries were created, and dormant ones revived (wood stoves, for example).

Can the Customers' Demands be Predicted?

The customer is thus always changing, both in tastes and identity. To what extent can the marketer predict consumer behavior? In the individual case, the task is probably not worth the effort. We need too much information to do the job. In terms of groups of customers, of definable segments, the task is quite manageable, must in fact be undertaken. We have learned a great deal about how the market is segmented, and how each segment reacts. Many of these segments change consumption patterns very slowly, even though the identity of the occupants of the segments are in constant flux.

SUMMARY

All transactions originate in the desires of the customers. A handful of psychological concepts can serve to aid the understanding of how these desires arise and impute value to the satisfaction of these desires.

All purchase decisions are shaped by three groups of automatic responses, or habits: the mental habits of perception and of attitudes and the physical habit procedures involved in product usage.

Customers select only those offerings for attention which are perceived as promising satisfaction of the topmost desire sets in their hierarchy of desires. Because all of us have an almost infinite number of unfulfilled desires, all desires exist in some kind of temporary hierarchy. Those perceived as having the greatest immediate value are at the top of the hierarchy of desires.

All perceptions are shaped by three kinds of patterns which may differ from objective reality. Differences in such stimuli as offering benefits and prices are recognized as substantive only when they exceed a significant value known as the j.n.d (just noticeable difference). People try to organize everything which they perceive as part of a given situation into a single meaningful whole. They may add details suggested by the context and proximity to arrive at their own concept of that meaning. Finally, some details which are actually present in a situation will be ignored as "ground" (background) in order to determine what is meant by the rest(the important "figure" of the situation).

Attitudes are sets of generalized reaction tendencies which form the basis for judging value. They involve a set of beliefs, a set of feelings compatible with these beliefs, and a set of possible actions which would flow from the other two elements. All three elements must be perceived as in balance, called "cognitive consonance." When this balance is disturbed by any event which changes any of the three components (action, beliefs, or feelings), the resulting "cognitive dissonance" causes the person to find some way to bring the system back into balance. Since the design compromises of most purchases tend to result in such internal conflicts, they often seek reassurance of the values bought.

All purchases are the result of mixed approach and avoidance motives, if only because all require some sacrifice. Physical use-system procedures are acquired only through long practice and effort. Changing them takes more than twice as much effort. Thus prospects will tend to avoid offerings which require habit relearning, are much quicker to adopt new offerings which fit into the same routines.

All of these automatic reactions tend to resist the forces of innovation which are the lifeblood of marketing competition. These are offset by five factors facilitating entry of new competition: design compromise and satiation of salient desires, the changing pattern and diversification of demand as offerings pass through their market life cycles, customer turnover within market segments and the existence of eternal searchers, the drive for stimulus variation, and finally, the ever changing social, economic and political environment of marketing.

FOOD FOR THOUGHT AND DISCUSSION

CIGARETTE PRICES: SOFTENING THE TAX BLOW

Cigarette taxes have long been a useful source of Federal revenue. For decades the tax on a package of cigarettes was more than the cost of the ingredients. From 1959 to 1982, while the price of nearly everything, including cigarettes, tripled and quadrupled, the tax on a pack of cigarettes remained at 8 cents. Facing a huge 1983 Federal deficit, Congress voted a doubling of the tax in the summer of 1982, to take effect the following January (amid industry howls about what it would do to their sales and to the poor tobacco farmer).

Early in October, Philip announced an immediate wholesale price increase of 4 cents a pack. Other producers followed suit. The announced reason: to soften the effect of the coming increase in January. At the time, cigarettes cost the consumer less than 60 cents per pack at some points in the Carolinas (with almost negligible state taxes on cigarettes) to much more in states that taxed cigarettes heavily.

1. Why should raising the per pack price in two steps in a four month span make any difference in the effect of the total 8 cent price change?
2. What do you think the real short term effect of the price rise, however it is handled, have on sales volume? Why?
3. What do you think the long term effect of a price rise of 8 cents could be? Why?

TONI TEACHES THE WOMEN TO CURL THEIR OWN HAIR

One recurrent fashion cycle is for curly hair-dos. This raises problems for those whose hair cross-section is too round to curl. For generations, the only answer was to curl strands of the hair around a hot iron, which would temporarily flatten it enough. The only problem was that such a curl would, at best, last through one day.

Then the electrical hair permanent machine was developed. This gave the hair a wave that lasted until the growth of new straight hair required a new treatment - usually from 3 to 5 months. The machine, so-called, consisted of a bank of curling electrodes attached to a hooded stand. A skilled beauty operator wound strands of hair around the curlers, and baked the hair for about one-half hour.

Although some other lotions and supplies were used, the electrical permanent was essentially a set of more effficient curling irons, operating in a single bank. There was another difference: the curling had to be done by a skilled beauty operator. The beauty parlor business boomed from the middle 1920's on.

In the early 1940's, a machineless permanent was developed. The new entry consisted of some pads impregnated with a chemical which heated up when wet. This new thermo-chemical pad was wound with the hair around curlers, then moistened. The machines were obsoleted, and the machineless permanent replaced them in the beauty parlors.

Seeing the possibility of doing such a permanent at home, a firm introduced "Charm Curl" kits in the stores, at $1.25. At the time, the beauty parlors charged from $5.00 up to $25, depending on the reputation of the operators. A small Minnesota wholesaler of beauty parlor supplies, the Harris family, decided that this might be a good added market, and developed a similar kit, pricing it at $1.00 retail. They decided to force distribution by the lower price and some advertising.

The Harris venture backfired. The advertising used up the firm's working capital and produced no sales. Shortly afterward, Charm Curl also dropped out of the market. The thermochemical method worked well under trained operators, but not in the home.

Then, just as World War II drew to a close, a true chemical permanent was developed. This consisted of a mild alkaline solution which deformed the hair when it was wound around curlers with a pad and kept wet for some period. Charm Curl reentered the market with the chemical product, but with no substantial advertising.

The Harrises decided on a new market entry, but with a different strategy than before. Perceiving that their real competition was the beauty parlor $5.00 plus price, their new entry was to be priced at $1.75 to generate promotional funds. The initial distribution was confined to St. Paul, Minnesota, and to be branded "Toni". An initial supply was made ready, then salesmen called on every cosmetic counter in the city. An initial inventory was left with each retailer, on consignment, if necessary. And the salesgirl behind the counter was given a free kit to try out herself. With all stores stocked, full page, long copy newspaper ads broke the news to the public.

The timing was accidental, but perfect. With the end of the war, many families had more claims on their purses than money in them, especially the 15 million veterans returning to set up their homes. No major home appliances had been available for nearly five years, and no automobiles. Even the household linen supplies needed replenishing. Families were seeking ways to stretch incomes in a period of rapidly rising prices. Curly hair was the style, and the beauty parlor bill looked high in terms of 1940's dollars and in the light of the host of home furnishing demands on the family pocketbook.

Moreover, the free kits to the cosmetic counter salespeople had worked. When women asked about the product, most salespeople could give it their own testimonial, in person. Reorders started coming in, and money.

Now to establish an advertising budget to follow up the initial success. The rule was simple: all net returns were to be poured into radio and newspapers (TV was not yet a mass medium). The Harrisses were aware that market growth would not be automatic. Most women would still have to be convinced that the product gave a good-looking permanent, and that they really could do it themselves. This would take an overwhelming promotional effort, and the small size of the individual sale precluded any direct person to person sales effort.

Fortunately for the Harrises, toiletries are a no-capital-cost, high margin class of products. Contract manufacture was readily available, and ingredient costs were a minor fraction of the selling price. By limiting their effort to a single market, and pouring all promotion into that market, they mounted a saturation radio campaign, as much as several times a day, nearly every day of the week. Quiz shows were one choice, when available.

The theme was simple: you can do it yourself. This was presented partly in the form of "the Toni Twins", featured in the print advertising, and to audiences of the quiz shows. This consisted of presenting identical twin models with identical hair-dos, and the question,"which is the Toni?" This was supplemented by drawing women from the audience who had been identified as Toni users, and asking about their experience with the product. These testimonials were unrehearsed and spontaneous, with sometimes unexpected results. On one occasion (when the market had been expanded to enough cities to justify national network) a woman who was questioned about her Toni replied:

> "When I went to get the train to get here, I did not have time to
> get to the beauty parlor. Just as I was boarding the train, a friend
> thrust this package in my hand. I didn't know what it was. When I
> opened it on the train, it was a Toni kit. So I went to the ladies
> lounge and gave myself a Toni."
> [M. C.,"How did it work?"]
> "Well, it wasn't easy!"

The strategy worked. Within months, the St. Paul market was saturated, with Toni getting three-fourths of the home waving market and an added half of the beauty parlor business. Then, and not until then, did Toni start distribution in next door Minneapolis (despite the overlap of their broadcast advertising). Success in the neighboring Twin City was equally quick, and was followed up by a city-by-city expansion of the national market, reaching New York at the end, three years later. Only after national distribution was achieved did any significant competition enter the market. Toni was always able to keep ahead of new brands, and maintain market dominance.

1. What elements in the environment opened the opportunity for the Toni success?
2. What elements in their strategy do you think made that success possible?
3. The toiletry industry is highly competitive, even cutthroat. Why do you suppose no major toiletry company entered the market until Toni was well entrenched?
4. What likely later events, other than direct competitors, do you think could set back their sales?
5. What was the key benefit in their offering which attracted buyers? Why did it have a high perceived value at that moment in time?

IF HANDED A LEMON, SHOULD YOU MAKE LEMONADE?

Reputations, whether of people or products, are nothing more than habitual perceptions of what to expect from the holders. From the standpoint of those who grant the reputations, they represent sets of attitudes, negative or positive, toward the holder. As with all forms of habit, reversing a reputation is an extremely costly and difficult task. People who are the object of bad reputations have little choice but to make the extended effort required if they wish to reverse other people's perceptions of them. Sellers have another choice: they can abandon offerings and make a new start under new labels, under the assumption that it is easier to sell a new label than to refurbish a tarnished reputation.

Walter P. Chrysler tried both ways after he took charge of the faltering Maxwell-Chalmers Co. in 1920. At the time, Maxwell had begun to acquire the reputation as a "lemon", due to a weak axle. Chrysler first remedied the weak axle to get rid of the heavy overstock, then went on to improve sales, culminating with an attractive new model in 1924. Apparently deciding that this path was the less rewarding choice, he brought out a completely redesigned, 6-cylinder car under the Chrysler nameplate at the time of the January 1924 auto show, and had an instant success in the middle price class. In three years, profits zoomed from the respectable $4 million dollars he had achieved in 1924 to $46 million.

France's Renault suffered a severe setback as a result of consumer experience with its introduction of the 4CV and the Dauphine in the 1950's. The Dauphine, especially, was initially quite popular. Unfortunately, it was not built to meet American driving conditions, and the very volume of sales backfired. Sales dropped so rapidly that dealers dropped it. Attempts to gain distribution with better-designed economy models were unsuccessful until Renault made an alliance with American Motors and, through AMC dealerships, achieved some sales of its low-end Le Car model. At the end of 1982, its hopes were riding on the introduction of of somewhat luxury-oriented Alliance model to be made by AMC in the U. S A.

1. 1924-1927 was a boom period for the auto industry, but also a period in which GM made spectacular progress with new models, under Sloan. Why was Chrysler able to do so much better in the 1925-1927 years than in the previous years, which were also good?

2. Why did Renault have to wait nearly a generation, and even then have to buy its distribution through partial ownership of AMC?

3. What do experiences like these suggest as to the best tactic to win back market support which has been sacrificed through past mistakes?

4. What principles of human behavior explain such experiences?

THE MARLBORO MAN IS BORN

How do you break into a mature market with well established brands, such as cigarettes? Philip Morris did it with "the Marlboro Man" when they decided to go after the growing filter tip market in the 1950's.

Cigarettes are typical of a wide group of consumer products with so little physical differentiation that all blindfold tests have shown that buyers cannot identify their own brands without the label. Yet brand preference is relatively high, based on positioning. The economics of their marketing is such that the leading brand can defend its position with heavy advertising and still have a lower promotional cost per unit than any competitor.

Philip Morris decided to use a filter brand name, Marlboro, which it had acquired when it purchased the Benson & Hedges specialty operation. Originally made with multi-colored tips, Marlboro had a feminine positioning among those who knew it at all, but most smokers knew nothing about the brand. To give the introduction some kind of talking point, the firm developed a simple "hardpack" with a flip-open cover. This was not expected to provide any real sales pull, however. What was needed was a strong "image" of some sort.

Fortunately, not long before, the Chicago Tribune had commissioned a major psychological study of smokers and their motives, and the ad agency, Leo Burnett, Inc. studied this carefully. This study disclosed that the single strongest motive for smoking, among men, was to gain a sense of virility, or potency. This was not a conscious motive, not one of belief. It was a feeling which revealed itself indirectly in respondents' reactions to various psychological tests.

Based on this knowledge, Leo Burnett prepared a series of print and TV ads dominated by a large picture of a male model portrayed in some role popularly associated with the "he-men" stereotype: cowboys, sailors, construction workers, etc., all shown with well muscled arms adorned with a tattoo and faces well lined from outdoor activity. They were shown smoking, of course, but the only package shown was not part of the illustration, but an obvious montage at the corner of the illustration. The copy said nothing about the illustration, only "You get a lot to like in a Marlboro: filter, flavor, flip-top box," sung as a jingle in the TV ads.

Marlboro sales rose quickly, and within just a few years, became neck and neck with the best selling competitor. Subsequent research repeatedly showed that Marlboro had a very strong masculine image. Post-introduction research also revealed a surprise: women were contributing substantially to sales, and not because of the masculine image. The hardpack appealed to them - it kept packages from being crushed in the jumble of their purses.

One interesting postscript: Once Marlboro established its niche, a smaller filter brand, Viceroy, decided to develop a special image for itself. A $5 million campaign was launched under the banner of "the thinking man's cigarette." Well polished male models were shown in obvious outdoor activities, such as sailing, but pictured as engineers, scientists and book lovers, also. Both verbally and in print, the models talked specifically of smoking a "thinking man's cigarette." Subsequent market share statistics did not show any gain from the campaign.

1. Dozens of cigarette brands have been launched with heavy promotion, especially in recent years. Most have failed, and Marlboro is the one exception which achieved equality or near equality with the leading popular brand of the same type. What elements in the strategy do you think made this major success possible?

2. Which of the tactics used in carrying out the strategy made the strategy successful, and why?

3. Why was the Viceroy campaign so ineffective?

THE INDIVIDUAL SEARCH FOR STIMULUS VARIATION: BRAND AND FLAVOR SWITCHING

Fashion and fad cycles are social manifestations of the search for stimulus variation. If this search is a universal drive, we might expect to find some kind of individual buyer manifestations, also. What about the following?

A marketing executive, who decided to take a breather from the corporate world, took over a laundromat operation. His habits of watching consumer reactions followed him however, so he did more than manage revenue and expenses. Commenting later on his experiences, he noted that many women switched detergent brands from time to time, more from a desire for variety (brown granules instead of blue) than for any dissatisfaction with performance.

A woman of the author's acquaintance, with a keen nose for perfumes, regularly changed her face soap purchases about once in three months. She noted that after that time, she no longer smelled the perfume (which all major brands have), and had to have a brand with a different fragrance.

A major seller of cake mixes produces a very wide variety of flavors. The policy is to produce a couple of standbys regularly, but rotate the other flavors, never selling more than a half dozen at any one time. Their market position is excellent.

1. What other drive seems to be involved here?
2. What does this suggest as to the best product policy for a retailer or distributor? For a manufacturer of offerings with little objective differentiation?
3. What similar phenomena have you observed?

CHAPTER 4. HOW CUSTOMERS CLUSTER: MARKET SEGMENTATION

Market segments: a useful concept, not a set of pigeonholes
Demographic segmentation
Cultural segmentation
    National and regional differences
    Social class segmentation
    Social role segmentation
      The critical importance of role transition periods
    Lifestyle segmentation
Functional segmentation
    The differences between ultimate consumers and the six
        functional segments
    Industrial markets
    Institutional buyers
    Commercial customers
    Agricultural markets
    Professional prescribers
    Governmental customers

HOW CUSTOMERS CLUSTER: MARKET SEGMENTATION

4

The planning of a marketing strategy must start from the identification of a group of market segments that are open to an offering which the seller is in an advantageous position to make available.

All markets are segmented in the sense that different clusters of potential buyers are seeking to satisfy substantially different bundles of desires. Buyers vary widely in the values they perceive in any given component want within that bundle. Thus even the segment clusters contain possible subdivisions.

Markets can be usefully segmented in several directions. Most segments are essentially cultural in their origin, but some are based on economic function and others on personality factors. Among the various types of measures used to identify and measure them are such demographics as residence, income, age, and sex, direct correlates of cultural factors such as social class indicators, nationality, and geographic region, lifestyle factors, and the economic purpose served by the purchase. Segment boundaries are blurred, blending into adjacent boundaries.

Market Segments: Not a Set of Pigeonholes

To some degree, market segments are a creation of the economics of standardized mass production. Variations in desire sets arise from such diverse sources that it hardly extreme to speculate that the number of possible segments might be as great as the number of possible buyers. Only universal custom production could hope to come close to meeting everyone's desire sets. Customers, however, are aware that custom production would involve such high unit costs that few could come into the market. So buyers settle for some benefit bundle/value compromise made available through mass production.

The inevitable consequence of this variation is that any market segment is a mix of potential customers. Each segment consists of a core group whose desire sets are as close as possible to complete fulfillment, and a surrounding fringe whose desire sets are less well met in varying degrees. At the edge of every segment will be customers who are equally dissatisfied with all available offerings.

Market segments are therefore not analogous to the segments of an orange, with sharply defined boundaries and a relatively uniform content. They are more like the color bands in a rainbow, with one color shading into the adjacent bands. The variation is multi-directional because of the multi-faceted nature of the different desire sets and their manifold origins.

As with the rainbow's bands, identifiable clusters are obvious, the result of the finite number of major forces creating the different desire sets. These forces are of two general types. The more important, and most easily identified and measured, are external to the individual. The rest are largely related to personality factors.

Most of the external forces are more or less correlated with available objective information, permitting useful estimates of the relative size of the segments. Internal personality variables manifest themselves in action and market patterns which permit some rough identification and even quantification. Their greatest value is in product and promotional planning.

The numerous underlying forces tend to conflict. Customer resources are always limited in some degree, and choices must be made. Those choices will be a product of the variables of current resources and the perceived value of satiation of dominant desires. However strong any single underlying force, all of those identified by the segment label will not be equally committed to purchase.

For purposes of strategic planning, it would seem most useful to define a market segment as a mining engineer might define a promising ore body: an identifiable cluster of prospects promising a high assay of profitable customers.

No mining engineer expects to discover any ore body which is a solid vein of 24-carat gold or pure iron, of uniform quality throughout. What he seeks and hopes to find is a large ore body of varying quality that, with the proper mining tactics, will yield a substantial profit. The marketer can hope for no more: only a large group of prospects composed of a profitable proportion of possible buyers. If some method of classifying people identifies such a high assay group of prospects, it is useful to label it a market segment. One of the most widely useful set of segmenting measures are the so-called demographics: the kinds of information available from official censuses. These do not designate markets directly. They are indices of specific physical bases of needs and wants, or synonymous with underlying social and cultural patterns which set general consumption patterns and choices.

Because of the wide variation even within subcultural consumption patterns, sellers have increasingly sought additional indexes which relate to clusters of personal variations in taste and consumption. Various labels have been applied to these personality clusters, the most recent of which is "lifestyle".

However segments are designated, most useful segmentation is defined in

terms of five classes of underlying indicators:
- Pure demographic: variables which are related to physical differences of place, time, age or other quantifiable personal characteristics
- Cultural variables, such as social class, ethnicity, religion, etc.
- The variable of social role
- Personality factors
- The functional economic role of the purchase: personal, professional, commercial, or industrial

Demographic Segmentation

A very useful form of market segmentation for a wide variety of offerings—industrial and commercial as well as final consumer—is furnished by the demographics available in the various official and private censuses. In the case of consumers, the variables of age, sex, place and type of residence, marital status and family age and composition, occupation and income have obvious relationships to the choices people must make.

Likewise, for industrial goods, market potentials can be estimated by use of such measurable characteristics as size of operation, industry, character of the workforce, location, and other census data.

For many planning purposes, such demographic measures are adequate. At other times, they need to be supplemented with added data, of which by far the most important are indicators of cultural patterns. The same family or individual income level, for example, will include people from several different social classes within the population and different roles in the family life cycle. A master plumber may well have an income as good or better than that of a well-paid professional family. But the proportion of his income spent for housing will be much less and the furnishings bought for the house will probably differ both in kind and taste from those of the professional family at the same income level.

Cultural Segmentation

National and Regional Cultures

The general culture and subculture which governs the daily life of any group sets the basic proportioning and content of personal and group consumption patterns everywhere. Cultural standards define what possible items of consumption are valuable, and how valuable, what is unimportant and thus less valuable.

Conformity to culturally determined values of consumption is enforced directly by the actions of the groups to which the individual looks for approval. It is reinforced indirectly by the limits on what sells in adequate volume, and is thus available in the market. Such cultural values operate at a number of levels of generality: national, regional, ethnic origin, social class, and in some cases, religion. They may modify over time, but only in terms of generations, not mere years.

GERBER GIVES UP IN BRAZIL

The Gerber baby is a familiar sight in every supermarket in the U.S., but won't be any more in Brazil, according to a **Business Week** story in the Feb. 8, 1982 issue. The problem: "We never convinced the housewife here to use baby food as an everyday feeding item," commented Donald Filshill, president of PAISA, Gerber's joint venture with the Brazilian Industrio and Commercio Atlantis Brasil Ltd. She would use the prepackaged baby food only when she "visited mum or went to the beach."

It was not for lack of trying, for eight years. PAISA's advertising campaign was an award winner. Its theme: mothers would have more time to show affection to their infants if they were not bent over a sink preparing food. But Filshill admits that they underestimated a cultural factor: "Brazilian mothers are not willing to accept that prepared baby food is a good substitute for fresh food prepared by themselves"—or, more likely, by their live-in maids, since most women in Brazil who can afford to buy prepared baby food can afford to have a maid.

Gerber officials appeared to be puzzled by the failure in Brazil, and a similar failure in Argentina. They had done well in Mexico and Venezuela.

U. S. CITY CONSUMERS NOT LOOK-ALIKES

Mediamark Research, Inc. regularly surveys consumers in the 10 largest cities of the U.S. concerning their buying in 1,000 product categories. Comparing the use or ownership with national averages (=100), they found the following, among many differences:

Relative percentage owning:

Chrysler made cars		Cadillac		Toyota	
Cleveland	179	Washington	171	Los Angeles	222
San Francisco	42	Boston	53	Cleveland	41

Alcoholic Beverages used in the preceding 6 months:

Ale		Tequila		Bourbon	
Philadelphia	309	Los Angeles	274	San Francisco	148
Los Angeles	40	New York	49	New York	42

Pills used in the previous 6 months:

Sleeping Pills		Vitamins		Diet pills	
Washington	122	Los Angeles	134	St. Louis	140
Cleveland	84	St. Louis	79	Washington	60

Ignoring the nuances of such cultural patterns can bring marketing plans to naught, as Green Giant learned when it tried to introduce its popular corn "Niblets" into Great Britain. Except for corn flakes, which the British did eat, corn itself was not perceived as a food for people, only for chickens.

The attributes which lend high value to an offering in one country may be discounted in another. In the United States, convenience has been a strong selling point for offerings ranging from instant mashed potatoes to riding lawn mowers and automatic dishwashers. But General Electric's International Division learned that a different appeal had to be made in Germany: the practical point that the machines could do a better job of sterilizing by using water too hot for hand washing. Initial attempts to sell electric blankets, electric can openers, and electric bottle warmers all failed. The German culture frowned on purchases for purely personal convenience.

NOR ARE EUROPEAN CONSUMERS LOOK-ALIKES, EITHER

PER CAPITA CONSUMPTION Of SELECTED FOOD AND
BEVERAGES, WESTERN EUROPEAN NATIONS

COUNTRY	FOODS (Kilograms/capita/yr.)		
	Bread grains	Meat & fish	Butter & fats
France	109	96	28
Italy	142	58	8
Netherlands	87	66	19
Great Britain	94	126	21
Germany	91	84	29
Sweden	85	87	39

	BEVERAGES(liters/capita/yr.)				
	Beer	Wine	Soft drinks	Coffee	Tea
France	40	114	14	251	5
Spain	31	68	55	70	12
Italy	12	111	25	144	—
Gt. Britain	93	5	41	72	306
Germany	111	17	31	248	9
Sweden	48	—	32	799	16

Source: European Marketing Data & Statistics, Vol 8, 1971,
European Marketing Consultants (Publications) Ltd., 125
Pall Mall, London SW 1, England

Wide regional variations of the general national pattern can be found in almost any country. American travelers in Scotland who get hungry in late afternoon, discover that "dinner" is not served until about 9 P. M., but that a "high tea" is served at the same hour as Americans eat supper, and that it is a meal in itself, with a meat course. In the English portion of Great Britain, they find no high tea. The menu served in Northern Italy varies greatly from that served in the southern part of that country. Any one who has traveled much within our own country soon discovers the wide differences in consumption patterns of many kinds covering every aspect of daily living from food and dress to recreation, and even investments.

Moreover, the specifications of the same item of purchase will differ in different regions. Coffee is widely used in every part of the United States, but each region has its own favorite blend and degree of roast. Garment chains have found it necessary to depend on the judgment of local managers on what to stock. Favorite colors and other approved details of garment designs vary greatly.

OCCUPATION AND SOCIAL CLASS IN THE UNITED STATES

The social class "pecking order" is so thoroughly embedded in the culture that it changes little over long periods. A survey of the prestige ranking of 90 occupations, repeated in 1963, found the new sample gave almost identical rankings to those assigned by the sample surveyed in 1947 (Siegel and Rossi, 1966):

In the top quartile, positions which would generally be recognized as requiring a relatively high level of education and usually some degree of responsibility, none that would be designated a manual labor: Supreme court justice, scientists, State governor, U. S. cabinet member, college professor, Congressman, chemist, lawyer, diplomat, physician, dentist, architect, county judge, psychologist, minister, mayor, priest, civil engineer, airline pilot

In the second quartile, more white collar occupations requiring considerable education and carrying responsibility, but at a lower level, plus (near the borderline) three skilled labor occupations: Banker, biologist, sociologist, school teachers, army captain, accountant, small factory owner, building contractor, recognized artist, symphony musician, fiction author, international labor union official, county agricultural agent, owner-operator of a print shop, railroad engineer, electrician, trained machinist

In the third quartile, lesser professionals, small businessmen, skilled labor jobs, and some semiskilled occupations; Farm owner-operator, undertaker, welfare worker, newspaper columnist, policeman, newspaper reporter, radio announcer, bookkeeper, tenant farmer, insurance agent, carpenter, small store manager, labor union local official, mail carrier, railroad conductor, traveling salesman, plumber, automobile repairman, playground director, barber, machine operator in a factory, lunch stand owner-operator, army corporal, garage mechanic, truck driver

In the bottom fourth, lower-ranked semiskilled positions, 1 skilled "dirty" job(coal miner), unskilled and menial positions: Fisherman-boat owner, store clerk, nightclub singer, filling station attendant, dockworker, railroad section hand, night watchman, coal miner, restaurant waiter, taxi driver, farm hand, janitor , bartender, clothes presser in a laundry, soda fountain clerk, sharecropper, garbage collector, street sweeper, shoe shiner

Some of the food differences clearly originated in climatic limitations, The emphasis on corn in the south and wheat and oats in the North reflects the crop capabilities of the regions. Likewise, the preference for lettuce in the North and the coarser greens in the South represent the original

availabilities.   But the people carry these preferences with them when they
move into the opposite climate.   The character of the fresh produce which
could be sold, in a local supermarket serving an upper-middle-class Los
Angeles neighborhood, changed radically when upper class blacks from the
South moved in.

The subculture of social class tends to cut across regional differences
while conforming to the basic outline of the region.

Cultural Factors: Social Class

Every society has some form of class structure: some pattern of social
relationships which grants greater prestige to some segments of the
population than to others.   In the western culture, and particularly in the
United States, class is defined mainly in terms of the occupation of the
individual, closely correlated with educational level and type of residence.

Class, everywhere, is far more than a mere matter of social status. Each class has its own subculture - a different set of standards of to what is valuable in consumption and what carries a lower priority, what is good taste and what is not. Studies have shown that the status of a given occupation is recognized both within and outside the class, and that the status of a given occupation tends to be stable.

Within the United States, the upper classes are a very small part of the market except for a very few items. The rest of the population can be divided into five major class segments in terms of the broad occupational classifications used in censuses and other official summaries:

1. Professional, official, and proprietors, making up the upper middle classes
2. Clerical and sales, approximating the lower middle class
3. Skilled workers: the aristocrats of the upper lower (read: "blue collar") class
4. Semi-skilled workers
5. Unskilled laborers, at the bottom of the hierarchy

SOCIAL CLASS DIFFERENCES IN TASTE

The **Chicago Tribune** sponsored a number of studies into the relationship between social class and reactions to offerings and to advertising. The following class differences in taste were discovered (Pierre Martineau, **Motivation in Advertising**, McGraw-Hill, 1957):

In home design: blue collar workers disliked the ranch style houses and two-story colonials then popular among the middle and upper classes.

In furniture: the middle and upper classes were buying the plain functional designs, blue collar families favored the "heavy commercial, highly overstuffed styles."

In clothing and clothing advertising: Upper-upper class women were attracted by styles and fashion advertising denoted by such adjectives as "aristocratic," "well-bred," "distinguished." They bought classics, avoided the fluctuations of current fashions.

Lower-upper class women responded to advertising using such terms as "chic," and other terms suggesting "sophistication." Clothes described as having "glamour" were avoided - to them this meant "cheapness."

By contrast, middle and lower class women were repelled by any suggestion of high style as being too extreme. The best styles were those described as "smart," like those worn by movie stars, who had "glamour," meaning "femininely pretty" to them.

Many of the professionals in the upper middle category receive incomes significantly lower than most skilled workers, as do nearly all clerical workers.

Regardless of income level, there is substantial consistency in the allocation of spending within social classes, and substantial differences between classes.

Such tabulations of amounts of money spent only hint at the real differences in consumption standards. The style and nature of the offerings bought differs even more widely, as numerous studies have revealed.

Early studies conducted by the Columbia Bureau of Social Research led to the conclusion that the differences in tastes between upper and lower classes could be characterized as follows:

UPPER CLASS PREFERENCES   LOWER CLASS PREFERENCES

Bitter,dry tastes   Sweet chocolate tastes
Irregular weaves & fabrics   Rubbery fabrics
Less pungent fragrances   Sweet fragrances

Lazarsfeld concluded that, in general, upper class people preferred the "weak stimuli". lower classes the stronger stimuli. Myers and Reynolds, quoting the results of a study of leather grain vinyl upholstery materials for automobiles, found a similar result. Lower class respondents tended to prefer the coarse grain effects, while upper class respondents preferred the finer grain textures (James H. Myers and William H. Reynolds, **Consumer Behavior & Marketing Management,** Houghton-Mifflin, 1967).

Although the details of the taste differences change with the fashions, the differences between classes is practically constant. Even within social classes, relatively wide ranges will be found in consumption. Some are accounted for by differences in the social role or family life cycle position at the moment. Others arise from differences in personal interests.

Social Role Segmentation

Shakespeare was a pretty good social psychologist when he noted, "All the world is a stage," and all the men and women actors on that stage, playing many parts over their lifetime. Indeed, we all play many roles at any given moment in our lives, a different one in each of the groups and organizations, formal and informal, to which we belong. Our actions of purchase and consumption are shaped by our perceptions of each role in any particular situation.

The same person, in two different roles, may make two different kinds of purchase choices. As a purchasing agent for a large corporation, the individual may buy or lease one make and model of automobiles for the field sales force, as a private citizen seeking a new car for the family, buy a quite different make and model. A housewife without outside work, may limit purchases of highly processed convenience foods. With her last 6-year-old off at school, and a job of her own, she may well turn readily toward purchases of both convenience foods and convenience appliances, such as a microwave oven, to enable her to devote less time to household chores.

FIGURE 4–1. FAMILY EXPENDITURE LIFE CYCLE: The Percentage Distribution
of Spending for Each Class of Spending, at Each Stage

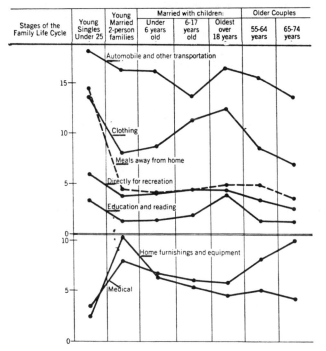

Stages of the Family Life Cycle	Young Singles Under 25	Young Married 2-person families	Married with children:			Older Couples	
			Under 6 years old	6-17 years old	Oldest over 18 years	55-64 years	65-74 years

(Estimated from U. S. Dept. of Labor surveys of consumer expenditures

Role Transition Segmentation Roles inevitably change over time – most of
them in a reasonably predictable course. Role transition periods are usually
times of tension and anxiety, as the individual leaves well understood
situations to enter new relationships in which new rules must be learned.

Such transition periods mean new kinds of choices, new purchases, new
purchasing habits to acquire. Infants, of course, are fully dependent on the
family, begin to acquire some contacts with choices as they approach school
age. Once in school, children became part of peer groups who come to
dominate many of their choices well up into adolescence.

Probably the transition of greatest tension is adolescence, as youths strive
to assert a growing independence, at least from the family and those a little
older than themselves. Partly because of the high anxiety of this period,
this is a time of extreme conformity to the peer reference group standards,
even to the details of the brand of apparel worn.

Emergence from adolescence into young adulthood brings a measure of true
independence, as group contacts diversify and multiply, often cutting across
age group lines. Now, nearly every purchase decision becomes the

individual's own, in the last analysis. The period of late adolescence becomes the time when many patronage loyalties are first developed and become part of the routines of the individual. It is also the period during which individuals start through their own full-fledged family life cycle of consumption, with its changing roles over the years.

Organizations and Managements as Role Players Role playing and role cycles are not limited to individual final consumers. Organizations play roles within their industries. Managements play roles within the organization, roles which change over time, with different guiding personalities at each stage.

Within most industries, it is easy to identify the leaders, the innovators, and those searching hard for a niche of their own. Recent management literature has noted the different roles which top management plays at different periods in an organization's life cycle. The early stages are governed by the innovative entrepreneurs, who must give way to administrative management as the organization matures.

All of these role changes affect industrial and commercial buying, as much as role changes affect individual consumption. Like other buyers in the beginning of their independent consumption cycles, it is the organizations just carving out their own niches who are most receptive to new ideas and new processes. For organizations as for individuals, transitions mark critical marketing situations. They also mark periods of opportunities, when prospects passing through them are making new decisions without guidance from habit.

The Critical Importance of Role Transition Periods For both individual consumers and organizations, role transitions represent times of intense search for satisfying offerings not previously part of their habitual consumption. The heavy buying final consumer segment is the 16-25 year age group for many items of personal consumption, from beverages to cosmetics, toiletries and fashion goods. During this period, brand preferences are established and become part of the automatic routines. Within organizations, it is the struggling new firm which seeks for and establishes trusted sources for many items.

During any role transition period, both individuals and organizational managements are passing from situations in which they were able to follow habitual consumption patterns with no conscious thought. They are entering new areas of consumption in which the availabilities and the rules are imperfectly perceived, cannot be handled with habitual routines. They are thus forced to spend a great deal of effort in learning what to do.

Role transitions are periods of trial and much error. Psychologists tell us they are also periods of intense anxiety, and pressures to conform to somewhat dimly perceived new rules. In no instance is this more apparent than in the problems of adolescence and the transitions of early adulthood.

Young couples with their first home of their own, their first baby, and other firsts are wide open to suggestions from authoritative sources.

What is being conformed to, however, may not be the standards of the more mature. Young firms, struggling for a marketing niche, soon learn that they must gain some kind of substantial advantage over the established sellers, become open to sources which can help them establish that advantage.

Even previously well entrenched organizations may be faced with traumatic transitions, with new and aggressive competition which seems to spring from nowhere and take over large segments of their markets. Such was the case of the Detroit automobile manufacturers, who woke up in the late 1970's and early eighties to a loss of the the smug dominance they had enjoyed for decades. R & D was not only expanded in long neglected areas of engine innovation, but the services of small outside research specialists sought out and financed.

It has long been observed that wide differences in consumption patterns exist within segments defined by many of the more objective cultural factors. Subcultural clusters, with their own special sets of values, can be discovered. The current label for such groups is "lifestyles".

Lifestyle Segmentation

Any level of cultural grouping is accurately described as a lifestyle. In current popular usage, however, the term is reserved for smaller subsegments of the market. Some of these patterns are subsegments of one social class. Others cut across social class lines. All of them are definable in terms of a narrow class of benefit values being sought in (largely personal) offerings—usually perceived psychological associations only tangentially associated with physical attributes of the offerings.

As with the larger cultural groups, lifestyle subcultures consist of interwoven systems of shared values. For research purposes, they are usually measured by respondents' answers to a list of attitude, interest, and opinion ("AIO") items. (See **Miller Beer** at end of chapter.)

Such value systems not only determine what kinds of new offerings will attract attention and patronage. They also determine the best form and content of the communications necessary to get favorable attention. Knowledge of such value systems are especially important in devising competitive brand strategies for product categories in which brands differ very little in objective benefits. Their special importance is in defining the copy appeals and forms of presentation.

One of the earliest studies to focus on the relation of such value systems to product adoption was Opinion Research Corporation's Tastemakers study (1959). Seeking to pinpoint groups of early adopters of a wide range of new products, ORC rated the commitment of respondents to 44 different value items. Cluster analysis grouped the answers into 12 value areas:

- Personal and family life
- Emotional life
- Spiritual Life
- Outdoor life
- Business and career
- Health
- Food
- Travel
- Recreational pursuits
- Education and culture
- Drinking and smoking
- Politics

Correlation of these ratings with adoption of 75 products in the previous 10 years produced some unexpected associations. Adoption of exotic coffees was much more closely related to a strong commitment to politics than to food interests:

    Of the exotic coffees (Turkish, expresso, etc.) adopters:
        75% had a high commitment to **politics**, none had a
        low commitment
    Only 43% had a high commitment to food interest, and 14%
        had a low commitment

Adopters of boating and sailing did have high commitments to sporting events and outdoor life, as expected. But such people adopted boating and sailing only when these interests were combined with a high level of commitment of the whole family to a set of other interwoven interests in the family, recreation, the children, and food. Such adopters, indeed, adhered to a complete set of subcultural values.

ORC referred to such value systems as "lifestyle", but did not attempt to find any definitive system of generally applicable cluster categories. More recent studies have made such attempts, fitting groups into such designations as "price conscious", "child-oriented", "art enthusiast", etc. based on answers to AIO questionnaires constructed with as many as 300 items (W. D.Wells and D. J. Tigert, "Activities, Interests and Opinions," **Journal of Advertising Research,** April 1971, pp.27-35). Recent experience has raised questions about any generalized single classification scheme, applicable to every marketing situation. Urban society is probably not that simple (P. Bernstein, "Psychographics is still an issue on Madison Ave", **Fortune,** Jan. 16, 1978, pp.78-80). On the other hand, pinpointing the lifestyle attitudes in relation to a given type of offering has proved useful in planning every aspect of offering, pricing and communications strategies and tactics.

In our dynamic society, new forms of lifestyle are not uncommon. One major change has been the emergence of the two-income family as an accepted norm. The increasing acceptance of a career outside the home has had far-reaching effects in markets of many kinds.

Those who people any segment are constantly changing. However stable the segment itself, most segments are simply a brief stretch during the individual's life.

CONTINENTAL MAIL ORDER: SHOULD WE CHASE AFTER LOST CUSTOMERS?

Continental Mail Order (a disguised name) thought it had a problem. It had to drop about one-fifth of its customers each year because they had quit buying. Not that business was dropping: Continental's customer list was still growing, as new customers sent in orders from neighbor's catalog. But the statistic bothered them. Robin Edwards, the head of Sales Planning, asked the Marketing Research Department to find some answers.

The MR department decided to ask some former customers. After some careful thought, the analysts put together a questionnaire, secured a list of "expirated" customers in a small city at a convenient distance from headquarters, and assembled a team from its own ranks to spend a day interviewing. Respondents were asked about their buying of various kinds of goods of the general types listed in the Continental catalog: from whom, how much, etc. Interviewers identified themselves under a cover research agency name so as not to prejudice the answers.

The results: none of these old customers were doing much buying, from any source, of the types which would justify sending them a catalog. They had quit buying from Continental because they had quit accumulating the general merchandise items which made up Continental's main sales. This seemed a reasonable conclusion to the research staff, and enough in line with probabilities that no further research would be worthwhile.

Edwards was not satisfied, however. If he could just find a way to recapture these lost customers, what a feat that would be! After mulling over the problem for a year or so, he developed his plan, and persuaded management to give it a try. In one of the larger states, catalogs would be mailed to every expirated customer. These catalogs would be seeded with some very special buys at deep-cut prices, but otherwise appear the same as the catalogs sent the rest of the customers. No special attention would be directed to the bargains. It was felt that catalog users would peruse the new books and stumble over the prices, causing them to order again. Continental would know whether the scheme worked by spotting the specially keyed order blanks and tallying them.

Very few orders were received. The total operation lost more than the normal annual Continental profit.

In our mobile society, those currently in any one segment remain there for a limited period of time, moving on as they age, change roles, etc. They enter a period of heavy use of particular forms of offerings, then move on and out. Patronage decisions are usually made at the onset of heavy usage. The most effective efforts at winning new customers are made at this time. Much the same is true of organizational customers.

Because of the many roles any one individual plays at any one time, individuals may be parts of more than one segment for a given class of offerings, buying differently in each role. This can happen if the end reasons for the purchases relate to different functional roles.

Functional Segmentation

Important components of the benefit bundle sought are related to the economic function the offering serves for the buyer. Many common household products are also bought by organizations, but the core satisfactions sought are different. The ultimate core values sought by individual consumers and households are subjective psychological satisfactions. Organizations purchase offerings primarily for their direct contribution to the value of the organization's offerings, or to maintenance of organization and its ability to continue production of its own offerings.

Many of the attributes sought by households have no meaning to industrial, commercial and other institutional purchasers. Households may value toilet tissue which is colored and perfumed, and pay little attention to the sheet count. Institutions are fully aware of the sheet count, and will pay nothing for color and perfume. Both housewives and commercial bakers buy flour from the same millers, but in different quantities and choose makers for different reasons. Even small computers sold to professionals for home use and to small businesses require a different kind of approach as well as different "software".

In terms of purposes to be served and channels of communication and distribution, we can distinguish seven classes of markets. For some offerings, all seven may represent attractive segments. Each of the seven will have to be treated as a separate market. These are:
- Final consuming households
- Industrial purchasers
- Commercial buyers
- Institutions
- Agricultural customers
- Professional prescribers of purchases by others
- Governments

Each of the six functional markets are themselves split into definable segments. All share some general characteristics, but each might have its own periodicals and its own special channels of sale and distribution. Because goods pass through many hands before the final consumption, and some goods are used up, the total volume of marketing activity and sales is greater for the functional market segments than for the more visible consumer markets we are all familiar with.

The relationships between buyers and sellers also tend to be much closer in the functional markets than in the consumer markets. However strong brand and patronage loyalty may be among consumers, they seldom feel that their personal interests are closely bound up with those of the sellers they patronize. For large purchases and key items, functional buyers and their sources usually recognize strong mutual interest and mutual interdependency.

Most major purchases are made under implicit or explicit commitments for substantial periods in advance—normally a year. Buyers generally expect close technical service on equipment and supplies, when appropriate.

In general, the best communications mix is quite different than for final consumer sellers. Advertising usually plays a lesser role, although far from useless. Because of the large size of many purchases, personal sales is more feasible and normally the dominant element in the mix. Sales personnel frequently serve a technical service function, and are backed up by a special technical service staff. Exhibits and fairs are major promotional tools. The value of publicity is probably much greater than in the consumer field, is more widely read, even looked for.

Industrial Markets Industrial organizations typically purchase all sorts of items in order to produce their own offerings: raw materials, semiprocessed goods, processing supplies, component parts, maintenance, repair and operating (MRO) items, major plant and installed equipment, accessories, auxiliary equipment, both of standard and specialized design, special services (employee health benefits, insurance of several kinds, outside auditors, etc.) and increasingly, outside management and research expertise. A few of the items may be sold to a single type of buyer: some raw materials, special catalysts, and special-duty equipment. Some items are purchased by a wide variety of industries: items such as word processors, lubricants, forklift trucks, abrasives, etc.

Some items have dual markets: sales to original equipment manufacturers (OEM sales), and also sales to the aftermarket, independent distributors of spare parts.

Whenever the item is of major importance to the buyer, buyers usually prefer to have more than one source, as a matter of insurance of continued supply, but normally no more than a second or third source. Relationships between buyers and sources are normally quite close and stable, because each is very important to the total business of the other. In some cases, suppliers may build special facilities to serve a few buyers or even a single customer. Very often, the technical service of the supplier's representatives is a major part of the total bundle of satisfactions purchased.

Sales outlets for smaller purchases may be similar to those for consumer goods: industrial distributors selling wide assortments of related items bought in relatively small amounts, either to single industries (such as oil field stores selling oil production items in small quantities). Generally, large volume purchases are sold directly by the factory, the small purchasers buy through either company-owned or independent distributors.

Purchases of any financial significance, made by large organizations, typically involve concurrence of several individuals. Major plant and installed equipment may involve all divisions of the top executive hierarchy and even the board of directors.

Usually, auxiliary equipment purchases can be made at the functional level involved. Even then, the department or division head who signs the order may have to listen to others who will be using or depending on the equipment or item.

The dominant core satisfactions sought are cost-in-use and dependability of supply, delivery and of quality level, as well as the quality of any technical service needed. Cost considerations include the cost of using the item in production, in storage, or in shipping. Ability to add value to the finished product is a plus.

Even industrial markets sometimes are susceptible to fringe value considerations. Some purchases are made to enhance executive ego, others to be in fashion in the industry. Many kinds of consultant services have been sold on the basis of fashionable labels without demonstration of a real benefit, and organizations with plush offices often do no better than those operating out of spartan headquarters.

Commercial Markets Commercial buyers purchase equipment, supplies and even services to supply services to others. They would include the taxi service and the rent-a-car agency, the insurance agency office and the large insurance company, accounting firm, and the janitorial service.

Buying motives would be similar to those of the industrial customer, except that some items may be purchased mainly because they impress customers rather than for the functional value they deliver.

Institutional Buyers Institutional buyers are also producers of services: hospitals, eating places, hotels and motels, and other organizations buying equipment used in providing or even producing services.

Many of the items bought have a surface resemblance to ordinary consumer goods: furniture, food, and cleaning supplies, for example. The volume of many items is large, however, the buyers reasonably expert, and their specifications often more stringent than those required for items selling to the general market.

The two offering attributes of greatest importance to these buyers are low cost per unit of service sold, and attributes making their service more attactive to their customers in some way.

Such buyers regularly pay premium prices for quality reflected in durability or in relatively higher value perception in their customer's eyes. One leading supplier of "contract furniture" was known to demonstrate the chairs he sold by throwing them across the room and slamming them down on cement floors. He also gave a five year warranty on his products. Coffee specifically blended for the restaurant trade has always sold at a much higher price per pound than that purchased at the supermarket by housewives. Restaurants are often judged by the quality of their coffee, and the special blends also yield far more cups per pound than normal retail brands.

Any item minimizing service occupations is welcomed by such organizations as hospitals and nursing homes: disposable diapers and hypodermic needles, for instance, and even disposable "linen".

To avoid labor administration and also get economies of scale in purchasing and expertise in administration, institutions such as schools, hospitals, and even industrial plants have become major markets for feeding services.

The Agricultural Market In many ways, the major agricultural market resembles the industrial market. It is really a large number of different industries. In each, the major enterprises are concentrated in one or a few small regions or areas. The major portion of the market is highly capitalized, and the buyers are expert. They are businesses, and run as such. The number of important buyers is relatively small: less than 20,000 farms of all kinds account for a large share of the total production. Each major segment of the industry has its own periodicals.

Family operation is the one major difference from most larger industrial operations. Even most of the largest farms are primarily family operations, using no permanent outside employees. One unusual facet of the farm market is the tendency to do much of the major purchasing of supplies and even some equipment through their own cooperatives.

There is another, numerically large farm market: roughly a couple of million small farms, no more than half of them commercial producers in any significant volume. Although many also buy through the cooperatives, much of their purchasing of supplies is in small retail lots, bought much as final consumers buy household items: hand-to-mouth, with considerable reliance on established brands.

Professional Prescribers The professional prescriber markets are made up of people who do little or no buying in their major roles, but decide what others will buy: physicians, professors, consulting design engineers, architects, building code authorities, and other authoritative advisors. These either specify the specific offering, or write specifications so narrowly that only a limited number of alternatives will be considered. They do not pay for the purchases and may pay only limited attention, if any, to the price. Selling in any market in which their advice is influential requires selling them, not the actual purchasers or users.

The main interests of such prescribers are the various aspects of offering performance, as perceived both by them and by their clientele. If cost performance is not insisted upon by the clientele, they may pay little or no attention to price. A major consideration is continued acceptance of their professional expertise by possible clients.

Sales communications to such prescribers need to be highly informative and impartial, or at least seem to be. The prescriptions and designs they purvey are, of necessity, individualized, to fit the unique elements of the situation. Prescribers need to know a great deal about the uses and limitations, both the advantages and disadvantages of each new offering considered. Keeping abreast of the stream of new offerings and solutions appearing on the market takes more study than many have time for. They tend to depend on sales communications to bring them to their attention and furnish credible information about their attributes and limitations. Plowing through the technical literature on every new drug, every new building material or system, or reviewing every new textbook is time-consuming drudgery. A relatively close personal relationship is necessary between the "detailmen" or "bookmen" (as salesmen may be called) in such situations. This requires well-informed sales people, and well-prepared, balanced publicity and advertising.

When judging the presentations, such professionals tend to depend on some special clues in the buying situation: the reputation of the supplier, as perceived by them, and of other sources of the offering. In drugs, physicians tend to discount the value of brands sold under the label of firms who also push over-the-counter proprietary drugs, especially cold remedies, even when the medication is identical to that sold under the name of an "ethical" (prescription drug) manufacturer. The well publicized adoption by a major clinic or a local medical leader may furnish the assurance that the prescriber is not experimenting.

Likewise, in textbooks, a "brand name" authorship may secure at least initial adoption more readily than the writings of a newcomer. The identity of the publishing house may also swing decisions. The personality of the sales people often influences the judgment. If the latter is perceived as well-informed and credible, the supplier behind will be so perceived.

Such professionals, like the rest of us, follow fashion trends in their fields. Medications fitting well into the currently accepted fashion of treatment is assured of much more favorable attention than one which goes against the current trend. The textbook whose title seems to suggest adherence to current dogmas is likely to be viewed more favorably than one pioneering a new trend. Whoever the architect, it is usually easy to date a building by its design. To a considerable extent, such fashion adherence is the result of the perceptions of the clientele, who are inclined to judge advice by its cosmetics.

The Government Market However measured, the government market—national, state and local—is big. The total is awesome even when personnel costs are subtracted from the total budgets. Governmental purchases range from mundane off-the-shelf items purchased by any organization (paper clips, typewriters, stationery, light bulbs, etc.) to innovative Research and Development of exotic weapon systems.

Selling to governments can be more cumbersome than to most other organizations, especially when the purchase is large and faces competition. With legislative bodies always looking over their shoulders, the bureaucrats must often follow very rigid rules and procedures. Quite often, the lowest bid must be accepted and specifications so written as to include as many competitors as possible. This may result in awarding the contract for something less than the most appropriate design. Industry sources have charged that the Federal purchases of data processing equipment have tended to consist of designs which are obsolescent, as suppliers have bid low to rid themselves of inventories of outdated systems.

Legislatively mandated procedures often burden sales with much added paperwork, often irrelevant when applied to minor purchases from small suppliers.

Large government purchases can often be quite lucrative and the lifeblood of whole organizations, especially when the item is non-standard and requires new design. A whole series of gatekeepers must be sold, not only on the item, but on the organization itself. Among such gatekeepers will be the influential committee chairmen in the appropriate legislative body(ies), and even the opposition leaders, the directors of agencies and programs, and sometimes the technical people who must use the results.

With all of these complexities, segments are to some degree the creation of sellers who have enough innovative insight to perceive sufficiently large groups of unsatisfied prospects and who can design offerings for them.

SUMMARY

1. The starting point for strategy planning must be the identification of a group of target segments in need of offerings which the organization is in the best position to create.

2. Segments are identifiable clusters of potential customers, a large portion of whom might be attracted by a given offering. The specific design would come as close as possible to meeting the desire sets of those at the core of the segment. Those at the fringes will consist of possible customers who find no single offering coming close to filling their wants.

3. Segments are designated by definable descriptive characteristics which correlate reasonably well with probable desires. Five general classes of measures are used to estimate segments: demographic factors, cultural factors, social roles, lifestyles, and the economic function to be served by the purchase.

4. Demographic factors consist of the kind of population data found in censuses. For the ultimate consumers, these consist of such information as age, sex, place of residence, occupation, marital status, and income. For non-consumer markets, they would include such items as the type of business

or industry, size of establishment, workers employed, location, sales volume.

5. Cultural factors are usually indicated in terms of countries, regions, and social class.

6. Social roles are defined as the place of the individuals in the various groups in which they participate, and by their stage in the family life cycle.

7. Lifestyles are personality related special subcultures which may cut across other cultural boundaries, usually identified in terms of the individual's system of values, interests and opinions, as related to consumption of specific types of offerings. This system of segmentation has its greatest value in the design of communications.

8. Because many products are sold both for ultimate consumption and for those serving buyers, there are 6 different kinds of functional segments: industrial, commercial, institutional, agricultural, professional prescribers, and governmental units. Each has it own distinctive distribution channel needs and communication needs and systems.

FOOD FOR THOUGHT AND DISCUSSION

CONTINENTAL MAIL ORDER: THE CONTRARY SAMPLE

The last of the World War II textile limitation orders was finally dropped, near the end of 1946. For five years, the amount of fabric used in ladies' dresses had been severely restricted. Now the designers could go where the customers wanted. Continental's fashion buyer came to the research department with a problem. Could they help him forecast the relative demand in a line of dresses? Asked if he wanted a sales forecast, he said no.

His problem was much simpler. Because he was permitted to buy only a fourth of his initial season estimate, he could estimate total sales, even by line, well enough. His difficulty lay in estimating the relative sales within each single price line of the same type of dress, usually 6 to 8 dresses. Lacking any information from customers, the best estimate he could make was that sales would be about the same for each number. However, sometimes half of the orders would be for a single item, resulting in a rush of orders too big to handle, even with backordering. It took six weeks to get a reorder filled. Moreover, he would most certainly, in that case, be stuck with a large oversupply of one or two of the other items in the line and have to job them off at a high loss.

The analyst was assured that he could have planographed proof pages of a new special catalog, featuring 4 new numbers, for use in any tests. Returning to his office, the analyst prepared a simple questionnaire to be sent to sample customers, saying that the enclosed pages showed fashions the firm was "considering for inclusion in a new catalog," and asking for the respondents' choice. To determine how best to prepare any future samples, several alternate forms of sampling the customer file were to be used. In addition, the analyst reasoned that since the firm had a large female workforce with income levels not far from those of the customers, they too should be sampled in the same way. If this proved to be a useful sample, it would save substantial time and the mailing costs. Accordingly, a sample of supervisors and clerks also received the questionnaire, in person.

When the returns were tabulated, the customer samples all were in reasonable agreement in ordering the relative preferences among the four items, ranking them in an order which can be simplified as A, B, C, and D. The employee sample, however, ranked the same fashions in exactly the reverse order, and by almost the same percentage values! The later sales results corroborated the validity of the customer answers.

1. How could two samples of women, from the same region of the country for the most part, with similar income levels, differ so much in taste?

THE MAJOR NEW LIFESTYLE: THE TWO-INCOME FAMILY

Anthropologists and sociologists have long noted that the all elements of the culture are influenced by the ways in which the people gain a living. In the United States, and to an increasing extent in all industrialized countries, this has been undergoing a number of revolutions. One of the most important has been the new dominance of a new lifestyle: the two income family.

According to the studies of the U. S. Bureau of Labor Statistics, the proportion of women of working age in the labor force crossed the halfway mark in 1978, and the percent of dual husband–wife wage earners reached 50% by 1980 and will continue to increase at a relatively rapid pace. These increases include substantial proportions of women with children of preschool age as well as those with school children. These changes reflect a major reversal in attitudes of families toward the place of women in the structure of the family.

Traditionally, women have viewed themselves as marginal workers, coming into the workforce only temporarily, until they had a home established, and the husband had a reasonably assured income. They left the workforce whenever their jobs conflicted with child–rearing. As late as 1970 (when 3 out of 7 were already in the labor force), they averaged only a little more than 21 years in paid employment in their lifetimes, compared with more than 37 years for men. By 1977, the figure had already risen to 26 years, and is still rising rapidly. During the 1970's, women began to postpone childbearing until careers were established, took shorter maternity leaves, and more and more, returned to work while children were young.

Polls have confirmed that these statistics represent a basic change in attitude. A Harris survey in late 1975 found the following shifts in the short period of 5 years:

- A sharp decline in the proportion working "to bring in extra money": from nearly half to only 39%, and a like drop in those working to simply "keep busy" (from 9% to 7%)
- Practically no change in the percentage working "to support their families": about one–fifth
- A steep rise – from 23% in 1970 to 37% in 1975 – working to support themselves
- An accompanying shift in attitudes toward day care centers: from just under half of the men in 1970 to 61% approving in 1975, with women changing from 63% to 72%
- Younger, more affluent families were now inclined to believe that "a woman was not fulfilling herself unless productively employed"

Among the more obvious results of this trend has been a growing gap between the incomes of dual- and single-earner families: about one-fourth more, after taxes, for the dual-earner families. The extra employment is not without its costs in extra transportation and clothes. A National Bureau of Economic Research study in 1980 indicated that the two-income family spent over half again as much for clothing then the single-earner families, 45% more on such durables as cars, home furnishings and appliances, and a little more on food and services.

At least one of the major factors helping bring about this revolution in lifestyle has been the inflation of recent decades, but the trend started long before, and continued during the period of relative monetary stability in the late 1950's. Economists attributed the gains during this early period to the shortage of labor during this period, causing employers to pay young married women better.

However that may be, the trend is a logical outgrowth of the shift from a country over half rural to one predominantly urban, accompanied by the shift of women's traditional in-home employment in food processing, garment making, and cleaning tasks. On the farm, women always have had, and still have, a major economic role. In the city, bakeries, commercial canneries, and electric home appliances drastically reduced both the volume of their traditional tasks, and their contribution to the family's real income. It required only a change in attitude, brought on both by spending pressures and job opportunities, to start the trend toward paid employment.

An important symptom of the permanency of the attitude change has been the increasing tendency of women to enroll in higher education. Since 1959, women high school graduates have increased about 39%, and college graduates came close to doubling (88% increase). Completion of advanced professional degrees was almost spectacular between 1969 and 1980: from 8% to 24% in medicine, from 7% to 28% in accounting, and from 3% to 23% in business.

1. Changes in the total spending usually mean changes also in what it is spent for, including matters of taste. How many industries can you think of as likely to be affected by this change in lifestyles? What kinds of changes would you expect in each case.

2. What might be the affect on a common woman's purchases such as cosmetics?

3. What might be the effect on their political "spending" (voting) attitudes and other habits?

4. What categories of family spending would you expect to be changed in both quantity and quality, and in what directions? Why?

MILLER BEER: TURNING A SPECIALTY ITEM INTO A MASS MARKET SHARE

When the Surgeon General's Report on Smoking threw a fright into the cigarette trade, cigarette companies began to look for diversification shelters. Philip Morris looked for acquisitions in fields requiring much the same advertising expertise which gave the firm a strong position in cigarettes: primarily packaged consumer goods in which brand strength is important. One of its major acquisitions was Miller Beer, in 1969, to which it added Lite Beer in 1972 when it purchased the brand names and distribution network of Meister Brau, Inc., of Chicago.

Beer is a product in which brand differentiation is largely psychological, achieved through positioning. Confirmed beer drinkers can usually detect some difference in taste between brands in true blind tests, but are seldom able to identify their favorite brand without the label. Positioning is achieved through advertising which succeeds by associating a brand with their own lifestyle and use pattern.

To get a major market share, a brew must win the heavy using segment. Although something over half of the adults drink beer at least occasionally, 80% of the output is consumed by only 30% of the beer drinkers. Numerous studies have shown that heavy beer users are a strongly family–centered, tradition–oriented group, strongly interested in such sports as football and baseball, and other traditional outdoor activities.

Anheuser–Busch and Schlitz had the number 1 and number 2 positions in the market in 1969. Anheuser–Busch brands had a solid hold on the heavy–user segment, continually reinforced by every element of its publicity and advertising, from the well–publicized draft horse teams to its baseball connections. Christmas commercials featured such illustrations as a horse–drawn sleigh driven across fields to a family Christmas gathering.

Schlitz had been slipping. Part of the reason was a change in formula and some apparent slippage in quality control for a while. The advertising was also a little off–beat for the traditional blue–collar drinkers. One sports background commercial, for example, featured ice–boat racing. A Christmas commercial, run opposite the Anheuser sleigh production, showed an apparently hilarious Xmas tree trimming, outdoors in the woods!

Miller Beer was long advertised as "the Champagne of Beers", and much of the advertising featured the beer in a special occasion setting. Patronage loyalty was strong within a small, occasional user group, giving it a 6% national market share. The Miller High Life bottle was the only clear glass container used in the industry. This container could be used because Miller was produced with its patented malt extract method, conferring good shelf life without protection from the effects of light. Commercials were more in line with the High Life theme – often depicting upper middle class family scenes. Miller was considered a high quality beer. Miller's users were loyal, but not heavy users.

Philip Morris' main target was the volume market. The problem was how to win this without sacrificing the current segment. The first step was to remove all people from the advertising illustrations for a period. Advertising featured outdoor landscape scenes which anyone could identify with, such as a bubbling mountain stream, flowing over rocks through the woods. Then gradually, scenes depicting real workers, doing traditional heavy outdoor work, were shown, relaxing in groups after work with "Miller Time: a time to enjoy the best tasting beer you can find." The new slogan was "If you've got the time, we've got the beer." Partly to induce sampling, a 7–ounce non–returnable "pony" bottle was introduced – just enough for one glass, and small enough to remain cold until the last sip. By 1975, Miller's market share had risen from 7th place to fourth. By 1982, Miller was in a strong second place, and Schlitz far behind. A substantial part of the total was the Lite brand, first introduced under the Miller trademark in 1973, and marketed nationally since 1975.

Low calorie beers were no novelty when Miller acquired the Lite label in 1972. None, however, had achieved any real market acceptance. They were too much associated with dieting, and beer drinkers are not addicted to dieting. In addition, they lacked a characteristic beer taste. Research, however, revealed that the heavy beer drinkers would welcome a beer that was "less filling", but had a "real beer" taste. In addition, various studies, long before, had shown that the heavy user tended to prefer a somewhat lower alcoholic content.

Miller brewmasters spent a year in devising and testing new formulas aimed at fewer calories but maintaining a rich flavor with an alcoholic content over 3.2

percent. The new Lite was introduced into 4 test markets under the now well-known slogan, "Everything you always wanted in a beer. And less." It caught on well, and was rolled out nationally in 1975. Lite proved to be what the heavy user wanted. To quote one Wall Street analyst, "It's the sin without the penalty," – an excuse to drink more. One independent test also showed that it had the lowest alcoholic content of 14 beers tested: 4.3% as compared with 5.1% for Budweiser. Numerous imitators soon crowded into the market, but Miller Lite still outsold all the others in 1982.

Quality control is extremely strict for the whole line. Any stock over 4 months old is removed from dealers' and distributors' shelves and destroyed. Distribution is as strong as possible, but still does not equal that of Anheuser-Busch.

The large market share gained did not come without cost. During the introduction of Lite, Miller was reported to be spending an estimated $6.50 per barrel on advertising, compared with an industry average of $1 per barrel.

1. Without question, the advertising presentations played a key role in gaining a heavy user segment for Miller Beer. Do you think advertising alone could do the job? Why, or why not?

2. If not, what other elements were important in achieving success, and why?

3. To what extent do you think a similar approach could be used to gain a substantial market share for some quite different kind of offerings – for example, an automobile, such as American Motors?

HAZEL BISHOP SUDDENLY COMES TO LIFE AGAIN

During the 1960's Hazel Bishop was one of the top, heavily advertised cosmetic brands. But it withered under the pressure of competition and its own lack of marketing imagination.

Frank S. Berger, a former top marketing executive at Seagram Co. acquired it under a leveraged buyout in 1981, for what was reported to be "a very modest figure", according to a story in the March 15, 1982 **Business Week.** Berger chopped down fixed cost, closed the manufacturing plant and contracted out the production to a private-label manufacturer. Although he admits, "I don't know much about cosmetics," he tripled the sales in less than a year. Capitalizing on a still recognizable name, his strategy was to position it as a budget-line item at about 89 cents—approximately half the price of other low-end items. He has excellent volume in Revco, Zayre, Thrifty, Woolworth, and Caldor chain outlets.

Although sales had not yet reached the $65 million level Hazel Bishop had in 1969, Gerber expected to build it into a major cosmetics name. He is quite aware of the power of better financed competitors, but feels that his low margin strategy would make it too expensive for them. At Seagram, he had himself used financial strength to push its brands to the top, and is using some of the lessons he learned there in merchandising Hazel Bishop. He claims that all lipsticks are the same, whether for $10 or the 89 cents his sells for. "My own people get annoyed when I say this,but its all the same junk," he asert. "Wine and spirits, soad and cosmetics all are parity products tha sell on image—the sizzle, not the steak."

Berger has made no changes in quality, but has brightened up the brand image by replacing gaudy display racks with black and chrome designs, introduced clear lipsticks and new colors with exotic names and atttractive packaging.

Other industry people express doubts about how far Berger can go with Hazel

Bishop, and comment that he must be getting his trade from older women who remember the name, and teenagers with little to spend. But the market has been changing. Long dominated by department stores with lavish, glamorous displays, department store share of market has dropped since 1977 by an estimated one-third. Drugstores currently dominate the trade, with food and mass-merchandising stores rising rapidly.

1. What do the shifts in the cosmetics market seem to imply about the perceived attribnutes now being sought and bought in cosmetics?

2. What changes in the nature of the cosmetics-buying market segments might be responsible for such a shift?

STANLEY WORKS: DISCOVERING A GROWTH MARKET FOR AN OLD PRODUCT

The homeowner do-it-yourself market first sprouted in the late 1940's, in home decorating. Building craftsmen's wages started a steep climb, feeding on a sustained building boom, lot of new families were just getting started, as the WWII veterans came home, and paint manufacturers had developed the first water-based latex paints—much easier for the amateur to use than the older oil-based finishes. It grew rapidly, with the development of relatively inexpensive power hand tools. To many observers, it was labelled a fad, but as one colleague retorted, "A fad? Have you tried to hire a plumber recently?" The building supply industry, long used to dealing almost entirely with professional builders, was slow to respond, but new mass building supply merchandisers began to sprout, and by the early 1970s major lumber yards were beginning to convert to building materials and building tool supermarkets, catering to homeowners buying in small retail quantities.

Black and Decker early started designing their power drills and other power hand tools to the needs of the do-it-yourselfer. By the early 1970s, the new chairman of Stanley Works, Donald W. Davis also noticed the trend.

Stanley was a well-known name in the field of carpenter and other building craftsman tools, and in builders hardware. In its century-plus history, it had, one analyst is quoted as saying, "grown complacent, fat and lazy." He credited Davis with pulling "it into the 20th century." Noting that homeowners were beginning to buy the hammers, screwdrivers, saws, and other tools the company sold, he concluded that do-it- yourself was no fad, but an "evolving lifestyle of Western society," and started aggressively developing the market. By 1978, half of Stanley's sales came from do-it-yourself homeowners.

To get this business, Stanley had to change many of its product lines and redesign many of its hammers, measuring tapes, planes, and other tools, developing less expensive lines for amateur use. It launched a well-financed television and print advertising campaign to promote its tools and encourage new recruits to the do-it-yourself ranks. From 1976 to early 1979, the overall ad budget rocketed 73%, with TV spots alone doubling to a 1979 budget of over $5 million. Stanley did not forget the dealers. It developed displays and merchandising aids for both tools and such builders' hardware as it line of quality locks, now designed for easy installation.

Some ads promoted the do-it-yourself trend generally, Others pushed specific Stanley items, others do-it yourself projects for which it furnished plans—and which took tools to build. A how-to-build a dollhouse ad drew a half million requests for plans.

To meet the needs of the new market, some manufacturing operations were consolidated and automated to provide for the high-volume production needed.

(Based on "Stanley Works: Capitalizing on the homeowner do-it-yourself trend," **Business Week,** Feb. 26, 1979, pp.125–6.)

Stanley's original market was an older type of industrial market somewhat unusual in these days—a market of individual professional artisans. The items offered both the professional market and the do-it-yourself market are very similar.

1. How would these markets differ?

2. What differences would be needed in the design of tools needed by the professional carpenter or other tradesman and the homeowner?

3. How would the trade channels differ?

4. How would you expect the communications mix to differ.

5. What other differences can you think of which which need a different kind of marketing organization and operation for the two markets?

CHAPTER 5. PRODUCT LIFE CYCLES AND THE PROCESS OF MARKET GROWTH

The product life cycle: key framework for strategy
The basic life cycle concept
    The stages of a full life cycle
        Conception
        Product development gestation
        The critical infancy of market development
        The rapid growth phase
        The competitive turbulence of maturization
        The plateau of market saturation
        The final decline
The diverse forms of real life cycles
The four fundamental life cycle types
The intangibility of product
The learning requirement and its prediction
    Low learning products, missing link products, and fads
Market growth: the social diffusion of innovations
What we know about the diffusion process
    Product adoption roles
    Who are the early adopters?

PRODUCT LIFE CYCLES
& THE PROCESS OF MARKET GROWTH

5

The Product Life Cycle: Key Framework for Strategy

Success in marketing management requires a workable strategy. Continued workability requires a dynamic strategy, based on an understanding of the marketing implications of the various stages of the product life cycle and the different forms it can take.

Strategic plans are imperative in a mass consumption economy because current profit possibilities are the result of plans and actions formulated months, more often years, before. Organizations and industries which simply react to current events sooner or later fall into real trouble. Managing the marketing effort involves estimates of what lies ahead, well down the road.

Any strategy must be flexible and dynamic because every new offering goes through some form of life cycle. Each stage in that cycle results from an evolution in buyer perceptions of the values being received and from the changing competitive climate.

All types of product life cycles have a few surface simlarities in common: a period of growth, a peak of saturation, and an eventual decline. But cycles are extremely divergent in their speed of development and in their total life expectancies. The appropriate strategies vary just as much. The differences are due to the kinds of benefit advantages perceived by buyers, and the extent to which getting those benefits require much learning.

Product life cycles are also unit profit cycles, with the greatest gains coming during the growth and early maturity phases. Recognition of this fact has given rise to interest in the portfolio concept of the product mix.

The Basic Life Cycle Concept

The complete product life cycle is generally considered to consist of 8 stages: conception, product development, and a market life cycle of 6 stages:

1. Introduction of the offering and market development
2. A period of rapid growth and market expansion
3. Market maturization and competitive turbulence
4. Market saturation and maturity
5. Decline
6. Death and replacement

FIGURE 5-1. THE COMPLETE PRODUCT LIFE CYCLE

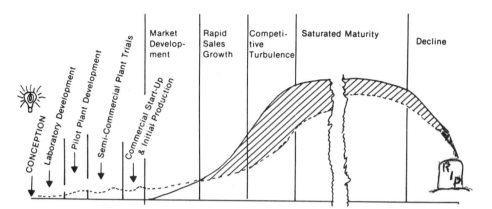

Reprinted from Chester R. Wasson, **Dynamic Competitive Strategy & Product Life Cycles,** 3rd ed., Austin Press, 1978, by special permission of the copyright owner.

Conception. Whether through planning or by accident, offerings are born out of a mating between a set of product attributes and a perceived set of market needs. As with any birth, the potentials for future health are limited by the quality of the match between the product attributes which a developed and the unfulfilled desire sets they are intended to satisfy. As with all infants, survival and viability are heavily dependent on the financial and human resources available to carry the offering through its early life. If the parents lack the adequate means, the idea should, if possible, be turned over to better equipped foster parents, organizations capable of and willing to support the concept through the incubation period and the market development phase. Even the most promising offerings need careful nurture during the early stages. The prematurely born mammal or offering lacks independent vitality.

The Offering Development Gestation Period. All offerings start out as mere ideas. At the start, they are either some simple performance concept without form or substance as yet, or some physical offering whose perceivable attributes are imperfectly predictable. Market life becomes possible only when a producible benefit bundle is developed which is capable of satisfying a set of physical and/or psychical desires of some substantial segments of potential buyers, then properly delivered into a favorable marketing environment.

Generally, the best results come when guided by well-planned research into the total performance attributes needed to fit the highest valued desire sets and the identity of the most interested market segments. Once the character of the offering becomes apparent, marketing plans should be developed to insure favorable birth conditions. Premature delivery before either the offering or market are prepared can be dangerous to the health of both the infant and the parent.

The Critical Infancy of Market Development. Revolutionary new offerings usually tend to start life slowly. Sales income, in such cases, lags behind market development expenses because the public needs education to perceive adequate value in the benefits offered. Commonly, also, the potentialities for user satisfaction are not clearly foreseen at the time of introduction. The introductory period can be a time of learning about the values perceivable by buyers, and the marketing niche the offering can hope to gain.

Once launched, customer experience with the new offerings needs to be watched closely for possible weaknesses and defects which could sicken the market. Just as important, this experience will furnish knowledge as to just what benefits customers are finding in the offering, and thus guide both efforts in improving design and in widening the market.

Such market development introductions are specialty offerings, perceived by buyers as having no close substitutes. A single basic model is likely to satisfy all early adopters because the core functional attributes are the focus of customer interest. The market has yet to be segmented in any significant manner.

If early market development really is slow, direct competition will not be a problem—the obvious deficits and lack of surging demand are more than enough protection. Promotional costs needed to establish a foothold will exceed expenses. Some form of personal sales push will be needed, of the most intense kind. The low sales volume and need for hard selling will dictate limitation of distribution to a selected few, highly aggressive outlets, who will be expecting to receive a large portion of the sales price.

If the market really is in need of what the offering promises, sales will begin to grow at an increasing pace sooner or later. If and when such a growth phase starts, competition will not be long in following, and the seller must be prepared in advance to meet it.

The Rapid Growth Phase. Sales curves all start from zero. Whether growth comes early or late, full momentum takes time to develop. When growth does start, it tends to be at a steady, increasing speed. The whole market climate begins to change. Profit margins begin to exceed promotional costs, distributors begin to seek the product. The ballooning market attracts competitors like clover draws bees. With widening public understanding of the offering comes diversification of the desire sets and the need for offering variations.

Potential competitors will now be alert to the possibilities. They will take advantage of any gap in product line offerings, in distribution coverage, or any too wide unit profits to carve out a piece of the action. At this stage, customer loyalty does not exist to any significant degree. Most of the added sales are coming from newcomers to the market. For many, the item will be a shopping good, no longer a specialty item. They will be looking for designs to fit their own special desire sets and prices to fit their purses. Distribution will have to be widened and intensified, both to reach final customers better before someone else does, and to satisfy dealers who might otherwise actively seek additional sources.

Promotional emphasis and content needs revision at this point. The growing sales are proof that customers have been well educated on the offering concept. The purpose of promotion is to entrench the seller's brand in their hearts and affections.

All of this takes advance planning and an ear close to the market. To wait until the growth is visible is to risk loss of the market to more aggressive competition. The first to enter the market can be the first to lose it. The innovator must have already started to develop a strong niche, or others will reap the end results in a coming shakeout.

The Competitive Turbulence of the Maturing Market. One of the most poorly remembered absolute truths is that nothing keeps growing at a constant rate. Certainly those experiencing the glow of fast-rising new product markets nearly always forget it. At some point, market growth has to slow down—the supply of new customers is limited. The appetites of all customers become satiated, just when every seller is expanding capacity.

As the new excess capacity begins to develop, a competitive scramble ensues. Unit profits decline and a battle for survival results. Those who have not already carved out a solid niche drop by the wayside early. Even strong leaders can suffer if they have not kept up with the changing diversification of demand. The customers, both ultimate and the intermediaries, are now beginning to call the tune. Market positions need to be reinforced and preparations made to profit with thinner unit profits in the coming mature market.

R & D to constantly improve the offering is still a must. But the more innovative and entrepreneurial elements of management need to be turned to developing new offerings. With the novelty values disappearing, the offering is beginning to lose some of its perceived value, and the perceived differences in offerings may be diminishing. Distribution will be a key element in market strength.

This is the point to start paying close attention to continuing reviews of the product line. Any gaps should be closed. Line elements which do not strengthen the seller's market position need to be dropped. Cost controls should be tightened. The promotional and after-sales emphasis should include elements intended to reduce the cognitive dissonance of buyers. Buyers may need to be reminded of the value of the purchases made.

The Plateau of Mature Saturated Markets. Sooner or later, new customers become scarce, their numbers offset by disappearance of old customers, except for population growth. Although some sellers will have a far greater market share than others, large portions of the market will have little brand loyalty. Perceived differentiation (and the actuality itself, most likely) will have decreased greatly. Other and more exciting offerings will be gaining public attention. The potentials for major product improvements will be disappearing. (But some possibilities will still exist, so long as customers must make any kind of design compromise choices.)

The offering is now becoming "yesterday's breadwinner", and resources need to be devoted to developing tomorrow's. Competitive threats will not have disappeared, but they will come from unexpected quarters: from outside the industry, and usually from new types of offerings which satisfy some of the same core desires and eliminate some of the design compromises. If any of these begin to gain a foothold, decline is on its way.

The Final Decline. Like everything else mortal, products die at some point. Few enjoy more than a generation of popularity, some yield no more than a few years of profit, and fads die out in months. Once a market has hit the downtrail, there is neither wisdom nor profit in prolonging the agony. The offering should be milked of whatever profit remains, then put quietly to sleep.

The Diverse Forms of Real Life Cycles

The above description of cycle phases is essentially correct whatever the type of cycle. But there is no immutable cycle course. Not all introductions pass through all eight stages. Most introductions skip any significant market development stage. One particular type of cycle—the fad—wilts suddenly at the very peak of its sales curve. The concept is not very useful if treated as a prediction of the probable course of sales of every kind of introduction.

We need, first, to distinguish between the degrees of innovation being attempted by product introductions. At one end of the spectrum are new product forms, such as the automobile in 1896, the radio, when first introduced a little later, and the computer in more recent times. At the other end is the introduction of a new brand of coffee, or other familiar product which differs little from offerings already well-established, except in the label and the seller. Even the emulative brands have their cycles, but if well-conceived, most require no substantial period of market development because they ask customers to learn little more than the name of a new source of a familiar satisfaction bundle.

FIGURE 5-2. COMMON VARIANTS OF THE PRODUCT LIFE CYCLE

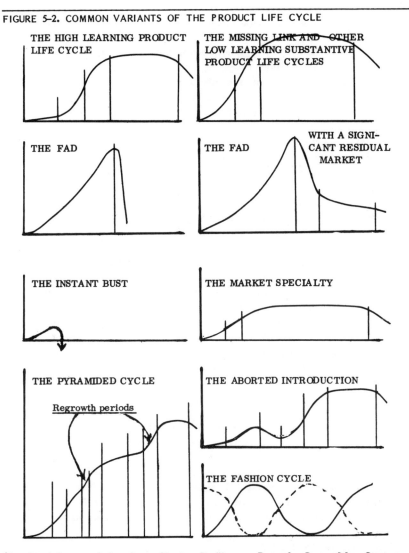

THE HIGH LEARNING PRODUCT LIFE CYCLE

THE MISSING LINK AND OTHER LOW LEARNING SUBSTANTIVE PRODUCT LIFE CYCLES

THE FAD

THE FAD — WITH A SIGNIFICANT RESIDUAL MARKET

THE INSTANT BUST

THE MARKET SPECIALTY

THE PYRAMIDED CYCLE
Regrowth periods

THE ABORTED INTRODUCTION

THE FASHION CYCLE

(Reprinted by permission from Chester R. Wasson, **Dynamic Competitive Strategy & Product Life Cycles**)

We need to discriminate between at least four points in this spectrum:
- The product category (such as powered wheeled transportation)
- The product form (individualized motor transport: the automobile)
- The product variant (sports car)
- The brand (Ford)

(Likewise, we might have a spectrum like: tobacco usage, ready-formed smoking products (cigars and cigarettes), filter cigarettes, and Marlboro.)

But even revolutionary new product forms, such as the automobile and the computer experience a wide range of really different life cycle curves. Figure 5-2 illustrates some of the obvious variants which even superficial observation will reveal. Some products surprise even their optimistic sponsors with a rocket-like ascent to popularity. Among these are fads, which trap the optimists with their sudden collapse at the moment of greatest sales. Others, with a similar fast growth, like the automobile, become a deeply entrenched part of the culture. Still others, like color television, gobble up large amounts of promotional capital before the public takes them to heart.

Many products die at birth. Others—we call them fashions—seem to rise spontaneously, enjoy a significant period of popularity, then fade away, only to be reincarnated a few years later, and time after time.

The time it takes to reach a growth phase take-off is extremely variable, even among those introductions which follow the classical 8-stage life cycle. It required a full generation to develop growth momentum for electric typewriters. The so-called personal computers took no more than three years after designs with adequate capacity became available.

One revolutionary introduction, like hybrid corn seed, requires years before the market begins to bubble. Another, like broad spectrum antibiotics and insecticides, rise to peak volume with no perceptible period of market development. Most fads die out completely at the peak of their growth. Other obvious fads retreat just as quickly from peak volume, but stop short of extinction and continue to serve some narrow market. Some revolutionary products seem to level off at successive plateaus, only to enter new growth phases as either inventive consumers or perceptive marketing management uncovers new satisfaction potentials which make them, in effect, new products.

If the product life cycle concept is to furnish any useful guidance, we must cut through the numerous variations to discover underlying patterns. Analysis seems to indicate that various combinations of four fundamental life cycle forms can explain all of the observed fluctuations (see Figure 5-3).

The Four Fundamental Life Cycle Types

It looks like we can sort out all the varying real life cycles into examples or combinations of four specific life cycle patterns, each of which requires a distinctive course of marketing management:

1. The classic 8-stage cycle experienced by any offering whose net added benefit values are offset by a need for substantial relearning of automatic reactions by nearly all prospects

2. Cycles which skip any prolonged market development stage because prospects need little education as to the values offered and have

already developed use–systems into which the offering fits without change in any of their automatic response patterns.

3. The sky–rocket rise and quick burn–out of the true fad
4. The oscillations of the fashion cycle, with its wide swings of opposing trends

FIGURE 5–3. THE FOUR BASIC LIFE CYCLE FORMS

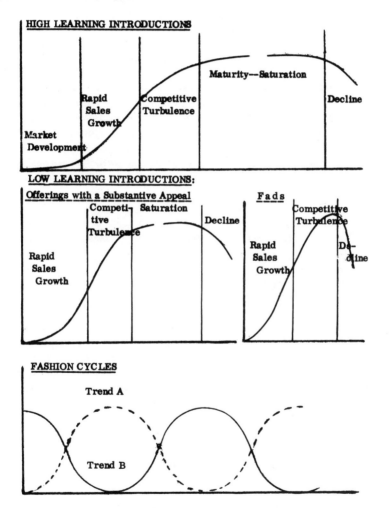

(Reprinted by permission from Chester R. Wasson, **Dynamic Competitive Strategy & Product Life Cycles**)

Of the 9 observed types depicted in Figure 5-2, 4 are examples of the basic types in their uncomplicated forms. The others are obvious combinations of the basic four.

The fad with a significant residual market is simply an introduction which fits the need of a wide public for novelty, but also fills a salient need for some narrow segment. Thus it is a combination of fad for a large part of the initial market, and of a low-learning offering for a narrow market segment.

The instant bust is an offering which finds no receptive market, either because the design does not, as introduced, fit a salient need, or because the marketing plan or the resources behind it were inadequate.

The market specialty cycle is just that: an offering meeting the needs of a small segment (and thus probably a low-learning one of necessity).

The pyramided cycle is one which develops new benefit patterns as customers learn the possibilities. It may start life as a low-learning product (as the automobile did) or a high-learning offering (as did color television, which some believe is entering a new growth stage).

The aborted introduction would be one which was initially launched with an inadequately developed design (as the water-jet boat was originally) or an inadequately targeted or financed marketing plan, and the error corrected before the market was lost entirely.

Fashion cycles are unique in at least three respects, as we shall see later:
- They are not full-fledged separate kinds of products, but essentially cosmetic aspects of an extremely wide range of offerings
- They are recurrent, with, normally, wide pendulum-like swings from one extreme to the opposite. They are thus a combination of two or more opposing fashion cycles.
- They seem to be rooted in the psychology of the buyers themselves, sometimes developing with no aid from any seller.

Manifestly, before an appropriate plan can be developed for any introduction, we must have a reasonably correct forecast of the character of the probable cycle it is entering. High-learning introductions require provisions for sustained deficits and entirely different promotional mixes and distribution arrangements than do low-learning introductions. Riding a fad market requires more perceptive market horsemanship than is required by entries into a fashion market.

To make such a forecast, we must first be clear as to what all the customers involved—distributors as well as ultimate consumers—are buying. We must also understand the relationship of any offering to the customers' established automatic response tendencies. First of all, we must be aware that however concrete the form of the offering, it is really, from the buyer's point of view, a bundle of intangibles.

The distinction commonly made between selling the concrete physical items we call "products" and the marketing of so-called intangibles is an optical illusion. In the buyers' perceptions, they are receiving a bundle of promised services. They expect to fill a cluster of desires with this one purchase by plugging it into some use-system, preferably an established one, requiring no learning.

THE CASE OF THE CAMOUFLAGE COSMETIC

A girl born with a disfiguring facial birthmark developed an effective pancake make-up. Believing it would help others in a similar situation, she had it packaged under a trade mark, NO-Mark. The human interest aspect of her problem and inventiveness cornered long publicity write-ups in even the largest metropolitan dailies whenever she went into any market, and she easily sold it into large department stores.

Unfortunately, the product died on the shelves. Too few women had facial birthmarks.

Some time later, a direct-selling firm, looking around for new promotions, learned of the product and its history. Considering the product's promotable capabilities, they reasoned that a different angle could sell it to a wider market. If the product would camouflage a birthmark, it could also camouflage minor facial flaws like pockmarks and acne scars, which many more women were concerned about.

Together with their ad agency, they developed a 15-minute beauty advice TV program. 13 of the 15 minutes were devoted to the proper use of cosmetics. The end 2 minutes contained the commercial, which asked, in essence: Did you ever wonder how Hollywood stars achieved their flawless good looks? Did you ever see a star without her make-up? They then showed a close-up of a woman with the pancake make-up, and the same model, make-up free, with obvious minor blemishes.

The program drew profitable sales from the first showing. The sales level continued to hold up so well that NO-Mark went back into the stores.

The physical item purchased is simply a necessary nuisance—a required clue that the customer has acquired a key element the use-system lacks. What is the automobile buyer looking for? Ideally, probably the following performance attributes:

- Immediately available transportation at whatever time desired, with no element of discomfort, no limitations of available roads, no learning to operate
- Unlimited capacity for whatever luggage or cargo needed on any specific trip
- Clear evidence, visible to all bystanders, that we own this marvelous possession
- Complete freedom from maintenance of any kind: no repairs ever, no cleaning, no storage space between the occasions to use it
- No operating cost
- No depreciation, no hunt for scarce parking at the destination

---

INDUSTRIAL AND MILITARY BUYERS PURCHASE PERFORMANCE, NOT HARDWARE

The time was the spring of 1941. France was on the verge of collapse under the Nazi blitzkrieg, America was desperately pushing a transition from a peacetime army of 125,000 men, armed largely with World War I equipment. The War Production Board was trying to gear up for full production of modern weapons. In the Military Requirement Branch of WPB, a young economist had been told, "Find out how much nickel we might need. The answer seems to be here in the specifications for the M3 tank. He was handed a thick book, labelled "Bill of Materials," listing the various shapes, sizes and alloy designation for each piece of steel going into the construction of the Army's M3 tank. Most of the specifications were expressed in terms of S.A.E. standards, a book of which he also had available. The standards gave the percentage of alloying elements, if any, including nickel. But one item, weighing more than the rest, was listed with a reference to a U. S. Army Dept. of Ordnance specification: the tank armor.

Going down the hall to the Army's Ordnance office, then in the same building, he asked for the specification. When he explained his reason, he was told: "Here it is, but it won't do you much good." ("Why?") "Because it is a performance specification. It simply specifies what size and velocity of shell it must stop." (But you must know what is in it!") "Not necessarily. They can make it of sawdust if it does the job."

When asked where he could find out, he was referred to one of the colonels in charge of procurement. The latter did have information on the alloys being used by the suppliers – 29 of them. They used 29 different alloy mixtures.

Being realistic, we all compromise for a lot less than this. Just which limitations we accept depends on who we are, and which of our use-systems are perceived as most in need of the purchase. In any event, what we have bought will simply be a cue that we can hope to satisfy the specific use-systems. What we are willing to pay reflects the value we perceive in whatever degree of satisfaction that cue appears to be promising us.

Some of the actual physical performance potentials of the purchase may be part of the perceived values, but not necessarily all of them. Indeed, they may be incidental or not even relevant. A good perfume should smell nice, but a nice smell alone does not bring the kind of prices well-accepted perfumes bring. In fact, what we perceive as an attractive odor is not necessarily an objective fact for all peoples. It is defined by the culture which set the purchaser's perceptions and standards.

To justify the price received by any leading fragrance requires more than an accepted odor. The price can be obtained only when the perfume suggests an end result that the chemist cannot embody in the physical product. For much of the world, that attribute is "glamour", romance. (Although, with the changing roles of women in western society, this seems to be changing in some respects, and for some market segments.)

Even these illustrations are generalizations not applicable to all purchasers. A considerable portion of the perfumes purchased for the use of women are not bought or even chosen by them. They are bought by others as gifts deemed generally acceptable, and the price may be a sought-for attribute in itself, as a cue to the degree to which the giver "cares."

All offerings are thus simply perceived sets of promises that the buyer will be able to complete some specific sets of use-systems. The use-systems are the sources of the sought-for satisfactions. The interest of potential buyers in any introduction will be inverse to the degree to which established use-systems and the related automatic responses must be changed – the degree to which to which prospects perceive the need for some relearning.

The learning requirement is the key to predicting the initial market reactions, to the degree of newness in a new product.

The Learning Requirement and its Prediction

To predict the initial reception of any introduction, we must estimate to what extent the customer may have to modify or change established automatic response patterns to use it. All of us have had enough experience with the problem of changing some established habits of body or mind to appreciate the difficulty.

FIGURE 5–4. A CONCEPTION OF THE HABIT RELEARNING PROCESS

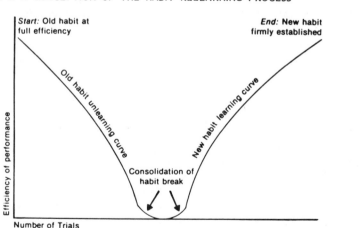

(Reprinted by permission from Chester R. Wasson, **Dynamic Competitive Strategy & Product Life Cycles**)

An old but still valid laboratory experiment with rats can help us visualize the process as well as the problem (Hunter, 1922). Hungry rats were started at opening of a simple T-maze. When they reached the point where they had to turn left or right into one of the two arms, they got a cue from a light. If the light was on, the food was in the right arm. If the light was off, the food was in the opposite arm. On the average, the rats required 286 trials to make the proper choice without error. Then the pattern was reversed: the food was in the left arm when the light was on, in the right when not lit. Relearning the new pattern required 603 trials, well over double the work of learning the initial response.

Rats, of course, are not people (although some seem to think they are smarter). But anyone who has ever had to go from a manual typewriter to an electric model, or attempted to break a smoking habit, will recognize the three steps needed to change a habit:

1. Gradually bring the automatic impulses of the old habit to the level of consciousness and keep blocking them
2. Consolidate the blocking of the old impulses
3. Build the new habit into an unconscious automatic response

As the rat experiment suggested, the process of substituting a new automatic response pattern for an old one is more than twice as arduous as simply learning a pattern which does not conflict with a previous one in any particular. Developing any new pattern is energy- and time- consuming, and a substantial price for whatever satisfaction is obtained. But a changeover is far more frustrating.

Most use systems are deeply embedded complexes of physical habits, positive value perceptions, and habitual role perceptions. It follows that market acceptance of any offering which demands any significant turnaround in automatic responses can be expected to be slow, initial buyers few and expensive to reach and sell.

There is one exception: an offering which eliminates a step which is repeated often, but resented as a nuisance, and thus not really automatic (such as having to stop regularly to fill the fuel tank of the car, and pay for the contents).

No kind of forecasting bats 1.000. The best sellers can do is to estimate the probable market reaction in terms of the use-systems and the benefits which appear to be foreseeable, in the light of the use-system learning or relearning the analysis seems to suggest.

Predictions of the extreme cases are not likely to err often. As outlined later, the prediction of the effect on physical use-systems can be reasonably objective, and the effect on mental habits reasonably discoverable. The major sources of error concern difficulties in predicting which market segments are likely to be in the early adopter groups, the kinds and levels of values buyers will perceive once the product is in hand, and the use-systems into which they will perceive the offering as best adapted.

In any case, careful preliminary analysis can forewarn of any problems ahead and help limit use of a seller's developmental resources to those kinds of offerings it is best equipped to see through any market development period. For any seller with limited resources, this inevitably means low-learning offerings.

Low-Learning Offerings: Missing Link Products and Fads.

Products designated as "new" range from the revolutionary new offerings resembling nothing on the current market, to emulative and adaptive introductions which are new only to the seller presenting them. Technically, if they succeed, even the emulative and adaptive represent added perceived value for some segments. The only learning required is that of a new source for a somewhat improved, already acceptable offering. If launched by an accepted seller, or by almost anyone during a growth period, the financial resources required for success would be minimal. But there is another kind of low-learning introduction which gains ready acceptance: the missing link, or **systems-completing** offerings.

Systems-completing offerings. Some revolutionary new offerings can be perceived as psychologically familiar and find the system waiting for them. Such was the case with paved highways in the 1920's, when a waiting public was eager to vote funds to get them, and with the expressways and super-highways in the 1950's and 1960's. They added a higher perceived value to the already highly valued system of private automobile transportation.

Likewise, black-and-white television never required any customer learning. Perceived as free movies at home, the sales growth was almost vertical, at a time when broadcasting was limited to a few evening hours and network facilities had not yet been created.

The history of the spreading use of computers has demonstrated the value of introducing missing link offerings. IBM was not the inventor of the first computers, nor the first to enter the market. What gained the market for IBM was the development of "software": libraries of standard programs fitting some of the most obvious needs of users. The early programs were proprietary, fitting only the seller's own computers.

Much more recently, the rapid development of large capacity small machines of a number of makes has opened markets for independent software systems for a wide variety of uses, which can fit a large number of makes. The early success of the Apple computer was apparently due largely to the openness with which the manufacturer revealed the architecture of the machine, enabling a wide range of independents to tailor special programs of all kinds for use on the Apple.

Small hobbyists with few resources other than their own time and labor have reaped profitable markets. The item sold is nothing more than a manual and a program disk. To develop similar programs for their own use, users might have to work for as long as a year, even after they became adept at the tedium of programming. The computer user can buy one for less than $500, and some for less than $100, and need never learn to do the programming. These, in turn have made it easier for new competitors to launch emulative offerings, since vast libraries of software were avaliable to their customers.

MISSING LINKS ARE WHERE YOU FIND A NEED THEM

Missing link offerings are added items or services which make it easier for buyers to fit the core offering into their established habit patterns, or into use systems they are ready to develop or are developing. They may be accessory items, like rubber tires for tractors. They may be ready made programs which have continuously broadened the market for computers. They may be elements in the promotional effort which help interested prospects gain a quicker understanding of the nature of the benefits, or a new type of distribution link which renders the product more available.

Their distinguishing mark is that they suddenly broaden the market by bringing in prospects not otherwise likely to buy soon.

Automotive sales growth started to level off from a spectacular climb about 1920. Until that point, most intercity roads were really little more than ungraded paths between fields. Then the good roads movement, backed by the auto industry, began to take hold in a flurry of road construction, and auto ownership resumed its climb for a period. The new road systems widened the utility of the automobile. Until then, its main value had been confined to local errands. Even a cross–state trip had been a major adventure, under substantial handicaps of weather and road conditions. Similarly, the development of radiator anti–freezes changed the automobile from a mild weather vehicle into a dependable year–around transportation necessity. (Well into the mid–1920's, many owners simply drained the radiator for the winter, and stored the car until spring.) Those who did brave winter freezes, drained the radiator at any stops prolonged more than a couple of hours, and then refilled when ready to go again.)

People have always wanted to do as much of their food shopping as possible in a single trip. Before the automobile, a clustering of sellers in a single market place or a nearby central market district served well enough, especially when the lack of adequate refrigeration dictated nearly daily shopping for many items. Then the automobile reduced the need for markets close to hand. The mechanical refrigerator made fewer trips necessary, but larger volumes on each trip. Parking became a problem, especially with store to store shopping. Supermarket development fitted the need so well that chains of them rose rapidly to dominate the food distribution system.

As noted later, the adoption of hybrid corn seed was extremely slow at first. Early distribution was through ordinary farm supply merchants, by the Pioneer brand. Then DeKalb, originally a farm buying cooperative, developed its own strains, and appointed key local farmers as dealers, selling personally to their neighbors. The personal sales effort of these local leaders gave the benefits the needed credibility, and sales started their swift rise, carrying DeKalb to industry dominance.

Emulative and adaptive offerings. Any rapidly growing market inevitably attracts swarms of new competitors. Because of the growing number of new prospective customers, market entry is easy and takes only limited initial resources. Distribution is becoming more readily available, and many of the new customers are shopping around, especially if (as is usually the case) sellers are not aggressively downpricing their offerings to pass on the savings of new volume sales. Most of the new offerings are emulative or adaptive. Many are low-end or at least low-margin offerings to take advantage of the broadening market.

Tull has distinguished between the emulative offering, introduced by new competitors, and the adaptive: new models launched by an existing seller to broaden the market and meet or preempt new competition. (Donald S. Tull, "The relationship of actual and predicted sales and profits in new product introductions," **Journal of Business,** July, 1967, pp. 233–250.)

Both the emulative and adaptive enter the market when growth is quite visible. Both succeed when they offer noticeably better value for some substantial segment of the market.

Emulative and adaptive entries may be offered even in the saturated phases of the cycle, adding little or nothing to the total market volume, but taking market share from some of the weaker or sleepier competition. When this is the case, the seller must usually be well-financed, and willing to spend heavily for promotion. But they can succeed, especially when the gross margin between production cost and sales price is high (as is normally true in such consumer areas as beverages, toiletries and cosmetics, and cigarettes). Procter & Gamble has done it time and again with toothpaste (Gleem and Crest), shampoos, and other toiletries, and even peanut butter. The Philip Morris successes with Marlboro cigarettes and Miller Beer are excellent examples. Emulative and adaptive offerings are basically marketing opposites, both designed to win new market segments among those not fully satisfied with current offerings. Not infrequently, the adaptive product is a defensive move, a design to ward off competition which is threatening to fill a market gap. To succeed, the entry must be perceived by some segments as better values than otherwise available.

The fast growth of fad markets always attracts large number of emulators. Winning at this game takes some very precise timing.

The fad: the empty offering. There is some element of fad purchasing in practically every fast-rising growth market. Some degree of "over-adoption" takes place because of the novelty aspect of any popular new offering, including fashion. Some buyers quite clearly purchase items not well fitted to their substantive desires.

Buyers of true fads, however, neither expect nor receive any benefits except the excitement of novelty. Psychological experiments have long demonstrated that some sort of drive for new or different experiences exists among all sentient beings.

The lack of any substantive benefit other than novelty is the distinguishing mark that dooms such introductions to an early sudden death. The novelty is gone once the market is saturated, and the market itself vanishes.

Some kinds of true fads do retain a much smaller residual market. This can happen if the fad interests a very narrow age segment, especially that of young children, whose attention span is very short. Then successive generations may adopt the item themselves for short periods. Some form of the hoop is always around, and skateboards have been around for generations, with some ebb and flow in interest.

Many armchair hobbies and games manage to retain a small market among the forcibly idled, especially invalids. The time–killing attributes of such offerings have substantive value for such customers.

There is a tendency to lump all currently popular purchases, including true fashions, as fads. In 1900, a large part of the population treated the automobile as a fad. It is still here, passing through its own variants of the fashion cycle. Fashions do have substantive benefits to offer.

True fashions eventually fade, but never have the fiery rise and fast plunge of the fad. They are a very complex aspect of many facets of the culture, given the more extensive treatment required in the next chapter.

The shape of the market cycle of all introductions results from a recognizable social process which has come to be labelled as the **diffusion of innovations.**

Market Growth: the Social Diffusion of Innovations

Whatever the public readiness for an offering, the spreading sales take some period of time even for the hottest fad. Most people agree with the the 17th century poet, "Be not the first by whom the new is tried." Even under the most intense advertising barrage, few of those "exposed" to it pay attention. Even among those who do, only the very few actively seeking some such satisfaction bundle risk trying the offering. Only after these venturesome innovators validate the claims do their acquaintances start to buy. We have learned that the spread of any innovation is brought about by a chain of example and word of mouth testimony, by a social diffusion process. The greater the cost of change, the slower the diffusion.

What We Know about the Diffusion Process

Real understanding of the diffusion process dates from the 1940's, when American rural sociologists analyzed the course of the adoption of the use of hybrid corn seed, which revolutionized Corn Belt agriculture during the 1930's.

The adoption of hybrid corn followed the classic model of life cycle growth. Early sales were hard to come by. Only 6% of the farmers tried hybrid seed in the first 6 years. At that point, adoption speeded up. By the end of the second 6 years, 80% of the farmers were using hybrid seed.

Research revealed that the adopters could be classified into 5 groups according to the stage at which they adopted, each with a different attitude toward new offerings:

- Innovators
- Other early adopters

- The early majority
- The late majority
- Laggard skeptics

Innovators, the first 2% or 3% of adopters, are perfectionists, always seeking out better methods and offerings even before ready for release for general use. They are so far ahead of their neighbors and associates that their main value to the seller is in their cooperation in testing pilot offerings

Early adopters (variously labelled by some as tastemakers, peer group leaders, opinion leaders, key communicators, influentials). These make up the early market, about the first 12 to 15%, when the innovators are included. Their expertise in the areas of the specific kinds of offerings is respected by neighbors and associates, and their contacts in the community are relatively wide. They are looked to for assurance that the promised benefits exist. Their approval is the impetus for adoption by the rest of the **early majority:** those who bring sales up to the halfway point of saturation.

The entry of the **late majority** in the market signals the slowdown of the competitive turbulence ahead. They constitute about one-third of the eventual market.

Skeptical laggards finally come on the market as it reaches saturation, and usually are the last to abandon during the decline.

Who Are the Early Adopters?

At first blush, this would seem to be a key question. In the field of farm practices, members of each of the adopter groups seemed to fit a characteristic pattern:

- Early adopters had large farms, high income, were risk takers, usually under 56 years of age, actively sought new ideas in farming, and participated in groups outside the local community.
- The majority groups had average size farms and income, tended to be between 50 and 60 years of age, were not actively seeking new ideas, but were receptive, and participated in local groups.
- Late adopters had small farms and low income, were security minded, usually over 60, skeptical of the new, and seldom participated in local groups.

Such information can be valuable to those whose offerings are directed solely to career agricultural interests. Innumerable attempts to find parallel descriptions for quite different types of offerings do not seem to have found any single clear answer. The answer may not be as important as it appears at first glance. Certain factors do appear to identify people likely to be first adopters for some kinds of offerings, but only those promising credible benefits fitting the value systems to which they are most committed.

THE ADOPTION OF HYBRID CORN: A CLASSIC HIGH-LEARNING OFFERING

A grain of hybrid corn looks like any other corn. It is planted, cultivated and harvested in the same manner as any other corn. The only differences are in a higher degree of uniformity of quality, in substantially higher yields per acre, and in one fact of extreme importance to the way corn farming had been carried on up until the introduction of hybrid corn. Corn from one crop cannot be saved for planting the next year.

That single difference meant that the whole operation was no longer as self-sufficient as before. Instead of saving some of the best of his previous crop and replanting it the following year, the corn farmer who adopted hybrid corn had to purchase seed every year – seed that cost quite a bit more than he had received for the same amount from his crop. This took a lot of soul-searching and relearning. The result was a slow and difficult sales operation for hybrid producers for a half dozen years.

From the first release of hybrid seed, farmers were fully aware of its availability. They were constantly informed of its benefits, from sources which carried as high credibility as any claim can hope for. The farm journals, which nearly every farmer took and read, were full of authenticated reports of the better yields. The Agricultural Colleges and the local Agricultural Extension personnel actively promoted its use.

Despite the continuing stream of favorable publicity, only the most venturesome even gave it a pilot trial. During the first 6 years, only 6% tried it at any time. Then usage started spreading, and by the end of the twelfth year, 80% of the corn growers were seeding their fields with the hybrids. Today, any other kind of seed is difficult to find.

Of the numerous studies published, nearly all have focused on a single type of offering. One, however, did cover a wide spectrum of introductions among a single group of families: The Tastemaker studies conducted by Opinion Research Corporation (ORC) in 1958 (Opinion Research, Inc., 1959).

The ORC studies surveyed a group of suburban families concerning their adoption of 75 widely different kinds of new products released on the market between 1940 and 1958. Included in the survey was an in-depth analysis of family characteristics, history, and interests. In the analysis, families were scored on a mobility index, on the hypothesis that wide mobility may make people more receptive to new ideas. As indicated earlier, families were also classified on the basis of their value systems.

The principal findings of the Tastemaker study were significant:
- In 6 out of 10 new introductions, purchases during the first half of the market rise came entirely from the 27% of the families with the highest mobility rating, but none were early adopters for every item.
- Nearly a fourth of the early adoptions came from low-mobile families
- Early adoption of any specific introduction was directly related to the lifestyle commitments of the family members, and the intensity of the commitment.

- As indicated earlier, the lifestyle value leading to early adoption was not always one associated with the product

This last listed finding goes far to explain the difficulty met by anyone who attempts to predict market potentials for proposed new products. The benefits buyers are going to perceive cannot be foreseen with any accuracy.

All of the studies do seem to point to one characteristic of real value to marketing people. Early adopters are actively seeking some kind of new satisfactions in line with their major interests. This seems to indicate that buyers will find the product if publicity is wide enough to reach the special communications media touching on their interests. Once they start buying, early research can identify their definitions of the offering. This can then be used to target advertising and sales efforts.

Discovering the values sought by early adopters would seem to be especially valuable for fashions of all kinds, where many of the values sought are psychical and personal.

SUMMARY

1. Any workable marketing strategy is dynamic, based on an appreciation of the implications of the product life cycle.

2. The classic model of the product life cycle consists of 8 stages: conception of a marketable offering, product development, and six marketing stages—market development, rapid growth phase, competitive turbulence of maturization, the mature saturated market, decline, and death.

3. Real life cycles do not follow this neat outline. Most do not go through a market development period of any significant length. Fad cycles die out quickly at the very moment of reaching saturation. Fashion cycles go through successive reincarnations. The product life cycle concept is applied to four different types of market introductions: new product categories, new product forms within a category, product variants, and brands.

4. The wide diversity of actual cycles observed can be analyzed as combinations of four fundamental cycles: high learning offerings which follow the classic 8-stage cycle, low-learning cycles which start on a rapid growth phase early, fashion cycles, and fad cycles.

5. The differences arise in the buyers' perceptions of any offering as an intangible mix of services which promise to fulfill a complete set of desires, by completing an established use-system.

6. If the offering fits established use-system habits and perceptions, no prolonged market development period is likely. If acceptance and use requires modifying such automatic response patterns, the learning required will hinder sales for a shorter or longer time, depending on the kind and degree of learning.

7. Successful management of high-learning introductions requires both patience and a substantial supply of patient capital. Accordingly, most

sellers are limited to launching low-learning introductions: emulative or adaptive offerings, or systems-completing offerings. Systems-completing offerings can be especially rewarding.

8. Fashion cycles and fad cycles are not variations of the same kind of market cycle. Fads die quickly because they offer nothing but novelty. Fashions gain popularity because they promise substantive benefits.

9. All offerings gain markets through a process of social communication which has come to be designated as the diffusion of innovations. Only a small percentage of initial innovators adopt solely on the basis of sellers' communications.

10. After the innovators have validated the benefits promised, the reaction of the rest of the market depends in part on the recommendations and examples of others who have adopted the product.

11. The identities of the key innovators varies with the kind of offering, although such influentials or tastemakers seem to have certain personality characteristics in common: usually wider contacts. The key to the adoption is the value system into which the offering is perceived as belonging, and the degree of commitment of the adopter to this value system.

FOOD FOR THOUGHT AND DISCUSSION

THE DIFFERING INTRODUCTORY EXPERIENCES OF FROZEN ORANGE CONCENTRATE AND OF INSTANT COFFEE

Frozen Orange   Instant Coffee
Concentrate   Equiv. 000,000
00,000 gal.   2-oz. jars

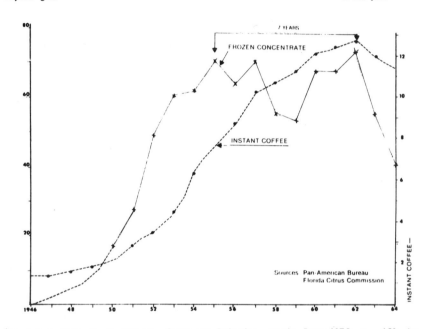

(Reprinted from C. R. Wasson, **Consumer Behavior**, Austin Press, 1975, p.   159, by special permission of the copyright owner)

Both frozen orange concentrate and instant coffee hit the general market shortly after the end of World War II, both of them a result of capacity built up to supply military field rations with powdered beverage concentrates.

The market response, however, was quite different, as the chart above indicates. In fact, the shipment data understate the early demand for the frozen orange concentrate.   Refrigerator cars capable of proper protection of the concentrate were inadequate to keep stores stocked, and Florida orange production insufficient to furnish the volume required during the first three years.

The orange concentrate was a modification of the dry powder used by the military.   The reconstituted powder had proved to have too sharp a taste.   When mixed with an equivalent amount of fresh juice, and frozen in sealed cans, the product had a flavor within the range of the fresh juice, but had to be stored and shipped at temperatures below 15 degrees F.

Frozen orange concentrate was a sales success from the day of the first radio commercial introducing it. There were no market development problems, only a scramble to create adequate shipping facilities and to bring orange groves into production.

Instant coffee, as can be seen, was no instant success. It was, in fact, not a completely new product except for general consumer use. In the form of one-cup packets, it had been sold for institutional use since at least the late 1920's. Despite this modest head start, sales barely rose for nearly four years. Even the rapid growth phase was muted, and a second brand was not attracted to the market until 1951.

In terms of convenience, instant coffee was a simpler product than the orange concentrate. At a time when home refrigeration was still short of universal, it posed no special storage problem. The flavor was well within the range of that produced in most homes. But most housewives shunned it for a long time.

1. How might you account for the different introductory experiences of these two convenience products?

2. What trends since might explain the eventual market growth?

EVALUATING OPPORTUNITIES IN THE MUSHROOMING PC MARKET

Prof. Reynolds Carson really did not set out to study the booming market in small computers. He was merely looking for a simpler solution to a task he had set himself: getting out a specialized management text which he felt he would have to publish himself. He was not a complete novice at the publishing game. Besides 3 other books published for him by textbook firms, he had put out one narrow market specialty volume on his own. In that case, he had used an IBM Executive model electric typewriter, equipped with a special No. 2 Bold face and carbon ribbon. Right hand margins were left unjustified (ragged, not flush). University presses frequently did this with specialized books. This enabled him to prepare "camera-ready copy" which could be used to produce cheap paper offset plates adequate for short runs. Computer developments led him to believe an even simpler production sequence was now available., which would produce a more finished product.

Operating as he had before did keep costs down, and by-passed a typesetting step and two proof-reading tasks (galley proof and page proof), thus cutting down on both time and errors. But it still was cumbersome, and involved getting a more highly skilled free lance typist than he had yet discovered in his new location. He still had to make a readable draft which a skilled typist would put in final form with his IBM. She had to have the ability to catch typos and spelling errors in his original manuscript. Some errors popped up in the transcription, at best, and these had to be corrected. And Carson also had to find an experienced editor to review for errors he missed in the various reviews. From his reading, he obtained the impression that the new personal computers would simplify his job substantially, and greatly shorten the preparation of a final manuscript without significant outside help. The answer seemed to lay in the new, more powerful personal computers and the available word processing and editing programs which these machines could use.

It seemed to Carson that he would be able to work out a finished draft on the computer monitor, check his spelling with a dictionary program, transfer the draft to storage discs, and print it out in a form ready for photographic reproduction. From what he could read in the computer periodicals, a number of more powerful programs would enable him to lay out the printing, number the pages automatically, print out the result on a suitable typewriter quality printer in proportional spacing, and justify the margins. Checks with a consulting colleague in another city who had some experience with a similar setup confirmed his impressions of the capabilities available. Various news stories on the growing market for the personal computers also indicated that a substantial part of that market was among authors, as well as accountants and engineers.

Carson carefully defined his needs before shopping around. The setup he sought must handle proportional spacing, and justify the margins. It must work with one of the the word processing programs which had these capabilities, and which also would handle incremental line spacing (so as to allow more "white space" between lines than the standard typewriting spacing of 6 lines to the inch, for readability).

Carson ran into his first surprises when he started to shop computer dealers. They were all ready to show him how the computers could handle accounting and financial programs. They knew little about the word processing uses, and did not even know what he meant by proportional spaced typing. The monitors of the most popular personal computers exhibited only 40 characters horizontally, and to read the rest of the line, they had to "scroll" the printing, raising problems when reviewing and editing the work. The standard typewritten line is 65 characters, and for a number of reasons, the best dimension is 80 characters, which some of the more expensive machines displayed.

In addition, the local price on the appropriate typewriter quality printers was more than the remainder of the the equipment: more then the total for the computer, the terminal and keyboard, and the disk drives combined. Since such a printer is simply an electronic typewriter minus a keyboard, he could not understand why it should cost $3,000, or twice as much as some good typewriters. Picking up a hobbyists magazine, he discovered that mail order houses were charging less than $2,000 for the same printer. Furthermore, when he called a couple of the mail order houses, using their 800 numbers, he discovered that they were better informed than the local people, and gave more useful information.

Carson finally settled on a portable unit with its own self-contained small monitor and double disk drives, sold as a package with one of the most widely used word processing programs, a mailing list merger program, the best known financial planning program, and the most widely used operating program. The monitor displayed only 52 columns (characters), but this seemed to be the best deal within the pocketbook restraints. The dealer was positive it met all of Carson's other objectives, the writeups on the machine had seemed promising, and the word processing program was one listed in the reviews as accomplishing all that he asked for.

Carson decided to order a printer by mail, and it took a little while before he had it. Meanwhile, he sat down to educate himself on the intricacies of the equipment, and get started on typing out a draft of the first chapters, which he had already worked out in rough form. When the printer arrived, he received another surprise: he could not find a print wheel of the kind he needed, and had to buy one intended for financial printouts to test the machine. Finally locating a distant mail order source, he received one some weeks later. Meanwhile he had completed a final draft of one chapter, thoroughly checked and edited.

Up until the arrival of the proportional spacing print wheel, printing posed no trouble. But when the new print wheel was on the machine, and the switches set for proportional spacing, everything went wrong. After more than a week of frustrated trying, Carson went to the dealer. The dealer called in his technician, and a couple of suggestions were made. They did not work. Then the dealer asked to let his senior technician work with the machine for a few days. The technician could not find the answer. It developed that he, too, was ignorant of the kind of programming task proportional spacing called for. Finally, Carson called the word processer seller. The latter disclaimed any responsibility, saying that the computer manufacturer had simply bought the program and "then modified it to fit his machine." Calls to the technical support people at the computer manufacturer finally revealed that there was "no way" that a proportional spacing program would work on the current model. The firm was expecting to produce an update some months hence which would take care of the problem. That was no help.

Carson finally took the machine back to the dealer, reminding him of his assurance that it would meet his specifications. After some discussion and a couple of days, the dealer agreed to take back the machine at a discount. He had no alternative package that would meet the buyer's needs.

Just about then, two new small computers came on the market, and one of them, another portable, seemed to be an answer. It had 65K of internal memory, used double density disk drives and a more readable monitor. With liberal use of long distance calls, Carson learned of a local dealer handling it. Investigation proved that this dealer's main sales were to small businesses, and that the partners who ran it had 15 years of selling and servicing small computers to businesses. They also were a source of supplies for the printer he had, and could be called on for service. The new dealer was better equipped with software, but hardly had a wide variety. He did have a word processor intended for use with long documents and proportional spacing type.

Partly to assure himself of a local service source, Carson bought the computer through this dealer, and also the word processor he had.

When he started to use the word processor, he again had trouble. He soon learned the validity of the comment made by one periodical expert, that manual instructions were not well written for new users. Again, Carson could not make the proportional spacing aspect type out properly. This time, however, he knew that the problem was not in the computer or the printer. Again he took the machine to the dealer. The technician partner, an extremely experienced man, himself took two days to find out the answer.

Finally, everything was working as it was supposed to. But then Carson discovered that even this program had its problems. The technicians who had devised it had developed the instructions for use in preparing technical manuals, not textbooks, magazine articles, or any form of narrative writing. The standard treatment of headings and spacing of sections were excellent for a technical manual, terrible from the standpoint of textbook layout. Carson finally worked out a method of doing what he wanted, but it involved far more instructions to the computer than he thought should be necessary.

He went ahead with his writing, but also on the side started thinking about what was needed to serve growing segments of this expanding market.

Certain defects were apparent in the entire approach of the industry to its markets. The programmers were obviously more attuned to the logic of mathematics and subjects based on numbers than to an understanding of the diverse needs of the potential markets. Financial programs, engineering graphics programs, and games were finely honed. Word processing was thought of mostly in terms of ordinary typewritten letters and memos (including form letters and components). The needs of authors were not understood well by anyone except a few producers of dictionary editing programs. Dealers were clearly jumping on the bandwagon of popular electronic games, which took no great amount of selling or understanding, and the tried and true uses of financial management. They were poor sources of any other kinds of essential software, and not capable of helping customers buy for any other purposes. Margins for some of the peripheral equipment and supplies were clearly based on much more limited sales volume than the current level. (The first dealer was charging $60 for 10 disks of a widely used brand. The same brand could be bought by mail for about $26.)

As some of the popular magazines were saying, quite a bit seemed to need doing to meet the wider market. To Carson, it looked something like the situation in the home appliance field just after World War II. The public was scrambling after the goods, but the pricing and dealer structure was still geared to serving a narrow market which did not question markups. That was, as he remembered his history, when the home furnishings discount houses got their start, both with lower prices, and with well-informed service. He began to think, "What kinds of services and distributive institutions should develop out of this?"

1. How would you answer Carson's question? How many kinds of opportunities do you see in this situation, and which would you expect to see develop soon, and why?

WHY DO SOME VALUABLE PRODUCTS TAKE SO LONG TO GET TO MARKET?

Passive Solar Construction. It has been about 5 decades since a Chicago architect, Keck, accidentally stumbled on to the winter heating savings possible through some simple design details. Helping supervise some workers finishing up a heavily glassed building for the 1933 Chicago World Fair, he found the inside workers shedding their coats and shirts on a bitterly cold day, in an unheated structure, because of the trapped sunlight. He then began to design homes for upper middle class customers making maximum use of the solar heat to be trapped by concentrating large window areas on the southern exposure, with a roof overhang which shaded the higher summer sun. Over the years, others occasionally produced similar designs, and the literature on building methods regularly published the data needed on overhangs and the benefits to be obtained.

The benefits to be obtained are substantial and come at very little, if any extra construction cost. Furthermore, they require no different methods of construction for the various crafts involved, only a different placing of window openings and sizes. Esthetically, the resulting designs seem to be pleasing, and there is no evidence that any of the homes so designed had any sales problems. Nevertheless, few houses in any part of the country were designed or built in this manner until the beginning of the '80's, and only a few builders were offering such designs even then.

What do you think is responsible for this lag?

Automotive Design Improvements The 100th anniversary of the American automobile industry is only about a dozen years away, and designs of today do not resemble the horseless carriage of the 1890's. Yet despite all of the design refinements of the decades past, some that could have improved the efficiency of the present offerings have gathered dust on the shelves for years. Some are now reaching the public, some are not visibly on their way.

Detroit became aware of the need to reduce wind resistance as early as the 1930's, when highway speeds above 50 miles per hour became common. The vertical windshield, a prime producer of drag was then dropped, but little more was done to reduce wind resistance until the designs of 1982 and later. Yet the techniques had long before been worked out in the aircraft industry, and the use of wind tunnels routine in aircraft design. It cost no more to produce a "slippery" body design than some of the elaborate sheet metal sculptures regularly launched in model changes.

The "stratified charge" engine, developed by American engineers in 1925, outside Detroit, was never adopted until Honda designed such an engine in the late 1970's. Electronic ignition accessories were being bought by automobile owners on their own as late as early as the late 1950's, but only found their way onto production models of a few makes in the middle 1970's. Their value in reducing ignition maintenance costs and improving engine performance was well-known among auto buffs.

How would you account for these lags in adoption?

What other instances of lagging adoption of seemingly valuable offerings can you think of in:
- Items of everyday household usage?
- Major consumer purchases of any kind?
- Offerings in other areas, such as any industry you are familiar with, organizations of any other kind, etc.?

PRODUCT LIFE CYCLE EXAMPLES

1. What offerings that you can observe appear to be well started on a rapid growth phase:
- In the area of everyday consumer purchases?
- In recreation?
- In education?
- In industry of any kind?
- In non-profit areas such as health care, religion, etc.?

2. What examples can you think of, of offerings well along in their mature phases and possibly heading for decline?

3. What kinds of offerings, still available, seem to be in a definite decline phase? What is taking their place, and why?

4. What offerings now coming on the market seem to you to be ready to start a rapid growth phase, and why do you think so?

CHAPTER 6. FASHION AND FAD:
THE RESTLESS SEARCH FOR STIMULUS VARIATION

The wide scope of fashion and fad phenomena
Fashions and fads: the distinguishing differences
Don't designers tell us what to wear?
The psychological foundations of fashion and fad fluctuation
       Desire sets and design compromise
       The hierarchy of needs and the priorities of satisfaction
       The principle of satiation and subsequent restructuring of
         priorities
   The normal process of social diffusion of innovations
   Over-adoption: acceptance for social reasons
   The predictable classic
The complex strands of fashion trends
The place of fashion in the market life cycle
Cultural limitations on style recycling
Fads: the empty offerings

FASHION AND FAD:
THE RESTLESS SEARCH FOR STIMULUS VARIATION

6

Fashion and fad values are present in such a wide variety of transactions that they merit attention for that reason alone. In addition, the insight they permit into the adoption of new offerings in general would justify much more intensive study than has been devoted to these two related but quite different phenomena. Both represent a large part of the value of offerings involved, often greater than the value accorded to the core physical function of the offering.

Both fashions and fads permeate our personal lifestyles, the economy itself, and politics. They are easily detected both in commercial transactions and in the acceptance of offerings with no tinge of commercialization.

Fashions are not fads, nor are fads short-lived fashions. Their market life cycles are entirely different. Fashion trends have proved to be predictable to some degree. Fads do not seem to have any degree of predictability.

Despite a widely held belief, fashions are never the artificial imposition of authoritative designers. Close observation of the experience in specific cases indicates no basis for such a belief.

Fashions and fashion cycles can be completely explained as the combined result of four basic buyer tendencies: the need to compromise the satisfaction of several related desires in a single transaction, the existence of a hierarchy of needs, the effect of satiation of a dominant desire, and the structure of the social diffusion of innovations.

Any given fashion usually is a complex mingling of several item fashion trends.

Fashions are a cosmetic aspect of any class of offerings, an aspect which appears well along in the growth phase. Its importance sometimes seems to disappear as offerings become an established part of the culture.

Although fashion elements tend to repeat regularly, some design elements are unlikely to be repeated within a given culture because of incompatible changes in the culture which are relatively permanent.

Unlike fashions, fads have no substantive attributes: they are pure novelty. They have no significant mature phase, only a swift rise and complete collapse. Profits can be good only with minimal investment, a very early entry, and exquisitely timed withdrawal from the market.

IS LOVE SUBJECT TO FASHION?

Falling Back in Love with Love (Joan Beck, **Chicago Tribune,** August 25, 1981. Copyrighted©, Chicago Tribune, 1981.)

...romance is making a remarkable comeback in a country where love songs have long been drowned out by disco and where courtship is often limited to, "Your place or mine?"

...The current publishing phenomenon is the mass market paperback romance with the formula format that calls for heroines to be virgins, passions to run high, but nothing more explicit to happen than the clinch at the end. The appeal of the genre cuts across age, education and income lines. The sexually liberated young buy the books by the bunch as avidly as lovelorn housewives.

Romance is Fashionable
   Romance marks much of the fall fashion, too.... There haven't been so many puffed sleeves since Judy Garland was 12. The ruffles, the shawls, the flowered skirts, and the new cosmetic colors are sending out messages deliberately different from his-and-hers brief cases and his-and-hers MBAs.

   Touch dancing is resurging here and there, as the disco generation discovers that moving to music can be more romantic and less athletic than they had assumed. Along with dancing chic-to-chic, there's fresh interest in big band sounds of more sentimental times.

   ...the romantic appeal of getting married is growing....The 2,442.000 marriages during the year ending with May—30,000 more than the year before—set an all-time record for the United States.

Weddings are Back
   What's also blooming as never before are weddings—with the expensive splendor of lavish bridal gowns, musical comedy costumes for males, and all the traditional trappings. Never mind that the bride and groom may have lived together for a year...Wild flowers and do-it-yourself vows in the park are now passe. Lohengrin and Mendelssohn are back, hang the cost...

The Wide Scope of Fashion and Fad Phenomena

   The subject of the Fashion supplement of any newspaper is almost entirely women's apparel, and this corresponds to the general connotation of the term **fashion** to most people. Yet we all recognize fashion in apparel of all kinds, for both sexes, in automobile design, and in architecture, especially family residences. If we stop for a moment to consider, most of us would also recognize fashions in methods of child rearing, in the management of corporations, and, in fact, of TV program popularity, music styles (especially popular music), in women's hair-does, and in masculine facial hair as well as haircuts.

   There are clear fashions in public attitudes toward religious ideas, easily measurable in the content of religious publications, as a colleague once demonstrated for himself. There are even fashions in academia, in social and marketing research techniques, and in political coloring. Anyone who follows the stock market news cannot help but be aware that the principal element in the value of any security is whether the industry represented is currently a fashionable investment or otherwise, with limited relevance to the current "fundamentals".

Although many of these forms of fashion fluctuation could plausibly be attributed to someone's profit-motivated promotion, some are totally free of possible commercial taint.

FASHIONS IN ENTERTAINMENT?

One does not have to be a dedicated TV viewer to realize that TV shows come and go. Some of the dropouts certainly result from poor quality, but most of it has a pattern, one that has all the appearances of a fashion cycle geared to the popular culture of the moment.

A case in point was the comment column of the TV–radio critic, Gary Deeb, in the March 13, 1980 release published in the Chicago Tribune, headlined, "CBS may show ABC that teens don't rule airways." That the headline was news was obvious to anyone who tuned in even occasionally during the previous decade. Deeb noted that after the close of the Olympics in the previous February, CBS adult–oriented shows had clearly taken over the top spot ABC had previously been enjoying with teen oriented programs. Listing the top 30 programs in cumulative rated audiences, he noted particularly CBS' "60 Minutes," heading the list, "M*A*S*H," "Dallas" and "Archie Bunker's Place," on the CBS standouts. The list certainly supports his point. Of the first 10, 7 were CBS shows with a definite adult appeal, 2 were ABC shows, and one was NBC's "little House on the Prairie." All of the shows in the bottom 10 were ABC entries, and the majority seemed to appeal more to the teens.

Don't Designers Tell Us What to Wear?

There is no better example of the difference between human perception and objective reality than the deeply entrenched myth of dictated fashion. Even the most cursory reading of the seasonal fashion news reveals a wide selection of designer offerings, most of which fall by the wayside. Moreover, the "hot" designer this season is seldom the popular one next season. If designers were as powerful as even many professors believe, then the task of the merchandise buyers would be a simple one. As the accompanying experiences indicate, those who are most in touch with the markets have relatively low batting averages.

It cannot be denied that once the market reveals a beginning trend, all designers hop on the same bandwagon. Of course they do: what other choice do they have?

It would seem more fruitful to look at what we know about buyer psychology for an explanation. The answer does not seem to be very complex.

THOSE WHO SELL FASHIONS CAN'T PREDICT WHAT WILL SELL!

If designers or anyone else on the sales side of the counter could tell people which styles to choose, the merchandise buyers would most certainly be in on the secret. On the record, they are not, despite their wealth of industry information and months of study before making commitments. Any harried, long experienced buyer will readily admit as much.   Their oral testimony is corroborated by 21 years of experience in a mail order company which the author was privileged to analyze: a comparison of the feature treatment given individual women's dress outfits in the catalog with the actual and relative sales of the items.

The obvious rule in advertising is to put your best foot forward: to allot the most and best space to the numbers you believe will attract the most customers. In a catalog, the outside and inside cover pages are carefully chosen. They are usually given only to a single item thought to be especially attractive.   Other means of featuring are single item/page, 2 items/page, and added space on a page containing more items.

If the industry could make customers buy any special style, any such featured item should sell well above the average for all dresses shown in the catalog. Even if the industry could not, the experienced buyer might be thought capable of identifying most of the better sellers after his careful advanced study.   The table below shows that he cannot: about 2 times out of 3, the featured item did worse than average (ranging from a disastrous 10% of average item sales to 90%). (It should be noted that this is still better than chance, since the buyer must choose from a total of 60 to 90 items per season.   The average number of featured items per catalog were about 4.)

Item sales, relative to average, of featured dresses, 21 seasons, in a major general merchandise mail order catalog

Treatment	Number of items		
	Total	Below average	Above average
Front cover	4	4	0
Inside cover	6	4	2
1/page	11	2	9
2/page	20	12	8
Added space	55	41	14

The Psychological Foundations of Fashion and Fad

It is possible to find a satisfying explanation of the fluctuations in design popularity, and the directions these fluctuations take, by looking at the implications of the combination of four basic tendencies already discussed:

- transactions as attempts to fulfill clusters of desires and the resulting necessity to compromise on design
- the hierarchy of needs and the priorities assigned to specific satisfactions
- the principle of satiation and the resulting restructuring of priorities

- the normal process of social diffusion of innovations, by which successive waves of buyers depend on the authority of earlier adopters

Desire sets and design compromise. The cluster of desires with which all buyers approach any transaction inevitably includes some physically incompatible attributes. Some desires will get less than full satisfaction if others are fully met.

The hierarchy of needs and the priority assigned to each desired satisfaction. At any given moment, the satisfaction of certain desires will be given greater attention than the others in the cluster. Generally, these will be those which have experienced the least satisfaction for the longest time.

The principle of satiation and the subsequent restructuring of the hierarchy of desires. Once a priority desire is satisfied, its place in the hierarchy is taken by a different, much less well satisfied desire, and the drive for fulfillment of the new salient need begins to grow.

The effect of the normal process of diffusion of innovations Only a few tastemakers search for the new on their own. The rest depend on the advice and example of these influentials in determining the likely best purchases. Thus the acceptance by the early adopters determines what is socially acceptable, and therefore popular.

An adequate explanation of fashion must include a parallel explanation of two related phenomena: the existence of over-adoption and the existence of the classic design.

Over-adoption: acceptance for social reasons

Any major fashion trend is almost certain to result in some over-adoption by some of the later adopters. The miniskirt, which could look attractive on an immature adolescent female was purchased by women with better developed figures, on which it achieved a somewhat different result. Farmers often adopted new machinery with far too much capacity for their operations, and offices bought computers which did some tasks more slowly and at greater cost than the clerks they displaced.

Over-adoption occurs because many of the later adopters are more concerned with conformity, to that which they perceive as the socially approved, than with a careful search for what fills their own objective needs. The progress of any fashion might be described as follows:

1. Any fashion requires some learning of the ability of an offering to satisfy the salient desires. Every one carries some risk that it may not. Initial adoption will be by a few innovators and early adopters. These will always be those who feel freest from the group pressures to conform, those at the top of the pecking order in the given culture.

2. Once these early adopters validate the claims for the new offering, through their own trial and adoption, they will be imitated by those

only a step below them in the pecking order. Step-by step, the innovation will be adopted by those who depend progressively more on social approval for purchase decisions.

3. Later adopters will be responding more to a need to conform to the group than to their other personal felt needs. Among these later adopters will be some to whom the offering is poorly suited, from any objective point of view. With the coming of full maturity of the fashion cycle, most adopters will be buying either from reasons of conformity or through lack of any perceived choice, or both, with the added help of the need for stimulus variation.

4. Once a fashion has reached virtually full acceptance, those who adopted early will no longer perceive it as filling the need for stimulus variation, and will be moved to look for something else new. The acceptably new will be a design which contains attributes satisfying the least well satisfied desires in their desire sets, and thus inevitably, virtually the opposite of the now reigning fashion. The fashion pendulum will be starting in the other direction, a predictable change in any cycle.

Fashion is generally a pendulum, swinging from one side to the opposite, with one exception. That exception is the **classic**: the style which is always in style with a substantial segment of the market, with only minor changes.

The predictable classic.
Most fashions are predictable in the sense that the general character of the next reigning style can be forecast as some opposite of the current one. Even its onset can be discovered, at least a short time in advance, through research. Sales of the classic can be predicted accurately enough without any research. The demand is relatively stable.

Experienced sellers in any field can name the classics with no difficulty. They are rarely the reigning style, always sell in relatively high volume. Most are long established, but new styles sometimes achieve a classics niche. One such was the dressy pants suit and its derivatives, for women.

What makes a classic? If we visualize fashion fluctuations as a pendulum, then something which is stable must be dead center. Looking at certified classics, this neutral position seems to be an apt analogy. The standard woman's pump is such a classic: nearly every woman owns a pair, it generally is second in sales year-in, year-out. There is nothing exciting, and nothing displeasing about it: plain simple lines, suitable for either formal or informal wear. The heels are neither high nor low, but a comfortable, walkable "medi-heel" moderately wide surface, about mid-height. It is a quiet, quietly attractive style which goes well for almost any buyer, with almost any costume. So also is the tailored suit, the simple two-story colonial house, an automobile painted in the near-white range, and any other classic we have been able to observe.

RECIPE FOR SUCCESS: White Castle Thrives Making Hamburgers as It Has for 61
Years, by Michael King
  (Reprinted by permission of The Wall Street Journal, © Dow Jones & Company, Inc.
1982)

COLUMBUS, Ohio —... A few blocks down the road from McDonald's here is a White
Castle, and quite a contrast it is. The Depression–era porcelain–steel building has
dents in it from repeated rammings by automobiles. Inside, blue–topped stools and
stainless–steel tables add to the impression the place conveys of a mission–district
soup kitchen.
  White Castle sells hamburgers. And "White Castle is no frills," says E. W. Ingram
III, president of the family–owned company, whose 170 restaurants are concentrated in
the Northeast and upper Midwest. "You don't go to a White Castle because of the
atmosphere or the broad menu selection....We stick to what we know." Which is
selling cheap little (two–inch wide) hamburgers and precious little else....
  In 61 years, the White Castle system hasn't changed appreciably, and that is part
of its appeal.... It maintains a severely limited junk food menu in a sparsely
appointed environment while franchisers – like McDonald's, Wendy's and Burger King –
race to expand menus and improve ambience....
  "Four generations of my family have eaten at White Castle," says Stephen Simon,
an instructor at the University of Minnesota Law College of Law. "There's very little
permanent in the world. But in October, when I am 40, I can go back to White
Castle and have the same kind of hamburger I had when I was 5 – 35 years ago."...
  [Other comments:] "I've been eating them for 50 years," says William Grosse, an
architect's assistant. "It's good meat and good flavor."....Larry Bynum, a Detroit auto
worker visiting Columbus, isn't much of a fan. I ain't crazy about them," he says,
wolfing down a whole burger at one gulp. "It's just something to eat."....
  Sharon Mulvehill, a graduate student at Ohio State University, says that she, too,
likes White Castle's consistency. "When you go into a White Castle, you know what
you are going to get".... "there is something that keeps people coming and makes
people want to try their product," an official of a major hamburger chain says.
White Castle's restaurants have an average annual sales of $1 million each; that puts
them second only to McDonald's on a per–establishment basis.... (WSJ, Sept. 2, 1982)

Since the classic is seldom the dominant style, we must assume that its
strongest appeal is to one particular market segment. That segment would
have to be one which is least concerned with complete conformity: self–
confident buyers less concerned with the stronger "image" aspects than with
the more substantive core functions.

If these observations are accurate, then a classic can be identified even
when it first appears. If would be a quietly pleasing design which performs
the central functions of the product form superbly well, but generates little
excitement. The seller who concentrates on a classic offering is unlikely to
be the dominant factor in the industry, but will generally be profitable with
stable earnings.

Even classics can be expected to experience some variations in design
details, such as fabrics in clothing classics. The reigning fashion is not a

single element design, such as a dress silhouette. It is a composite of several different strands of fashion trends.

The Complex Strands of Fashion Trends

Any fashion is a complex combination of several elemental fashion trends. The most popular dress is made up in the currently most popular type of fabric, in a fabric design which is currently most popular. The most popular new house is built with the currently most popular facing materials, window structure and facing, in the most salable location. There seems to be some interdependence between these strands, but also considerable independence of the cycle for many of them.

Observation of what was bought over a fashion cycle seems to indicate that, for a given type of offering, certain kinds of traits seem to cluster. When low heel shoes are the style, the toes are always rounded or squarish, never pointed. The uppers tend to have some kind of ornamentation: leather work, bi-color leather, bows, fringes, or similar adornments. When the style swings to high heels, the toes are always pointed, the uppers tend to much less ornamentation.

Shoes themselves are an accessory item, and high heels sell best when the current clothing exposes considerable leg, the low heels best when the legs are emphasized less.

Within such clustering, however, there are clear degrees of independence of the general core style. The degree of patterning and even the kind of textile itself will vary over the mature phase of any given fashion trend in dresses. These details may have their own cycles.

Any fashion may be viewed as an innovative offering in itself, with its own market life cycle. But all fashions are, to a considerable degree, surface aspects of some basic product form. Shoe styles of every kind come and go, but some form of foot gear is a constant in any industrialized society--an item of dress which no major segment goes without. Furthermore, the fashion component of market value varies over the life cycle of many kinds of offering categories. Where does fashion fit?

The Place of Fashion Value in the Market Life Cycle

Although the fashion empire has wide boundaries, its rule is not absolute.

Some simple offerings, which fulfill a single functional purpose, experience changes only when technology displaces them. Thus the means of fastening the framing elements of buildings has shifted over time, but not in any cyclical manner. In large structures, steel skeletons, riveted together, replaced massive masonry and cast columns permanently, when steel technology became adequate. More recently, the rivets were replaced with bolts when the bolt-making technology improved. Nylon displaced silk even in its oriental home, because nylon could do a better job, at less cost.

Even in apparel, the rule of fashion is rather limited outside of formal and semi-formal wear, whenever the cosmetics are not dominant.

In automobiles, styling was not a significant element of value until the mid-1920's, when quick-drying lacquers made color variations possible. More importantly, by this time, a few wealthy movie stars were paying a Cadillac dealer, Don Lee of Los Angeles, to completely refashion the bodies and chassis of their purchases, creating sleeker lines. A visit to Don Lee by the Cadillac general manager brought this effort, and the designer, to the attention of GM, and helped found the first styling department.

STYLING AND THE AUTOMOBILE LIFE CYCLE

The first commercial sale of automobiles in the United States was in 1896, the first real production line was in the Oldsmobile factory in 1902. Sales rose rapidly from the first, and the rapid growth phase did not begin to flatten out until the mid-1920's. By that time, as Sloan notes in his MY YEARS WITH GENERAL MOTORS, the cars began to be purchased for everyday travel and business, rather than mostly for sports and pleasure, as the early cars had been.

Also up until then, open cars had dominated the market, and the lines of all were about the same. Everyday use, however, dictated less exposure to the weather, and closed cars gained popularity. The first ones were quite high and awkward in appearance, due to the practice of building the chassis as a separate unit, then mounting a closed body on top. Alfred P. Sloan, president of General Motors, apparently had felt that cars needed a lower look for some time, having his first Cadillac delivered with wire wheels to get a smaller wheel for that purpose. In a 1926 letter to Bassett, general manager of Buick, he stressed the need for more attention to appearance, and indicated that "At the present time one of our very important lines is being revamped from the appearance standpoint..."

Sloan's reference was to the LaSalle, introduced in March, 1927, by the Cadillac Division. The LaSalle was, according to Sloan, "the first stylist's car to achieve success in mass production." The design was the work of Harley Earl, who had been hired as a consultant the previous year. Earl had been customizing cars for movie stars in Hollywood, and was brought permanently to GM to head a new "Art and Color Section" as the styling staff was called then.

Acceptance of styling was slow at first, but became a major factor in differentiation by the early 1930's.

[Ref.: Alfred P. Sloan, **My Years with General Motors,** Doubleday & Company, Inc., 1963]

By the 1940's styling became the dominant method of differentiation and primary element of value in American automobiles, and held full sway during much of the the 1950's. By the end of the 1950's, a substantial segment of the buyers began to abandon style changes for more functional foreign models, with much fewer style changes and style differences, in the interest of driveability and economy, and parkability. The segment continued to grow, and Detroit has begun to move in a direction putting less emphasis on styling. As with all fashion cycles, the decline in the popularity of the heavily styled has been gradual. There is still a substantial segment which pays well for styling differences, but it seems to be declining. Engineering values are definitely on the increase, especially among the less conformist segments.

Observation of similar trends in home appliances and other mature life cycles seems to indicate that fashion comes in only when the market is well along in its growth curve, and diminishes in value as the market becomes thoroughly mature and consumer interest shifts to other kinds of purchases. Fashion seems to fill a permanent niche only in such places, like dress wear, where the cosmetic values are inherently the central values.

The fashion cycle is a repetitive phenomena, but certain types of fashions die a permanent death because of major cultural changes.

Cultural Limitations on Fashion Recycling

That museums are the best source of fashion inspiration is no secret. Fashions do tend to repeat periodically. But not all of them. The wheat farmer is unlikely to return to the hand sickle. The hat industry has been unable to promote the general use of male head coverings, and even women seem to have continued lukewarm toward the hats which once dominated their interest. Nor is the high-bodied automobile with vertical windshields ever likely to become popular again, despite the belief of one student of fashion.

The reasons are basic changes in the culture and technology. Hand harvesting methods are uneconomical and unnecessary. In temperate climates, at least, head covering no longer serves any positive function, and is even a nuisance in an automobile-driving, central-heated society in which most work is indoors. The vertical windshield is completely unacceptable because of its wind resistance in vehicles driven at modern highway speeds.

Nor are we likely to see a return of the hoop skirt, the bustle, or the hobble skirt, in any quantity, even among the upper class. They are not compatible with a the active economic lifestyle of the 20th and quite likely the 21st century woman. Any fashion must be compatible with the general culture, and woman is no longer, in any class, the means of exhibiting the family wealth and leisure status.

Fashion is, indeed, a complex phenomenon, one which deserves more detailed study than it has received, or is getting. By contrast, fads are essentially simple, single dimensional types of offerings which share their only value with fashion--their novelty value.

Fads: The Empty Offerings

Fads and fashions, despite their linkage in both scientific literature and common usage, are quite different types of of offerings. They do share one attribute in common-- they furnish stimulus variation and both are social phenomena, the currently accepted way of doing things. But fashions have a substantive value, and decline because of the inevitable compromises in any kind of design. Fads have no discernible value other than novelty, and suffer sudden death when the novelty evaporates, as it must. Fashions have a perceivable, predictable relationship to the fashions which precede and those which will follow. Fads have no discernible relationship to any fad past, and no predictable successors.

Both fads and fashions can be identified in their early stages. Fashions take hold slowly, fads enjoy fast-growing popularity from almost the first day. The differences in speed of acceptance require quite different marketing strategies.

Because of the explosive growth curve, the introducer of any item which develops a fad appeal must move very fast on both production and distribution. Competitors are certain to flood the market given any opportunity, so dealers must be supplied quickly and kept supplied. Since the market life will be very short, production should be at the the highest volume possible in the very beginning, and contracted out unless idle capacity is available. No substantial investment in production facilities can be justified.

Probably the most crucial decision is when to stop production and phase out. Because sales will collapse at the moment of peaking, the ideal is to arrive at zero inventory throughout the distribution channel at that moment. This implies stopping production sometime before the peak: a rather difficult forecasting task.

The recognized fad is simply the extreme example of products whose value is primarily novelty. This is true of significant portions of the introductions in a number of industries, such as popular music, such items as snack foods, and even flavors in such things as cake mixes.

Whenever it is possible that the major appeal may be novelty, marketing plans should include contingent elements to check early on the nature of the initial response. When it is known in advance that novelty is the most likely appeal, the strategy should assume a short market life. One major seller of cake mixes, for example, keeps only a couple of classic flavors in constant production (angel food and chocolate), and rotates production of the wide variety of other flavors, no more than a half dozen at any one time.

SUMMARY

The understanding of fashion and fad acceptance gives us valuable insight into the process of acceptance of any new offering.

Fashion and fad attributes contribute substantially to the perceived values of all kinds of offerings, both commercial and otherwise, ideas as well as physical products.

The evidence is clear that the demand for any fashion, like that for any other new offering, arises from within the buyers, is not imposed on them from the outside.

Fashion fluctuations are the consequence of four factors: the design compromises resulting from the desire of buyers to fulfill a whole cluster of desires in one purchase; the hierarchy of desire priorities by which the least well satisfied desires get first attention; the effect of satiation of the topmost desire in restructuring the hierarchy; and the social process of diffusion of innovations, by which adoption starts with the few innovators and gathers momentum through a chain of conformist purchasing by those less sure of their own judgment.

Because of the conformist nature of later adopters, some degree of over-adoption results, with many accepting offerings not fitted to their needs, and thus left unsatisfied.

Classics--styles that are never out of style--are an exceptional aspect of the fashion cycle. Their dominant characteristics seems to be that of a stable, midpoint compromise, placing heavy emphasis on the core values in the desire set, and accepted by those who place little value on stimulus variation.

Any fashion is a complex of fashion strands, some of them with cycles independent of the core trend.

Most fashion elements are periodically repeated. Some, however, go out of style never to return, because of an incompatibility with changes in the culture and in technology.

Observation seems to indicate that for many product forms, fashion tends to come in well along in the growth phases, and to later diminish in value as maturity becomes well established.

Fads are offerings whose sole perceived value is novelty--a value which vanishes at the peak of popularity. Management of fad cycles requires early recognition and aggressive early entry, low investment, and a quick phase-out short of the peak of sales.

FOOD FOR THOUGHT AND DISCUSSION

MODS: A NEW MAJOR YOUTH CULTURE FASHION?

Youth cultures seem to have fashion cycles of their own. Within the current generation, the most sweeping was probably the hippie movement, whose trademarks were scruffy clothing, unisex styles, drugs, ear-splitting rock music, and a plethora of "anti-" activist movements, opposed to anything sponsored by the decrepit "over 30" population. The more extreme elements of this culture burned out in the 1970's, as the sponsoring generation itself became over 30, and had to adapt themselves to the "materialistic" realities of everyday existence.

Now, if the following news dispatch out of Hollywood is significant, we may have a new kind of youth culture style. [Excerpted from a syndicated Los Angeles Times story by Ann Japenga. Copyright ©, 1982, Los Angeles Times. Reprinted by permission.)

Mods Find Fashion in '60's Fad

HOLLYWOOD — (The O. N. Klub, on Sunset Boulevard on a recent Friday night)…. was filled with mods, a new breed of well-behaved young people whose trademarks are shiny Vespa scooters. These are the kind of kids who say "excuse me" to pass in a crowded club. Before going out, they ask their mothers if their sweaters and slacks match.

Parents and police aren't sure what to do with the new youth movement. The mods are not protesting anything. They are not into drugs.

They are hard to understand.

John Irvin was 14 when he saw the movie that would change his life. The movie was "Quadrophenia," starring The Who. It is a look at a group of mid-60's British youth who called themselves mods and dressed fashionably in reaction to motlier youths.

Before he saw "Quadrophenia," Irvin was drifting. "I wasn't a hippie or nothing., I didn't wanna be a punk," he said. "Punks are slobs. They are not even brought up right."

What Irvin and thousands of other upper-middle-class youth saw in "Quadrophenia" that led them to become mods remains a mystery, but it certainly had something to do with style, with class. Now Irvin is 18; he has seen the movie more than 200 times, and mod style figures in everything he does.

And mods spend a lot of time talking about what is wrong and what is right, style-wise.

"I went through it all," Irvin said. "It took me time. Now I know what is right. There are just some things you gotta know. For instance, my scooter. I would never put round mirrors on it. It's not right."

So Irvin sent to England for $75 oblong mirrors and a set of tassels to hang from his handlebars. The right scooter is a Vespa or Lambretta. You would no more try to get by with a Suzuki than you would substitute a trench coat for a parka.

And mods like Irvin will never make substitutions. This night Irvin was wearing a peach-colored sweater over a Fred Perry shirt and a thin tie. Even on the hottest nights, he wears a parka with a Royal Air force bulls-eye insignia on the back. His hair is half-inch long and curly.

His black bowling shoes are an inspiration borrowed from the No. 1 mod band, the Jam, "but mods don't all wear bowling shoes," he said. "I don't want people to think just because they wear bowling shoes they're mods."

So what's the philosophy behind the mod movement?   For that first time in the conversation, Irvin paused.

It is something he has not considered, he said.

Neither has Claude Grimes. Grimes parents worried when he got his hair cut short, started coming home from thrift shops with bags full of old clothes and formed a band, the Untouchables.

But to his parent's surprise, Grimes in his mod attire looked more conservative than they did.   Soon he was making friends with older people who were pleased with his neat look.

Eventually, Grimes invited his family to the O. N. Klub to witness the mod movement he and his friends were largely responsible for starting.   Grimes said a lot of the "ace faces," the sharpest guys and gals, were there that night.   Grimes grandmother got up and danced.   "My family thoroughly flipped," he said.

Almost every night now, there is a mod scene somewhere.   The men are the peacocks in this bunch.   They own the scooters and the clothes, but the women contribute new ideas in dance, Grimes said.

Part of being a mod is to shop cheap.   "It's an economical scene, very economical, Grimes said.   "It's perfect for the 80's."

[Special footnote to the above: an October 16, 1972 story in the Charlotte Observer noted that Charlotte barbers are getting a lot of requests from high school athletes for mohawk and crew cuts, and quotes a high school principal as noting a trend to shorter haircuts since the first of the year.   "Hair is much shorter than it was five or six years ago," he noted.   "all that long stuff seems to be out.   Not only are boys wearing short haircuts but the girls are wearing skirts and dresses and I think it's real nice."]

Could this refer to a related development?
[From a Sidney Zion news story syndicated by **The New York Times** August 16, 1981.
© 1981 by The New York Times Company. Reprinted by permission.]

Is Rock 'N' Roll Here To Stay?
Between the rock and the hard disco, the melody began to slip back in. A piano bar here, a big band there, a touch of Gershwin, a spot of Kern. In gay places and in out-of-the-way places.   Exuberant, but a little wary, like a gambler with a short bankroll.

And disc jockeys are spinning Sinatra, Ella, Bennett, Benny. Radio stations—752 of them—are playing big band music, according to a list compiled by Ray Anthony, the head of big band 80's, an organization of band leaders across the country.   Suddenly, it appears, the Return of Style is at hand.   Songs that swing or carry the torch or conjure up dinner dates and flowers.   Wit, charm, savvy, romance.   Music by Rodgers, lyrics by Hart. A blue piano, a swaggering trumpet.   Frank Sinatra serving orange juice for one.   Ella Fitzgerald scatting with the Basie band.   Bobby Short fighting the old ennui.   Fred Astaire doing anything at all.

Style.

For nearly three decades the music has been keyed to the young, one Hot Tuna after another Who....

So a question begs about this resurgence. Is it the real thing or simply a bash? I spent the last year talking with people in all corners of the entertainment world...

Something was happening, and it quickly became clear that more than fortunes were involved. I felt like a cop who happened on an accident and begins to suspect a crime. What's everybody so upset about?

The American popular song has undergone significant changes since it came into its own as a native music around the turn of the century. But the changes were gradual, the links strong— melodically, rhythmically, lyrically. People born on the lip of World War II...connected naturally with everything from ragtime to pop, from the waltz to the Lindy hop....

Kids were singing these songs and their sophisticated offspring... and dancing to them at high school proms as late as the mid-1950's.

Within a couple of years, the younger brothers and sisters of these kids couldn't hear that music. It was still in the air, but it was Swahili to them. They heard Bill Haley, Little Richard, Elvis Presley, Chuck Berry and later, the Beatles, the Rolling Stones, the Jefferson Airplane, the Grateful Dead, the Clash. It didn't seem to matter if a young person was on drugs or not. if he was sexually active or not, ... or even if he was fighting in Vietnam or participating in an anti-war demonstration —the music was still rock'n'roll....

Most people saw it—and still see it—as a grassroots revolution, a spontaneous breakaway by teenagers and pre-teenagers looking for their own kind of music. The radio stations and the record companies, according to this view, noticed that a giant generation was developing its own kind of music and seized the opportunity to expand their profits to unheard-of limits....

A couple of years ago, however, rock found itself in trouble. The attributed reason was disco. When discomania died, rock was back, or so said the record companies. But the record industry is experiencing difficulties....The platinum record is becoming harder to attain and a double platinum is now something of a rarity....

Many reasons are heard for this trend: inflation, recession, the end of the baby boom, bootlegging and home taping of records. But something more fundamental may be at work.

Rock 'n' roll is 27 years old, which is a long time for a musical genre—the Swing Era lasted only 10 years. And swing was the music of the whole nation, not just the younger set. So perhaps rock simply overstayed its welcome, or, if you will, its need.

"There is no future in rock 'n' roll, only recycled past." So said, of all people, Mick Jagger, lead singer of the Rolling Stones in an interview last summer with Rolling Stone magazine....

Slumping record sales, depleted box-office revenues at rock concerts and a small but discernible radio trend away from rock, particularly on the AM band, are among the indicators that the rock may indeed be nearing the end of its spectacular roll....

Though some big record companies haven't yet acknowledged the resurgence of the old sounds, the radio stations are starting to. In New York, the switch from soft rock a year ago at WNEW–AM, the flagship of Metromedia, was the beginning....Since then, the WNEW format has been picked up by stations across the country....

1. Do you perceive any common thread between the observations in these two news stories? If so, what is it?

2. Is there any perceivble connection between them and the "Falling in Love with Love" item by Joan Beck, and/or the changing popularity of TV programs noted by

Gary Deeb? If so, what is the basis of that connection?

3. Is what you perceive in any of these a sign of changing fashions? If so what consequences would you expect to find in the demand for apparel? What other kinds of developments do you foresee?

4. Have you noted the signs of any other kinds of fashion changes in any area, recently? What are they? What kinds of market opportunities do you see opening up as a result?

5. Does the White Castle story belong in this chapter? Why or why not? If so, what is its significance?

6. How can White Castle continue so profitable over such a long span of years, without improving its ambience, with very little or no advertising, and without adding to an extremely limited bill of fare?

PART III. PLANNING SUCCESSFUL STRATEGY AND TACTICS

Consistent success in marketing management begins with a carefully worked out flexible strategy. That strategy will be based on a realistic appraisal of the seller's strengths and weaknesses, relative to actual and potential competition. It will aim at the service of those segments it is equipped to serve better than probable competition.

The chosen strategy will set the guidelines for product policy and product development policy. The resources and skills available will define the degree of innovation sellers should attempt and the points in the product life cycle in which they are best fitted to operate.

Pricing has both strategic and tactical aspects. Both are complex, include many forms of perceived value moves, and typically involve chains of money prices and offering design and distribution decisions aimed to affect buyer perceptions of both value and total cost. The role and meaning of price moves at all sales levels changes over the market life cycle.

Distribution management centers around consideration of what services are best performed by intermediaries and which by the seller. Distribution intermediaries are always customers with some degree of independent decision. Like all other customers, they are segmented. The strength of the channel relationships depend on compatibility of the assortments offered by the seller and those assembled by the distributor. Compatibility of the marketing capabilities of seller and distributor is also crucial.

A major portion of the marketing effort is necessarily concerned with the mix of communications required to bring buyers and sellers together. Personal sales and the various mass communications play different roles and must be coordinated. Administration of the personal sales effort is usually the costlier, and a complex separate effort of its own.

Mass communications can and should involve a coordinated mix of advertising, well-planned, persistent publicity, and some of the wide variety of efforts labelled sales promotion.

The usefulness and forms of every aspect of marketing management shifts with the changing phases of the market life cycle. For most offerings other than fads, and for most sellers, the bulk of the sales volume and total profits are generated by offerings in the mature phase of the cycle. Flexible competitive tactics require special attention in this phase.

CHAPTER 7. STRATEGIC PLANNING: CHARTING A PROFITABLE PRODUCT
POLICY COURSE

STRATEGIC PLANNING:
CHARTING A PROFITABLE POLICY COURSE

7

Organizations often achieve even sensational market success without any thought out marketing strategy. Others start with a strategy well fitted to the initial market, but suffer later because the strategy is inflexible, does not adapt to changing markets.

If the organization aims for an indefinitely long, healthy life, it must plan a workable strategic course. Strategic plans are often labelled as mission statements. But not all mission formulations are true strategic plans: only those founded on a clear-headed appraisal of the competitive environment and on the strengths and weaknesses of the organization and its position relative to that environment. Workable strategic planning consists of a decision as to the strategic direction for its total mix of offerings, a basic direction for each "strategic business unit" (SBU) if its mix is large and varied, and for each product in that mix.

The results of pursuing the plans must be monitored and both strategies and resources constantly readjusted in the planned direction to meet changes which develop in the competitive environment and which develop at each changing phase of the market life cycle in:

1. The buyers and their desire sets
2. The competitive environment
3. Other factors affecting profit possibilities

Because the possible span and type of attention of any executive or executive group is limited, the strategic plan needs to be sharply focused on an offering mix which requires a consistent form and type of attention and similar skills. The plan must be capable of fulfillment within the resources of finance and personal capabilities available to management.

The proper objective is a portfolio of offerings which will yield a maximum of returns for the management effort which is allocated and include substantial potentials for future returns.

Strategic Plans versus Strategic Planning

Most of the strategic plans and mission statements which organizations actually use can be grouped into three classes:

GETTING RID OF INDIGESTIBLE ACQUISITIONS

The merger binge of the 1960's and early 1970s was often marked more by lack of product policy than guided by one. The result was the typical morning-after indigestion of any unbridled binge. By 1975, the business news was full of moves to dispose of misfit acquisitions. The April 21, 1975 issue of **Business Week** noted "An urge to purge" such misfits. Consolidated Foods had put up its Fuller Brush subsidiary for sale, "one of a forest" of "for sale signs" then sprouting up all over the corporate landscape. One merger broker had noticed that over half of the merger pronouncements during the first quarter of the year had "pertained to the sale of a product line, division, or subsidiary of a parent company." Another merger consultant stated that "Every major company has something they would like to get rid of—at the right price." One manufacturer is quoted as saying that he was hearing from "two companies a week wanting to sell us something."

Some of the sales were proving hard to make, as corporations were developing a "wariness of straying into unknown areas." Toy maker Mattel, Inc. still had not found a buyer for its Ringling Bros.-Barnum & Bailey Combined Shows and a partly built Circus World park near Orlando, Fla.

- "Dear Santa Claus" plans
- "Model T" plans, based on a correct appraisal of the initial market, then set in cement
- Navigational plans, charting a feasible course subject to variations to adapt to the market weather

"Dear Santa Claus" Wish Lists

Far too many organizations, of all sizes and types, have approached planning in much the same spirit as young Western children approach Christmas. They draw up a wish list of marketing positions, sales, and profits with no real analysis of the possible in terms of resources and opportunities, and no consideration of the competitive climate. The textbook publisher may seek a major share of a competitor's popular textbook, decide that is what they would like to have. The firm then looks for an author and a manuscript with the identical appeal, turning down manuscripts which do not look like the competitors. (One well-known publisher, who sought early on for an offset to Samuelson's "Economics", admits turning down the McDonnell manuscript, which became another best seller, gaining a market which found Samuelson too heavy).

During the great conglomerate boom of the 1960's, too many firms, with the resources to expand by acquisition, simply glanced at the market share and balance sheet of candidates without investigating the fit to the organization's other product lines and it management methods. For the last decade, hardly a week has passed without news of the spinning off of such acquisitions which had turned sour because they were misfits.

THE CSU DEAR SANTA CLAUS PLAN

[The names below have been disguised for obvious reasons. The facts have not.]

Central States University (CSU) was established as a non-degree granting Normal School at the end of the 19th century, with the purpose of training school teachers for the rural area surrounding the small rural county seat and industrial center. Like many other normal schools, it became a degree granting teacher's college in the 1930's and diversified its curriculum to some degree. Noting the success of Central Western Teachers College, at the other end of the state, which had successfully lobbied the state legislature for university status, it launched a drive for university status in the 1950's, and succeeded toward the end of the decade.

At the time of being named a university, it had an enrolment of something over 4,000 students, a good portion of them from the nearby suburbs of Lakeport, a major metropolitan center whose suburbs were, by that time, reaching within 20 miles of CSU. It does not appear that either the faculty or the administration paid any attention to that fact, nor to the certainty that such would continue to be the case. They apparently thought that, like CWU's, the new students would be mostly resident students, with the bulk of the hoped for 25,000 student body requiring dormitory rooms.

But CWU was in a truly rural area, whereas the CSU major potential within the four county radius was from the Lakeport metropolitan center, and would be commuters, in effect, even if they chose life in the dorms CSU started building. (It has been the almost universal experience of colleges of every kind that the majority of the student body comes from a radius of approximately four counties surrounding the school.) No one apparently gave any thought to the wisdom of relocating the university nearer to the student potential, in the nearby growing suburbs.

[Even though most of the student body already came from the Lakeport suburbs, most of the tenured faculty apparently viewed a trip to the fringes of the suburbs as an adventure, and the city itself as an inaccessible foreign country. The Business dean, at that time with over a dozen years at CSTC and CSU, admitted to a new faculty member that he had never been to Lakeport. He also saw his mission as "training students for the businesses of the local county." Those businesses never had more than a half dozen openings, and the dean was then granting degrees to about 500 each year. When another faculty member mentioned to the Dean of Women a recent performance of the New York City Ballet he had attended in Lakeport with his wife, that dean inquired, "How long did it take you to get there?" The reply: "A little more than an hour!" She was veteran of more than 10 years on the campus.]

Within a half dozen years after CSU got its University charter, the state gave university status to the other teacher's colleges, and set up a Higher Education Governing Board to apportion duties of the various schools. One of its first projects was to get a mission statement for each school, and each was asked to submit its suggestions. Although over half of the degrees granted by CSU were still in Education, the Arts College had the majority of the faculty because of the service courses at the freshman and sophomore level, and they dominated the Senate.

Had the faculty known more about or conducted any serious study of their own area and academic realities in general, the location and the competition in the Lakeport area offered some real potentials. There was, at the time, no established state University in the area. The strong land grant University was in a rural area far from Lakeport or any major metropolitan center. The only engineering schools were in higher tuition private schools (and engineers, as a class, go to schools close to home.) Business students also go close to home, as a rule, and the only local programs were in private schools. Arts students, including those majoring in the pure sciences, on the other hand, tend, if they leave home at all, to go to a more prestigious school, which in this case meant either the top Lakeport schools, or the State University, or outside the state.

The plan as drawn up, however, reflected the departmental ambitions of the dominating clique in the Senate: CSU was to concentrate on becoming a major center for the Humanities and the Arts and Sciences. No provisions were made to even consider an Engineering School (which would have indirectly built up the Science faculty). Because the school already had a Business Education program, this was made into the Business School, with the Business Education Department head as the new Dean. Early on, the school was given permission to establish a few doctoral programs. They chose to do so in English, History, Political Science and Physics: all fields in which the applicants always outnumber the demands for jobs in their own field. Business students who wished to do doctoral work were allowed to take an Ed. D. program (which has no value in that field). The faculty was beefed up in the arts to the extent that, by the end of the 1960s, when the school had 20,000 students, the Arts College had 51% of the faculty, although granting less than one–fifth of the degrees, Education had 20% of the faculty, but half of the graduates still, and Business, with only 9% of the faculty, was accounting for more than a fifth of the degrees. A tabulation showed that Physics had a faculty of 6 of professorial status, but graduated only 5 students per year, and no doctorates.

By the middle 1970's the new community colleges were taking over much of the freshman and sophomore service course load. The disillusionment which had set in concerning the career values of the Arts courses and the cutback in public school teaching opportunities flooded the Business School with applicants. That faculty was already stretched so thin that the Business School put an absolute limit on enrolments. At the same time, the CSU administration had to face up to the fact that nearly the whole of the regular Arts faculty had long been underemployed, but also had tenure, even though they often faced no more than 5-10 students per year per instructor. Not excluding the State University, with many expensive graduate programs, CSU had the highest cost per student in the State. There were some grumblings in the legislature. Educational appropriations were the second largest category of state spending.

The Model T Approach

Other organizations analyze the opportunities and competition correctly, plan within their resources and limits, and gain a strong market position as a result. Unfortunately, they then treat the plan as graven in stone on Mount Sinai, and later fall victim to the changing desires of the customers and a competition which adjusts to them.

The outstanding example, of course, was Henry Ford Sr. and his vision of a dependable car which could be produced in volume to sell for less than $500. The introduction of the Model T (aimed at $500, but originally priced at $850) changed the entire market from a class basis to a mass market. For the time, the roads, and the market, it was close to an ideal offering. It created a rural market which did not previously exist, and won the hearts of the world for more than a decade. As late as 1921, Alfred Sloan of General Motors, looking for an entry into the low end, concluded: "with Ford in almost complete possession of the low-price field, it would have been suicidal to compete with him head-on. No conceivable amount of capital, short of the United States Treasury could have sustained the losses required to take volume away from him at his own game." (Sloan, 1964)

But Sloan also perceived that other game plans were available by then, brought about by the maturing of the automobile market and changes in desire sets being ignored by Ford, then making plans to continue on the identical path as before. These were:

- Growth of the trade-in, used car market (which Ford was actually warning his dealers to avoid)
- Growing use of instalment credit (which Ford continued to resist for 4 more years)
- Growing interest in closed body models for all-weather comfort (for which the model T chassis was too light)
- The natural growth of model changes

Hence, just as Ford was pouring his entire resources into the River Rouge plant to build more Model T's even more efficiently, Sloan was initiating a market strategy which doomed the Model T to extinction and wrested top market position from Ford in 1925 (the first year in which Sloan was able to bring his new models to market).

Ford lost out because a near-perfect initial strategy was frozen in place, and the market, as always, changed. Sloan's GM won because he had developed a marketing strategy flexible enough to change with the market as tastes diversified and competition broadened.

Strategic Planning as a Navigational Course

No ship leaves port, and no aircraft takes off without a clear destination and a carefully plotted course or flight plan. In both cases, the actual course of the trip may well be modified to avoid navigational threats (for example) not seen in advance, or to take advantage of favorable circumstances which improve the trip to the same destination.

Like the pilot's flight plan, strategic planning is a well-thought-out guide to everyday management at all levels—a guide to the course to follow, subject to adjustments to threats and opportunities. Writing 4 decades after formulating the first GM product policy, Sloan noted that "the new policies never materialized precisely in this form", yet remained the basic direction which gave General Motors its competitive advantage.

Strategic planning must be a continuous process, with plans continuously modified to meet the opportunities and threats which continuously develop as a result of changing consumer desire sets and changing competition. The basic direction should be defined in terms of a particular form of offering mix, a target market niche composed of defined types of buyers and their desire sets, and a competitive niche in relation to known and foreseeable potential competition. It must envision regular improvements and changes in the offering mix, and regular reallocation of resources to take advantage of evolving trends.

The Tripod of Strategic Planning: Analysis of Opportunities and Threats, of Competition, and of Capabilities

Strategic planning must stand on three legs. The first is an accurate, objective analysis of market opportunities and threats as defined by potential customers and their desire set trends. The second is a similar analysis of actual and possible competition, and their strengths and weaknesses. The final support is a careful, cold-blooded weighing of the organization's own special strengths and skills, and its resources, physical, financial, and personal. With this foundation, objectives can be chosen, aimed at the opportunities revealed by a situation analysis.

THE PRODUCT POLICY THAT BUILT GENERAL MOTORS
(Excerpted from Alfred P. Sloan, **My Years With General Motors,** Doubleday & Co., 1964, pp. 54–67, by permission of the copyright owner.)

[In the 1920–21 period, General Motors passed through a financial crisis, from which it was rescued only through the help of the du Pont interests, and a marketing crisis, from which it was rescued by a clear product policy, of which Alfred P. Sloan was undoubtedly the chief author. The following excerpts outline the policy and its rationale.]

General Motors then had no clearcut concept of the business...Mr. Durant had established the pattern of variety in product in the seven lines...Nevertheless there was then in General Motors no established policy for the car lines as a whole. We had no position in the low-price area, Chevrolet at that time being competitive with Ford in neither price nor quality...

The spacing of our product line of ten cars in seven lines in early 1921 reveals its irrationality...Superficially this was an imposing car line...In total output of vehicle units and in dollar sales, General Motors was second to the Ford Motor Company...Our net sales totaled $567,320,603 as compared with Ford's total of $644,830,550.

From the inside the picture was not quite so good. Not only were we not competitive with Ford in the low-price field—where the big volume and future growth lay—but in the middle, where we were concentrated with duplication, we did not know what we were trying to do except to sell cars which, in a sense, took volume from each other... The lack of a rational policy can be seen especially in the almost identical duplication in price of the Chevrolet "FB", Oakland, and Olds... The hard fact is that all of the cars in the General Motors line, except Buick and Cadillac, were losing money in 1921...General Motors in 1920 had enjoyed 17 per cent of the U. S. car and truck market; in 1921 we were on our way down to 12 per cent...It was clear that we needed an idea for penetrating the low-price field, and for deployment of the cars through the line as a whole.

...on April 9, 1921, The Executive Committee set up a special committee of the

Continued on Page 144

The Situation Analysis

The opportunities: what do we know about the product area and industry?
- Where are they in their market life cycles?
- What satisfaction bundles are currently available?
- What is the demand now, in terms of component satisfactions?
- What new trends in tastes and desires seem to be developing?
- Which kinds of desire sets seem to be least well satisfied currently? What relevant trends are developing in the economy and in the culture?

The Competition
- What are the market shares of current competitors?
- How brand loyal are the buyers of each?
- What are the weaknesses of current offerings, in general, and of specific offerings, in terms of total customer desire sets?

BANQUET FOODS FINDS A MORE COMPATIBLE PARENT

One of the more glaring misfit acquisitions was RCA's purchase of Banquet Foods in 1970 for stock worth $140 million. After 10 years, RCA finally discovered that the frozen chicken pot pie business did not mix with its main interests in high-tech electronics and show business. It sold Banquet Foods to ConAgra, an agribusiness firm, knowlegeable in the farm commodities trade, for $45 to $55 million, depending on future profits, according to a Wall Street Journal report of Feb. 8, 1982. The editor and publisher of Frozen Food World is quoted as saying that RCA officials "were thinking of Skylab when Banquet was talking chicken pot pies," and that he remembered hearing from Banquet officials who noticed "a glazing of the eyes" when RCA had to discuss food operations."

They never understood the farm commodities business with its thin margins and dependency on the weather, and were slow to make commitments to new products. When a single-serving pouch was being considered in 1978, RCA "agonized over the decision" and "pulled the advertising" at the last minute, scuttling the program.

ConAgra officials wasted no time in rejuvenating the firm. Shortly after the purchase, Conagra executives "came in, sat down, rolled up their sleeves and said they were committed to grow" by financing new efforts and broadening the distribution. They drew on their knowledge of the chicken business to reduce the mortality of Banquet Food's chicks, installing a system which monitored chicken-house temperatures and feed formulas. Quality-control experts were added to reduce the reputation for inconsistent quality and plant managers were given responsibility for maintaining the standards. Costs were kept under close watch, and price increases resisted. Both Banquet Foods and ConAgra were looking for more improvement, profit margins were growing. Banquet now had a 3-year operating plan, instead of the year-to year plan under RCA, and was reformulating major products to increase market share.

-   What are the competitor's biases, strengths, and weaknesses?

Us
-   What aspects of management in general, and marketing in particular, are we best at, compared to competitors: what are our skills?
-   Which of these skills fit into niches not already well occupied by competitors?
-   For which of the apparent opportunities do we have the resources to develop and market?

Setting Strategic Objectives

Realistic objectives will vary with the organization, with its capacities and interests, and with its opportunities. Most commercial organizations aim to maximize the financial returns on their resources. Trade associations usually hope to attract all or most of those in the industry or profession. A symphony orchestra hopes to become a leading cultural entertainment in the community and attract enough donations to put together a quality assemblage.

Such general basic objectives have to be translated into more specific terms, into terms which take into account the constraints and opportunities revealed by the market analysis. GM's general objectives of a high return on investment were translated into the specific objective of covering every significant segment of the market for mass produced automobiles, with offerings which sold at the top of their price class.

The strategy adopted, then, must be further translated into a product/mission formulation. This **mission statement** defines the offering mix to be produced, the market segments toward which the mix is targeted, and the types of desire-sets which will be emphasized.

The Product Portfolio Concept

The product portfolio concept of strategy has received substantial corporate attention in recent years. The concept has proved valuable in directing attention to the position of items in their market life cycles and to the need to apportion efforts in relation to future growth possibilities.

The concept emphasizes the importance of proportioning resources and efforts within the offering mix--the need for a constantly adjusted portfolio of offerings. As envisioned, the ideal portfolio consists of a balance of products approaching a growth phase, maturing products and an early identification of products on the decline.

Each of these stages requires a different level and kind of management. Each has its own characteristic profit potential. Unit profits tend to be least in the market development stage, greatest in the rapid growth phase, and tend to decline thereafter.

The need for aggressive marketing is normally greatest in the introductory and growth stages. The value of cost and production management can be greatest in the mature phase. The decline stage repays only the minimum of management resources.

The Product Portfolio Matrix.
The general validity of these considerations has, in recent years, given rise to a number of useful simplified prescriptions in the form of portfolio matrixes. Generally, the firm's offerings are analyzed in terms of a four box matrix. The best known is that originally promoted by the Boston Consulting Group, presented in terms of market share and estimated industry growth.

This scheme divides an organization's offerings into 4 groups (Fig. 7-1):
- **Stars**--A high market share in a high growth situation. These are candidates for maximum effort and attention
- **Dogs**--the opposite of stars: low market share in a low or no growth industry. Candidates for elimination
- **Cash cows**--high market share, low growth. Candidates to be "milked" of cash to support current and potential Stars
- **Problems**--low shares in a high growth industry. Should be converted into Stars, by improving market share, or recognized as potential Dogs

FIGURE 7-1. PORTFOLIO MATRIX

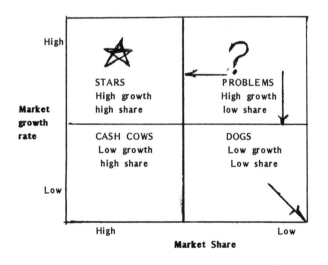

Variations of the portfolio matrix promoted by other business consultants share the same simplicity and the same assumptions. Vigorously promoted by their sponsors, they have been useful in focusing management attention on their product policies and cleaning out past diversification mistakes, especially those made during the merger binge of the late 1960's.

With some modifications, they can still serve as useful frameworks for reviewing the product mix and allocating an organization's resources (see **Fortune,** Nov. & Dec. 1981).

The Weaknesses of the Original Portfolio Mix Frameworks. The weakness of the too literal use of the portfolio approach lay in its too simplistic assumptions about cost performance, market shares, and the nature of competition, and also in the overall assumption that the star--cash cow--dog mix can be varied at will, and by any organization.

These major assumptions were:

1. Market share is a precise, meaningful measure of market strength
2. Price is the most important competitive variable
3. Experience determined production costs are the most important cost variables

FIGURE 7-2. THE EXPERIENCE CURVE:
the tendency of process cost to decrease at some constant percentage rate for each doubling of cumulative production experience. As B below indicates, the decrease per unit production is a diminishing absolute amount.

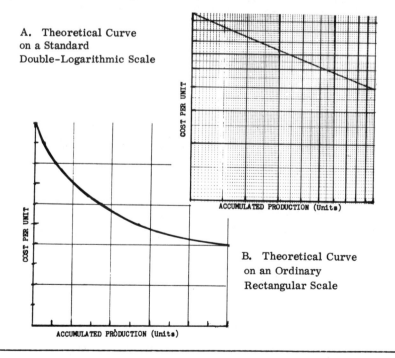

A. Theoretical Curve on a Standard Double-Logarithmic Scale

B. Theoretical Curve on an Ordinary Rectangular Scale

4. Production costs are the major basis of competitive advantage
5. Because of the experience curve (see Figure 7-2) the larger the market share (and thus the production volume), the lower the production costs
6. That any organization always has the capabilities for launching growth introductions, the marketing ability to pioneer, and suitable opportunities to do so when it chooses

Unfortunately, all of these assumptions are open to question for most forms of offerings, most organizations, and much of the time for all.

Market share has precise meaning only for commodities: those offerings for which the market can perceive no significant difference between vendors. These are also the only offerings for which **price competition** can be the major form of competitive advantage.

Commodity offerings are a very small part of the marketing scene. Primarily, the only commodities are industrial raw materials and standardized components, and not even all of these can be so classified. The total product mix of the vendor can be a means of differentiation. It is no accident that the Boston Consulting Group(BCG) formulated its matrix on the basis of studies in the paper and electronic components industries.

Contd.
From
P. 139

Advisory Staff... to look into our product policy...its work came under my jurisdiction...On June 9 I presented our recommendations to the Executive Committee, where they were approved...The recommendations outlined the basic product policy of the corporation, a market strategy, and some first principles...

...we on the special committee first idealized the problem. We started not with the actual corporation but with a model of a corporation, for which we said we would state policy standards...Our aim we said was to chart the true best course for the future operations of this model corporation, recognizing that present actual conditions necessitated sailing off the recommended course temporarily...

The product policy we proposed is the one for which General Motors has long been known. We said first that the corporation should produce a line of cars in each price area, from the lowest price up to one for a strictly high-grade quantity-production car...second that the price steps should not be such as to leave wide gaps in the line, and yet should be great enough to keep their number within reason...and third, that there should be no duplication of the corporation in the price fields or steps...

Having set forth these concepts, we then approved the resolution of the Executive Committee, which had been passed on to us to study, to the effect that a car should be designed and built to sell for not more than $600; and that another car should be designed and built to sell for not more than $900. The special committee further recommended four additional models, each to be kept strictly within the price range specified...(and)...that the policy of the corporation should be to produce and market only six standard models...

Having thus separated out a set of related price classes, we set forth an intricate strategy which can be summarized as follows: We proposed in general that General Motors should place its cars at the top of each price range and make them of such quality that they would attract sales from below that price, selling to those customers who might be willing to pay a little more for the additional quality, and attract sales from above that price, selling to those customers who would see the price advantage in a car of close to the quality of higher-priced competition...

Production cost of the individual item is obviously improved by volume experience. However, cumulative volume experience is not necessarily the only factor in low cost. Also, since the experience curve is a diminishing exponential curve, the difference comes close to vanishing in a long established industry. GM was clearly much further down its experience curve than any other car maker in the world in 1980, but its costs were substantially higher than those of the Japanese.

At best, the major experience advantage is gained during the growth phase of the product life cycle, when technological and work organization advances are rapid. In mature markets, nearly all competitors have equal access to the same basic production methods and technology. The advantages of scale of production also have limits. Cost advantages in mature markets tend to derive largely from marketing and managerial skills. The low cost firms tend to be those with the best cost control management, keeping overhead down and getting high labor productivity, or keeping unit marketing cost low. Whenever mass promotion is the key to marketing advantage, volume sales can be the major cost advantage, but only when they result from a clear knowledge of what the market is seeking.

Whenever buyers perceive substantial attribute or quality differences between competitive offerings, neither cost nor price confer the determining competitive or profit advantages. What then counts is the **consumer franchise,** obtained by shaping the offering and the communications to the desires of a given set of market segments. The premium offering is seldom the best seller, but nearly always the most profitable regardless of production cost. Moreover, the direct profit contributed by a given item in the offering may be less important than what the inclusion of that item in the mix does to sell the whole mix.

Pioneering is Not for Everyone

Launching new kinds of offerings, even major improvements, can be a special skill lacking in even some of the largest organizations.

A high official of one of the larger textile fiber producers was discussing some of his experiences. "We are not very good at being number 1," he said. "We do much better as number 2." He related an example of quite a few years previous.

When polyester textiles were first produced, they had a gray cast, were not a true white. His firm's R&D finally achieved the desired white by means of a fluorescent dye. When the sales force talked to manufacturers about it, however, they got a very unenthusiastic response. Four months later, a large competitor launched a similar product, with heavy promotion, labelling it an improved version IV, and gained a strong market. Everyone else, of course, followed.

Finally, **introducing innovations** requires special entrepreneurial skills possessed by only a minority of organizations. Furthermore, the opportunity to get into growing markets is not universally available to all, or at all times, especially during periods of economic stringency. Even when the economic climate is favorable for growth, and new technology favors it, the opportunities may well lie outside the capabilities and commitments of the organization.

Despite these flaws, there is substantial merit in the concept of the product mix as a form of investment, to be managed as a portfolio of securities might be managed. The approach has to be more than two-dimensional.

A More Generally Useful Portfolio Framework.
Clearly, any strategic planning must follow some basic framework in auditing the current state of its product mix. Just as clearly, whatever framework is used should relate directly to the basic objectives of the strategy. If we define "profit" in terms of those objectives (financial profit, membership strength, community influence, or whatever the objective), then one dimension must be that "profit", not market share or production volume alone. Probably the best indicator, applicable to any situation, is the depth and extent of the "customer franchise," which should always be an indicator of the the profit potential, direct or indirect.

Industry growth is always important, provided that the opportunity is one fitted to the organization's capabilities.

If we use the customer franchise, industry growth, and fit to the organization's strategies and executive interests as the key to classification, then we might redefine the matrix boxes as follows:

Stars   offerings with a strong customer franchise, in a growing market, well fitted to the capabilities of the organization and the interests of its executives

Cash Cows   offerings with a good to strong customer franchise, a stable or slow growth market, requiring minimum marketing effort and executive attention, reasonably well fitted to the organization's capabilities and interests

Problem Children Offerings with a questionable customer franchise, contributing little to the organization's strength, and not clearly within the organization's capabilities, nor eliciting much executive interest. Need to find a profitable niche and a useful role in the offering mix, or be classed as potential "dogs"

Dogs   Industry growth past or in decline, or organization's sales lagging industry growth, and customer franchise weak or essentially non-existent. No significant foreseeable contribution to profit, direct or indirect, and no help to the offering mix. Should be disposed of and the resources put to more profitable use.

Ideally, it would seem, any organization should maintain a constant alert for potential stars--offerings well fitted to the organization's capabilities in a potentially growing market. But there is nothing wrong with a barn full of well cared-for "cash cows", provided the organization has the skill and the knowledge to find replacements, and knows when to get them. These may well be some other organization's dogs--needing only better attention and a more carefully supervised cost diet.

Because every life cycle has an end, and consumer tastes are always changing, all offerings become dogs sooner or later. The wise organization keeps a careful watch on the vitality of its offerings, and does not prolong the death agonies.

SUMMARY

Any seller's continued success depends on the development and constant adaptation of a sound, workable strategic plan fitted to the capabilities and interests of the seller.

Actual strategic plans are of three types: "Dear Santa Claus" wish lists, formulated without regard for opportunities, capabilities, or the competition; Model T plans, which are excellent initially, but never changed to meet changing conditions; and navigational plans, which set a good course, and adjust it continually to meet current conditions, yet keep aimed at the same goal.

True strategic planning requires a thorough analysis of the opportunities and the threats, of the competition and the environmental trends, and of the internal strengths and weaknesses of the seller.

The general form of the strategic objectives will differ with the type of seller. It must be translated into objectively stated specifics.

The widely promoted portfolio concept is essentially a simplified scheme for auditing the offering mix of an organization in terms of the place of each item in the market life cycle, and its prospects for contribution to profit. Most of the more widely used portfolio schemes make too simplistic assumptions about the freedom of action of any seller, about the factors in cost, and the nature of competition. Especially weak are the assumptions that price is the major form of competition, and that the experience curve is the major element of cost.

The general portfolio concept is valid, however, if recognized as a simplified approach to auditing the offering mix, provided that the measures used are more generally applicable. It is suggested that the classification be based on the strength of the consumer franchise, industry growth, and the fit of the offering to the capabilities and interests of the organization's executives.

FOOD FOR THOUGHT & DISCUSSION

BIG RETAILER SEEKS PROFITS IN DISCOUNTING

MINNEAPOLIS—In the past decade, Dayton Hudson has transferred itself from a dowdy regional department store chain into one of the nation's largest retailers.

The company's decision to pour money into new stores certainly contributed to its success. But another factor was its strategy of finding new money makers long before its other businesses started slowing down. Now, the company thinks it has found another winner.

After studying the idea for several years, Dayton Hudson had decided to enter the $5 billion dollar off-price market. It expects to open three off-price outlets in the Los Angeles area next spring and two more in the fall. Analysts in San Francisco will be told about the plan today, and the Dayton Hudson board is expected to approve the move next week.

Upper-Income Bargain Hunters

Off-price retailing involves buying brand-name merchandise below manufacturers' wholesale prices and passing the savings along to consumers. The field is already crowded, but Dayton Hudson figures there will be room for it if it caters to the growing number of upper-income bargain hunters. "These customers don't want cheap steak," says Aldo Papone, a vice chairman. "They want steak cheap."

The company's commitment to strategic planning spawned Target discount stores and B. Dalton Bookseller in the 1960's and led to the acquisition of Mervyn's apparel stores in 1978. Today, those businesses contribute about 75% of the company's revenue, up from half five years ago. The contribution from department stores has shrunk by half.

Last year, a miserable period for most retailers, Dayton Hudson's profit rose 15% from a year earlier to $159.5 million, or $3.33 a share. Revenue increased 23% to $4.94 billion. Long range planning sets Dayton Hudson apart from some other retailers, experts say. Instead of worrying about quarterly sales and earnings, Dayton Hudson focuses on long term return on investment. (Its target is a 15% return.) And while competitors concentrate on existing businesses, Dayton Hudson executives set aside a day each month to ponder ideas that may not pay off for a decade. "I'm certain this is something no other retailer does," says a former Dayton Hudson executive who is now at a competitor.

Kenneth Macke, Dayton Hudson's president and chief operating officer, says: "There's no magic about the process. We spend a lot of time reaching no decision." They also reject many ideas. They decided against electronics retailing and financial services—two businesses that attracted other retailers—because they didn't think they had enough expertise.

Some of the ideas have turned out to be flops. The mail order and cosmetics businesses started in 1971 were dumped the following year when it became clear they wouldn't amount to much. In 1973, the company sold a catalog showroom named Sibley after only a year, taking a $1.8 million write-down....

Even profitable businesses have been dropped. Three years ago, the company sold its highly profitable Lipman's department stores because it figured the chain would never be large enough to affect the bottom line...

Promising ideas are followed up by intense market studies and field trips by the top brass. Mr Macke says he and the company's chairman, William A. Andres, examined nearly all of Mervyn's 40 stores before acquiring the company.

Off-price retailing was discussed in strategy sessions for years before it took hold. Like all serious projects, it had a sponsor... and a secret code name... A 100-page research paper completed last fall confirmed the market was ripe, and Edwin G. Roberts, a former Dayton Hudson executive who is now a Los Angeles consultant, was called in last February to head the project...

[Author's note: Dayton Hudson is the result of a merger several years ago of The Dayton Co., high end Minneapolis department store with a trade covering a wide area from Western Wisconsin through the Dakotas, and Hudson's, the largest department store in Detroit.]

1. What seems to be the timing, relative to the market life cycle, of the Dayton Hudson entry into any new field of retailing?

2. What seems to be the logic behind this timing?

3. How does the choice of the kind of entry fit in with previous history and executive skills?

WARNING: DIVERSIFICATION CAN BE DANGEROUS TO CORPORATE HEALTH

Prescription drug maker A. G. Searle is a good example of some of the problems which arose during the merger binge of the 1960,s and early 1970's. With an excellent balance sheet as a result of a strong position in the market for The Pill, Searle pushed ahead with a wide variety of acquisitions over a 10 year period. By 1977, it had piled up a heavy load of debt financing, and was losing $28 million on sales of $749 million.

Acquisitions were wide ranging, including surgical drapes, medical instruments, and record forms. For a time, the stock price climbed, selling for $40 per share in 1973, then started dropping, reaching a low of $12 per share in 1974, recovering to $26 in early 1975, then sinking quickly to $15, and continuing to fall to $11, and staying in the $11 to $12 range until 1978. At that point, a new management was brought in. It found a drug R&D in disarray and under a cloud for presenting false test results on proposed drugs.

Rumsfeld, the new CEO, sold off 30 businesses and cut corporate staff to less than half. R&D staff, however, was beefed up, from 1,000 to over 1,600 in 1982. The businesses left were of two types: pharmaceuticals, and Pearle Vision, a chain selling prescription eyeglasses. By the end of 1981, earnings were back to $2.60 a share (as compared with a peak of $1.60 during the early part of the diversification move). Prospects were bright for stronger increases later. One contributor: a new table top, low calorie sweetener finally approved for sale in late 1982 by the FDA: aspartame, to be sold over the counter under the trade mark of Equal.

The Pearle Vision centers were also doing well, having tripled in the 5 years to 966 in 1982, with plans to expand further via the franchising route. It was expected that many of the franchisees would be qualified optometrists. Pearle was succeeding where drug store chains were having difficulties. Some attention was being given to expanding into a chain of dental service centers. Individual units started by independent groups in shopping centers appeared to be doing well, and Searle was testing the waters through purchase of a three-store retail dental service operation in Tampa.

Searle was also interested in further expansion in the drug business. It missed out to Dow Chemical on the acquisition of the Richardson—Merrill prescription spin—off by Vick's Chemical. The firm would like to find a German or Italian drug firm merger to get a foothold on the European markets.

1. The acquisitions cited seemed to have some relationship to the health care field. Why did they go wrong?

2. How does an over—the—counter sweetener fit in with the main Searle business?

3. What strengths does Searle bring to the optical prescription business which justify its place in the total strategy? To retail dental care centers?

WHITE CONSOLIDATED: A WHOLE KENNEL FULL OF PROFITABLE DOGS

The May 7, 1979 **Business Week** noted that a home appliance manufacturer almost nobody recognizes—White Consolidated—and which had not been in the business as late as 1967, had become the third largest seller, with brands everybody recognizes, including the venerable Frigidaire. Furthermore, White was making a profit on its output which had eluded the previous owners of the brands: giant corporations like GM (who had owned Frigidaire since 1918), Westinghouse, Ford (Philco), and American Motors (Kelvinator). All had gone through years of low returns and often large losses because of the "brutal price competition that has long ruled the appliance trade."

The price competition itself had resulted from lack of any consumer perception of any significant difference between brands. White did not, however, consolidate brands, considering the brand franchises and dealer networks as the most valuable parts of its acquisitions. Instead, White achieved a "drastic increase in the efficiency of plants, people, and equipment" by a "Scrooge—like obsession" with cost cutting measures, and a recognition of marketing trends.

Operations were streamlined. Marginal models were discontinued. When White took over Westinghouse's Columbus, Ohio operations in 1975, it reduced the number of models from the over 40 then being produced, to 30 which represented 85% of sales. This doubled production runs on each model and eliminated costly downtime.

Management is decentralized, with each of the 15 plants a cost center under its own president. Each plant focuses on a limited number of products. White has no expensive executive "perks". Offices are "Spartan." The headquarters is in an old factory building in Cleveland, in which the company chairman "lines up with everyone else for lunch at White Consolidated's gymnasium—like cafeteria."

White has the reputation as a tough bargainer with labor, and is willing to take strikes. Because several plants make each of the major types of products, White can make up for a walkout at one plant by increased production at another. When it acquires a company, it also streamlines the executive overhead. When it took over the Mansfield, Ohio, plant of Westinghouse, it pared the salaried staff by 39%.

Advertising battles are avoided by selling about half of its output under the private—label brands of mass merchandisers such as Sears, J. C. Penney, Montgomery Ward, Gambles, and Western Auto. R&D concentrates on productivity improvements, such as redesigning appliances for lower production cost without sacrificing efficiency in use.

Starting out in 1967 as a $400 million per year seller of industrial equipment and sewing machines, White had become a $1.7 billion maker of appliances, and viewed as "an awesome competitor" by the remaining appliance sellers.

WHO BUYS CORPORATE LOSERS?
(Reprinted by permission from **FORTUNE,** Jan. 26, 1981, p.60)

...even the mangiest mongrel has its admirers. A couple of entrepreneurs bought Helena Rubenstein, the cosmetics company, even though Colgate–Palmolive lost $50 million on the business in 1979. Another business man bought the Remington electric–shaver operation from Sperry Corp. in 1979 despite losses of $30 million in five years. And three partners who knew little about the field unhesitatingly snapped up Squibb Corp.'s ailing Beech–Nut baby–food business, which was suffering from falling birthrates and vicious price wars....

Helena Rubenstein's new buyers were convinced that the company's reputation as a corporate dog was greatly exaggerated. The cosmetic company was troubled even when Colgate–Palmolive acquired it for $142 million back in 1973, and it lost money in 1978 and 1979. Colgate decided to sell the company, but [three attempts fell through and]...Albi Enterprises bought it last July for $20 million—a down payment of $1.5 million, with the rest payable over 15 years....

The new owners looked at the business differently from Colgate. They saw that in many markets the company was doing just fine...Even in the markets where Rubenstein was in deep trouble...the damage did not seem irreparable...

Colgate, like many large companies, emphasized volume and so was reluctant to cut back operations. Rubenstein's principal outlets were department and drug stores, but it sold three products... to chain stores. Burack and Weiss found these mass–market products inconsistent with Rubenstein's high–fashion image. They sold the brand names....

In the hope that volume would soon increase, Colgate had been holding onto factories that were operating well below capacity....Burack and Weiss ...have shut down and closed plants... This year, according to the owners, the company will be solidly profitable...

Seemingly small changes in strategy can bring a longtime loser out of the doghouse. When Victor Kiam paid some $25 million to buy the Remington electric–shaver business from Sperry Corp. in 1979, Remington had been losing money for years....A marketing man, Kiam...was convinced that Sperry's error was to consider technical innovation, no matter how minor, to be of paramount importance. [Says Kiam], "You can do something every three to four years, but not every six months." Kiam cites Sperry's decision to add an internal recharging unit to Remington's model 3000. "I stopped that," he says. "We were not going to obsolete our best seller."... The Remington 3000 is now called the "Microscreen," a name he says is more descriptive....

Remington's market share is up significantly. Last year, the company had a pretax profit of $2.6 million.

The initial idea Frank Nicholas had to transform Beech–Nut baby foods flopped almost immediately. In 1972, the year before he bid for Beech–Nut, Nicholas and two partners bought Baker Laboratories, an infant–formula maker. "If we could persuade the mother to buy our formula," Nicholas figured, "we could then link her to our food." He bought the company from Squibb in 1973 for $16 million. During the first year the company lost $6 million. The next year, Baker Laboratories quit the infant–formula business in the United States.

[Later] Nicholas came up with another marketing brainstorm...In July 1976, Beech–Nut ceased adding sugar to its fruit juices and started selling them in glass bottles rather than the cans that had been the industry standard...With babe in arms, a parent could quickly screw a nipple directly on the jar. Almost immediately, Beech-Nut's apple-juice sales quadrupled.

The next January, Beech-Nut announced that it was purging salt and most of the sugar from its strained foods. Nutritionists cheered. A relentless promoter, Nicholas toured the country preaching the no-salt no-sugar gospel, appearing on radio and television talk shows, and earning the nickname "Mr Natural."....Sales shot up to $65 million [from a low of $54 million in 1973]....

In late 1979, Nicholas and his partners sold the company to Nestle', the Swiss food giant, though he still runs it. Strained carrots without sugar and salt turned out to be worth their weight in gold. Nestle' reportedly paid about $35 million, more than twice what Nicholas and his partners had paid for the company....

1. By no means every corporate loser repays the new owners, but the examples quoted here are not alone. None of the 5 examples given in this chapter (the 3 above, plus the Banquet Foods and the White Consolidated stories) were products from the growth phase. Can you perceive any common explanation of what might cause a lot of corporate dogs?

2. Do you perceive any common principles in choosing those for rescue, and the kinds of treatment which brings them to life?

CHAPTER 8. PRODUCT DEVELOPMENT AND PREPARATION FOR INTRODUCTION

NEW PRODUCT PRACTICES: The Booz-Allen Studies

All of the quantitative information in this chapter, and as indicated, much of the specific information on best practices, derives from **New Products Management for the 1980s** by Booz-Allen & Hamilton Inc., 1982, a summary of the latest of 5 studies of company new product practices conducted by Booz-Allen over the last 25 years. The information comes from "a comprehensive mail survey of corporate executives and product managers of **Fortune** 1000 companies..." [supplemented by] "more than 150 interviews... with leading new product executives in the United States and Europe."

"More than 700 U. S. manufacturers responded to a questionnaire on current product practices. Their responses provided information on over 13,000 new products introduced over the past 5 years. Sixty percent of the respondents represented industrial goods companies in the information processing, instruments and controls, industrial machinery, chemicals, power generating equipment, OEM components, and textile industries; 40 percent represented consumer goods companies, divided equally between durables and nondurables."

All of the information is being quoted by permission of Booz-Allen & Hamilton Inc., copyright, 1982.

PRODUCT DEVELOPMENT
& PREPARATION FOR INTRODUCTION

8

No organization can escape the effects of the dynamics of the market, fueled by the constant changes in the identity of customers, in their tastes, values and interests; by the changes in the kinds, types and levels of competition; and by the changes in the culture, the economic environments, and in the legal and political environment. Most larger commercial organizations have learned this lesson in recent years, and have developed permanently organized new product processes. Far too many non-commercial organizations do not seem to have followed suit, as yet.

Introducing new offerings is always risky to some degree. Recent years have seen outstanding gains in the cost and efficiency of getting new products ready for successful introduction, but apparently no substantial reduction in the mortality, once introduced. More than a third of those introduced fail to live up to expected success.

Despite these risks, there is only one certainty: sellers who neglect the development of new offerings face erosion of their vitality over time, and in the long run (not always very long), they face extinction. This is just as true of non-commercial operations producing services, as it is of commercial manufacturers of tangible goods.

The new product introduction process consists of 7 steps. The ratio of successful new products to those accepted for development has been drastically reduced in recent years by increased emphasis on the early steps: development of a product strategy, idea generation in accordance with the strategy, screening and evaluation, and the business analysis. The result has been to lower the amount spent in the expensive final, commercialization, step.

The type of organization used depends on the level of innovation attempted. Both free-standing, autonomous, units and functional units may be found in the same organizations.

Successful product development must include a vital value difference from competitive offerings, and a minimization of the learning requirement. A well-organized testing phase includes carefully analyzed pilot tests and test production runs and some form of consumer tests of the developed offering to determine what customers will perceive its greatest values to be.

"UNEASY LIES THE HEAD THAT WEARS THE CROWN"

It is still true: any roll call of the leading corporations of 10, 20 or 30 years previous finds most of them them no longer there, or at least anywhere near the top. Dominance seems to anesthetize management, or at last stifle innovation. A comment column in the February 4, 1981 Wall Street Journal ("Corporations: A Perilous Life at the Top," by Paul Ingrassia) reminds us again. He points to the history and present problems of 3 once giant Chicago firms—Swift, Pullman, and International Harvester.

International Harvester's history dates back to the early 19th century, and dominated the farm machinery scene until not many years ago, but has been passed by Deere & Co in the last couple of decades, and is still teetering on the edge of bankruptcy as this is written, saved only because, apparently, its creditors cannot afford to let it die.

When the railroads dominated transportation, Pullman was the second largest transportation equipment maker in the world—exceeded by only Ford Motor Company in 1917. When the railroad era waned in the 1940s, Pullman seemed to be unable to find a profitable niche, and was bought out by Wheelabrator, "an obscure New England Company only one-third its size" in 1980.

Swift dates back to Gustavus Swift's butcher shop on Cape Cod, in 1855. The real start was his later move to then booming Chicago, where it occurred to Swift that it made more sense to slaughter the beef from the prairies in Chicago, and ship the beef east, than to send the live cattle on the long journey east to be slaughtered there. By 1916, Swift was paying $31 million in dividends, and by 1920, was being sued for antitrust. But it was more innovative competition, not the lawyers who brought Swift down. And they were simply modernizing Swift's original idea: cutting shipping and labor costs even further by moving closer to the farms, and shipping out "boxed beef" (major cuts rather than whole carcasses). In 1980, Esmark,the overall modern Swift conglomerate, spun off its fresh meat business to look elsewhere for profits.

The three Chicago companies mentioned were no exceptions. Woolworth and A&P could been added to the current list. Any reading of corporate history finds every leader in trouble sooner or later.

Why? Alfred D. Chandler, the noted Harvard business historian, attributes the problem to the difficulty people have in changing. He is quoted as saying,"When you're number one, you get stuck in your ways. It's a complicated process, but the key point is that you have investments in equipment and in people that do things a certain way. Then how do you change?"

The Seven Key Steps in the New Product Introduction Process

An organized new product introduction process consists of 7 key steps:
1. Development of a product strategy
2. Generating new product ideas in harmony with this strategy
3. Careful screening and evaluation of each idea in relation to established criteria for consideration
4. A business analysis of each idea
5. Development of the offering

6.   Testing the offering and its marketability
7.   Commercialization

The Proven Value of a Product Strategy Process

The process of developing strategies has already been discussed. Full-fledged development of a carefully worked out product strategy is a relatively new development in most organizations, but one that has drastically improved the efficiency of product development investments.   The addition of this key step has increased the ratio of successful introductions from from a reported 1/58 in 1968 to 1/7 in 1981, according to parallel studies made in 1968 and 1981 by Booz-Allen & Hamilton, Inc. "The percent of total new product expenditures allocated to products that are ultimately successful has increased--from 30 percent in 1968 to 54 percent today." (Booz-Allen, 1982) Thus by spending more in the preliminary steps of screening, organizations have greatly improved the payoff of their product development dollars.

The purpose of the new product strategy, and the strategic plan of which it is a major part, is to identify and define the role which the development of new products is to play in maintaining the vitality of the seller and any expected growth.

Any rational new product strategy has to start from a series of analyses of:

- Existing markets and their estimated growth potentials or otherwise
- Emerging new markets which the seller could serve, and new products needed by those markets
- The present strengths of the organization, present weaknesses, relative to serving present markets and relative to entering any new ones
- The existing management style and new product experience

Only after this analysis is completed is the seller ready to formulate a new product strategy.   That policy will identify those markets to which the seller will confine his search for new product ideas, set performance criteria guidelines and measurement criteria for new product performance acceptance thresholds to be used in screening.   A key element of that policy will be the definition of the level of innovation the seller will undertake.

The Levels of Innovation To Be Sought
"New product" is a label which covers a wide spectrum of innovational content, from the revolutionary new type of product, with a high learning content, to the new-only-to-me offering, added to fill an offering mix lack, to a mere promotional repositioning of an existing offering. In analyzing the 13,000 1976-1981 new product introductions reported by the 700 firms in its 1981 survey, Booz-Allen found that they divided as follows:

- **New-to-the-world,** creating completely new markets (10%)
- **New product lines,** to gain an entry into an established market (20%)

- **Additions to product lines,** supplementing established lines (26%)
- **Improvements in/revisions to existing product lines and replacing them:** better performance or greater perceived value (26%)
- **Cost reducing:** products giving similar performance at lower cost (11%)
- **Repositioning:** existing offerings targetted to new markets or segments (7%)

With the exception of repositioning, the list above is in roughly a descending order of risk, and over half of the surveyed companies avoided the high risk new-to-the-world revolutionary types of introductions.

The opportunity to introduce the revolutionary depends, of course, on the industry involved and the maturity of the technology the seller is capable of working with.   Furthermore, few organizations are equipped with the combination of technological skills and marketing expertise to succeed with the truly revolutionary.   But the more risk which is dodged, the less the chance for profit.   Low risk markets are low margin markets.

Repositioning can be a low cost operation, or a very high investment operation.   Both the cost and the risk can be substantial.   Philip Morris' repositioning of Miller Beer was a very expensive operation, requiring as much patient capital as do many revolutionary market development introductions.   Such would almost always be the case when the attempt is to secure a major position in a well-established market.   But there are also times when the offering can be repositioned in an attractive market vacuum.   The case of the NO-MARK makeup, in an earlier chapter, was such.   In such cases, the risk is low, since the product is a no-learning offering, with minimal promotional costs.

The level of innovation to be sought obviously gives a sharper focus to the choice of new product ideas to be entertained and influences the sources of those ideas.

Sources of New Product Ideas

Any new offering starts either from the market side or the technological side: it is either a concept of some marketing opportunity or of some offering which could be produced if the market could be developed. Development requires a compatible mating of the two.   The ideas themselves may come from within the organization, or from the outside.   While most useful ideas will result from systematic internal search efforts, anyone in the organization or its marketing system may furnish excellent ideas, from the assembly line worker or clerk to the chairman of the board, and including distributors and even final customers.

External sources would include free-lance inventors, stylists, and designers, observation of competitors and their offerings (both the mistakes and the successes), published news and technical literature, both of the industry or trade, and of a general character, and merger brokers and finance institutions (for some kinds of acquisitions).

NEW PRODUCT IDEAS: TREND WATCHING

Woolworth: Population Watcher

Woolworth's success as a pioneer of mass merchandising was solidly based on a sure sense of location and merchandise appeal. Really the first discount operation, he understood what his market was. In 1890, when the chain had little more than a dozen stores, he made his first buying trip to Europe. Just after returning, he wrote the following to his store managers:

"I have been looking over a census of the United States and I am convinced that there are one hundred cities and towns where we can locate five-and-ten-cent stores and we can sell a million dollars' worth of goods a year!"

As his biographer notes: "The great tide of immigration to the United States was just setting in, and during more than a quarter of a century thereafter the growth of population was a study which absorbed Woolworth as a hobby. He maintained elaborate charts which revealed to him how towns and cities were growing. As the curve of immigration rose, so did the curve of his ambition. The immigrants would be his customers! All those millions with very little money could afford to trade at the five-and-tens, even the poorest."

[Woolworth reached his million dollars a year five years later, in 1895, with 28 stores. The chain continued to expand to around a thousand stores by the time he died, in 1919.] (John K. Winkler, **Five and Ten**, McBride, 1940,p. 102)

Toni Anticipates a Trend

When the Toni Home Permanent kit was introduced, the fashionable hairdo was curly. Aware that fashion was a fickle goddess, the firm's research department took no chances. Like others selling through mass merchandisers, they subscribed to store audit services to keep track of current retail sales trends.

But they wanted more than past sales data: they wanted a fix on where sales would go in the future. Consequently, the marketing research department instituted a monthly telephone survey of several thousand randomly chosen women a month, asking them what they were going to do about their hair **the next time** they went to a beauty parlor. As the 1950s gave way to the early 1960s, they detected a trend toward more casual hair styles. The firm then developed products better adapted to this trend, and when it developed, put them on the market early. When the decline in curly treatments started to show up in the retail markets, Toni sales held level, and the entire decline was absorbed in competitors' losses.

Internal Idea Sources

Among the 700 manufacturers surveyed by Booz-Allen, those most successful in new product introduction relied on internally developed offerings as the primary source of growth. The major potential sources of new offering concepts should be those in close contact with the markets (sales forces, technical and other customer service people, distributors, and repair personnel), product planning and marketing research staffs, and the R&D staff. Marketing personnel can and should be a source of ideas about felt market needs, especially improvements and revisions of current offerings, and about line additions which could improve the attractiveness of the offering mix.

Planning and marketing research people should be assigned the task of the continuing analysis of market, industry, and customer trends of every kind which could open opportunities for new kinds of offerings, require revisions in current offerings and offering mixes, and pose threats to existing offerings. Such analyses of trends should turn up both possible modifications of existing offerings and ideas about completely new types of products or product lines. If such research personnel work closely with the R&D staff, as they should, the liaison should help develop concepts of market-oriented applications of newly developing technologies. Their analyses of important design compromises being required of customers should also be a stimulus to the R&D personnel.

Marketing research could do more than is usually attempted in uncovering design possibilities, sometimes of an even very substantial character. Some years ago, a rug manufacturer commissioned some research into consumer preferences in rug weaves and designs. The researchers discovered that consumers placed a high value on the texture of the Wilton velvet weave, but disliked its tendency to show foot tracks. Under prodding by the researcher, the company and the industry first developed a looped weave, and then the "sculptured velvet" weave which became very popular for a number of years. A number of private studies have also demonstrated that field research with customers can uncover taste trends among consumers long before they show up in the market, particularly in fashions.

EMERGING TECHNOLOGY: BOTH THREAT AND OPPORTUNITY

The growth industry of the 1970s and 1980s has been in solid state electronics. Products which performed timing and calculating functions have been pushed aside by "Silicon Valley." Watchmakers and the manufacturers of electro-mechanical calculating devices have been major losers.

The financial news of November 13, 1982 chronicles one result: Assuag, the leading watchmaker in Switzerland (Longines, Certina, and Rado brands) announced a loss of $67.5 million for 1982, assertedly because of the depression and the **increasing popularity of digital watches.** The board president, Peter Ringgli, noted that the firm faces a "very worrying situation."

What the item did not note was that the use of electronics in watches was originally developed by the Swiss watchmakers, but not pushed by them. They were the first to develop quartz crystal regulation, but never put much effort into marketing them, and ignored the possibilities of the digital movements, entirely. They apparently felt that their finer quality mechanical movements would continue to be more profitable, and let others exploit the market.

Likewise, NCR, which held a near monopoly of the cash register market, ignored the transaction recording and accounting gains possible with computers until it almost lost out completely before abandoning its mechanical manufacturing facilities and making an all out fight to regain some foothold in the market it had lost. All of the leading makers of calculating machines made the same mistake, and none are among the current leaders in the electronic machines at any level.

R&D personnel can be the source of concepts for: new kinds of offerings capable of fulfilling known desire sets, new processes and new technologies which open up possibilities for less design compromise or for fulfillment of new desire sets through market broadening modifications, new materials, mechanisms or services which could add substantial values of some kind to the offerings.

NEW PRODUCT IDEAS: COMPETITOR WATCHING

The Fashion Knock-off

The ladies garment manufacturer was describing industry practice to a visiting professor:

"Take that three-piece knit suit that was so popular last year—a jacket, blouse and skirt. As soon as So-and-So brought it out, we could see it was selling well. We got to thinking: why make a whole blouse? So we put out a similar outfit for less—a jacket, a dickey, and a skirt. But Blank, down the street had an even smarter idea. He knit a jacket with a contrasting insert, still cheaper. He sold a lot of them."

GM Knocks Off a Ford Design

When the first volume sales of foreign cars started cutting deeply into Detroit's market share in the 1950's, each of the Big Three made crash production moves in 1958, cutting the normal 3-year design lead to 2 years to put the first major American compacts on the market: Ford with the Falcon, Chrysler with the Plymouth Valiant, and GM with the rear engine Corvair.

The Falcon sold the best of the three, although at the expense of other Ford models. The Corvair stumbled at first, then the Monza model gained a popular specialty market, but nowhere near the Falcon volume. The Corvair was a success in that most sales were a plus, not at the expense of other Chevy models. But GM thought it would be nice to have part of the volume compact market in addition. Their answer, the following year was the Chevy II.

Looking over the new model when it first appeared, the author noticed some familiar lines. Talking about it to an engineer MBA student, who was with the Fisher Body Division, he remarked, "It looks to me like a Falcon with crisped-up lines. The engineer simply said, "no comment," with a smile.

Stealing General Mills' Cookies

General Mills is in a business where new offerings are a way of staying in business. Some years back, they developed a prepared breakfast item to be warmed up in a toaster, to be labelled Toast-Ems, and duly put it into test markets before release for general sale. The test marketing operation came to the immediate attention of Kellog's, who are also in the breakfast food business. Convinced by the early sales that this could be a winner, Kellog rushed development of a package and a similar product, registered the name, Pop-Tarts, and contracted with the Keebler Biscuit Company for immediate volume production. Before General Mills could analyze its test marketing data, Kellog had a national campaign in full swing and captured the market.

Valuable as internal development normally is, ideas from outside sources and acquisitions can both represent opportunities for profits which should not be passed up.

External Sources of Profitable Ideas

There are 3 important external sources of new offering ideas:
- Observation and analysis of competitors' offerings and their experiences
- Published news and technical literature of both a general or popular form or specific to the industry, trade or technology
- Acquisitions of specific ideas or partially developed offerings

Observation of competitors and their offerings. One of the oldest of new offering ideas is still an important one: competitor watching. Sellers can and do profit both by competitor's mistakes and their successes. Smart competitors spot omissions in segment coverage. The most common use of the information so gained is, in industry slang, "the knock-off": the quick production of a copy of competitor's successful offerings. But learning of a competitor's errors and omissions can be at least as profitable, and analysis of a competitor's designs can suggest possibilities for strategy.

The **knock-off** is virtually a way of life in industries in which the novelty attribute is a significant component of perceived value: fashion, jewelry, and toys, especially. It is much more widely practiced than most observers realize, and even includes some forms of industrial goods. It works best when used either to preempt a market by moving faster than the competitor, or, conversely, when the design and pricing are intended to appeal to a segment excluded by the originator's marketing plan. In the latter case, it is a real service to the market, and probably needs to be more widely practiced than it is. The knock-off cannot work unless some segment gains perceived values, in some form. The added value, of course, may be no more than the inclusion of the item in an offering assortment already under consideration.

No organization should neglect the lessons to be learned from competitors. But sellers who depend solely on the initiative of others will sooner or later miss out to more innovative competition. The most dangerous competition is not the most obvious, as the Japanese taught Detroit's big three when they limited their analysis to each other's plans.

Published news and technical literature sources. The really fundamental new-to-the-world offerings come from a knowledge of advances in technology and changes in populations and their lifestyles, paralleled with an imaginative analysis of the needs these create and the desires which become possible to fulfill.

The best sources of such knowledge comes from reading, both the news in general publications, including newspapers, in the various censuses, and in the interest-oriented press of popularization, of the trade, of industry, and of technology.   Watching the various trends which these depict can suggest the point at which a demographic change or a development of the state of the art is ripe for new offering development.

One of the great advances and marketing successes of the 20th century has been duPont's development of synthetic fibers, beginning with nylon. Although duPont had been moving to become something more than a maker of explosives for some years, no other development has done so much to transform the company.   Like many such advances, the end product was not in view in the early 1930's, when duPont saw that the development of giant long-chain molecules was ready to come out of the laboratory, and hired Carrothers to develop the possibilities.

Likewise, it was imaginative insight into the the need for a one-stop shopping facility with parking spaces which led a few independents to originate the first supermarkets in 1932, uniting the trend to automobile transport and better home refrigeration, and changing the shopping habits of the world.   It was not the giant computer firms who saw the possibilities in the mini-computer, but hobbyists who saw the market application of the new powerful new computer chips and put the Apple and other "personal computers" on the market.   Probably more than any other industry move, these changed the whole character of the industrial and commercial market for computer devices, a move the giants had to hurry to catch up with. The Apple was so successful because other hobbyists had insight into what such a computer could do for various segments, and developed standardized programs that enabled the Apple to fit their needs with little learning.

Such spectacular successes do not come down the pike every day or week, but those on a lesser scale are reasonably frequent.   The financial and market leverage they permit have built many a large business from modest investments.   The founders of the businesses have often profited best by being acquired.

The Acquisition Route. Very large organizations are often apt to shun the risks of major innovations.   They are often quite open to acquiring offerings in which some of the risk and time delays have been removed by partial development by others.   But large sellers are not the only ones to profit by acquisition.   Often rather small entrepreneurs have made spectacular gains by acquiring and building up businesses started by others.

Acquisitions are of four general forms:
- Marketing rights acquisition
- Acquisition of offerings needing some further development to be market ready.
- Acquisition of healthy businesses in established markets
- Acquisitions of others "dogs"

Acquisitions can be good investments **if chosen for their fit to the seller's well-considered strategy,** and the plan for their exploitation is compatible with the skills and available resources of the acquiring seller.   As compared with internally developed offerings, they can avoid many of the uncertainties and costs of development. They also can reduce the time needed to get to market. How well they do any of this depends on the future potential of the acquisition, its current position in the market, and whatever resources accompany the acquisition.

Profitable acquisitions can be made at any stage of the product life cycle, from an early point in the development stage through maturity to offerings on the decline. Any acquisition assumes some special strengths in the acquiring organization which the selling organization lacks.

The acquiring organization may expect to improve the profit situation through one or more of the following:

- Fitting the offering into a more compatible product mix
- Applying greater marketing skills and strengths in sales and advertising, an established customer franchise, an established distribution system, and/or more imaginative market analysis
- Supplying better financing
- Applying better development facilities and skills
- Using tighter cost controls

Further growth of some kind is the obvious goal: growth in sales, in market share, and, of course, profit. This would seem to rule out offerings in the mature and decline phases. Observation reveals excellent examples of profitable acquisition in both phases.

Acquisitions of offerings with established market niches have several advantages. The acquirer has or can easily get relatively accurate knowledge of the consumption systems involved and the values being sought by the customers. The established market base furnishes a foundation on which growth can be built. Four conditions must be met if the acquisition is to live up to expectations:

- The offering should not have a negative image in the market, should have a neutral reputation, at least, and preferably a positive one with some significant market segment
- The offering must be adaptable to the overall strategy and objectives of the acquirer, be in line with executive interests, and have a potential volume adequate to justify continued interest and attention
- The acquirer must have some sound reason for a belief that the market for the offering can be made more profitable in some manner. This could be through promotion changing the offering image to fit a broader market segment, through providing access to an established customer franchise base, access to stronger and wider distribution, improvements in production costs and quality control, and/or improvements in design, packaging and display.

Growth phase offerings are available when the sellers realize they do not have the resources to develop a strong market niche, and are willing to take a profit on their development efforts.

Market development offerings require strong finances, combined with marketing skills of a high order, that only a strongly financed organization can provide. The acquiring organization must be one accustomed to seeing offerings through to market success.

Product development offerings become available because the innovating developer has become aware that he lacks the managerial resources to bring them to market success.

The book publishing industry, for example, generally depends on authors to develop ideas and bring them through to the manuscript stage. Most manuscripts require some further development, ranging from a complete rewrite down to minor editorial polishing and some graphics design.

By selling at the manuscript stage, the author is assured of some return from the moment of the first sale, with relatively little cash outlay on his part.

Since nearly all publishing costs are front end, the publisher assumes the risk of too little sales volume to cover breakeven costs, and furnishes the sales and advertising facilities and management. In return, the author's manuscript development has reduced a large part of the initial development time and cost. Rarely, if ever, has any major textbook publisher, for example, been able to make a profit by financing the entire manuscript development cost.

"Dogs" can sometimes be attractive candidates for acquisition, when the seller possesses the appropriate marketing and/or management skills and resources. Many "dogs" have a prize show potential. Carefully chosen, they can reward generously the buyer who understands the market and production management needed and furnishes the tender loving promotional care and attention. Many became "dogs" simply because they were misfits in their previous ownership.

Dogs can be cheap acquisitions, often available as leveraged buy-outs, with the seller putting up minimum direct purchase capital.

Whatever the type of acquisition, it should receive just as careful screening and evaluation as any other new offering idea, and meet the same criteria.

Criteria for Screening and Evaluation

Thorough screening of new product ideas is a major key to success. That screening should include at least 4 basic sets of criteria:
- The fit to market needs and the estimated level of offering advantage of any kind to any key elements in distribution and consumption
- The fit to the seller's overall strategy
- The specific role the offering would play in the seller's strategy
- The type and nature of the financial performance expected

The **strategic roles** assigned to acceptable new product ideas by the firms reporting to Booz-Allen were classified under 2 main types and 8 subheads,

as follows:
- **Externally Driven**
  - * Defend market share position
  - * Establish a foothold in a new market
  - * Preempt market segment
- **Internally Driven**
  - * Maintain position as product innovator
  - * Exploit technology in new way
  - * Capitalize on distribution strengths
  - * Provide a cash generator
  - * Use excess of off-season capacity

The role assigned will affect the level of investment and the risk this entails. These two factors will then affect the type of financial performance and its minimum level for acceptance. The 3 most widely used criteria of financial performance are the estimated contribution to profit, the sales volume expected, and the estimated return on investment. Over half of the firms also considered the expected payback period, and a minority used the internal rate of return or net present value. Most firms use more than one criterion.

When using these criteria, it should always be kept in mind that the most carefully worked estimate is a rough guide at best, subject to the unforeseen reactions of customers and of competitors, as well as unforeseeable external events.

Once an idea passes a screening, it needs to be assigned to some form of new product organizational unit to oversee development and preparation for marketing. Whatever the form of that organization, it should include a product champion to see it through.

New Product Organization and Management

New product development, production and marketing tend to upset the habitual routines of operating people in both production and sales. The oversight of the development and market preparation thus needs to be the first priority of some person or group especially assigned to the task. Two general forms of organization are used: **autonomous units** reporting to no functional branch of the organization, and **functionally based units**, that are permanent parts of existing planning, marketing, R&D or engineering departments. Both types may exist side-by-side in a complex organization. The more revolutionary new ideas may then be given to the autonomous unit, and evolutionary units fitting into the existing business structure assigned to the functional unit most affected.

Autonomous units may consist of interdisciplinary joint task forces (usually containing representatives from R&D, marketing, and production), separate new product departments, or venture teams.

Under venture team plans, some highly interested corporate manager or technical staff member is given leave to explore an approved new idea, usually with rather restricted resources, requiring the manager to exercise ingenuity and initiative. If the promise of success develops, assistants from the various functional groups may be added: from research, marketing, finance, and production. If adequate sales and profits develop, the operation may become an independent unit of an established division of the firm, or even a division in itself. The venture team manager is a powerful extension of the product champion concept.

The Role of Product Champion

Product champions have come into being because really new product ideas are seldom welcomed with open arms by the operating personnel in any organization, commercial or non-commercial. The returns they promise are in the distant, intangible future. The disruptions in comfortable habitual routines their development occasions are here and now, quite tangible. Most new products require a strong, enthusiastic sponsor, with the full backing of upper management, who takes the responsibility for the disruptions and the risks on himself, expediting the course of development, and preferably seeing the initial commercialization through at least a year, until the offering becomes an accepted part of the established routine.

Setting Goals for Development

The estimates on which the screening and evaluation were based assumed, or should have assumed, the delivery of a specific bundle of satisfactions, to be perceived by a specific set of market segments as significantly more valuable in some specific attributes than any available otherwise. These performance specifications become the goals for product development. Just how specific these goals can be will depend on the level of innovation being attempted.

At one end of the extremes is the occasional **research innovation** type of development project, such as the assignment given Carrothers by duPont in 1932: to explore the developing art of long chain molecules for some chemical which could be put to volume use. At that point in the state of the art, no one could have perceived the emergence of nylon. Such assignments are so rare as to be outside the limits of the chosen strategy of all but a few extremely well-capitalized organizations.

Somewhat more common is the **new-to-the-world idea** perceived as being within the capabilities of the current state of the art. In this case, it should always be possible to define the ideal characteristics of the foreseeable end product, and set up milestone review points to check on the progress being made toward the specifications.

The formulation of those specifications should be a joint effort of the engineers, who best know the possibilities, and the marketing people, who should be best informed about customer perceptions and values. Continued collaboration between marketing and R & D is needed as the limits and the possibilities become more obvious. Even in such cases, the goals may have to be modified, and milestone reviews scheduled in advance to decide whether further investment is justified, or a different set of performance specifications set.

Product improvement goals can and should be quite specific, and should look forward to a level of difference over current offerings in the market as to be really noticeable. That difference may be in the physical product itself, or in some of the marketing and promotional attributes, or a combination of the two. At least 6 definite goals for product improvement are nearly always worth trying for:

- Simplification of the use system by which the satisfaction is obtained (such as reducing all the editing commands in a word processing program to individual symbols, rather than a string of symbols)
- Eliminating or at least minimizing, to the greatest extent possible, any tangible characteristics which have no perceived positive value: weight, size, odor, thickness, poor handling qualities, difficulty of service access, etc.
- Building flexibility into the offering package , so that the buyers may tailor it more closely to each one's special desire-set (such as using modular construction)
- Minimizing the maintenance required, or the individual adjustments
- Improving the storing and sales qualities of the offering for the benefit and profit of the intermediaries through whose hands the item must reach the market. Any aspect which makes storage, stock picking, pricing or price marking, display, or handling more efficient, or gives better customer information, makes the intermediary's job lighter and more profitable, and thus more readily available to the final buyer.
- Carrying the performance of some key attribute one noticeable step higher (such as doubling the memory capacity of a computer).

Eliminating or at least minimizing the learning requirement should be a performance goal for any level of innovation. This requires an analysis of the kinds and degrees of learning any aspect of a design calls for.

Predicting and Minimizing the Learning Requirement

Failures or major problems in new offering introductions stem from many causes. One of the more important, can, however, be foreseen with some degree of accuracy, and largely prevented: the neglect to forecast the physical or perceptual habit relearning required by the new offering, and by the specifics of its design and marketing. The neglect is serious whether the neglect results in an underestimate of the length of the market development period needed, or a too cautious estimate of the speed of acceptance. The first leads to financing problems, the second to the risk of being overrun by drooling competitors in hot pursuit of fat profits.

The Four Kinds of Automatic Response Relearning

An introduction may require any or all of four kinds of physical or perceptual relearning before acceptance:

1. Physical habits: changes in the physical use-system
2. Value-perception learning: learning to perceive enough added value in the offering to justify an added cost
3. Role-perception learning: learning to accept a changed and somewhat downgraded social role with respect to the use system involved
4. Use-perceptual learning: learning to perceive an apparently quite different source of satisfaction as a reliable and improved fulfillment of a specific desire set

Predicting physical habit changes. Few forecasts are as cheap or as reliable as those which can be made concerning the amount of physical habit change the use system for a proposed introduction will require. Nothing more is needed than a drafting stool, some paper, a pencil, and a careful step-by-step analysis of the use systems required by the offerings to be displaced and the one proposed, in the form of a simple flow chart. A couple of minutes of visual inspection will reveal the differences in routines, and their character.

The character of the changes required will indicate the extent of the problem rather well. Nuisance steps are an added value to the offering. Any other kind will pose problems of acceptance.

Value perception relearning and its prediction. The prices of some introductions require the purchaser to perceive some new added attribute as worth significantly more than purchasers have been valuing similar attributes in the past, in other contexts. Such changes will inevitably require a prolonged market development effort to gain acceptance. The outstanding example was the introductory experience of color television.

The initial reception of monocolor (black-and-white: B&W) television was a runaway success, as Figure 8-1 shows. Typical of such rapid growth sale periods, scores of makes flooded the initial market. The whole industry expected a similar experience with color TV when the FCC finally approved the RCA technology in 1954, and major makers started preparing to enter the market. Sales were so rare that all but RCA withdrew before the year was out. RCA had little choice but to continue, and sustained 8-figure losses each year for 8 years before sales took hold and started a rapid growth.

The reasons need not have been obscure, even before sales were initiated. B&W TV experience should never have been considered a history which would be repeated. The initial perceived values were quite different. B&W TV was perceived as a familiar and widely popular entertainment medium, in a much more convenient form: movies at home in the parlor, available as the turn of a switch, with no significant cost once the set was bought.

Color TV added only one added value, and that one at a high money cost and somewhat less convenience. It added color--to only a few programs. The shows were the same, and most did not benefit from color. The color itself was not very faithful, and required rather frequent adjustment. Worse, the set was priced at 3 times the level needed to replace the the B&W set which most families already owned, in good condition. Finally, evidence was readily available that few people valued color that much. Most movies still did well in B&W. Most film sold for cameras was still not color.

FIGURE 8-1. THE CONTRASTING GROWTH CURVES OF COLOR TV AND MONOCHROME TV

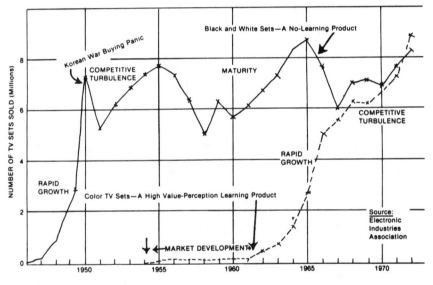

Had RCA conducted no more analysis then the above, the firm might have adopted a quite different and less costly introductory marketing program, knowing that initial demand would be light and costly to get.

Predicting the value perception learning requires an analysis of three items:

- The key attributes in the satisfaction bundles of the offering(s) being displaced, compared with the satisfaction bundles being promised by the introduction, and a determination of the main added attributes with significant perceivable value.
- An estimate, usually based on market values of similar attributes in other offerings, of the likely level of valued perceived in these added attributes.

To some degree, such an estimate should always be an element in the initial price quoted in any event. In a major case, like that of color TV, it can mean an entirely different kind of introductory marketing plan.

Role-perception learning and its prediction. Other new products may imply a change in the perception of the prestige level of the social role of some active participant in the use system. If it downgrades that role, some substantial period of market development may be required before sales commence to grow rapidly.

An example already cited earlier was the introduction of instant coffee, which cast a shadow on the need for housewifely skill in the kitchen. The instants made good progress only as the housewife began to see her main role outside the home, at some paid work.

The introduction of computer typesetting was greatly slowed by strong union opposition. Typographers had been one of the elite groups in labor, with a job rated as highly skilled. When the "cold type" of computer typesetting replaced the "hot type" of the linotype machine, they resisted the substitution, perceiving themselves being reduced to little more than mere typists—not a highly paid occupation. Much of the success in getting the new process into use consisted of physically transferring the work itself to non-union establishments.

Prediction of this effect is not at all difficult in the kind of industrial situation represented by typesetting. In the case of consumer goods, it usually means only some rather simple attitude research. This need not be very extensive, since what is involved is a basic set of cultural values which are widely and rather uniformly held.

Use-perception relearning and its prediction. Some new product designs are enough different from the established offerings of quite similar benefits that potential buyers find it difficult to perceive the promised satisfactions as both reliable and as improvements over the familiar. The smaller foreign-type automobiles were viewed by most automobile owners as probably lacking adequate room and being uncomfortable, even though many actually seated passengers better and more comfortably. They were judged on the external dimensions, compared with the Detroit models. It required a decade for the market to grow to a dimension that gave American automobile makers any great concern. Most apparel fashions gather momentum slowly at first, are tried out only by the most assured, until other buyers learn that they may offer attributes they seek. New types of building materials, even when they fit current trade practices well, are slow to gain markets because of this skepticism and the desire to avoid risk. It can generally be assumed that if an offering looks different in any attribute considered important to performance, it will meet some market resistance.

Minimizing the Relearning Requirement

Whenever possible, it is best to so design the offering and its promotion as to minimize any foreseeable habit or perceptual relearning need. Tractors were available as early as the first automobiles, and were built in commercial quantities almost as soon. But the early tractors were huge machines, weighing tons, and gained acceptance only on the virgin western prairies of Canada, which needed powerful, large capacity machines to break huge expanses of tough prairie sod. They began to win a real mass market only after light weight machines were offered which did about the same work as a team of good horses. The giant machines were not adaptable to the operations of farms averaging about 150 acres each. Only when most really important commercial farms grew to much larger sizes were the powerful machines sold today accepted--some four decades later. Originally, they were viewed as a substitute for horses, requiring less attention and able to work longer hours. Only later did they become a tool for spreading the span of operations per farmer.

Once the kind of reception is known, and the development of the offering has proceeded far enough to envision the end product, preparations can be made for the introduction.

Preparing to Market: Production Runs and Pilot Tests

It is seldom wise to move directly from the laboratory to introduction. Seldom is either the offering or the promotional plan fully ready at this point. Production runs use different equipment, personnel, and procedures than laboratory production. What appears, on paper, to be a flawless promotional plan may convey the wrong impression of the offering. Buyers may find flaws, with their methods of use, the expert cannot develop under his skilled trials. Indeed, buyers may define the offering as fitting a different use system than the one envisaged by the seller.

Provision needs to be made to check for all of these possibilities. Where physical production of a tangible offering is involved, pilot plant runs and semi-commercial runs should normally be made before any attempt to put on general sale. When possible, customer use tests should be conducted. Promotional plans and themes should be given market tests unless some degree of secrecy or timing forbids.

The degree of advance physical product testing necessary and advisable obviously varies with the amount of technical innovation built into the introduction. If an offering is basically a minor variant of the known, very little may be needed, and perhaps none advisable, to avoid alerting potential competition.

Conversely, offerings with major construction innovations and made with unfamiliar processes should always be thoroughly use tested by non-expert final users, and nothing sold until proved in a commercial or semi-commercial production run. The use tests are needed to establish the real appeals of the offering as well as uncover design defects which could sour the market before it gets established.

RUSHING INTO THE MARKET TOO SOON CAN BE FATAL

The Coal Stoker Blunder

For decades, most homes in the more populous areas of the United States were heated by coal in hand-fired furnaces, a dirty, not very efficient process. Then residential size coal stokers came on the market in the 1930's, and began to make headway, especially after World War II. Looking around for new products fitting its steel fabricating skills, the A. O. Smith Co. developed a design of its own. The construction of such a stoker required no really new state of the art. So when the prototype model showed good results, Smith tooled up for full production, and started selling.

Initial sales were reasonably good—unfortunately. In ordinary users hands, the production line model revealed a number of minor "bugs". All were rather simple to remedy, once revealed. But by the time Smith learned of them, so many stokers had been sold that the stoker had acquired a reputation as a lemon. After reviewing the situation, further production was scrapped and the product withdrawn from the market. Officials were convinced that the reputation could not be salvaged.

If Things Can Go Wrong, They Will

One part of the AC Chemical Division's business was the development of industrial finishes and paints. A recent trend had been to get away from solvent based and oil-based paints into latex emulsions. At the time, there was not yet a good latex enamel on the market. Division chemists finally developed what looked like a good one, using a special form of epoxy resins. It gave just the desired results in the laboratory. It was sent to production to try out—with surprising results. When put on the usual production equipment, what came out was not a smooth emulsion, but a lot of hard marbles. The laboratory went back to work.

Market tests also have a role to play. Generally speaking, their purpose is not to test the offering, but to firm up and correct any flaws in the introductory marketing plan. The design is pretty well set at this point, subject to only minor corrections, and the production equipment backed up with a substantial investment. Only the purely marketing aspects of the introduction are susceptible to much modification: the pricing, distribution, and promotion. This is one of the few major points in the market life cycle in which much elbow room is available for pricing decisions.

SUMMARY

The well-planned new product development and introduction is a 7-step process, starting with development of a product strategy, generating new offering ideas consistent with this strategy, and carefully screening and evaluating each idea on the basis of established criteria. These first three steps are the keys to success. They are followed by a business analysis, actual development of the offering, tests of the offering and its marketability, and final commercialization.

The degree of innovation ranges from offerings new to the world (only 10% of the total) to the mere repositioning of an existing offering to reach new markets or segments. Less than half of the firms studied ever attempted the really new.

Ideas for new offerings can originate from the outside or internally. The most successful organizations rely primarily on internally developed offerings.

Externally derived new offering ideas come from 3 principal sources: observation of competitors and their offerings, publications, and acquisitions. Thorough screening of new ideas utilizes 4 basic kinds of criteria: the fit of the offering to market needs and the level of competitive advantage it promises; the fit of the offering to the organization's overall strategy; the specific role the offering is expected to play in the seller's strategy; the type and nature of the financial performance expected.

Formal new product organizations are of two types: autonomous new product units, and units based in specific functions of the organization. Many organizations have both types. Autonomous units are usually assigned to collecting and developing ideas of a more revolutionary type. Functionally based units are expected to develop items fitting into the existing business structure of the functional unit.

Product development and introduction succeeds better when guided by an assigned product champion.

Product development goals should be as specific as the level of innovation permits, be expressed in terms of performance specifications, directed at a specific market segment or set of segments.

One major development goal should be the elimination or minimizing, so far as possible, of any learning requirement in the product design.

Offerings can require any of four kinds of automatic response relearning on the part·of buyers: physical habit changes, value perception learning, role perception learning, or use-perceptual learning.

Generally, once development is well along, the offering should be submitted to some form of consumer testing, to determine whether the possible buyers will perceive the performance to be as expected, and to learn what use systems buyers perceive the offering as fitting.

Developed products also need to be tested on production runs before release.

FOOD FOR THOUGHT AND DISCUSSION

DAYTON-HUDSON: AN INTERESTING QUESTION

Richard L. Schall, a vice chairman of Dayton Hudson (see story on page 148), characterized the dropping of the highly profitable Lipman's department store chain as "one of the decisions I'm proudest of." Given what we were told about the Dayton-Hudson strategy, why should he be especially proud of this decision?

THE SCHMOOS PUZZLE: WHAT HAPPENED?

The Keebler Co. is a large baker of packaged biscuits and cookies, many of which are used as snacks. Looking over this aspect of their product mix, officials decided that Keebler should try to gain a substantial share of the market for one item not in their line: potato chips, a large volume item because of their principal use in connection with dips.

Potato chips are of two types. The most common form is chips made from thin slices of fresh potatoes, sold principally in plastic bags, requiring frequent direct store service. Other potato chips are made from reconstituted dehydrated potato flakes or granules, formed into thin chips and baked. If put in sealed boxes or similar packages, like shelf cookies, these can be sold like snack cookies, without direct store delivery and would fit into Keebler's distribution channels. This second form has another attribute: the shape is not governed by the shape of the potato, and can be formed into any shape desired. General Mills has long sold such chips, and P&G's Pringles brand makes use of this characteristic to put theirs into a compact tube package.

Keebler recognized that the potato chip market was essentially mature, and that some attention-grabbing attribute or appeal would be needed to carve a niche in the market. The decision was to exploit the appeal of a cartoon character, the Schmoo, created in some episodes by the then widely read Li'l Abner strip produced by Al Capp. The Schmoo had been a fictional creature which bred prolifically, was boneless, tasted like chicken, and just begged to be eaten. Like all promotions of this sort, this required paying an appropriate license fee to Capp. In addition, Capp was induced to resurrect the Schmoo in a new episode to appear during the introduction of the new chip. Since the Schmoo was depicted as a rather balloon-like creature, the shape was no problem.

As is usual with such consumer introductions, the new chip was first placed in test markets with appropriate advertising and promotion, and, of course, parallel audits on consumer purchasing. The stores stocked the item, as desired, and initial sales appeared good, but had dwindled off to insignificance before the end of the test.

In reviewing the research data on the test, the marketing research people noted that sales were really on target during the first 6 weeks, including repeat business. Then the sales curve just seemed to drop quickly.

1. Hindsight is always better than foresight. But could such a result be foreseen, and why? How might Keebler have designed the offering so as to sustain a good level of sales.

THE U.S. DEPT. OF AGRICULTURE: INTRODUCING A NEW SERVICE

The primary mission of the USDA is the promotion of the welfare of the farmer, especially farm income. The primary way of securing income gains is through development of more efficient methods of agriculture, and of more efficient methods of marketing agricultural produce. A primary means of improving the income from marketing is the promotion of trade use of standard grades for farm produce, assuring the farmer who produces quality the premium his output should earn.

The department thus spends a substantial amount of energy in developing market oriented grading systems, and in then selling those who trade in agricultural produce on using them. Use of such grades is voluntary on the part of the trade, so the department measures the success of its operation in terms of the proportion of the trade which uses the grades. Developing a grading system requires considerable research into possible measures which can be rather simply applied and yield consistent results in terms of the attributes by which the market judges quality. Once developed, department representatives mount a concerted effort to educate the trade in the value of the standards, and also educates graders in the use of the grades. Most of the promotion is in the form of personal contacts with members of the trades involved, usually in groups.

Meat, and especially beef, has long been graded in terms of quality as defined by buyers, and this has helped farmers who produce high quality beef get a price reflecting the quality produced. From the standpoint of the retail butcher, however, quality grades are only half of what he needs to know when purchasing carcasses to cut into the steaks and roasts he sells. Beef animals, like humans, come in a variety of builds. Some carcasses yield a higher proportion of steaks and the other profitable cuts than others. From the butcher's point of view, two carcasses of the same quality grade and the same weight may differ as much as $100 in the total value of the cutting yield.

To control costs, retail organizations, especially supermarkets, have long inspected the carcasses before purchase, and set rigid judgment standards on what is bought. They have periodically conducted careful cutting tests to reinforce their judgment, in addition. Since the butcher is buying from a meat packer, not the farmer, and buying on the basis of his own judgment, the farmer who breeds cattle for yield was not likely to get a proportionate return on his effort.

Aware of this problem, the USDA spent substantial effort in a search for simplified means of estimating cutability on the hoof, and after slaughter. By the middle 1960s, officials were convinced by long experiments that they had solved both problems. Grade standards and methods of using them were published in 1965, and the USDA Extension Service set out to gain trade usage. Within each quality grade, cattle and carcasses were assigned one of five cutability grades. By referring to the price per pound, the buyer could judge the value to him of a carcass in any of these grades. Buyers did not have to stick with a single grade, since a simple calculation would tell them the profit on the carcass of any cutability grade, given the price per pound.

With the new grades, both cattle buyers and the butcher trade would be able to make sure of how much yield value it was getting without the cost of personal inspection. Carcasses could be bought by phone, without inspection, with a certainty of the cutability value being obtained. Furthermore, buyers would not have to search for a single ideal build, but could buy whichever grade gave the best price on the current market. In the long run, those who bred for best cutability would be rewarded and the market itself would be better.

The USDA keeps regular reports on various statistics of production and marketing, including the volume of beef sold under Federal inspection. Figure 8–2 shows the progress of the use of cutability grades by quarters, from mid–1965 through 1973. It will be noted that after an initial spurt, the volume yield-graded remained almost stationary for nearly a year, then began to grow at an increasing rate, reaching a very rapid growth stage in late 1972, early 1973.

Figure 8–2. The Volume of Beef Sold on A Yield Grade Basis, 1965–73
(00,000,000 lbs. per quarter)

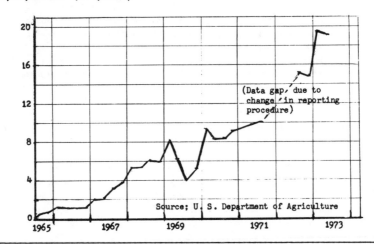

1. The benefits to be derived from the use of this system seem to be obvious: it greatly simplifies the work of buying beef, making it almost routine, and certainly less costly and more trustworthy. Yet it is obvious that very few organizations made any attempt to use the grades for quite a long period. The answer was not in awareness—the USDA has long cultivated contacts with the trade, and has a good reputation, as well as well honed skills in getting out information.

How would you explain the slowness with which this system gained acceptance?

FEATHERBONE: THE PRODUCT IS LONG DEAD, BUT THE MAKER PROSPERS

Edward K. Warren was a thrifty Michigan merchant of the 19th century who hated to see things thrown away. Like turkey quills, discarded when the feathers were used to make a popular household implement of the day—the feather duster. So he invented featherbone: quills wrapped in cotton binding, to be used as stays in women's highly sculptured garments of the day, and quickly took over a major share of the market previously held by whalebone. The famous actress, Sarah Bernhardt, is said to have sworn by Warren's featherbone, and Warren garnered a fortune. But styles change. Simpler ladies garments took over in the 1920s and 1930s, styles which fit in better with a motoring nation. And a new, cheap flexible material came on the market: rigid plastics. Officials saw that in their rigid form, they would be a real threat to featherbone.

But they also saw that the non-rigid form of plastics looked like a great new material: light and flexible, waterproof, acid-resistant. After some brainstorming, they conceived the idea of making plastic baby pants, to replace the heavier, hotter, latex rubber baby pants then on the market.

Today, featherbone is just a memory. According to The Wall Street Journal, Warren Featherbone is now "one of the top bottom-outfitters of the country", turning out some 6 million pair of baby pants a year, as well as other baby clothes. Priced in the medium to upper ranges, they are sold under the Alexis and Warren labels to retailers of all kinds, and under Sears own label. Now located in Georgia, President Whalen sees its recent growth as due to the efficiencies of operating from a single plant, with a low labor turnover, and to having "zeroed in our market—we see ourselves as producers of clothing from newborn to 24 months, and that's it." He adds, "our ability to make a product at reasonable cost is very good." Observers say that it has an almost religious commitment to quality. New employees come through its own training school, and individual sewing machine operators put its clothes together. Everything, including the cheapest baby pants line, is personally inspected.

The move to Georgia came when it outgrew the Michigan plant, and added to its line by acquiring an established producer of fancier baby clothing. When disposable diapers became popular, it began offering "diaper dress–ups": unlined pants worn over the disposables.

1. Warren Featherbone is a small–to–medium 440 employee company, so the top officials are as much as it has in the way of R&D. How does such a firm keep its product assortment dyanamic?

2. The present product line is a far cry from the offering it started business with. Do you find any consistency in the way it was developed, or any other policies which made it a logical choice, or utilized any of its previous strengths? If so, what?

3. How is it that a small firm like this (no more than 200 employees a decade ago) escapes the blight that hits the really big firms with vast resources, like those mentioned in the WSJ story on International Harvester, Swift, and Pullman?

CAN A&P REGAIN ITS FEET?

When giants fall, they fall hard, and once dominant A&P is no exception. The first and the largest food store chain in the United States until 1973, A&P has dropped fast and hard since. And as Business Week indicated (in "A&P looks like Tengelmann's Vietnam", Feb. 1, 1982), the food industry has grave doubts about its rehabilitation. Even the optimism of the German owners who bought controlling interest in 1979 has been sobered.

The problems that brought it down had long roots, but boil down to two: it failed to keep up with changing customer patterns, and its management failed to move with changing customer demands.

When customers moved to the suburbs in the 1950s and 1960s, it did not follow to the new shopping malls, and was left with stores much too small, buried in the inner cities. Heavily involved in making its own dry groceries, A&P failed to stock the heavily demanded national brands and many of the new merchandise items. Management got the reputation of being smug and complacent, of feeling that "they were the only people who understood the grocery business," as one observer puts it. A former food processor salesman is quoted as remarking that "When you called on A&P, they'd treat you like you were trying to take bread out of their mouths."

They obviously concentrated more on their dry groceries department than on the meat and produce which are at the top of most middle class shopping lists. A grape grower once told the author that "It's easy to deal with A&P. All they ask is 'Do they look like grapes?'" And a member of a meat supplier firm noted that in a major purchase of cured products, they looked only at price, and would take lower quality.

By 1974, it was obvious even to its own directors that grandma was in deep trouble, and they hired the first outsider, Scott, to turn the company around. Scott brought in his own management and began closing unprofitable outlets. Unfortunately, no attempt was made to shrink market coverage, so that the distribution network became a burdensome overhead. Losses and internal morale continued downhill. Nevertheless, Erivan K. Haub, a deep admirer of the U. S. and head of Tengelmann, a highly successful German retailer, bought a 42% interest in 1979, clearly expecting to turn A&P around, and continued buying until he had a controlling interest.

As losses mounted, Scott was replaced with James Wood, a Grand Union veteran. Wood had to continue closings, but did withdraw from some markets, and has started to refurbish stores, replaced some New Jersey stores by purchasing a chain of 10 large supermarkets in New Jersey, and opened a chain of 21 large multiproduct Family Marts. The trade is still skeptical about the ability of A&P to make it, but Haub is in so deep it will be hard for him to withdraw.

1. Why is it so hard to turn such large organizations around with better planning?
   2.Why does it seem to be so especially hard with a major retailer?
   3. Can you think of any way A&P could make the job easier for itself?

.

DEVELOPING AND LAUNCHING A NEW HOSIERY OFFERING
(From a report on a speech by William F. Kambach, V.P. of Marketing, Hanes Hosiery, before The Advertising Club of New York, as reported in **Marketing News**, November 14, 1980, under the heading, "Underalls success due to 'flanking strategy,' product idea, positioning" p. 11. Reprinted by permission.)
...Panty hose sales boomed in the late 1960s and early 1970s because of the popularity of the miniskirt...During that period, Hanes emerged as a leader in the branded panty hose market with its department store brands and L'eggs....

But then a fashion trend negatively affected the sales of this new product category. "As dress habits changed during the mid–1970s, an increasing number of women began to wear slacks...They switched from panty hose to knee–high stockings or they wore no hosiery at all. The panty hose market suffered..."

"If a woman chose not to show her legs, manufacturers believed she would not wear panty hose. So they dismissed pants wearers from their market... This all related to our perception of our own business. What business were we really in?" In 1974, Hanes "opened its eyes"... If Hanes could position panty hose as "an **accessory**, as a product to improve a woman's overall appearance rather than just a way to make her legs look pretty, substantial advances could be made..."

To test this concept, Hanes relied on focus group research. Consumers were presented with three concept statements:..."Of cooler/no cling, slim/smooth look, and built–in underpants, the latter generated the greatest interest,"...but women could not visualize the product...

"Hanes developed a built–in underpants garment. A product also was developed with a smooth look benefit." Hanes wear–tested the built–in underpants garment in–house..."Prior to wearing the new garment, even our women employees were skeptical....Remember, Hanes was asking them **not** to wear panties, probably for the first time in their lives. After wearing the garment for several weeks, though, it appeared that we had identified a new need segment...Comfort—fewer layers of clothing—and appearance—panty lines disappearing under slacks and dresses—were the major pluses..."

Hanes presented four product positionings to panty hose wearers in general, and not to just pants wearers. These consumers were asked to rate the concepts and the garment. The positionings were:

1.   Appearance—the elimination of panty lines under slacks and dresses;
2.   Comfort—due to fewer layers of clothing;
3.   Economy—because there would not be a need to buy panties; and
4.   Logic—no need to wear panties

...The appearance positioning was deemed strongest and adopted. Most critical was the decision to market the garment as a separate brand, since the positioning was "radically different" from that of existing products....

"Hanes was ready to embark on a new product offering: Underalls, panties and panty hose all–in–one would eliminate panty lines. We rolled into three test markets with three different levels of advertising...(stressing) the no–lines message. After five months of test marketing, Underalls achieved a 24% share of the department store market...."One year later we knew the initial success had not been a fluke. Underalls had achieved awareness and trial levels comparable to the market leaders. Underalls continued its success when launched nationally, spawning a host of imitators. In fact, the panty and panty hose all–in–one market is the now fastest growing segment of the hosiery market."

1. Kambach's presentation indicates that Hanes was seeking to change dress habits. Yet Hanes seems to have succeeded without much more effort than would normally be taken to introduce a new fashion design. Why?

CHAPTER 9.   THE KEYS TO PRICING:
BUYER PERCEPTIONS & REACTIONS

The facets of buyer price perceptions
> Monetary cost
> Deficits in the timing aspects of availability
> Deficits in the place aspects of availability
> Time spent in using the offering to gain the benefits
> Search effort costs
> Risks of dissatisfaction
> Learning costs
> Design compromise

The structure of buyer perception of value and price
> Right price reference points
> Traditional prices and price lines
> Price/quality imputations
> Price/use bracket judgments
> Noticeable difference and quantum expectations
> Price aura effects
> Reverse price-difference perceptions
> Price terms quotation effects

Engineering to a price

THE KEYS TO PRICING:
BUYERS' PERCEPTIONS AND REACTIONS

9

Pricing the offerings of mass production in modern differentiated markets, and the effects of pricing moves, are far more complicated than most classroom discussions indicate.

As even the most simplistic textbook recognizes, all value is in the consumers' eyes, is a matter of perception. Those eyes look beyond the figures on the price tag to the totality of the resources which must be sacrificed to gain the results of possession. The values perceived have at least 8 dimensions, and the negatives in the transaction have at least 8 sides. All of them must be considered in designing an offering and deciding on the price to be asked.

The Facets of Buyer Price Perception

Any understanding of the needs of price decision must start where every experienced seller has learned to start: with the buyers' perceptions of every negative aspect of the offering. Buyers view any obstacle to gaining the satisfaction sought from an offering as a price, any kind of cost. Eight principal costs must be recognized (Figure 9-1):

1. monetary cost
2. deficits in the timing aspect of availability
3. deficits in the place aspects of availability
4. time spent in using the offering to get the benefits
5. search effort costs, to locate the offering
6. risks of dissatisfaction
7. learning costs
8. design compromise

Together, these eight aspects combine to form the buyer's perception of the total cost, the sum of the barriers to gaining assured satisfaction.

Money cost, alone, is not very informative, and has different meanings at different stages in the market life cycle. Even the most elementary economics text indirectly recognizes recognizes **"time and place utilities"** as parts of the offering. Since these are always less than the desired immediate here and now, they are negative aspects, and perceived as part of the price.

FIGURE 9–1. THE COMPONENTS OF BUYER PERCEPTION OF PRICE

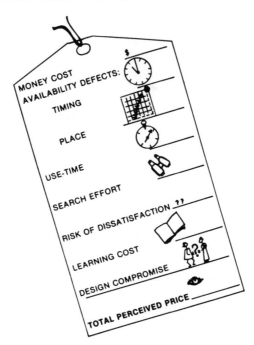

Reprinted from Chester R. Wasson, **Dynamic Competitive Strategy & Product Life Cycles**, Austin Press, 1978, by permission.

Time costs of any kind often loom larger in buyer perceptions than the money cost, especially the time cost of gaining the end satisfactions. In the modern well-advanced industrial civilizations, with their relative affluence, the time available to very many buyers is much less elastic than the monetary income. Substantial numbers of buyers can increase their monetary resources significantly, if needed. None can add a microsecond to the hours in the day.

The history of the competition between public transportation and the automobile well illustrates the value put on time. The flexibility and often the total time of commuting has been so much better than surface transport caught in the same traffic jams that most surface commuting systems have steadily lost patronage, despite significantly lower total costs. On the other hand, speedy mass transit, traveling frequently on privileged rights of way, have returned many autos to the home garage, even when the marginal costs of mass transit were higher.

Likewise, the quickly prepared convenience foods have gained major supermarket space, often despite some decline in quality, since the two-income family became the norm, and the housewife's kitchen time severely limited.

Search effort costs involve both time and energy, and are one aspect of the time and place values perceived by buyers. The dominance of the supermarket concept in all forms of consumer retailing is clear testimony to the value buyers place on reduction of the search effort cost, as catalog shopping has corroborated.

Some search effort requirements are unavoidable. They can be minimized by making supplies available in as many and as diverse outlets, close to buyers, as possible. Intense advertising and other communications efforts offer another way of reducing search effort by informing possible buyers when and where an offering is available. There is an obvious trade-off between intensive distribution and extensive promotion about availabilities.

Risk costs are an inevitable aspect of any purchasing decision. The primary risk is that the desired satisfactions will not be obtained from the purchase. Buyers seek information clues which help them evaluate the degree of risk, and ways of avoiding it. The less well known the offering or its source, and the less certain of the guarantee of the seller, the more the buyer will discount the other prices asked. The risk price is the major problem of the new, untried brand in an established market, and the major barrier to entry once the market matures. Risk price is the reason for the substantial discount of the off-price brand, the lower tag on the private brand retail item, on the local brand of gasoline. The risk of maintenance service on durable items handicaps the seller whose distribution is weak.

The risk of uncertain supply is very important to industrial buyers, especially, but not ignored by end consumers. Most of our purchases assume, directly or implicitly, that we can continue to get the same consistent quality without trouble in the future. The risk of an uncertain supply is the driving force behind patronage loyalty.

Dependability of the source of supply is so important to industrial buyers that they will ignore substantial price premiums in times of easy market supplies in order to be assured that the supply will be there when markets are tighter. No manufacturer wants to close down a million dollar assembly operation while waiting shipment of a 10 cent screw. Just as important is the assurance of consistent quality, another reason for patronizing the same sources.

New competitors seeking an entry into markets in which maintenance service is important must locate buyers to whom the unique values in the offering are perceived as so valuable that the risk of supply and service interruption is less important. The first European sports cars and small sedans imported in the 1940's were the purchases of auto buffs who put a high premium of the sensitivity of their handling attributes and were willing to pay a high price in possible out-of-service interruptions to gain the attributes.

Any relearning effort required is a major price barrier which can, as already noted, make the offering introduction a costly, lengthy one. Initial buyers will be scarce and must be hunted down and sold personally. Even then, they will be those to whom the learning requirement will be less than that perceived by the rest of the market. Not infrequently, the early buyers will be those who have to learn the use of whatever alternative is chosen--the new buyers in that market.

Some degree of design compromise is part of the price of every purchase. The buyer can seldom hope for more than to find an offering with the least amount of compromise of his own particular desire sets. Even custom production to order does not entirely eliminate the need to compromise, since the buyer nearly always is looking for complete fulfillment of a set of somewhat incompatible desires.

Large segments of the buyers of any mass produced item are sure to perceive a substantial amount of design compromise price. Painful as it may be to the production engineer, the economies of the single-model design must give way, early in the growth phase, to selection from a variety of differentiated models. Henry Ford I lost his market dominance to GM in large part because he refused to recognize that tastes had become differentiated.

With at least 8 types of price variables available, the seller must design an appropriate **price mix** side of his offering mix to appeal to his target segments. One seller may develop an intensive distribution system to make the offering as widely available as the market system permits. Another, perhaps a later comer to the market, unable to attract a really wide distribution network, may sell through high volume mail order distributors whose wide selections and lower margins make them attractive to a different segment. A third seller may find it necessary to utilize the intense selling effort of a restricted number of selected distributors, and compensate for the number of limited outlets by heavy local and national advertising.

Sellers with intermittent supplies must aim at fringe segments who are more interested in the monetary price than in dependable supplies. Each price mix must be tailored to the forces of customer value perceptions dominant in the segment which can be sold, and have meaning in terms of the specific phase of the market life cycle and in the current economic atmosphere. The seller's choice of pricing strategy is far from open most of the time. The successful choice is one which takes account of the competitive niche and customer expectations.

The Structure of Buyer Perception of Value and Price

Experienced sellers find little mystery about the way buyers judge value. They can point to at least 9 basic buyer reactions and perceptions:

FIGURE 9–2. THE 8 PRINCIPAL DIMENSIONS OF BUYER PERCEPTION OF VALUE

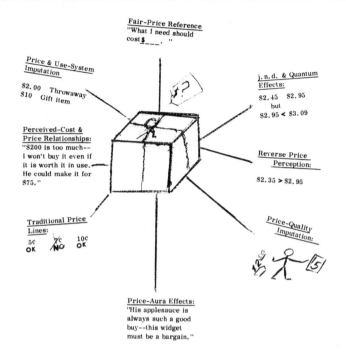

Reprinted from Chester R. Wasson, **Dynamic Competitive Strategy & Product Life Cycles,** Austin Press,1978, by permission.

- The widespread use of "right price" reference points in judging prices
- Traditional or price-line slotting
- "Reasonable" cost/price relationship judgments
- Price/quality imputations
- Price/use bracket judgments
- Noticeable difference, or quantum expectations
- Price "aura" effects
- Reverse price-difference perceptions
- Price quotation effects

Reference Price Evaluation of Offerings

Real demand curves seldom look like those in textbooks. Especially in mature markets, one very common form is what the economist calls a "kinked" curve. Sales do not decline at progressively higher price quotations but are greatest at some specific price level, and less at prices both above and below that point.

In established markets, buyers seem to feel that experience indicates that prices below this level are of inferior quality, prices above do not bring a proportionate degree of satisfaction. Such judgments sometimes occur when the offering is new, but seems, to buyers, to be analogous to a different offering whose prices are known to them.

Academic attention to this right price reaction is rare, but experienced merchants have long been familiar with it. A great deal of the skill of the buyers for any merchandising operation is their ability to recognize the probable level of this reference price for any proposed new item. Known reference points are also the normal focus of new product and new model development in every major industry, leading to the standard practice of "engineering to a price" (discussed later).

THE PRICE MUST BE "RIGHT"

Buyers for a hard lines retail chain thought that a standard item they offered was not moving as it should. Suspecting that the 94 cent price might be the reason, the firm conducted a controlled sales test, dividing test stores into 3 groups. In one group, they priced the item at 89 cents, in a second group at $1.29, and in the third group at $1.29. The sales volume was significantly better at $1.09 than at the old price of 98 cents, or at either 89 cents or $1.29.

Tull, et al, reported a similar result in an laboratory experiment with students. Students were told to assume that a specific price was the one they "usually paid" for the purchase of a familiar consumer item, and then given the chance to make a simulated buy at other prices above and below this point. They bought more at the "usual" price than at levels above and below. (Tull, et al, "A Note on the Relationship of Price and Imputed Quality," **Journal of Business**, April, 1964, pp. 186-191).

A firm which experimented with introducing horticultural perlite to retail buyers, when first introduced, had some problems in determining the best price structure. Experience finally showed that the best sales volume for the standard 4 cubic foot sack was at the price of a 50-pound sack of fertilizer. Perlite was and is sold in the same department as fertilizers, although not a plant food, but a soil conditioner which stimulates growth through better soil texture.

Traditional Pricing and Price-Line Slotting

Two somewhat similar buyer reaction patterns are the widely observable buyer expectations of traditional prices, and of the closely related practice of distinct and relatively uniform price/quality lines.

Traditional pricing is most obvious in popular confections such as candy bars and chewing gum, which have always sold in some multiple of 5 cents. The most extreme example was chewing gum. Come inflation or deflation, a 5-stick package was always 5 cents, from early in the 20th century to the early 1970s, with no change in the package contents or size. When rampant inflation and soaring ingredient costs finally forced a boost in prices, the price level had to jump to 10 cents, for a 7- or 8-stick pack.

Candy bars of whatever recipe always sold for 5, 10, 15, 20, or 25 cents per package. To adjust to the often wildly fluctuating ingredient costs, candy makers have to adjust prices by varying the size of the bar. When this adjustment ends up with a bar too small, the jump has to be to the next price line higher--some multiple of 5 cents.

Price-lining is virtually universal in the merchandising of mass-produced items in which a wide variety of perceivable quality levels is both possible and demanded. By price-lining, we mean the familiar practice of selling similar products at widely separated, sharply defined price quotations. Each such price line represents a quality level perceived as substantially different from that of the price lines above and below it.

Price lining is most apparent in apparel of all kinds, but is to be observed in consumer items, especially, from processed foods to automobiles, TV sets, and such hardware items as tools of all kinds.

Once price lines become an established part of the market for an item, buyers tend to shun items priced at any level substantially different from the customary ones. Such odd price levels leave them without clues to expected quality.

THE MISFIT LINE

The son of a men's clothing merchant was discussing experiences at his father's two stores. "We handle two main price lines in our men's suits, in the moderately better price ranges. However, we have one other line in our store that is a real buy, quality considered. But we have difficulty selling it. The problem is that it is priced in the middle between the customary price lines. Those normally buying at either the lower or at the higher price lines will not look at it. Those buying the lower price line will not pay more. Those buying the higher price line will not consider a suit with the lower price tag."

"Reasonable" price/cost relationships

Even when buyers approach a price quotation with no established reference points in mind, they tend to make decisions as to the "reasonableness" of a price in terms of what they perceive to be the cost of production, and act accordingly. Generally speaking, the mature buyer expects the seller to make a profit, but within limits. If buyers seem likely to judge the price as substantially out of line with their perception of relative cost, then the seller must expect to have to spend strong promotional effort and funds to reeducate potential buyers. It would probably be well, also, to reexamine the design cost targets. Such buyer doubts open opportunities for competition to bite off substantial segments of the market.

SELLERS SHOULD TAKE ONLY A "REASONABLE" PROFIT

Most tractor manufacturers were getting an added $200 for power steering when it first became a popular option. One maker's engineers, however, developed an ingenious design which competitors estimated would cost the firm no more than $12 to produce. When the time came to set the final price on the line, the sales department said their experience indicated that farmers would not pay anything like $200 for this as an option because of the obvious mechanical simplicity of it. It was decided to make power steering standard equipment and use it as a selling point.

Standard bolts are relatively inexpensive items turned out on automatic machinery. Some "specials," however often have high production costs. Among the specials are some critical high alloy bolts used on aircraft. For these, the quality inspection costs alone are quite high, since nearly absolute perfection is necessary. Under usual pricing formulas, one such bolt would have normally sold at $300 per unit as a replacement item. The aircraft firm, however, discovered that even its sophisticated customers considered $300 as an outrageous price for such a simple item, and had to lower the price.

Price/Quality Imputation

The tendency to judge quality by the price has long puzzled economists. A common example is perfume selling at $50 per dram, which can be produced to sell at a fraction of that cost, but does not sell well when it is offered at the lower price. On its face, buyer reasoning seems to be circular in such instances.

There really is no puzzle, however. The phenomenon usually occurs only in the context of well established markets. Also, such judgments are made only when most buyers cannot readily judge quality by mere observation. In such circumstances, long experience has taught consumers of every kind that higher quality is to be had only at a significantly higher cost. They have learned that offerings which may appear to be similar may not be equal in quality.

IF IT COSTS MORE, IT MUST BE WORTH MORE

In a brand loyalty experiment, W. T. Tucker offered 42 housewives a choice of four bread loaves on 12 daily visits in succession. Loaves were identical, identically packaged except for the "brand label"—a single capital letter(L, M, P, or H). No suggestion was made about any possible differences. The position of the "brands" on the tray was rotated, so that no one brand appeared in the same position on two successive visits.

Nevertheless, sometime after the start, half of the housewives confined their choices to a single brand at least three times in succession. After the third such choice, a penny was taped to the brand she had selected least often, and an additional penny each day until she switched, or until the end of the 12 visits. None switched for a single penny, and more never switched than did, even for the maximum of 7 cents at the end of the test. In an oral report on the test, Tucker quoted one housewife as exclaiming,"No wonder you have to pay people to eat those other loaves!"

At times, of course, what is being bought is the price tag itself, either as a recognized status symbol (by those who feel the need for some objective label of high status), or because much of the item is bought as a gift (which is true of well-known, expensive perfumes). [One does not give a recognizably cheap gift!]

IT'S WORTH WHAT YOU PAY FOR IT [THE RATS AGREE!]

Some years ago, the author was escorting a group of students on a tour of a major general hospital. When the tour reached the optical department, the tour guide opened a drawer. Pointing to it, she said, "See—it's empty!"

She then explained. "We used to give the glasses free, but so many people never returned to pick them up that this drawer was always full, waiting for them to return. Then we put a nominal charge on the glasses and the drawer is now empty."

Rats seem to have a similar point of view. Carter and Berkowitz reported on a laboratory exercise with rats given free food for a period, then a choice of the same food free or identical pellets which could be had only by pressing a lever. They preferred the "earned" food when they could get it with one or two presses of the lever. They returned to the free food only when the "price" became "too high": ten presses of the lever for a single pellet. (Carter and Berkowitz, "Rats Preference for Earned in Preference for Free Food," SCIENCE, Feb. 27, 1970, pp. 1273–4.)

Whatever the reason for buying, the higher price will be obtained only so long as substantial segments of the market perceive a significant difference in level of quality, whether that difference have a physical basis, or be due to socially recognized prestige value.

Price/Use Context Judgments

Price/use context judgments are closely related to price/quality judgments. Disposable items, of course, are expected to cost much less than those which are expected to have repeat usage. The other side of that expectation is that a low price implies disposability. Even when not disposable, a low price bracket indicates everyday utility use, a substantially higher price bracket, "company" usage.

PRICE IS CUE TO THE USE SYSTEM

Looking around for an item on which to build a business, an advertising executive developed the TIKI–TORCH, a kerosene flair to add novelty to backyard barbecuing. Seeking to diversify offerings, he hit on the idea of a TIKIBACHI—a firepot of baked clay in the form of a grinning pseudo–Polynesian god, topped by an iron grill.

Experiments at a number of outlets yielded scant sales at $2.95, but a significant demand at $4.95. A little inquiry revealed that most sales were made by wives as a gift to husbands. The maker's wife commented, "Of course. Nobody buys a gift that costs much less than $5."

Offerings bought primarily for their novelty must be relatively low in price. Higher prices call for more discrimination and care in purchase. Casual wear garments are expected to have neither quality workmanship nor a price much above a moderate level. A gift, however attractive, must not be perceived as truly inexpensive--if it is, it shows that the "giver does not care enough to give the very best." Accessories and supplementary items (such as a supplementary textbook) must cost less than the central item.

EVEN THE COST OF MONEY HAS ITS TRIGGER POINTS

During 1981 and up until August, 1982, the residential housing market was virtually dead. "For Sale" signs stayed up so long they had to be refreshed. With new mortgage money costing 16-1/2% to 19% there were very few lookers, and almost no buyers.

Meanwhile, the bank prime rate on short term loans of any kind had been slowly dropping, from a high of over 21% to 15%. Suddenly, in August, the official rate on VA and FHA loans was cut, to 14-1/2%. Further cuts were made, reaching 12-1/2% in early November 1982. The drops had not been foreseen. As late as July, The National Association of Home Builders had predicted that "mortgage rates aren't going to come down very much, even under the best scenario," and all of the economists were in agreement that the same was true of interest rates in general.

When the prime rate dropped below 15% in mid–August, the stock market suddenly sprang to life, posting all–time record daily and weekly volumes. The downtrend that had dropped the Dow Jones industrial average to a low of 770 the previous week was reversed. Within a week, the averages were a full 100 points higher, and continued up to reach an intra–day high of 1078 before pausing for breath in mid–November.

When mortgage rates dropped to 14-1/2%, real estate offices came to life. People started looking, although buying was not yet brisk. When they hit 12-1/2% it was, a North Dakota builder is quoted as saying, "like a light bulb turned on." His third quarter starts totalled 89 units, compared with 11 units the year before.

Similar reports of a sudden boom came from other parts of the country. According to **The Wall Street Journal** of November 23, 1982:

- Builders from all parts of the country reported sales were up 20% to 50% in the last 2 months, and the biggest builders were reporting third quarter sales up from 21% to 107% compared with the same period a year earlier
- Building starts nationwide were up 31% in October to a seasonally annual rate of 1,120.000 units from the depressed level of 854,000 in October, 1981. October permits...climbed in every geographical region to a rate of 1,180,000, up 60% from 738,000 a year earlier...
- With lower fixed–rate mortgages available, home–seekers were swarming over scores of tract projects in Southern California. In San Leandro, 1,200 potential buyers registered to bid for 27 entry–level units owned by the Bank of America. All were sold within the first 30 minutes of this month's auction "at roughly the original asking prices."

Noticeable Differences and Quantum Effects

Perceptions of price differences are, as already noted, subject to the **j.n.d.** principle. Merchants long ago learned that prices must differ by a substantial amount to make any difference in sales volume. [Did you ever see a clearance sale shouting "Bargains! 2% off!"?] Indeed, as every merchant knows, any difference less than 10% is not normally worth touting, and even 20% can be marginal.

Noticeable difference effects seem to revolve around round-number quantum points. Supermarket merchandisers, for example, have found that a price just under $1.00 will move far larger quantities than a price somewhat above $1.00, even when the higher priced package is a better buy on a unit content basis. The Osborne mini-computer apparently owed a great deal of its success to a price of $1795, perceived as less than $2,000 for computer, drive and screen with a substantially complete software package.

A perceived j.n.d. is proportional to the total, both in the psychological laboratory and in the market place. If something around a 50 cents difference becomes noticeable on prices near $5, then something close to a $5 difference is needed to become noticeable on a $50 tag, and a $600 difference needed to be noticed on a $6500 automobile.

Whenever there are substantial differences in the perceived satisfaction mix of closely competing brands (as in automobiles, for example), the brackets defining the price line will be relatively broad, as Alfred Sloan noted when he first formulated the GM product policy in 1920.

When a large portion of the buyers perceive little or no really significant differences between brands (as in general purpose laundry detergents), the seller has very little elbow room on price. Substantial numbers of consumers may habitually buy a specific brand, but only so long as the price is not noticeably different. The prices of the leading brands must be close together, and any success in developing some degree of preference pay off in a larger market share and less promotional cost per unit of sale.

The Price Aura Effect

Buyers' judgments of the quality of an offering often derive as much from the context of the the offering and its promotion as from the performance of the core offering itself (although the latter must also be perceived as of the right quality level). This is especially true of the premium level offering. The Cadillac or the Lincoln Continental must, of course, be perceived to be as fine a mechanism as American mass production can build, and must include mechanical niceties not sold in lower priced offerings. But they must also be sold in showrooms that spell luxury and attention, and the after sale service must be of the highest quality (and of course, high priced).

The expensive perfume must be available only at cosmetic counters in the "best" stores, be enclosed in an obviously carefully designed package, spelling the best of good taste. Both the advertising and the fragrance itself must have some degree of tasteful subtlety.

The retail outlet for such items must clearly cater to those with discriminating taste as well as bountiful spending power. A tailored mink stole would not sell in John's Bargain Store.

Assortment associations help reinforce the aura effect. Customers generally seek to buy an assortment of satisfaction bundles from the same source. Some of the items in the assortment are salient to the buyer's needs--they are purchases felt to be of top importance, and the closest of attention is paid to both cost and quality. The prices and quality of the other items in the assortment bought will then be perceived as parallel to the perceived quality and prices of the salient items. The perceived quality and prices of the salient items determine the segment that will be attracted. Thus the price decision is always a **price-mix pattern decision,** and must be designed to fit the perceptions of a specific set of market segments.

Reverse Order Price Perception

This aspect of price perception defies logical analysis, but merchandising experience confirms its existence.

Certain prices seem to be viewed by buyers as more attractive than quotations which are mathematically lower. A $2.45 price may move less goods than a $2.95 price tag, a 24 cent price less than a 29 cent tag.

Some form of round-number interpretation may be involved. The widespread use of odd-number pricing ($4.95 instead of $5.00, for example) may accustom buyers to perceive 29 cents as a 30 cent quality item, and thus better than a 24 cent item, perceived as 20 cent quality. The same phenomenon may explain why a bin of packaged apples labelled "3 for 90 cents" may do well alongside a bin of loose apples of the the same type and quality priced at 29 cents per pound, despite the opportunity the loose apples afford to pick and choose.

The Effect of Method of Price Quotation And Regularity of Payment

The same real price quoted three different ways can attract three different levels of demand. This is especially true of big ticket purchases often bought on the instalment plan.

Credit sellers long ago learned that the habitual credit buyers practice "budgetism." They tend to regulate their purchases of credit items almost entirely on the basis of the level of the periodic payment without regard to the total cost required. Given the same periodic payment, neither interest costs nor premium price tag seem to have much effect on sales.

Similarly, major costs incurred only after long intervals get less attention than the prices of frequently purchased items. Television programs which require purchase of a $500 receiver are thought of as "free." A doubling of the 60 cent/gallon price of gasoline in the 1979-80 period appeared to cause far more public pain than the same rate of increase in car prices during the preceding years.

After the rebate form of price reduction seemed to have lost its effect in the 1980-82 recession, GM discovered that a well-promoted interest rate cut, no greater in value, was effective.

Also, the persistent, regularly billed price may get far more attention than one which occurs irregularly, and often for different total quantities. With the sharp rise in oil and other fuel costs in the 1979-82 period, customers grumbled some at the doubling of furnace oil costs, but paid them. Through the public regulatory agencies and the legislatures, however, they fought tooth-and-nail against paying utility bill increases, of a lower percentage rise, occasioned by the same fuel cost increases.

Because of all these reactions of final buyers to what they perceive as the price, the pricing discretion of sellers is extremely limited. Most of the time, sellers must engineer their offerings to an estimate of what the market segments they are targetting consider a fair price.

Engineering to a Price

In a mass production, mass distribution economy, products must be designed to sell, with a profit, to a specific set of market segments. The price, when introduced, must be one the prospects are expected to consider favorable, within a restricted range of volume. The production planning which parallels the designing is predicated on that target price.

Changes in major material and labor costs which affect the entire economy may modify the actual final quotation, but only if all price brackets in the industry change. The $7000 price sticker on the new basic car line was set 3 years before, subject only to changes in the economy in the interim. It was the primary specification, accompanied by specific performance attributes desired.

The dress in the show window, whether a casual tagged at $49 or an exclusive tagged at $4900, was designed to sell at that price before the designer set pen to his pad.

In essence, this means simply that pricing is really a product decision. There is nothing new about this procedure. Henry Ford's introduction of the Model T, and the innovative engineering which went into producing it, were the result of a goal to produce a dependable car for $500 or less. When Alfred Sloan set out to rationalize the GM line in 1921, he was setting price goals for each element in the line. The ready-to-wear clothing market has never operated in any other way, nor could it.

Even in the field of agricultural commodities, the beef cattle raiser decides on increasing or decreasing his herd according to the price he expects at the time the resulting steers will hit the market, more than two years later.

Even the engineering of offerings to a price is more complex than this, since that price is subject to the economic weather and changes with time and the competitive environment. Moreover, the decision involves every other item in the offering assortment, and must allow for payment of distributor discounts. Pricing is a multi-dimensional decision.

SUMMARY

From the buyer's point of view, the total price to be paid is far more then the money asked. At least 8 components make up the possible total price.

Money cost is, of course, one of these, but it has different meanings at different points in the market life cycle.

The availability in terms of time often looms more important than the monetary cost, and the time required to gain the result through use is equally salient.

Like time, place availability is usually treated as a "utility." From the consumer's point of view, it is always somewhat negative, since neither form meets the desired perfect here and now.

Search effort costs involve both time and energy resources of the buyer, and can be a real barrier to purchase.

All purchases involve some degree of risk of not obtaining the satisfactions sought, and some offerings carry a risk of uncertain supply in the future. The degree of perceived risk is also a price.

Learning requirements, and especially relearning requirements, often prove to be the major cost barrier for new introductions.

All purchases carry some degree of design compromise for almost all purchasers, and for those in fringe segments, a high degree of necessary compromise.

Buyers approach all buying situations with at least nine different kinds of perceptual sets which influence their reactions to each of these price components.

Probably the foremost of these sets is the disposition to interpret the asking price in terms of a predetermined reference point for that kind of purchase.

Well established markets generally have some form of traditional prices or well understood price line structures. Price lines generally correspond to perceivable quality lines. Buyers tend to shun offerings not fitting these price line patterns.

Whenever buyers feel that they are in a position to judge the cost of production, they resent any price they consider out of line with such costs.

In mature product form markets, buyers look on price as a cue to quality.

The price level can also be perceived as a cue to the level or type of use the product has been designed for.

Because buyers are interested in assortments, and sellers offer them, buyers tend to judge the level and quality of all items in the assortment on the basis of those items they have experience with.

Perceptions of price differences obey the laws of j.n.d. Minor variations in price are viewed as essentially non-differentiating.

Some price comparisons seem to reverse the mathematical logic, with the higher quotation interpreted as more attractive.

The reactions of buyers to the monetary price can be influenced by the method of quoting the payment terms.

Because of these perceptual sets, sellers must engineer their offerings to a price specified before beginning work on the design.

CHAPTER 10. PRICING DECISIONS AND MANAGEMENT

The nine varieties of pricing decision
Market entry choices: cost-plus and return on investment
Market niche strategy pricing: price/quality level choice
Offering mix strategies
      Traffic items
      Merchandising to a profit
      Offering-mix pricing: a product acceptance standard in practice
      Pricing the internal-competing assortment
Trade discounts and other dealer attracting devices
Price quotation timing: leader or follower?
Managing price changes
Tactical price competitive maneuvers
      Temporary price concession tactics
      Why not just cut the price?
      Combination deals
      Offering premiums with the purchase
      "Blocked currency" premiums
      Using package size perception to gain market advantage
Bid pricing and competitive bidding strategy
Commodity production decisions and price
The "legal department price"

PRICING DECISIONS & MANAGEMENT

10

Pricing management involves far more decisions than the simple textbook "What shall we charge customers today?" Sellers must sell to and through a chain of intermediaries as well as the final buyer. They must consider the reactions of both actual competitors and those whose could become competitors, if profits are allowed to become too attractive. They must be concerned with long term patronage relationships, study buyer price expectations before they even design offerings, and change tactics to meet the changes in consumer value perceptions over the market life cycle, as well as meet exigencies resulting from unforeseen economic events and from new kinds of competition.

What final customers in the target market segment will find attractive is the starting point of any pricing decision, but only the starting point, with the exception of those minority of cases in which sales are made directly by the producer officials to the final buyers. In all other situations the producer gets only part of that price, often less than half. The remainder goes to pay the intermediaries for services necessary to the final buyer. The margins allowed such distributors are essentially buying prices for these services.

Furthermore, both producers and merchants are pricing assortments, not single items independent of other components of the assortment. Each item in the assortment has a role to play in selling the whole mix and must be priced according to that role.

In reality there are at least nine varieties of pricing decision.

The Nine Varieties of Pricing Decision

Those administrative decisions we call pricing run the gamut from very long range product introduction choices to the temporary tactical price maneuvers made to meet the exigencies of competition and of economic conditions. At least nine thoroughly different kinds of decisions and actions have been grouped under the single label of "price:"

- Decisions on market entry, based on cost-plus and return on investment
- Long run decisions as to market niche--the price/quality level decision
- Offering mix and merchandise mix decisions
- Distributive discount structure decisions and other dealer-attracting devices
- Decisions as to price quotation timing and methods

- Tactical price-competitive maneuvers
- Bid pricing
- Anti-trust avoidance decisions
- Commodity production decisions

Cost/plus and price/quality decisions are choices of whether or not to enter markets, given the prices customers are estimated to be willing to pay.

They are strategic decisions based on a given price structure: "go or no-go" offering decisions. Choices of offering mix patterns are also strategic decisions--decisions on the offering assortment emphasis designed to attract a specific set of market segments. To the extent that such a decision deals with individual items in the mix, it does so only in terms of the relative margins to be sought for classes of items.

Superficially, distributive discount structures are quotations of prices at which distributors must buy. They are, but they are offered prices, not asking prices. Trade discounts are an allocation of the expected returns from final buyers, to be surrendered for the services which distributors can best make to the satisfaction bundles desired and needed by final buyers.

Tactical price maneuvers, however expressed, are truly actual price quotations for goods in being. But their effectiveness in gaining a temporary market advantage usually depends on some modification of the offering itself.

One way to modify buyers' perceptions of the values offered is through the terms and timing of payments.

Bid pricing is the only form of price quotation of a directly competitive offering, since the buyer sets the offering specifications. But even in this case, the buyer may perceive differences in the values offered by different bidders.

Organizations which dominate their industry sometimes set price quotations based more on what they perceive to be acceptable to antitrust lawyers or other regulatory officials than to market conditions or competition.

Those who produce true commodities must accept market prices, but must then vary their plans for the future based on their estimate of future prices and profits. The assumptions underlying traditional economic theory really apply only to such commodity producers, but they must, like all others in the market, be concerned with plans for the future about which they can do something, rather than the present about which no seller can do very much.

Market Entry Choices: Cost-Plus and Return on Investment

The nature and purpose of both of these two pricing criteria are sources of a long standing disagreement between businessmen and economists--a controversy which cannot be settled because the two sides are discussing different decisions. The economists are correct in believing that cost-plus makes no marketing sense in setting prices for goods in production and being. The same can be said for return on investment, because by the time production takes place, investment is a sunk cost.

But no businessman consistently uses either method when the time comes to make a sale, even when he views it as his standard (as many job shop operations do). They are used, however, as market entry decision benchmarks and in setting price targets for designs. Even so, they are not item-for-item measures, and the prices asked at the time of sale are adjusted to the realities of current demand.

Cost-plus is even an erroneous label. Actually, the standard is market oriented, and should be called **price-minus.** What every businessman does who uses this system is to first estimate the price at which he thinks the offering will sell to the segment he is targetting, then subtracts the prospective cost, at the volume expected, to determine whether the profit so estimated meets a standard he desires, or at least can live with, in that market. Such is the actual procedure whether the seller is a merchant confronted with a possible new item, a manufacturer considering an addition to the line, or a foundry operator bidding on a casting. Price is the initial decision, with any design effort tailored to the cost and price situation.

If the seller is a merchant, he first judges what market price his customers would pay for the item, subtracts his estimated acquisition cost, then decides whether the margin is at least equal to his standard for that category of merchandise in terms of his normal price/merchandise mix. The final decision is a product decision: whether or not to add the item to his merchandise line.

If the seller is a manufacturer, planning a line to be made and sold 3 years hence, the price/cost ratio is simply a design target, with the cost calculated on a standard cost basis. Manufacturers skirt the problem of estimating actual cost, which depends on sales volume, by using standard cost--the long run average cost of operating at an assumed capacity level.

If the seller is a job shop operation, like a foundry or a printshop, the actual bid will be based on the seller's need for volume and the probable level of competition. The margin the bid would allow may be measured against some arbitrary percentage, but may nevertheless be quoted even when that margin is a loss, under tight business conditions.

Return on investment is really a similar standard, applied to a whole line.

Both return on investment and price-minus are based on rough estimates of cost, at best, and every experienced user knows it. In the case of return on investment, price is also, by necessity, an extremely inaccurate figure, since it deals with a future market reaction which is impossible to pinpoint. Both cost plus and return on investment estimates rest on some assumption of market volume. Except in the case of a job bid, this is an unknown which cannot be estimated with any degree of accuracy. Future costs are decision costs, not accounting costs.

FIGURE 10-1. THE BREAK-EVEN CONCEPT

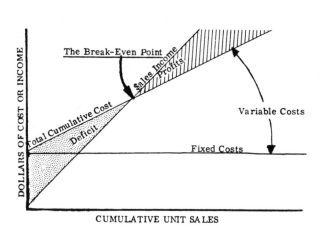

CUMULATIVE UNIT SALES

The break-even concept is essentially a yardstick useful in judging the feasibilty of plans and the profitability of a price level. The break-even point itself is, that level of cumulative sales revenue which just covers all costs incurred up to that point, both attributable fixed investment and overhead and the unit variable cost of production. After this point profits begin. Their level will be approximately the difference between unit sales revenue and attributable unit variable (and sometimes, semi-variable) costs.

The basic concept is graphed above. The calculation is simple:

$$B\text{-}E = \frac{\text{Fixed costs}}{\text{Unit revenue} - 2(\text{unit variable costs})}$$

Fixed costs: investment in R&D, directly attributable production facilities, administrative overhead, initial promotional commitments made ahead of sales, and any other expenses not directly linked to sales volume.

Variables costs: All costs directly proportional to units sold: raw materials, direct labor, packaging, manufacturing supplies, sales commissions tied to sales volume, etc.

Breakeven cost estimates are commonly used to decide on market entry by organizations which must regularly launch new offerings whose reception is difficult to estimate in advance: book and recording publishers, for example. Such organizations hope to break even, at least, on every new offering, and gain major profits from those which exceed the breakeven point. A decision to add the offering will normally be made if the breakeven volume seems to be less than a conservative estimate of possible sales, and the margin after breakeven is attractive. As Figure 10-1 indicates, all fixed costs plus all variable costs will have been recovered at the breakeven point, and profits can mount rather quickly afterwards.

Even the cost estimates of the breakeven point are far from solid, especially the fixed costs. Normally, the fixed costs include elements of previous capital investments which have few alternative uses, and are therefore sunk costs. Moreover, most of them are joint costs shared by existing products already, and not directly attributable to the added entries.

It is possible for a seller to put too much weight on the sharing of such joint costs. This can leave the market open to a competitor who is not hampered with such a fixed cost estimate.

Contribution to overhead is usually a better basis for market entry decision. When this is the cost standard, each item can be judged on the basis of what it will add to total profit. The go, no-go decision then can rest on either the direct contribution to profit, or the indirect contribution made by strengthening the total mix in the perceptions of the market segments targetted.

Market Niche Strategy Pricing: Price/Quality Level Choice

The price line positioning a seller chooses is a determining factor in defining its niche relative to competition. Once established, it is difficult to change. Although often referred to as a choice between pricing "below the market," "at the market," or "above the market", the emphasis is on perceived quality level, not price. (The correct terms are low-end, middle range, high end.) Even were offering aspects other than price objectively the same (which is seldom, if ever, true), the very fact that the policy succeeds indicates that the market is imputing higher quality.

In practice, the offerings are far from identical in objective respects other than price and the satisfaction source. An offering with a Marshall Field or Nieman-Marcus label carries warranty implications not conveyed by a discount store label. Even the physically identical private brand offering, from the production line of the seller of a well-accepted brand, is not necessarily cheaper from the buyer's standpoint than the same item with the known label. At the very least, it lacks the assurance of a specific level of quality and dependability which the label connotes.

No seller of any kind has completely free choice of product/quality level. A seller who wishes to follow a premium end policy must be able to design, produce, and deliver an offering which prospects will perceive as of truly prestige quality. The promotional communications must convey a feeling of quality. The channels of distribution must be of a type buyers associate with quality. If the market is well established, there must be a substantial segment of buyers who do not perceive any established seller as filling the bill.

If any one of the elements in the marketing mix does not fit buyer expectations of high quality level, a premium level program will not succeed.

Similarly, penetration of the low end market must meet the standards of the segments sought. Low end offerings are not simply items missing some costlier details.   They are specific designs and specific merchandise mixes designed for a very specific set of market segments.

Quality may be lowered or the attribute itself eliminated on those aspects of the offering in which the buyers see no value.   The buyers of low end dresses may not look for the finer points of tailoring and stitching.   But they will expect much more ornamentation than the buyer of exclusive designs finds acceptable, and will respond to more flamboyant advertising. The purchaser of low end cut rate gasoline may not care whether the brand has numerous stations nationwide, but he wants them readily available on his route of travel and at all hours of the day.

Generally speaking, a low end policy concentrates on offerings in which some high-cost attributes may be missing because the buyers do not perceive much value in them.   In some kinds of offerings, the lower valuation may derive from the inability of the less well informed to discriminate quality details.   But some low end product sell to heavy users who are interested in the functional core values and not susceptible to the appeal of fringe values.   Typically, cut rate motor fuel, for example, sells best to middle class long assistance drivers and truckers.   The stations offer gasoline and oil, are well located on high traffic routes, and offer none of the fringe maintenance services of some neighborhood service stations.

The price/quality level choice is always part of a merchandise mix strategy aimed at a specific set of market segments.

Offering Mix Pricing Strategies

Most pricing decisions, even tactical ones, have to be taken in the context of an offering mix strategy.   Pricing of a single offering without regard to other items in the mix is relatively infrequent and can compromise the strategy itself.   Buyers are typically seeking to purchase an assortment from the same source.   Their interest is in conserving search effort and shopping effort as well as money, by getting as much as possible of their desire sets from a single source.   They thus hope to build up a stable patronage relationship with some supplier who comes closest to their perceived assortment needs in both satisfaction content and value.   Sellers' real offerings are their assortment of related merchandise and services, each with its own relative price and margin goal--what producers think of as their product line and merchants as their merchandise plan.

Specific items in the mix will be intended to attract specific market segments, segments which are likely to perceive a high degree of salience in the satisfaction bundle of those items.   Each buyer in the segment may differ somewhat in the breadth and content of the specific items in the assortment.   The importance of price and quality will probably differ somewhat from buyer to buyer.

All of the segments targetted must seek some related core values which the chosen seller has to offer.   The identity of the core values which a seller is perceived as offering forms the so-called "image" of the seller. That image needs to be sharp to be successful. It can be blurred by trying to attract too wide a spectrum of segments, and will fail if blurred.

THE PRICE/QUALITY MIX DETERMINES THE MARKET NICHE

The offering/value mix is the principal factor in determining the segment which will patronize a given seller. Where the buyers have the ability to judge the quality, both patrons and non-patrons will probably agree on the level of quality being sold. This was one clear conclusion of a study of the food shopping pattern in the Fox River Valley suburbs west of Chicago, conducted by Bell and Wasson in 1971. The 5 established supermarkets in the Geneva–St.Charles area presented an opportunity to observe the results of 4 different price/quality merchandising policies in a middle class and upper middle class community, with a wide range of age groups and family composition. The results were tabulated from 1427 questionnaires handed to Saturday afternoon shoppers at the 5 stores, and returned by mail.

These showed that 2 of the five stores dominated the trade of the area, almost equally: the independent Blue Goose Market, and the Eagle chain market. Between them, these two stores attracted almost 70% of the shoppers. Both their regular patrons and those who did only supplementary shopping at these two stores agreed on the perceived quality of their merchandise mixes.

The Blue Goose was rated as having the best selection of meats, fruits and vegetables, bakery and delicatessen, and frozen food items of all 5 stores. Few thought their canned goods selection and quality were as good as the other stores. [Observation indicated that the selection on meats and produce were quite wide, and the meat prices obviously higher per pound, but in line with the grade.] The store was not heavily promotional. It ran a few specials, but largely as a result of special buys, and obviously used only a moderate advertising budget.

The Blue Goose attracted a disproportionately high number of childless and single person families, and also of the families in which the oldest child was 18 years or more.

By contrast, very few respondents rated the Eagle's selection of meats, produce, bakery and delicatessen as a reason for shopping there. But the Eagle outranked all of the other stores in canned goods. Eagle followed a "low price everyday" policy: no specials except when it made a "bonus buy" and passed it along. The chain advertised in the metropolitan papers, stressing its regular prices.

The Eagle attracted more of the married couples with children and also the greatest proportion of the families with children under 12.

All of the other stores had mostly a local shopping clientele. They also adcertised heavily in the metropolitan dailies, featuring weekend specials at prices substantially below their regular level.

At the time of the study, the Eagle was in a relatively small store, with poor parking, in an older, established part of town. Shortly afterward, the Eagle moved into a new, much larger supermarket in the midst of a development with new, young families, and prospered even more, apparently drawing off some of the local trade the two Jewel Tea Stores in the area had been getting. (Wasson, **Consumer Behavior,** pp.337–344.)

The necessary differences in offering mix strategies explains why any business district or shopping center draws heavier traffic if it has more than one "anchor merchant" and why all of the "competing" stores in the mall prosper, each with a clearly definable clientele of its own. Each seller offers those specific assortments desired by specific market segments, as they perceive their desire sets. Each must also price the offering mix, as sold, at a profit if it desires to stay in business. Each will therefore give greatest emphasis to the price/quality combination most attractive to the patrons in his core segment, in those special items highest in the hierarchy of their desire sets, while aiming to attract fringe buyers whose choices are not well matched by any seller. One of the devices used to attract these fringes is the promotion of special buys in **traffic items.**

Traffic Items

Some items of frequent purchase are part of nearly every buyer's desired assortment. They must be carried by all competitors at approximately the same level of perceived quality. Usually these are essentially commodities: sugar and the most popular soup brand in the supermarket, standard grade women's nylons in the apparel store, standard carbon steel nuts and bolts in the industrial market, the hamburger at the meat counter.

The trade labels such offerings as **traffic items.** Their role in the marketing mix is to draw customers who can be expected to buy the more profitable items in the offering mix. Sellers must usually "meet the market" for them because perceivable differences between sellers is low or non-existent and purchase is frequent and in substantial volume. Because of their drawing power, they are promoted heavily regardless of normally thin or non-existent profit margins. Any price significantly above competition tends to be seen as an indication that all of the seller's lines may be high-priced, because of the "price aura" effect.

Because of the necessary presence of traffic and other low profit items in the mix, any seller must perform a delicate balancing act, offering some items for which a higher than average profit margin is available to offset margins on other offerings which are lower than an acceptable average. This balancing act is known as "merchandising to a profit."

"Razor blade pricing" is a variant of the traffic item--selling the necessary durable component at a profitless price to create users of the supplies (so-called because the disposable blades potential were what led Gillette to develop his razor). IBM long followed this policy in its rentals on card sorting equipment. The high speed card sorters were precision machinery which cost, it is reliably estimated, around $30,000. They were rented for $15 per month. Any machine user bought a great many cards, and IBM stood ready to sell a very high quality card.

THE PROFITABLE PART OF THE MIX MAY LIE IN THE MAINTENANCE

When a durable item market reaches maturity, the real profit may lie in the supply of spare parts and maintenance. A good illustration is the situation of the Ford Motor Company in the early 1920's, when Ford began to feel the competition from Chevrolet. Model T prices were cut to the bone. Net profit of the Company on cars sold in the year ending February, 1924 was only $4,110,000, approximately $2 per car sold. Financial analysts at the time estimated that the net revenue on sales of spare parts was about $29 million, or better than a third of all Ford profit from all sources. The same estimates indicated that the retail purchases of spare parts per Ford owner per year were about $40, of which $28 were sold by Ford and his dealers. (Nevins and Hill: **Ford: Expansion and Challenge, 1915–1933**, p.237.)

At that time, when the main touring car model had been cut to $295 f.o.b. Detroit, it would have cost a Ford owner well over $1,000 to buy all of the parts needed to assemble a Ford. Dealers were getting 40% of this price (as compared with 15% on the car itself). Such spare part price relationships were quite common throughout industry. To some degree, the buyers are a captive market. Although some independent parts suppliers are inevitably attracted to such markets, their offerings do not carry the official label, and suffer the image of being low end.

Merchandising to a Profit

How does a seller achieve such an offering mix balance?

First, the seller quotes prices which provide a margin which is adequate, volume savings considered, on a core group of items whose quality level and design are salient for the core patronage segment. Profit is expected to develop as a result of high turnover by a heavy user segment. Second, he can obtain higher margins on those items in the assortment which have a lower frequency of purchase and lower attention value for the segment served, and also on attractive specialties not readily available elsewhere. Finally the seller may add items which are normally in some assortment bought by patrons, but usually sold in higher margin outlets, and sell them at what, for him, is a very high margin, but average or even low for the competing type of outlet. An obvious case in point is the sales of toiletries in food markets.

The resulting mix should make the seller appear to the core patrons as a lower-cost supplier, quality considered, than other possible suppliers.

By the same token, other segments will most certainly find the mix of designs and margins out of line with their desire sets. They will be patronizing or seeking a supplier who emphasizes a different set of items and designs.

Offering mix pricing thus requires a carefully managed price mix which takes three factors into account:

1. The salient desire assortment of target market segments, in terms of items, designs, and quality, and the degree of salience of each item

in the total mix.

2.   The usual frequency and volume of each purchase, the extent to which it is a part of the desire sets of all segments, the degree of standardization and, as a result, the price sensitivity of buyers in relation to the item.

3.   The turnover of the item when purchased by the target segment.

The resulting policy standards are then:

-   Price traffic items at or very close to the level quoted by competition. Expect no significant direct profit from them.

-   For significantly differentiated items demanded by and selling in good volume to the seller's core segments, quote prices which yield a satisfactory margin over cost, but a price which enables those to whom the item is salient to perceive the offering as giving a high value in relation to cost.

-   Seek high margins on items carried as a convenience for target patrons, but not particularly salient in their desire sets, and not bought frequently or in high volume.

-   Set high margins on specialties that are attractive to the core segment

Offering-Mix Pricing: A Product-Acceptance Standard in Practice

The offering mix of many merchants runs in the thousands of items, and that of many producers in the hundreds. Such an offering mix can change through additions and deletions monthly or even weekly. Clearly, no such organization is going to call an executive committee meeting every time there is an item change.

In practice, such sellers classify items by category of margin objectives, then use these margins as rule-of-thumb for pricing, making temporary adjustments to temporary competitive situations.

The rule-of-thumb margin then becomes the standard with regard to decisions concerning additions of new items to the line. If the margin objective appears unobtainable, the item is not added.

The general policy with respect to margin objectives may be subject to so little attention over time that no current executive may ever have given any thought to it, so long as it worked. The initial decision on margin standards is definitely a price decision, but it becomes a product acceptance standard.

Sellers of big ticket single item purchases must also develop an offering/price mix pattern.

Pricing and The Internal-Competing Assortment

Even when the purchaser is buying a single item such as an automobile, house or other big ticket item, the seller usually must usually offer a range of models at a range of prices. In order to maximize the profits on their line, such sellers must also offer a price/quality mix covering a range of margins. Models must usually conform to some kind of price line pattern, so prices of all models must fit into the same relative pattern.

Generally, the perceived differences between models are either quality level, or perceived use and benefit bundle, or both. Generally, also, the perceived quality differences between the high end and the low end are far greater than the production cost differences. Segment fringes are usually interested primarily in the core functional attributes, not the refinements that may differentiate the offering for the core segment being served.

The low end is thus distinguished from the high end by the differences in design niceties, as buyers evaluate them. The price mix is made profitable by:

1. Designing a "stripped model" low end offering with adequate functional attributes but so few amenities as to be relatively unattractive to most buyers, and to promote the price of the stripped model to get traffic into the showroom. This model will yield a very narrow margin, and may even be offered in such limited quantities that the buyer must pay a waiting price to get it.

2. Designing a standard line line with most of the attributes sought by the bulk of the core segment, priced to yield something like the target profit margin (on a standard cost basis). This line will constitute the major production volume.

3. Design a "luxury" line with all the options the most enthusiastic might wish, to yield substantially higher margins. They will be expected to sell in significant volume, and will always be as available as possible at the retail level.

Designing the margin structure for any type of offering assortment always requires a complex balancing of target customer value perceptions against the need for a specific average profit. The initial steps are the determination of a feasible average profit margin target and the decision as to the assortment necessary to serve the segments whose patronage is sought. The salient items these segments seek in this assortment must be identified both as to kind and quality, and these will carry the average margin. Possible traffic items must also be identified, and priced to project a competitive image. Finally, items whose prices need not be competitive should be identified to help offset the low margins on the traffic items: specialty items or others not part of the central patronage decision.

Determining the prices to be quoted for final buyers is only the beginning of the price structure design for producers who must sell through distributors of any kind. The contributions these can make to the final satisfaction bundle sought by the final consumer must be paid for through a discount structure.

Trade Discounts and Other Dealer-Attracting Devices

Producers must start their pricing decisions with a determination of how much the final buyer is willing to pay, but they do not get all of this price. A substantial portion--often more than half--must be allowed distributors in the form of discounts or commissions. Such distributors are themselves producers, adding some of the most costly services to the satisfaction bundles sought. These include inventory availability, tailored to local tastes and needs, various communications and sales services, and often some shaping of the offering to meet individual customer needs.

Much of the value perceived by the final end user is in the services contributed by those in between the initial producer and the final buyer. Normally, most of the intermediaries are independent businesses whose services must be attracted by offering them a chance to make a sound profit. The slice of profit is offered by producers in the forms of **discounts**, which the distributors think of as their **mark-up.** (These terms are exact synonyms and are calculated in the same way: by dividing the discount or margin allowed by the total price received by the distributor.)

Such trade discounts are truly purchase prices: the offering of a given portion of the customer-perceived value in return for adding significant values to create the satisfaction bundle desired.

Deciding on the correct discount structure is easy in the case of many established types of offerings. The seller has little choice but to accept the habitual trade practice for that category of offerings, as it exists in each channel through which his offerings must move to reach the market segments targetted.

Dealers and distributors in any one kind of channel usually follow a standard basic mark-up practice for each of a few general categories of offerings handled by them. This structure is one that has become established as workable by long experience. It yields the margin objectives of distributors when the merchandise assortments they handle are well managed. So long as the sales through these channels, and their relative strength, remains stable, producers do not find it wise to try to alter the established trade habits.

Sometimes dealers must be offered more than just a discount. Offerings which must pass through a market development phase to gain acceptance require a special kind of aggressive sales effort which can be obtained only through some restriction on the number of outlets in a given market area. Producers with a relatively weak market share often must offer a similar inducement at any stage of the market life cycle.

During mature phases of the cycle, dealers may also be offered additional margins or incentives to cooperate with a strong promotional effort: free goods with volume purchases, or many of the same incentives given sales forces (contests of various kinds, for example).

In established markets, distributor discounts are subject to relatively rare reviews. The final price itself, however, often requires constant review because of the fluctuation in competition, both direct and indirect, and in economic conditions. When the organization has a significant share of the market, it often must chose whether or not to be a leader or follower in price changes.

Price Quotation Timing: Leader or Follower?

The forces determining production costs and buyer value perceptions can be expected to change regularly. In our industrial society, most prices are quoted ahead of their effective date. Those who do the quoting must consider the quotations made by competition of all kinds, both direct and indirect, and the reactions of competitors to their own quotations. Since prices affect profits, a high degree of anxiety can be expected among those who make the decisions in those periods in which price increases become necessary or even workable.

The most popular anxiety-avoiding measure is mutual agreement among sellers. Were it not illegal, as in the United States, it would be much more widely followed than it is. History has long shown that such agreements break down sooner or later, and usually sooner. Customers, for obvious reasons, do not like to cooperate.

Nevertheless, when costs really squeeze, prices must and do go up. The only options sellers have are how to go about raising prices, and the delicate question of "who moves first?" A similar set of questions arise when costs move downward, and prices should follow.

Price leadership in some industries tends to rotate among major producers (automobile and banking are cases in point). When it does rotate, some interesting maneuvering often ensues, each producer hoping to let others be known as price raisers, or to gain the image of being low price for themselves.

In most larger industries, some one dominant seller tends to set any upward moves, and others follow quickly. Only a seller with a strong market position can assume such upward price leadership. Any with a significant market share can lead prices down.

Leading price changes, especially on the upward side, is a not a role which is easy to carry out properly. The role carries with it substantial responsibility for the competitive position of the seller and of the industry itself--a responsibility not always recognized by those carrying out the effort. The leader must be careful to avoid raising an umbrella price which automatically gives everyone a margin which tempts added competitive capacity or opens the door for substitute offerings.

The dangers of competition from other kinds of offerings, or even new sources of similar offerings, are far too easy to overlook. When the possibility of such competition is ignored, the industry may find itself starting a decline phase which could have been retarded otherwise. Once such competitors gain a toehold, the added volume may yield a cost-lowering advantage they would not have experienced so early.

Furthermore, once the customer switches, he is hard to lure back (as Detroit discovered in the early 1980's). Customers will have passed the hurdles of learning, are no longer held back by the risk of trying something new. The old must now prove to be better than the new--usually almost impossible.

Those quoting prices must consider the method as well as the amount by which prices will be changed.

SOHIO THROWS AWAY ITS UMBRELLA

When the Supreme Court broke up the Standard Oil empire in 1911, the Standard of Ohio remnant had about a nine-tenths share of the petroleum products market in Ohio. For the next 17 years, executives attempted to hold prices at levels guaranteeing their idea of a fair profit. Under this benevolent Sohio umbrella, competitors flocked in. By 1928, Sohio's share of the gasoline market had dropped to 11%. Changing course, Sohio then did its best to adjust a statewide price to conform with current conditions in the general petroleum market. In the next two years, Sohio pulled back to a 30% market share.

In 1933, the federal National Recovery Act decreed retail prices assuring wide dealer margins. Sohio conformed, only to see its market share shrink to 20% by 1936, when NRA was ruled unconstitutional. With the death of NRA, Sohio began to regain market share. In 1938, Sohio modified its competitive stance even further. Statewide pricing was abandoned in favor of pricing by distributive areas according to local market conditions. By 1941, market share was back to 30 per cent and continued stable for decades.

An interesting result of conforming its price leadership to competitive conditions has been the relative freedom of Ohio from the gasoline price wars most other areas experienced periodically.

Managing Price Changes

Sellers have a choice of how to put price changes into effect, and the results will be affected by the method. Basically, there are five methods of managing price changes:
1. Wait until the need becomes critical, then make the change in one quick jump (up or down).
2. Make periodic small changes over a period of time.
3. Maintain stable quotations until they become obviously untenable, then raising or lowering them to another stable level.
4. Maintain stable nominal quotations, but ignore or include special charges already in the published list, depending on market demand.
5. Keep the per unit price quotation steady, but vary the contents of the unit quoted to parallel costs.

Cutting prices in very large jumps can be very effective in stimulating demand, as merchants long recognized (Clearance! Prices cut from 30% to 50%).

Such drastic cuts draw attention, and sales.

Raising prices in one big jump, however, can be just as effective in stunning the customer and cutting demand. Such moves have a traumatic effect, often enough to make buyers consider alternatives and change buying habits permanently for some. A series of small raises may cause some irritation, but if they are less than a j.n.d., have no significant effect on demand, even when the total over time is as great or greater than the single large jump.

Maintaining a stable price level over long periods despite large fluctuations in demand, is widely followed by those selling industrial raw materials. Such a policy enables the industrial buyers to forecast their costs with some certainty, a real boon from their standpoint. In fact, one reason for the growth of the market for man-made fibers in this century has been the practice of maintaining relative stability of price. Those using the natural fibers had to contend with prices which could fluctuate even hourly, and had to undertake hedging or other practices to be able to plan at all.

Such a stable price policy raises some problems if there are periods in which demand outruns supply. Producers meet this problem by asking for an indirect offset. They ration buyers in periods of shortages according to their purchases in periods of plenty. This shifts the burden of demand fluctuation onto marginal sources of supply.

FIGURE 10–2. PRICES OF PRIMARY AND SECONDARY ALUMINUM INGOT, 1953–68

Price: cents per pound

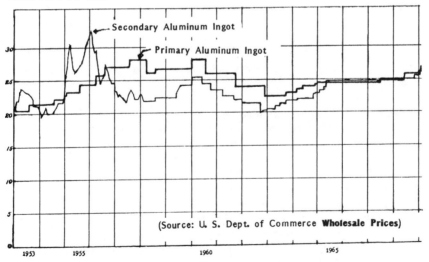

(Source: U. S. Dept. of Commerce **Wholesale Prices**)

Reprinted from Chester R.Wasson, **Dynamic Competitive Strategy & Product LifeCycles,** Austin Press, 1978, by permission.

[Rationing was a major element in the price of aluminum ingot from the end of World War II until the middle 1960's--see Figure 10-2. Most aluminum is used in the form of alloys, sold to users in ingot form. All such alloys are made from a mixture of scrap metal and primary, sold by both the primary aluminum producers, and secondary metal processors. Ingots are produced to the same standard specifications by both sources, and this is well known by users. But the primary producers are the dominant source. Demand grew rapidly from the end of World War II, and during some periods, expansion of primary capacity could not keep pace. During shortages, primary aluminum producers rationed supply, and the price of the secondary soared. During periods of plenty, buyers stayed with primary producer sources, and the price of the secondary plummeted.]

The steel industry followed the policy of maintaining nominal book prices over long periods, but varying the "extra" charges. Steel is produced in a very wide variety of shapes, sizes, alloys, and special qualities. Price quotations are in the form of a base price for large lots of a single shape and specific size, usually of plain carbon steel.

The actual price is the base price plus extras for chemical (alloy) differences, other shapes, and other sizes, as well as for such items as the "cold-heading" quality needed by makers of industrial fasteners. In times of easy supply, however, large users, especially, simply are not billed for some of these extras. When supply is tight, even those who buy overruns at a discount lose their discounts and are often charged for extras of no value to them.

Finally, many producers of consumer goods find it easier to vary contents of a package than to change prices directly. This is especially true of candy bars, and can be observed in consumer paper goods such as paper towels and toilet paper. Such changes rely on the observed fact that many consumers tend to buy by the package without attention to the contents statement.

Whatever form of pricing policy is adopted, variations in the competitive climate often require temporary price tactical maneuvers., intended to gain a competitive edge or defend market share, or to open new markets.

Tactical Price Competitive Maneuvers

Pricing is primarily a tactical competitive tool: the means of rapid response to day-to-day competitive pressures, especially product oriented pressures. Price is the only element in the marketing mix which can be put into effect on a moment's notice. All other aspects--offering design, promotion of all kinds, and new distributive arrangements take time to effectuate, from hours to years between planning and market exposure. A direct monetary price change takes no more than a phone call.

The speed with which a straight price change can be put into effect is also its weakness. Competitors can, if they choose, counter just as quickly. As soon as it is announced, the competitor down the street can match it or go one better. Consequently, it is usually wisest to plan reductions in such a form that competitors must take time before they can match them. This usually means some change in the offering. Whatever the form of the change, if intended as temporary, it must be made in such a manner as to make clear its temporary character. Otherwise, consumers may expect it to continue as the standard price.

BRISTOL MYERS LEARNS HOW BRIEF THE ADVANTAGE OF A PURE PRICE CUT IS

The pain killer market is large and profitable one. For years, aspirin was practically the only reasonably safe one. Patents on it expired decades ago, and competitors were plentiful. The strongest niches were held by Bayer, the original introducer, by Anacin (a combination of caffeine and aspirin), and by Bufferin, a buffered form intended to avoid the stomach side affects some people suffer from pure aspirin. A later entry was Bristol Myers Excedrin, differentiated from the others simply by containing twice the standard dose. Private brands and generic packages were widely available at very low cost, and undoubtedly held a significant market share.

Then McNeill Laboratories, a subsidiary of Johnson & Johnson, introduced acetaminophen, under the trade mark of Tylenol. Tylenol promised to be usable by people who had problems with aspirin. McNeill entered the market through physicians, detailing them heavily, and getting Tylenol sold on a prescription basis. By this means, they endowed the offering with the mystic of professional endorsement (although it could be bought without the prescription), and captured a substantial segment of the whole analgesic field. (Although Johnson & Johnson has 100 subsidiaries, Tylenol is reported to have yielded 7% of the total profit in 1981.) Acetaminophen is not patented, although Tylenol is, of course, trade marked.

Bristol Myers obviously was attracted by the profit, and decided to reach for a major share of the market. They registered the trade mark, Datril, decided to price it at half the price of Tylenol (which carried a price much higher than the costliest aspirin), and prepared a series of TV spots with a pure price appeal. Quite bluntly, they portrayed Datril as the same as Tylenol, at half the price.

Johnson & Johnson was not napping. J&J immediately protested the advertising to the TV networks, even before it appeared, and blocked much of it, getting future presentation changed. But it did not stop there.

The McNeill sales force was small but J&J's was not. Rather than cut the wholesale price and wait for the effect to work down to the stores. Johnson and Johnson cut prices all along immediately, and sent its sales force to cover the retail outlets, get the price marked down, and refund the difference at the dealer's cost of current stock directly, so the dealers would not lose. Many of the stores were reached before Datril was stocked, and Datril never reached full distribution, nor gained the market share hoped for.

Temporary Price Concession Tactics

Price reductions intended to be perceived as temporary can take many forms. The simplest and most common are the "cents-off" deal and the temporary bargain pack ("four bars of soap for the price of three"), clearly labelled on the pack and in the advertising to make sure the outlet passes on the deal. Such deals are self-restricted to the run of packages so prepared. Since the reduction requires some special packaging, some time advantage is gained. Competitors, if they match it directly, must themselves prepare the added packaging and distribution. A variant is the price allowance coupon--a money substitute limited to the quantity printed, and to any expiration date.

The primary value of these forms of temporary reductions are to gain sampling by new buyer segments by lowering the price avoidance reaction, or to hold customers for a while in the face of an extra-attractive competitive offering or heavy competitive promotion.

Such promotional pricing can prove useful in getting buyers to absorb an otherwise unwieldy inventory, or to gain increased consumption, where that is possible. Generally, such a promotion takes the form of specials for multi-unit purchases. When the immediate target customer is a dealer or distributor rather than the final user, such a deal is called a "free goods offer" ("one extra carton free with each order of 10"). The aim, of course, is to stimulate dealers to load their inventory in order to get an extra margin. Thus loaded, it is expected that the dealer will promote the offering more heavily to reduce his inventory, and will pass on part or all of the reduction to the final buyer. Even when dealers pass on the entire savings, they can gain by using the special price to get themselves perceived as price-aggressive, and thus a source of bargains.

Recently, two other forms of temporary reduction have become popular: some form of direct rebate at time of purchase, or delayed rebate, such as a mail-in coupon with proof of purchase. The direct rebate is really not essentially different from the "cents-off" coupon, except that on credit sales of such big-ticket sales as automobiles, it is a way of reducing the immediate barrier of the down payment (or the monthly payment, when offered in the form of a below-market interest rate). The mail-in rebate tends to cost less than appears on the surface because many who purchase neglect to redeem the rebate coupon, and the cost is delayed in any case.

Why Not Just Cut The Price?

From the arithmetic of accounting, all of these forms of temporary reductions would seem to be identical in value: all merely reduce the price paid. The end results are not the same, at least at any one given moment. When automobile rebates seemed to have lost their effectiveness by the beginning of 1982, an interest rate reduction kindled new sales. Some years previous, when the Florida orange growers faced a new season with a swollen hang-over of frozen juice from the previous corp, a test showed that a "one free with six" offer moved far more cans than a straight price reduction did.

A study of coupon returns showed that 85% of coupons mailed to homes were redeemed by new buyers, as compared to a new buyer gain of only 35% of those picking up a "cents-off" pack. The mailed coupon apparently penetrated the selective attention of non-users better than the pack in the store.

Other, more intricate deals also have advantages. They include combination deals and what the economist would call "blocked currency" deals: offers of a whole range of premiums from a catalog.

Combination Deals

. Some of these other forms of temporary price reductions really involve some modification of the offering itself. The coupon good only for a multi-unit purchase is a change in the size of the basic unit as well as the unit price. Sometimes this is done by means of packaging, banding together the four cakes of soap for the price of three, for example. Sometimes it may be a combination of a sample size unit with a standard size, with the offer: "Try the sample, and if you don't like it, return the package for a full refund." The intent in this case is to use the free sample to get substantial numbers of buyers to try a full package. This could establish a habit break more effectively than would the short time use of the sample itself.

A combination deal may also tie together two disparate but use-related items in a single offering: "Free: 25 gallons of our premium grade gasoline to everyone who buys a set of 4 of our tires during the sale!" The aim may simply be to dramatize a simple price reduction by combining the gift of a certain-to-be-used premium (gasoline) with the item to be purchased. Or it may serve an auxiliary purpose of getting non-buyers to sample the "free" product (our **premium** gasoline).

Sampling the gift may be the primary purpose of the offer (a free gift of our new superedge razor blades with our new super-adjustable razor at the low introductory price of the razor alone!").

Offering Premiums With The Purchase

. Combination deals of any kind are less vulnerable to matching than a straight price cut. They are also less easy for buyers to compare and evaluate directly. Even less easy to evaluate are unrelated premiums offered with a purchase, such as a toy in a box of Crackerjack, a cocktail glass with a tankfull of gasoline, or a special pack of the offering in a reusable container.

The premium may not be sold directly with the offering, but available if ordered with box tops and a nominal charge. The premium may actually be "self-liquidating": the seller may recoup his own direct cost, but the value to the buyer be perceived as the much greater normal retail price.

PREMIUMS AS A DIFFERENTIATING ATTRIBUTE

One of the more competitive areas is that of mail order vitamins and health foods. On standard items which constitute the core volume, there can be little differentiation. The vitamin has to meet specific standards, whatever the source, and the contents clearly labelled as to potency, in standard terms. Major sellers in the field necessarily use some aspect of pricing as their basic appeal. GNC's Natural Sales Co. Division, an industry leader, persistently used some of its own products as premiums for a long time, plus various novelties, the amount depending on the size of the order. In 1982, however, Natural Sales switched to a "$25,000 'Health & Wealth' Sweepstakes" with the following prize list:
  - First prize: $10,000 cash, or new car, or cruise for two
  - Second prize: GE 45 inch big screen color TV ($3500 value)
  - 75 third prizes: GE digital scales (a $50.00 value)
  - 600 fourth prizes: $13.95 Aloe Vera beauty kits—4oz. each of Aloe Vera Moisturizing Cream and Cleansing Cream, and 8 oz. each of Aloe Vera Freshener and Super Rich Body Lotion.

Also in the December, 1982 issue of **Prevention** magazine, Biorganic Brands, Inc. was offering:
  - A Phone Caddy with super clamp for memos with every order
  - A Simmer Ring: anti scorch heat diffuser, with a $12.00 order
  - A Bed Light with adjustable hanger and swivel head, with a $27.50 order
  - All three "gifts" with any order of $35.00 or more

Stur-Dee Health Products, Inc was offering a pocket magnifier with every order, the choice of a 4 cup thermal pitcher or a 1 lb. whole wheat raisin bran fruit cake with a $12.00 order, a "DeLuxe 'Leatherette' Health Library" container capable of holding 12 issues of **Prevention** with an $18 order, the customer's choice of any 3 of the above with a $27.50 order, and all 4 gifts with a $34.50 order.

Barth's featured an extensive list of merchandise in a 1-cent sale, and in addition, a set of 4 stainless steel knives with a $7.50 order plus a fruit and vegetable press if the order was $30 or more.

Smaller houses simply offered a limited list of limited quantity packages of volume selling items at deep cut prices. (All advertisers offered some "specials").

[To see how varied the deals and offers can be, see any city Sunday paper advertising stuffers, and the Thursday food sections of the same.]

"Blocked Currency" Premiums

Finding specific physical premiums with a universal appeal is not easy. Even when one which has a nearly universal appeal is found, buyers reach a point of satiation with additional purchases, and lose interest. Any family has a limited need for cocktail glasses, sewing scissors or kitchen canisters. If only a brief effect is desired, this may not be a major problem.

If only a brief effect is desired, this may not be a major problem.

Sometimes, however, the aim is to promote a sustained patronage habit and perception of lower price, over an extended period. In such a case, it is crucial to keep a high level of interest in the premium, do it in such a manner that competitors cannot directly match it easily because the buyers view it as "something extra", not that of a lower price for the offering. A common method of achieving a more enduring and more widely accepted premium is to offer a catalog of premiums, available in proportion to total purchases, measured in the form of cash register receipts, coupons, or, commonly, stamps. Such catalog forms of premium offers can be effective over considerable periods because buyers perceive them as something different from price concessions, and because effective counters take time to arrange. If they succeed, however, they will be countered, sooner or later in some manner. In addition, however broad the list of offerings, most buyers soon have enough of everything offered which they desire.

Whatever the intention, the effectiveness of such premium offers is temporary. In addition, they can become perceived as part of the total offering, and abandonment may cost substantial patronage, as makers of coupon brand cigarettes discovered.

The packaging of an offering may also be changed to either conceal price increases or to emphasize permanent price cuts. These are usually a matter of market entry price strategies or defensive strategies.

Using Package Size Perception to Gain Market Advantage

Whenever package sizes have become relatively standard across an industry, some seller may take advantage of consumer perceptions of package contents to enter a new market with a concealed higher price. Others can and have used knowledge of perceptual processes to block an entry by means of a well-timed sudden decrease in price emphasized through a change in packaging.

Toilet paper was long sold to the consumer market primarily in 1000 sheet rolls, with a few at plainly marked 500 sheet rolls. Then fluffier types of tissues were developed, and introduced with a mere 625 sheets in the roll, sold at a similar price because the package looked to be the same size as the 1000 sheet roll, giving the seller a very substantial cost advantage (which could easily be used to finance heavy promotion).

The 12 ounce jar of peanut butter was long standard. When P&G decided to add peanut butter to its line, it discovered that consumers disliked the square inside corner of the jar, between side and bottom, so used a jar with a rounded corner--but put only 11 ounces of peanut butter in the jar, gaining an 8% contents cost advantage which all except those rare buyers who read the fine print perceived as the standard size (thus making use of the j.n.d. principle).

Similarly, when P&G decided to launch a cooking oil of its own, the standard containers had long been straight-sided glass bottles. P&G developed a wasp-waisted bottle which did offer advantages of grip on an oil-slick bottle. But apparently noting that their design, in a 24 fl. oz. bottle, was perceived as having the same capacity as a 32 fl. oz. straight side bottle, introduced their oil in the pint-and-a-half bottle at about the same price as the competitor's quart bottles, giving them a hefty 25% contents cost advantage, which could finance an advertising blitz.

By contrast, P&G lost out to a competitor's fast footwork when it tried to invade the water-based hair spray market, then dominated by Alberto-Culver's product. Noting all of P&G's preparations, Alberto-Culver was able to anticipate the timing of the P&G entry through information available in normal industry sources. Just as P&G was starting to distribute its initial stocks, Alberto-Culver increased the single dimension of can height, and stocked stores immediately. With P&G's adherence to standard container size, the contrast was so great that the P&G promotion died on the shelves.

Even such permanent packaging unit changes confer only a temporary advantage. If the move succeeds, surviving competitors adopt the new unit as standard.

All of these indirect price competitive maneuvers gain time advantages because they require some offering change as a counter. The advantage seldom is as long lasting as would be one gained by giving the buyer that which he desires: more perceived real value. All of them are subject to more or less effective counterattack in time, and can lead to burdensome price or promotional wars as costly as those initiated by direct price cuts.

Some apparent price reductions, of course, are not intended to be temporary, nor the sale planned to gain direct profit. The offering may be aimed at selling something which yields a continuing profit. Razor holders have always been offered on very moderate terms because the blades generate a stream of cash and profit. Both Eastman and Polaroid cameras were promoted to sell a continuing stream of film. Card tabulating equipment was long rented at prices far less than real cost because of the volume of card sales they generated. In such cases, no profit from the low priced item is ever expected, nor is there any intent to raise prices later.

Marketing strategies based on pure price appeal alone tend to be self-defeating in the end, because price has meaning for the buyer only in relation to perceived value. Value comes from offering something fitting the desire-sets of substantial segments of buyers.

In one type of pricing decision situation, the producer has very little or no choice of offering design. The buyers themselves specify the core of the design very precisely in the case of major sales on the basis of competitive bids.

Most major construction projects, and many other parts of the GNP, involve sales in which the buyers formulate rather precise specifications, and often the design of the offering, and award the purchase to the lowest bidder. In such cases, the seller must first decide whether or not to consider making a bid, decide on his objectives with relation to any bid to be made, estimate the probable bidding procedure of competitors, and estimate the probabilities of achieving the objectives. Quite often, competitor's moves are guessed at, and the tendency is probably to underestimate the level at which others will bid.

The basic process of competitive bidding strategy is quite simple, and uses the same kind of information normally used. It yields dispassionate numerical comparisons of the **profit position** of any bid which might be made: a figure which takes into account both the estimate of actual profit at a given level, and the uncertainty of landing the bid at that level.

The data necessary for the calculation are:
- A list of those competitors considered likely to bid
- Past bids made by each potential competing bidder on jobs on which the subject bidder has past estimates of his own
- The subject bidder's own cost estimates for each of these past jobs.
- The size of the winning bid in each case
- The general state of business in the industry involved, relative to capacity

The calculation rests on three assumptions:
- That the estimating and bidding procedures of each competitor are reasonably consistent.
- That the cost estimating procedures of each possible competitor tend to yield **parallel** (but not necessarily the same) results as those of the subject bidder.
- That when only the winning bid is known, the bids made by others were nominally larger than the winning bid.

The central calculation is the preparation of a probability distribution of the likelihood of winning for each possible bid within the range being considered. In many cases this can be done graphically, as the description below suggests. On those few occasions on which past experience is more voluminous, the same steps would be followed on a computer. The basic procedure is as follows:

1. Assemble the available information on past bids made by each prospective bidder.
2. Choose from this list those **n** number of bids which are judged to have been made under circumstances and on jobs roughly comparable to the present one.
3. For each of this list of **n** bids, list the subject bidder's own estimate of cost at the time the bid was made.

4.   Using the subject bidder's own cost estimate as the estimate competitors were using, estimate each competitor's percentage margin objective in the instance of each of these past bids.

5.   Rank each competitor's margin objective according to size, thus producing an initial array for each competitor, of the estimated values of his percentage margin objectives **m**.

6.   Convert this array into an estimated cumulative probability distribution of **n + 1** bids, composed of **n** bids plus the next, unknown bid by plotting the known values at the midpoints of **1/(n+1)** fractions of a 100 per cent probability distribution, starting with the highest margin as the lowest point of probability.

7.   Plot this cumulative frequency, preferably on normal probability paper, and draw the smoothed cumulative frequency curve which seems to best fit the plotted points.

8.   Repeat this process for each of the other competitors.

9.   Develop a set of tables showing cumulative probabilities for each competitor by interpolating the data plotted on the initial first estimate curves at some convenient round number levels of bid percentage profit objectives (for example, −10%, −5%, −2%, 0%, +1%, +2%, +5%, etc.).

10. Develop a table of combined total cumulative probabilities that all of the competitors will enter bids higher than that indicated by each point. (For example, if the cumulative probabilities of each of 3 competitor's bids at 10% or higher are, respectively, .19, .20, and .18 the combined probability that **all** 3 will bid 10% or higher is (.19 x .20 x .18) = .00684. (This probability is so much lower than the chance that any specific one of the trio will bid 10% or more margin because bids are assumed to be independent of each other.)

11. Develop a cumulative probability curve for the win probabilities by plotting a smoothed distribution of this table.

12. Determine the profit position of each of a number of proposed bids within the range meeting the firm's objectives by multiplying the absolute profit of each such bid, if won, by the probability of winning with such a bid as shown on this curve.

13. Plot these profit position values on another graph to estimate the best profit position value bid, and obtain a picture of the distribution of profit position values.   (Chester R. Wasson & Richard R. Shreve, 1975)

The calculation does not directly indicate what bid to make. That will depend entirely on the objectives sought. The profit position figures simply help the bidder compare the values of possible bids objectively, and thus make a decision on other than grounds of anxiety. Neither does it make a prediction of which bid will win. All of the probabilities which can be estimated are less than certainty, and most are far less.

The principal value is in substituting an objective criterion of bid choice for an emotional one. In at least one series of bids that has been studied, the long run effect can be greater profit on the bids won, according to an unpublished study by one of Donald S. Tull's students. He analyzed an actual set of bids made in the ordinary manner by an oil drilling contractor. The results indicated that if competitive bidding strategy calculations been followed, "the same bids would have been won and lost, but, for each one won, a higher price would have resulted." (Letter to the author from Donald S. Tull.)

Commodity Production Decisions and Pricing

If standard textbook models of price have any practical value, it would be in the field of commodities produced by a multitude of small producers, none of them large enough to affect the market. Even here, it does not depict the kinds of decisions made because it omits the problem of time lag between the price incentive and any resulting supply.

Agricultural economists long ago discovered regular cyclical fluctuations in the production of meat animals: a 7 year cycle for beef, a 3-1/2 year cycle for pork, for example. In all cases, the cycle is tied to the relative return from the meat animal in relation to the cost of feed (the so-called corn/hog ratio in the case of pork). The length of the cycle is a reflection of the time it takes to breed an increase in herds and bring the offspring to market weight. What clearly happens is that the decision to increase production is occasioned by a very favorable ratio of meat prices to feed costs. The resulting supply, however, hits the market much later. Obviously, producers trend to assume continuance of whatever price trends are current.

Their decision on production thus does not differ in essentials from the decision of industrial sellers, who base market entry on estimates of what customers can be expected to pay. Their major problem is the use of the kind of naive forecasting method almost always used by eager competitors during the growth phase of any market life cycle. They make a straight line projection of future demand without considering the certainty that there will be a turning point ahead. The result is the same in both cases: industry production exceeds supply when the expanded capacity all comes on stream, leading to a shakeout of the weaker sellers.

One other form of pricing decision has no clear relationship to market forces: pricing decisions based on what the organization's lawyers believe will be the attitude of the anti-trust lawyers in the U. S. Department of Justice.

The "Legal Department Price"

One of the anomalies of modern price making is the effect of the legal twists which have been read into the Sherman Anti-Trust act by government lawyers. Although the law is specifically aimed to "protect competition", anti-trust lawyers have regularly acted to do the opposite: protect competitors, as they see it. (The result has often been the reverse of even that goal.)

The result has been to keep the actions, especially the pricing decisions, of dominant producers in every industry under constant surveillance. Naturally, such organizations are capable of, and do, hire strong legal staffs of their own, and some pricing is the result of their interpretations of the possibility of anti-trust suits, with no recognizable relationship to market demand patterns. In the nature of things, sometimes they guess right, sometimes not. (It is difficult to overestimate the ability of lawyers of any kind, including anti-trust lawyers, to generate volumes of business for themselves.) In any case, some introductions are priced at what officials of one big organization has labelled an L.D.P.: a "legal department price," aimed to be moderate enough as to not be seen as putting a squeeze on competitors.

Since such prices have no demonstrable basis in market demand or consumer perceptions, no attempt will be made here to find the rules which govern lawyer's perceptions.

SUMMARY

Pricing is a term applied to nine different varieties of decisions on avoidance attributes of the offering.

Cost-plus--more accurately labelled price-minus--and return on investment are standards for entering a market, given the prices buyers can be expected to pay.

Market niche strategies include decisions on the price/quality level to be offered to attract targetted market segments.

Product mix and merchandising mix pricing strategies involve the balancing of margin objectives on different categories of the offering to achieve an overall margin objective. Some categories will be offered at minimum margins to attract buyer traffic. Others, expected to constitute the bulk of the purchases by the target segments, will carry margins close to the objective set. Some specialties and items carried for customer convenience will be priced at wider margins. Once the categories are set, the margins available on new offerings are compared with the standards to determine their inclusion in the line.

Sellers who must reach final buyers through a chain of distribution must allow substantial trade discounts in order to gain the important services these distributors furnish to buyers.   Such trade discounts and commissions are really purchase offers for the services.

Sellers must consider both the timing and the method of price changes which become necessary.   A major timing decision is whether to be a price leader or a price follower.   Price leadership on the upside requires a dominant market position, and carries responsibility for the effects of the industry price structure on the competitive situation.

A large portion of the pricing decisions are part of tactical competitive maneuvers, intended to meet a temporary situation.   Such temporary price concessions are best made in some indirect manner that requires time for competitors to counter.   Such temporary maneuvers may include special bargain priced packages, combination deals, premiums, and permanent changes in packaging units.

When the producer must obtain business through competitive bidding, his only means of differentiation is usually price.   The use of a technique known as competitive bidding strategy can optimize the returns on the bids made by providing an objective basis for comparison of all bids within a range which will meet the bidders objectives.

Because of the various inconsistencies which have arisen in the enforcement of the antitrust laws in the United States, dominant sellers in any industry must often quote prices according to what the attorneys believe will be permitted by antitrust lawyers.

FOOD FOR THOUGHT AND DISCUSSION

SELLING ROLLS-ROYCES

Transco, Inc., in High Point, NC, is the only Rolls Royce dealer in North Carolina, selling about 30 Rolls per year, plus some Bentleys on the side.   Geoffrey Eade, the British general manager, may experience whole months without a sale of his handmade offerings.   About half of the sales are new Rolls Royces (starting at $111,000, up to $165,000). The other half are "previously owned."

Lyles Chevrolet, across the street, is the owner of Transco, but the two dealerships are quite separate, and the sales programs quite different.

The stock of Lyles Chevrolet stands in long rows in the open lot.   Any interested passerby can stop, open the door of any of them, sit in it, kick the tires.   But not with Transco's Rolls. The $million plus of inventory is all indoors.   Car doors are all locked.

Transco runs no blaring newspaper ads, never appears on television, runs no year-end sales.   In fact, Rolls makes no yearly models.   The newest model appeared in 1981, the last one previous went on sale in 1973. A new model is already in the works, however.   It will be more fuel efficient.   But not because customers complain of the present mileage of 15 to the gallon.   Whoever buys a Rolls does not worry about the cost of petrol.   The more economical Rolls will be available for "social reasons."   Affluent buyers have some concern about fuel shortages.

Advertising consists of a single annual letter, each one individually typed and hand–signed, sent to a card file of 1,200 names selected from the Yellow Pages and Dun & Bradstreet listings. They include every physician and lawyer in the state. There are no follow–up letters. Eade explains, "It's not hard sell. It's just to let people know we are here."

Transco does not finance cars. Rolls buyers do not ask the dealer for loans. The firm will lease cars, with the option of applying the payments to the purchase.

Eade seemed pained when asked about parts. Yes, they carry parts. Occasionally—only occasionally—a Rolls needs one. "Once in a while, one will fail to proceed." [A story from a different source relates of the reported experience of a Rolls which broke an axle while traveling the Pennsylvania turnpike. Rolls flew in a crew of mechanics, replaced the axle on the spot. Asked about the charge, they are said to have remarked, "What charge? Rolls Royces do not break axles!"]

About his customers, Eade says, "The only thing they have in common is the ability to write a check."

Recently, Transco added another make to its line: the Avanti. Selling for $23,000 to $30,000, it is handmade from the dies bought from Studebaker in 1964. The Avanti has only 15 dealers world wide, sold 191 cars in 1981.

(Based on a profile, **Transco Inc.**published in **Business: North Carolina** Volume 2, No. 10, p. 41)

1. Why do people buy new Rolls Royces? Used ones?

2. Why is the entire promotional program so different than that for a mass production automobile?

3. Why not finance the sales? Most of the buyers are going to borrow the purchase price, not pay for the automobile out of their current bank balances.

3. Why add the Avanti to the line? How does it fit into the merchandise mix?

4. What is the general pattern of the sales approach? What are its various elements, and what is the rationale behind all of them?

APPLYING MERCHANDISE MIX PRICING TO A FRANCHISED SERVICE

It has long been accepted as good public policy to grant exclusive franchises to services which can be carried out more efficiently as monopolies: telecommunications, public transit, etc. The latest of these is the cable television franchise. Cities have adopted somewhat more sophisticated requirements to the granting of such than was exercised in the past. Those hoping to gain such franchises have also come up with some innovative bids in order to gain highly desirable franchises. Among those in 1982 was the offer which won the Boston franchise for Cablevision Systems Development Corp.

Cablevision's winning bid offers the 240,000 Boston households a full 52 channels of basic television service for only $2 a month: not only far less than the usual base rate of $8, but a fee that will guarantee a loss if that is the only service the households buy in the 5 years for which the rate is guaranteed. In addition, Cablevision promised to turn over to the city and to a non–profit corporation 8% of gross revenues, and at least one full cable of 50 channels which the non–profit corporation will be permitted to use to establish its own competing pay television channels.

The $2 basic fee includes 3 popular services—Cable News Network, a sports programming service, and USA network, as well as a variety of independent stations around the country. Cablevision is gambling that a substantial portion of the subscribers will want a number of additional services. Home Box Office will cost them $7 a month, 20 added channels costing $6 will be required to get special movies and sports channels. Other channels will cost $8 each. Financial analyst familiar with the industry believe the operator will need to get at least $20 to $25 a month from large numbers of subscribers, and may not do better than break even at that.

The real profits will come if a large number of cable users spend the $40 to $50 dollars per month that some industry people believe may be reached by 1990. In that case, the wide market base opened up by the low rate may be very profitable.

(Ref.:**The Wall Street Journal**,"Boston Award May Overhaul Cable TV Rates," p. 17, August 17, 1982)

1. An official of a losing competitor, Warner Amex, is quoted as observing that "In that city, half of the households have under $15,000 income...We think their estimate that the average household will subscribe to more than 4 extra services, for $44 a month, in unrealistic." What do you think?

2. Customers will still have to pay a monthly bill, rather than to make a good aerial installation which could draw in from a wide area. Why should the $2 rate get a really wide base?

3. If the rate does prove very attractive and gains a really major part of the Boston households, what advantage can that be other than the possibility that more will eventually add services.

4. Can you perceive any other sources of advantage from establishing the city of Boston franchise?

FOODTOWN: CUTTING PRICES TO THE BONE—TO MAKE PROFITS

Supermarkets make their profits on fast turnover and on high dollar sales per purchase by customers. Since the usual payment terms are 1% discount for payment within 10 days, they can sell fast turnover items before payment is due, and still get the cash discount. Heavy sales per customer purchase reduces checkout cost, a significant component of any store's cost.

Foodtown, Inc. is a dominant supermarket chain in the central Piedmont area of the Carolinas and Western Virginia. It was not always thus. Originally a single family food store in a small city, the business grew slowly in the first 10 years, adding a few small stores in other Piedmont towns, but not making any spectacular gains. To some extent, it was not sure of its competitive niche, and profits were far from exciting. Then the firm decided on a drastic move: cut the retail prices on a long list of the dry grocery items carried in their own warehouse to the wholesale invoice price. These totalled over 500, included offerings from disposable diapers to peanut butter and toilet tissue. They coupled this with a low price every day policy (no specials except a pass-on of special buys). At this writing, Foodtown has an abnormally low total gross margin—16-1/2% recently, compared with a normal 21% industry wide. It is also the most profitable large chain in the area. Part of the reason is a personnel policy that gives employees close identification with the firm's interests, and a group of other policies which keeps pilferage to an astounding low 1/2 of 1% level. The main reason, however, is the heavy turnover and the very large sales per customer. A large portion of those lined up at the checkout counter are pushing shopping carts loaded to the brim.

1. With prices so low on such a broad line, how can Foodtown be so profitable?

2. What market segments does the Foodtown policy seem to be aimed to attract?

3. Why should this be a good segment to build a supermarket business around?

4. In the Fox River Valley study, the Blue Goose seems to have had a quite opposite price policy from that of Foodtown. From all appearances, the Blue Goose was also quite profitable. Why did it attract so much traffic, and what was the basis of its success, so far as can be inferred from the brief description given here?

COAXING OUT A LARGE SUPPLY OF SECONDARY PLATINUM

During the Korean War, it became necessary to expand the supply of very high octane gasoline for use in the fighter planes of the time. High yields of such grades of gasoline were then obtained by "platforming" the crude oil in the refining process, as the platinum catalytic refining process was called. The process does not use up the platinum, but needs it to tranform the crude oil.

This need called, in turn, for an immediate increase, for one year, of 100,000 ounces Troy of platinum. This did not sound like much until it was discovered that the annual production of platinum for all uses was only 400,000 ounces a year outside the Iron Curtain, and Russia was not exporting. Further, it was discovered that nearly all of the new supply was by-product production from two sources: International Nickel Corp.'s production in Canada, and the South African gold mines selling through the Johnson-Matthey interests in England. Since it was a very minor by-product production, expansion of the newly mined supply could not be expected. The Metals Branch of the U. S. Office of Price Stabilization was given the task of finding a way to get more supply.

At the time, the legal ceiling price on platinum was $93 per ounce. The producers were not hostile to a raise in price, but voluntarily commented that it was doubtful that they would charge customers more even if the ceiling were raised. In any case, there was not much they could do to increase supplies. Talking with other elements of the trade, the economists learned that most of the uses of platinum were non-destructive. As a result, it was thought that about four-fifths of all the platinum ever mined, since its was first discovered in Russia in 1820, was still available somewhere in the world: a total of 8 million ounces. [The first use platinum was put to, after its discovery, was the counterfeiting of silver coins!]

Industry trade sources also noted that some of this platinum periodically appeared on the secondary market, when the price was right. Some months before, in the fall of 1950, prior to the passage of price ceiling legislation, quite a bit of it appeared for sale at $103 per ounce.

On the basis of this history, a price regulation was prepared amending the price ceiling to $105 per ounce. Suddenly, opposition appeared from an unforeseen sector. A major use of platinum is in spinnerets for forming glass fibers, and a principal producer had some 50,000 ounces on loan from the U. Government stockpile to produce fiber glass for the military. They were adamantly opposed to the change in ceiling, and had enough political influence to stop the signing of the order for a period. Eventually, the order was signed, more than enough platinum appeared on the secondary market, and the refiners got their catalysts.

1. Why did the price need to be set so high? Why could not more platinum be had for $98 or $99 an ounce? Since this material was already available, why not just try small raises until enough became available? Isn't that what traditional supply

curves say will happen?

　　2. Why should the primary producers be reluctant to raise their own prices?

THE TOYOTA TERCEL PRICE MIX

　　Leafing through a November 1982 newspaper, the author's eye was caught by a full page ad for the Toyota Tercel line. He had previously seen TV ads touting the Tercel as the lowest priced front wheel model for sale in the United States, at $4998. This ad, however, depicted all four models of the line, with the $4998 offering highlighted, together with the EPA mileage rating of 40 hwy., 32 official. The line, with prices and descriptions were as follows:

　　- 1983 Tercel 3-door liftback............$4998
　　- 1983 Tercel 5-door deluxe liftback.....$6058
　　- 1983 Tercel 3-door SR5 liftback........$6618
　　- 1983 Tercel 4WD SR5 Wagon..............$8148

The full copy indicates that all models use the same engine, have similar mileage, and the same suspension system. Presumably the body shell is the same for the $4998 3-door liftback and the $6618 3-door SR5 liftback. A check with the dealer indicates that the SR5 is an options package which includes a 5-speed transmission and quite a few other niceties. The 5-speed transmission can be purchased separately on the other models as well.

　　Toyota has copied most of the sales practices and adapted much of its design to American tastes and practices, the pricing practice included. Clearly, with the exception of the wagon's 4-wheel drive and body, all models share all major components.

　　1. Why the big gap in price of the regular 3-door liftback, and the SR5 liftback models? In the light of your answer, why should the $4998 model be so heavily promoted in the advertising?

　　2. Check around some showrooms for other cars, and for major appliances. What similar practices do you find? Do some "shopping" for one of these. How does the salesman treat the low end model?

　　3. What is the psychology of this treatment of low end models, in the promotion and on the salesroom floor?

CHAPTER 11. MANAGING OFFERING AVAILABILITY

The services rendered by distributors
Adjusting disparities between producer's offerings and buyer needs
    Disparities between producers' and buyers' locations
    Disparities between scales of production and consumption
    Assortment disparities
Completing offerings to meet individual needs
Multiple distribution channels to serve multiple market segments
Distribution requirements for intangible services
The interdependence of producers and distributors
    The basis of mutual interest
        Assortment compatibility
        Marketing effort compatibility
Distribution policies: intensive, selective, exclusive
Channel systems and channel leadership
        Pull strategies
        Push strategies
    Leadership and the customer franchise
The channel choices
    Direct sales
    Using integrated intermediaries
    Working with independent intermediaries
Developing coordinated logistics systems

DISTRIBUTION:
MANAGING OFFERING AVAILABILITY

11

From the buyer's point of view, part of the price of any offering is the degree to which availability is limited. All forms of availability are limited in time and place to some degree. No offering is ever always here and now when we want it.

Making offerings available to buyers when, where, and in the forms and amounts they wish usually requires a systematic development of a chain of intermediaries. Only a small portion of exchanges are made between actual producers and final users today. (Little more than a century ago, this was the primary system for most offerings, even in the more industrialized countries.) Even what is called direct selling today usually involves at least one set of intermediaries: the sales force of the seller. (As will be seen later, even the salesmen employed directly by the seller are, to some degree, independent intermediaries.)

The functions of intermediaries today are far more complex than those of the merchants of previous centuries. The interdependence of initiating sellers and intermediaries is certainly greater. The earlier 19th century merchants served mainly to bridge the distance between producers and users, and to finance production. The relationship between producer and merchant was mainly that of seller and customer. Normally, the merchant was the only "market" the producer was directly familiar with.

Today, of course, the distributive intermediaries are still customers, and still think of themselves as such. They are also what today's producers perceive them to be: an integral part of his distribution channel to the final user. They become part of his price (the search effort required) and also part of the seller's production system--providing services which are needed to complete the offering the final customer buys.

In turn, the producers become part of the distributor's management system, furnishing promotional and other kinds of services, as well as the profit opportunities the distributor seeks.

The Services Rendered by Distributors

Initiating sellers depend on these semi-independent intermediaries because of a number of disparities and deficiencies in the offerings as they leave the producer's hands. They also need the distributors because the latter can handle certain aspects of promotion and finance more efficiently than can the producer, and can be an important source of market intelligence on final customers needs and on competition.

Adjusting Disparities Between Producers' Offerings and Buyer Needs

In the modern mass production economy, the offerings of nearly all producers suffer at least 3 disparities in relation to the needs of individual final buyers, and often even, of final sellers:
- Disparities between assortments produced and those sought by buyers
- Disparities between the scale of production and the scale of consumption
- Disparities in location

In addition, many offerings need finishing touches of some kind to fit them to customers needs. Many also need added services, including personalized information at the point of final sale, to make them attractive or even useful.

Moreover, distributors can often handle local promotion more efficiently, and they are a source of financing for suppliers. Being closer to the customers, they can have a clearer understanding of customers' wants and needs.

Disparities Between Producers' and Buyers' Locations

The most obvious disparity in our modern mass production economy is that of location. Physical production and at least some managerial functions of planning and control are most efficiently carried out in a few centralized locations. Customers are dispersed over wide regions, whole countries, and even the entire globe.

Rarely if ever is it efficient to attempt to centrally plan inventories at all points customers would desire, or to direct service operations from a central location. As modern centralized economies have clearly demonstrated, the necessary bureaucracy becomes far too unwieldy and insensitive to buyers' needs. In addition, intermediaries help finance the production and distribution through their purchases and creation of local inventories, and also by handling credit arrangements further down the channel. Their superior access to knowledge of indirect customers is critical.

Disparities Between Scales of Production and Consumption

Large scale production needs to be moved away from the point of fabrication in truckloads, carloads, and even trainloads. The scale of transactions needs to be comparable, to maintain efficiency of paper work. (Anyone who has ever had to get an address or an error corrected by an automated computer run operation learns the inefficiency of mass handling of clerical operations.)

For some portion of the channels utilized, the disparity of scale between initial seller and final retailer is often too great to bridge directly,. Distribution channels have to be longer, with more intermediaries. (In some of the less developed countries, where aspirin tablets are often sold in lots of 2 pills at a time, common consumer items may pass thorough a string of wholesalers, jobbers, subjobbers, and even sub-sub-jobbers to some parts of the market.)

The greatest and most common disparity is between the offering the customer is seeking and the total offering the initial seller can produce economically. Such disparities include those of the assortment made and the assortment purchased, the problems of custom fit, purchase-risk reduction, and after-market service.

Assortment Disparities

Customers rarely, if ever, approach an exchange situation seeking a single satisfaction. As already noted, buyers approach any purchase with hopes of fulfilling a substantial bundle of desires. They also prefer to purchase a number of related offerings in a single transaction, from as wide a choice of possibilities as possible.

Any consumer who has limited time available soon learns that doubling the number of stops nearly doubles the shopping time for the same number of items. Only a little more time is needed to buy and pay for a cartful of groceries than to buy 2 or 3 items. Similarly, industrial buyers long ago learned that it takes little more time to handle the purchasing of 10 items than the buying of a single offering. Dealing with two salesmen always is more costly than dealing with one.

Consequently, markets have always tended to present an extended assortment of related offerings available in a compact area or through a single transaction of some kind. Since dim prehistory, sellers have developed arrangements of various kinds to facilitate some kind of one-stop shopping, from the itinerant peddler and his pack, through the central market place or plaza, to the modern supermarket and department store and the industrial trade show.

Production, whether of tangibles or intangibles, is best carried out with some degree of specialization. Although most producers produce a line of offerings, the relationships between items in the line are dictated by similar production considerations of some kind.

Relationships between items in the assortments desired by buyers, on the other hand, are consumption oriented, and differ from one buyer of any given offering, to another. This is true whether the buyer is a middleman or a final user.

This disparity between the assortments desired by buyers and the assortments which sellers can provide tends to exist at every step in the channel of distribution.

To the extent that buyers perceive the disparity as a salient cost, a profit opportunity exists for an intermediary who will bridge it. On the other hand, if the disparity is not perceived as very great, two stages in the channel of distribution may merge into a chain operation. The greatest part of the assortment will then move through the channels under common ownership.

Even in a chain operation, some elements in the desired assortment must be assembled from different sources. Thus the local supermarket receives the great bulk of its assortment from a central warehouse, but obtains such items as dairy products and fresh bakery items from separate sellers. For a wide variety of minor items ranging from pet supplies and spices to panty hose, the store will depend on rack jobbers to keep its shelves stocked.

Similarly, the largest steel producer in the United States, U. S. Steel Corp., must go beyond its own product line for such items as aluminum shapes and sheet to supply its chain of steel service centers, set up to sell to machine shops and other smaller steel consumers.

A PROBLEM OF A PAIR OF SHOES

Some kind of rationing of apparel became inevitable during World War II because of the heavy demand of the military for clothing and the facilities to make it. The problem was not severe in men's apparel because 15 million adult males were subtracted from the civilian population for military duty. In ladies apparel, the problem was met by limiting the amount of fabric which could be used in dresses and suits. In shoes direct rationing was imposed. Ration stamps were issued limiting each individual rather severely in the number of shoes which could be purchased in a year's time. Rationing must be "just": every person must get identical treatment. In this case, it meant that every person received the same ration.

One of those 15 million men who were given uniforms was a buck private sent with an infantry division to the Hawaiian Islands, on a training assignment preparing for amphibious assault. While there, Pvt. Smith (as we shall call him), had the good fortune to be detached from his outfit and assigned to a base command headquarters operation. Pvt. Smith had a special personal problem: his feet were inclined to perspire heavily, which led directly to a severe problem with athlete's foot, especially when wearing standard issue army shoes, with their high tops. During basic training, he had to change his shoes twice a day to get by. To his delight, he discovered that headquarters personnel were permitted to wear oxfords, if they purchased them themselves. Also, he discovered, Hawaii had no shoe rationing, even though it was part of the U.S. So many of the natives seldom wore ordinary shoes that no one had been able to design a rationing system to fit.

So Pvt. Smith headed to downtown Honolulu, as permitted, on his free time. He had only one problem: his feet were on the larger end of the normal size ranges, and most Hawaiians had small feet. He had real difficulty finding a pair coming close to his size. A tour of all the shoe stores finally located a pair that pinched only a little bit.

In any line of trade, the assortments demanded by similar market segments will vary from one locality to another. Market segments differ in the kinds and variations of assortments they desire because of differences in physical need (climate, age distribution, size of organization in industrial markets, etc.), in taste patterns, and in significant cultural characteristics. Thus all assortments must be tailored to the local market, a task best carried out by those familiar with these submarkets. Generally, too, some final touches may be needed to fit the offering to local needs.

Completing Offerings to Meet Individual Needs

Physical requirements and tastes of individual buyers differ so widely that the advantages of mass production are blocked by any attempt at central production of every detail or aspect of any kind of offering, including services, Consequently, the initial seller's offerings usually cover only the common core parts of the design needed to cover a substantial range of demand. Before they are ready for the individual buyer, they usually need additions and/or alterations to fit customer needs.

The maker of men's slacks ships most of his product with the bottom of the leg left unfinished, long enough to cover a leg of any length. The local retailer usually finishes them off to suit the legs of the buyer. The meat packer ships whole meat carcasses, or major cuts at least, and the local store reduces them to steaks, roasts, chops and hamburger, cut or prepared as the local trade desires.

Additionally, many modern offerings need added service availability at the point of sale: maintenance and repair parts and services, local warranty service, displays, and personal instructional help in many cases.

The customer, at all stages of the channel, looks to the sales contact to provide help in making choices and to thus reduce the effort and risk in buying. Not unusually, buyers depend on previous experience with the vendor, or on the vendor's reputation if the personal experience is lacking, as an efficient substitute for careful evaluation of all possible choices. This so-called "consumer franchise" can be the most valuable asset any seller has.

In most industrialized countries, the buyer has come to expect the local outlet to help correct or avoid errors through exchanges, and to be the ultimate guarantor of satisfaction. Moreover, the customer depends on the intermediary's people or advertising and displays to have offerings available for inspection. They expect the sales help to further their understanding of the exact use-patterns of the offerings, and the contained services.

In all of these efforts, the intermediaries are an essential part of the seller's sales communications systems.

Because the same or similar offerings often are bought by quite diverse kinds of buyers, many producers must sell through multiple channels to reach their full potential.

Multiple Distribution Channels to Serve Multiple Market Segments

Multiple Distribution Channels to Serve Multiple Market Segments

The segments served, the assortments desired and the appropriate channel contacts of most of these segments usually differ too widely for any line to be sold through a single channel, even for physically identical offerings.

The tire manufacturer sells the new car buyer through the automobile manufacturer (the OEM: the original equipment manufacturer channel). Replacement tires are sold through several channels: specialized tire dealers, gasoline service stations, chain auto supply operations, and perhaps a mail order retailer, probably under a different, "private brand" label.

The steel mill sells automobile and appliance makers direct, local machine shops through "steel service centers", petroleum production operations through "oil field supply stores." The building materials manufacturer may sell large operative builders direct, smaller local developers through wholesale lumber yards, and the do-it-yourself home improvement market through large building supply supermarkets (who may buy direct for their own wholesale yards, or from other wholesale yards), and smaller materials dealers, who would buy from regional distributors.

Sellers of intangible services also have a distribution management need.

Distribution Requirements for Intangible Services

Service producers have both location and time availability distribution decisions to make. In many respects, the larger ones are mass production operations whose problems are no different in most respects than the mass producers of more tangible bundles of satisfaction. Such is certainly the case for insurance companies, bankers, security underwriters, university systems, and health service operations.

In one sense, all of these are essentially distributors themselves. **Insurance organizations,** particularly those in life insurance, gather the savings of their customers, and distribute them as loans through various channels to those who can put the savings to productive use. Much of this distribution of savings goes through multiple channels to the final users of the loans or capital investment. Some is made available to mortgage bankers, who process loan applications in various localities and collect payments. Some of the money is "sold" directly to large borrowers such as real estate developers and builders of large commercial structures. Some goes as loans to large manufacturers, buying up their commercial paper. Other amounts go indirectly to organizations through bond purchases, and some goes directly into equity investment through stock purchases.

In all of this, such organizations are performing banking functions, sometimes in direct competition with similar services provided by banks. Indeed, savings banks in Massachusetts have been writing life insurance policies for most of this century. [As this is being written, the rather arbitrary legal boundaries between all sorts of financial institutions are being eroded and may well be abolished completely within a decade.]

The funds of insurance organizations of all sorts come from the mass production of risk evaluation and risk offsetting services. In their usual form, these are insurance policies for which they collect premiums. But the risk management function for very large customers may involve only an actuarial and administrative service operation at what might be called the wholesale level.

In order to make risk management available to the smaller retail customer, most of the industry has long depended primarily on a system of independent agents, distributing their own assortments of various kinds of policies issued by a number of companies. Within the last 50 years, an insurance industry version of chain retailing has come into being: firms known to the industry as "direct writers," whose agents are exclusive sales offices for the one insurance firm.

Even in those jurisdictions in which branch banking is not permitted, **commercial banks** also form distributive systems. Large "wholesale banks" have served to channel funds received by smaller correspondent banks to the investment community. As the number of services have proliferated, with credit cards, debit cards, and other new instruments, the larger organizations have had to develop special well located retail operations or arrangements to handle their services.

With the coming of national banking systems not too far off, banks will have the problems of any chain organization: what kinds of units, where, what assortment of services appropriate in each location.

Universities are both producers of information and the tools of intellectual skills, and distributors of intellectual services. Until the current generation, this was mostly a simple single location operation, aimed at a narrow set of market segments: the traditional full-time student in the late teens and early 20's, attending daytime classroom and laboratory instruction.

The missions of universities expanded rapidly after World War II, and led quickly to the establishment of statewide university systems providing a broad assortment of educational services in multiple locations, at many hours of the day, and often off-campus. Colleges, normally having only the instructional mission, have also seen themselves having to broaden both their market appeal, and their offering assortments. The new mission has often required careful thought as to location.

Even the branch channels have been multiplying. Traditional classroom instruction is offered on-campus, off campus in other kinds of school buildings, and off-campus on the premises of large commercial operations, for their own employees. Special short course seminars and executive development programs have been developed, particularly by the business schools. The growth of courses especially tailored for older students is a major trend. Among the assortments offered by some universities are computer networks of instruction tied into large instructional programs.

Health organizations are just beginning to consider their service assortments and the question of location for each. In the larger cities, the whole range of services is still available at one central location. The more specialized services will continue to be centralized. But the same organizations are sponsoring, or at least encouraging, a number of limited service operations, needed more frequently, in neighborhood locations: neighborhood clinics, centers for emergency service, even simple surgery centers of types not really requiring a hospital stay. In addition, paramedic units provide emergency service in mobile units.

SELLING THE VALUE ADDED WITHOUT OWNING THE OFFERING

The major function of the banking community is to assemble the savings of the community and distribute the funds as loans to those who can put them to productive use. The usual process is to collect the savings from various sources, and lend them in the bank's name. But North Carolina National Bank found (NCNB) a different way to sell its services when it discovered that its resources were not sufficient to make a real mark the usual way in the field of international loans.

NCNB is the largest banking system in the Southeastern region of the United States. But when NCNB decided to expand its horizons to include international business, the officials discovered that its resources were not great enough to win a leading or even strong supporting role in underwriting the usual forms of international loans.

After some investigation, NCNB officials discovered a niche not being well served by available financial institutions: the financing of container shipments out of Great Britain. Such loans are short term, secured by the shipping documents. NCNB, however, did not loan its own funds. Instead, it found private investors who would make the loans, with NCNB collecting a fee for the placement. In a relatively short period of years, NCNB was financing a major part of the container business out of Great Britain.

Insurance companies are also in the business of collecting small amounts of money—insurance premiums—to distribute to those who meet with specified kinds of losses. In this way, none of those at risk have a very large loss. But some organizations are large enough that they can and do self-insure: their risk base is great enough that the premiums are not worth paying.

Insurance companies, however, have an expertise in the administration of payments most such organizations still need and lack. INA, a large insurer, sold that middleman expertise itself on a big project in 1947. The Erie Mining Company was undertaking the development of a taconite (iron-ore) treatment process in the Mesabi Range, involving a $300 million dollar project in which 245 contractors were to construct 74 miles of railroad, two large docks, a dam to hold 10 million gallons of water, and a town of 1,200 houses. Erie needed an insurance program providing general and workmen's compensation for the Erie Mining Company and all of the contractors and their employees.

Assigning a resident staff to the project, INA provided safety engineering to cut losses and handle claims promptly. Known as a retrospective rating plan, INA charged the insured its own losses, the cost of administering the protection, the expenses of claims handling and safety work—all for a fee.

In service operations of every kind, organizations are having to give thought to the same considerations as must those who distribute tangible goods to a widespread population. About the only problem not faced is that of the location of physical inventories. In a sense, this may not be as much of a difference as first appears. In service operations, the inventory is in the form of knowledgeable people, and the problem then becomes as to where and when they will be available, and what depth of knowledge and skill is needed at each type of location. This may well raise some of the considerations of producer-distributor interdependence and channel leadership as does the distribution of tangibles.

The Interdependence of Producers and Distributors

Quite a bit has been written about channel conflict, as though producers and distributors were natural adversaries. Short-sighted management can create frictions and conflict. But well managed distribution systems are like the relationships in all good marketing operations, a symbiotic relationship. Both sides of the transaction need and have much to offer each other.

TWO TROUBLED AUTO MAKERS RESCUE EACH OTHER

In the 1957–59 period, American Motors was riding the crest of the enthusiasm for compact autos, and so was France's Renault with its Dauphine import into the United States. Twenty years later, both were in trouble in the American market.

The Dauphine had sold too well—it was poorly designed for American driving conditions and habits, and lacked an adequate service network. Repeated efforts to revive the American market for better designed Renault cars had failed—despite relatively heavy advertising outlays, Renault could not attract distributors. It had only 340 dealers in 1977, and sold just 13,000 of its LeCar model. Outsiders estimate that Renault lost $5 million on its American operation that year. In France, it still dominated the market, and finances were not its problem.

AMC, too, had fallen on hard times. Never strongly financed, AMC had made some product mistakes and was losing $1 million a week on its passenger car operations. It did have a strong position with its unique Jeep line, and still had 2100 dealers. AMC lacked the funds to develop the new fuel efficient designs demanded by the 1970s and 1980s, and had been searching for a partner for some time.

The two got together in a partnership agreement in mid 1978. Renault lent AMC $50 million to help retool the Kenosha, Wis. plant in preparation for an American version of the Renault R–18: an attractive compact design to be released four years later. Meanwhile, AMC dealers would begin to sell the Le Car model until the Alliance version of the R–18 was available.

Not yet a merger, it did marry Renault's financial and design strengths, badly needed by AMC, with a dealer network Renault without which it was getting nowhere in the American market. [The financial stringencies of the early 1980s made it necessary for Renault to buy into AMC before the promising Alliance came on the market in late 1982, by which time the partnership was essentially a marriage.]

Producers can offer much more than just quantities of the physical offering sold to distributors: advertising support, some degree of consumer franchise, merchandising help, and often some kinds of management guidance.

On their side, distributors bring valuable assets to the partnership: the creation of a customer-desired assortment which brings traffic to buy the producers' output, offering completion services, local promotion and display and personal communications, inventory financing , knowledge of the specific customer segments served. The distributor is the first to hear customer complaints, or learn of their satisfaction. Distributors are often the first to learn of moves by competitors. They are also first to sense the effects of competing offerings on demand.

The Basis of Mutual Interest

Relationships within the distribution channel should be truly marketing operations. Both sides are seeking bundles of satisfactions which are more than the immediate transfer of physical offerings for some money. Both need and want an enduring relationship.

Buyers are seeking dependable profit opportunities which can come from the ability of the physical offering to enhance the value of the distributor's assortments in his customer's perceptions. Other profits may come from the services the producer renders or aspects of the offering which simplify operations and cut their costs.

Sellers are seeking a set of outlets which are building assortments attractive to the set of market segments most valuable to them. They desire outlets whose assortments match their own assortments as closely as possible. They also desire distributors whose total marketing effort is compatible with their plans and the needs of the current stage of the market life cycle.

Assortment compatibility is the foremost objective of both the seller and the buyers within a channel. Sellers want buyers who purchase as many as possible of their full line, and who handle items compatible in type and quality. They want as few "cherry picker" customers as possible.

Buyers want suppliers who can furnish as many lines as possible of items fitting their merchandise plan. Buyers want to avoid the cost of dealing with more sources than necessary. Such assortment compatibility obviously implies a common set of market segment targets.

Marketing effort compatibility is another goal of both buyers and sellers. Both need to have the same understanding of the proportions of the communications mix and the role each is expected to play. This role will have to involve the type and degree of distribution selectivity necessary at the current stage of the product life cycle.

Distribution Policies: Intensive, Selective, Exclusive

A producer's intended distribution policy can vary from the intensive and extensive, through selective to exclusive. Which is best depends on the phase of the market life cycle, the nature of the offering itself, its degree of differentiation or specialty attributes, and on the competitive position of the producer.

An exclusive or selective policy is an absolute necessity if an offering is such that potential buyers must undergo learning to use, and the market must go through a development period before take-off. In addition, the producer must allow a very substantial discount to the proper distributors and be prepared to back up distributors' efforts with an investment level of mass communications. In return for this package of incentives, the distributor must be able and willing to field the aggressive sales effort needed to find early adopting prospects and get them to try the offering. The selective policy is his guarantee that others will not reap what he sows.

Generally, an exclusive policy covers a large geographical area, not much less than a single major metropolitan trade area, sometimes even more. A selective policy protects the dealer in a smaller area, but one large enough, considering the nature of the demand.

Exclusive distribution is also used to make certain that enough sales of a specialty offering will be available to the dealers carrying it, and that they will give the offering the kind of effort and atmosphere needed for success. Rolls Royce sales in the United States, for example, of around 1,000 per year, dictate a policy of permitting only a very few dealers in the entire country. At the same time, the dealers chosen must be perceived by potential buyers as "Rolls Royce types."

Selective distribution also helps concentrate the local sales volume of the smaller, limited-line producer and thus make the line attractive to those dealers selected. Even during the mature phase of the cycle, these dealers, too, must get a longer margin than average for the type of offering.

A policy of the most extensive and intensive distribution possible is necessary to gain a strong market share for any mature phase offering of a type viewed by buyers as a convenience item in which differentiation is low. During the rapid growth phase of the cycle, attainment of as intensive a distribution as possible is the best insurance for survival during the coming shakeout period.

Obviously, the degree of channel leadership possible, and the identity of the leader, affects the degree of selectivity.

Channel Systems and Channel Leadership

The distribution channel should move more than offerings from the initiating seller to final buyers and payments in the opposite direction.

Efficient channel operation also requires a two-way flow of information of 4 kinds:
- The character of market demand and the expected demand fluctuations for the services embodied in the offerings
- Competitive developments which could influence that demand in any way
- Promotional communications plans and developments
- Production and merchandising plans

These information flows may follow different paths from the flow of offerings from producer to end user. The paths taken depend on the relative access of the various channel members to market information and the ability to assume leadership in planning both promotion and the flow of offerings. Some one member must do the overall planning for any one channel and single offering, and there must be some understood hierarchy of leadership.

The overall leadership may fall on any member of the channel: the initiating seller, one of the intermediaries (wholesaler or retailer), or even the final large customer, when the latter originates the designs and sells on bids. Just which member achieves the key position depends on several factors:
- The relative financial strength of the various members
- The relative market strengths of channel members
- Their relative access to overall information on customer demand patterns
- The planning lead time available and required
- The communications emphasis best suited to the sale of the offering

The two extremes of channel leadership are often characterized in terms of communications strategy:
- "pull strategy," in which the initiating seller "pulls" the offering through the channel by means of heavy mass promotion of the brand
- "push strategy," in which the downstream members are expected to handle most of the customer persuading communications

These terms are most apt when applied to mass market consumer items. The **pull strategy** is also frequently referred to as "selling over the head of the dealer." By this is meant that the intense mass promotion used is expected to develop enough consumer interest that retailers must stock and sell it.

Pull strategies are most appropriate for standardized offerings designed for broad mass market segments with little need for individual fitting. When such is the case, the initiating seller has an opportunity to:
- Develop an efficient centralized mass media promotion around a single theme
- Undertake marketing research to discover the appropriate appeals
- Gather intelligence on competitive standing and on competitors plans

Pull strategies are the common approach in toiletries (soap, shampoos, detergents, hair dyes. etc.), soft drinks and other beverages sold by dominant firms through mass outlets. The latter are especially susceptible to psychological differentiation based on knowledge of consumer attitudes toward the offering category.

TONI LEARNS THAT PULL DOES NOT WORK WHEN PUSH IS NEEDED

Toni's creation and dominance of the home permanent market was a major success story of the late 1940s and 1950s. Realizing that a single product producer is vulnerable to changing tastes, Toni went on to develop a number of other hair care products—shampoos and hair conditioners in particular—with substantial success. The line still was not as broad as desired, however, and Toni decided on broadening out of toiletries into cosmetics.

A quality lipstick was developed and launched with the same blizzard of advertising that had captured the hair care markets. But this did not work. Toni neither succeeded in getting much distribution, nor an adequate market share. Research finally turned up the answer. All premium quality cosmetics got their major promotion from the clerks behind the counters in key department stores. These clerks were carefully trained cosmeticians receiving a large part of their income from the commissions on sales which were made available by the producers. The heavy user segment for cosmetics tends to be the 16–25 year old group, and this segment tends to be concerned with the specific adaptation of the assortment of cosmetics available to their skin and personality. They are thus susceptible to the persuasion of the well trained sales people.

The push strategy required took an entirely different kind of promotional technique than the pull strategy which worked so well for toiletries. Reviewing the situation, Toni decided that cosmetics marketing was not their cup of tea, and dropped the lipstick.

Push strategies must be used by even otherwise strong channel leaders for any offering requiring substantial personalized fitting, demonstration, or instruction at the point of sale: high fashion apparel, automobiles, boats and other big ticket mechanical offerings, premium cosmetics (lipsticks and related offerings). In such cases, the end seller tends to be franchised by and identified with the initiating seller and channel leader, even when legally independent. The channel leader tends to have de facto control over management methods and promotional designs down to the last point of sale. **Push strategies** are a symptom of downstream leadership for 3 other types of offerings:

- Offerings which are characterized by significant differences in locality and regional tastes, on which the final seller has the best information (fashion apparel is one such case)
- Offerings produced by non-dominant sellers, even though standardized and aimed at mass markets
- Offerings which have a limited potential for significant perceived differentiation and tend to be bought on the basis of the dealer's

Under pure push strategy conditions, the offering may or may not carry the initiating seller's brand or be otherwise identified with that seller. If it does, the brand may carry little meaning for the buyer, or be a significant factor in the choice. Frequently, it may carry a wholesaler's or retailer's designation.

Leadership and the Customer Franchise

Channel leadership is closely related to the possession of a strong customer franchise, or the ability and the funds to develop one. Initiating sellers working through a number of channels may have a different leadership potential in each.

No dominant seller of automobile tires, for example, can expect to exert a leadership role in the sale of original equipment tires to General Motors who resells them as part of the Chevys they deliver to customers. The same tire producer may be a strong leader in the sales of own brand tires through independent replacement market dealers, and relinquish both the brand designation and the leadership to a powerful retail chain, selling under its own brand in its own automobile service centers.

On the other hand, a maker of a lesser brand of tires may relinquish leadership even for its own brand products to selected strong independents or to an oil company with strong market franchises.

Initiating sellers create their consumer franchises through an effective mass communications mix, reinforced by wide distribution. An intermediary merchant creates such a franchise best through a well-designed merchandise plan which develops strong patronage relationships with important market segments.

Some degree of relative size is required to assure the resources vital to develop and exercise leadership. Size alone does not guarantee leadership. Size must be accompanied by the will and the interest, as well as organizational and marketing expertise.

When perceived physical differentiation is not substantial, some degree of leadership can be exerted by developing merchandise plans and aids to simplify the promotional efforts or dealers, or otherwise make their selling job easier. Any effort which increases the profit potential for the dealer helps strengthen the distribution channel.

Distribution channels vary in length, and any seller has only limited freedom of choice in building them.

The Channel Choices

Planning distribution requires making 3 choices:
- What type of operation is to be used at each stage of distribution
- Whether to attempt to sell through a wholly owned channel or through independent intermediaries at some or all stages

- To what degree sales outlets shall be limited, especially at the final buyer stage

In most sales situations, the initiating seller is limited by the types of outlets available, and by the degree of promotional support needed or useful at that stage of the market life cycle. The commonly used channels which might be open to choice are discussed in the appendix to this chapter. No definitive list, complete in every detail, is possible. As with all other aspects of marketing, distribution channel design is subject to the effects of imaginative innovation. Elements may be combined into producer-integrated channels, into wholesale integrated chains, or be independently owned at each step in the chain of distribution.

Any such list is necessarily somewhat simplified. Thus a real estate agent or broker represents the seller of tangible real property, but also may act to place mortgage loans (an "intangible") for a mortgage banker in order to facilitate sales. Operative home builders quite often arrange directly with banks and insurance companies to obtain mortgages wholesale, and, in effect, sell the mortgages as part of the assortment offered to home buyers, as traffic items at little or no margin for themselves.

As already noted, the oldest form of distribution to distant buyers consisted of chains of independent merchants, each buying for his own account, and selling to the next link in the chain. Most goods and services were produced locally and sold directly from craftsman or farmer producer to the customer, with no specialized sales personnel in between.

Neither form of distribution is important today in industrialized countries. Even the independent merchant has to be part of an organized system of patronage relationships, and what is known as direct selling involves some form of intermediary--a force of professional salesmen, or an advertising agency or internal professionalized advertising department.

Direct Sales

Direct personal sales to user organizations is common for industrial goods when the quantities bought are quite large and buyers relatively concentrated. Such is the case for most raw materials and semifabricated materials, major industrial components, and capital equipment purchased by large organizations. (Smaller industrial customers tend to be supplied by special industrial wholesalers.) Many such purchases require after-sales service or occasional technical service, which require the personal contact. Usually, such personal selling is supported by catalogs and special literature. Substantial reorder quantities are often purchased directly by telephone or mail.

Direct in-person selling of mass market items is feasible under either of two circumstances:

- The value of the individual order is relatively high, and personal sales effort can both stimulate perception of value and crystallize a buy decision which might otherwise not be made. Insurance, fine china, silver ware, and vacuum cleaners often use this channel. It is especially useful during the market development, growth, and early maturity phase of the market life cycle.

- Some market segment(s) perceive in-home buying a real convenience and the assortment bought makes the order large enough to justify personal sales cost. Such has proved true for young mothers with pre-school children, in the purchase of cosmetics and toiletries and even some household supplies, as well as home delivered bakery and dairy products. The same segments are profitable targets for catalog sales by mail and telephone, when the offerings are well-established and standardized.

Mail and telephone order sales by catalog or descriptive brochures are feasible when:
- The offering needs no significant individual fitting to the buyer's needs
- Buyers understand the benefit bundle well enough that a good catalog description is all that is needed, or at most, needs to be supplemented only by small samples (such as small swatches of cloth)
- No substantial after-sales mechanical service is required, or else such service is supported by adequately located service centers

For at least some major part of the market, most industrial operating supplies require some kind of intermediary stocking in key locations in order to assure quick delivery, and often also supplementary items in the buyers' desired assortments.

Constant availability and wide assortments are especially important in consumer offerings, so that direct selling tends to be a minor channel for most consumer goods.

In both situations, producers must choose between some degree of integrated channel and independent distributors.

Using Integrated Intermediaries

The independent distributor can have a lot to offer--**if** the right one is available. Such, unfortunately is not always the case, and the producer may have to develop one or more links of the distribution chain himself.

The independence of distributors also means that they are free to follow their own plans, not those of the source. This is part of the price the source pays for the services they may provide: access to a well-developed patronage franchise, financing, the development of a strong assortment of items not supplied by the source but desired by the buyers, etc.

In some situations, the values added may not be worth the price. This is true where no available distributor attracts enough of the right market segments, or when the promotional efforts of no available distributor is strong enough to gain an adequate market share. It may also be the case when the assortment produced by the source does not match a major part of the assortment the distributor would need to assemble.

In all of these circumstances, the producer may find it wise to integrate forward in the channel to whatever degree is necessary to achieve the market share perceived as available.

Channel integration can be forward, as when the producer creates or acquires his own wholesale or retail operations. It can also be backward, as when wholesalers or retailers, or both, acquire their own captive sources of supply. Such integration makes good economic sense when the assortments are fairly well matched and the quantities handled not too far apart.

BACKWARD INTEGRATION OF DISTRIBUTION

Most chain operations, especially in the food field, tend to avoid producing their own merchandise. In addition, a number of chains do process some high volume items whose processing requires no very high level attention. Many chains roast their own special coffee blends, which tend to be sold at attractive prices, as traffic items. A number do some of their own production of baked goods. In recent years, developments in agriculture have led some to get into production of dairy products and eggs.

In the case of milk and eggs, the situation is the same: industrialization of the process on a mass basis. One West Coast chain was said by competitors to derive its entire net profit from its dairy operation. An operation which can sell its entire production as fresh milk can be very profitable because milk sold by independent producers gets a blend of price: the average of the price for milk going into fresh milk and cream usage and a lower price for that going into manufacture of butter, cheese and other "manufacturing" uses. West coast dairy farms are highly mechanized operations, with large herds penned up and fed from hay and grain imported from distant farming areas.

Chains in a number of parts of the country now get their eggs from their own industrialized henneries, housing as many as 500,000 to I million feathered assembly line producers in cages, feed from moving belts. They started doing this when caged production became the mode by which nearly all eggs were produced.

Previously, eggs had been produced as a common source of income on farms in every part of the country, usually in flocks of 500 or 1,000 birds. The eggs from such operations were sold to assemblers called country buyers, who put together the production in the local community to be shipped out in truckloads. When caged production became dominant in the late 1950's, the minimum flock size quickly became 5,000 hens, with each flock producing enough eggs to by-pass the local buyers. Production quickly concentrated in the hands of a few specialized "factories." The new type of egg producer did not raise his own laying flock, but bought almost-ready-to-lay pullets (young hens) at 20 weeks of age, caged them through the heavy producing first year, then disposed of them to make room for some more pullets.

Egg production became a relatively predictable factory operation needing no very high level of judgment. A flock of 500,000 could supply all of the eggs needed by a large chain, and save some distribution steps. Large chains which did not directly own their egg producing sources tended to contract with a local operator for his entire supply.

Some degree of actual or de facto integration is almost inevitable when the assortment st the lower level parallels a large part of the assortment made available by the source. Then one major reason for the distributor's independence disappears: the need to make his own choice of which items in the mix to promote most heavily, and how.

Such is commonly the case in item sales so large that they get very careful consideration by buyers: major plant and equipment in industrial markets, passenger automobiles bought by final consumers, sales of homes by large operative builders, major raw materials and industrial components bought in quantity. In such cases, the distributor becomes a company representative in effect. The only real choice is between company-financed sales operations and privately financed, company franchised operations. In either case, the working relationship cannot be at arm's length--it must be very close.

An absolute matching of assortments is rarely possible. If the match even comes very close, integration is almost certain. The savings in transaction and promotional costs alone are substantial, especially when the added administrative costs are not large. Production cost savings made possible by close scheduling can also be attractive.

Integration has its hidden costs. To be sure of adequate supplies, large merchants have often had to create their own sources. They have nearly always spun them off when the producing industries involved became more mature. Production and merchandising administration do not tend to mix well. Also, merchandising profits depend heavily on constant readjustment of the merchandise mix to follow customer trends. The objectives of production are normally to keep costs down by avoiding as much change as possible. Merchants who own their own sources, or are owned by them, thus face an internal conflict of interest not faced by those who are independent.

Both complete producer- to- consumer integration and complete independence of every step in the channel together account for only a minor volume of the total transactions in our economy. The common choices concern the degree and type of interdependence and cooperation.

The producer naturally desires the enthusiastic inventorying, display and promotion on the entire line by every distributor. The extent to which this is wise for the distributor depends on the degree to which the content and quality of the assortment desired by the distributors' customers matches the assortment produced. It also depends on the importance to the distributor's merchandise plan of the line offered by the producer. The producer can make the profit possibilities more attractive by the right price discount, advertising allowances, and promotional activities.

The most important elements in maintenance of close cooperation is a mutual compatibility of interest in the same market segments, a common understanding of what is needed to serve that market, and complementary abilities in serving it.

Really full cooperation means that the distributor parallels the source's general advertising efforts with local promotion, features the source's planned sales events, makes full use of whatever training help the source offers. Cooperation involves serving actively as the source's local market intelligence, feeding back information useful in planning offering improvements, better service arrangements, any aspect of marketing strategy and tactics, and efficient production scheduling.

THE AUTOMOBILE INDUSTRY'S DEALER REPORTS: WHY NEEDED

Automobile dealers 10-day reports on sales and inventories are steady news items in the financial press. They are also what they started out to be—a vital feedback of market conditions, necessary to keep production in line with sales. They arose out of the problems GM encountered when duPont and Sloan took over GM in the early 1920's. Up until 1924, each division of GM set its own production plans, quite often on the basis of the optimism of its own sales people. Sales had been so good in 1923 that production could not keep up. As often happens even today in many industries, the divisions made their production plans on the assumption that the boom in sales would continue.

By early March, 1924, when the figures for the previous November–January sales became available, GM headquarters got some hints that production was already outrunning sales at GM, and also probably in the whole industry. Some cutbacks in production were ordered, but the full extent of the industry overproduction did not become apparent until Sloan and another official made a trip in May to talk to dealers about other matters, and it became apparent that the cutbacks had been far too small—that the dealers were overloaded for months ahead. Production was drastically curtailed, but it took several months to work off the excess dealer inventories.

As a result, as Sloan related it:

"We worked out in 1924 and 1925 a system of statistical reports to be sent by dealers to the divisions every 10 days. The core of these reports was the information on dealers' sales of cars and trucks to consumers and the number of both new and used cars in dealers' lots. Used car inventories were important because if they backed up in the hands of dealers they would block the sale of new cars. With this information in hand...the divisions and headquarters staff were then able to take corrective action and make forecasts with greater accuracy."

On the source's part, cooperation requires careful planning of advertising and promotion, with close attention to the coordinated timing of promotion with the placement and distribution of any inventories and supplies needed for the promotions. It requires developing of sound training programs for the distributor's sales personnel, and of management aids which will make the distributor's entire operation more efficient. It means developing a logistics program which places the minimum financial load on the distributor while ensuring top quality customer service.

Developing Coordinated Logistics Systems

Mass production and mass distribution of offerings of every kind has its own costs:

- The cost of the scheduling and moving of offerings from relatively centralized locations to outlets properly located to best serve a widely dispersed market.
- The cost of maintaining the opposite flow of information needed for adequate scheduling and coordination of the timing and location of the offerings through the outlets, and the concomitant timing of the intricacies of all aspects of sales communications required.

Until recent decades, the outflow and inflow were handled quite independently in most organizations. Even storage and transportation were separate assignments, resulting in substantial inefficiencies. Total costs of a logistics system are often best kept down by trading off more costly shipping against the cost of keeping larger inventories.

The really central trade-off is between customer service time and convenience and the cost of furnishing it. Solutions are often intricate enough to require substantial computer capacity, but are theoretically rather straight-forward, once a feasible objective is determined.

The problem is to determine what the level of service should be. Even casual observation of the kinds of service choices people make would indicate that the answer depends on the target segment, and also on the state of the supply/demand balance at the time. Costs themselves change with changes in the economy and in interest rates.

For all these reasons, whatever solution is adopted must be constantly reviewed. Fortunately, recent technological advances in transactions recording and communications have greatly speeded up the flow of the information needed to streamline inventories and the order flow. Electronic point-of-sale equipment makes it possible to transmit up-to the-minute information on demand and sales back up the distribution channel.

When full advantage is taken of these advances, including the UPC (Universal Product Codes) on products, many of the operating costs of distribution will be diminished. The same advances will almost certainly change the relationships within channels, creating an even greater interdependence of all members.

SUMMARY

Most offerings today move from producer to final consumer through intermediary distributors. These intermediaries are needed to bridge 3 kinds of disparities between the producer's offerings and the customer's needs: assortment disparities, differences in the scale of production and the scale of consumption, differences in location.

Distributors also frequently complete the total offering to better match the needs of their customers, help in the financing, handle a substantial portion of communications, and serve as sources of market intelligence.

Producers' distribution policies can be anywhere in the range from intensive through selective to exclusive. The best policy depends on the phase of the market life cycle, the character of the offering, and the competitive position of the producer.

A distribution channel is also a two-way information conduit, yielding knowledge about market demand, about competitive developments, information on promotional plans, and on production and merchandising plans.

Some one member of the channel must take the leadership for that channel and the specific offering. Just which member assumes the leadership depends on relative financial strength, relative market strength, relative access to information on customer demand patterns, the planning lead time, and the needed form of communications.

The extremes of leadership position are characterized in terms of two polar forms of communication strategy: push strategies and pull strategies. Pull strategies require upstream leadership. Push strategies are associated with downstream leadership.

Channel leadership is also closely associated with the strength of the customer franchise possessed by the specific seller.

In any specific situation, the sellers' choices are limited by the outlets available, and the degree of promotional support useful at the specific stage of the marketing life cycle.

In general, channels fall into one of three classes: direct sales, integrated intermediaries, and independent intermediaries.

Efficient production and distribution requires a well-coordinated logistics system, designed to produce the optimum balance between customer service time and the cost of providing service.

FOOD FOR THOUGHT AND DISCUSSION

FOREMOST–McKESSON: TURNING A DOGGY DIVISION INTO A STAR

By all of the rulebooks on portfolio management, the large distributor conglomerate, Foremost–McKesson, should have gone ahead and dropped its drug wholesaling operation in 1976, and it almost did. Return on equity was a measly 5.9%, and growth really negative—profit growth was a nominal 2%, far less than inflation, according to a writeup in Business Week ("Foremost–McKesson: the computer moves distribution to center stage," Business Week, Dec. 7, 1981). Instead, officials decided to bring the business into the late 20th century, to apply computer technology to operations, with the aim of making Foremost so valuable to its manufacturing suppliers and to its retail customers that they could not afford to bypass the firm. Apparently they succeeded. By 1981, profit was growing at a 20% per year rate.

Foremost accomplished this by using the computer to automate its own operations and by making its data processing so useful to both suppliers and customers that it became part of their marketing operations.

One of the important early steps was to computerize its own procurement operations. Starting with a single computer link to a drug manufacturer in 1976, it had links with 32 by 1981. This enabled the firm to handle double the volume with only 13 people in its pharmaceutical purchasing staff, compared with 140 in 1976.

Through computer analysis of its own sales data, Foremost is aiding manufacturers to manage inventories, collect and analyze market data, and plan sales campaigns and even new product development.

For its retailer customers, Foremost has leased electronic ordering equipment to them, hand-held machines used right in the aisles, developed and set up a computerized accounts receivable program that helps pharmacists offer charge accounts to their preferred customers, and made available a microcomputer system which enables them to do their bookkeeping and analyze their markets.

On top of this, Foremost has a prescription card system which companies can give to their employees to obtain prescriptions at 41,000 drug stores across the country, at $2 per prescription. Foremost acts as a clearing house, collecting the charges and billing the corporations, then distributing the payments to the drug stores. While a fee is collected, the major value is the tight tie the system makes with the retailer.

Among the other important ventures were:

- Creating a 1,000 person rack jobbing service for retail stores, which saves stores labor and brings marketing knowledge to the sales of costume jewelry, cosmetics and other small items to the retailer.
- Designing drug stores for retailer chains
- Taking waste products for recycling, as well as finished goods, from chemical manufacturers.
- Researching new uses for products it gets from manufacturers.

The rack jobbing grew out of a realization that the drug stores were not doing a good job with the jewelry line it was selling them. Investigation convinced them that store employees were doing a poor job of stocking the racks. Foremost persuaded some store owners to let them service the racks with their own crews. When sales went up by 80%, they expanded the operation nationwide, and store owners appeared happy to save the labor and get the job done right.

One of the major projects was a joint marketing venture in 1979 with Monsanto, on the Monsanto chemical preservative, potassium sorbate. It was expected that the principal market would be Foremost's food processing customers, but some investigation indicated that cosmetic makers might also be interested in the ability to extend shelf life of their products. The result was a "dramatic jump" in sorbate sales.

The lessons learned in the computerizing of the drug wholesaling operations have been used to streamline Foremost's own chemical operations, improving ordering and invoicing procedures, and develop customer profiles. Centralized inventory analysis of the 1200 products moving through its 72 chemical warehouses makes it possible to serve regional rather than local markets.

A similar system installed in its wine and spirits division was expected to identify changes in consumer tastes quickly, for use by both retailer customers and by manufacturers.

1. What implications do you see in this kind of development for the future of distribution in general: food, hard lines, fashion apparel, etc.?

2. Distributors of industrial goods face a different kind of market. What aspects

of the techniques outlined above might have implications for industrial distributors, such as distributors of industrial supplies, or distributors of materials and tools to small fabricators such as machine shops, fiber glass fabricators, automobile service garages, etc.?

NEW DEVELOPMENTS IN THE DISTRIBUTION OF BANKING SERVICES

The 1980's will doubtless be marked by historians as the era of the big financial services revolution. The first skirmishes probably date from the mid 1970s, when stock brokers started experimenting with ownership of insurance companies. Merrill Lynch & Co. acquired the small Seattle-based Family Life Insurance Company in 1974 and started testing the feasibility of selling insurance to its clients out of 14 of its offices. The previous year, Dean Witter started training some of its brokers to sell life insurance and moved to acquire Surety Financial Corp., a Salt Lake City life insurance holding company in 1976. At that time, the brokers' moves seemed to be little more than another way of capitalizing on their relationships with some obviously excellent prospects for insurance.

Meanwhile, with the rising interest rates of the late 1970s and the early 1980s, money mutual funds, many affiliated with brokerage houses, attracted a substantial portion of the liquid savings funds of the nation, much of it at the expense of the savings and commercial banks. These money funds began to carry out some of the checking account business formerly largely reserved to commercial banks. By the late 1970's the Savings and Loan Banks also went after the checking deposits with NOW accounts. Commercial banks were then permitted to offer NOW accounts at the beginning of 1981. Meanwhile, both types of banks were losing business to the money funds.

Finally, Merrill Lynch merged the money fund concept with their brokerage accounts with their Cash Management Accounts, and other brokers started to follow.

Banks themselves had meanwhile taken over much of the short-time retail credit through their Master Card and Visa Card efforts, and some started to issue debit cards which permitted customers to use their checking accounts without bothering to write checks. In these latter services, banks apparently felt that they had services somewhat less vulnerable to the competition from the brokers.

The governmental climate was getting more favorable to the idea of a true national banking system, with banks operating across state lines, but the smaller institutions were exercising strong political influence to block or retard this movement.

Then two 1981 events changed everything: a merger of American Express, the largest issuer of credit cards and traveler's checks, with the brokerage house of Shearson Loeb Rhoades Inc., and the grand merger of Dean Witter, a major broker, Sears, Roebuck, a retailer which had a well established insurance subsidiary in Allstate Insurance Company, and the large real estate firm of Coldwell Banker & Co., with the avowed aim of becoming "the largest consumer-oriented financial service entity," making use of its nationwide retail stores to handle these financial services. Both of these mergers were capable of providing services very similar to those of banks, without having to submit to banking regulation restraints.

Just how successful the Sears, Dean Witter alliance will prove will take time to find out. As a Wall Street Journal story on the merger indicated, the Street's old guard was skeptical, and a little condescending: they immediately dubbed the merger "Socks'n'Stocks, reflecting a belief that merchandising and brokerage did not mix.

One of "Wall Street's most powerful investment bankers" is quoted as "solemnly intoning" that "People will buy fertilizers and washing machines from Sears, but not stocks and bonds." (**The Wall Street Journal,** "Socks'n'Stocks: Sears attempt to link retailing and investing raises brokers' doubts," Nov. 19, 1982)

Actually, Sears was not rushing to put brokerage offices in all of its over 800 stores. Centers were set up in eight metropolitan areas, in locations near obviously well-to-do residents: Cupertino and Costa Mesa, California, Fairfax, Va., Chicago, Houston, Dallas, Denver, and Atlanta. The store financial counters are "centrally located and highlighted with bold design features to attract customers." They were staffed with Dean Witter brokers, a representative of the Sears long-time insurance affiliate, Allstate Insurance, and by a real estate representative from Coldwell Banker & Company.

For the most part, Dean Witter would continue to operate out of its 348 offices. Dean Witter did claim, however, that the Sears counters had proved effective in getting new business, opening more new accounts than the average Dean Witter office.

The major asset Sears brought to the business was felt to be its 25 million charge customers. The retailer claimed that a computer check showed that of the 9.5 million households doing business with any big board member, 7 million were Sears customers.

Initial efforts to use the Sears mailing list for investment promotion drew mixed results. An attempt to promote the Dean Witter IRA account through stuffers in a Sears mailing bombed out. The Dean Witter chairman felt that that was not the best kind of product to sell by mail—it took person-to-person explanation, he felt. But Dean Witter did raise $400 million for the Sears U. S. Government Money Market Trust through sales to Sears customers.

Part of everyone's hopes, obviously, was a carry over of Sears image of reliability and safety, going back to its standard mail order policy of unquestioned refunds on purchases. But one investment analyst wondered about this, "Just because they'll come and fix the washing machine they sold you doesn't mean they'll take back an investment that turns sour in a down market."

Nevertheless, there were some hints that the Sears consumer franchise did carry some aura. One local business man walked into the Cupertino center and left $3 million in cash and securities with the Dean Witter broker there. And at another outlet, "an elderly woman" spoke out at length to the broker stationed there about her distrust of all brokers. When he mentioned that he himself was a registered stockbroker, she is reported to have corrected him, "No, you're not. You are a Sears employee," and opened an account with him.

******

However much the brokers may have sneered at the merger, bankers were not sneering at these developments. They were worried that their turf would be taken over by such financial giants before the regulatory wraps were taken off their freedom to compete. They were especially concerned about the entrance of the credit cards, already competing with their own Visa and Master Charge accounts. According to a Business Week report of January 18, 1982, key executives from a "dozen of the largest U. S. and Canadian banks" flew into Chicago's O'Hare airport for a secret meeting the month before, and this was only one of a dozen of such meetings which had been held to talk over the sharing of their automated teller machines (AtMs) is such a way that any of their customers could go to one with his debit card to obtain cash.

A number of such ATM networks were being formed, with the hope of consolidating retail banking services in the same manner that consumer credit services had been organized by the Master Card and Visa interbank credit cards. Visa itself was pushing one such network. With the debit card (which has a superficial appearance of a credit card), a customer could go to any participating ATM and make an electronic withdrawal of cash, make a deposit in a checking or savings account, transfer funds between accounts, or make a balance inquiry. The networks foresaw a day when they would be expanded to include electronic transfers from home or from some merchant's point-of-sale terminal, to pay for purchases. In fact, some banks were already experimenting with in-home terminals.

Many banks, however. were resisting the Visa and Master Card networks, not wishing to share their ATMs with local rivals. One problem the banks currently have is the fact that they are still forbidden to conduct retail operations outside their own state boundaries (and in some states, such as Illinois, even outside their own neighborhoods). The banks are afraid that such outside financial enterprises as those represented by recent mergers would have captured much of the business before 1985, the earliest date that Congress appeared likely to repeal the 1927 McFadden Act prohibition against interstate branch banking.

****

1. Considering, first, the Sears mergers and any others like it that might occur, what investor segments are likely to make use of the Sears store outlets, and which will probably not? Why? Is it likely to add to the size of the total individual investor market, or simply share it? Why? If it does add, what other types of financial institutions are likely to lose out, and why?

2. What types of brokerage services are likely to get attention from the segments who would deal through Sears store outlet, which ones are likely to get little attention from these segments, and why?

Looking at the banking networks, let us think about what can be learned from credit card experience:

3. The situation currently is that 3 general charge cards dominate the scene: American Express, Visa, and Master Charge. Two others have not done so well: Diner's Club and Carte Blanche. What seems to have given the 3 strong ones the ability to attract customers which the other two, started no later than Visa and Master Charge did not?

4. To some extent, the 3 dominant cards have also displaced many of the more specialized cards, such as oil company cards. Why?

5. There is no question that both Visa and Master Charge have been aggressively marketed, but so was Diner's Club and Carte Blanche. Why do so many people carry the three dominant cards, especially those that seldom or never borrow beyond the billing date (about half of the cardholders)?

6. Assuming that debit cards eventually become the dominant method of handling consumer banking and perhaps other transactions services, what will the kinds of customers who will make up the early growth portion of the market want in a card and network arrangement? Why? Think carefully about what bankers proposing them are thinking of, and whether that fits the needs of the kinds of segments who might adopt such cards early?

7. What market segments are most likely to be among the early majority in adoption, and why?

8. Why should these developments be placed in discussion with this chapter?

NOW: GET YOUR TEETH AT YOUR NEARBY FRIENDLY SEARS STORE!

"Retail dentistry" is very much in the news. A January, 1981 story in Business Week called attention to the growing movement, and the Feb. 21, 1983 Fortune called attention to an inevitable consequence—the mushrooming growth of retail dental franchises. Some of the earliest were in stores of Montgomery Ward, Sears, regional chains and discount stores, and pharmacies such as People's Drug Stores in Washington, D.C. They appear to have no problem getting customers.

According to Business Week, it was already a $100 million business by the end of 1980, and growing fast.

While it was originally thought that it might attract people who would not otherwise go to a dentist, and was often heavily advertised on price, this has not proved to be the case.

What obviously does attract a clientele is the hours (8AM to 9PM), the acceptance of credit cards, the ability to combine the trip with shopping, and the ability to walk in and get instant care. People do not seem to care that they do not always get the same dentist.

The development was made possible by a Supreme Court decision of 1977 and the following FTC rulings which abolished the professional bars against advertising. Dental societies have tried to erect barriers against the practice, but have been stymied by the oversupply of new dental graduates, the ability of the new enterprises to advertise, and the high cost of establishing a new practice.

Generally, the franchise organizers promise to oversee every detail of managing a dentist-franchisee's group practice—site location, leasing and improvement, helping to hire the staff, and conducting the ad campaign to get in the first wave of patients. By law, the franchisee must himself be a dentist.

As the head of one franchise puts it, "We tell the doctor what day to show up and start practicing dentistry, and he arrives and has a full book." The franchisor continues to supervise the operation, supplying a standard management and accounting system, and the owner of the franchise becomes mainly an administrator. The attractions for the staff are obvious. The typical dental graduate owes around $50,000 for his education, and must raise an additional $100,000 to establish an office of his own. As a franchise employee, he can be sure of an income of from $30,000 to $45,000 immediately, or at least 20% to 30% more than he could hope for on his own. Even the purchaser of the franchise need only put down from $7500 to $50,000, and he can hope for a 15% to 20% profit after all expenses.

The costs to the patients tends to be about 10% to 15% less than the normal individual practice yields, but price has not proved to be an allure for patients. To some extent, price advertising tends to be associated with a perception of low quality, so this approach is being abandoned. Shopping mall locations are favored, and patients are often furnished beepers to take with them into the stores around while they wait their turn.

Meanwhile, other professionals are considering similar ventures: optometrists (Searle's Pearle Vision Centers are already a large chain), podiatrists, chiropractors, and hearing aid specialists.

1. What social changes, might have made this system of distributing dental services an attractive one for many segments?

2. What trends in the life styles of American people could have contributed to the perceived value of a professional service distributed in this manner, and why?

3. What elements in the offering, other than location, would seem to give it special value and why?

4. What implications do you see in this development for the distribution of other forms of professional service, which ones, and why?

5. Why would a patient trust an unknown dentist in a franchise?

CHICAGO RAWHIDE AND SCM: PRODUCERS TURNED DISTRIBUTORS

Chicago Rawhide's name dates back to the earlier days when rawhide packings were used to keep lubricants from leaking from driveshaft bearings. Later, as the various rubbery compounds became available, they developed packaged oil seals of these elastomers and metal to do a better job. CRI earned a reputation for quality among producers of all kinds of machinery and equipment, from automobiles and road machinery builders to the aircraft industry.

Looking around for new products, CRI executives thought they saw an opening in what seemed to be a growing market in hydraulic seals, something which might take advantage of CRI's expertise in designing products with synthetic rubbers. Investigation turned up one interesting item: O-rings (so named because of their kind of thin doughnut shape).

Survey of the industry revealed quite a few producers already well established, including one firm which made a very high quality product, but had a weak marketing effort and little industry penetration. They made an agreement with this producer to take on sales of his line, and duly cataloged it.

******

As did other typewriter manufacturers, Smith-Corona had long made and sold a line of typewriter supplies: ribbons, carbon paper, etc. The line was not unprofitable, but SCM finally decided to streamline its operation and abandon the manufacturing. The production facilities were spun off to a separate corporation, with the proviso that SCM would continue to sell them under its own label.

1. Why should a producer of an offering give up or avoid production of a line and act only as a distributor, under its own label?

2. Why should some other organization take on production of an offering which is not sold under its own label?

THE DISTRIBUTION PLAN THAT FLOPPED

A certain large general merchandise mail order firm we shall call Rural Mail Order (RMO) sold entirely by mail until after World War II, unlike some of its competitors who had retail store chains. As a result its losses during the war were especially heavy.

All merchants of every kind suffered from severe merchandise shortages and uncertainties during the war. The mail order firms were especially hurt because they would list items in their catalogs, prepared months before the receipt of their purchases, and then not be able to fulfill the orders when they came in. The problem was magnified by the fact that the missing items were those most heavily ordered, as consumer's searched desperately to get wanted items. A cancelled order costs as much to handle as one that is filled, and incurs a return postage cost in addition. All mail order firms lost money during the war, but none were hit harder than RMO. Besides lacking store chains which would not have been hurt so badly, its prewar business had been based entirely on consumer credit, which credit restrictions killed.

Deciding that it would have to get into chain store operation after the war, RMO used the tax advantages of its accumulated losses to purchase some going ladies apparel stores. Unfortunately, MRO's managerial decision system was highly centralized. Buying for the chains was centralized at headquarters, and every store was allotted the same lines and inventory. It was felt that the extensive card tabulating operation which had been acquired with the purchase of the chains would be an adequate control.

The diversification into chain retailing did not work out. Although the chains purchased had been profitable when bought, the average unit sales in the stores went on a decline, with the average ticket going down steadily, in a period when prices in general were rising. Eventually, MRO spun off the chains at a loss and got out of the chain store business.

1. Both MRO's experience and Pvt. Smith's shoe problem cited earlier point to one obvious lesson: different localities have different merchandise tastes and requirements. What does this tell us about the management needs of any distribution system?

2. How can a chain operation best handle this management problem?

APPENDIX: THE RANGE OF DISTRIBUTION CHANNELS

The list below outlines the commonly used distribution channels of distribution. As with everything else in marketing, the definitions are not very precise because there are constant variations due to the innovative imagination of people who find a way to make profits by rendering some new kind of service for which someone feels the need.

There are also some ambiguities. Are OEM buyers customers, or a channel to reach their customers: in other words, is General Motors simply a customer for the tires on its cars, tires which carry the name of the tire manufacturer? Or is GM a major channel for the manufacturer?

Similarly, when a manufacturing firm, in order to round out its assortment, chooses to buy some items from others and sell them under its own label, is it a channel or a customer? The practice is common. For example, a steel company which dominates the manufacture and sale of the widest line of industrial fasteners (nuts, bolt, rivets, screws, etc.), nevertheless purchases "specials" (low volume items made to tight specifications) from others, to sell as part of its line.

Is a manufacturer who makes a commitment to carry out the entire wholesaling operation for some market segments not well covered by another firm, selling under the other firm's label, with its own sales force carrying related assortments, is it a wholesaler?

Marketing is a circular process. Once we reach adulthood and become a part of the total economy, we are all both producers and customers, and to some extent, nearly all of us are to some degree distributors of offerings produced by others.

The usual institutions of distribution can be grouped into six logical classes:

- Direct sales operations
- Markets and fairs
- Sales negotiators
- Intermediary sellers, wholesale and retail
- Franchisees
- Licensees

Direct Sales Operations

Without intermediate sales representation: direct from producer to buyer.
Usually either: (a) very large scale sales between large organizations and implied or explicit long term contracts, or relatively small scale operations, especially of a personal service nature—handicraft, custom production, medical or legal services, etc.

With some kind of personal sales or other professional promotional aid
Through salesmen calling on prospective and present customers. An expensive channel on a per call basis, which requires an adequate return to cover the expense. A necessity under a number of circumstances which require some kind of dialog or other personal sales service, outlined in the chapters which follow this one.

Telephone sales, usually aided by some kind of catalog or other descriptive advertising. Best suited to relatively standard, well understood items for which the customer needs little more information than is furnished by a printed description and a price list.

Telephone sales without supplementation with literature. Generally requires some familiar form of offering, with sales responsive to some degree of short personal presentation. Most useful in soliciting contributions for non-profit enterprises.

Catalog sales by mail or computer link. An economical channel especially adapted to standard familiar items and quite common for reorder of frequently purchased items.

Sales through independent sales representatives (manufacturers representatives, food brokers, etc.) For the producer, the operation is not essentially different from one using the producer's own sales force. Representatives act as regional sales offices, working on commissions mutually agreed to, covering defined market segments in an exclusive territory.

Generally, such representatives carry related non-competing lines of other sellers, making up an assortment needed by the market segments with which they have developed contacts. They are especially useful for very limited line producers, for covering territories in which the demand would be too thin to justify use of the producer's own sales force, and/or getting quick access to new market segments in which they have experience and well-developed contacts with the major buying influences. A channel mainly useful in industrial markets and in contacting wholesalers or large retailers.

Markets, Fairs, Shows

An extension of one of the oldest forms of one-stop merchandising. Under whatever title, the market or fair brings together competing sellers or their representatives, provides facilities for exhibiting the offerings in some manner, and by its size and range of choice, acts as a magnet for interested buyers.

Still exist in the original form in many of the less developed areas of the world, and, in the form of "flea markets", even in the advanced areas. In addition, markets, shows and exhibitions are important forms of sales promotions for many kinds of industrial goods, and a wholesale channel for other kinds, such as toys, furniture, and apparel. A major sales channel for heavy industrial goods in major international markets.

Sales Negotiators

The above is not a standard term, but seems to be the best fit for a group of important channels comprised of sales agents, commission merchants, auctions, and merchandise brokers.

Sales agents take on the responsibility of selling the entire output of a producer on a continuing basis, often combining the lines of related producers to produce an assortment attractive to a market. Clients can be small manufacturers or seasonal producers. They often extend such management assistance as product planning, financing, and credit and collections.

Commission merchants accept lots of goods on consignment for resale. They do whatever warehousing may be necessary, and handle sales and collection efforts. They were long the dominant channel for farm produce and livestock, and many of them were and are agents of farmer cooperatives. Their role has diminished greatly in recent years because of the dominance of large farms selling in volume and the use of direct telephone sales to large buying organizations.

Auctions accept offerings for public sale on competitive bids. They are most important in the public exchange of items in which the no individual seller or buyer is dominant and the market wide and fluid, as in investment securities and in major raw natural commodities. They are also important in other areas in which each item sold may differ in value to some degree from other like items, such as the market for used items and for leaf tobacco. They are a principal means of wholesaling of used cars between dealers.

Merchandise brokers are professional negotiators representing either the buyer or seller, collecting a fee for the service.

Intermediary Sellers

Wholesalers
Wholesaler is a term applied to those merchants who sell offerings produced by others, to buyers who are either resellers themselves, or will use the offerings in production processes.

Although they usually purchase and sell in lots larger than the normal final consumption unit, some of them sell in quantities no larger than, or even smaller than, those bought by some final customers.

Wholesalers are of a number of kinds, classifiable into two major groups: full service wholesalers, and limited function wholesalers. Full service wholesalers include consumer goods wholesalers (including chain warehouses), and industrial distributors. Limited function wholesalers include drop shippers, "service wholesalers" also divided into rack jobbers and wagon jobbers, assemblers and collectors.

One other form is hard to classify: the advertising specialty wholesaler.

Full Service Consumer Goods Merchant Wholesalers

Full-service merchant wholesalers purchase a wide assortment of offerings to match the assortment requirements of their retail customers, warehouse them, and deliver them on order. They grant credit to their customers, usually maintain service on merchandising, store layout, and promotional plans, and set up accounting systems for customers.

The core function of such wholesalers is to search out sources for an appropriate assortment, to maintain stocks for quick delivery, reduce the number of sources with which a retailer must deal, and also the number of outlets the sources must work with. (A typical supermarket handles 8,000 items or more, of which a large portion comes through some wholesale warehouse. In most cities, salesmen for the goods the wholesalers handle need to see no more than a half dozen buying offices.) Such warehouses can be independent suppliers, or a local chain headquarters.

Chain warehouses are wholesalers serving specific groups of retail outlets of the same type, usually doing business under a common name. Their legal structure may be that of the corporate chain, they may be voluntary chains, or they may be retailer—owner cooperative wholesalers. The only real difference is in ownership. Corporate warehouse chain retailers are owned by the corporation (although the same corporation may also supply "associate stores" owned by independent proprietors). In voluntary chains, the retail units are independently owned, operating under the same name and following the same merchandising practices. The retailers served by retailer—owned cooperatives also usually operate under the same name. An exception is the largest one: Certified Grocers in Southern California, whose members include some very large chains operating under their own names.

In practice, chain operation is the same regardless of the pattern of ownership. Buying decisions are made at wholesale headquarters, with individual retail outlets making minor variations in the merchandise mix to fit local assortment needs. Special sale items and promotional plans tend to be centralized, and the headquarters maintains a staff of supervisors who give aid in merchandising and display and make sure of some degree of uniformity in planning. Central headquarters helps in store design and layout, and establishes uniform accounting systems.

Industrial Distributors

Industrial distributors exist to assemble assortments of items purchased by specific industrial market segments and provide quick delivery in the quantities needed. In general, their customers buy in smaller than mill quantity lots, but in the case of some major supply items, they may maintain inventories needed by even the largest consumers of major supply items such as abrasives. Some serve very narrow vertical markets, as do the oil field supply stores and barber and beauty shop distributors. Others may serve a broad spectrum of industrial customers needing some common assortments, such as janitorial supply sources and steel service centers. Usually they maintain some kind of field sales force.

All full service wholesalers pay for the inventories they carry, and grant credit to customers. They thus serve to help finance the distribution of offerings by the producers. So also do other title—taking resellers who carry out more limited functions.

Title—Taking Limited—Function Wholesalers

Limited—function wholesalers include cash—and—carry wholesalers, drop shippers, assemblers and collectors, rack jobbers, and wagon distributors (both of the latter also known as service wholesalers).

Cash-and carry wholesalers are designed to serve the very small retailer: the so-called "mom-and-pop" stores whose trade does not justify economic delivery service, credit and personal sales costs.

Warehouses are self-service, the customer shopping in much the same manner as the householder buys in a supermarket. By limiting the service to assortment availability, such wholesalers can help the small operator buy at prices which enable the small operator to survive.

Drop shippers deal largely in such standardized staples as coal, coke, lumber and other construction materials. They maintain no inventory, deal only in carload or truckload lots, shipped directly from the producer to the industrial buyer. They do take title to the shipments ordered, and are responsible for its sale once purchased, if it meets specifications.

Assembler and collectors bring together the small lots produced, usually, by small producers, concentrating them in lots adequate for large scale shipment. They normally do some sorting and grading of the items before shipment. They were once a key link in the distribution of farm commodities of nearly every kind, bringing together the small lots of milk products, eggs, meat animals, etc., to be forwarded to processors. As country elevators, they are still important in the grain trade, but have virtually disappeared in most major producing areas for most other products because of the concentration of farming in the last generation.

As collectors of secondary materials, especially scrap metals, they are important sources of supply for a number of industrial materials, from paper to platinum.

Rack merchandising has been a growing channel as retail outlets have broadened their merchandise mixes. The rack merchandiser typically furnishes a well-designed display rack, positioned in an appropriate location in the outlet. The rack is stocked with the right assortment of items, checked and put in order regularly, and kept filled with price-marked merchandise. The retail outlet does not buy the merchandise, but is given a substantial margin out of the price of the merchandise sold. In essence, the operation amounts to leasing an outlet's floor space for a percentage of the sales.

Rack jobbers may be an integral part of the original producer's distribution system. Hanes opened the supermarkets to it L'Eggs line of pantyhose by establishing its own rack merchandising operation. The rack merchandiser may be a subsidiary operation of a full-service wholesaler, as the Foremost-McKesson reading above indicates. The health and beauty aids displays in many stores are rack merchandise operations, as are the housewares sections, pet supplies, spice assortments, and periodicals sold. Stores welcome them because they are profitable and take none of the store labor. The only inventory is on the shelves or rack.

Wagon jobbers sell fast-moving perishables and some specialty items from an inventory carried on trucks handled by driver-salesmen. The line carried is narrow, comprised of offerings which cannot be inventoried in quantity because of limited sale or short shelf life: potato chips, oleomargarine, specialty pickles, cheeses, etc.

An Ambiguous Channel: Advertising Specialty and Premium Wholesalers

This group of wholesalers exists to sell items which the purchaser is going to give away, or sell with little or no margin. Probably as many ball point pens reach users through this channel as through normal sales channels. Any novelty with some sort of broad appeal and low cost may be so distributed, imprinted with the giver's name and advertising message. The distributors are really a branch of the advertising industry, and are equipped to design giveaway campaigns.

Premium houses are a somewhat related group of wholesalers, specializing in goods to be used either in sales promotions as self–liquidating premiums, or in goods to be used as sales incentives. Some manufacturers, such as Eastman Kodak, have premium divisions.

Retailers: The Point of Direct Contact with the Consumer

We are all reasonably familiar with the various and changing classes of retailers: supermarkets, department stores, hard lines stores, specialty stores of many kinds (apparel, sporting goods, fabrics, etc.). Some mention should be made of three types of retail outlets for physical goods: consumer service establishments, lease–operations, and the institutional market.

Consumer Service establishments
Barber shops not only cut hair—they constitute an outlet for a small but significant share of the market for hair care products. Similarly, beauty shops form a retail channel for various toiletries and cosmetics.

Lease Operators
Although most of us have often patronized lease operations, we were probably unaware of it. They are common in department stores, especially. These operators help expand the assortment available in the establishment of which they appear to be a part. But they are not under the management of the store—they simply lease the space for a percentage of the revenue. Most of them are personal service operations to some degree, or handle specialty lines which the parent establishment would not find it easy to merchandise. They include such operations as optical departments, beauty shops within stores, key duplicating services, millinery departments, and restaurant operations.

The Institutional Retailer
Institutions such as motels, hotels, schools, restaurants and hospitals have become increasingly important retail outlets for foods in special packaging, and many other kinds of goods packaged to meet their needs, and sold as an integral part of the services they render customers.

Many of these retail operations, and some wholesale operations also, are franchised outlets: a specialized type of channel in itself.

Franchised Operations

Franchising as a means of gaining distribution has advantages for both the franchiser and the franchise owner, when the operation is well managed. The franchiser is enabled to expand operations faster and farther than would be possible with the initial capital resources available, since the franchise purchaser must furnish much of the initial capital. In return, the franchiser is obligated to furnish management aids in getting started and a common identity which makes promotion easier. Since the franchise owner gets all profits less a royalty, such franchise owners have the incentive of any entrepreneur to produce results.

Good management of a franchise should always include substantial training in proven operating procedures, site selection service, a standard design which is both efficient for operation and a badge of identity with recognized value in the consuming public's perception, equipment and supplies purchases which pass on the advantage of volume buying, and a strong, effective promotional campaign. Franchising can be used at any level of operation. Regional Coca–Cola and other soft drink bottlers have always been franchise operations, essentially at the wholesale level (although they do some processing). Everyone is familiar with many service operation franchises at the retail level: MacDonald's, Holiday Inns, Howard Johnson's, to name some well–known ones.

A strong supervisory service is imperative to maintain the value for all franchise owners, holding them to a standard level of service quality.

Licensing as a Method of Distribution

The line between licensing and franchising is a thin one. Licensing usually is primarily a means of gaining both production and distribution, with the help of the licensee's capital investment. Frequently, it is the preferred path to international expansion of an operation, conferring the advantages of operation by native personnel familiar with the market, and a native identity which can be a real political protection at times.

As with franchising, the licensee must be carefully chosen, well trained, and the operation and product quality supervised.

CHAPTER 12. COMMUNICATIONS: GETTING BUYERS AND SELLERS TOGETHER

COMMUNICATIONS:
BRINGING BUYERS & SELLERS TOGETHER

12

The Role of the Communications Mix

Communications are the ties that connect sellers with buyers. Potentially attractive offerings and competitive pricing attract buyers only when well targetted communications penetrate the protective screens of selective attention and selective perception. The two sides get together only after buyers:

- are made aware of offerings which might promise to satisfy some salient desire set,
- are brought to understand the value of the satisfactions promised and convinced of their desirability, and
- are finally persuaded that those values are attractive in relation to the prices charged

Since the marketing effort aims at a continuing relationship, those who purchase need to be constantly reminded and reassured they are receiving the values they sought.

Each element in the communications mix, and the system as a whole, involves four variables:

- the intended audience(s)
- the message
- the media used to carry the message
- the perceived source of the message

Commonly, sellers must reach more than one audience, with messages tuned to the salient needs of each one. To reach all of the intended audiences, sellers must normally use a mix of personal sales, the mass media of advertising and publicity, and of the miscellaneous class called sales promotions.

The Multiplicity of Audiences to Be Addressed

Except for the lone craftsman selling his wares direct, most sellers must address a number of audiences, each with a different set of salient unfulfilled desires. Each such audience will probably need a different

message, delivered in different media. Large sellers may have to reach and convince as many as 8 classes of potential audiences:
- **Fabricators and/or industrial, institutional, or commercial buyers and users.** These need to perceive the seller as the most profitable source of items contributing to the value of their own offerings.
- **Merchants and distributors.** These need to perceive the offering as a potential source of added value for their own assortments.
- **Financial institutions and other investors:** need to perceive the organization as a worthwhile investment. (In the case of non-profit organizations, this would include potential contributors.)
- **Prospective employees, particularly in scarce categories:** need to perceive the organization as offering the most attractive job opportunities.
- **Current employees:** need to be convinced that the organization's best interests are their own best interests, worthy of their most productive efforts.
- **Various segments of the general public, especially active voters and politicians:** need to be brought to perceive the organization as a good citizen whose activities and needs are worthy of their support.
- **Designers, counselors, and prescribers:** need to be persuaded that the offering is an attractive means for solving the needs of those whom they serve as professional advisers.
- **Final buyers:** need to perceive the offering as the preferred source of satisfaction for their desire sets, and be persuaded to develop and continue in the habit of seeking out the offering.

These various audiences fall into 3 interest groups;
- **Direct users** of the offering, either personally as final consumers, or industrially as a supply item. Both are seeking the direct benefits of the offering itself, to satisfy specific desire sets.
- **Fabricators and other resellers**--seeking an opportunity to profit through improvement of their offerings and assortments.
- **Others interested in the seller and the seller's operations:** financial institutions, seeking investment profits; current and prospective employees, seeking attractive personal opportunities; contributors to non-profit organizations, seeking to improve the quality of life in some manner; political interest groups--seeking to enhance, or at least maintain quality of their economic or physical environment.

Even though the actual benefit sought may be different, a single aggressive promotions campaign sometimes is effective in reaching more than one of the audiences targetted.
Knowledge of the weight of a forthcoming ad campaign may convince merchants and other distributors to place orders for offerings fitting their assortments. If the sustained promotion of an offering helps to build strong

potential employees may find a well-known employer more attractive. Securities markets quite clearly pay a higher price for the earnings of well-known organizations.

Similarly, the university or college which is high in the preference of student applicants also is a stronger magnet for contributors.

In most cases, however, the communications mix best for each audience must be different: a different message, carried in different media.

The Message: Its Role and Some General Principles

Effective communications help to sell offerings, but seldom do the whole sales job. Any sale is the end product of a series of communications tasks, using different communications tools and often diverse messages at different points in the communications process.

Various authors have proposed somewhat different labels for different aspects of the communications task, most of them carrying essentially the same meaning. One of the most easily remembered set of labels is keyed to the title of the well-known opera, AIDA:

- Attention (or Awareness of the message and the offering)
- Interest (created by comprehension or understanding of the benefit being offered)
- Desire (aroused by a conviction that a salient desire set will be best satisfied by the offering)
- Action to buy

A fifth step needs to be added to these four: persistent reassurance of the value of the benefits the buyers are getting, after the purchase.

People pay attention to those messages, and only those, which clearly touch on the possible satisfaction of key felt needs in their desire sets. Since desire sets differ, we might expect to find, and we do, that different audiences respond to different messages. Much of the uncertainty and frustration of selling comes from the problem of making prospects aware of the values offered. At best, attention is difficult to gain.

Gaining Attention

The very fact that some of the audience does pay attention is proof that the message has aroused some kind of interest in the offering, and in some aspect of the benefits perceived as promised. Attention does not necessarily lead to action. Research on the diffusion of new products has consistently shown that even early in the product development stage of high learning products, awareness can be very high, but only a few pioneer innovators buy, and then often only on a trial basis.

For offerings requiring much habit change, the initial communications must be directed to the search of those with active, unsatisfied desire-sets: the more likely innovators. The message delivered must strike strongly at the core of the satisfaction lack. Once some trial purchases result, the offering must be perceived as delivering the benefits promised in the communications. The tryers then become part of the communications media.

GETTING ATTENTION, BUT TO WHAT?

A common method of testing ad copy effectiveness is the determination of the degree to which the ad has been remembered by those who had a chance to see it, and how many can recall what was advertised. The copy chief of a large agency was reviewing a set of ratings of this kind before a marketing group. One of the ads was a full center spread in a girly magazine, the entire diagonal of which was a "bathing beauty". The ad had a near perfect "remembered seeing" rating, but a zero rating on what was advertised (men's sox).

The Media Alternatives

Media split into two basic classes: the personal dialog and the mass monolog: the give and take of individual explanation delivered through sales personnel and the mass one-sided presentation of the printed or broadcast media. (Perhaps a third class, consisting of the trial of the offering itself, is worth noting.

Personal sales. Both sellers and buyers place a high value on the services of sales personnel. The expenditure for personal sales, however measured, is several times the combined total for all other marketing communications, testifying to its high standing with sellers. By the same token, the clear results which sellers get from the personal sales effort is strong testimony to the value buyers place on the personal sales contact.

The dialog made possible by personal communications makes them the most flexible and most effective means of fitting the message to the information needs of each individual prospect. Moreover, no other form of marketing communications can yield as complete and as rapid feedback on the identity of prospects, on the specifics of their desire patterns, and on the benefits of the offering as perceived by buyers after purchase.

Personal communications media include, besides the seller's own sales force, independent representatives employed by the seller, and the sales forces of the distributors. Some forms of group selling must also be included: seminars, "talks" by representatives, demonstrations, etc. Outside of the control of the seller, but quite important, are the satisfied buyers and users. The information they pass on to friends and acquaintances are valuable at any time, but especially important during the early phases of the market life cycle.

Because of the immediate feedback from prospects, the salesman need not guess at the proper content of the message.

Unfortunately, personal sales is by far the most expensive form of marketing communication, per prospect contacted. Estimates of the per call costs vary, but as of this writing, the lowest average published is nearly $80 per call. A .300 average is as good in selling as it is in major league baseball. This rules out much personal sales effort at the final retail step of distribution, except for big-ticket sales.

Once an offering is well established and its use-system widely understood, the need for personal selling becomes much less, and other forms of communication may be more cost-effective.

Even during the early stages of the market life cycle, the one-on-one character of personal sales is too slow a process for gaining wide market awareness, and the mix usually needs the support of the mass promotional media of publicity and advertising

The Special Values of Publicity. Only advertising and publicity can provide rapid wide coverage of the market during the introductory period for any kind of offering, whether high learning or low learning. Of these two, publicity, carefully prepared, is by far the more persuasive form of communications during the introductory stage.

Publicity and advertising share many similarities, but differ in three important respects:
- Advertising is paid for by the seller, and the cost is proportional to the coverage. Publicity is not paid for, and its cost (which is largely internal) bears no relationship to the coverage.
- With advertising, the seller has full control of the message, the timing, the media in which the message will appear, and the frequency of its appearance. Publicity is published at the discretion of the medium, the medium controls the content of the message and its timing, and the same story will not normally appear more than once in the same specific medium.
- Advertising is signed by the seller, and the seller is perceived as the source--a source which is not impartial. Publicity, even when published as issued by the seller, appears in the news items, and is perceived as coming from the medium itself, an impartial and often perceived as authoritative source. As one result, publicity gets far more attention than the same story in an advertisement, and the message carries far more credibility, has a greater potential for creating conviction.

Publicity can be an especially valuable communications tool for the non-profit institution whose activities carry a high degree of community interest, such as schools, hospitals, and symphony orchestras. The media virtually welcome items from such organizations with open arms, provided that it is prepared with an eye to its news value. An understanding of the satisfaction attributes offered by the organization can be convincingly presented to various audiences by means of a steady stream of well-chosen publicity prepared by a competent small staff with both an eye for newsworthiness and an understanding of of what these audiences are seeking.

While the for-profit business enterprise has less easy access to publicity, the opportunities are there, and the advantages justify a competent professional effort not always given.

For the public institution, publicity may fulfill most of the mass communications needs very well. Normal business enterprise must leave most of the task to advertising.

SANDY BUYS A CAR

When people switch brands on something as important as a new car, how do they make their choices? The answer may be far from simple, as the following episode indicates.

The train of decision really starts with Charlie, who wasn't directly involved. Charlie really got hooked on front wheel drive cars long before they became as popular as they are now. In addition, he did a lot of driving, and was always reading the driving test writeups in the automobile magazines. The car he had been driving was getting to the trade-in point when he read an article on the Subaru, a Japanese model then coming on the market. Since the new models of his current make were getting beyond his pocketbook, he looked one over at a dealers. Not long afterward, he had to make a quick buying decision, located a Subaru he liked and purchased it. His wife already owned another front-wheel drive car, an Audi, she liked very much and on which she put in a lot of mileage covering a number of schools as a psychologist.

Sandy was one of Charlie's wife's close professional and personal friends—a special education supervisor covering a widespread suburban school district. Sandy was a big woman, large framed, over 6 feet high, and a husband to match—the kind you expect to drive really big cars, and that was what they owned at the moment. But one night Sandy called Charlie's wife, saying she had to get a new car. She asked about Mrs. Charlie's Audi, and was told,"I really like it, but I have to go to—— (a suburb 30 miles away) for service. Why don't you look at the Subaru—my husband likes his." Sandy called again the next night: to announce that she had bought the subcompact Subaru! Furthermore, when it came time to replace it, she got another Subaru. Although it looked small, and was, externally, both she and her husband were sold on the leg room.

The Solid Virtues of Advertising. Advertising communications takes up where publicity leaves off. Publicity items cannot be repeated in the same medium, or to the same audience. Their appeal is as news, and stale news is no news. Advertising works best with substantial repetition, reminding buyers what they have received, attracting the attention of newcomers to the market. Advertising can be timed precisely, to coordinate with distribution. Publicity must stick to expository writing, although some degree of emotional appeal can be achieved with personal interest items.

Advertising can make use of psychological devices to appeal to the affect side of motivation when such an appeal is the best one.

Advertising should be teamed with publicity to reinforce awareness and to start the next steps, building interest by providing comprehension of the benefits and stimulating desire. Advertising also strengthens the impact of personal sales presentations in building desire.

Advertising alone is relatively weak in securing action, in producing sales except on established and very low-learning offerings.

When personal sales efforts must be minimal, sales can be stimulated by attention-attracting labelling and display, and a grab-bag of tools with the ambiguous label of "sales promotions".

Labelling and Display. In this world of increasing self-service, display, well-conceived labelling and good package design are often the only tools available for promoting sales, especially of low value items. This is nothing new—it dates back to the first large scale self-service merchandiser: F. W. Woolworth and his Five and Ten stores, one hundred years ago.

Labelling has two main roles: (a) to identify the contents in a way to catch attention and stand out from the 10 thousand other items competing for the shopper's eyes in the same establishment, and (b) to convey an attractive message about the desirability of those contents. Tactically, the label may also advertise, prominently, a "sales promotion" offer to add further stimulus to sales: a premium, a "cents-off" offer, a coupon offer, for example.

Sales Promotion Devices. Sales promotion is an unfortunate term used to encompass a diversity of sales stimulating tools which are not advertising, publicity, or personal sales (which are also sale promotion tools). However, it is the only label used for a wide variety of means that serve the whole range of promotional roles, from creating awareness to gaining action.

Even a list of the objectives of such promotional forms is a lengthy one:
- To stimulate consumer sampling
- To generate buyer traffic for dealers and distributors
- To counter a competitor's promotion or new product advantage
- To stimulate heavier than usual purchases
- To familiarize prospects with the offering and educate them in its values
- To induce trial of the offering
- To get buyers or future buying influences well started on a habit of using the offering or brand
- To induce dealers and distributors to undertake more promotional effort
- To aid salespeople, distributors and/or dealers in carrying out their tasks more efficiently and profitably
- To develop a closer relationship with members of the distribution

channel and thus get them to perceive the supplier as a favored source
- To stimulate salespeople, distributors and dealers to more concentrated sales efforts, either on specific elements in the line, or to do more full line selling
- To create a price advantage in such a manner that it appears to be a product difference, and thus not as likely to copied quickly
- To keep reminding dealers, advisers, and customers of the organization and its offerings
- To gain favorable attention from the next generation of consumers
- To draw attention to the offerings in a setting which draws heavy traffic of probable prospects and some opportunity for dialog.

Examples of the major tools will be discussed later, but no list can be definitive. As with all other aspects of marketing, imaginative innovation is the road to success.

The same tool may serve different objectives under different market conditions, and the same objective may be served with quite diverse tools. The place of each element in the mix will vary with the seller and the situation.

The Importance of the Perceived Source of the Message

The ability of the message to attract attention, and the degree to which it will be believed, are strongly influenced by the perceived source of the message. Messages clearly identified as coming from the producer, a known partisan, naturally attract less attention and carry less credibility than messages perceived to originate from others with some perceived degree of independence of judgment.

Part of the importance of the intermediary audiences addressed (designers and prescribers, merchants, and OEM customers) lies in the perception of some degree of independence attributed to them.

The advice of a physician, dentist, architect, school counselor or even the beauty shop technician, will carry more weight than the identical message from the seller. The mere fact that an offering is sponsored by a respected merchant or other reseller can strengthen the promotional efforts of the producer. Endorsement or claimed usage by famous figures is sought by advertisers for this one reason.

One basis for the greater effectiveness of salesmen, especially trusted sales people, is the acceptance of them as advisers.

Likewise, the advertising of a highly-reputed organization gets more attention than similar advertising by a less-well-known competitor.

The high attention value and credibility of publicity is due to the fact that the perceived source is a publisher, and one already accepted by the publisher's audience.

Proportioning the Communications Recipe

The proper role of each element in the communications mix, and its proportioning, will be determined by:

- The character of the offering, the nature of its demand, and its cost to the buyer
- The resources of the seller and the opportunities to make use of specific forms of communication
- The skills of the seller in the use of specific communications forms
- The competitive situation
- The stage of the market life cycle
- The degree of perceived offering differentiation between sellers
- The structure of the distribution channels and the importance of the offering to the members of the channel

Many of the limits are obvious. Labelling and packaging are not useful tools in promoting heavy construction machinery. Items sold through the mail waste no funds on attractive packaging, but spend much effort on attractive advertising and copy. High value prestige items are not sold by couponing, and sampling is not likely to promote the sales of items in the decline of their market life cycles. It would be difficult to get much publicity for a particular seller of wheat, although the flour market as a whole, and even a brand, can use recipe columns and baking contests with success. Personal sales efforts will not pay off in promoting two-bit ball point pens to final consumers, but it would require far more persuasive power than advertising carries to get the nation to stop smoking cigarettes or to start using home nuclear plants.

On the other hand, many sellers obviously overlook the values of adding some types of promotion to their accustomed sales efforts. Probably the most overlooked means is publicity. Business firms far too often appoint a relative of the president to the job of public relations director because the relative has no talent for much of anything. Schools too often think any amateur can generate publicity items, and that marketing knowledge is not relevant. Then they wonder why even those who live near the campus know little about the school, and why donations are hard to come by. Even as successful a firm as IBM long overlooked the value of any tool but personal sales, as the accompanying story shows. Successful communications requires an understanding of the possible values of each tool, and what is required for their management. As in everything else in marketing, each seller must come up with the best answer for that seller, even with the best of understanding. Both Avon and Revlon have been highly successful in selling cosmetics. Avon stressed personal sales, and used limited advertising. Revlon used a heavy advertising budget, but added it to the personal push of those behind the cosmetic counters and in the beauty parlors. The Hazel Bishop brand was revived by a seller who modernized the display and packaging, and pushed sales at a low end price in mass outlets.

The most widely used, and most effective medium of communication, is that of personal sales. Because personal sales is by far the greatest part of the promotional budget of most organizations of any kind, proper management of this medium is critical.

SUMMARY

Four elements make up the communications mix, intended to attract buyers to the seller: the audiences, the messages, the media, and the perceived source(s) of the message.

Most sellers must reach a number of different audiences, falling into three main groups: direct users, fabricators and other resellers, and audiences interested in the seller and/or the seller's operations. Sometimes the same communications will deliver the required messages to more than one of these audiences. Generally, different media and different messages must be used to reach the separate audiences.

The total mix must accomplish four different tasks: gain attention to the offering, stimulate an interest in its promised benefits, arouse a desire to acquire it, and galvanize the prospect into action, to buy.

Media can be grouped into two main classes: those conducting a personal dialog with the buyer, and mass media conducting a monolog.

Direct sales personnel are the principal conveyors of the personal communications, but some other forms of communication may contain a personal element. The feedback made possible by the dialog makes personal sales the most effective of the media, but also the most expensive.

Of the mass media, publicity carries heavy weight because an independent outsider is the perceived source. Since no payment is made to the medium carrying publicity, it is the least expensive mode of communication, one especially useful to many kinds of non-profit organizations perceived as rendering a community service.

Advertising's major strength is the wide coverage possible and its ability to reinforce the other elements in the mix, especially in creating awareness and interest.

Labelling and display are useful in attracting attention and stimulating interest.

A numerous catalog of other devices under the common label of sales promotion serve many kinds of support objectives

Successful communications generally requires a combination of the various modes, unique to the individual seller and the sales task to be carried out.

FOOD FOR THOUGHT AND DISCUSSION

SANDY BUYS A CAR

1. Thinking back over the elements that went into Sandy's choice, what did Subaru and its American sales agency, Subaru of America, do to obtain that sale?

TIMBERLAND CO.; TURNING WORK BOOTS INTO A PREMIUM PRODUCT

When the Swartz brothers, Herman and Sidney, joined their father's Boston shoe firm, Abington Shoe Co. in 1956, its only product was unbranded cheap work boots, sold to department stores and other retailers to resell under their own labels. Marketing was a simple proposition of dealing directly with a handful of chain store buyers—no advertising or other promotion. But by the time their father was easing out of management a decade later, this was getting to be an uncertain business with a downhill look. The Boston factory was cramped, expenses high, workers unreliable, and customers getting fewer and "fickle", according to a story in the Aug. 24, 1981 Wall Street Journal.

The Swartzes moved operations to Newmarket, New Hampshire and started rebuilding. Strengthening their private label business, they started thinking of finding a niche of their own in the market. Herman Swartz, the president, says, "We noticed college kids buying work boots" and they decided to throw their resources into developing a top-of-the-line boot that could tie in with the college fashion and the current boom in hiking and backpacking. Their father designed a waterproof boot for which the injection molding machinery used for work boot soles was well adapted. Selling a branded item to consumers, however, proved to be a much more complex job than the selling they had been doing.

They engaged a Boston advertising firm, and it came up with a name, Timberland, to give it an outdoors image. The agency also persuaded them to hire an experienced sales executive, which they did—Stanley Kravetz, later made executive vice president. Kravetz decided to use a force of manufacturers' representatives rather than an in-house sales force. Full-page color advertisements were placed in magazines like the New Yorker and Playboy, making bold use of humor playing on the outdoors use and waterproof qualities. With ads in hand, the representatives went to the kind of stores the reader of the magazines shopped: Saks Fifth Avenue, Bloomingdales, and others of the same level, convincing them to stock the boots.

Advertising appropriations run 7% of sales—about triple the industry average. While the Timberland boots were getting established, the firm took on just enough private brand business to keep the factory busy. When marketing started in 1973, only 3,000 pairs of the half million boots made were Timberland. Total production remained the same through 1975, but Timberland was then 80,000 pairs out of the total. A new factory in 1978 enabled them to make 625,000 pairs, three-fourths of which was Timberland. With the brand name and reputation established, the Swartzes were working on boat moccasins and other products to capitalize on the name.

1. What moves were necessary to create a brand image in this case, given a favorable market climate?
2. To what audiences was the original advertising addressed?

IBM DISCOVERS ADVERTISING AND PUBLICITY WORK

IBM achieved dominance of the data processing equipment market through a strong personal selling effort by its well-trained systems-selling sales force plus well-organized educational efforts. Until 1959, it was inclined to feel that "advertising has a very minor influence in our marketing and that nothing can replace the effectiveness of a direct sales call," as an official at that time was quoted as saying.

However, some careful research IBM commissioned in that year changed its point of view. In that year, IBM introduced a new product line: magnetic character-sensing equipment to enable banks to sort checks electronically. Coincident with the introduction, IBM decided to test the ability of each of four kinds of promotional efforts in accomplishing the four stages of the sales process: creating **awareness** of the product, developing **comprehension** of its benefits, establishing the **conviction** that it was worth buying, and inducing a prospect to **order.**

The four promotional efforts to be used were:
- **Personal sales** by its data processing sales force
- **Advertising** in trade journals, general news magazines, and newspapers
- **Education** through bankers' meetings, in-bank seminars, and IBM schools
- **Publicity** through news releases and articles

IBM perceived the potential for sales was in the 500 largest U. S. banks. A representative sample of 185 of them were chosen for a study to be conducted about 6 weeks after the market introduction and the start of the sales campaign. The interviewers were to interview the bank officer which the bank designated as the person most influential in the decision as to whether or not to invest in such equipment. IBM was not identified as the sponsor of the study, and the questions asked concerned equipment sold by others as well as IBM. The primary aim of the questions was to establish the stage in the buying process each respondent had reached when interviewed, and pinpoint the media which had brought the banker to this stage.

The results were a real surprise. Direct selling had reached only 7 out of 10 of the influentials, advertising had reached 4 out of 10, and educational efforts and publicity had produced results between these two figures. More revealing were the results for each stage of the sales process:
- Advertising and publicity, between them, accounted for about four-fifths of the awareness creation, personal sales and education only about one-tenth each.
- Education led in developing comprehension of the benefits, accounting for about two-fifths of the result. But advertising and personal sales each contributed about one-fourth.
- Personal sales began to come to the fore in establishing conviction, getting credit for about 45% of the total, but advertising was not far behind, with well over a third of the results. Both education and publicity accounted for less than 10% each.
- Personal sales was, as expected, dominant in securing an order, credited with 7 out of 10 cases. But each of the other three modes of communication accounted for an additional 10% of the total.

(Ref:"Advertising Saves Sales Calls." **Business Week,** Dec. 5, 1959, p. 69.)

1. This study is over 20 years old now, and concerns a large equipment

installation. One of IBM's more recent products is a minicomputer, also known as a personal computer. To what extent would the results of the study have been applicable to this introduction? How would the communications mix differ for an offering such as this?

2. What aspects of the magnetic character-sensing equipment (used to sort checks mechanically and to route them: a new system then coming in) would have influenced the kinds of ratings the various communications modes received?

3. The offering being sold was a highly technical, very expensive piece of equipment—definitely not something bought on impulse or whim. It was also something that would result in some reorganization of the buyer's clerical operations, and probably affect some middle management level positions.

Nevertheless, 3 out of 10 of those who were ready to buy were doing so as a result of either a communications mode with no direct selling (the educational efforts) or one or the other of 2 completely non-personal, one-way modes of communications: publicity and advertising.

a. What factors in the situation do you think produced such a readiness to buy?

b. What sort of persons do you think those were who bought on the basis of publicity or advertising, or, for that matter, as a result of seminars and other educational efforts?

CHAPTER 13.   PERSONAL SALES MANAGEMENT

The unique strength of the sales dialog
The roles of personal sales
        The customers' viewpoint
        The sellers' viewpoint
        The viewpoint of the sales people
     The range of personal sales duties
     Personal sales and the market life cycle
     Types of sales responsibilities
Building and managing the sales force
     The limitations faced by sales management
     Recruiting and selecting the sales force
        The importance of self selection
        The avoidance factor barriers to choosing a sales career
        The attractions of selling
        Formal recruitment and selection programs
     Training the sales force
        Initial orientation and training
        Continuing education for the sales force
     Organizing the sales operation
        The span of sales attention possible and needed
        The types of customers and their need for special treatment
        The position of the offering in the market life cycle
        The need to develop new markets or serve thin markets
        Breadth and depth of the mix offered similar customers
     Allocating sales force assignments
     Directing the sales force
     Controlling sales force activity
     Sales analysis and evaluation
     Compensating salesmen
        Determining the target income
        Relating pay to effort
        The four basic requirements

PERSONAL SALES MANAGEMENT   **13**

The Unique Value of the Sales Dialog

Personal sales is the one two-way communications link between buyers and sellers, one which can serve both sides of the transaction. Because of this potential for dialog, personal sales is by far the most persuasive mode of marketing communications. No high learning offering introduction has ever succeeded without some element of personal sales during the market development phase of the market life cycle.

The per sale cost of personal selling is inevitably high. The total expenditure for personal sales exceeds, by far, the total spent for all other forms of communication.

Selling is really many kinds of jobs, ranging from the mere transaction recording of the supermarket checkout clerk to the task of the full-service systems sales engineer, who may help a customer design a production process or a management informations system. Even the common title of "sales" may ignore many whose main task is selling.

All true sales jobs have one element in common: the sales people are viewed by buyers as possible problem solvers and the personal embodiment of the sellers they represent.

The useful role of personal sales changes with the course of the market life cycle. The role differs from offering to offering, from one competitor to another, and from industry to industry. Within any selling organization the sales job will differ from one customer type to another for the same offering.

Because the strength of the sales operation depends on the exercise of personal initiative in each situation, management of the sales operation has to be somewhat indirect. The principal means open to the manager are careful selection, thorough training, well-designed methods of evaluation, guidance, and motivation.

The Roles of Personal Sales

The personal sales effort dominates the communications budget when and if a flexible two-way conversation is needed. Sales people are the real "middlemen" in the transaction. Both the buyer and the employing seller expect to be represented by them.

The Customer's Viewpoint

Customers perceive the sales people as potential problem solvers. Buyers expect help from them in arriving at a wise purchase decision. Sales people can succeed in this role by knowing which of their offerings best fit the desire sets of customers, and helping customers understand how and when they fit. Trusted salesmen often help establish and reinforce that trust by frankly telling buyers when their offerings do not fit customers' needs, and guiding customers to better solutions.

Because each customer's needs vary somewhat from the needs of others, the problem solving role demands a frank dialog only a personal contact can provide. The customer wants the salesman to be on his side.

WHAT DO CUSTOMERS WANT?

The media buyer for a large advertising agency relates his experiences with two salesmen on the same day.

The first salesman, representing a group of newspapers, presented an idea that interested the buyer very much. But when he learned that the advertising campaign proposed was out of his territory, he let the matter drop without either looking to see how other newspapers might be worked in, or what other campaigns the idea might fit.

The second salesman, a TV representative, stopped in to ask about the fall effort for a seasonal male-oriented offering. Some decisions had already been made. 60% had already been allocated to national media. The media for the remaining 40%, to be spent in key markets, had not been definitely chosen, but the media buyers were inclined toward radio because of 6 criteria for their choice:

1. important reach against a specific audience
2. audience selectivity, including the elimination of waste coverage
3. budget limitations
4. the requirement for a highly flexible pattern
5. cost efficiency
6. adaptability to the creative approach already decided upon

Knowing the nature of the the agency thinking, this salesman nevertheless indicated that he thought that the right television package could meet the specifications and do as good a job as radio. He took the overall objectives back with him, contacted the stations he represented. Explaining the objectives and specifications to these stations, he asked them what they could do to meet the needs.

Putting the results of the stations' replies together, this salesman came back to the buyer with a package which he could show met the rating point goals within budget, and met the key flexibility requirement, provided the stations were given some leeway to move spots on extremely short notice. Although the latter was not normally permitted by the ad agency, the presentation was so persuasive that the agency decided to test the effectiveness of television against radio in selected markets.

The Seller's Viewpoint

Sellers perceive the duties of their sales people as that of finding potential customers and persuading them to to buy profitable assortments. Sellers may give some guidance as to the best kinds of prospects to locate, but it is up to the sales people to seek them out and find those most ready to buy on a continuing basis.

The Viewpoint of The Sales People

Sellers generally train sales people in the benefits of their offerings, as the seller's perceive them. But the salesman must translate these benefits to prospects in terms that fit customer habitual perceptions and habitual use systems. Sales people must satisfy both sides of the transaction, and do so in such a way that both sides find a continuing relationship attractive. If either side of the transaction finds the transaction unprofitable, a sale has been made, but has not blossomed into the marketing relationship both buyer and seller hoped for.

The degrees and kinds of problems to be solved naturally differ widely as between buyers, between offerings, between types of sales situation, and at different stages of the market life cycle.

The Range of Personal Sales Duties

The degree of sales service needed and expected in the sales situation covers a very wide range. At one end is the mild suggestion selling of the health food store clerk, "Have you had your vitamin C today?" At the opposite pole is the task of a computer representative who helps a major customer design a management informations system, remaining with the customer for as much as two years full time to aid in the installation and "debugging."

Only limited personal sales service is needed or wanted by buyers of well established offerings fitting into the established use-systems of regular buyers. In fact, if anything beyond personal service and routine reorders are needed, the need may be fully met by an 800 telephone number, backed up by a telemarketing station at headquarters.

By contrast, offerings being bought for new and unfamiliar use-systems obviously require substantial sales service (even when the offering may be well-established in other use-systems). The new-user prospect needs substantial sales help. The well established user may prefer **not** to be so treated.

The elements of the sales job mix might be arrayed roughly in the order of complexity and skill about as follows:
- transaction processing(taking orders, etc,)
- stimulation of buyer attention and interest
- offering presentation and offering assortment fitting
- market and prospect exploration and definition

- market development: discovering what the market is, what satisfaction bundles will attract the early adopters, designing satisfaction bundles adapted to the needs of different prospects, arousing attention to and stimulating interest in these bundles, and developing a comprehension of the values being offered
- after-sales service of many forms, from simply maintaining customers' awareness of the values they are getting from their purchases, to correcting any transactional problems (order-filling errors, delivery schedules, etc.), and training of employees, finding new uses, training distributor and dealer employees in carrying out their sales roles, or developing installation details
- liaison and intelligence feedback: learning the needs and whims of individual customers, developing a personal relationship which gives the seller some personal meaning to the customer, discovering and feeding back information on customer needs and problems, on new product possibilities, and on competitive developments.

Of course few, if any salesmen, have all of these responsibilities. Some types of selling do not involve taking orders: drug "detail men," publishers' college department representatives, industrial abrasives salesmen, among others. Very few salesmen are really equipped for market development. It would be a rare individual who could cover the whole range well, and even rarer the sales job which required it.

Different personalities, different sets of habits and skills are needed for the full-service missionary salesman, the routine sales clerk or driver-salesman, the liaison representative, and the telemarketing sales force.

However limited the sales aspect of the position, training those assigned pays off. Even over-the-counter suggestion selling can repay some degree of sales training and even incentive reward. Such personnel can be furnished with enough skill to perceive when hesitant shoppers can be helped to perceive their needs and helping them find the answers. Many routine outside sales position take about that level of skill.

Higher levels of retail selling benefit from training in sensing customer needs in the types of products being shopped, then locating the offerings best suited to the customer's desires and helping the customer understand the benefits in the choice. Such skills can be useful in selling major purchases such as fashion goods, appliances, furniture and house furnishings, automobiles, and sports equipment. The interest stimulation skills required in such efforts are similar to those needed in any selling job.

The after-sales function can be quite complex and require substantial knowledge and skills. Much of the task may require working with people who are not directly influential in placing orders or making sales themselves. The job of the sales representative covering food store buying offices may require working with the home economist, suggesting food recipes to fit in with a proposed promotion, calling on store managers and giving them valuable help in arranging display space in general (not just for the representative's product), and putting display materials to optimum use. These, and similar personal services build up the personal relationship helpful in developing intelligence feedback as well as establishing a rapport that leads to sales efficiencies later.

A JOB DESCRIPTION FOR ONE KIND OF SALES POSITION

Major electric appliances have been in mature markets for many years. As in all mature markets, distributors are not likely to change sources, and new dealers are not frequent. What, then, do the sales people who contact the distributors do? According to the job description of one such major seller a few years ago, they have enough to keep them busy:

- **Analyze** each market to determine customers' shopping habits
- **Recommend** adequate retail distribution to provide convenience for the consumer and maximum profit opportunities for the dealer
- **Encourage** dealers to take advantage of store identification, display and floor-plan programs to display merchandise for greatest impact and keep display cost and investment in line with potential sales volume
- **Counsel** with dealers to maintain a balanced inventory of (the firm's) major appliances, television and stereo in order to provide adequate delivery. Counsel with dealers to obtain optimum inventory turnover.
- **Advise** on retail and wholesale credit arrangements available for the firm's products
- **Guide** dealers in the use of the firm's advertising funds
- **Provide** dealers with and assist in the development of promotion ideas and advertising programs which are timely and effective
- **Make sure** that dealer sales personnel have thorough knowledge of mechanical and sale features for all of the firm's major appliances, television receivers and stereo. Hold regular in-store training meetings (and invite dealer sales personnel to group headquarters for sales-training meetings in principal markets)
- **Counsel** with the dealer in maintaining proper customer services including delivery, installation and repair service
- **Review** the dealer's inventory on each call. Help him forecast requirements and assist him in ordering proper display and back-up stock.

To the extent that any significant part of the job involves much more than handling transactions and after-sales duties, some amount of market exploration and market segment discovery work should be an understood, even required part of every outside sales job, and even inside sales at any retail level position dealing with shopping goods. Good sales management, of course, involves giving salesmen as much guidance as possible on who the customer segments are. The old practice of sending salesmen out on "cold calls" without much guidance is highly inefficient, and an imposition on those hired for the task. But there are often unsuspected opportunities not visible in the broad statistics with which headquarters must work, and newly developing segments best uncovered in the personal sales contact. Salesmen need training and incentives to dig for these, and feed back the information.

Many of these developments result from the changes in demand patterns over the life cycle of products. The same dynamics of the life cycle changes the role of personal sales over time, for any offering.

WHEN DO CUSTOMERS WANT SALES HELP?

A then-new plastic resin was about to be launched by a number of companies, including the one George, a chemical engineer, worked for. The new resin had some interesting new applications, and also would be competing in some uses with established resins. This would, he thought, put an early limit on the price. The market for current plastic resins was mature. They were selling at such low levels that the profit margins were vanishing for the larger producers.

Much of the pressure on prices came from some new sellers who had entered the market as it reached maturity. They fielded no sales forces, operated with a price list and a telephone, handling only the volume items. The major original producers still fielded sales forces and offered technical assistance, putting them at a cost disadvantage.

George was aware that the market positions of these major producers had been won by the technical service when the resins were new. Users then needed and welcomed help on the uses and processing of the resins. But from his observation, resin purchasers were no longer welcoming the technical service, in some cases not even allowing the sales personnel to work with the production people. Most users now needed no advice on working with plastics, and some, at least, seemed to think that they had developed some know-how which they did not want salesmen passing on to their competitors. As George saw it, the proper strategy was to make heavy use of technical advice in the beginning, but phase it out as the market became competitive and put the salesmen to work in other areas, on other offerings. In that way cost could be lowered to a point where a reasonable profit would be available in maturity also.

Personal Sales and The Market Life Cycle

The high learning, market development offering always requires a high level of sales service, a great deal of sales hand-holding. The customer has old habits to break and unfamiliar routines to learn. The market maturity offering requires little more than routine procurement service--primarily negotiation on terms and the expediting of a smooth flow of deliveries. The declining offering will never repay any significant expenditure for sales service.

As the phases of the market life cycle advance, the point of focus as well as the amount of sales service needed will shift. The high learning product in its early market development phase will need intensive personal promotion directed at both the final buying point and at the distribution intermediaries. By the time market growth begins to speed up, final buyers will need less service and intermediaries will require the maximum of attention and service to attract and hold the stronger ones needed to survive the coming shakeout.

Once the market matures, the major focus is on routine order service needed by distributors, to ensure thorough customer availability. Even at maturity, some minor market niches may remain open for some minor degree of personal service. Some specific market segments may reward the seller who brings the store to them, in effect. Such is the case with catalog teleservice ordering, in-home sales of cosmetics, toiletries and cleaning supplies, the truck distributor salesman of tools to small garages and machine shops. The amount of dialog is not usually much more than is given by merchants in a fixed location.

As already indicated, offerings on the decline have to be left to coast, without any significant sales help.

Clearly, sales management has a major major task in recruiting and selecting the kind of personnel best fitted for a given type of selling, training them at the start, and retraining them as the needs of the job change.

Building And Managing The Sales Force

The Limitations Faced by Sales Management

Sales management can only be classed as one of the more complex people management tasks. The sales manager must recruit people for a job which requires some degree of independence of both judgment and action. Satisfactory tests for the required skills have yet to be developed. The accomplishments of the sales people are difficult to evaluate accurately, and what measures are available are often misleading.

Sales people must be, to some degree, independent entrepreneurs, working as much for the buyer as for the seller. Direct oversight of the job is impossible. The capabilities required are hard to define, and when defined are hard to measure. The measurable output—usually dollars of sales—often results in some part from factors over which the salespeople have limited control.

Recruitment and selection is obviously a critical task.

Recruiting And Selecting The Sales Force

Personnel recruitment for any job requiring personal skill and judgment is far from easy. Usually, however, some degree of objectivity is possible: the requirement for certain credentials and experience helps. Generally, any one position is very similar between different employers, and even more so within any one organization.

Defining the position is far more difficult in selling. Because the offerings of all successful firms are different from the offering mix of every other in the same industry, the selling job also differs. Even within the same organization, the sales situation differs substantially from market to market, the sales effort needed is different for new lines than for established ones, and the task varies over the economic cycle, and shifts with the market life cycle.

Nevertheless, successful sales forces are closer to being the rule than the reverse. One possible reason is that the attractive features of the job of selling and the repelling features are so clear and strong that a substantial amount of self-selection of recruits occurs, and that the poorly fitted discover it early and get out.

The value of self-selection. Even the most limited of observation reveals that most people in selling aimed at quite different careers in the beginning. Many came into sales from other positions within the firm, or from management trainees whose original goals did not include sales. They chose sales eventually because attracted by the job itself, after some degree of observation and exposure. Many others were experienced in some kind of sales under some other employer, then chose to apply for the present position after gaining familiarity with its operation, either as a competitor, a supplier, or customer.

Such self-selection can be a very efficient form of test, especially when the attractions and the negative factors are as open to observation as are those of selling. The avoidance factors seem adequate to discourage anyone not strongly motivated.

The Avoidance Factor Barriers to Choosing A Sales Career. The main avoidance factors in selling are the general social attitudes toward selling in our culture, and the conditions of work in most selling jobs.

Socially, the position of salesman carries a low status image relative to the level of ability, initiative, and skill required. Confirmation of this impression rests on a study of the perceived prestige of 90 occupational groupings made in 1947 and repeated 16 years later, in 1963. The results were almost identical, across the board. Insurance agents and salesmen ranked well below the middle of the 90 occupations listed--far below engineers, electricians, and merchants, and only barely above plumbers and auto repairmen.

No one is likely to be unaware of such generally held social attitudes. Social climbers do not enter selling, but many engineers do, despite the comedown in social status.

The working conditions are, in themselves, enough to discourage many others. For the outside salesman, travel and irregular working hours can limit family and social life. Frustration is at least as common as success. In general, the batting average is about the same as in big league baseball: .300 is extremely good in landing accounts.

Only those who value the other aspects of the position will apply, or if placed in sales, stay in very long.   What is attractive about the job?

The Attractions of Selling. The avoidance factors seem to be a high price to ask of people of the needed ability and initiative.   The attractive values are apparently such as to attract the types of people needed.   What kind of people are they?   Research has indicated that all types of sales people share two personality characteristics: "empathy" and "ego drive".

By **empathy** is meant the ability to perceive and understand the point of view of other people.   The empathetic salesman has the ability to understand the buyer's desire sets, and translate the benefits of those offerings in his assortment which fit the desire sets.   In plain English, the good salesman tends to like people, to understand their problems, and to help to solve them.

"Ego drive" is another bit of psychological jargon for the drive for personal accomplishment and recognition of that accomplishment. Salespeople out on the job have no superiors looking over their shoulders, know that they are on their own.   When they make a sale, they know that they have accomplished a feat of some importance.   And they know that the credit will go to them.

Empathy is a necessary attribute of the marketing oriented salesman. Empathy enables the salesman to do a good job for both the seller and the customer.   The chance to work with people rather than shuffle papers draws such individuals to selling.

Likewise, those who must work on their own must have a strong ego drive--a desire for visible results and recognition.

Thus the very working conditions which keep many people out of selling attracts the kind of personality selling needs.

In addition, while the engineer who stays at his desk may feel superior, his colleague who joins the sales effort earns far more, with a much higher ceiling.   Furthermore, he usually is in a far better position to advance to the higher echelons of management than those who stay in production.   For all of these reasons, the element of self-selection has been efficient in drawing the right kind of people into selling.   Recognition of its value should be an implicit factor in any recruitment, selection, and training program.   Most of the numerous small sales forces probably can get by with no formal recruitment, other than to fill vacancies.   Larger ones must, of necessity, maintain a constant program of recruitment and selection.

Formal Recruitment And Selection Programs.   Only a continuing mass recruitment campaign can fill the sales ranks of organizations fielding several hundred or more sales people--such as insurance firms, drug firms, large investment brokers, and major consumer product firms.   Where the sales efforts require a relatively high level of general ability, as some of those mentioned do, the organization may have a choice of making the initial recruitment one aimed specifically at sales, and one that is part of a general management training program in which sales exposure is a part.

The advantages of merging the sales recruiting with a general management trainee operation are worth considering. The importance of sales to any such operation justifies exposing every trainee to the sales operation of the firm, whether or not they are ever likely to be part of the sales force. If the training program makes room for a period of field experience in sales, some will find it to their liking and sooner or later elect to transfer to sales. Those who do not will get some taste of the problems of the sales division and get a better understanding of them. Initial recruitment for the training program will not be handicapped by the uninitiated's low status perception of sales.

Organizations who choose to recruit separately for sales training often find it wise to cloak the sales operation under a euphemism which avoids the sales stigma: "underwriter" (insurance firms), and "account executive" are popular terms, and probably succeed.

In either case, some form of initial screening is necessary, especially for the sales-only type of program. The usual means of screening are detailed application forms, personal interviews, and the use of some standardized psychological tests. Analysis of the **written application form** is a widely used part of the screening program. A structured questionnaire covers the applicant's school record, hobbies, and attitudes toward past experience and performance. Answers are compared with those on the applications originally submitted by the best and poorest salesmen still in the force. While many organizations seem to find this procedure useful, none have ever been subject to a true controlled test of validity. (Proof of validity would have to require employment without regard to any screening procedure, and then observing performance after a substantial period of employment.)

Personal interviews permit the applicants to inform themselves about the exact nature of the opening and the opportunities that will be open to them. An interviewer who has enough insight and professional skill can gain insight into the applicant's personality. (But it is doubtful that many interviewers have that much psychological expertise.)

The interviewer often summarizes his impressions on a rating sheet, covering items such as initiative and leadership in past activities and consistency and clarity of goals.

The record of **standardized tests** on personality characteristics, when used for any purpose, is one of statistical validity at best. All of them are subject to manipulation by a smart, ambitious applicant. All of them hit wide of the intended mark on substantial proportions of those tested.

Most organizations use a variety of screening methods. In the process, they undoubtedly screen out the poorest of applicants, and experience or the training program itself must do the rest.

R-O PHARMACEUTICALS: CORRECTING AN ATTITUDE PROBLEM

Not long after Vic took over as Marketing Research Director for R-O Pharmaceuticals, he sat in on a conference of the regional and district sales supervisors. They presided over the field work of 500 salesmen, known as "detail men" in the industry. The salesman's job is to visit physicians and "detail" them on the company's offerings, especially, but not limited to, the newer introductions. This involves explaining the "indications" (the symptoms and circumstances for which each one is effective) and also the "counter-indications"—the side effects and the circumstances under which caution should be exercised.

During the discussions at the meeting, a number of supervisors complained that they had problems in selecting new salesmen—they were not as able as they wished to separate the more promising candidates from those who later proved to be rather ineffective. After the meeting, the sales director talked to Vic about it. "Vic," he commented, "I wish you could give us some help on this selection problem. I don't have a good answer, either. I have done the usual things: compared and analyzed the application blanks of the best and poorest, and I can't find any differences."

After some thought, Vic decided more information was needed. Vic knew that all of those hired had one characteristic in common: they were all pharmaceutical graduates, with a good understanding of drugs. He got approval for, and hired a group of professional psychologists, teaming each one up with a salesman, and travelling with the salesman for a period of time. The psychologist's assignment was to observe the interactions of the salesman with each person he came in contact: the receptionist in the physician's office, any nurses, and the physician himself. Each psychologist took detailed notes on his observations, and also on anything learned in casual conversations with the salesman.

When the psychologists returned, and their notes were analyzed and discussed, the answer seemed clear. The typical pharmacy school graduate has been a student whose ambition had been to study medicine, but who had, for one reason or another, been unable to realize that ambition. When dealing with physicians, many of them were suffering from an inferiority complex: they were being asked to instruct the man who "lived in the big white house on the hill."

Vic's recommendation was to hire a new training instructor, a professional trainer rather than one of the salesmen, and teach the detail men salesmanship. The recommendation was adopted and the problem subsided.

Vic's solution was not the only alternative. Another firm, some years ago, decided to hire experienced salesmen instead of pharmacists, and teach them about the drugs. Apparently it worked very well but almost too well. Informants say that after a period of time, the sales department began to have substantial turnover, as the new type of salesmen often moved out of sales into upper management, one of them eventually becoming president. They went back to the old system.

Training The Sales Force

Two types of sales training programs are needed: an initial orientation program and continuing education of the veterans.

The orientation program has the obvious goal of preparing the prospective salesman for the job ahead. When well designed, it provides the trainee with a clear understanding of the job and the working conditions, and some initial technical training.

Continuing education is a necessity to sharpen skills and to update the sales force on changes in strategy and in the product line, and in market conditions and competition.

Initial Orientation and Training

Formal orientation programs attempt to build knowledge of four kinds:

- The organization, its history, structure, operations, promotional and price policies, and its offerings. Knowledge of product or other offerings tend to get strong emphasis
- The customers and the potential: who are most likely to buy, and under what circumstances
- The necessary routines of the job: the routing of calls, preparation of expense accounts, order processing, required reports, personal relationships and protocol within the sales force, servicing customers, reporting on competition
- Salesmanship

All aspects except some of the salesmanship training are necessary components for any type of selling. To the extent that salesmanship is narrowly defined to mean closing sales and getting orders, the need is not universal. As already noted, some kinds of selling do not include either one.

The methods used include on-the-job training, lectures, group discussions and conferences, and correspondence lessons.

On-the-job training is almost universal. In some smaller sales forces, it is all the formal orientation attempted. Requiring some on-the-job experience prior to any class work can be productive of better understanding of the classwork.

Descriptive material is most often conveyed in lectures when the number in training is substantial. Recently, some organizations have been experimenting with videotaped recordings, which would appear to have substantial advantages over straight lectures. Lectures are commonly supplemented by manuals and other printed materials. Discussion seems to work best for those aspects of training, such as salesmanship, which are intended to establish new attitudes. Active participation is encouraged by role-playing, case analysis, and problem-solving.

Continuing Education of The Sales Force

Even the most experienced sales people need continual updating on the organization's offering, competitive situation and other developments which could affect sales operations, including strategic and tactical plans. Generally this is done through discussion groups and conferences of salesmen, both at the local or regional level, and at the national level. Probably as important as the formal program is the informal getting-together which meetings and conferences make possible.

The quality of the training program direction can make or break it. It is an all-too-true cliche that putting training into the hands of a former star salesman is likely to "lose a good salesman and get a poor teacher." The knowledge of how to sell is not necessarily related to knowledge of how to teach others to sell. It is a fact that the father of professional selling, Patterson of National Cash Register, was never a salesman, but developed a successful sales training program that has long been a model for the whole profession, and was carried over to IBM, to build that organization's dominance. John H. Patterson was a coal dealer and owner of a general store who had taught briefly after graduating from Dartmouth.

Organizing The Personal Sales Operation

Sales management is, first of all, management, with the same functions as any other aspect of management: setting objectives, communicating them, structuring organizational relationships in conformance with the objectives, evaluating their execution, and instituting controls to make sure the objectives are carried out. The structure of the organization is influenced by the current strategy of the seller and the nature of the market situation:
- The amount of personal sales push needed by each offering in the total mix and the possible span of sales attention
- The types of customers targetted
- The levels of distribution which will be approached in person
- The position of each offering in its market life cycle
- Any need to open new markets
- The relative market strength of the seller
- The breadth and depth of the offering mix

The Span of Sales Attention Possible And Needed

Personal selling is a greedy consumer of time. The number of sales contacts possible in a day is limited. The clock is a fairly good measure of the degree of attention given to any one offering. Consequently, the number of offerings any salesperson can push is limited by the degree of sales attention and emphasis devoted to each--ranging from a mere mention to a full-service presentation. Generally, only one major item or line will get major emphasis with any one customer.

Types of Customers And Need for Special Treatment

Many offerings are bought by a wide range of customer types, often for quite different purposes. Some kind of sales force specialization is needed in such cases, with a different kind of sales force for separate markets.

Tires are sold to auto manufacturers as OEM, to retail distributors, to fleet buyers. The buying decisions are different in each case, as are the buying procedures.

A minicomputer may be bought by an accounting firm or small business, by an engineering firm, by an author or publisher, or by a family with teenagers. Each is seeking a quite different benefit package. The accountant is seeking a means of financial record keeping and analysis, the engineer to handle design problems and graphics, the author for a sophisticated word processor to handle both manuscript and editing, the suburban family an entertainment device. In each case, the sales people must understand the special needs of each in some detail, be able to understand what it is the customer is asking for, what software is needed and compatible with which models, and translate the capabilities of the various offerings in ways the customers themselves may not have previously understood. This can be asking a lot of one person.

The Position of The Offering in The Market Life Cycle

Offerings which must be guided through a market development period demand the exclusive attention of the assigned sales force and intensive field service.

In mature markets, offerings usually need little more than routine sales attention and very limited sales service. The same sales force can then cover a broad line, or even several related lines of mature offerings.

This usually means a restructuring of the sales force as offerings move into maturity. Once necessary separate sales forces to different departments become a "duplication of effort." A large part of the orders previously handled by an outside sales force may be serviced very well, and much more economically by a telemarketing operation.

The Breadth And Depth of The Mix Offered to Similar Customers

The longer the line handled, the less attention can be devoted to any one item. So long as the assortment is matched to the needs of members of the same market segment, the line takes on value with length, and selling cost per item is less. But if assortments bought differ much between customer segments, the sales force may need more specialization.

The Need to Open New Markets Or Serve Thin Markets

Organizations entering markets new to them face a selling problem more difficult than those fielding high learning market development offerings. They need to become acquainted with a new set of customers and their needs. They must also gain this knowledge fast, and in the face of competitors whose offerings are accepted and part of the habitual sources used and trusted.

One solution is to hire a sales force which has established acceptance with the same set of buyers—an outside firm of manufacturer's representatives or food brokers. Part of the value being paid for in using these independent sales organizations is their established contacts with the buyers they normally cover. Although technically classified as "limited function wholesalers," their relationships with their "principals" are not very different from those of a wholly integrated sales branch. They need the same product training and close contact with the sales department as the internal sales force.

RALSTON PURINA BY-PASSES ITS OWN SALES FORCE

Ralston Purina already had a well-established sales force which called regularly on food company buyers in connection with their extensive line of breakfast cereals. Then Ralston Purina decided to add dog food to its retail lines. The firm had plenty of experience in feed formulation, selling lines through farm supply dealers; so the production of the dog food was no problem. Retail sales of dog food, however, was highly competitive, and would require a heavy advertising campaign, backed up with strong food store distribution to gain immediate market impact. As well known as the Ralston Purina sales force was around food store buying offices, it was not known to the buyers of pet supplies in those firms. Rather than hire an additional sales force, Ralston Purina selected 70 food brokers carrying lines bought by the same buyers, and got the quick distribution it needed.

Such sales representatives are especially valuable as permanent additions to sales organization of limited line producers, and even of those with broader lines, but covering territories in which the demand for the producer's line is very thin and scattered. Organizations with a highly seasonal demand pattern often turn to such sales firms.

HENRY PRATT CO.: THE VALUE OF A LIMITED DEMAND LINE TO A SALES REPRESENTATIVE

The Henry Pratt Company produced a line of very specialized valves, mostly custom designed: rubber seat butterfly valves, 20 inch or larger, used mainly in water or steam lines. The firm supported only one sales office of its own, in New York City. The mission of this office was to work with the half dozen consulting engineering firms specializing in utility designing, all of them headquartered in New York City. They bought nothing themselves, but wrote the specifications of whatever equipment was to be purchased for the systems they designed, and Pratt's engineering salesmen worked to get these specifications such as to favor their offerings.

Sales in the rest of the country were assigned to a number of manufacturers representatives, each one covering a region. These representatives sold other lines of valves, of types used more widely in industry, motor valve controls, and similar related lines bought by industrial purchasers. One such firm operated out of Kansas City—an area with a limited number of industries, and therefore a very thin market for Pratt's line.

Discussing the value of the Pratt line to his business, the Kansas City representative commented, " I sell only about two Pratt valves a year. But I carry a line of expansion joints and a line of motor valve controls. Whenever I sell a Pratt valve, I can usually sell 2 expansion joints and a motor valve control."

Occasionally an organization's own marketing effort is so weak that it is well advised to turn the entire operation over to a sales agent who has a strong marketing franchise. If this course is chosen, the seller can avoid the need for sales management.

Allocating The Sales Force Assignments

Getting the most for the sales dollar requires a careful, rational assignment of sales personnel to specific set of sales prospects. Assignments should require about the same amount of effort. The more common bases of allocation are geographic, by product lines, and by customer class.

Nearly all customer assignment plans are territorial at some level in the plan. Product line organization is the usual major division whenever the product lines differ substantially in the kinds of buyers and in the nature of the selling effort. Thus IBM's Data Processing sales force was long separate from its Office Products sales force, handling typewriters for the most part. The addition of IBM's minicomputer and its use in word processing forced a reevaluation of this division in 1982. The minicomputers were competing with typewriters, and also to some degree with larger computer usage.

Division of the sales force by customer class is common when:
- different classes of customers are buying for substantially different use systems and require a different kind of knowledge of the customer and his systems
- the actual form and/or quantity of the offering purchased is significantly different and necessitates a different sales approach.
- the purchase channels in the buying organization are different

Thus an industrial abrasives seller would use one sales force to reach industrial users of any size, a different one to service non-industrial consumers through retail outlets. The industrial salesmen would need substantial engineering knowledge and would be capable of rendering some substantial technical production service to major end users. The retail channel force would have little need for technical expertise, but need substantial knowledge of merchandising methods. There would be no account overlap between the two sales forces.

On the other hand, an organization selling industrial precision gauges or process control equipment might have two different salesmen calling on the same buyer. One might be servicing the production division. The other might be calling on the R&D laboratory personnel, whose precision demands were more exacting, and whose needs were for smaller scale equipment.

Whenever the purchasing responsibility is subdivided, as in a general merchandiser or in a food chain, different sale forces may be needed to contact the frozen foods buyer (for example) and the pet supplies buyer. Even a line as unglamorous as industrial fasteners (nuts, bolts, rivets, etc.)

will be bought on one basis by the production department--usually on a "participation" basis (splitting the order between a limited number of suppliers on some ratio basis). The maintenance department will be ordering separately, usually from a single, and often different supplier who makes ordering small quantities convenient. The production department will consider price closely. Maintenance may be ordering out of a lump budget and be little concerned with price, as such.

Directing The Sales Force

Sales force direction necessarily consists of setting objectives, giving guidance and information on sales opportunities, offering incentives, and utilizing performance controls. The emphasis has to be on spelling out the what, where and why of the task. The nature of the sales task leaves the how to do it up to the salesman in each individual sales situation.

A major part of the training programs (including meetings) is devoted to outlining the best sales opportunities compatible with the organization's strategy, and the approaches which seem to give the best results. Internal house publications and other literature emphasize this knowledge in various ways--often in the form of success stories.

The allocation of customer types and territories implies some degree of sales emphasis. Sales analysis helps pinpoint current opportunities. These are then often translated into specific forms of customer focus, such as a specified call frequency by classes of customers. Call reports are then used as a control device, both as a reminder to the salesman, and as some check on performance.

CHANGING THE SALES FOCUS THROUGH INCENTIVES

The Ditto Corp. was having profit margin problems. At the time, Ditto was still an independent company with a single line of offerings: a spirit duplicating system that was one of the two quick simple ways of reproducing typed copy quickly, and by far the least expensive. Xerox machines had not yet taken over. Almost anyone who had any kind of office work, even a small business, used them for everything from restaurant menus and interoffice memos to research reports. Business volume was good, but margins had been shrinking. The primary source of sales revenue and profits was the supplies—primarily the special duplicator carbons. The business in these had become very competitive, since no producer had a patent. The business of larger users was often on a bid basis.

The incentive portion of salesmen's pay was based on dollar volume. Ditto finally changed the incentive pay to a total gross margin basis. Before long, company sales declined and total profits increased. Salesmen quickly discovered that sales to smaller buyers, for which competition was much less keen, paid off in gross margin, and in their paychecks.

The sales compensation system, including contests, special recognition, and prizes, direct sales attention to specific kinds of effort, and can be varied to secure the kind of emphasis fitting the organization's marketing strategy.

Field sales supervisors exercise a more personal form of direction, largely through on-the-job training and morale boosting.

Controlling The Sales Activity

The form of control open to sales management is that of modern management in its purest form: the setting of performance objectives, accompanied by analysis of selective information on operations and performance. The reports required of salesmen serve as an important source of some aspects of the performance measurement. They also serve as a reminder of the objectives management has set. Reporting has to be kept to the minimum essentials, however. No good salesman is a desk person. Requiring excessive detail can lead to careless or deliberately false reporting. Reports must be supplemented by analysis of other information indicating performance.

Sales Analysis And Evaluation

The seller's own records of sales, margins, and costs are the most widely used basis for control and evaluation. Sales, margins, and costs are commonly analyzed in terms of:
- the sales organization unit: division, region, branch, individual sales territory
- the offering and line
- the type and class of customer and/or distribution channel
- the time period

Common comparisons are between sales organization units and between periods of time for the same unit (this month vs. the same month last year, for instance).

Caution is needed when interpreting such comparisons. Territories vary widely in their sales potential, both one from another, and in the same territory from one period to another. The factors which can make for such differences must be investigated and allowed for. The salesmen. out on the firing line, will be all too aware of any such factors, and judge management's directives accordingly.

Compensating Salesmen

The sales compensation system has to be the primary means of directing the sales emphasis. Most good compensation systems have a monetary portion and a personal recognition portion. Money is, without question, one of the major incentives drawing people into selling. Recognition of effective efforts is a necessary ego-reinforcement for those whose task is often discouraging. (It may also serve as a substitute for the lack of social recognition sometimes accorded this key communications effort.)

The standards for a really fair and stable compensation system are easy to state:

- The pay should be high enough to attract the quality of personnel needed for the specific sales task
- Every sales person should be paid in relation to the effective effort put into the organization's sales operations

Unfortunately, quantifying these general standards is harder than stating them.

Determining The Target Income

Theoretically, the market for personnel determines what must be paid to get competent sales people. The problem is determining what that market is for a given sales force.

Internal information is seldom adequate. The great majority of sales forces are too small for an experience base--30 salesmen or less. Only the very largest sales organizations employ enough sales people to get adequate turnover information. Even comparison information from other organizations is hard to evaluate. The selling job is seldom closely comparable, the role of the personal element in the communications mix may well differ significantly, the organizational structure is probably not the same. Probably the best test is whether the pay is enough better than the applicants could get in some other position to attract them to selling.

Relating Pay to Effort

Superficially, the solution would seem to be to base the pay on sales, since the task is aimed at creating sales. Such, indeed, is the standard for some kinds of selling jobs, but primarily in those cases in which the individual is not committed to a full time effort for the one seller. Such a flat commiSsion system is the logical one if:

- The sales objective is sales volume alone, without regard to sales margins, customer service, or other tasks important to future customer relationships
- Sales efforts pay off in quick orders
- Sales volume is related almost wholly to the individual sales person's efforts

Conditions such as these hold in a relatively small fraction of sales organizations. Even when they do, such a choice may not be wise.

Paying for sales in total disregard for future customer relationships is not marketing, but a confidence game which can backfire. The job of the sales people is to create customers. not just immediate sales. Customer service takes time, often without adding to sales volume immediately.

Even in terms of immediate sales, a flat commission may lead to less profitable results: dollar volume can be racked up by pushing the low margin items.

In most sales jobs, the really profitable sales volume results from long run efforts at market cultivation. In addition, sales may depend heavily on elements beyond the control of the sales personnel, such as the level of after-sales service provided by the selling company, and the level of mass promotional communications. In industrial, commercial, and institutional selling, especially, the volume of sales is a derived demand, depends on the sales of the buying organization.

Then why do a minor, but substantial proportion of organizations pay on a straight commission basis? Many do so simply because they always have, and no executive has ever given thought to better alternatives. The rest generally fall into one of three types of operations:

- Sales operations are conducted primarily through independent sales representative or agents, usually representing other sellers at the same time (food brokers, manufacturers representatives, insurance agencies)
- the sales force consists primarily of part-timers, usually with ill-defined or undefined territorial or customer list assignments, and after-sales service is considered relatively unimportant (your Avon Lady, Amway, etc.)
- Young enterprises without established reputation or capital sufficient to insure the stability of income and employment established sellers can guarantee, paying generous commissions to attract those willing to take a chance

There are few alternatives to paying commissions to the independent sales organization. Such representatives divide their time and effort between sellers according to conditions as they find them. The level of commission is the only control management has to influence their choices. The level is subject to individual negotiation, and is sometimes variable, depending on volume. Also, any such established representative has a substantial investment in his customer contacts. The main asset of such representatives is the goodwill established with regular customers--plenty of incentive to carry out the service responsibilities.

Insurance agents get commissions on renewals, usually without much further effort, so that their main aim is a continuing relationship.

Most part-timers work with only the barest of supervision, and commission plans are the only real control. Also, turnover is normally very high.

Young organizations with limited capitalization seldom have the resources to do other than hire what amount to sales partners until they get established.

From the sales person's point of view, the flat commission lacks any assurance of income stability. Moreover, income tends to be poorest at just those times when the greatest sales effort is needed. Except when overly generous, the flat commission is unattractive.

From sales management's viewpoint, sales commissions fail to provide incentives to carry out important market building and patronage maintenance activities. Activities needed to build business and strengthen patronage relationships may include:

- do extensive prospecting
- handle adjustment problems, and even arrange for repairs
- expedite orders or track down shipments
- furnish technical advice and other help to customers which may not promote sales of the offerings, as well as help that does promote them
- do other missionary work
- Collect and feed back market intelligence

To pay for such efforts, most compensation plans incorporate some kind of guaranteed salary or other monetary income, plus some kinds of incentive payments, both monetary and non-monetary.

The four basic requirements of a good pay system are control, incentive, flexibility, and easy understandability.

Control is achieved through some kind of salary-type base income, whatever it is labelled.

Straight salaries are the preferred compensation for about one organization in four. Usually, these are non-consumer goods selling, in which sales are not easily traced to individual effort. Organizations routinely add some perquisites appropriate to the job, which can have substantial monetary equivalence—an automobile, for example, needed on the job, but available for family use off the job. Business expenses are fully covered.

Monetary incentives may be in the form of some kind of commission scale, or bonuses, or a combination—usually as a smaller part of the total. If commissions are paid, they may start after a specific level of sales, or vary by line or item. Bonuses may be based on sales, or on meeting some other management objective, such as full-line selling, minimizing expenses, servicing customers, missionary sales work, or other objectives.

Non-monetary incentives may includes contest prizes, special privileges, internal or advertised publicity, and/or other special recognition of high-level accomplishment—the "Million Dollar Club," in insurance or real estate, for example.

Flexibility is needed because of the inherent differences in the potentials of assigned territories or customer lists, and also because of the difference in experience and skill levels (such as a lower base pay for beginners in need of further training). When quotas are so used, care needs to be taken that they are based on sales opportunities.

Easy understandability and perceived fairness are Siamese twin requirements. Without them, the plan serves no purpose and management has no control. Without control, there is no management. This can happen, and sales appear to be satisfactory, because the task depends on personal initiative, and draws people to it who are independent enough to wish to exercise that initiative.

SUMMARY

Personal sales is many kinds of jobs, but all share the common factor of maintaining a flexible two-way communications between seller and buyer.

The salesman is a true middle man: representing both sides of the transaction to their opposites. Customers expect sales people to help them solve their problems. The seller expects them to find prospects and persuade them to buy. Sales people know they must translate the needs of each side to the other.

The breadth of the sales job varies widely, from mere order taking to the developing and servicing of markets, and different skills are needed for each type of position.

Only a strong personal sales effort will develop the market for high learning offerings. As offerings pass through their growth phase to maturity, the role of personal sales diminishes and changes from that of missionary to that of routine customer service. Offerings on the decline should get no sales attention at all--it cannot pay off.

Management of the sales operation is a difficult task. The complexities start with the important task of recruiting and selecting the proper personnel. Really objective guides and tests do not exist. Nevertheless, most sales forces are staffed with competent personnel,

One reason is the high degree of self-selection on the part of applicants in the light of strong avoidance characteristics of the job, and the character of the offsetting attractions. Most salesmen aimed for other careers originally, came into selling because of the attractions.

On the negative side, the profession is somewhat low in social status, and the working conditions often a strain on family and social ties.

On the positive side, selling attracts people who like to work with people, and to see positive objective accomplishment. The pay is higher than those of similar abilities earn in non-selling occupations.

Many sales forces are relatively small and fill their openings from voluntary applications from those inside the organization, or from the outside. Very large sales forces must maintain a continuous, strong recruitment and selection program. Screening of applicants in such formal programs tends to be based on the contents of written applications, followed up with personal interviews. Some organizations make use of some standardized test, in addition, but none of the tests have more than statistical validity.

Sales training is a major responsibilty, consisting of some form of initial orientation, often accompanied by field experience, and a necessary continuing education of several forms.

The organization of the sales operation is influenced by the overall strategy of the seller, and the nature of the sales operation. Among the determining factors are the span of attention possible and needed to carry out the assigned tasks, the types of customers dealt with and any need for special treatment of customers, the position of the offerings in the market life cycle, the breadth and depth of the offering mix, and the need to do missionary work in new markets.

Much of the efficiency of the operation depends on rational allocation of sales assignments. Most assignments have some kind of territorial basis. A further division by customer class or type of line, or both, is common in organizations with a complex offering mix.

Direction of the sales force is necessarily indirect: the formulation of objectives, guidance on opportunities, and incentives of several kinds to reward efforts most valuable to the seller.

Evaluation of the efforts of sales personnel tends to be based largely on sales analysis, and this needs to be done well.

Compensation usually consists of two parts, with the combination aimed at a feasible target income thought necessary to attract salesmen of the caliber needed. Part of the pay is intended to provide a stable income base. The remainder is a reward for specific kinds of effort. Some of the more important parts of the compensation consist of non-monetary personal recognition of several kinds.

FOOD FOR THOUGHT AND DISCUSSION

DEVELOPING AN IMPROVED BASE FOR INCENTIVE COMPENSATION

Fred Benton was a graduate industrial engineer who started to work for the PQR Abrasives Corp. in production, was transferred to an assignment in technical service. After 4 years at this, he requested and was given a sales assignment. PQR produces a full line of industrial abrasives, from papers to industrial diamond items. Most items are standard, but some wheels, particularly, are built to customer specifications. Abrasives have so many applications, some competing with other forming methods, that customers frequently need engineering advice on the best selections.

The majority of the sales go through local distributors who handle the PQR line exclusively, ready for quick delivery to industrial customers. Some very large accounts are sold directly by PQR, by agreement with the distributor. The salesman's responsibility is to contact all users, whether direct accounts or distributor accounts, giving engineering advice and correcting problems of any kind. When the salesman feels the need for extra help on a particularly tough customer problem, technical service is called in.

His other duties were to work with distributors, check on their performance, and advise PQR of any actions needed in connection with distributors: special sales promotional campaigns, distributor salesman training, factory visits, or other sales stimulating provisions. He could even, if market share remained below expectations, recommend changes in distributor appointments—a step not taken lightly, however.

The bulk of the sales were to the really large industries in any sales district. These large buyers split their business among a small number of sellers, based on some percentage distribution which could be changed from time to time in accordance with the buyer's perception of the quality of the sales and distribution service received from each. In any given year, the "participation rate" was usually stable. Changes were never sudden. About the only way a salesman could influence sales in the short run was to find some new accounts. The chances for this were rare.

Fred received a base salary and incentive bonus based on the total sales in his territory, whether direct or through the distributor. Bonuses were awarded on what was designated as a "quota performance percentage." The basic division of his income seemed reasonable to Fred, but not the method by which the incentive portion was calculated. He felt that too much of the quota variation was due to irrelevant factors. The calculations for district and territorial quotas were as follows:

1. A national forecast of PQR sales for each quarter was prepared, based mainly on a forecast of national industrial production.
2. "Base period sales" were calculated by averaging company sales for the preceding 3 years.
3. A "base quota" for the territory was calculated as the percentage the territorial sales had averaged during the base period, plus an arbitrary 5%.
4. The "forecast quota" was then this adjusted percentage times the national sales forecast for the quarter.
5. After actual sales reports for the quarter were in, an "actual quota" was calculated as the same adjusted percentage of actual sales.
6. The critical "quota performance percentage" was then the total territorial sales for the quarter divided by the "actual quota."

Fred had no quarrel with the forecast of national industrial production as a basis for production planning. But he felt that the assumption that all districts would have even a approximately stable relationship to this total overlooked some major factors. He cited an instance in which a district had won a contest for increased quota performance solely because the steel companies which accounted for nearly 80% of the abrasive sales in that district had been on strike the year before, giving the district an abnormally low base period percentage. In addition, metal forming techniques were changing, and such technique changes in the plant of a major customer could substantially affect the sales potential in a district.

At the time, Fred was just finishing work on an MBA at a local school which required a thesis for graduation. He submitted a plan for investigation of the sales potential structures in the territories in his regional district, and it was approved. The data was readily available in his district office, since distributors summarized and reported sales by customer.

What Fred hoped to show was that it would be possible to get a good industry-by-industry forecast for any specific territory by using the forecasts of the major customers themselves in a given territory. Analysis of the data showed that even though the least industrialized territory contained over 200 customers, the bulk of the sales came from a few big customers. Typically, about two-thirds of a territory's sales came from 10 accounts or fewer. In some territories, 90% of the sales came from 2 or 3 customers. Moreover, the proportion of the business accounted for by such major accounts was remarkably stable over long periods of time.

His conclusion was that it would be possible to get a forecast of the coming period by simply getting the internal forecasts from these major customers (which the sales force easily could do), and apply their historical percentage for the territory to get a territory forecast which the national office then could use. This system could work for a whole series of companies who sold any major industrial supplies, such as cutting tool, drills, taps, reamers and other expendable supplies. A comparison of the quotas that would have resulted, with the quotas actually used showed that the results of such a built up forecast were substantially more accurate than the current method.

Fred also suggested that the incentive portion of his pay should be based on a "participation percentage change" rather than on dollar sales: for each increment in the purchase percentage won by his firm, the salesman should get a special bonus.

1. What do you think is the effectiveness of the present compensation system?

2. There is no hint that sales turnover is very high, indicating that salesmen stay on the job and produce despite any flaws in the current system. If many other sales people are likely to view the system as unfair, why do they stay, and why does it not affect sales production visibly?

3. PQR is a dominant producer and has been in the business for a long time. Presumably, most top officials must be aware of the buying habits of major customers, especially the participation method of allocating sales. Why do you suppose they have adhered to the current basis for compensation for so long?

4. Fred's interest in the subject seems to go beyond writing a thesis, perhaps hoping to get PQR to change its system. How easy do you think this will be, and why?

5. Under what circumstances might a district be highly disadvantaged for a long period ahead, under the current system?

6. A minor sidelight on Fred's job and his outlook: he told of a day on which he had no pressing appointments. Fred used the time to survey the businesses in an industrial district, knocking on every door, without exception to find out what kind of abrasives they might use, and for what purposes. One that he called on was a paint manufacturer, hardly an obvious prospect, as he himself saw. To his surprise, the firm did have one use: a small grinding wheel which helped blend pigments. It turned out to be one of PQR's own wheels, but the manufacturer was sending clear across the country, to San Francisco, to get it, unaware it was in stock locally.

How would you reward this kind of activity?

OCEAN SPRAY: BROADENING ITS MARKET

Ocean Spray Cranberries, Inc. is the sales arm of a cranberry growers' cooperative with 700 members. For a long time, the cooperative simply sold its output during the holiday season, plus canned cranberry sauce.

Then disaster struck in 1960. The federal government announced that a herbicide used on cranberries caused cancer in animals. (The herbicide has since been banned.) The business for that year was ruined, and remained poor for several years.

After that, Ocean Spray began developing year-around products: newly formulated cranberry juice and juice blends, grapefruit juice, and a tomato-vegetable juice.

Sales multiplied ten-fold, from $30 million in 1963 to $302 million in 1981, and more products are in the offing. Ocean Spray is strong in food markets, and in some parts of the food service field, but had little toehold in the national restaurant chain business until recently. It developed a "paper bottle,"--a paper package for juices to appeal to the institutional market. This package required no refrigeration and cuts costs of production, shipping, and storage.

To reach food service outlets, Ocean Spray uses a field force consisting of 20 food service brokers and 25 other brokers covering both retail and food service outlets--not enough to do a thorough job with restaurants. The coop was handicapped in the food service field by the necessity to ship in less-than-truckload lots.

In 1981, Ocean Spray moved to strengthen it foothold in the institutional markets by means of a cooperative agreement with H. J. Heinz. Heinz would add the Ocean Spray line to that carried by its 150-man institutional sales force, with Ocean Spray paying a commission on sales, and Heinz handling, delivering and collecting on the sales.

E. F HUTTON: AN AGGRESSIVE SELL FOR INVESTMENTS

In recent years, E. F. Hutton has moved up fast to become second only to Merrill Lynch in the brokerage field. It has won its spurs by a strong emphasis on sales training and incentives instead of painstaking research or brilliant speculation.

Hutton has accomplished this by spending three-fifths of a $2 million training budget on teaching experienced brokers new sales tactics, according to an account in the January 19, 1981 Business Week. Outside analysts say that Hutton's brokers average per-capita incomes higher than the average of brokers at other publicly held firms. The average commission earned is 40%, better then in most public securities brokerages. When Hutton has a push on for some special product such as life insurance or tax shelters, it pays a 50% commission. As a consequence, Hutton's brokers are quick to adapt to new products and new markets.

When the municipal finance department introduced a new type of housing revenue bond in 1977, 30-odd brokers went through an intensive seminar, then fanned out as a so-called 'SWAT team' to make more than 700 sales calls in 3 weeks. Business Week notes that "within two years it was the undisputed leader in housing revenue bond sales."

The training program teaches brokers to identify their selling styles and adjust them to the client. One is reported as saying he was able to turn three recalcitrant investors into clients in the first week after taking the course.

Observers note that Hutton is willing to take risks to create product which attract affluent clients: the first to build a tax shelter department, and an originator of a personal finance planning service whereby a financial advisor will, for a fee, counsel an individual investor on his investment and insurance portfolio.

Hutton is aiming at being a major factor in investment banking. In 1980, it won the underwriting of $125 million worth of variable-rate tax-exempt bonds from U.S. Steel at a time when the bond market was not at its best. It devised a novel twist for the rates that made the bonds appear attractive, and quickly sold $105.5 million of the bonds. It managed or co-managed $5 billion of corporate financing in 1980. Competitors concede that the U. S. Steel issue was a feat, but are skeptical as to its success in "the exclusive and gentlemanly club of investment banking," with its hard sell tactics.

1. What segments of the investing community are likely to be susceptible to the hard sell approach that Hutton is using?   Why?

2. Defining as retail those customers investing as individuals, what is the most attractive retail segment?   What might substantial numbers of them be looking for in a broker?

3, If better honed sales skills pays off as well as it has for Hutton, why are their competitors so slow to follow suit?

4. A stock broker has to prove a relatively high level of technical knowledge to pass his license exam.   What does the Hutton success tell us about the relative importance of technical knowledge and sales knowledge in recruiting and training people for other positions requiring a substantial technical knowledge of some field and its products?

5. What would be your opinion of the possibility of Hutton gaining a significant foothold in investments banking?   What strengths do they have which could help them do it?

INTERMEDICS: AN AGGRESSIVE SELLER IN THE MEDICAL IMPLANTS FIELD

According to Business Week, Intermedics Inc. "is the second largest manufacturer of heart pacemakers in the world, with 14% of an $876 million market" growing at 12% to 15% per year.(**Business Week**, "Intermedics: out to be no. 1 in the medical implants market", January 18, 1982).

Intermedics got its major push when it introduced the lithium-battery pacemaker in 1976, extending the life of a pacemaker from a previous 2 years to 6. Intermedics also acquired Intraocular, Inc. in 1976, which makes implantable lenses for cataract patients.   Intraocular has grown at the meteoric rate of 130% per year.

The pacemaker market is hotly competitive, and what has won Intermedics its strong position is its aggressive sales organization.   As a medical industry analyst has noted, an effective sales force is second only to reliable technology in that market, and "a stress on incentive is what separates Intermedics from the rest of the industry."

Other pacemaker manufacturers have their own internal sales forces, but Intermedics chose to offer sales people from other companies an opportunity to set up their own businesses selling Intermedics products.   It provides marketing and educational support for them and their 183 sales representatives working on straight commission.   As Intermedics president Chambers is quoted as remarking, the commissions give "them a hell of an incentive to sell."

These sales representatives also serve as an intelligence network for the Intermedics diversification program.   According to Chambers,"that sales group is out in the field and aware of what's going on every day.   If they see a new product we're not in that they're excited about, they'll let us know because it could mean money in their pockets as well as the company's."   Intermedics moves fast when it spots such opportunities.

1. How is the sale of something like the pacemaker decided upon?

2. Presumably, the sales representatives are essentially detailmen, as in the rest of the medical field.   How can the representatives affect total sales volume?

3. How is the operation usually paid for, including the pacemaker implant?

4. Considering your answers above, can you think of any problems which might

possibly arise from the kind of high sales pressure implied in Intermedics' form of sales organization and sales compensation?

5. The intelligence function is certainly worth pushing. How would you provide adequate incentive to pursue it to an internal sales force with a stable base income plus some incentive pay?

6. What form of training would you install to develop a similar ability in sales trainees in other areas in which they call on professional advisors, such as those covering architects for building materials, or college "bookmen"?

A SALES REPRESENTATIVE AND HIS CUSTOMER FRANCHISE

For historical reasons, manufacturers' representatives who sell to food stores are known as food brokers, although some of the offerings they represent may well be non-foods. The line any one carries normally is confined to the lines purchased by a single chain buying department.

One such broker was Art. As is true of many brokers, Art gained his experience with a major food store chain—in his case, the leading Detroit chain, becoming a chain supervisor, working out of chain headquarters. His close acquaintance with the store managers and headquarters personnel provided Art with an initial acceptance which paid off for his principals.

The product Art represented were not glamorous: they included such items as barbecue supplies. But they went to the same buyers Chuck Carsons hoped to sell a new pet supply his firm was introducing—a supply the supermarkets were not yet handling. Chuck made a number of trips to visit Art, and with him, the chain headquarters. Talking to Art, Chuck asked about how he would go about getting a new item in a store. Art replied: "If they seem reluctant to buy outright, I usually ask them for permission to drop ship to any manager who wishes a supply, and they will usually do it. Then I go around to the managers and get orders. I know most of them well, and they have taken my advice on stocking and display in the past. They will usually take my word on any product I am willing to put in my line. Then I take the orders back to the buyer and ask him: 'Do you want me to drop ship these, or put them through your warehouse? They order them for the warehouse".

On one trip, made on a Monday, a remark of Art's illuminated the reason for his acceptance among store managers and owners. He noted that he was a little tired. He had spent the weekend helping the owner of a 3-store chain get ready for a new store opening. "Like everyone else, he had so many items, he was having trouble getting enough shelf space. I helped him decide on the shelf spacings that would work best for each item." No more than 3 of the items in the store were in Art's line, and they would have been minor ones. Most of his weekend labor had gone to help the store owner plan sales of items not remotely related to Art's line.

1. Art was an independent food broker, but his task was really no different from that of a salesman in the employ of some food processor, calling on supermarket warehouses. How would you stimulate the kind of activity Art was carrying out, and how would you evaluate and pay for it in such a case?

Chapter 14. Managing Mass Communications

Mass communications: prerequisite to reaching broad markets
      The door opening and support roles of mass communications
      The limits on what mass communications can do
Leveraged communications: publicity and public relations
      Generating publicity
Advertising management
      The questions to be answered
            What role should advertising play in the mix?
                  Variations in the role
                  Relationship of the role to the types of offerings and
                        to the nature of prospect segments
                  Advertising and the market life cycle
            What are the campaign's objectives?
            What segments should be targetted?
            What benefits should be emphasized?
            What is the best way to impart credibility to the claims?
            How much shall be spent?
Sales promotions and their management

MASS COMMUNICATIONS MANAGEMENT

14

Mass Communications: Prerequisite to Reaching Broad Markets

Modern mass marketing and the mass communications of advertising, publicity and sales promotions were born and grew up together. Neither could have developed without the other. Personal sales is too slow a form of communications to reach large numbers of buyers within reasonable time limits, and much too expensive to handle the initial steps of creating awareness and initial interest in an offering. Cyrus McCormick, as indicated earlier, was the inventor of the first true mass marketing effort. It was his shrewd blending of personal sales, constant publicity, aggressive advertising, and the sales promotion tool of demonstrations which gained market dominance in the face of strong competition.

Each of the three modes of mass communications makes a unique contribution to the marketing effort. Publicity is by far the strongest of the mass tools for gaining early attention and providing credibility for the benefit claims. Publicity is also by far the most cost effective tool, one that cost so little that even the lowest budget non-commercial organization can make extensive use of it. But publicity is outside the control of the user, and can tell the same story to the same audience but once.

Advertising has the advantage of seller control and repetition, and can continue to remind buyers of benefits long after all news value is gone.

Sales promotion is a label covering a wide group of types of efforts whose only common thread is that they are not personal sales, advertising or publicity, but a means of support for any or all of the other modes. Some promotions are attention-getting devices, some a means of conveying an understanding of the benefits, and a number of them are basically pricing devices, used to stimulate trial or counter a competitor's moves.

The usefulness of these modes of communication and the appropriate mix changes with the shifting phases of the market life cycle. Expenditures for sales promotion are at least equal to the more visible total for advertising. Spending for publicity and public relations cannot even be guessed at, but are certainly far less than those for any other mode.

Mass communications can be extremely cost effective in drawing attention to offerings and stimulating interest. They prepare the way for sales personnel, and reinforce the relationships after purchase.

The Door-Opening And Support Functions of Mass Communications

The value of mass communications in smoothing the path for the sales effort have been graphically depicted in an ad run periodically by **Business Week** magazine. Full page, it centers on an executive leaning forward on the arms of his swivel chair and coldly informing an unseen caller:

> I don't know you
> I don't know your company
> I don't know your product

The implication is clear. The salesman, if he even gets that far, will have to spend a lot of expensive time educating such customers before he can hope to deliver a sales message. Even were his offering potentially of real interest, the probabilities of success would be much poorer than if a persistent mass communications effort had cleared the path for him.

Mass communications also serve to remind customers between sales, maintain customer consciousness of the offering and its benefits, Finally, advertising, especially, can keep reminding actual buyers of the possible benefits they have gained.

All of these benefits can be obtained from advertising for nickels or dimes per contact, compared with $100 or more per contact in industrial selling. But mass communications also are limited in what can be done with them to gain the sale itself.

HOW MANY OF TODAY'S ADS CAN YOU REMEMBER?

Research has established that the average middle class person is "exposed" to over 700 advertising presentations of all kinds in a 24 hour period (some, of course, on pages flipped over without looking).

Manifestly, none of us could take the time to study any substantial number of these, and we don't. But none of us can escape at least a glance at some of them—the billboards on the route, the commercials sandwiched in between TV programs, etc. How many make even a short-time impression?

The author has tested this on a number of student classes with from 20 to 50 students at a time. When asked to raise their hands if they could remember even one ad seen in the last 24 hours, no more than 2 students in any section could do so—sometimes none. Those who did noticed only those promoting something they were interested in, and it was as likely to be some small poster as a large ad when they did.

The Limits On What Mass Communications Can Do

Mass communications can be extremely cost effective when:

- the right message is delivered
- in an appropriate manner
- to well-targetted segments of the market

- to accomplish an objective which is within the limits of a monolog

They can be a waste of money, at best, and even hurt sales, if even one of these conditions is not met reasonably met.

Entrenched habits seem to be immune to one-sided presentations. Offerings which require substantial relearning require something more than advertising and even publicity to sell. No mail order seller has ever broken open the market for any offering requiring even a moderate degree of habit relearning.

Any form of mass communications is a monolog, with all of the limitations of any conversation lacking questions or other feedback.

Indeed, in the absence of specific research, we cannot know whether:

- anyone paid attention
- those who may have listened received the same message the seller intended to send
- the message was one which really interested the target audience
- the audience who did receive the message was the right target

The one exception to some of the above is direct response (mail order, etc.) advertising. Even in this case, the results need added analysis to determine the full effect of the effort.

As with all forms of mass production, mass communications must deliver a standardized product, with only a minimum variation, for mass segments of the target market. Some initial degree of potential interest must already exist, or the effort is screened out by the process of selective attention. The message conveyed must be one the audience already understands and is fully ready to accept.

Fortunately, most of the messages we hope to deliver involve offerings which are already established, or are otherwise low-learning. When this is so, we can discover the proper audience. We can get excellent information on the media which reaches these audiences. And we know, or can find out, what benefits the important core audiences are seeking. The rest is up to the professionals with a sound understanding of marketing and the skill and experience to formulate the messages in a manner best suited to attract attention and be believed.

Both marketing knowledge and communications expertise are essential. Modern marketing became possible only when the communications specialists were professionalized. The need for seasoned professional help is especially acute for the communications tool which is critical to both the non-profit community service organization and the introducers of high-learning introductions: publicity and public relations.

Leveraged Communications: Publicity and Public Relations

Publicity is any message concerning the offering which appears in the news context of the medium and which lacks any designation as being a purposeful selling effort. Publicity and the related public relations could be characterized as low profile, low cost messages about the seller which carry the impact of news. Because of its low profile news character, many sellers who might take advantage of it neglect the effort needed to generate publicity and make certain that it carries a needed message. The cost is low because the space or time in which it appears is not charged for. It is not charged for because those giving it space or time consider it part of the news. It is believable because those receiving the message perceive the source as the medium itself--as a trusted third party, not the seller.

Publicity is not without some cost: the cost of careful planning and skilled presentation. But that cost is rewarded many times over by the effectiveness of the results. No form of openly sponsored, paid communications can even begin to match the value of well-directed publicity.

Publicity's greatest value is to exactly those sellers most in need of a low-budget effort: those trying to sell high-learning offerings, and those community service organizations whose activities carry an inherently strong potential for wide interest: schools and colleges, hospitals, symphony orchestras, governmental service activities, etc. Their most marketable activities are generally also those with the highest news value.

High learning new offerings with a real long run potential are also news, and publicity is by far the best vehicle for creating awareness of the benefits being offered. Even well-established, blatantly commercial offerings can find ways to benefit from well-planned and directed publicity efforts, and get them published. In that case, however, the effort's main value is as a reinforcement of the other communications modes.

Publicity can be generated, but not freely controlled. Publication depends on its news value, as perceived by media editors. (Although it can also get published if it is inextricably tied to a newsworthy event. The advertising panels on the front of the spectator stands at athletic events, for example, which get into the TV pictures of the event, and the names of sponsors of automobile racing events, and even of the teams.)

Stale news is no news, so a given item can appear only once in a given publication. Keeping a story before an audience requires both imagination and the skill to find different newsworthy ways to present the same basic message.

As with any other aspect of marketing strategy, the p.r. effort must be focussed on a message, an audience which will perceive substantial benefit in the offering being publicized, and on benefits which are salient in their desire sets. The same aspect of the basic theme must be highlighted in everything the seller does which can be turned into a news item. In other words, there must be a clear strategy, and a clear definition of the place of p.r. in that strategy.

THE PINKERTON STORY: A WELL—MANAGED COINCIDENCE

When I picked up my March 4, 1982 Charlotte Observer, I found a feature article on page 1 of an inside section headed, "Pinkerton Agency Has Chased Outlaws for 13 Decades." Under the by—line of Michelle Iroff of the Smithsonian New Service, was a lengthy review of the history of the Pinkerton Agency, from its establishment in 1850., mentioning its part in some savage union management battles of the 1890's, but emphasizing its more colorful detective exploits.

Then I turned to peruse my Wall Street Journal. Lo and behold, on page 10 was a quarter page ad with the bold type headline, "WHY YOU SHOULD INVESTIGATE PINKERTON," noting its long history. Subsections were headed, "We give you investigative expertise," We give you premium service," and "We give you peace of mind."

Generating Publicity

Any organization may get some publicity by accident, and at least some of it may accidentally be useful. But efficient, really effective publicity must be planned.

Sound planning must start with a general marketing strategy: an audience to be reached, a benefit bundle perceivable as valuable by that audience, a message about those benefits which has proven value in getting their attention, and a total communications plan in which the publicity mode has a well defined role to play.

If the organization is a personal service operation, all responsible members of the organization need to understand and be a part of this plan. Much of the news must come from them, or the p.r. director will be empty-handed. In turn, this requires a widespread educational program on what normal events and activities make good news items.

Special events with good publicity potentials can also be created deliberately. Among the possibilities for community service operations the following examples are common:

- appointment of newsworthy individuals to auxiliaries and advisory boards, or any other events linking such individuals to the organization
- The initiation of special programs of general interest, such as special classes and special clinics. Also any event which highlights a program of general interest which is not yet well known: the graduation of the first class in a relatively new program, special accomplishments of those connected with a program, etc.
- Human interest stories about participants in a program, especially those of volunteers.
- Sponsorship of newsworthy on-premise events put on by other organizations

Established commercial organizations can generate publicity by sponsoring various community service or other high-news-value special programs discreetly tied to the general theme of its communications strategy for an offering or for the organization as a whole.

The primary role of publicity is as a trailbreaker for the personal sales and advertising efforts, and a continuing reinforcement of both. When utilized in connection with new offerings, the follow-up burden must be carried by advertising and/or personal sales. When utilized by a community service operation, publicity may carry the brunt of the mass communications effort, but commonly should be followed up with timely advertising and tied in with such personal sales effort as that conducted by the "admissions office" of a college.

Advertising Management

Although advertising lacks almost all of the mystical persuasive power for which it is mistakenly given credit, advertising is potentially the most cost-effective means of presenting a persistent story about the benefits of an offering and developing a wide interest in and understanding or those benefits. Advertising is the only widely available tool for differentiating low-price consumer items whose objective physical differences are relatively minor (beverages, toiletries, cigarettes and other packaged consumer goods, for example).

Advertising is also the most frustrating mode of communications. Costs are highly measurable and known to the penny. The results cannot be even roughly approximated in advance. Even after the fact, measurement of the effectiveness in forwarding the sales is only roughly approximated at best. Sometimes, the results are not visible at all, even when effective. Someone once commented that "half my advertising is wasted, but I don't know which half."

Advertising expenditures are easy to waste, or worse. (There is some experimental evidence that some proposed or actual themes have cost sales.) All that is needed to waste money is a major mistake in the receptive audience, in the campaign appeal or copy execution, or a failure to coordinate the advertising effort with a well-conceived marketing strategy. Most such waste that occurs (and it does) stems from a failure to gather and use the objective information needed for good planning. Innovation is a major ingredient in advertising, but a disciplined innovation, which starts with a knowledge of the market and the benefits being sought, then designs a program which is coordinated with the total strategy.

An effective advertising strategy starts with careful thought to the answers to a number of questions:

- What is the role of the communications mix in the total marketing strategy?

- What role can advertising best play in the communications mix?
- Which segments offer the greatest potential?
- What media reach these audiences with the least waste and the greatest impact?
- Which of the possible perceivable benefits of the offering are prospects seeking?
- In what form are these benefits best communicated?
- How much shall we spend?

The Possible Roles of Advertising

The **general role** of advertising in the communications mix is simple: to develop attitudes favorable to the offering and/or the seller, among any or all of the specific market segments the seller must reach to succeed. These necessarily include, in addition to the final customer, all direct and indirect customers in the various levels of distribution.

Also included are others whose cooperation and/or patronage are important to the seller's vitality: those who specify the use of its products or recommend them in any way: investors and financial institutions, potential employees (especially in scarce categories), potential contributors, politicians and voters, esp. at the local level.

The **specific roles** for a seller's advertising will vary with the special marketing skills of the individual seller, with that seller's communications needs at the moment, with the nature of the offering and its role in the offering mix, with the size of the individual purchase and the system under which it is bought, and with the number of potential buyers.

The useful role of advertising changes with the phases of the market life cycle.

Individual variations in the role. We need only observe the world around us to see variation in the role of advertising in the communications mix.

The cosmetics field is one example. Revlon and other premium cosmetics have built strong market positions through heavy advertising coordinated with the promotion by sales-trained, commissioned cosmeticians in franchised departments of major department stores. Avon built a major volume with door-to-door sales with no advertising originally, and only limited advertising later. The advertising that was run was to build up the image of the "Avon Lady," and certainly, in part, to keep the ranks filled with more of them.

In household supplies, Amway promotes its own line to a similar market--young housewives tied down at home. Amway's major advertising is directly aimed at Amway's major sales problem--securing a continuing supply of "distributors". (Turnover of sales personnel is very high in door-to-door selling.)

Some insurance firms sell through local agents, backed by TV and print advertising. Others have no agents and get sales through direct mail advertising.

Advertising's best role also differs with the position of the seller in the distribution chain.

The relation of advertising's role to the kinds of offering and the types of prospects. In the sale of mass produced, low-priced packaged consumer goods, advertising tends to play the dominant communications role. The possible audience is large and widely spread across the landscape. Product benefit expectations are relatively simple and rather easily discovered. The unit of purchase is small and the offering tends to be regarded as a convenience item by many in the market, justifying very little shopping effort.

In the sale of higher-priced items such as automobiles and major appliances, advertising plays an important but subsidiary role. The same item may satisfy quite different desire sets for different customers. Many of the customers are shoppers, tend to consider several competitive offerings, and are subject to some degree of personal sales persuasion. The price makes personal selling feasible.

By contrast, advertising's role tends to be relatively modest for most major offerings to industrial, commercial, and institutional buyers. Markets trend to be concentrated and the number of customers is relatively limited. Purchases are large, patronage relationships are relatively close. Using the offerings often involves substantial personal contact and personal service.

Advertising And The Market Life Cycle

The appropriate mission for advertising shifts with the changing phases of the market life cycle.

For **high-learning offerings** starting through a market development phase, advertising must alert potential innovators and early adopters to the availability of benefits that interest them. Advertising can also attract possible early adopting fabricators or strong, entrepreneurial distributors. In all cases it should help pave the way for personal sales and arouse the kind of interest which will lead to intelligent questioning of the sales people.

The general task in the market development phase is to promote the basic offering benefits. Since there will be no effective direct competition, brand identification is secondary.

Competitive differentiation is a major task for the advertising in the **growth phase,** helping to build strong patronage relationships at both the intermediary and the final consumer stage.

Once the **market matures,** the main task is to find ever-freshened ways of reminding current customers of both offering form and brand values they are receiving, to forestall both brand competition and potential cross-product competition from new forms of offerings.

When the **decline phase** appears, advertising as well as all other promotional expenditures have no role to play. The funds and the resources should be put to work where they can produce profits for the future.

What Should The Campaign's Objectives Be?

Successful advertising requires a specific set of objectives. The specific set will vary with the distribution level of the advertiser and with the market circumstances.

Producer advertising generally aims to develop a specific perception of the benefits to be expected from the offering: to give it an image and position it with respect to competition. The benefits promoted may be physically inherent in the offering, or they may be intangible benefits which the best potential customers are prepared to associate with their use-systems involving the offering.

While nearly all **merchant advertising** features specific items, those selected (and the form of the copy) have the primary aim of creating traffic of a specific set of market segments. Thus one supermarket will feature, at attractive low margins, items whose heaviest buyers are working class families with a number of small children. Another may feature quality meats and produce, and a breadth of variety not readily available in competitors' stores, to attract an upper-middle class professional customer segment.

A substantial amount of producer advertising is intended as much for distributor and dealer attention as for final user attention. The "merchandising" aspect of such promotions achieve their purpose **before** the advertising is finally published. The proposed campaign becomes a selling tool for the sales representatives contacting distributors and dealers.

Organizations who must regularly recruit numbers of highly skilled specialists of some kind may run ad campaigns featuring their research activities (for example) in media widely read by the audiences sought.

Which Segments Should Be Targetted?

Cost efficiency demands that the advertising be directed to attract those specific market segments who offer the greatest potential available for the specific seller. The total cost is directly proportional to the audience of the media purchased. The unit cost is inversely proportional to the buying response obtained: the numbers who act, and the size of their purchases. The aim is to attract the profitable customers. Advertising to the rest simply reduces the profit.

When the identity of the most profitable segment, and of the desire sets to appeal to them is unknown, the best advertising appropriation contains the funds to find out.

What Benefits Should Be Stressed?

Generally speaking, effective communications zero in on some single specific appeal. That appeal should be the one which objective evidence and research has shown to be dominant for the high-potential audiences which the specific seller can hope to attract. It is often very easy to "armchair" the appeal thought best. It is even easier to be wrong, in the absence of some directly analytical evidence of who the customers are and what motives impels them to buy.

HOW YOU PRESENT IT IS IMPORTANT, TOO

The ad agency was discussing an account they never said much about. It consisted primarily of placing direct response TV ads run by a couple of entrepreneurs. Generally, the advertisers themselves prepared much of the advertising, one series at a time. Each series consisted of an advertisement making a "limited offer" of some specialty or novelty, one ad per week, bought one week at a time. The series would be run as long as the ad paid off, then dropped, and another started when the partners found an item which appeared suitable. Since the TV time was purchased on short notice, the placement depended on open availabilities. Most of them appeared on such programs as the Late-Late Show or on low-rated shows.

One such item was a salad maker. The commercial consisted of a demonstration of the cutter working, showing only the tool and the hands of the demonstrator, accompanied by his voiced sales pitch. The demonstrator was a street corner pitchman type, with the voice to match. Sales were profitable, but along with the orders, stations were getting a substantial stream of complaints about "that awful commercial." These were forwarded to the ad agency, with queries about whether they could do something about it.

Finally, with the client's consent, the agency decided to erase the voice track on the filmed commercial, and substitute the same spiel, read by a professional soap opera announcer. The complaints ceased and the sales doubled.

How Best to Impart Credibility to The Benefit Claims?

Copy preparation is an art, requiring a high level of experience, skill, and imagination. These need to be wedded to an understanding of the customer psychology in general and of the specific social psychology of the target segment in relation to the product form.

Any reasonably complete discussion of all of the behavioral principles involved requires more space than can be devoted here. However, a few basics, which are sometimes sometimes ignored, should be mentioned.

First, any advertising is perceived and makes its impression as a whole. The audience senses the layout, the typography and the illustrations as part of the message which is intended for them. They will then try to make sense out of this whole, as perceived by them. If, as indicated much earlier in the case of the Marlboro Man, the illustration seems to say something not mentioned in the copy, they will search their own habitual perceptions patterns for one that seems to fit. If none is found, the message is discarded as meaningless. But if one fits, that one is the message. By the principal of closure, discovering that connection tends to convey conviction, **even when a cognitive statement would be rejected as silly.**

Second, established product forms fit into specific life-style patterns for those in the heavy-user segments. Messages about them register only when presented in terms of the life-style context expected.

For some offerings, the life-style relevant for heavy users is a traditional pattern, as opposed to an innovative life-style. (This is true of the heavy beer user.) For others, the heaviest consuming segments are upward-striving in a role transition situation (cosmetics, fragrances, high fashion clothing, among adolescents and young adults in their transition to full adult status).

Thus all successful copy for offerings with little physical differentiation (and for some that have substantial differentiation, such as sports cars) appeals to the role-system values and also the perceived use-systems of the offerings.

What Media Reach The Target Audiences

The media question is the one for which the most objective measures are available. Each medium attracts a specific audience, and most media of any importance regularly develop information on that audience and make it available. What attracts the specific audience is the "editorial" slant of the medium. This bias can be discovered through an analysis of the editorial content itself (when print or TV) and confirmed by an analysis of the other advertising attracted to that medium.

Moreover, media covering extensive markets often run separate editions for different regions of the country or different areas of a metropolitan region. The advertiser can buy a single such market. When a direct mail effort is a possibility, a mailing list of almost any desired major segment can be purchased or prepared.

How Much Shall Be Spent?

This is the really hard question. The only simple answer gives little help except in rare instances: as much as is profitable.

Direct action advertising is the only form normally producing even an approximate answer, and then only by running a test. If the test proves profitable, the advertising is run until the last ad barely pays off.

Even in this case, the amount needed depends on the skill, imagination, and insight into the nature of the demand which is embodied in the presentation.

No other advertising situation yields any good answer as to the pay-off in sales. Nor should we expect such direct sales pay-off, or measure of it.

Advertising is only one element in the total promotional mix, and the promotional mix is only one factor in the marketing mix. The effect of the total mix is affected by the actions of competition. As already indicated, advertising is relatively weak in producing actual sales. The primary factor is the offering itself--the offering as perceived in the context of its use-value relative to competing offerings. Predicting the actions of competitors is obviously risky, and there is always the problem of knowing what the indirect competition will be.

What advertising does best is to influence the perceptions of the offering and attitudes toward it. Attitude research is a relatively imprecise tool, which can give an approximate reading, but not the kind of advance reading needed for planning.

Because of these difficulties, most advertising plans use one or more arbitrary rule-of-thumb standards which may have some actual validity in specific situations. Most budgeting decisions belong to one or more of 5 general methods:

1. All that we can afford
2. Match the competition
3. Percentage of expected sales, or some specific amount per unit sold
4. Objective-and-task method
5. What we have always spent

The all we can spend school has something to be said for it when applied to low or moderately-low learning offerings in the introductory period, especially new start-up enterprises. In such a situation, the aim is to establish as strong a market position as possible in the minds of both distributors and final buyers, before competitors can gain a foothold. When this is the aim, the promotional expenses are an investment in future market strength. The value of that investment depends on the size of the expected potential. If the real potential is very substantial, the investment may be cheap at any price.

Matching (or attempting to beat) the spending level of competitors has at least some superficial appeal for offerings highly responsive to advertising pull. However, any validity it has assumes parity of advertising quality and perceived parity of competing offerings among similar market segments. In addition, it must assume that all competitors are in the same phase of their offering life cycles. Such assumptions obviously narrow whatever validity this standard can claim.

All sales-related measures share the assumptions that advertising should **follow** sales volume, and that the sales estimates are reasonably good. This standard also implies advertising when sales are easiest to get and cutting back when customers need extra coaxing.

WHEN SHOULD YOU ADVERTISE? THE CHEVY TEST

Delorean's rise in GM was based on his accomplishments in turning around the Chevrolet operation, which was apparently in some trouble in 1970. One of the areas on which De Lorean focussed was the advertising. In this effort, he made use of the professional expertise of Dr. Thomas A. Staudt, recently brought into Chevy by GM President Ed. Cole, from Michigan State University, where he had been Chairman of the Dept. of Marketing and Transportation.

One of the practices which De Lorean questioned was what he designated as the "strike—while—the—iron—is—hot" method of advertising appropriation: spending heaviest on advertising when business is easy to get, and cutting back when sales were difficult. GM based the advertising appropriation on the beginning of the year production estimate, allotting a specific amount for each unit produced.

Staudt and De Lorean questioned this practice, and scheduled a market test during a year when sales were down.

Three similar markets were chosen: a control market, where no plans were changed, a second market in which a special promotion planned in Detroit was launched, and a third market in which the same special campaign was reinforced by dealer effort, with showroom placards, banners, and dealer promotion. The program was run for several weeks. In comparison with the control market, the second market sustained a sales increase of the order of one—fourth, the all—out effort in the third market about a 60% increase.

(GM top management subsequently refused to allow a change in the method allocating ad expenditures for the Chevy division as a whole.)

[Ref: J. Patrick Wright, **On a Clear Day You Can See General Motors**, pp.182–3, Avon Books, 1980]

However, this standard does make sense as a limitation rule for new offerings. The standard can also be one founded on experience of the organization with similar product forms in the past, or a means of limiting the budget to what the market seems likely to justify.

Objective—and—task methods are logical. The problem is in estimating the value of the objective and the costs of carrying out the tasks.

Objectives for a campaign are set in terms of discoverable communications goals: specific changes in brand and message recognition and recall, benefit awareness and comprehension, favorable attitudes, etc. To state the objectives is to disclose the difficulty of putting dollar values on them in any planning. Some degree of evaluation can be determined through time-consuming tests. Even then, the assumption must be made that competitive efforts will fail to nullify the effort.

Obviously, there are no simple answers, if what we seek to do is to establish a fixed budget in advance, and expect to know what the effects will be. Even the best and best analyzed of past experience does not permit this. But it is possible to get an idea from experience and specific tests as to approximately what might happen, then to monitor results as the campaign proceeds, and modify both budget and execution to fit the circumstances. No kind of market forecasting of any kind is ever even approximately accurate. There are too many unknowns, of which the greatest are the reactions of competitors and customers. Forecasting advertising effects shares all of these difficulties.

SECOND CITY MAKES BID FOR MORE TOURISM WITH GAME, AD PROMOTION
(From **Marketing News**, Nov. 12, 1982, p.7, by permission)

The Success of the "I Love New York" campaign has inspired other cities to market themselves, and the latest entry is the City of Chicago.

The "My Kind of Town" marketing campaign kicked off recently with an "instant win" game and will get into high gear later with a nationwide cooperative promotion between city, state, and private sector. Efforts are being directed by the Chicago Promotion Council (CPC), a not-for-profit umbrella organization.

"One of the most heated marketing battles being waged in this country today is that between cities and states for a greater share of the convention and travel market," according to restauranteur Don Roth, CPC Chairman..."we've developed a unique approach that we believe will help us stand out in the marketplace."

"Two major objectives of the promotion are to provide opportunities for our visitors to experience more of what Chicago has to offer, and to help add to the excitement and enjoyment of a visit...

Fast food restaurants ...and other businesses have had considerable success with "instant win" game cards, and that inspired the adaptation for the city promotion.

Visitors rub off an area on the card where three of a possible nine city names appear. If all three squares read "Chicago," the ticketholder wins one of 50 weekly prizes, ranging from free hotel accommodations to tickets to cultural events or other attractions.

If the ticket is not a winner, recipients can fill them out with their names and addresses and drop them off at designated locations for a second-chance drawing. Round-trip air fares to the city, shopping sprees worth up to $500, and other prizes designed to draw the visitor back to the city at a later date are awarded in these drawings....

Print and radio advertising is being used to promote the game, and a national campaign on behalf of the city will start later, using magazines,TV, print and radio.

United Airlines is committed to airing the "My Kind of Town" commercial in its key markets in the United States....

The national campaign seeks to promote the city as a business and travel destination and will provide opportunities for cooperative and tie-in advertising by businesses. CPC officials are negotiating for the rights to the song, "My kind of Town," and they hope to make the promotion self-financing through licensing arrangements and sale-for-profit of "My Kind of Town" merchandise.

Sales Promotions And Their Management

Sales promotions can be defined only in negative terms: they are any form of marketing communication or sales stimulation which is not included under the definitions of personal sales, publicity, or advertising. This is a very wide range of devices indeed, and one that gets wider every day.

Whatever their specific forms and objectives, their role is to reinforce the other communications efforts. Total expenditures for all forms is an unknown. The total for trade shows and exhibits alone have been estimated to be about the same as the total advertising bill, and this is only one form.

The nature of each form is different. Some, such as point-of-purchase (p-o-p) displays are a form of attention-attracting advertising. Others, such as trade shows, contain many of the elements of personal sales. Those which are designed to get sampling may accomplish objectives which no form of verbal communication alone can effect: give the customer some direct personal experience with the benefits of the offering.

No complete listing of all of the devices is possible. The limits of the list are the limits of creative imagination, and new forms are regularly developed. Even the list of major objectives is long:
- create sales directly
- create store traffic
- stimulate attention at the point of sale
- stimulate extra effort by salespeople and/or dealers and distributors
- help stimulate demand for the product form
- help stimulate demand for the brand
- help develop acceptance of the seller as a general source for a wide line of offerings
- create or improve a perception of the promised benefits in an offering
- arouse curiosity and prepare the way for a sales person
- stimulate heavier or more diverse usage by current buyers
- induce consumer sampling
- develop a closer relationship with distributors and/or buyers and thus get them to perceive the seller as a favored source
- counter a possibly damaging move by a competitor
- keep a constant reminder in front of possible buyers
- enhance the value of the offering in some manner

A list of the more common forms of sales promotions would have to include:
- special displays and display devices
- packaging and labelling with a positive communications and/or benefit content
- temporary price reduction devices such as combination deals, discount ("cents-off") offers, coupons, "free goods," ("11 for the price of 10") made to distributors and dealers.
- value enhancing extras such as premiums, sweepstakes, store games, unusual guarantees, etc.
- trade show exhibits and demonstrations

- sampling of various kinds
- educational efforts: training of distributor's sales people, of possible users of the offering (IBM courses, for example)
- "specialty advertising" give-aways: from calendars and ball point pens to T-shirts and beer steins
- Special scholarships
- entertainment: clowns, choral groups, etc.

Sales Promotions and the Market Life Cycle

As with all other aspects of marketing, the utility and appropriate forms of sales promotions are related to the phase of the life cycle.

Sampling is clearly an important aid for the promotion of understanding of the benefits offered by any high-learning offering passing through a market development phase.

Trade show exhibits can also be extremely valuable in introductory promotion. Such exhibits are often needed adjuncts to the personal sales operations on a continuing basis. They develop traffic by the combined draw of all of the exhibits and thus a broader exposure to potential market segments than would normally be available otherwise.

New brand introductions in low learning categories normally find special deals essential to early market penetration. Even in the maturity stage, they prove useful as a quickly implemented countermove to an unexpectedly attractive offering by competitors.

Special displays are often a necessary means of getting into retail markets or even staying there in the mature phase.

Special display racks serviced by the seller or a jobber may be the only means of distribution for some kinds of offerings, such as spices, hosiery, pet supplies, etc.

Sales promotions are often the most effective competitive tool in the mature phase of the market, a necessary component of a well-rounded communications mix.

SUMMARY

Mass marketing and mass production need the support of mass communications.

Each of the three modes of mass communications performs some unique tasks best.

All of them prepare the way for personal sales efforts, and help support them afterward.

All are limited by the problems of any one-way communication. None are very good at changing buyers habits, or selling any but well-established offerings.

Publicity is a leveraged form of mass communications whose possible effectiveness is far greater than the cost of preparing it. It is the most effective means of gaining early awareness of the benefits of high learning offerings, and an extremely available, as well as effective tool for community service sellers. Its content is not fully controllable, but a stream of publicity can be generated by those with both a sensitivity to news values and the marketing skills to generate the appropriate events.

Advertising's greatest value is the controllability of its contents, its frequency, the method of presentation , and the media, with the consequent ability to present the same message repeatedly, concerning an offering's benefits. Advertising is the only mode available for developing psychological differentiation for low-cost consumer packaged goods with insignificant physical differences.

Advertising planning must find useful answers to 7 key questions: the role of advertising in the communications strategy, the segments to be targetted, the media to be used, the benefits worth promoting, the method of presentation of the benefits, and the amount to be spent.

The appropriate relative role of advertising in the promotional mix varies with the communications skills of the seller, with the nature of the offering and of the buying system, the position of the seller in the distribution chain, and the type of customers. Advertising plays a more dominant role in the sale of consumer goods than in the sales to industrial, commercial and institutional buyers.

The useful role of advertising is also dependent on the phase of the market life cycle.

Some advertising is directed at more than one audience: some consumer advertising is aimed at distributors as much as at consumers.

The method of presentation can affect the result as much as the content does.

The media decision is based on the most objective information, once the target audience is known.

None of the usual methods of determining the advertising budget yield optimum answers, and some have no logical basis. The factors which influence the results are not knowable in advance. The only way to ensure cost effectiveness is to set a budget on the basis of the best available research and experience, then monitor the results closely and adjust spending accordingly.

"Sales promotion" is a catch-all label covering a wide range of supportive communications aimed at an extended diversity of communications objectives. Some, such as display and packaging are supplementary forms of advertising, some, such as trade shows and demonstrations border on personal sales, and the various forms of sampling are a means of providing buyers with some personal experience with the offering none of the other modes provide.

FOOD FOR THOUGHT AND DISCUSSION

ADVERTISING OBJECTIVES

Most Wall Street Journal advertising is obvious financial advertising. But two ads which appeared in November 1982 issues were not so, at least on the surface.

1. A full page spread by International Harvester Company, in the November 19, 1982 issue. At the time, International Harvester was teetering on the edge of bankruptcy, held back only because its creditors could not afford to let it be declared bankrupt. Yet it appropriated the funds to pay for a full page ad promoting the International 2375 truck, billed as the only tractor that could average over 8 miles to the gallon pulling a trailer with a 65,000 lb. load over mountain roads.

Some truck owners probably subscribe to the Wall Street Journal, but they would be a small fraction of the total subscribers IH was paying to reach? What could be the purpose of such an ad?

2. A double page spread for the Ford Motor Company, in the November 22, 1982 issue. The top three-fourths of the page was a photo of a California Highway Patrol Special Pursuit Mustang, with a bold type headline below: "This Ford Chases Porsches For A Living." The rest of the ad proclaimed an order Ford had won for 400 Special Pursuit Mustangs, and gave the specifications and special features. The copy ended with the note that "There could be a Mustang in your future, too. Even if you don't chase Porsches for a living."

What do you think the objectives of this ad were?

TYLENOL: FIGHTING BACK FROM DISASTER

The $1.2 billion market for pain-killers is highly profitable and highly competitive. For decades, aspirin had almost the entire market for over-the-counter sales, and most of the professional market as well. Although aspirin is not the official chemical name, the courts long ago ruled that the name aspirin was in the public domain, so that there were many brands of aspirin, as well as combination pills under other labels, such as Alka-Seltzer, Anacin, and Bufferin. Aspirin was widely proclaimed as one of the most effective and safest remedies ever developed. But one flaw showed up over time: significant numbers of users developed a sensitivity to aspirin, with adverse stomach reactions.

Then McNeill Laboratories, a division of Johnson & Johnson, introduced another drug, acetaminophen, under the trade mark of Tylenol, and entered the market via the professional route, detailing Tylenol to physicians as an answer to the reactions to aspirin. Physicians began prescribing it by the trade name, and Tylenol, with $450 million in sales at non-competitive prices, and 37% market share, was yielding $80 million in profit, 17% of J&J's total earnings.While some other brands were on the market, they had only minor sales and poor distribution. Tylenol had the cachet of medical approval, and the generic designation of acetaminophen, in fine print on every label, meant nothing to the public.

Then disaster struck out of the blue. In October, 1982, 7 people in the Chicago area died mysteriously, and the deaths were traced to Extra Strength Tylenol capsules in which someone had substituted deadly cyanide for the drug. It was quickly established that the substitution was done after the capsules left the factory, but Johnson and Johnson quickly ordered an immediate withdrawal of all wholesale and retail stocks of the capsules across the country and cooperated fully with federal authorities in the massive task of testing all batches. None were found outside the Chicago area. Only the capsules were involved--the regular strength pills did not lend themselves to such easy tampering, and their sale suffered only briefly. Many observers were ready to write off Tylenol as dead. But J&J was not ready to give up on the extra strength market.

From the first, every effort was made to reassure the public. James E. Burke, J&J chairman set the policy, "We do not do anything to make it seem we haven't taken every step to ensure public safety." In a complete turnaround from normal J&J policy, officials made themselves freely available to the press, the public relations staff meticulously answered thousands of inquiries, and a toll-free telephone line was set up that handled more than 350,000 calls. Chairman Burke himself appeared on "The Phil Donahue Show" and "60 Minutes."

To maintain vital shelf position and space in drug stores, the McNeill sales force was expanded and retailers offered a 25% discount if they purchased the same number of Tylenol products they had been buying before the disaster. All but a few responded.

The strenuous public relations effort apparently bore fruit early. The disaster struck on the eve of Halloween, and an independent survey immediately after indicated that 43% of the users said that they definitely would not use Tylenol again. Within 2 weeks, at mid-November, the percentage had dropped to 9%. Johnson apparently had similar information from its own private surveys. It started flooding the country with 40 million Tylenol coupons worth $2.50--the price of a small bottle--to forestall the possibility that previous users would replace with a different brand. The move apparently worked--the J&J share of market started moving back up, without the help of the capsules.

To revitalize the capsules, a tamper-proof package was needed. Johnson aimed, and succeeded , in being first on the market with such a package. The J&J package incorporated three safeguards: an outer cardboard container for the bottles that had to be torn open, a plastic seal on the bottle itself which had to be cut or torn off, and an inner paper seal across the top of the bottle. Then came the question as to how to launch the new package. Marketing research had indicated that people thought J&J should speak out (it had withdrawn all advertising at the same time as the capsule withdrawal.) A number of executives suggested a heavy advertising campaign. Instead, the company called what amounted to a nationwide press conference Besides the main in-person conference, there were piped-in presentations in main cities across the country. The package and the story got excellent coverage despite the competition of a space launching on the same day. Plans were made to launch a heavy advertising backup in January.

1. As you see it, what was the central element in the comeback strategy which was responsible for the swift rebound?

2. How did the other elements in the marketing mix fit to make this successful?

HURRY! GET YOUR ENTRIES IN FOR THE NATIONAL FARM-RAISED CATFISH COOKING CONTEST!

The Wall Street Journal does not normally pay much attention to cooking contests. But the 1983 Farm-Raised Catfish Cooking Contest made it in the December 23, 1982 issue.

It seems that this was the eighth year of the event, held annually at a shopping mall in Jackson, Miss., headquarters of the Catfish Farmers of America trade group. A panel of experts (catfish cooking experts, we assume) would sift through the recipes entered before Feb. 28, 1983, to pare the list down to five finalists, whose expenses would be paid for a trip to the June 4 finals. More than 1,000 entries were received in the 1982 contest, and past winners included catfish Kiev, catfish Caribbean en papillote, Mandarin catfish, and catfish Eldorado de Colorado. The contest winner would get $2,000, and the judges included no less than Craig Claiborne of the New York Times.

The idea behind the contest , according to Carolyn Ann Sledge, the coordinator, is to get people away from the old southern perception of catfish as something you just fried in "the black pot" and served "with hush puppies." According to her, there were "endless" ways of serving catfish.

The cook-off is part of the industry's attempts to upgrade the image of farm-raised catfish: catfish which taste better than the wild variety because of "the exquisite environment" provided by the raisers, who sold 266 million pounds in 1982.

The association also has its eyes on the European market. Talks were under way to supply catfish to several prominent restaurants in Europe, who planned to serve it as a "gourmet item."

1. If this promotion is to succeed in opening up a larger market for farm-raised catfish, what chain of marketing and communications processes would have to be forged to persuade consumers unfamiliar with catfish to try it and start buying?

2. Why should the group approach restaurants first in order to introduce their product into Europe?

WHY REVLON'S CHARLIE SEEMS TO BE READY TO SETTLE DOWN
(Reprinted from **The Wall Street Journal**, Dec. 23, 1982, © Dow Jones & co., 1982)

...Now Revlon Inc...has decided to let the woman in its Charlie fragrance commercials have a serious romance. She may even get married.

That's a big switch for an advertising character who was introduced nine years ago as the quintessential liberated woman. Charlie, as Revlon calls her, was single, had a job and wore pants to the office before it was fashionable, She went into bars unescorted, signed the check in restaurants and dressed in tuxedos at night. Her walk--a long stride, with arms swinging--bespoke independence, confidence and a touch of insouciance.

Most of all, she didn't need a man. Men were bit players in Charlie ads. Charlie wore cologne not as a part of some husband-hunting scheme but because she liked the stuff.

Suddenly, in the latest Charlie commercial, there's a wholesome-looking fellow proposing marriage and hinting that Charlie should put their relationship before her career. Revlon spent nearly a year preparing this commercial, carefully analyzing public opinion research. What is the perfume maker trying to tell us?

Advertising is a meter of social and cultural change. Unlike the ERA or Betty Friedan, advertising is rarely controversial. Only when a new idea no longer is threatening do marketers move in to exploit it through advertising. They oversimplify and stylize the idea in order to sell products and make profits....

In the new Charlie ad, Revlon has replaced actress Shelley Hack, who has starred in the campaign since 1975.... In her place is actress Tamara Norman, a woman with a more rounded figure. She is wearing a strapless gown, not pants.

The 30-second commercial opens with Charlie and her date leaving a party. "Nice party," she says. An announcer sets the scene: "The best part of the party is when the party's over."

Standing under the orange neon sign of a late-night restaurant, he nuzzles her ear lobe. "Mmm, Charlie?" he inquires. She answers:"Uh huh." They then approach two huge stone lions. He pops the question: "Would you cancel your trip to the coast if I proposed?" She ignores him: " I wonder how much this lion weighs?"

As dawn approaches they stop to buy rolls at an Italian bakery. He is persistent: "Listen, I'm serious about what I said before." She continues to fend him off: "Eat your breakfast."

They stand outside her brownstone. A jogger passes by and milk bottles--an anachronism--wait on the stoop. "Even my mother thinks it's time for you to settle down," he argues. Grinning, she replies: "Your mother's right."

Did she agree to marry him? Or does "settle down" mean live together. And what about her trip, presumably for business? Will she skip it and risk ruining her career? Has he had enough of liberation and decided to trade her job for marriage and a family?

"Charlie hasn't changed," says Sanford Buchsbaum, Revlon executive vice president for advertising. "The world has changed." He insists that the ad character won't give up her career, but "has proven her independence" and is ready for "another dimension to her life." Everything else about the commercial is purposely ambiguous, designed to make viewers pay closer attention perhaps debate possible endings with friends. "I hate to call it a commercial," says Mr. Buchsbaum. "This is really a minimovie."

Revlon has been modifying the campaign subtly over the years, he explains, to stay on "the leading edge of where people's emotions, psyches and intellects have been going." In 1979, for example, Charlie got a boyfriend who appeared briefly in an ad as she playfully kissed him on the nose.

Now Revlon's research indicates that it's safe to advance Charlie's romantic interests further. Yankelovich, Skelly & White Inc., a market-research concern that Revlon and other big advertisers rely on for advice about social trends, says there's more interest in traditional relationships, marriage and families....

1. Why is it important for advertisers such as Revlon to "stay on the leading edge of where people's emotion, psyches and intellects have been going?"

2. For what kinds of offerings would such sensitivity to social (and economic) trends be important? Why?

3. What kinds of social trends might non-profit service organizations such as colleges have to take into consideration, if any? Why?

4. Besides provoking possible speculation, what might another psychological purpose of the ad's ambiguity be?

SAFEGUARD BUSINESS SYSTEMS: A SERVICE PROMOTION?

Safeguard Business Systems designs and sells the materials for accounting record systems, especially for small business. It also sells a data processing service to accounting firms serving small businesses.

The nature of Safeguard's services and some of its promotional activities were sketched in the Report to Stockholders for the 3rd quarter of 1982. The material below are direct quotations from that report.

More than 225,000 small businesses and professionals use our products and systems because their accountants recommend Safeguard....Approximately 15,000 accounting firms rely on Safeguard for products and services, representing a 35% share of the estimated 43,000 firms in the U.S. today.

Successful accountants know that they must meet the need of the client for fast, accurate record keeping systems. Safeguard provides manual one-write systems that can help businesses and professional practices cut record keeping time by up to 75%, eliminate transposition errors and provide immediate, up-to-date and accurate financial information.

The systems also help accountants themselves work more efficiently.... Safeguard currently offers more than 200 one-write system variations. We are constantly working to develop new special applications to meet the needs of specific businesses. Examples include specially tailored systems for restaurants, construction firms, real estate management firms and law offices.

Safeguard also serves the accounting community through its computerized Financial Reporting Program (FRP). Approximately 8,000 accounting firms use FRP to provide data collection and financial reporting procedures for nearly 47,000 of their clients...

Many small businesses, professionals and other entrepreneurs rely heavily on their accountants for financial advice and counsel, with the practitioner serving as a de facto chief financial officer and record keeping supervisor for these enterprises....

At the beginning of the 1982 business year, Safeguard announced long range plans to introduce microcomputer-based management systems to its general business, accounting practice, and health care practice markets...Orientation and training programs for our independent distributor organization are now underway, and we expect to enter these markets in full force in early 1983...

Safeguard launched a major private sector initiative during the third quarter on behalf of America's smaller businesses. The company formed the Safeguard Advisory Group on Small Business Issues, which is composed of 12 independent distributors based in key geographic areas across the country; and joined with the Institute for Constructive Capitalism at the University of Texas at Austin to conduct three surveys of businesses employing 10 or less people. The thrust of these surveys is to identify and define the problems facing this vast and important economic segment, and to explore practical solutions. We will report to you in the months ahead on our progress with this important and worthwhile program.

1. What is this Advisory Group? An act of charity, or an information channel for Safeguard to get a look at special problems they are not aware of? Could it have a promotional value in itself? If so, what would that value be?

MOST ADVERTISING UNPRODUCTIVE, SAYS ONE WHO SHOULD KNOW

Gus Priemer, the advertising services director for S. C. Johnson Co. is no outside amateur in advertising. He oversees an ad budget of $50 million a year at Johnson, and has spent 29 years in the business at Procter & Gamble and Johnson. His opinion of advertising (as quoted in the Wall Street Journal of Apr. 9, 1981): "Most advertising today is unproductive. It has become a kind of routine, an habit, a custom." Ad budgets, according to him, are based on faith. "Executives go on the assumption that advertising is doing something, just like praying or going to church is doing something." Further, a common belief is: "If sales are okay, then advertising must be working. If sales are bad, the advertising must be bad," neglecting the effects of distribution, sales promotion, product design, packaging, or pricing.

His solution: ask "What am I trying to make happen with this advertising that wouldn't happen without it? What evidence do I have that a campaign is working?" Specific, measurable goals should be set for a campaign, then tests made during the campaign to learn when the advertising needed to be changed or stopped.

Priemer cites an example of a competitor's campaign he could observe: P&G's test marketing of Pert shampoo, introduced in Milwaukee and Nashville in 1979. From his own analysis, he assumed that P&G's goal was to get across the Pert benefit claim: "bouncin' and behavin'" hair. Polling women from the day commercials began, he asked whether they could identify a shampoo that made this claim. When the ad recognition peaked, he assumed that the advertising had completed its job, and he noted that although P&G spent heavier on advertising in Nashville, the market share was less than in Milwaukee. To him this meant that the higher level of advertising was not productive. Advertising should stop when it has nothing new to say, he says. Once consumers buy, it is the product performance which counts.

1. Priemer's plan seems to make sense for a packaged consumer item like a shampoo or furniture polish, during an introductory phase at least. But how would you test the budget level for an offering in the mature stage, with relatively stable market shares but an intense competitive atmosphere, like beer or chewing gum?

How would you test it for an expensive piece of industrial machinery?

CHAPTER 15. SYNCHRONIZING STRATEGY WITH THE MARKET LIFE CYCLE

The Market Life Cycle: Foundation of Strategic Planning

Any meaningful strategic plan is shaped by the position of each offering mix in its market life cycle. The main purpose of that plan is to outline the moves necessary for the market situations coming with changes in the phases of the cycle.

As previously noted, buyers' perceptions of the desired benefit bundle values shift with the course of the cycle. The kinds and degree of competition change likewise: from none of any significance for high-learning introductions in a market development development phase, through increasingly intense competition for any offering passing through its early growth, to a turbulent competition which eliminates weaker competitors during the slowdown of late growth, to the relatively stable competitive structure of the saturated market, and a weakening of competition as competitors abandon the market during the decline.

The primary purposes of a strategic plan is to shape current marketing operations to the requirements of the current phase and prepare for the coming of the next phase. The nature of those requirements are definite and knowable. Prediction of the precise timing of phase changes is impossible, but not necessary. Continued strength of position in any phase depends heavily on both plans laid and actions taken during the previous phase. Whenever the phase shift starts, the foundation is set for it. Especially critical is an accurate forecast of the probable character of the initial introductory phase and an introduction plan compatible with the degree of market development effort which may be necessary. Only a small percentage of all new offerings require habit relearning and a major market development effort. Those that do must be identified because of the major resources required to see them through to profitable market growth. For such introductions, the possibility of significant competition is negligible during its introductory phase.

On the other hand, when the analysis indicates a probable low-learning introduction, the planned introduction must be prepared for the aggressive competition typical of the early growth phase which comes quickly for such introductions.

Whatever success is achieved during the initial phase, whatever its character, the seller can sustain it only by keeping ahead of developing competition in product design and in distribution strength, bolstered with a promotion mix which helps cement patronage loyalty of both distributors and final buyers.

The prescription for survival of the turbulence of the late maturity stage is a secure market niche based on a previously established patronage loyalty and a strong distribution network. Profits will probably suffer during the phase, as a result of the almost inevitable industry overcapacity and the scramble to survive. It is an opportune time for market broadening moves.

When the shakeout ends, competitive pressures will subside and not seem important. Market shares will tend to be stable, not subject to easy change. The primary threats will be relatively invisible: the threats posed by market opportunities left open for outsiders. The most dangerous threats will come from unforeseen changes in tastes and life styles (possibly created by the success of the initial offering), and from so-called cross-product competition: offerings of a different kind meeting the same core desires.

Sooner or later, such cross-product competition will gain a foothold and grow. The decline is then well started. Major resources should be withdrawn to better uses, the offering milked of profit possibilities and withdrawn when dry.

Each of these market cycle stages requires a different kind of management and a different allocation of resources. Strategic planning requires identifying the cycle phase for each offering in the seller's mix, making sure that each gets treatment appropriate to that phase, and preparing for the contingencies of the next likely developments.

Of all the contingencies, foresight of the climate and problems at birth are the most critical. Many an innovator has stumbled and lost a chance to capitalize on his ideas because of a failure to foresee the learning needs posed by his introduction, and the resources needed to gain acceptance. The innovator who brought the attention of the later promoters of the Toni Home Permanent to the market failed to understand the intense promotion needed to develop credibility and acceptance. He passed from the scene early, without gaining any significant market.

Other innovators have lost out because they they were unprepared to meet the early onslaught of competitors eager to get in on the highly visible profits of a low-learning introduction. Of the two kinds of errors, this should normally be the easier to correct, since the profits in this period are adequate to finance any nimble-footed seller.

The appropriate strategy for any phase takes the probable competition into account, first of all, then develops the five management and marketing policies and efforts to meet market needs and conditions:
- offering design and mix
- pricing
- distribution

- the promotional mix
- the marketing research and intelligence efforts
- the character of the management itself

Introductory Strategies for Market Development Offerings

Those introducing offerings which require any significant consumer learning must be prepared to finance a substantial period of deficits. Promotional and sales cost will be high and sales come slowly. Without the honey of quick visible profits, competition will be notable by its lack, or at least, insignificance. In the really rare case that some does develop, it will only help bear the cost of market development.

Such high-learning offerings should be designed to minimize the learning costs. They should be cost-engineered to sell at a price appropriate to the spending patterns and perceptions of the most profitable receptive market. The personal sales element in the promotion must be dominant, which means that distribution must be restricted to protected, aggressive dealers. Marketing research should be focussed on identification of the best early adopter segments and on their use-systems. Management must be both entrepreneurial and technical at this stage.

Design of The Market Development Offering

Product design at this stage should be relatively simple, usually confined to a single model. Initial buyers will be seeking the core function, not variations. Design standards should:

- Be use-system engineered to require the absolute minimum of possible habit change, value perception learning, and user-role change
- Within these limits, yield the optimum of new satisfactions
- Be cost-engineered to sell at a price appropriate to the spending patterns of the most receptive market segments
- Contain as few use-system or quality defects as possible. Any discovered after introduction must be corrected as quickly as possible

The early adopters must be able to perceive as complete satisfaction as can be provided. Their recommendations will be the foundation of market growth. All diffusion research has revealed that awareness of high-learning offerings and benefit claims are widespread long before sales begin to take off. Most prospects depend on the adventurous early adopters to validate the claims before they will buy.

Pricing The Market Development Offering

The end-user price needs to come as close as possible to the level such receptive segment end-users might expect to pay for some similar, but inferior satisfactions in a familiar form. (The first mass market tractors sold at approximately the price of a good team of draft horses, and handled about the same work load.)

SELLING COLOR TV: THE BIG DIFFERENCES IN DEALER PUSH

The year was 1959, and RCA was not doing too well with the sale of color TV which it had introduced 4 years before. Deficits were running in the low 8 figures annually, just to keep some color programming on the air until enough sets were out to interest advertisers. One of RCA's employees, an MBA student in nearby Philadelphia, decided to do his term project on finding out why color TV sets were not moving.

His research plan consisted of shopping all of the dealers in town, posing as a buyer interested in a Color TV set. This was a goodly number, since RCA had adopted an intensive distribution policy, selling color sets through any dealer with an RCA franchise.

Interestingly, all dealers but one quickly steered the "buyer" to the black-and-white models, even though most had a sample color set on the floor. For some reason (the student thought it was the service problem), they did not want to sell the color set.

The one exception was Mort Pharr, then the most aggressive discount and volume appliance dealer in the city. When the shopper asked about color, he was immediately steered to a special room with several, all tuned in and in perfect adjustment. He also learned that Mort Pharr had gone beyond waiting for customers. When a program with special interest to physicians was scheduled, he arranged to place a set on consignment in each of the homes of 10 selected physicians, installing it with his own crews, who made sure of perfect adjustment. Only 4 of the sets were returned—the other physicians bought.

Distribution Policy

Distributor appointments should be limited to the strong, aggressive few, under either exclusive or selective arrangements giving some territorial protection. They will be expected to conduct an active selling effort, with a high degree of personal sales involvement. Generous margins must be provided to give them an incentive to undertake that aggressive level of sales promotion.

Promoting The Market Development Offering

Market development phase promotion has two primary objectives:
- Identification of early adopter prospects and persuading them to give the offering an adequate trial
- The creation of a widespread awareness of and interest in the new offering and development of some degree of understanding of the benefits offered

A strong personal sales effort is by far the most efficient means of ferreting out the identity of possible early adopters and of tailoring presentations which can persuade them to give the offering a trial. An aggressive, searching personal sales effort is needed at every level of distribution. Distributors themselves will need to be sold on the profit possibilities.

Publicity is by far the best tool for developing awareness and interest in high-learning new offerings, and should be pushed to its limits. Fortunately, when managed with experience and skill, publicity is readily available. Offerings with benefits revolutionary enough to require some learning are commonly also unusual enough to be news.

The publicity needs to be reinforced with informational advertising in media most used by probable early adopters and their friends.

THE HARVESTORE: THE VALUE OF THE PERSONAL SALES PUSH

Anyone driving through the corn belt or the major dairy areas of the north could not help but notice the large number of shining blue silos with a trademarked name, Harvestore, on the side. This is a patented silage storing system developed by the A. O. Smith Company of Milwaukee. Their construction of enameled steel has two advantages: they permit a relatively tight seal at the top, by a vinyl cap, and the smooth sides let the silage slide easily into an automatic unloader at the bottom.

This author first heard of the Harvestore around 1951, in talking to an official of A.O. Smith who was fairly enthusiastic about its potential. More costly than the ordinary silos, it paid off by keeping cattle penned up in a feed lot, out of the pasture, where they would have tramped down and spoiled twice as much forage as they ate. They were then fed out of the silo, which was kept full through regular cutting of the forage. In this way, a farmer would get 3 times the yield of feed from his land.

Nothing much was heard about the Harvestore for 3 or 4 years—for a good reason. Smith had turned it over to farm implement dealers to sell, and they were not selling many. The problem was that the Harvestore meant a complete change in the habitual system of livestock management, and required a change in buildings and equipment in most cases. Farm implement dealers function much as auto dealers do—they wait for customers to come in.

Believing that prospects were out there, Smith then took the Harvestore out of the hands of the dealers, and started appointing distributor-contractors who had to invest $250 thousand in erecting equipment. Assigned exclusive sales territories, they went out after customers. The results are plainly visible throughout the midwest, and elsewhere.

Introductory Phase Marketing Research and Market Intelligence

Marketing research needed to guide the introductory phase needs to be initiated long before the offering is launched. In fact such research needs to work shoulder-to-shoulder with the product development effort, estimating the marketability, investigating needed performance specifications, checking consumer reactions to proposed concepts and design compromises. Once the offering begins to approach prototype completion, some marketing research should be focussed on gathering the kinds of information needed to make an estimate of the probable market acceptance pattern. Key information needed is:

- What kinds of prospects are likely to be interested?

THE COOPERATIVE EXTENSION SERVICE: A MODEL MISSIONARY SALES FORCE

If someone were to ask you what organization is the most effective sales force the world has ever seen, would you name the U.S. Cooperative Agricultural Extension Service? You would have a hard time finding one with a more spectacular record of "sales", of sales of really high-learning products.

Look at the record: In 1910, more than a third of the population was working on farms. Today, only 1 person in 25 lives on a farm, feeding the whole country and much of the world besides (and one-fourth of those are producing 9/10 of the total).

The surface reason has been the development of better seeds, better methods, and better machinery, in large part by the scientists at the 50 land grant colleges and universities and in the federal government. But the work of these experiment station scientists did not get into much use from the time that they were set up by Congress, under the 1885 Hatch Act, until after 1914, when Congress set up provisions for local "county agents", and the Cooperative Extension Service was established. They were looked on as theoretical "longhairs" by practicing farmers.

Agents appointed by the State Extension Service at each land grant college, with funds matched locally, had a single assignment: convert the farmers of their counties to the use of better farming methods. It was up to each local agent to decide where to start. The rule was: "start where the people are". By this was meant to find some problem considered a major one in the community, and work with the farmers to solve it. Usually, this was done by arranging for a small scale trial demonstration by some more innovative farmer. Changing the farming habits of experienced farmers did not prove easy. Some of the more innovative would adopt, but progress with the rest of the community was difficult.

So the Service decided to work also with the young, who had no well established farming habits yet. 4-H clubs were set up, each member of which had a single project: such as raising a pig, or a steer, or a demonstration plot of some crop. At harvest time, there were contests at the county fair between those on similar projects, and at the state fairs, given wide publicity and usually resulting in some kind of scholarships. The social and agricultural activities of the 4-H clubs were well publicized. In addition, county agents regularly wrote articles for the local press on various farm topics of local interest, as did the county Home Demonstration Agents who joined the office to work with the homemaking side of farming.

Land grant schools supplemented the work with short courses, held in off season periods, where free practical instruction was available on specific farm management topics.

County agents' duties included helping those farmers who would cooperate to establish purchasing and sales cooperatives to improve their business position. In all of this, they received backup assistance from specialists of every kind at the state level, much as industrial sales people can call on technical support personnel. State specialists worked closely with the publishers of the farm papers practically every farmer subscribes to, developing articles on topics of interest to their readers, spreading the word of new agricultural discoveries.

The early years were not easy. Many farmers resented the proffered help, even as late as the 1930's. But when World War II, and the reconstruction that followed, needed the produce, the farms were ready to deliver. The amount of land per farm has doubled, the population needed to work it has been cut to about 1/8 of what it was in 1910.

- What attributes of the proposed offering evoke the highest interest?
- What are the specifics of the use-systems into which they are likely to be fitted?
- Are these existing use-systems such that the offering fits them well, or does the offering seem likely to require habit changes in some essential detail?
- How does the likely price fit into the value perceptions of prospects? If the cost of some attribute is substantial, are prospects likely to be willing to pay extra for it?
- How does the new introduction fit the perceptions of users of their social status or other roles?
- How does it fit into existing distributions structures, or will somewhat different distribution structures have to be built?

Whatever the conclusion reached on the basis of this research, plans should include contingencies that the forecast could have missed some vital aspect of buyer reaction. Forecasting of any kind is always subject to some error. Part of those contingency plans should include plans for a quick reading on the nature of demand and the market reaction after the introduction. Specifically, four groups of information are needed, quick:

- 1. Who are the buyers? Are they typical innovators, or do they, even at the start, include some members of the expected early majority? What market segments do the most interested prospects seem to belong to? Are the segments those originally thought to be the most receptive segments, or are they a somewhat different class of buyers?
- How do the buyers perceive the offering: what values are they seeking? What does this reaction imply for offering design changes? what does it tell us about the promotional mix, themes, and media? What does it seem to forecast as to the character of the market life cycle ahead, and the likelihood of early competition?
- Into what use-systems is the offering being fitted? What do these use systems imply for product revision, for product promotion, for pricing, for distribution?
- Are there similar offerings being introduced by competitors? If so, is the product succeeding as well as the sales seem to indicate, or is it simply being tried by rotating groups of buyers, then rejected as not really offering a noticeable added value? If so, can the offering be repaired, or should it be phased out immediately?

As much of the information possible should be collected through formal provision for quick feedback from any sales personnel at every stage of the distribution channels. These people are certain to be the recipients of both complaints and compliments. They are also in the best position to observe all those interested to any degree in the offering. Guidance and encouragement in using and summarizing their experience are directly valuable in helping them to carry out their own selling task. Leads developed from such feedback will help the marketing research people to formulate whatever added research is needed.

Answers to these questions will permit a more accurate estimate of the nature of the introductory phase, and the degree and types of learning involved. If the introduction is a high learning offering, further research can then be designed to pinpoint the prospects more exactly, and to discover what may be needed to minimize learning requirements and to correct any offering defects immediately, before they ruin the introduction. Once the initial effort is well on its feet, both the research and intelligence feedback should focus on possible new use-system developments which suggest a need for offering variations. Any such need will tend to forecast a more rapid growth of sales. Early need for diversified models can also be a symptom that the growth period is not far away. Similarly, the attitude of distributors outside the chosen channels needs to be watched. A growing demand from such distributors is a certain signal that any market development period has succeeded and is shifting into a period of rapid growth.

Marketing Development Stage Management Needs

Looking over the history of successes and failures, it seems clear that revolutionary offerings fare best when guided by a management of relatively high technical competence, which is also market oriented. The market orientation is needed to sense the probable needs of a major segment of buyers not currently being served. The technical competence is needed to develop offering bundles not previously available. Without the technical insight, the offering will lack the innovational characteristics required. Without the marketing insight, the offering may be aimed at a market that is inadequate to support production.

The entrepreneurial temperament is the need of the moment: a bent toward innovation, and the willingness to risk the uncertainties of venturing beyond the well-tried and obvious. A certain degree of looseness of administration does not seem to be a handicap, if it permits the flowering of ideas. Competitive costs are no problem at this stage. Finding ways to deliver new and better values to buyers is the road to success.

Rapid Growth Phase Strategies

Only a very small fraction of new offerings involve enough relearning to require a costly market development period before real market growth can start. Most of those which succeed enter a period of rapid rise in sales within a relatively short period after introduction.

At whatever point in time the sales curve starts to move with less effort, the seller can be sure that competitors will start sprouting like crab grass in July. Every seller who hopes to survive to the calmer waters of the mature phase must establish and secure a unique brand market niche. The niche must be made secure through a strong distribution network and a firm consumer franchise.

That market niche will be secured and protected by being the **first** in three aspects of strategy and tactics:

- Covering as many as possible of whatever potential large volume variations are needed to fit developing consumer desire-sets and new use systems by use of flexible offerings and modular design
- Maintaining quality and improving appearance
- Keeping buyer cost moving down in line with decreases in unit costs resulting from production experience

Timing is critical during this phase. Most buyers are new to the market and the offering. **The first offering they find** which satisfies their initial desire sets stops their search and consideration of competing offerings and establishes a basis for future patronage habits. If this prescription is faithfully followed, competitors will have difficulty finding attractive gaps in the market offerings by which they can gain a foothold.

The offering and pricing moves must be paralleled with strengthened distributor relationships, but distribution margins can be much less than in an introductory phase. Because of the rapidly growing buyer demand, distributor costs will be less and the value of the line to distributors' merchandise mix will be increasing.

At this point, strong distributors will seek and push the offerings of those sellers who:

- have a quality offering with good consumer acceptance and good customer service
- back the offering with strong mass communications and helpful promotions
- give dealers the best on-time delivery service
- furnish the best merchandising aids and sales training, if needed

Rapid Growth Stage Offering Needs

The growth stage is inevitably characterized by a growth in market segmentation, as different kinds of buyers come into the market, with diversifying perceptions of fringe attributes desired in the offerings. Sellers must find a niche for themselves which they can fill better than any current competitor, and design a flexible mix of models to serve the types of segments occupying that niche.

Some of those models will be for new use systems developed out of customer experience and imagination. Some of those use systems may impose strains the original design was not equipped to handle well. The seller needs to provide for quick feedback and a sensitivity to these needs in order to adapt offering designs to the demand pattern.

THE RISE AND DECLINE OF FORD AND THE MODEL T

The history of Henry Ford and his Model T is a classic of a brilliant marketing idea which built an industry, then declined because the market moved, and the product and management did not.

As early as 1903, Henry Ford was aiming at a car for $500. The original Model T carried a retail tag of $825, but Ford was able to boast that "No car under $2,000 offers more, and no car over $2,000 offers more except the trimmings." Historians agree he was accurate, For the roads and needs of the time, it was a revolutionary design. Using the best of the then known metallurgy, he had been able to cut the weight down to 1200 pounds, built a car with a dependable magneto ignition, built high to clear the ruts in the mud roads of the day. The 10-gal. capacity gas tank was generous for the short trips permitted on the existing primitive road systems. The simplicity of the two-speed planetary transmission was well fitted to a population just getting acquainted with driving. It quickly gained a reputation for dependability, something most cars of the day lacked. Some defects showed up as time went on, and up until 1916, at least, Henry Ford and his associates listened, and corrected them.

Organization was very loose, although there was never any question about who was the ultimate boss—Henry himself. But in those early days, he encouraged the initiative of a number of able associates. Problems began in the post-war period from 1919 on. Ford began to resent independence, and some of his ablest associates left or were fired. Among them, Knudsen, a brilliant production engineer moved over to General Motors to head up the Chevrolet Division, and Norval Hawkins, who had built the Ford dealer organization, also to GM.

The Model T was built for pure utility. By the 1920s, drivers wanted something more. Road building was well under way, trips were becoming longer, and the Model T's shortcomings were being exposed. The thermosyphon cooling system, lacking a pump, heated badly on warm days. The planetary transmission required drivers to

---

During this stage, a seller must keep in the forefront of changing design possibilities, in order to preempt any possible opportunities for new competitors.

Rapid Growth Stage Pricing

The speed of market growth depends in part on decreases in consumer cost. Lowered consumer cost can open up market segments not previously interested. The growth in production experience and sales volume open up possibilities for substantial production cost decreases. By this time also, industry suppliers of components are becoming numerous and searching for business. The combination of all these factors opens up opportunities for new competitors. They will seize them quickly unless the original entrants preempt the moves by keeping all kinds and levels of pricing moving down in harmony with the cost reduction possibilities, anticipating any advantages of market broadening to lower price to get it.

This applies to prices paid to distribution as well as those charged the fi-

hold their feet pressed on the shift pedal all the way up any steep hill. The gravity oiling system could get clogged from bits of the transmission band linings, and burn out the bearings. To check on the gasoline supply, the driver had to lift the front seat cushion and drop a gauge stick to measure it. A whole industry had sprung up to build missing accessories needed for the traffic and driving conditions of the 1920's.

People now wanted more comfort, women were beginning to drive, and were interested in appearance and styling. The closed car was displacing the open touring models, and although Ford built some sedans and coupes, his Model T chassis was too light for them. The replacement market was beginning to be important, and with it, a trend to trade-ins--a trend which Ford tried to discourage his dealers from following. Buyers wanted credit arrangements, and Ford discouraged the dealers from arranging it. Buyers were looking for a 6-cylinder motor, but Ford fired Kanzler who suggested it.

By 1926, dealers were apparently going broke or leaving in large numbers, and by this time, there were other cars in the Ford price class. Some of the best dealers went over to General Motors, whose dealer organization soon was to become the best in the industry. [DeLorean, in his account of his Chevrolet experience written up by Wright, flatly said that "General Motors is more successful than Ford, Chrysler, or American Motors...today because its almost 13,000 dealers are more successful...the single identifiable reason GM dominates the American automotive industry is its giant size as best expressed in the breadth and strength of its dealer body." [Wright, **On a Clear Day You Can See General Motors** Wright Enterprises, 1979, p. 136]

Sales dropped so drastically that at the beginning of 1927, a crash effort to design the coming model was initiated. Production of the model T ended in May, 1927, and it was to be a full year before the factory could put the Model A on the road. GM, under a professionalized management built up by Sloan, filled the gap with its Chevy.

nal customer. It also applies to perceivable use-system prices. Many of the newer buyers will be less tolerant of problems in fitting the offerings into their perceived use-systems then were the earlier adopters. They will expect more convenience and the seller who offers it first will capture a significant niche in the market.

Rapid Growth Stage Distribution Policy

The easier selling atmosphere of the growth stage lessens the need for a strong distributor push. The need to protect distributors is much weaker. Distribution should be broadened to whatever extent is required to make the offering easily accessible to the now bigger and wider market.

This implies the abandonment of any substantial degree of exclusivity of territories or customer lists. For some kinds of items, it may require an active courting of low-margin mass distributors. The latter move often tends to offend the initial distributors, who feel some proprietary interest in high margins. But those who can deliver the volume will stay anyway because of the warm attraction of the volume demand.

Moreover, distributor selling costs will have come down. Buyers are now seeking the sellers more often than the reverse. The need for the high margins is gone. Distributors now need something else that will greatly improve their profits: the best of inventory service and delivery. This is a must for the producer. By making certain that distributors can replace stocks quickly, the producer makes certain that sales lost to others will be at a minimum. A clear focus on such quality inventory service will also cement relationships with the distribution--a relationship which is essential to survival in the inevitable shakeout phase which is sure to come--often just when unexpected.

Rapid Growth Phase Promotion

By the time rapid growth becomes obvious, the need for the strong push of the personal sales communications is diminishing. The credibility of the offering benefit claims have long been established by the early adopters. Communications must now take on the task of forestalling or meeting the competition entering the market, and the potential competition getting ready to enter. The task is now to strengthen the brand preference of customers already won, and to attract the new customers coming into the market.

The primary emphasis will be on mass communications modes, primarily advertising. This needs to be buttressed with sampling and other forms of promotions at retail. Some personal sales efforts aimed at intermediaries will be needed, at least to broaden the distribution base. Sales personnel in contact with final buyers will need instruction and sales training in the unique benefits of the brand. Display will be very important.

Because the emphasis is now on the brand, publicity will be harder to come by, but still available to some degree. Major improvements in performance, including new kinds of models for new use systems, will still be news. Other forms of publicity can be generated by promotions tied in with newsworthy events which emphasize brand benefits-such as competitive demonstrations, when available.

Rapid Growth Phase Research and Intelligence

With the coming of real competition comes a need for intelligence on brand position in the market. This needs to include identification of distribution coverage gaps, gaps in line coverage, gaps in model coverage, and trends in specific kinds of demand.

Marketing research also needs to focus on emerging trends in use systems, for which new designs must be developed, and for other opportunities to expand the brand and offering coverage. The effort to uncover possible offering weaknesses needs to continue, as well of consumer satisfactions which suggest promotional approaches.

The Managerial Emphasis of the Rapid Growth Phase

Management of the rapid growth phase requires some technical knowledge, but the primary emphasis is on marketing management. By this time, most producers will have access to much of the technology and component suppliers will be established or be entering rapidly. The task ahead is to build an entrenched market position in preparation for the competitive turbulence of a certain-to-come shakeout phase: a strong brand franchise and the best distribution system.

Shake-Out Phase Strategies

The rapid growth in sales will begin to slow down just when everyone is convinced it will continue indefinitely--at just about the moment when sales have reached about half the final potential. Because nearly everyone tends to forget that all growth has limits, production capacity being built at that point assumes a straight line continuation of the previous growth rate for some period ahead, and the industry suddenly finds inventories backing up. A scramble for customers and markets quickly breaks out. In the process, profits are inevitably sacrificed in a battle for survival.

Some producers may drop out quickly, realizing that they can generate more earnings in some other endeavor. Many will simply be forced out because they do not have the customer franchise to maintain a viable sales position. At this point, distributors will cut back on the number of brands they handle. The survivors will be those sellers who have established a strong brand franchise and are well positioned in the sales of the stronger distributors.

Offering Strategy in The Competitive Turbulence of The Shake-Out Phase

Continued emphasis on product improvement remains important during this period. However, it must be paralleled with some tightening of the line: elimination of unnecessary specialized models, not delivering any significant differential value to market segments of any importance. Attention to styling and other elements of novelty start to become valuable as a means of stimulating interest and differentiating offerings: more flavors, more kinds of models (but made from the same basic components, with a keen eye to the cost structure of producing and marketing.)

Pricing for The Shakeout Phase

The shakeout phase leaves little room to be other than competitive in price, and there is something to be said to beating competitors to the draw on price cuts, to get to be known as the first.

But mere price cuts are not the full answer to the situation. Straight out price cuts can gain very little advantage in timing and probably almost

IMAGINATIVE PRICING IN A PRICE WAR

Federal banking regulations limited the interest banks could pay on deposits to relatively low levels for nearly 50 years preceding December, 1982. The original purpose was to strengthen the tottering banking system in the Great Depression, and the rate was knowingly set at somewhat less than large investors would normally obtain in gilt-edged investments.

That difference was not enough to lure small investors away from savings accounts until the steep interest rate increases of the late 1970s, when a number of Money Market mutual funds were created, with limited checking privileges, paying high rates of interest. This started a drain on banking deposits which weakened the thrift banks especially, threatening the mortgage structure they supported. Commercial banks also were seriously affected. The growth of the money market competition was one factor which helped get the banks moving toward support of deregulation of their activities. One of the major steps in that process was the abolition of interest rates on savings deposits in mid-December, 1982, to be followed by permission to pay any rate of interest on deposits over $2500, with very limited checking privileges.These accounts were to be covered by deposit insurance, which the money market mutuals were not. The interest was to be variable, pegged to Treasury bill rates—a yield just slightly under that which money market mutual funds were likely to experience.

Sighting a chance to regain large deposits, banks in every part of the country entered into a bidding war for new funds. Nowhere was the competition more intense than in Charlotte, NC, home of NCNB, the largest banking system of the Southeast, and a number of other statewide and large local branch banking systems. NCNB apparently overstepped the regulations in some manner in its haste to gain new money, offering 20% on funds for the month preceding the January thaw, and had to step back a little.

There were some limits to the bidding allowed to be paid on savings in the December 14 to January 15th period. Nearly every bank pushed as close to those limits as permitted. Each bank was naturally hoping to gain a substantial share on its own, in competition with the other banks. In any event, a mere direct pricing war is almost never profitable. What is needed is some way of making an attractive price cut which is not easily compared with those being made by competitors.

The Charlotte bankers proved they were not lacking in imagination. NCNB pointed its ads directly at the money market mutuals, offering 2% more than the 5 leading money market funds for that month. This, of course, gave no direct measure of the actual return. One S&L offered a free term life insurance policy: an unusual premium-with-each-purchase type of offer. The value would vary with the age of the individual, and would, in any case, not be a quantity that very many people could estimate with accuracy. Another S&L simply ran quarter page newspaper ads, with a screamer headline, **DITTO** in heavy block letters over 2-1/2 inches high. The copy simply stated that they were offering the same Money Market Deposit Account that everyone else was—that the others looked to them like theirs.

One bank offered no premium of any kind, out of its own pocket. Instead, it offered to loan 2-1/2 times the amount deposited, at 12-1/2% interest, so that the borrowers could take advantage of the other offers, and collect the interest difference over the month (about 3%).

none in market share in such a period.

But price cuts can be selective--made to open up new kinds of markets and broaden demand. This is the time for such moves. Various forms of temporary price moves have their value (see the next chapter). And prices can be cut to reach markets the brand alone cannot: the private label market, and the market for a superficially stripped model under another brand.

This is the time to use imagination in devising a perceived value difference which is attractive to substantial numbers in the market, beyond its cost, and not likely to be matched by other sellers.

Distribution Policy in The Shake-Out Phase

Any limitations on distribution policy should be abandoned at the first symptom of the shake-out. The distribution should be as extensive and intensive as the character of the offering permits. This should be coupled with every effort to build strong ties with all elements in the chain of distribution through efforts which make the offering more valuable to them. These include efforts and management aids which keep their inventory costs to a minimum and those which help them improve sales at minimum personnel costs through merchandising aids.

Communications Strategy during The Shake-Out

Communications objectives during the shakeout have three aims: reinforce the consumer franchise, attract whatever trade the failing brands might have won, and strengthen distribution ties.

Mass advertising will still carry the main load, but sales promotions will be needed at the final purchase level, and also at the dealer level (such as free goods offers). Sampling will be useful to attract those not committed to some other strong brand.

Managerial Focus of The Shake-Out Phase

The managerial style of the shake-out phase needs to reflect a transition from a market-building emphasis to a financial control emphasis, without loss of a sensitivity to market opportunities. (This requires a tightrope performance which cannot be avoided. Financial people tend to avoid the risks inherent in marketing moves.) Margins are likely to be thin from this point onward, and are easiest achieved by keeping cost down. But any neglect of market needs and trends will invite competition from inside the industry, at the expense of both market share and cost, or from outside the industry, from new kinds of competition, at the expense of the industry vitality itself.

Strategies for The Surface Stability of The Mature Market

The shakeout phase ends in a saturated, mature market. Market growth, beyond that due to population growth, is not common. Each of the remaining competitors tends to have its own niche. Market shares tend to be rather stable. If production required substantial capital investment, capital needs for entrance now become quite large and relatively unattractive. Habitual patronage patterns and distribution strength tend to minimize shifts in brand preferences. Consumers tend to have highly fixed perceptions of what to expect from each seller. Each seller thus tends to have his own set of core segments. Dealers have a clear idea of what their own customers prefer, and at what price level.

Because of the low potential for growth, the basic strategy is an active defense, on the constant alert for opportunities to improve the offerings attractiveness, to lower costs, to adapt the offering to market changes, and a sharp look out for threats from new kinds of offerings. Especially important is the alert to possible internal relaxation, to the tendency to go to sleep.

In this atmosphere of relative stability, minor shifts in market share are usually the result of shifting purchases by fringe segment buyers, stimulated by one of two causes:

- The search for novelty elements which are perceived as the only significant differences between brands. Such effects tend to cause short term rotation of purchases between brands, with little or no overall effect.
- A temporary response to sales promotions by individual sellers.

Major brand share shifts are normally managed only at a very substantial cost, except when one of the sellers makes a really major marketing mistake. Bringing about any such major brand share shifts usually requires one or more of the following moves:

1. Developing an offering benefit improvement perceived as major by substantial market segments
2. Major price repositioning moves (see the next chapter)
3. Major shifts in the distribution channel due to blunders by a competitor
4. Major market repositioning of a well-accepted offering with a secure but narrow market share
5. A quick move by one competitor to take early advantage of a newly developing use-system or newly developing desire sets which can pyramid the offering into a new plateau.

The Hidden Dangers of Mature Market Apparent Stability

Managements can very easily take this relative stability of the mature market as a signal to relax. Too often, the relaxation passes into slumber.

Then the market, which never stands still, develops trends which offer opportunities which new kinds of competition can use to gain a strong foothold before the older managements come fully awake.

THE DANGEROUS COMPETITION COMES OUT OF LEFT FIELD

Most sellers tend to wear blinders concerning competition. They pay attention only to firms making similar offerings. Once an industry attains maturity, the really dangerous competitors are other, growing industries, far too often ignored in their early stages. The displacement of major steel markets by aluminum is a case in point.

Until World War II, aluminum had a relatively narrow niche in the metals market, one which was of little importance to either the steel or copper producers. Its major uses were in pots and pans, and as part of the group of die-casting alloys. Volume was relatively small, and the price too high to pose any significant threat to either steel or aluminum.

The needs of the military for aluminum in fighters and bombers, in World War II, changed all that. Capacity was expanded several fold, and new producers encouraged to enter the market. With the end of the war, aluminum producers went aggressively after new markets, and prices were much lower, relative to other metals. Many of the attractive markets were using steel.

By 1950, aluminum had already made some inroads on steel because of some real advantages: it was almost immune to atmospheric corrosion, far lighter than steel,and could be made into structural shapes and castings much more cheaply and easily than steel. But the steel industry ignored any possible threat. Executives felt protected by the large volume of steel production: "Aluminum production is measured in pounds, steel production in tons," they said. They proceeded with business as usual, investing little or nothing in real product improvement or marketing research.

Meanwhile, aluminum had already captured a large part of the the metal roofing market because of its corrosion resistance, and aluminum casement windows were being offered at the same prices as steel casements. The aluminum ones were far more attractive to home owners: they sealed better than steel casements, and needed no painting. Later, aluminum foil coated paper cans took over part of steel's valuable container market. Oil companies adopted them quickly because their lighter weight cut shipping cost for oil in containers. Aluminum cans also began to displace tin plate sales. Much of the problems of the steel industry in the 1980's stem in part from losses of important markets to paper, aluminum, and pre-stressed concrete structurals. The rest was due to the ignoring of the cost advantages of new production technologies, opening the way for foreign competition.

Underneath every mature, superficially stable market structure are constant changes and shifts in:

- Consumer identities, as the human life cycle removes one "cohort" from the market to replace it with a new population who have no well established patronage loyalties
- Consumer life styles and desire sets, in response to a multitude of social and economic forces

- Changes in buying habits and channels of distribution, due in part to innovations in merchandising
- Newly developing technologies and knowledge of materials which can change cost potentials and design possibilities

In addition, somewhere out in the economy there is likely to be some cash rich organization looking to diversify its offerings and willing to invest patient capital in expanding the market for a previously well-received brand with a minor market share.

Such potential threats are compounded by the ease by which a long established industry can continue in the same traditional ruts of design, production methods, and offering mixes. The apparent stability of the market can lull such managements into some carelessness in cost management.

Meanwhile, there are always, somewhere in the world, some hungry entrepreneurs looking for market openings, and such opportunities are not left open forever, as the American automobile and steel industries, among others, learned in the late 1970s and the early 1980s.

The key to survival of the mature market phase is an active defense--a defense which recognizes the dangers and keeps a constant alert to weaknesses in need of correction before others discover the opportunities. In marketing as elsewhere, an effective defense is an active defense, based on a positive strategy. Such a strategy includes an active alert to opportunities to improve the perceived value of current offerings in any manner, and reduce the costs of their use. It means a constant search for opportunities for fresh promotional approaches and new channels of distribution which serve final buyers better.

Although mature offerings are generally classified as "cash cows," the cows must be kept sleek and well-fed by careful attention to appropriate R&D, market research, and attention to cost.

New Entries into Mature Markets

Despite the normal stability, entry of many new offerings and even some new producers are not impossible in the mature stage.

Entry is easiest for producers of offerings in which capital requirements are relatively low, for which fashion and design are the deciding element in buyer choice and for which brand preference is weak. (Apparel, cosmetics and toiletries are good examples.) In such situations, even the small entrepreneur can succeed with the right offering.

In the case of product forms for which brand preferences are strong, most new offerings are launched by well-established sellers to strengthen or improve market share by one or more of 4 methods:

- Expanding the variety of offerings to match the diversifying tastes of buyers. Generally, this takes the form of model diversification or the addition of brands.

- Significantly improving the performance or other quality features of the current offerings.
- Creating new fashion designs to match the changing trends of taste.
- Adding a novelty element to create interest.

Well-financed outsiders may succeed in a market invasion even when brand preferences are strong. They must be willing and able to invest heavily in brand promotion to gain a beachhead, and to wait some time for profits. They must also first find some substantial market segments not fully satisfied with current offerings available. Success rewards such efforts only when the new entrant studies consumer desires and buying motives carefully, and expects no quick results. Successful entrants have usually chosen offerings requiring similar marketing skills as their current offerings, or were producers of similar offerings in other markets.

A final type of new entrant is the outsider exploiting a newly developed technology capable of fulfilling the same performance attributes better, but which is being ignored by the current principal producers. Any technology which can create significantly better value for buyers can displace the present offerings and start the older sellers on the decline phase of the cycle.

Maintaining An Effective Mature Market Defense

The primary aspects of defense must be:
- constantly seeking ways to minimize the negative aspects of the offering and maximize its performance
- constantly maintaining a keen cost consciousness
- constantly improving customer service
- constantly maintaining a research watch for product improvement possibilities and for technological changes which need to be adopted.

As with any kind of defense, the problems of the mature phase are to be able to perceive the weak spots in the effort and find ways to strengthen them. All of us are inclined to assume that what succeeds needs no improving, and the sellers who survive the shakeout are no different. They tend to overlook the negative aspects of the compromises inherent in offering designs or at least assume nothing can be done about them. Having survived, they do not question their cost structure nor their customer service. At the moment of their survival, their technology was probably up to date, and they can not see over the horizon to new, quite different technologies which could make the one they are familiar with obsolete.

Questioning success is always difficult, but necessary. It is easy to travel the well-worn ruts, a jarring wrench to pull out of them.

Analyzing The Mature Phase Offering

Every successful offering has some kinds of defects from the buyer's point of view. Consider one example from recent history: the lowly can sitting on our kitchen shelf, and which long dominated many shipping and storing uses. These round steel containers were one of the more important uses of steel.

No shipping container has ever been developed which did not weigh something. But shippers do not like to pay freight on the container. Until something lighter comes along, it may not even occur to them to complain. But when a container becomes available which saves a significant percentage of the freight bill, they are quick to switch. The steel industry learned this when it took its can business for granted a little too long. Nothing substantial was done about the weight of cans until after the oil industry had switched to foil-lined paper cans, and beverages to aluminum cans to save freight. Then the industry did what it should long before have tried--built a can with thinner steel which did the job. The lost business did not return, but what was left was salvaged.

Prolonging the profits of the mature phase requires a constant scrutiny of the offering, and especially of its negative attributes. This applies to the customer and maintenance service elements of the offering, as well. These affect cost-in-use, both in time and money, and in recent years have become a major irritant. They are too often treated as a source of profits, without respect to the effect of their costs on buyers. Sellers need to become conscious of these costs and their effects on buyers.

Another type of cost needs watching--the costs imposed by the designs based on current technology.

Searching for And Adopting New Technologies

Looking backward, any modern technology is a marvelous emancipation from the cost of human labor, compared with what preceded it. The history of invention has been that of new technologies which reduced the cost of creating satisfactions: the match that replaced the making of fire with flint and steel, the water wheel which freed the housewife from the tedious mortar and pestle method of grinding grain, the reaper which abolished the back-breaking labor of cutting grain with sickle and scythe, and the modern combine which obsoleted the reaper.

But in their time, not every new technology was welcomed by those accustomed to working with the old. Cyrus McCormick had difficulty interesting the wheat farmers of the then dominant producers in the east with his reaper. The steel industry in the United States ignored the values of oxygen reduction technology long after its efficiency was proved. Typesetters clung to their "hot type" for a considerable period after photo typesetting equipment proved its reliability and much lower cost.

As with so many problems of management and business, the problem lies in habit. Designers stick with the familiar technology because that is the rut which is comfortable. Financial officers look at what has been spent for equipment, and its remaining "useful life," neglecting the opportunity costs of scrapping that and gaining a cost advantage. So the new technology is left for the outsider unencumbered with investments in the old, and the seller wakes up some morning to find the sales curve headed downward, with little prospect of turning around.

A sharp lookout for these various threats is the major task of marketing research and intelligence in the mature phase.

Mature Phase Marketing Research and Intelligence Needs

The best defense is preventive: the discovery and elimination of as many of the probable weaknesses in the marketing mix as possible, and knowledge of possible threats of all kinds before they become visible problems. A threat foreseen can often be turned into an opportunity.

Market threats and opportunities come from 3 directions in the mature phase:

- From competition with other members of the same industry
- From changes in customers and in their habits
- From outside the industry

Most sellers do pay a great deal of attention to inter-industry competition and the plans of competitors, with good reason. The immediate threat to sales does come from competing sellers and their actions. So major sellers gather information on market share and market trends, as they should. They also collect information from various sources which tell them much about competitor's plans.

The importance of such knowledge of the mature market competition cannot be denied. But such plans and actions work only when they give customers something they desire and are not receiving. A more basic kind of needed knowledge is that about customer changes.

The most obvious of customer changes are the changes that are taking place in the population composition: by age group, by place and type of residence, by occupational characteristics, and by other easily measured characteristics. These are measured by the census, and the trends are usually so stable that projections can be made for some period ahead. All of these trends are important to sellers of nearly every kind. Most sellers pay attention to them and to their more obvious implications.

Some of the meaning of these trends for consumers' habitual life styles may not receive the close analysis they deserve, however. One example has been the changes in the birth rate. Everyone foresaw some of the implications in trends some time after the peak in birth rates passed. But few analysts, even in official quarters, read the implications for the future rates in the details of fertility by educational level, place of residence, and workforce participation by married women until some time after the effects became noticeable. The importance of this kind of information lies in its meaning for consumer buying habits and the motivation underlying them, and this requires some analysis and additional field work.

Thus part of the marketing research needed concerns the habits, attitudes, and perceptions of major market segments—information usually summarized under the title of lifestyle.

Sellers of any offerings in which an element of aesthetic design is a factor need to keep a close watch on the social trends in taste we call fashion. These trends can affect a wide range of offerings, not excluding industrial sales items, and could easily be worthwhile for far more sellers than systematically investigate them through direct research.

Threats from the outside, unfortunately, get the least attention, and may deserve the most. Even the full buyer appeal of the foreign car invasion was not completely understood by the Detroit automakers until the end of the 1970s. Yet private studies, available to the industry, outlined a strong potential demand for the attributes offered by foreign designs as early as the early 1950s. Nearly all major sellers wear blinders with respect to the threats posed by new technologies, whether in retailing or in electronics. Yet no Ph. D. in electronics would have been needed to foresee the eventual attractions of the capabilities offered by silicon chips to buyers of offerings ranging from watches to cash registers.

Technological intelligence should focus on possible use-system gains, on developments with the potential to produce better, cheaper, or simpler means of meeting relevant desire sets, and on developments which could lower costs or increase value of current offering designs, including decreases in design compromise.

In the use of market intelligence, information is available in quantity for those who will learn from it. Such pioneers as McCormick and Marshall Field were able to anticipate developments with an almost insignificant set of information, compared with that available to everyone today. The problem is the lack of foresight to interpret it and look for implications for change. The difficulty seems to lie in the false sense of security stimulated by the apparent stability of the mature phase. The type of administration mature markets draw may be part of the problem.

Management Requirements for The Mature Phase

The mature phase needs a controls-minded management, but one which is also cost-sensitive and market oriented. Tighter organizational and financial controls are necessary during the mature phase. Unit profits are bound to be thinner than during the rapid growth phase. The novelty has worn off the offering, and demand has become largely functional, in a broad sense. No seller has any really significant technological or design advantages, and fringe segments with no sharp preferences are large, putting competitive pressure on prices. Any profit advantage has to be a cost advantage, due to the size and nature of the market niche the seller has won, and to internal economies.

Something more imaginative than mere administration is needed, however. It must be coupled with an understanding of current market needs, in relation to cost. The surviving sellers are usually few and large. Being large, some costs are allowed to creep in because they can be passed on to the consumer--for a time: fat official salaries, industry-wide wage sales far out of line with those the customers are getting, plush executive suites and perquisites. Temporarily, this works because the offering has become part of an habitual consumption system.

But the consumer's buying power is limited, and consumer interest in the offering is no longer at white heat. Those extra costs just open the opportunities for outside competition a little wider, and bring the inevitable decline a little closer. The White Consolidated case at the end of Chapter 7 is only one of many case histories indicating the value of a spartan management at this stage. The plight of the steel and automobile industries in the 1981-82 period were well publicized examples of managements who failed to perform as needed in the mature phase and suffered sales declines from which no complete comeback was in sight.

Decline Phase Strategies

Perhaps the major problem of decline phase marketing strategy is a form of sentimental attachment to an offering which once made important profit contributions: a reluctance to admit that the decline is terminal, and past reviving. Yet such a declining offering will be a drain on profits unless managed as a "milking operation." Only those efforts should be put into marketing such offerings as will yield a significant contribution to profit and overhead.

IT DOES NOT ALWAYS PAY TO ADVERTISE

The effectiveness of promotional effort of any kind depends on what part of the market life cycle the offering is in.

Promotional expenditures have their greatest value during growth stages of the market life cycle. Buyer interest in the offering is highest then, and the attention value of communications concerning the offering can reach a receptive audience. Sales gains made during this stage tend to mean the winning of a market share for well into the future.

During the decline phase, however, any promotional expenditures are wasted. Interest is at a low ebb, there are no new customers to win, and the old ones are not listening--they know what the offering means to them. An analysis of promotional experience by a firm with a substantial list of consumer offerings confirmed this very dramatically. Analyzing the experience with a score of offerings which had received some significant burst of promotion during the decline, it was found that there was an apparent temporary lift in sales in one case in four. But another list of about the same size in which **no promotion** had been used showed a similar coincifental temporary spurt in sales one time in five!

No promotion of any kind will pay off, nor design attention. Pricing should be held at a level contributing to overhead and profit, without respect to sales volume consequences. The offering mix should be trimmed to the minimum essentials. Distribution should be phased out, eliminating any outlets which become marginal. Marketing research should be concerned with one single question: when should the product be dropped?

Only the barest minimum of caretaker management should be given the offering, and that at a very low level.

Deciding When to Get Out of The Market

Offerings may be dropped at almost any stage of the cycle that an optimum profit can be realized, or the resources better used to some other end. History indicates that the high-learning offerings are more likely to come to market from small entrepreneurs than from the established organizations. But only the larger organizations can afford the resources to develop most markets, and if such a sponsor will buy, the small enterprise might well sell just as the market is developing, or even sell the idea before ready for market, to someone better equipped to develop it.

Selling out has disadvantages. The innovator may well be more aggressive in developing his offering and putting it on the market than is a large organization with other lines competing for attention. Moreover, larger organizations are often reluctant to take on anything really outside the established pattern. There may be no buyers, or none that will put the needed resources behind promotion of the offering.

If the resources are even marginally available, it may be wise to stay with an offering well into the growth phase. Theoretically, at least, the ideal time to sell out may well be at the point where the rate of growth is just starting to slip. Someone once remarked that the secret of most large fortunes seems to be to get on a fast-rising development, ride until it reaches its crest, then capitalize the operation as though the rise were to continue indefinitely, and sell out. Certainly, if the resources are available to get this far, selling out just as the market show signs of maturing has much to be said for it.

Even the well-capitalized firm, with a good market share, may shed an offering still in the growth phase if it does not fit its lines well. Union Carbide Corporation was a maker of radio sets in the earlier years, when vacuum tube sets required its Everready batteries for power. It dropped out when the alternating current tube made Union Carbide's Everready batteries unnecessary.

Dropping out is an individual economic decision which should be based on the principal of best economic opportunity. The seller should shed an offering at that point at which the prospect of a future profit is less than is personally acceptable, relative to other uses of energies and resources.

SUMMARY

The basic purpose of any strategic plan is to fit current marketing operations to the stage of the present phase of the market life cycle and lay the groundwork for the next phase.

The appropriate strategies are best summarized in chart form(over).

FIGURE 14-1. SUMMARY: COMPETITIVE STRATEGY OVER THE MARKET LIFE CYCLE

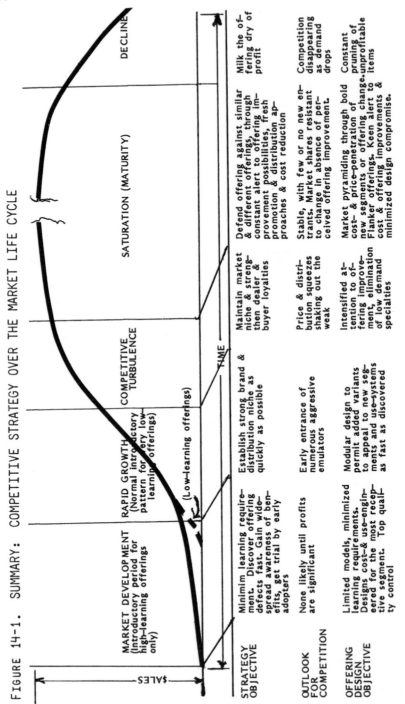

	MARKET DEVELOPMENT (Introductory period for high-learning offerings only)	RAPID GROWTH (Normal introductory pattern for very low-learning offerings) (Low-learning offerings)	COMPETITIVE TURBULENCE	SATURATION (MATURITY)	DECLINE
STRATEGY OBJECTIVE	Minimum learning requirement. Discover offering defects fast. Gain widespread awareness of benefits, get trial by early adopters	Establish strong brand & distribution niche as quickly as possible	Maintain market niche & strengthen dealer & buyer loyalties	Defend offering against similar & different offerings, through constant alert to offering improvement possibilities, fresh promotion & distribution approaches & cost reduction	Milk the offering dry of profit
OUTLOOK FOR COMPETITION	None likely until profits are significant	Early entrance of numerous aggressive emulators	Price & distribution squeezes shaking out the weak	Stable, with few or no new entrants. Market shares resistant to change in absence of perceived offering improvement.	Competition disappearing as demand drops
OFFERING DESIGN OBJECTIVE	Limited models, minimized learning requirements. Designs cost-& use-engineered for the most receptive segment. Top quality control	Modular design to permit added variants to appeal to new segments and use-systems as fast as discovered	Intensified attention to offering improvement, elimination of low demand specialties	Market pyramiding through bold cost-& price-penetration of new segments or offering change. Flanker offerings. Keen alert to cost & offering improvements & minimized design compromise.	Constant pruning of change-unprofitable items

PRICING OBJECTIVE	Match the value reference perception of the most receptive segment & impose the minimum of value perception learning. High trade discounts	Price lines for every taste & purse. Customary trade discounts. Aggressive promotional pricing—prices cut as fast as costs drop. Intensified sampling deals	Increased attention to market-broadening & promotional pricing opportunities	Defensive pricing to preserve category franchise. Alert for incremental pricing apportunities, including private label contracts to use full capacity	Profit level pricing without regard to market share.
PROMOTIONAL GUIDELINES Communications objectives	Develop widespread awareness & understanding of the offering benefits. Get trial by early adopters	Create & strengthen brand preference among trade and final users. Stimulate general trial	Maintain consumer franchise and strengthen dealer ties	Maintain buyer and trade loyalty, heavy emphasis on dealer &distributor service. Promote greater use frequency.	Phase out
Optimum media mix	Strong personal sales supported by heavy publicity and mass advertising	Heavy use of mass media Sales promotions, inc. sampling, personal sales, publicity, (in that order)	Heavy mass media Sales promotions at all levels Sales service to dealers, p.r.	Mass media Dealer-oriented promotions	Cut all promotion to the bone
DISTRIBUTION POLICY	Exclusive or selective, with distributor margins high to justify heavy promotional spending by them	Intensive & extensive, with dealer margins just normal. Special attention to rapid resupply of distributor stocks, heavy inventories	Intensive & extensive, emphasis on stocking dealers as well at low cost to them	As intensive and extensive as possible, with the best of inventory service to dealers and distributors	Drop outlets as they become marginal
MARKETING RESEARCH & INTELLIGENCE FOCUS	To identify the market segments buying and the use systems developing. Uncover any offering weakness or flaws quickly	Detailed attention to brand position, to gaps in model and market coverage, & to market segmentation possibilities	Attention to offering improvement, market broadening, new promotional approaches	Intensified attention to offering improvement needs. Sharp alert for potential inter-product competition & hints of beginning market decline	Look for more profitable uses for the resources involved

FOOD FOR THOUGHT AND DISCUSSION

PRICE ADVERTISING IN A PRICE WAR

1. Referring to the bank bidding war for customers in Charlotte, NC, in December, 1982, it seems reasonable to assume that the offers of each of the 3 different banks would appeal to somewhat different types of savers. What kind of customer segment do you think each bank was attracting with the kind of appeal used?

RCA's "BIG GAMBLE" NO WINNER

Feb. 25, 1981: In a splashy closed-circuit television presentation to 5,000 dealers in 74 locations, RCA placed what Business Week characterized as "its most audacious bet ever," launching its new SelectaVision videodisc player, backed up with a $22 million advertising and promotion campaign.

SelectaVision is a single function device: hooked up with a color TV set, it replays already recorded pictures and shows on the screen, much as an ordinary phonograph record plays music, and in the same way--with a stylus riding in a track on the record. At the time it came on the market, a much more sophisticated machine—the videocassette recorder (VCR) had already built an established market. The VCR could record shows from the TV itself, for later replay, as well as play prerecorded cassettes of movies or other events. Anout 800 thousand VCRs had been sold in 1980, at $600 to $2,000 each. Prerecorded tapes sold for $50 to $70.

The videodisc could not record, but RCA was counting on the lower price and simplicity of its offering to develop a mass market. The initial price was just under $500, and the discs available sold for $14.95 to $27.95. They claimed that their market analysis indicated about 2.4 million customers ready to buy.

Complicating the situation was the fact that another, and different videdisc system was already on the market, and a third system expected before the year was out.

RCA had lined up an impressive distribution system for the effort. Besides its 5,000 franchised dealers, Radio Shack, Montgomery Ward, Sears, Roebuck and J. C. Penney were committed to selling, as well as Sanyo, Toshiba and Hitachi. Zenith had agreed to sell RCA equipment until its own compatible system was available. All told, RCA claimed that dealers responsible for 60% of color TV sales were distributing the player.

David Henneberry, staff marketing vice president, was predicting that RCA would "sell everything we can make and wish we had more," but recognized "that the market is not waiting breathlessly for this machine, and we'll have to educate the public and market it very shrewdly. Capacity was 500,000 machines and 5 million discs at its Indianapolis plant.

Oct. 31, 1981. Headline in the Wall Street Journal: "Following a Slow Start, RCA Plans a New Push for Its Videodisc Player"

According to this report, only about 40,000 units had been sold up until then, although RCA expected to sell 100,000 by Christmas. Advertising expenditures during the Christmas season were budgeted at $20 million. But the Journal doubted that advertising alone would solve RCA's problems. The kinds of families RCA considered to be its market did not seem to understand what videodisc was, nor what it had to offer. Consumers were confused by the variety of video products: three different videodisc systems and video cassette players. In a test promotion in Atlanta on money-back guarantees, 2 of 3 players sold one day were returned the next and exchanged for videodisc recorders

May 18, 1982. Wall Street Journal headline:"Home Videodisk Players Sell Slowly, So Firms Look to Industrial Market"
    Less than 160,000 player had been sold, about evenly divided between the RCA needle player and the higher-priced, more sophisticated Laservision Model of the Pioneer--N. V. Phillips joint venture. RCA cut its price to $299, and would concentrate on selling discs to player owners. By the end of the year, RCA expected to have 400 titles to offer.
    Meanwhile, Pioneer had an industrial model, and Philips was introducing one in June. Sony already had built an industrial market for its $3100 model. When used for marketing and instructional purposes at Ford Motor, the head of Ford training and merchandising programs reported "unqualified success" with its use in training and sales. RCA was bidding on a potential order from Avon Products Co. for 25,000 to train its door-to-door sales force of about 1,2 million.

Wall Street Journal headline, Nov. 22, 1982: "Plan to Introduce Third Videodisk System into the U.S. Collapses Under Market Pressure"

February, 1983. Charlotte, NC, appliance dealers are advertising 4 models of the RCA player, for sale at prices ranging from $99 to $219, when bought with a coupon book for 50 disc rentals at $169, with a free disc club membership thrown in. Other reports indicate that disc clubs are flourishing, but player sales rather dull.

    1. Considering what RCA officials understood about probable consumer reaction before the introduction, how would you appraise the marketing program for its introduction, and why? Consider all aspects of it: pricing, distribution and promotion.
    2. The product design and the plans hint that RCA was comparing the possible market to that for record players and musical records, an industry in which it has long been a major factor. How good do you think the parallel is, and if you think it is not perfect, what differences do you see?
    3. What specific entertainment benefits do you see in this system, and how does it compare with other entertainment alternatives?
    4. Who or what would you think would be the consumer market for the player and the discs?

PERSONAL COMPUTERS: THE SHAKEOUT COMES EARLY IN THE GROWTH PHASE

    In the fall of 1981, the business press was heralding the personal computer market as a no-fail business. Sales were booming for Apple, Tandy (Radio Shack), Commodore International, and Atari, with rising record quarterly profits, depression or no depression. And 1982 continued to be a boom year, with the market for the 6-year old industry segment reaching $6.1 billion worldwide and projections for 1986 sales of $21 billion.
    But clouds were gathering over the fortunes of many of the pioneers by November 1982. Business Week magazine was featuring a review headed "The coming shakeout in personal computers." The price cutting, especially at the low end, certainly looked

like a shakeout symptom. What had happened at this early date in what seemed to be a real growth curve?

For one thing, a lot more companies had entered than distribution channels would support—at least 150 computer makers, and at least twice as many formed to supply the necessary "peripheral" hardware, software, service, sales and other support. Some of the newcomers were more aggressive in building distribution and marketing than the pioneers.

As Business Week saw it, the key to survival lay in three areas: low cost production, strong distribution, and a wide choice of software.

Adequate software is the primary prerequisite. The Apple was little more than the hobbyists toy it started out as until another hobbyist developed a spread sheet program of wide utility. Because Apple made its "architecture" common knowledge, a host of other programs helped build its usefulness and created a market both for the programs and for Apple.

Tandy also created a library of programs for its machines, including one version of the spread sheet program. Meanwhile, Digital Research's CP/M system was becoming an industry standard available for licensing on any machine, including those with 64K of internal memory, as compared with Apple's 48K, and a deep library of programs developed around it--so many that even Apple users were buying additional circuitry to tap it.

Apple started getting flanked in the market. At the low end were machines with much less capacity than the Apple, but suitable for simple applications and playable through a home television screen, at a fraction of the cost. Some were suitable for little more than video games, which boomed. Others had initial capacity, which could be expanded, to handle the simpler forms of word processing as well as the less demanding calculation programs--like the Texas Instruments 99A, selling for only $400, compared with the Apple of more than $2,000 without necessary peripherals. On the other end were 64K machines (compared with Apple's 48K), capable of more demanding programs, such as the better word processing programs, and in the case of the Osborne, selling a complete package of computer, disc drives and controller, and basic software for less than $2,000.

The Osborne, introduced in 1981, was an immediate success. Sold as a portable, it was a self-contained installation, unlike the Apple, which took a separate monitor and disk drives. The accompanying software included the popular Visicalc spreadsheet program originally designed for the Apple, an abbreviated version of the popular Wordmaster word processing program, and the CP/M system with a Basic program. Its monitor was tiny—a mere 5-1/2 inch diagonal, but it accommodated 52 columns (essentially a 52 character line, for those using it for word processing), compared with the 40 column Apple II.

But the Osborne was really only a packaging operation, as, in fact was also the Apple to a lesser extent. Both depended on microprocessors, drives, and other hardware produced by others, and software developed and sold by others. What they did could be done by others, and soon was.

By spring 1982, mighty IBM had put a 128K Personal Computer on the market, also an assembled machine, selling at only a little more than the cost of a complete Apple package. And others took direct aim at obvious weaknesses in Apple and Osborne. Anyone using the computer for writing, as many authors and offices were beginning to do, wanted an 80 column screen for the standard line length. Those using proportional spacing typing needed 64k machines, not the Apple's 48K, and disc storage of 190K to handle the program which the Osborne could not. Further, the tiny screen of the Osborne was completely inadequate for any prolonged use, and had to be supplemented with a separate monitor at least. In mid-summer, the Franklin Ace 100 was launched, using similar circuitry to the Apple, but compatible with **both** Apple and CP/M programs, and with 64K capacity, and usable with an 80 column monitor. The Franklin machine quickly gained distributors, who sold a complete package--at less than the Apple's price. On its heels was the portable KAYPRO II, produced by Non-Linear Systems, Inc., a components manufacturer, selling at the list price of the Osborne, with a quite adequate high-resolution 9-inch 80-column monitor, double density (190K) disc drives, and its own package of word processor and spread-sheet software. Both of these entrants pushed strongly for distribution, and by the beginning of 1983, Kaypro had reached a sales level already three-fourths that of the Osborne and was getting wider distribution in at least some areas. wider than Osborne's.

Distribution was clearly going to be a major key to survival and success. What was not so clear is what that distribution needed to be. Observers believed that as the price of computers came down (as they already were at the beginning of 1983--TI's 99A and Commodore's Vic 20 could now be bought for $169 in some outlets), mail order houses and department stores would be favored, especially for the home user. One analyst is quoted as saying that "retailers that are only specialty stores are vulnerable." But there are several market segments: small businesses, professionals needing something more than mass market game machines, for example.

Promotion, too will be important. Kaypro was developing a strong dealer coop ad campaign in early 1983, and dealers said it was bringing customers into their stores. Commodore was running a four-month promotional tie-in with General Mills in Canada, enclosing a coupon for its low end Vic20 computer in 125 out of 2.5 million boxes of Cheerio breakfast cereal. A chance to win a free Vic20 was also offered to new customers of the 20 largest branches of Toronto Dominion Bank, and similar promotions were planned for a soft drink bottler, a hotel chain, and a chocolate manufacturer.

Another distribution channel was so-called third party systems houses, packaging the computer, peripherals and software for specialized markets, such as insurance companies, brokerage houses, law firms, and health care agencies. Software producers might well dominate some of this business, since they have the know-how for tailoring their product for specific uses. Atari Inc. sold Chemical Bank of New York on basing its home banking service on the Atari Personal Computer, and Citibank has picked several computers to be used in a trial bank-from-home service.

That a shakeout is on the way is without question. Distributors cannot handle more than a half dozen makes at the outside. A California venture capital consultant is quoted as observing that by 1986, there would only be a dozen sellers in the field, and McDonald of Casio is quoted as foreseeing that within a few years the only survivors will be those with at least $100 million in revenue and a minimum 15% market share. To get the production economies, it is felt that the integrated producers of components will dominate.

1. A shakeout this early in the growth is unusual. Given the unclear structure of the eventual market, there must be some opportunities still open for innovators somewhere in the marketing chain. What possibilities can you see?

2. Several clear segments are already obvious in the personal computer market: household usage, educational markets, professionals both at home and in small offices, very small and small businesses. The professionals market is split into at least 3

segments of its own: accountants, engineers for calculations and graphics, authors for sophisticated word processing systems.

What kinds of distribution systems do you think would best serve each of these segments?

3. If you were one of the moderate-sized makers, how would you go about solidifying a niche in the market?

ROBBINS & MYERS INC.: BUMPING ITS HEAD ON CEILING FANS

Up until the end of world War II, about the only air conditioning available to most people were fans, of which the ceiling fan was the most efficient. Robbins & Myers had been making them since 1910, and bought out the original—the Hunter fan, Cadillac of ceiling fans—in 1949, just as electric air conditioners were beginning to obsolete them. Some sales continued, but the Hunter fans were just one of a number of lines until the mid-1970s, when nostalgia buffs rediscovered the 1942 Hollywood production, "Casablanca", in which ceiling fans played a prominent role in the romantic atmosphere. Suddenly, there was a rush to buy "Casablanca fans". Coincidently, energy experts discovered that ceiling fans used with air-conditioning lowered electricity costs 15% or better, and also reduced winter heating costs.

Robbins & Myers saw unit fan sales nearly double each year from 1975 to 1981 and saw its earnings rise 400%. Others, of course rushed in to cash in on the boom: about 130 U.S. manufacturers and importers joined the industry. A large portion were being imported from contractors in Taiwan. Many of them sold for less than half the price of the Hunter fan's lowest cost model ($175). A total of 7.4 million were sold in the U. S. in 1981, compared with 250 thousand in 1975. Most of the sales were being made to buyers who installed their own.

To maintain its position in the market, Robbins and Myers expanded its capacity from 50,000 per year to 900,000 in 1981, switching some whole plants from other lines, and eclipsing its other businesses in pumps, electric motors, and materials-handling equipment.

Then, suddenly, sales flattened out in 1982, and everybody was scrambling for business, some obviously selling at cost, trying to unload a heavy overload of inventory.

Robbins & Myers with prices far above the rest, were in the worst inventory position. To boost sales, it by-passed its own distributors in February 1982 to sell directly to large retailers and mass merchandisers in order to give them more profit margin, leaving its distributors with only the small accounts. Some of them dropped the line.

To stimulate sales further, R&M began offering customers a rebate, to the tune of $8.1 million. It sold fans—out of the dealer's inventories, who seized on the opportunity to unload their own inventories, and did not reorder.

R&M has finally cut back on fan operations, and introduced a medium-priced line under the "Comfort Breeze" label. While many are wondering what will happen to the ceiling fan market, R&M officials "think they're here to stay," and claim that "all the marketing research we've done indicates that." They believe that it has a place as a serious energy-saving appliance rather than just decoration, but that "It just won't be the leading growth market that it was."

1. If the fan is to have a significant future, it would have to be as an energy

saving device. How much do you think the fans needed to fully equip a home are worth as an investment in saving the energy in air conditioning and heating? How much would have to be invested to get this saving? Do you think this is enough motivation to support a sizeable market?

2. From the figures on sales growth in those 6 boom years, what would be your estimate of the total units already in use? How much more market is left, do you think? What would you base such an estimate on?

3. Given the history of the R&M share, and the trends in competition, How realistic was the extent of the R&M capacity expansion, even assuming the market would continue on the rapid growth curve of the past?

4. If the mass merchandisers were really important, as seems likely, how could sales to them have been handled without antagonizing the established distributors? Should a maker in the R&M position court the mass merchandisers? Why or why not?

5. Could R&M have anticipated the market glut earlier, or even in time to abort the expansion plans after they were made? If so, how and why?

6. What could R&M have done to insulate themselves against the contingency of a letdown?

A.O.SMITH: PLAYING IT SAFE DID NOT LEAD TO PROFITS

Like a lot of other companies, A. O. Smith has long believed it was safer to diversify internally, rather than by acquisition. As President John R. Parker is quoted in Business Week, "we want to expand peripherally from areas we know something about by taking a lot of little steps outside our existing businesses to spread the risks." And Chairman Lloyd B. Smith agrees, "That's a slower, but ultimately safer course to follow." (**Business Week**, A. O. Smith: 'Safe diversification that is endangering profits,' Sept. 21, 1981.)

And Smith's experience with at least one major diversification was certainly not happy: the purchase of the Armor Elevator Co., in 1969, a $40 million-per-year business. After four straight years of losses, Armor was sold at a $12.8 million loss, and Smith has almost entirely avoided acquisitions since.

Meanwhile Smith was living with a really big risk: nearly half of its volume, and a full half of its profits, came from one product, with one main customer: automobile frames sold mostly to GM, a business that at its peak was a $300 million operation for Smith, which had 40% of the market. And frame business and all, its profit growth was only 5% per year, much less than the average for the auto parts industry, most of whose members were diversifying away from dependence on Detroit.

Moreover, they have been aware of the risk of losing this business for some time, and their efforts at internal diversification were stimulated by this knowledge. But they had "an emotional commitment" to the frame business and "became zealots for frames," as Parker admitted. The trend to smaller cost-competitive cars since the mid-1970s had forced Detroit to shift to the frameless, unitized body. But Smith refused to see the handwriting on the wall. Officials worked hard to convince Detroit that the smoother-riding frames could be adapted to the smaller cars without a weight penalty. When GM brought out its unitized X-cars in 1979 (Chevrolet Citation, etc.), Smith spent $300 thousand to rebuild one with a separate frame, that weighed 7 pounds less, and "thought we had it made" when they tried the ride.

But GM, and the rest of Detroit was not buying. By 1981, 3 of the 7 frame plants in the U. S. had been closed, and the final blow came in Aug., 1981, when GM gave Smith notice that after 1983, it would no longer buy auto frames. Only a few luxury models would be using them after 1984 anywhere in the industry. Smith had been blind to the two major reasons for the switch to unitized construction. It facilitated robotized production to cut costs, and the unibody produces a more solid car. Separate frames are harder to fit to the rest of the car. Both gains were needed to compete with the unitized imports, especially the Japanese.

Nevertheless, Smith is still sticking to its internal diversification, spinning out new businesses from existing ones. It has begun rebuilding its auto parts manufacture with a new plant to produce trailing axles for Chrysler and GM front-wheel-drive compacts. Outsiders note, however, that this leaves them vulnerable to a wide list of possible competitors, because such axles can be turned out by any other stamping plant looking for a use for idle equipment. They have no special advantage in this business.

Most of Smith's other businesses are also tied to the cyclical durable goods, and have grown out of its welding and metal fabrication techniques. One of the earliest was in making petroleum pipeline pipe. Then the steel companies themselves got into the business, and cut the profits. Looking for a way to cut costs, they hit on a method of ceramic coating of the pipe to protect it from corrosion and speed the flow, but pipeline companies found electrolytic protection even less expensive. They then turned the ceramic coating expertise into the building of the Harvestore silos, a real success. The Harvestore division is a $140 million business and controls about a quarter of the on-farm feed grain storage.

The same ceramic knowledge was used to make the glass-lined water heater, in which Smith dominates the commercial market and is third ranked in the residential installations. More recently, it expanded the computer software and processing systems it developed for internal use into a data system operation marketing its service to such outsiders as electronic-funds-transfer processing for banks and computer engineering services to manufacturers.

There is some hint that even the Smith officials are looking more widely for diversification. A new technical group was formed in the spring of 1981 to coordinate a shift in the research budget into unrelated fields, such as robot software systems, combining its manufacturing and newly acquired software skills.

1. Why was Smith caught so flat-footed on the phase-out of frames? Any major industrial supplier like Smith maintains a close sales liaison with their few large customers. They are normally privy to the basic plans of these customers. Chrysler's Omni-Horizon compacts were in planning at least as early as 1974, and the GM X-cars no later than 1976. A supplier like Smith would normally had little trouble learning what the design thinking was, and why. How could they have been so blind?

2. How would you characterize the orientation of Smith's diversification policy, on the basis of past history?

3. To what extent does the move into software systems seem to be part of the same bias, or is it?

4. Smith is still laying its heavy bets on supplying the U.S. auto industry. How do you view the market life cycle position of tha industry, and its prospects as a future profitable market?

CHAPTER 16. COMPETITIVE TACTICS IN MATURE MARKETS

The economic and psychological bases for mature market stability
Factors weakening the stability in mature markets
Successful competitive moves in mature markets
    Nipping off a market share with a price pincers
    Other mature market opportunities
        Private and generic brands
        Price and offering design funnel opportunities
        Co-opting and image for a new brand in a time of changing taste
        Expanding from a class market to a mass market share
        Flanker offering possibilities
        Competing with cost control and productivity
Establishing a guiding anchor concept for mature market strategy
The timing and positioning dimensions of mature phase strategy
    The plan's time span
    Implementation of timing relative to competitive moves
    Implementation relative to the swings in taste
    The choice between rapid penetration and infiltration
    The brand positioning dimension of the mature market strategy
The limits imposed by industry structure and the size of seller
    The perils of size and dominance

NOTE: This author is indebted to the thorough research of Linden R. Brown, summarized in an unpublished doctoral thesis at the University of New South Wales, Australia, "An Empirical Study and Evaluation of Marketing Strategies Adopted in Competitive Consumer Markets", July 1975, for much of the conceptual framework in this chapter, and for the solid data underlying this framework. Studying grocery products in mature phase markets over the period from 1962 to 1972, Dr. Brown had full access to the Australian Nielsen data and the cooperation of executives in 9 firms whose products had been involved, and who knew the inside objectives of the strategies pursued in that period.

COMPETITIVE TACTICS
IN MATURE MARKETS

16

Managing offerings in the mature phase of the market life cycle tends to occupy most of the management attention and of the resources in nearly all well-established organizations. Rightfully so: current revenue comes primarily from such offerings, and tactical decisions have to be made almost daily on the promotional and pricing tactics aimed at improving or defending market share, and on the addition or discontinuance of short-lived brand variations.

The identity of competitors in a mature market remains relatively stable, and also their relative market niches. However, the stability is only relative. Each competitor constantly searches for opportunities to improve market share. Such opportunities arise because of the large numbers of buyers in fringe segments with no strong patronage ties. For these fringe segments, all of the available offerings fall short of reasonably complete satisfaction. Changes in consumer tastes and in the lives and identities of consumers add to this fringe. Moreover, constant changes in technology sooner or later permit new and more attractive design compromise possibilities which someone, within the industry or from the outside, can seize to restructure the market.

The mature phase industry structure typically consists of a loose "oligopoly" of a few dominant competitors, each with it own differentiated niche, and some market specialists, each of whom can potentially affect the market, plus some low overhead entrepreneurs. Most of the small entrepreneurs have no significant effect on the markets of the larger producers, but among them may be those who are sufficiently aggressive and shrewd to take advantage of any opening to seize a major share of market.

As a result of this uneasy equilibrium, each seller must find a competitive mode appropriate to his resources and skills and opportunities: offensive, preemptive, or defensive in nature.

In mass consumer markets particularly, a common tactic is the launching of new brands. Such a launch requires decisions on the positioning and on the entry strategy. Entry strategies may be either that of quick penetration or of infiltration. The positioning will include a choice of offering design, pricing, or some combination of both, and always involves a corresponding promotional theme and distribution.

Successful mature market strategies and tactics offer the buyer a readily perceived noticeable value difference: a better value/price ratio than current buyers perceive as available. Mere price cuts by new sellers or new brands are seldom very successful because of the tendency to judge quality by price, and also because of the speed and ease by which they can be countered. But combining price strategy with product and/or distribution changes can gain enough initial advantage to restructure market shares, and well-established brands can use any of several forms of price pincers to nip off a significant share of market.

The Economic And Psychological Bases for Mature Market Stability

Once markets reach maturity, the differentiation of offerings tends to be as much psychological as physical. All surviving brands are capable of serving the core functions reasonably well, customer interest is not very high, and many buyers have no strong preferences.

Market shares are usually not very fluid, for several reasons. Each offering has its own rather clearly defined niche, serving a specific core of habitual users. Distribution strengths established long before are an important factor in buying choices. Buyers have acquired rather well-entrenched perceptions (images) of the benefits offered by each of the competing offerings and of the relative value positions of each.

Generally, production is on a mass basis and the technology well established and pretty much available to all producers. The mass nature of the production and/or promotion sets the investment admission ticket high enough to discourage outsiders. Unit margin costs are also usually thin, furnishing little incentive to outsiders.

Consumer perceptions of value/price relationships are well established, so that the price of any unknown becomes a measure of the expected quality, not an incentive to buy it.

Fringe segment shoppers consist of those who perceive little differences between established offerings in relation to their desire sets. They are thus unlikely to be won over for the core segment of any offering. Share changes induced by purely promotional tactics thus tend to be fleeting, and not very profitable.

Nevertheless, the stability of the mature market can be upset due to other factors which make for potential instability.

Factors Weakening The Potential Stability of Mature Markets

Other factors are always eating away at the foundations of this surface stability, keeping all managers on the defensive, to maintain their relative market positions, and offering opportunities to the aggressive. At least 6 destabilizing factors are obvious:

1. Changes in customer identity.   Each segment of customers is a moving stream, not a fixed cluster. New ones are always coming into the segment and old customers dropping out. The length of their consumption cycles, and stay in the segment, varies with the type of offering, but none are really lifelong.

2. The constant cultural shifts in consumer tastes, standards, and life styles, creating new desire sets

3. Customer mobility: both final users and industrial customers are relatively mobile in our society. Such mobility changes the required distribution patterns, and frequently the physical needs and desire sets.

4. Technological changes affecting the industry, changing cost relationships, offering performance, and even the investment level.

5. The consistent appeal of novelty, especially in a period when many offerings are essentially on a par with competitors.

6. Design compromise, consistently leaving openings for some imaginative seller who can put together a different compromise which will attract substantial numbers in the fringe segments served by several offerings.

The frequency with which markets will undergo restructuring as a result of these destabilizing factors depends in part on the ease of entry into the industry, and the amount of perceived added value, including novelty, in any new offering.

A SEEDY GREETING CARD BUSINESS

Nature-loving Scot Alyn got tired of promoting soda pop , candy and other such unnatural things for big companies. He hoped to educate people about such wholesome activities as gardening and natural things. So he set himself up as president of the the Great Northwestern Greeting Seed Company of Oregon City, Ore., selling greeting cards doubling as seed packets for flowers, fruits, herbs, and vegetables.

The cards are printed with puns and colorful drawings similar to those on traditional seed packs. Among the best sellers: "Thanks....a bunch" (carrots, of course); "If we cantaloupe...let's just fool around;" "I'd like to hug you....till you're squashed;" "Happy birthday....for ears and ears to come," (popcorn).

Among his favorites, according to the August 20, 1981 Wall Street Journal, :"a friend like you.... is worth a mint;" "If I could dash away.... I'd spend my thyme with you."

Some ideas don't sell. People love to read, but do not buy "Quit stringing me along...plant your beans or get out of the garden." But one young woman wrote telling him, "My boyfriend got the message and we're back together."

Alyn's company is no threat to Hallmark as yet, but did sell a half million "greeting seeds" in its first year in business, distributing them through gift shops, garden centers and gourmet shops, with a retail price of $1.50 each. He guesses that maybe 1 or two out of 10 recipients plant the seeds.

Stability will probably be brief, and fashion oscillations the rule, whenever entry is relatively inexpensive and the novelty element a substantial portion of the perceived total. But costly entry is no bar to competitive entries when changes in buyers' tastes and life styles spawn a substantial unsatisfied segment of the market. Such appears to have been the case after World War II in the U. S. auto market, when Detroit designers went in the opposite direction from a substantial segment of the buying public. (A private study conducted in the early 1950s, by one of the larger research agencies, revealed that about one-third of the American buyers would be interested, even at that time, in the European type of small, highly roadable, fuel-efficient designs. Not a single U. S. model approaching such specifications was put on sale before the mid-1970s.)

Penetrating an established market requires a total set of strategies and tactics, just as any other aspect of marketing. The choice of emphasis differs with the situation, and with the seller's skills.

Successful Competitive Moves in Mature Markets

As with marketing efforts at any time, plans to gain a competitive advantage in mature markets succeed only when they offer prospects a noticeable level of perceived added value. The perceived value/price gain can be achieved by operating on either term in the ratio--by improving some aspect of the offering, or decreasing the perceived price in some manner.

The perceived value of the offering may be substantially increased through a change in some perceivable physical attribute of the offering itself, through a greatly improved availability of the offering, or through well-aimed promotion which creates a perception of a greater degree of some intangible benefit widely sought by users of the offering form.

Changing perceptions of either the tangible physical attributes of an offering, or developing perception of an intangible benefit through communications, is usually made easier by launching a new brand or changing the perceived sponsorship of the offering. An added brand avoids disturbing the demand from the core segment of the established market position. At the same time, any new offering sidesteps the need to erase any established perceptions in any respect. If the benefits promised appeal to any substantial segment, the segment will be set to listen with an open mind.

A lower price also improves the value/price ratio, but is normally effective in mature markets under only two conditions:

-   When the offering is an established one with well established perceptions of the benefits to be expected, and competitors do not follow quickly, which they usually can and do if the price change is a direct monetary reduction.

- If the entry is a new one, and is directly and obviously aimed at an uncovered low end market.

Any other kind of new entry trying to break open a mature market with a lower price than existing competitors operates at a disadvantage. The low price is initially perceived as connoting lower quality, not bargain, by the buyers in that market. And as J&J showed Bristol Myers when it tried this tactic with Datril, any established competitor can move in and nullify the advantage before the interloper can get a foothold.

A price move can succeed, however, if combined with some added perceived benefits in the offering, or if the price is in some other not easily compared form. A substantial improvement in distribution availability is one decrease in price that competitors cannot easily counter, for example. And as indicated in Chapter 10, there are other ways of decreasing price initially. Increasing package size can confer a time advantage necessary for success also.

One form of price cutting can be very effective under the right conditions, when the seller is in a position to accept a lower price permanently on a well-established brand: a price pincers move. This form of price repositioning can squeeze a competitor's market share if that competitor is reluctant, for any reason, to follow quickly.

Nipping Off A Market Share with A Price Pincers

Only established brands are in a position to use a price pincer maneuver. This tactic takes advantage of three common aspects of mature markets:

1. By the time any market matures, the various competing brands are grouped into a number of perceived price/quality lines—usually at three such levels. Prices of offerings at each level are closely bunched, often identical. The price gap between lines is quite substantial—usually far more than a j.n.d.

2. Buyers perceive very little benefit and quality differences between offerings at the same price line level, but very substantial differences in quality between offerings of any brand from offerings of any brand at some adjacent level.

3. Whatever production cost differences may exist between products at one level and those in an adjacent price level, those differences are far less than the differences in prices of the two levels.

If one or more sellers drop prices of offerings at one price level, buyers perceive the increased gap between that price and the price above it as lowering the attractiveness of the "better" quality product above. Such a move will draw some trade from a seller not previously viewed as in competition with the "pincher" by the sellers of the higher grade. Significant numbers of the buyers in the segment above will perceive the cost of the higher grade out of line with its quality difference.

Simultaneously, if there is a price level below that of the initiator, then sellers in that level will also lose sales to the aggressor, because in their case, the price difference is now less than the value of the quality difference of the grade above.

FIGURE 16-1. PRICE PINCER STRATEGIES

SINGLE PINCERS   DOUBLE PINCERS

Premium Price Pincer   Premium/Low Pincers

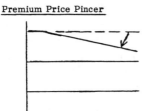   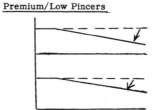

Medium Price Pincer   Premium/Medium Pincers

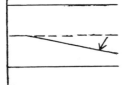   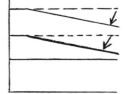

Low Price Pincer   Medium/Low Pincers

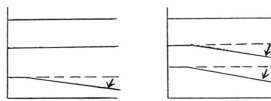

Adapted from Linden R. Brown, **An Empirical Study and Evaluation of Market Strategies Adopted in Competitive Consumer Markets.** Unpublished thesis, University of New South Wales, Australia, 1975.

It matters little whether others at the same price level move or not. (They probably will.) The gains sought come from sellers who do not perceive themselves as in competition, and they are likely to ignore the move long enough for it to succeed. Eventually, the entire market is likely to restructured at a new, lower level, but with a substantially larger share for the seller who moved first.

As shown graphically in Figure 16-1, there are 6 general forms of price pincers: three versions of a single pincer move, and three versions of a double pincers:

- **Single pincer:**
  - * **Premium price pincer:** a substantial price cut by one of the sellers at the premium level, putting the squeeze on sellers in the next level below
  - * **Medium price pincer:** a substantial price cut by some seller at the middle level, opening a wider price gap between his offering and those in the quality level above, and also narrowing the premium paid for his product in comparison with the level below
  - * **Low price pincer:** a substantial price cut by a seller at the lowest quality level, opening a substantial cost gap between his product and those selling in the price level above

---

SAS COMEBACK WITH A DOUBLE PRICE PINCERS PLUS OFFERING REVITALIZATION

Most airlines were losing money when Jan Carlzon took over as chief executive of the Scandinavian Airlines group in August 1981. SAS was no exception—the operating loss for the fiscal year ending in Sept. was $8.2 million. Carlzon wasted no time in streamlining the operation, He replaced 13 out of the 14 top executives and cut overhead by a fourth. But he knew that more was needed than mere cost cutting.

He invested $25 million to improve service and airport facilities, with special attention to the SAS hub airport, Kastrup International at Copenhagen, aiming to attract passengers from Lufthansa, KLM, Swissair and others for connections to other SAS flights. He succeeded in making SAS the most punctual airline in Europe, starting a rise in passenger preference polls. And in November, 1981, he launched the Euroclass program to gain a major share of the business travel, the cream of the passenger business. Euroclass gave the full-fare business traveler preferential treatment, extra service at standard coach prices—a service Air France and some of the others were charging a 20% premium for. Air France officials were so angry they blacked SAS out of its reservation computers briefly. They then matched SAS's prices in the markets both serve.

Then SAS worked the other jaw of their pincers, introducing discounts as high as 70% on the other seats, on a restricted basis. Carlzon's justification, according to Business Week: "When you want to fill the back of the bus, you have to cut fares enough so that they are noticed."

The discounts helped fill seats, but the major revenue gains came from the added full fare business. Total traffic in Europe dropped 1% in the year ending in Sept. 1982, but full fare traffic increased by 8%. Intercontinental traffic declined 2%, but the business class went up 16%. The total return per passenger mile improved 23%, and the airline earned $53.3 million profit for the year, on sales of $1.5 billion.

Double pincer plays:
  - * **Paired premium and low end moves:** simultaneous cuts in premium and low end offerings, squeezing the middle-range offerings.

* **Paired premium–medium pincers:** simultaneous decreases in the prices of offerings in the premium and middle ranges, putting a squeeze on the prices of low end offerings
* **Paired medium–low pincers:** simultaneous cuts in medium and low end offerings, putting a price squeeze on the premium end offerings

Brown's Australian researches revealed a number of such successful pincer movements, and a couple which backfired. The reluctance of those squeezed to retaliate is indicated by his finding that the widened gap could remain "for up to five years."

A danger of such moves may be too great a narrowing of the profit margin, not easily recovered. The form of pincer adopted, of course, depends on the quality level of the seller's major offerings. Because of the commonly better margins available to the seller of premium products, pincers involving the premium end would seem to have the greatest utility, especially since they tend to have a greater market expansion potential.

Such pincers moves are obviously supported by increased promotional efforts, but need to do nothing significant to the offering or its perceived benefits. Nearly all other forms of effective price competition in the mature phase are accompanied by some form of offering advantage. No better customer magnet can be found than a perceived product advantage. The effects will linger in the perceptions of buyers long after competitors catch up with the pricing.

Other Mature Market Opportunities

Most of the best market expansion opportunities in the mature phase involve tapping markets that, for one reason or another, contain substantial segments whose desire sets are not well matched by any well-established offering. At least four such opportunities frequently arise. Two of them involve inadequacies in coverage of the market by established brands: private brands and generic brand opportunities, and price and /or offering design range funnels. The other two involve the use of imaginative promotion of intangible benefits perceived as salient by major market segments: in one version, the promotion of a new brand during a period of some some structural changes in the market, by appealing to a desire discovered to be felt as salient by a substantial segment, but not clearly attached to a single brand. The other consists of expansion of the market of a well perceived premium brand with a small market share, to tap a very large market segment which seeks a highly specific intangible benefit.

Sellers of brands which move into the mature phase with strong distribution and a good consumer franchise, can capitalize on their positions to broaden their markets by the addition of related flanker offerings.

The mature phase gives greater importance to cost controls and productivity, because of decreased physical and perceived differentiation between the offerings of competing sellers, and the growth of uncommitted fringe segments.

Private and generic brands. A common price/product opportunity available in mature markets is the production and sale of private and 'generic' brands. The price, all through the channels of distribution to final buyer, is significantly less than for the strong recognized brands. They are profitable, however, because they utilize excess capacity, require no promotional spending, and they attract a market which the regular brand does not. They may be produced by the maker of a leading brand, or by a lesser producer who could not otherwise get into the market. Such is part of the strategy of White Consolidated, as described in Chapter 7.

Price and offering design funnel opportunities. The intense competition for market shares in a fully mature market tends to narrow the range of price and offering design open to buyers. The larger sellers, especially, all aim for the largest market segments. Eventually, large numbers of buyers find nothing on the market which clearly appeals to them: buyers whose desires and/or pocketbooks range outside the narrowing range of choices readily available.

When this occurs, sellers who understand the total market may find a market ready and waiting, with no immediate competition in sight.

That waiting market may all be at the premium end, if sellers have concentrated too strongly on price. Such was the history of the bread market in the 1920s and 1930s. In a competition for large market shares, all of the major makers allowed the quality of product to sink to the same low level. An obscure farm wife then started selling her home made bread to neighbors, and Pepperidge Farms bread soon secured a strong niche at the premium end of the market. Others found profitable niches at a quality level just below.

In the period just after World War II, the Detroit auto makers opened design gaps at both the utility side of the market , and at the luxury level, as every major producer aimed for the volume markets for large cars in the middle. The result was a well paved, red-carpeted invitation to foreign cars at both sides of the design range, filling gaps which Detroit refused to recognize until the imports had secured a well-fortified set of market positions.

As happened in both the auto and bread examples, such gaps in coverage permit the development of new competitors. Opportunities for promotional revitalizations, based on desired intangibles can be just as useful.

As already noted earlier, brand differentiation in many consumer goods areas especially, tend to rest on benefit images which have little objective relevance to the physical characteristics of the offering. In such instances, some major portion of the market may choose a brand because the brand is perceived as providing a greater measure of this psychological benefit. If a major segment of the market is seeking this benefit, and no one brand is strongly associated with it, heavy, well-designed promotion can establish a new brand, or greatly expand the market for an established brand with a good reputation.

Cigarettes and beer are two such products and both furnish examples of using promotional image creation to chew off a large chunk of the potential market.

Co-Opting An Image for A New Brand in A Time of Changing Taste. The structure of the cigarette market was getting more complex by the 1950s. The 100 mm. long cigarette had taken over much of the market from the once standard 80 mm. brands. Filter brands were becoming popular. And the Philip Morris company was looking to challenge the old-time leaders. The vehicle chosen was to be a new filter brand—a revitalization of an almost forgotten brand introduced in the 1930s by a recent acquisition, Benson & Hedges, a producer of a number of specialty brands.

The main Marlboro story was sketched at the end of chapter 3 ("The Marlboro Man Is Born"). As indicated there, what Philip Morris and their advertising agency, Leo Burnett Inc., did was to analyze available research on the market, discover that a salient motive of most cigarette smokers was the image of virility, and to attach this one image tightly to Marlboro, riding it to the top of market share standings. Other cigarettes have since latched onto this theme, of course, but as always in marketing, the first one there gets the credit, and the profits.

Expanding from a class market to a mass market share. The heavy user segment for beer has long been identified: a blue collar market which cherishes traditional family-centered values. Various beers have capitalized on this in some way or another, and Anheuser-Busch has done a shrewd job of winning a large market share through consistent promotion tied in with such values. Looking for non-cigarette diversification, Philip Morris saw a chance to enter by way of acquiring Miller Beer. Miller had an excellent reputation for quality, and as a beer for special occasions, which won it a solid 6% market share as "The Champagne of Beers." The quality reputation did not hurt, but a special occasion beer does not get the heavy user sales.

The Miller Beer story was also detailed earlier, in chapter 3. As noted there, the premium value was used as a base on which, gradually, promotional emphasis was placed on its everyday use by hearty drinking blue collar types.

Such promotional revitalization takes a well-filled treasury. but it can carry brands into the profitable cloudland of low per unit promotional costs, important to many consumer offerings with little perceived physical differentiation.

CHESEBROUGH (A): TRANSFORMING A SPECIALTY INTO A MAJOR BRAND

The C. H. Bass & Co. was a profitable maker of a small specialty line of shoes-the Weejuns brand--when Chesebrough bought it for $27 million in 1978, but Business Week notes that it hardly looked like a good risk. Bass was a small specialty producer in an industry losing out to foreign competition. It had a small market as a causal, preppie style among some college students, where it had become part of a status symbol, but it did not have the capital or capacity to expand and take on more customers.

In a little more than than two years Chesebrough tripled its sales to $80 million, with 1979 profits of $13 million. Manufacturing capacity was already 30% greater and plans were to add another 20% per year for 3 years. A new distribution center was built, two new shoe factories acquired, and a modern computerized ordering and inventory control system installed.

Previously sold largely in specialty stores on the basis of quality, Chesebrough was making a sales and promotional push into the larger department stores, where the competition would be stiffer. Bass 'Country Store' boutiques were installed in 20 department store chains and new point of purchase displays provided for smaller stores. The line was widened from 200 styles and sizes to 500 in 1981. To get away from dependence on the fall season sales, a line of spring and summer 'Sunjun' sandals was designed and grew to 42% of sales. Plans to expand into higher priced shoes and possibly leather bags were in the works.

Flanker offering opportunities. The strong distribution network which carries a seller through to the mature phase provides the base for broadening the offerings and profits through 'flanker' line additions: products which are use-related to the central offering and utilize the same promotional strategies. These are profit fatteners, because they use the same channels at little extra cost, and even can piggy-back on the promotional effort. Shampoos, hair conditioners and skin lotions are natural flankers for any firm with any kind of toiletries offering. The 3M Corp. developed its original Scotch masking tape to solve a painting problem of auto industry customers buying its abrasive papers. Gasoline service stations early added tires, batteries, windshield wipers, and other accessories to their petroleum products.

Competing with cost control and productivity. Both objective and perceived offering differentiation have declined greatly by the time the market reaches maturity. The size of the uncommitted fringe segments have grown greatly, as the growth of private brand sales shows. Some kinds of offerings have become commodities for a large part of the market, purchased on the basis of objective grade and price. Even when brand identity has some advantage, pricing tactics are obviously important.

Price cuts will cut too deeply into profits unless the total market is expanded, or costs are reduced in some manner. By definition, the maturity phase is one of saturated markets, so increased volume is unlikely to result from price cutting, as Ford discovered in the 1921-25 period. One alternative is to exercise tight cost control, from top to bottom, and step up productivity. Expert handling can substantially improve profits and put a seller in position to exercise pricing moves more readily. The White Consolidated case at the end of chapter 7 illustrates how effective this can be.

UNITED COATINGS: A BUSINESS GROWS BY ACTING LIKE A SMALL BUSINESS

Jules Knapp, a former paint brush salesman who founded and owns his own paint business, has a single formula: Simplicity. Run the business like a small business. His United Coatings Company is growing out of the small class—sales were $45 million when the Wall Street Journal interviewed him in 1982, up from only $25 million two years before. Moreover, this gain came at a time when the industry sales were on a downhill course. He started United Coatings in 1961 as a one man operation, selling paint to retailers by day and making it by night with a canoe paddle in leased space.

Offices are so simple that WSJ comments that to call them Spartan may be "unfair to the Spartans." Headquartered in an aging industrial district a few miles from downtown Chicago, it features painted concrete block walls, exposed plumbing and heating pipes, and metal-rimmed furniture.

Much of the profit comes from the things it doesn't do. It does not advertise much. Around 90% of its output is sold under the merchant's private label, directly out of factories in Chicago, Indianapolis, Los Angeles, Memphis, Jersey City, and Charlotte. Mass merchandisers like K-Mart, Wal-mart, and Zayre pick it up in their own trucks at the plant—United owns no trucks. All paint sold can be mixed from a single white base, so the factories do not have to be shut down for frequent cleaning.

The payroll, especially the administrative side, is kept lean. The entire executive staff is only 13: Knapp himself, five vice presidents and seven plant managers. None have their own private secretary, and every one answers his own phone. The entire clerical staff is less than 20—in fact the laboratory and quality control personnel outnumber the clerical. It does own a computer for payroll and billing. When new plants are needed, United looks for old inner-city buildings it can reclaim. And it buys used equipment whenever possible. Neighborhood good-will is built up by hiring from the locality and sponsoring annual "paint-up"days during which it gives away paint to anyone who calls around for it.

Customer relations are also kept simple. He claims to promise customers "good paint, on time, and at a good price. We make it clear that we expect to make money on what we sell." He thinks "no customer is worth shaving profits for." and relates an incident with Sears: "In 1980, we signed on Sears, and did about $6 million of business with them. The next year they wanted to cut my prices. I was going to ask them for an increase. I told them to go jump."

Knapp was starting to sell an interior latex paint under United's own label, with a 12 year guarantee, and an unusual feature: his own office phone is on the label. "If something is wrong with the paint, I'll want to know it."

The White Consolidated case also reveals some of the cost control problems of the mature phase, especially in the very largest sellers. Three of the four largest brands that White Consolidated took over were made by General Motors, Ford, and Westinghouse--all of them among the largest corporations in the country. They were not producing profits for the original owners because of too high overhead and labor costs. They are making profit for White, who cut overhead at all levels, and labor costs, and improved productivity, in part by eliminating low demand models. All of this suggests that as the larger sellers move into the seemingly calmer waters of the mature phase, the bureaucracies managing them get a little fat and sleepy. It is instructive that the problems of the Detroit auto makers also carried over to their main lines--their motor vehicles--where costs were permitted to get out of line with those in other countries, who also watched productivity closer.

None of these forms of mature market share expansion really rest on a single tactic or single aspect of functional strategy. All of the brand successes listed above involved a well coordinated campaign based on a single anchor concept, a specific differentiated appeal to a specific target segment.

Establishing A Guiding Anchor Concept for Mature Phase Strategy

Any formulation of marketing strategy necessarily starts with an **anchor concept**: a specific, differentiating action theme with reference to customer value perceptions. This concept or theme details the specific benefit attribute differences relative to competing offerings. The concept may include sub-concepts of offering, price, promotion, and /or distribution. Once the concept is chosen, each of the functional elements are designed to reinforce this key theme.

The differentiating elements in the mature phase necessarily involve the secondary benefits, the fringe attributes of the offering, since by this time, all competing offerings offer pretty much the same objective core benefits. All soap cleans, one bar about as well as another. Any one automobile takes us from here to there on our own schedule, without much difference, one make from another. The differences in soap may be the fragrance, or the color, or a deodorant additive. In automobiles, the styling, differences in handling, extra performance characteristics, minor differences in comfort, etc.

The anchor concept expresses something perceived by customers as a solution to some problem in relation to a use system, as an offering related desire not clearly satisfied by any other available offering.

The problem solution may be an all-in-one package of computer, drive, monitor and software, all in portable form, as the Osborne computer was designed to win a share in a market in which other sellers were simply offering separate components. It may be a low-cost, low maintenance dependability that the Subaru automobile used to win a loyal following in the U. S., and 5th place among imports: "Inexpensive, and built to stay that way."

The anchor concept may simply be a psychological perception of what it does for the user's personality, as exemplified by perfume advertising. (See the story on the changing themes for Revlon's Charlie, page 326.)

The concept can be availability: "Now finish that degree you neglected to get, in the evening and weekends, close to home." Or the availability may be curtailed, for a prestige item, to a few selected outlets with the right display policies and image (Steuben hand-blown glassware, with only 7 outlets nationwide, or Rolls Royce, with only 31.)

Price or price mix may be the central concept, as it is for mail order sellers of computer components, software and supplies. If so, all aspects of price and price perception must be in harmony. Generally, also, when low price is the focus, it should be accompanied with obvious offsetting benefits to make it a high value. In the case of mail order sellers, this inevitably means availability of a wide breadth of choice, or special, hard to find offerings.

Of course, price as an anchor concept can be at any level, including the premium level, provided that the offering, distribution, and promotion are perceived as consistent with it.

Whatever its form, the anchor concept aims at a perception as a solution to a satisfaction lack deeply felt by a substantial segment of prospects. Choice of an anchor concept is the necessary foundation for a rational strategy, but only a foundation. To give substance to the plan, four aspects of timing must be specified, and the character of the value perception positioning to be developed.

The Timing And Positioning Dimensions of A Mature Phase Strategy

Marketing plans for offerings in the mature phase are especially concerned with time dimensions: the **how soon or how long?, the when, relative to competition?, relative to taste and fashion cycles?, and with what speed of effort?** In formal terms, what the time span of the effort, what timing of implementation relative to competitor's moves, implementation relative to fashion cycles, and shall it be a high velocity full front penetration, or a creeping infiltration move?

The what of the plan is even more important: the kind of positioning to be attempted to gain added market segments.

The Plan's Time Span
Mature phase moves are necessarily either short term or medium term, if

we define short term as anything less than two years to complete and take
effect, and medium term as 3 or 4 years. Competition cannot be expected
to fail to react decisively over a longer period. Even the exact structure
of the competition is not foreseeable for any longer time span. As a
result, most brand cycles tend to be past their peaks within a medium time
span at the outside.

Implementation Timing, Relative to Competitors' Moves

Relative to the expected and suspected moves of competitors, the timing
strategies of competitive moves fall into three general types:
- **Offensive policies:** the aggressive pursuit of product improvement and
  promotional revitalization without respect to the plans of competitors.
- **Preemptive policies:** Aimed to hit the market ahead of specific
  anticipated moves of competitors.
- **Purely defensive.** More often a lack of policy rather than the reverse:
  a tendency to react to competitors' moves after they show up in the
  market.

CHESEBROUGH-PONDS (B): PREEMPTING COMPETITION

Chesebrough-Pond's was built on two old and successful brand names: Vaseline
petroleum jelly and Pond's Cold Cream. Since 1969, under the administration of CEO
Ralph E. Ward, it has been using its financial strengths and marketing savvy in what
one financial analyst has described as a textbook example of profiting from mergers
by using a bigger company's muscle to expand a smaller product line.

The first was the purchase of Ragu' Packing Company in 1969, then a $20 million
maker of spaghetti sauce. Until the Chesebrough merger, Ragu' was viewed as a low
growth product in a low growth industry—a food market expanding at 2% per year.
But Chesebrough saw an opportunity in the fact that there was no nationally
marketed spaghetti sauce. An aggressive national campaign was rolled out just as the
general public was turning to pasta products as a low-cost alternative to high cost
meat. By 1980, Ragu' had annual sales of $200 million.

In recent years, Chesebrough has had to fight hard to hold onto the 62.8% share of
market Business Week reported it had in 1980. When it observed Hunt-Wesson test
marketing a spicier product in 1977, Prima Salsa, Chesebrough immediately introduced
and went national with a spicy version of its own--Extra Thick and Zesty. Preempted
before its test was more than a month old, Hunt-Wesson never got more than a 9%
market share, and slipped back to 5.4%. When Campbell Soup tried to get into the
market with Prego in 1980, Chesebrough was practically 'giving Ragu away' with
coupons and truckload allowances, according to the Campbell vice-president of
marketing, in the areas where Prego was being tested.

Similar tactics were pursued to defend its position in its original health and
cosmetics lines. 2-for-1 offers and retailer incentives were used to meet twin
challenges to its dominant Vaseline Intensive Care Lotion, mounted by P&G with its
Wondra line and Nabisco with its Rose Milk lotion. Neither of the challengers got
more than a 10% market share.

In one sense, all three policies are defensive, with the offensive probably the strongest defense. At least one aim of all three is to maintain market share in the face of inevitable competitive moves by others. The independently aggressive policy and the preemptive policy attempt to gain the advantage of being first.

Being first confers a special advantage, as many studies have shown. Second place seldom pays off half as well, and sometimes pays nothing. Getting out of the starting gate first is useful, but not enough in the long run. To stay ahead, the seller must push forward with both marketing research and product development. The marketing research is needed to keep tabs on consumer experience with the offering performance, and to discover shifting tastes and unsatisfied segments. The R&D has the task of finding ways to increase user benefits, and decrease production costs.

Offensive strategies initiate market change by introduction of new lines or brands to win new market segments, by significant improvements in existing lines and brands, and sometimes by aggressive use of pricing initiatives, such as the price pincers previously discussed.

Preemptive strategies call for keeping a close intelligence watch on the moves of likely competitors, then moving to capture or hold specific segments at the same time, or just a little earlier, if possible, than planned by the competitor in question. The move usually has to be some simple, quickly executed change, as in packaging, pricing, or promotion.

Defensive policies are carried out by direct countermoves to any surprise action of a competitor, usually a matching, imitative one: an imitative brand, a similar sales promotion, or a matching price reduction.

(An occasional fourth choice is risky: do nothing.)

A seller with a dominant market position may be able to pursue a purely defensive tactics for some time, relying on the strength of the buyer franchise to maintain the advantage. Even such a seller lays himself open to a surprise flank attack from an unexpected competitor who moves fast. No weak firm can afford a pure defense.

However, no matter how aggressive a firm, it must always keep an eye on possible competition. No seller can ever be aware, in advance, of all moves by all possible competitors. So all must institute preemptive and even defensive tactics on occasion.

Shifts in consumer tastes can be just as dangerous as competitors, or even more so. Among those changes are the inevitable fashion cycles of many kinds, especially important in the mature phase.

Implementation Relative to The Swings in Taste

Fashion involves precisely those attributes of an offering which are the basis of design competition in the mature phase--the secondary attributes of styling and life style associations. These are always subject to change and are ignored at the seller's peril. Sellers have only three choices:

- Take the lead of any such change just as it is coming in, riding the leading edge.
- Wait until the trend is well established, then join in
- Concentrate on producing and selling only the classics

Each of these strategies attracts a specific set of market segments. Each carries with it its own special advantages and dangers. Although not mutually exclusive, the organization oriented to the wait-and-see policy is not likely to be able to jump on a leading edge gracefully.

The leading edge policy requires a sharp sense of consumer trends, and needs to be accompanied by the best of analytical research to identify and evaluate trends, screening out the fads from the more substantive. Initial sales volume will tend to be moderate, but initial unit profits high. Such a policy can sometimes result in gaining a hammerlock on a market segment before competitors are ready to move.

The wait-and-see what-is-developing policy will hit a mass market, if carried on consistently, but at a time when unit profits are likely to be less. And a fast developing trend can be overlooked until too late. The marketing research quality requirements are not nearly so great as with the leading edge policy.

Sticking with classics requires fewer changes, but attracts only a modest segment. Unit profits are likely to be only moderate. The customers seek no novelty values. But competition is likely to be modest also. A classics policy would seem to be compatible with a leading edge policy, as a line addition recognized for what it is.

Whatever the entry strategy, a choice must be made as to the speed by which the market is to be developed: whether by a heavy power play full front penetration, or a low profile steady infiltration.

The Choice Between Rapid Penetration And Infiltration

A rapid market share build-up through a forceful marketing effort may be the best course to plan if early competitive emulation or strong counter-promotion of any kind is to be expected. The type of fast national roll-out of marketing effort is manifestly open only to the well-financed large seller. It also assumes a very low-learning brand variant.

The infiltration strategy is the strategy of choice for the small enterprise seeking to nip off a substantial segment of a market dominated by larger sellers. Such a seller has to hope that the use of low profile promotional and distribution efforts will achieve a steady growth over time without attracting attention from larger competitors until well established with a market segment.

The infiltration strategy is also the proper course for even large sellers introducing a brand which initially appeals to a very limited segment, but which a larger group of customers, with some learning, will buy eventually.

The infiltration strategy is the appropriate strategy for three types of brand introductions:

- The premium priced **superior performance brand,** initially appealing primarily to a limited customer segment.
- The **specialty brand,** also normally premium priced, whose only likely appeal is to satisfy specialized needs of a small market segment.
- The **parity performance brand** introduced at a substantial discount from the prices of leading brands, by a small seller hoping thus to capture a limited market segment.

Dean's "market skimming price" strategy is simply one variant of an infiltration strategy involving a premium price. This strategy is as appropriate for the superior performance and specialty brands as for high learning offerings at the beginning of a market life cycle.

Using a discount price for a parity performance introduction is really a form of price positioning, as well as a timing strategy.

The Brand Positioning Dimension of The Mature Market Strategy

Both offensive operations and defensive moves involve one or a combination of the four forms of brand repositioning: **price image revitalization, price image change, perceived offering image revitalization,** and **perceived offering change.**

A **price image revitalization** differs from an outright **price image change** in the degree of price cut. In a price image change, the offering price is cut to the next lower price line. In a price revitalization tactic, the price reduction is enough to confer a noticeable price advantage in relation to previous positioning, but not sufficient to take it out of the range of the previous price segment.

One effective method of price revitalization is that which Alberto Culver used to fend off an invasion of its hair spray market share by P&G: increase the size of the unit package noticeably while holding unit price stable. Usually, this is accomplished to the accompaniment of considerable ballyhoo to bring attention to the new bargain.

A **perceived offering benefit change** requires a significant change in the offering itself which can be perceived by customers as a very substantial offering improvement. Brown points out such a move by Nestle in Australia, in 1969, when Nestle changed its powdered coffee product to a granulated form, perceived by consumers as yielding a stronger flavor benefit. (P&G later used the same tactic in the United States.) Similarly, when the 1960 Chevrolet Corvair received a tepid reception at the beginning, a luxury Monza model with bucket seats was introduced. To buyers at the time, bucket seats spelled 'sport car', and sales moved up quickly.

A **perceived offering revitalization** involves an offering improvement of lesser, but still noticeable degree—an improved package, moderately

improved performance, or improved intensity of distribution: the addition of
fabric softeners to laundry detergent, duly trumpeted on the label, was one
such move in the early 1980s. Facial tissue producers have regularly used
decorator packaging to this end.

Thus there are 6 possible brand positioning strategies:

1. price image revitalization
2. price image change
3. perceived offering benefit revitalization
4. perceived offering benefit change
5. the combination of a price image and offering benefit change
6. the combination of a price revitalization and offering benefit revitalization

---

CHESEBROUGH (C): INVADING A MATURE MARKET

The $40 million market for home permanents in 1979 had all the signs of late
maturity. Practically owned by two brands: Gillete's Toni and P&G's Lilt—it had
shown no growth for years. But Chesebrough thought it saw an opportunity, in a
lotion that produced a "soft" permanent and was odorless, which the competing makes
were not. Avoiding the risk of tipping off the competition, Chesebrough went
national without a test marketing operation, successfully. As expected, Gillette and
P&G responded with "soft" permanents of their own, but Chesebrough won a 27%
share of a market which the new products boosted to the $100 million level. Gillette
officials are quoted as admitting,"There's no denying [Chesebrough's] done a great
job."

Theoretically, we are faced with 72 possible combinations of mature phase
strategies: short time span, or medium term, 3 entry timing choices, 2 speed
of entry choices, and 6 brand positioning choices. But, as noted, the
choice is almost never that wide. The position of buyers and their
resources limit some sellers, the possibility for product change or
improvement may not be open, cost margins may be too thin to permit price
reductions, etc.

The market structure and the seller's position in that structure always
limit freedom of choice.

The Limits Imposed by Industry Structure And The Size of The Seller

The size of sellers relative to competitors, and the quality of their
respective market niches, influence the degree and kinds of strategy choices
they can make. Practically all industries contain a substantial range of
competitor size, with a few large sellers at one end, and significant
numbers of more specialized smaller sellers at the other.

Rather commonly, one or two of the larger sellers have a substantial
degree of market dominance, but the degree of concentration varies.

By size, sellers can be classified into 5 groups, with a typical form of competitive strategy in each group:

1. Large firms, dominating the volume markets. Generally follow penetration strategies in brand introduction, offering multiple brands to cover a wide part of the market. Tend to concentrate on brand development and non-price forms of competition.

2. Smaller sellers with a large enough market share to have an appreciable effect on the market. Such firms may adopt infiltration strategies, by offering a limited range of brands to one or more segments of the mass market. Their competitive tactics otherwise parallel those of the dominant sellers: brand development and non-price forms of competition. Examples might be the regional and weaker national beers in the beer industry: Stroh's, Lone Star, Coors, for example.

3. Market specialists: smaller sellers offering brands to specialized market segments using infiltration strategies. Competitive emphasis is normally on some form of non-price activity.

4. Low cost sellers: small or medium size organizations whose small size itself enables them to maintain a low overhead structure. Such sellers tend to produce offerings similar to those of the larger firms, but at a price discount with minimal promotional support. They may be a major source of private brands for mass merchants. They usually use low price penetration policies and in general adopt a price competitive stance. They frequently limit their activities to a regional market in a large country.

5. The Back Yarder, Garage, or Basement Office Operator. Such often literally operate out of the home garage or basement of their homes, normally in markets in which the cost of technology and equipment are low, and also the economies of scale. (Example: injection molded plastics.) Such operators have low rental cost, very low overhead in general, and usually pursue a price competitive strategy. They usually use low price infiltration strategies to gain strength in specific pockets of distribution. If they capture a wider distribution base, they are likely to adopt a low price penetration strategy.

The quality of market position may be, and often is, quite different from the size position of the seller. Market position quality has at least 5 identifiable dimensions:

1. The seller's market shares, relative to the market shares held by competitors.

2. The offering and brand mixes, and the market shares and profitability of the major elements in the mix.

3. The amount of initiative available to the seller.

4. The breadth of the product mix across market segments

5. The position of the seller's most dangerous competitors

Generally, the degree of initiative a seller can exercise would be expected to be more or less proportional to its market share. Such may not be the case if the seller neglects to develop positions with the growing market segments, or leans too much on emulation of the new developments initiated by others. A seller can get locked into declining market segments and extricate itself only with the greatest difficulty. This often happens to merchandisers. At least one shoe producer got so identified with work shoes that when blue collar labor declined, the seller could not shift over to dressier models.

The position of a seller's brands in the growing, static, and declining market segments is the most important quality dimension. Too great a conservatism in offering development has destroyed many a once dominant seller.

The market position of a seller's most dangerous competitors has obvious importance. The less dominant seller has to keep an alert to the plans of the dominant. Even the dominant worries about number 2. (GM has been reported as being constantly concerned about the plans of the Ford Motor Company.) The relative aggressiveness and innovativeness of less close competitors may also be a matter for concern.

The final dimension of problem market quality is the degree of reliance on one or two large brands or one or two offerings in related fields. When the market position is thus narrowed, the organization is vulnerable to competition using multiple brand strategies.

The Perils of Size And Dominance

The extent of market power which can be exercised, and the extent to which it tends to be so exercised, is much less than commonly supposed by the public in general, and by antitrust lawyers in particular.

Large organizations must have large markets in which to operate. Large producers cannot handle small jobs well, even when a future market may be large. The bureaucracy inherent in any large organization is disinclined to take risks. It tends to lose touch with the markets and changes in them, and to stick with trends long after the market has turned in a different direction. Theoretically, such well-heeled sellers are in a financial position to do more R&D than a smaller competitor. In point of fact, they usually prefer to wait until some smaller competitor proves out a market, and then try to enter. Sometimes they succeed in capturing a market this way, but not always. Their size makes it difficult to move fast.

For these reasons, and many more, dominant sellers of one year are missing from the list of the the large and powerful in later decades, their places taken by newer sellers, many of whom will follow the same path to decline later. Dominant sellers get their profits from mature phase offerings, and tend to follow those offerings into the decline phase, rather than follow the customers into new fields. As competitors, they can bring a lot of resources to bear, but tend to be short on innovation.

SUMMARY

Management attention tends to be heavily occupied with the tactics needed to maintain competitive position of the mature brands which constitute the main sources of revenue of established buyers.

The positions of most sellers in mature markets tend to be relatively stable because of their established market strengths and the effects of established consumption patterns among buyers.

The stability is vulnerable because new customers are always coming onto the market, the tastes of all consumers change, consumers move around geographically, the novelty values of the offerings have withered, technology can change, and necessary design compromises leave many consumers less than satisfied with all available offerings.

Successful competitive moves in mature markets depend on offering some substantial segments of buyers a better perceived value/price ratio than otherwise available.

While the value/price ratio can be improved by adding to the value or by cutting price, straight price moves seldom succeed because too easily countered.

One form of price move that does often work is the price-pincers strategy: lowering prices to compete in a lower price line range. Such moves work because they bring a seller into competition with a new set of competitors, ones not previously considered as competition by either buyers or sellers. In such a case, the new competitors may be slow to move.

Other mature market opportunities exist when offerings can be developed appealing to some segments of the market who were not adequately served by any previous offerings. Two such opportunities occur when the low end is uncovered, or when the offering design range narrows to a funnel, because of the concentration of all important sellers on a major mass market. In the latter case, opportunities may open up at both the low end and at the premium level.

A period of major taste changes may open another kind of opportunity--the opportunity to coopt a perceptual product benefit which much of the market perceives as important, but which is not strongly attached to a single seller or brand.

The addition of flanker offerings opens added profit opportunities for well positioned brands.

A high level of cost control and productivity can be a major source of profit in the mature stage.

Any mature phase strategy has to be formulated around a specific anchor concept: a theme detailing the specific benefit attributes to be emphasized, relative to competing offerings. The concept may include elements of promotion, offering, price, and/or distribution. This anchor concept must be perceived by potential buyers as a solution to some problem they have, relative to the purchase and use systems.

A mature phase strategy requires as many as 4 timing dimensions: time span, the when relative to competition, the when relative to taste and style trends, and the speed of full implementation.

Time span, as a practical matter, must generally be no more than four years. Competitive advantages will almost be certainly lost if it takes longer.

Relative to competitors' moves, strategies and tactics may be offensive, preemptive, or purely defensive. All are essentially a form of defense, but the first two aim at gaining the advantage of being first.

Relative to taste and fashion swings, 3 choices exist: leading the crowd in the direction of observed trends, waiting until a trend is already established, or sticking to the offering of classics. Each has its own advantages, and each attracts a different segment of buyers.

The speed of entry choice is between a rapid penetration strategy or an infiltration strategy. Only the well financed can afford the rapid penetration strategy, and the weaker competitors tend to choose the infiltration route. But for some specialties, all sellers may find the infiltration tactic most profitable.

Brand positioning strategies have four possible dimensions, with at least 72 theoretical variations. In practice, the number of feasible options is much more limited. The 4 primary dimensions are: price image revitalizations, price image changes, perceived offering image revitalizations, and perceived offering changes.

The industry structure and the relative size of the seller tend to determine the general form of mature phase strategy possible or likely.

Although large size means large resources, market dominance tends to make sellers too cautious and slow to change.

FOOD FOR THOUGHT

AIMING HIGH: American Greetings Cares Enough to Try Its Very Hardest
(Reprinted by permission from **The Wall Street Journal**, Mar.17,1982, ©Dow Jones & Co., Inc.,1982)

CLEVELAND—The Christmas television commercial, aired last fall, was soft and sentimental in its depiction of a grandmother doting on greetings cards from years past. The idea was to leave viewers with warm feelings about the happy memories that can be evoked by cards—and particularly by the cards bearing the logo of American Greetings Corp., the ad's sponsor.

Unfortunately for American Greetings, it was an idea whose time hadn't quite come. The company was using TV commercials for the first time in its long history; and when it later questioned viewers, it found that many thought the Christmas ad had been sponsored by American Greetings' archrival, Hallmark Cards Inc.

The setback illustrates the tough going for Cleveland-based American Greetings, long No. 2 in the $2.1 billion greeting-card industry, in its effort to narrow the gap between it and No. 1 Hallmark of Kansas City, Mo. Nevertheless, American Greetings officials remain undaunted. Morry Weiss, the company's president and chief operating officer, says that when it comes to greeting cards and related items such as gift wrappings and party favors, 'There isn't area that Hallmark is in that we don't intend to pursue aggressively.'...

Stressing Humor

With that positive frame of mind, American Greetings is now stressing humor in its television ads—a decidedly different approach from that taken by Hallmark's sweetness-and-light commercials. In one recent American Greetings ad, for example, a young couple in a restaurant are admiring a greeting card; a waiter peering over the couple's shoulder at the card, spills some food and precipitates a chain reaction of chaos; but the couple remain absorbed by the card, happily oblivious to the bedlam around them.

From now on, says an American Greetings official, comedy will be emphasized in the company's ads so that 'when you see them, you remember who the hell paid for them.'

It is all part of American Greetings' strategy to widen its penetration of Hallmark's upscale retail business by creating its own brand identity and raising the quality of its cards. As might be expected, it is also increasing its prices to match those of its rival, which at the end of last year were some 10% higher than American Greetings.

Vigorous Response

To help implement its strategy, American Greetings this month launched a corporate identification program that within a year will display the company name and newly designed logo of a rose, in about 80% of the outlets carrying its cards. While most stores that sell Hallmark cards have long been identifiable by a prominent display of the Hallmark name and crown logo, only a few American Greetings outlets carry the company name. (Although both companies own and operate a handful of stores, most of their outlets are independent retailers; and the vast majority of those retailers carry lines of either American Greetings or of Hallmark, not of both.)

David H. Hughes, Hallmark's executive vice president and chief operating officer says, 'We don't have a thing about American Greetings as American Greetings has for us.' Nevertheless, Hallmark's response to the challenge by American Greetings has been vigorous. It has increasingly been going after drugstores, supermarkets and discount stores--segments of the market where American Greetings is the dominant force. It has reinforced its defenses against attempts to steal its retail accounts. And it is trying to create a line of characters to license--an area in which American Greetings, with licensable characters such as Holly Hobby and Strawberry Shortcake, is already well in the forefront.

The intensifying rivalry comes after years of more or less peaceful coexistence. Both companies began similarly as one-man operations shortly after the turn of the century, but each soon carved a different niche for itself in the greeting-card industry.

Carriage Trade

American Greetings was founded by Jacob Saperstein, whose idea was to make relatively inexpensive cards for the masses and to woo retailers, not card buyers, on the assumption that consumers will buy whatever is most readily available. By offering to retailers such services as free shipment and return of unsold seasonal cards (neither being a service offered by Hallmark on its principal line), American Greetings garnered more and more outlets until today its cards are sold in about 50,000 stores--2-1/2 times the number of stores that sell Hallmark's lines.

Hallmark, on the other hand, has managed to grab about 47% of the card market, compared with only 28% for American Greetings. Its founder, Joyce C, Hall, decided to make quality cards for the carriage trade and to reach that market by consumer advertising; beginning in early 1950s, that advertising has included the sponsorship of the award-winning "Hallmark Hall of Fame" television specials.

Over the years, Hallmark grew to rule the department store trade in cities. When many customers moved to the suburbs, the company entrenched itself there as the leader in card and gift shops. And many Hallmark outlets made a point of offering a shopping ambience that appealed to women, who buy about 90% of all greeting cards. One Hallmark customer, Faye Jacuby of Brooklyn, N. Y., sums up: "Hallmark stores are specialty stores, they have a bigger selection and they have a pleasant atmosphere."

Miss Jacuby, a school teacher who says she buys at least 150 greeting cards a year, subscribes to Hallmark's longtime slogan: "When You Care Enough to Send the Very Best." She says she often buys "Hallmark's Peanuts and Ziggy cards"--heedless of the fact that Ziggy is a character featured on cards made by American Greetings.

The teacher's misconception has long been typical. Both Hallmark and American Greetings say consumer tests show that if consumers don't know what brand of card they are buying, they usually assume it is Hallmark. But American Greetings, after years of living comfortably (albeit anonymously) in second place, apparently began in the late 1960s to chafe at its always-a-bridesmaid status. "I mean, it wasn't the 'American Greetings Hall of Fame'" one American Greetings official said at a recent company gathering...

About five years ago, American Greetings began formulating a blueprint for making a serious run at Hallmark. It was a time when unit-sales growth of greeting cards were slowing. What's more, the two industry leaders had squeezed smaller competitors so much that there wasn't much left to wring out of them. (Industry sources say the next five largest companies combined have about 15% of the market, and some 300 other card makers grapple for the remaining 10%.)

But progress against Hallmark has come slowly, even though American Greetings has shown good overall earnings growth recently. In the fiscal nine months ended last Nov. 30, earnings jumped more than 20% to $23.3 million, or $1.71 a share, on revenues of $458.2 million....

Consumer Research

One of American Greetings' biggest challenge has been overcoming Hallmark's perceived quality advantage. Currently, American Greetings has only about 225 artists, including 50 free-lancers; by comparison, Hallmark's creative staff, mostly artists, numbers about 640. But the No. 2 company continues to concentrate on closing the quality gap by investing money in new machines and consumer research.

In the area of technology, American Greetings recently bought three Italian presses that cost $2 million each and turn out nine million cards a day....

The company's consumer research, undertaken with the aid of an outside concern, explore such topics as why people buy cards and what kind of artwork go with what sentiments. Such research now is helping to determine the size, shape and even the lettering on American Greetings cards.

(The company hasn't gone entirely scientific, however. Its 72-year-old chairman, Irving I. Stone, ... still regularly reviews each card before its release. Because he is aided in his review by a group of women employees, many of them historically elderly, the company's artists refer caustically to the review group as the "biddy committee"; but American Greetings says the committee provides an objective internal review of its cards.)

A Convert Speaks

American Greetings also is trying to wrest retailers from Hallmark. One recent convert is Terry Hood, the owner of Little Bits of Love card and gift shop in Toledo, Ohio. Mr Hood says that an elaborate sales presentation and promises of top-notch service persuaded him to switch. He adds, "I feel American Greetings works better with the retailer."

One area where American Greetings already has a definite edge over Hallmark is its appealing--and profitable--characters. The company's first successes were Holly Hobby and Ziggy, both created for greeting cards but later licensed for use as the basis for a wide range of items. The licensing arrangements proved so lucrative that five years ago American Greetings decided to create a character designed specifically to be licensed and only secondarily for use on cards.

The result: In 1980 American Greetings introduced Strawberry Shortcake, a little girl with red freckles, red hair, and a pink bonnet sprinkled with polka dots and strawberries. This year, Strawberry Shortcake will appear on around $500 million of children's merchandise, including bed sheets, sleeping bags and lunch boxes. American Greetings rakes in between 5% and 10% of the wholesale value of each item sold and hopes that other, newer characters such as Lemon Meringue (a blonde wearing yellow polka dots) will meet with similar success.

Meanwhile, Hallmark, which uses (but doesn't own) the Muppets and Peanuts characters on its products, is laboring to give birth to its own characters. To that end, the company has enlarged the size of its licensing department, consulted the retail industry for advice on marketable characters and test-marketed some potentially licensable creations. But it hasn't yet settled on a suitable challenger to Strawberry Shortcake. "Whether we will do as well or better than Strawberry Shortcake, I don't know," says a Hallmark official. "but we will do our damn best."

1. If American Greetings has more than twice as many outlets as Hallmark, why is Hallmark's volume so much better?

2. If people are not aware of the brand of cards they are buying, what purpose does the advertising and corporate identity serve? What are the objectives of the

Hallmark advertising?   Of the American Greetings advertising?

3. What determines the choice of outlet at which the heavy users of greetings cards buy?

4. What determines the choice of cards made, wherever purchased?

5. What part does the retailer play in the sale of greeting cards?

6. What would seem to be the best course for American Greetings to follow to increase its market share?

WHY SPIRITS SALES ARE SLIPPING A BIT

(Reprinted from the May 17, 1982 issue of **Business Week** by special permission, © 1982 by McGraw-Hill, Inc. New York, NY 10020. All rights reserved.)

During 1981, liquor sales posted their first decline since 1957, as consumption of distilled spirits in the U. S. slipped 0.13%. This dip, following 1980's slight 1% uptick, reinforces liquor's image as a slow-growth business and has liquor executives scrambling to grab larger shares of their market. "There is a very hostile environment out there," observes John Powers, senior vice-president for alcoholic beverages at Heublein Inc. "The consumer's disposable income is squeezed, making him more value conscious." Adds Alvin Ferro, president of Paddington Corp., which markets J&B Scotch: "Every beverage marketer is competing for gullets today.   And wine and Perrier are formidable competitors.   If someone orders a $2.50 Perrier with lunch, it's not likely he'll follow it with a $5 Scotch drink.

Indeed, BUSINESS WEEK'S annual scoreboard of brands retailing more than 500,000 cases reveals an industry caught by indecision.   Liquor executives seem unable to entice, or even hang on to their prime customers: drinkers aged 25 to 44, who are fickle customers.   Not only is this group choosing a wider array of drinks, running the gamut of wine, juices, beer, soft drinks, and bottled water, but it is also constantly sampling new items that are light and sweet or possess a cachet, such as cordials and brandy.

How U.S. drinkers' tastes changed in a decade:

Category	——Share of market——		
	1981*	1980	1971
	Percent		
Bourbon	13.5%	13.9%	21.7%
Scotch	12.9	12.9	13.6
Canadian	12.4	12.5	9.5
Blends	8.8	8.9	18.5
Other	0.3	0.3	0.3
Total whiskey	**47.9**	**48.5**	**63.6**
Vodka	19.1	19.0	13.3
Gin	9.6	9.5	9.8
Cordials	7.9	7.8	4.9
Rum	7.6	7.1	3.2
Brandy	4.2	4.1	3.7
Other	3.7	4.0	1.5
Total nonwhiskey	**52.1**	**51.5**	**36.4**

*estimated

Bourbon's decline. Glummest of all are marketers in the brown goods sector, particularly those in bourbon and blends, whose share is steadily dropping. Scotch managed to arrest that category's decline last year through copious promotion and advertising efforts. But Canadian products, which previously had seen increased sales, thanks to a perceived "lighter" taste than U.S. whiskey, showed a slight decrease.

While the total nonwhiskey area strengthened its grip on the market to a 52.1% share, vodka's momentum, beginning to slow last year, appears to have run out of steam. The consumer shift to rum, a flavorable but still mixable drink, has accelerated. Bacardi Corp. easily held onto its crown as the top-selling brand, and the company has buttressed its hold on the rum category by positioning its Castillo brand as a lower-priced alternative to the leader. Castillo posted a 23% gain.

The consumer inclination to shun products in the midprice range is forcing marketers to reappraise their product positioning. "I would hate to be a middle brand," comments Ferro. " As long as you're the cheapest or the best, you have a reason for being." Taking his own advice, Ferro says he is trying to lift J&B out of the lagging category with a new $15 million image-building ad campaign "and make it **sui generis.**"

Import magic. In fact , some of the best performers this year were brands that exploited the market's price polarization. Walter M. Haimann, president of Seagram Distillers, credits Crown Royal's steady increase to glossy packaging and advertising which omits the word Canadian and simply says import--a word that has worked its magic for several other brands, also.

Generally, liquor marketers are breaking little new ground in their struggle to vitalize a stagnant market. Ad budgets for premium products are being fattened; efforts to reposition slipping franchises are keeping Madison Avenue busy; couponing and contests are emerging as prime sales tools, and the shelf space battle intensifies.

Buckingham Corp., which raised its marketing budget 50% to $15 million in 1981 to launch a new campaign for its faltering Cutty Sark brand, has seen some encouraging results. The flagship brand, which recorded a 12.7% loss in 1980, recouped enough to register a 2.4% gain last year. Still, says Brian W. Dunn, senior vice-president for marketing: "We're cutting up a shrinking pie. The category will continue to decline, and competition will only intensify." To keep its progress smooth, Buckingham will increase its budget to $18 million this year, and where legal, undertake a large -scale couponing effort.

Pricing has become a touchy issue. In a slow growth market, all companies aim to wring the most profit possible out of their brands to make up for lagging volume. But tampering can backfire. For instance, 18 months ago, Heublein raised the tag on Smirnoff vodka 4.7% and saw the brand tumble. "It was like the sinking of the Maine," says Powers. "We're correcting that mistake."

While most liquor marketers merely bemoan the market's lethargy, a few are sensing new opportunities. The public's adventurous appetite for more varied drinks has propelled brandies, cognacs, and specialties to new popularity. Super-premium brandies rose a dramatic 17% last year, but were bested by E&J Gallo, which scored a smashing 60% gain for its low-priced product and landed in the sales derby for the first time. Gallo's success "cut into everyone else's share of the domestic market," says Melvin Chernev, president of Fromm & Sichel inc., which distributes Christian Bros. brandy. Gallo, he says, "merchandises brandy as if it were a wine."

However, the most astonishing results in 1981 can be credited to Bailey's Irish Cream, a liqueur that in two years has spawned numerous imitations and launched a new product category. Bailey's, a 34-proof whiskey-base drink blended with fresh cream, was developed in Ireland by Gilbey's, a subsidiary of International Distillers & Vintners, and imported into the U.S. in 1979.

A tenfold leap. From selling 50,000 cases the first year, Bailey's sold 525,000 cases in 1981. "We've got a tiger by the tail," exults Paddington's Ferro, its U. S. distributor. "We just don't know how high up is. We've only hit about a third of the drinking public." To satisfy demand, production facilities in Ireland are being boosted from a 2.5 million case capacity to 8.5 million cases by 1983.

Ferro predicts sales of "nearly a million cases this year." To ensure that it is not a pie-in-the-sky target, Paddington will put $8 million behind the brand, which it claims appeals to all consumer segments—provided they are well-heeled. Bailey's is an expensive product, retailing anywhere from $12 to $17 a bottle. "At that price, it's hardly a fad," says Ferro, disputing one criticism of the drink. To further enhance its upscale image and home in on the gift-giving market, Bailey's is packaged in a fancy gold foil box the year-round, and its ample ad dollars are spent in magazines that deliver a high-income public. Paddington positions Bailey's as a stand-alone drink, a mixer, or a cooking aid. The consumer seems to be finding a lot of uses for the product; Research indicates that the bottle is finished within 48 hours of it opening.

Riding a wave. This sort of popularity has hardly gone unnoticed. There are about 19 similar products trying to exploit the cream market. Most observers expect a shakeout to occur in the next two or three years. "Because of need and greed, everybody felt they had to be in this category," says Marvin Shanken, the publisher of several wine and spirits newsletters. "But they're riding a wave created by Bailey's, and when it recedes, there will probably just be three left."

At the moment, there are several brands in contention for place and show spots behind Bailey's. These include Renfield Importers' Carolans, which quickly followed Bailey's into the market; Fleischmann's Dunphy's, a made-in- the-U.S. product; W. A. Taylor's Venetian Creme, which uses Italian brandy as its base; "21" Brand's Emmett's, which is pursuing a low-price strategy; and Waterford Cream, from Buckingham, which is spending $2 million tying its image to that of the famed Irish crystal manufacturer.

Observers believe that Emmett's has the inside track to emerge a strong No. 2 because of its strategy to deliver taste parity at a lower cost. "We had to come up with a brand that would move the consumer and the retailer," says Kenneth W. Bray, marketing director at "21" Brands Inc., "so we priced it $4 to $5 less a bottle than Bailey's."

As the U. S. consumer's palate becomes more quixotic, all sorts of products are likely to prosper. Industry-watcher Shanken believes that it is the smaller, specialized beverages that will flourish. "Items like single-malt Scotches, imported vodkas, and cordials and liqueurs will grow 10% to 20% a year, while the mass market languishes," he predicts. The game now is the consumer's desire to discover new tastes—everybody's looking for brands they can associate with themselves, rather than those that have mass appeal."

1. Drinking patterns are in part a matter of fashion, and becoming even more so. To what extent was something like this foreseeable, in general terms at least, considering the age cohort (25 to 44) which is the main pace setter?

2. Vodka's fast rise in recent years has been due to the fact that vodka has no distinct flavor of its own: it is an ideal mixer with more flavorable ingredients.

Wines have grown to be a major beverage in the last two decades, and taken over some of the cocktail market in addition. Might these developments have suggested some of the recent trends? If so, in what way?

3. Although a whiskey still can produce other spirits, any established distiller has a substantial inventory of aging whiskeys on hand. What can such a distiller do to gain more profitable markets? What are all of the elements that would be needed to accomplish this end? How many sellers would be prepared to undertake such an effort?

SKIING LOSES THE BLOOM OF BOOM

By the fall of 1982, it was obvious that the ski resort business was in trouble, especially through the Rocky Mountain area. Part of the trouble had previously been laid to mother nature's fickle door—poor snow conditions in one area and another. But by the fall of 1982, the resort community was facing up to facts.

Business at the trendy area of Aspen had been flat since 1976. In the 3 years from 1979 to 1981, the sale of lift tickets had declined 15%. "Skiier days" (one skier, one day) dropped from 7.9 million in the 1979-80 season to 7.6 million in 1981-1982 for all Colorado resorts together. Although the number of skiiers apparently was still growing, the big resort area business was obviously in trouble everywhere, due to a change in population totals and to increasing competition both locally and abroad.

The average age of skiers had increased from 23 to 28 in the preceding 10 years, taking many out of the singles group. Many were now young parents with young children, and the older group was getting still older. The fast rising costs of air fares and hotel accommodations had hit just as the numbers of young and affluent declined. The strengthening dollar had put the European resorts into competition with the Rocky Mountain areas, especially.

Facing up to a marketing problem, the larger resorts which had been purchased by major corporations were changing management. [Many of the original resorts had been operated by veterans of the World War II Mountain Division—an outfit of trained skiiers whose interests were in customers of their own kind.]

Aspen had been purchased by Twentieth Century-Fox Film Corp. in 1978, and Aetna Life and Casualty Co. bought into the operation in 1981-82. They had installed a business school trained director of marketing and doubled the promotion budget to $2 million. Ralston Purina built and owned the Keystone resort in Colorado.

Many of the local resort residents and businesses were uneasy about the entrance of more aggressive promotion, seeing it as likening skiing to the selling of soap. The residents of Aspen were especially divided, because of the exclusive image of the past, which had been a drawing card. In midwinter of 1983, they were facing a referendum on imposing a local business occupancy tax on themselves to raise $1.5 million a year to help market and promote Aspen. Many were like the local restaranteur who felt that they should accept the no-growth situation and "just preserve what we have."

The Colorado and other Rocky Mountain area resorts were not alone in feeling the pinch. The New England Areas were also facing adjustment problems. The ski equipment manufacturing industry hit a peak in 1978-79 at 1.2 million pairs of skis, slid to an estimated 680 thousand for the 1982-83 season.

1. To what extent could this decline have been foreseen, and how?

2. What might have been done to prepare for it ahead of time?

3. What kinds of marketing programs might be undertaken to gain a larger market share during the inevitable shakeout?

4. What types of resorts are in the best position to retain strong positions in the maturity phase?

5. What measures might an equipment manufacturer take to hold on to or improve at least his market share?

PART IV. MANAGING THE INFORMATION NEEDS:
Marketing Research, Market Intelligence, & Operations Control

To plan marketing strategy and tactics, we must first make some forecasts of expected actions and reactions of customers, other consumers, and competitors. To make planning effective, we must maintain some kind of check on the results of the execution of the plans. Except in the smallest of operations, dealing with an extremely small customer list, both types of efforts require the collection of sample information, largely in the form of numbers or implying numbers, and the skillful analysis of their meaning for future action.

Forecasting is an art, a matter of judgment, whether in foretelling tomorrow's weather or tomorrow's markets. In both cases, forecasts can be improved by collection of data on the current situation, and the trends that have developed. In the case of marketing, detailed analysis of the trends in habitual patterns of market choice tells us a great deal about future likelihoods, because of the usual slowness by which habits change. The same is true of forecasting the actions of competitors, for they, too, have habits. But usual is not the same as always. Unforeseen events can cause sudden breaks in demand patterns. Skill consists of searching out the foreseeable possibilities from the unforeseen, and taking them into consideration.

The collection and analysis of information on markets and consumers is the sphere of **marketing research.** Collection of information on the modes of operation of competitors, and on the visible indications of their plans, is usually labelled **market intelligence.** The same personnel often handle both functions, at least in part.

Marketing information management must look backward as well as forward. Planning is an empty exercise unless the execution of the plan, and the effects of that execution, are carefully monitored. Provision for a flow of information must be part of any meaningful plan. So much of the information needed for control is useful for planning that the analysis of control information is frequently combined with the function of marketing research.

CHAPTER 17. MANAGING THE INFORMATION NEEDS

The information needs of sound planning
    Marketing research
    Market intelligence
Marketing research and rational planning
    The true role of marketing research
    The research process
    Sources of information
        The need for critical evaluation of available information
    Exploratory research
    Descriptive surveys
    Experimental research
Managing market intelligence information
    Evaluating the capabilities of competition
    Divining the intentions of competition
Requirements for marketing research and intelligence over the
life cycle
Market operations control information
    Purpose served
        PERT and critical path
        Sales analysis
        Purchased reports
        Formal and informal reports: internal
        Informal information: external
Using control information for planning

The Information Foundation Needs of Sound Planning

Marketing management is the process of discovering and taking advantage of opportunities in the seller's environment which promise a continuing monetary or other desired return. That environment includes:

- groups of potential customers with constantly changing, unfulfilled desire sets
- a shifting cast of actual and potential competitors hoping to attract the patronage of those same market segments
- changing social, political, and economic forces (both in the market and in places halfway around the world) which affects all parties to the transaction.
- changing technological developments which can affect both the opportunities and the customer desire sets.

Because marketing of any kind requires plans whose execution and results lie in the future, sellers must gather some kind of information enabling them to anticipate changes and to design strategy and tactics to meet them.

The information needed for planning is of two types: marketing research and marketing intelligence. The line separating the two is not sharp. **Marketing research** generally aims to discover:

- the unfulfilled desire sets of potential customer groups
- the trends in those desire sets
- the trends in numbers, distribution, and composition of actual and potential customer segments
- customer reactions to actual and possible offerings and to proposed promotional plans and tactics

The primary task of marketing research is to define the marketing environment for possible offerings. It is expected to give positive direction for all aspects of marketing plans and tactics. Commonly included is the analysis of continuous formalized flows of data on competitive position.

Data collection and analysis in larger organizations is typically the function of a specialized staff. Even then, other parts of the organization may have the responsibility of collecting some information, especially the sales staff.

Marketing intelligence more usually refers to collection and analysis of other more general environmental factors which reveal opportunities, constraints and threats: the capabilities and intentions of actual and potential competitors, industry trends and developments, more general social and economic trends, and political and other legal developments, and relevant technological trends. Responsibility for the market intelligence data collection and initial analysis is usually more diffused than the responsibility for marketing research, although the marketing research staff may be involved with part of it. In some of the largest organizations, much of the development of information affecting longer range considerations may be centered in a special planning staff.

Whatever the size of the operation, developing information for marketing research and market intelligence, especially the informal types, must be part of the consciousness of every part of management. All of those in the marketing operation, and responsible executives in other areas also, need to be on the alert for information of any kind revealing opportunities for, threats to, and limits on plans.

The supplier contacts, for example, or the purchasing executives are often the earliest sources of information on competitors' plans. The sales force can often spot developing desire sets otherwise likely to be overlooked. They also are in an excellent position to discover the initial marketing efforts of some competitor. Any alert executive can pick up important hints through trade and professional contacts, and clues to possible opportunities and threats in normal reading.

Marketing Research and Rational Planning

Especially in rapid growth markets, sellers can succeed and even rise to dominance without even a semblance of marketing research or market intelligence. However well such a seller fares initially, a blind marketing effort of this kind is almost sure to lead to a later stumble or even a fall in the absence of the guidance needed to fulfill ever-changing desire sets and counter better informed competition.

Although marketing research is often popularly perceived as synonymous with collection of survey data, survey research is seldom the core of any well-organized effort. At most, its main value is to fill in details needed to round out the analysis of other internal and secondary information.

The True Role of Marketing Research

Research is any attempt to analyze available and collected information and interpret its meaning for marketing plans and action. Good research is the art of interpreting the meaning of such information to develop innovative answers to planning problems. Occasionally, limited use of rather complex mathematical techniques can prove useful. Generally, however, the information available is too limited and too imprecise to permit the use of such finely honed tools, and the deadlines to be met by decision too early to permit doing better.

The mission of the research staff is to aid management in foreseeing and evaluating alternative courses to achieve objectives, and to arrive at the best judgments possible on the results of acting on each, within the often extremely short time limits available before action is to be taken.

The kinds of problems marketing research must help solve are as varied as the aspects of marketing itself. Research guidance best starts before the offering is designed, and sometimes before the offering concept is clearly formulated. The need for guidance disappears only when the offering is ready to be abandoned. The kinds of research which will prove useful obviously shifts with the changes in marketing problems to be met at each phase of the offering life cycle.

"QUICK & DIRTY," OR "WE NEEDED IT YESTERDAY"

Thorough research takes time--lots of it. Marketing people often don't have that kind of time to wait. The result is that a great deal of marketing research is of the 'quick and dirty' design--some experienced researchers have put the proportion at nine-tenths. Two incidents in one analyst's memories illustrate the situation.

The firm did a very large part of its business with credit customers. To handle the business, it borrowed money, and was, of course sensitive to changes in rates. One Monday afternoon, the top executives sent a hurry-up call to the research department. 'The Fed has just raised the discount rate, and we have a catalog going to the press on Friday. We must make a decision on whether or not to change our terms. You find out what would happen.' Overnight, 2 analysts put together a personal interview questionnaire, put it in shape immediately the next morning. Another analyst picked up some names of credit customers in a city near enough to get to by automobile. Some credit customers who had sent in orders were contacted by phone on what they would do under certain changes. Wednesday morning early, a carload of the senior analysts set off for the sample town, spent the day interviewing, talked over the results on the way home, wrote a report to be typed and duplicated on Thursday morning and turned it in that afternoon. Their conclusions: customers would spend the same amount of money per week, so that if the payment period were shortened with higher payments, sales would drop initially, but return to normal as the balance owed declined faster. That was enough information on which to act.

At another time, the research department foresaw that the firm might expand into acquisition of a certain type of specialty store. One analyst was given a sort of 'back-burner' assignment to study what standards might be used for choosing locations, just in case. When about half way through his analysis of available data, he got a call for immediate recommendation of a number of sites. When asked when they were needed, he was told that the real estate men would be out already if they had the list, so get it in that afternoon.

The Research Process

Research always requires analysis of data. But some of the most useful research requires no new data collection, and data collection is not, in itself, research. Given a problem, only the unseasoned neophyte rushes out to make interviews. The experienced professional has long since learned to spend some time defining the problem, and knows that primary data collection, if any, is only part of the fourth step in a six step process, and may be unnecessary. The full process consists of:

1. Analysis of the management problem to uncover the real research question which can lead to solution of the marketing problem posed

2. Analysis of the research question itself to decide on the kinds of information and the form of the research best adapted to developing an answer, and defining a standard of relevance for the data to be gathered

3. A search of the available information on the question to be answered and analysis of the kind of added information needed for an answer sufficient to meet the needs of the situation

4. Selection of an appropriate collection technique based on an analysis of the possibilities for obtaining the kinds of information desired and needed, and collection of this information

5. Analysis and interpretation of the meaning of all information collected to arrive at an understanding of the probable effects of actions planned

6. Presentation of the findings in a form which the operating executive will understand and accept

The problem question as phrased by operating personnel rarely reveals the real research question. Management's concerns are action-oriented (How much could we sell? Where should we locate a branch or an outlet? Should we launch the X offering?). Such action-oriented questions never show the way to the kinds of information and analysis needed.

The **research question** poses an **information issue**: "What factors determine customer choices?" "What kinds of customers can we attract, and where are they located?" "What satisfactions are customers likely to perceive as salient in product X; what use-systems does it fit; who are the likely early adopters, and what will they be seeking?"

The research question, and such subquestions as the above, then help the professional to decide on the types of information needed to get management an adequate answer, within the time and cost limits available.

The next step is to collect that data which is least costly in both time and money: available internal primary data and published external information and studies. Very often, available information is all that an adequate analysis requires. If not, the preliminary analysis will have narrowed the search substantially, and shortened the time span needed to arrive at a usable answer.

INTERPRETATION: GETTING THE MEANING STRAIGHT

A colleague was confessing some of his own previous sins as a neophyte researcher. Put in charge of a survey to investigate the potential of a then-new idea--a low suds laundry detergent, he concluded from his survey that "only 25%" of the housewives would be interested, and recommended against putting it on the market. As he noted in his own recounting, he overlooked the fact that no detergent brand on the market at the time had anywhere near a one-fourth share.

The real research effort just begins when the data is collected. Data does not yield answers, only that logical process we label analysis does: the grouping and regrouping and summarizing of information, its rearrangement into some kind of revealing order, and the relating of one piece of information to other pieces in such a way as to reveal interrelationships relevant to a specific problem. This is the essence of research, the aspect which requires the greatest skill and insight, and which is continuous from the beginning of a project.

However well done the analysis, researchers earn their pay only when they put their results together in such a fashion that the operating management understands the full significance of the findings and accepts them as a basis for decision. The presentation of the findings requires careful thought concerning the form which causes the least change in management's habitual ways of looking at its business. This may take more skill than the rest of the effort.

This last step clearly requires that the researcher's skills must include some degree of understanding of the skills of selling. Those who reject this idea ignore a major aspect of organizational life--its informal structures, not shown on the organization chart. Studies have long ago shown that all managers, especially at the middle level, spend about four-fifths of their time selling ideas to other managers over whom they have no control. The only difference is that the research executives have the toughest sales job: nearly every answer they come up with would require management to make some change in their habits of thought. Management, like the rest of us, prefers to get a change without changing habits.

Sources of Information

Information availability spans a spectrum as wide as the rainbow's. At one end, we can sometimes discover information already tabulated in a form in which it can be used as is for current objectives. At the other end lie survey results revealing the vague perceptions and attitudes of final buyers relevant to offerings they have never seen in concrete form--perceptions and attitudes they cannot consciously articulate and which can only be inferred from the use of indirect response techniques.

Relevance of readily available information also spans a spectrum. At the ideal extreme lie internal analyses of sales of the organization to current buyers. At the other extreme are general studies of life styles based on tabulated consumption patterns of a severely limited list of offerings, none of which include the category of products in which the seller is interested.

Combining the two dimensions of availability and relevance, we might group the sources of immediately available information in the following rough order of directly usable value:

THE DATA MAY ALREADY BE IN FRONT OF THE EXECUTIVE

The women's sportswear buyer for the mail order company had a problem for the research department: "Why can't we sell our sportswear?" An analyst was assigned to help find an answer. No expert on fashions of any kind, he had two questions immediately when he went to talk it over with the buyer.

"What", he asked, do you mean by 'sportswear'?"

(Buyer)"Well, I am not concerned with blouses and skirts—they are sportswear, too, and we do all right with them. It's these other items: sweaters, slacks, shorts, jodhpurs, etc. that you see on these pages (taking out his 'marked up' catalog, in which sales by sizes and item were kept)."

(Analyst)"What do you mean you can't sell them: none at all?"

(B)"Oh no. But I can never make more than 2 pages pay off?"

(A) "What makes you think that there is a bigger market than that?"

(B) "Well the other houses put in 4 or more pages and so must."

As they looked through the catalog, the analyst noted that the upper end of the size range ended at 18-1/2. He was already familiar enough with the catalog to know that the normal range for dresses went well above that. He asked,"Why do you stop at size 18-1/2?" The answer, "I don't know—we always have."

Thinking the problem over, the analyst noted that there could only be three reasons: the firm had the wrong assortment, the market really was not large enough to justify any greater attempt, or the firm's market niche was not the sportswear-wearing segment. It seemed that his last question to the buyer might be a place to start. So he took the buyer's record of sales by item and by size, and drew a simple frequency distribution . It was highly skewed toward the smaller sizes, and really tailed off at the 18-1/2 end, or the equivalent, for every item listed. Clearly, the buyer's size distribution made sense. How did it compare with the range for better dresses? The firm had a good business in dress fashions. Again, a set of simple frequency charts was drawn, and they could hardly have shown a greater contrast: dress sales were highly skewed to the right. Most sales were in the upper size ranges. Clearly, the firm's women customers were no diet faddists, and apparently thought that slacks, sweaters and swimming suits did not show off their figures to advantage.

Some similar analyses of a group of dress orders picked up for another purpose showed that geography entered also. But everything pointed to a simple conclusion which the sportswear/dress sales ratio by size indicated: the firm had the wrong kind of customers for sportswear items. The data had been there in front of the buyer all along. All that was needed was a very simple form of analysis, based on a search for a rational reason.

- Previous tabulations of internal information developed as a by-product of the everyday operations of the organization
- Sample tabulations of the raw data resulting from the organization's operations
- Experienced opinions of the seller's own executives, sales people, and others in a position to observe market operations and who also are forced to observe the markets closely and act on their observations
- Experience-based opinions of others in the marketing chain who have a similar observational basis with respect to the offering category
- Tabulations and other relevant information from trade associations, covering the offering category
- Library reference material: Government statistics, including but by no means limited to the voluminous censuses of several kinds
- Published periodical literature, both academic and non-academic, indexed by subject matter, in indexes carried in every reasonably well-equipped library
- Information on subscribers made available by periodical publishers of any importance
- Privately published analytical information made available only on subscription and usually not available in libraries (especially true of detailed financial analyses of some value in sizing up the competition)

Without question, the most important single source of data is the library of basic statistical information published by the United States government. Nearly all major marketing research must start with this treasure trove of official statistics, directly or indirectly, if for no other reason than to establish the base figures on population, industry, and other economic aggregates. The 1,000-plus pages of the annual **Statistical Abstract of the United States** contains a useful cross-section of available statistical data, with agency references giving leads to a wealth of detail available.

The need for critical evaluation in using available information. The use of any available information must be accompanied with a completely critical analysis of the meaning of the figures for the purpose at hand. A major problem with all such information is that it was gathered either for a generalized purpose with no one specific use in mind, or that the purpose it is intended to serve differs substantially from the decision situation which gave rise to the research.

Such is especially the case with the use of accounting results, particularly the use of cost data. The researcher does not need to be a CPA to challenge accounting data for his own purposes. (It may even be better if the researcher is not too habituated to conventional accounting measures.) Costs related to decisions to be made are almost certain to be different from costs as measured by conventional accounting practice. Much of the content of accounting cost consists of arbitrary and legalistic allocation of overhead costs. Standard accounting practice cannot take opportunity costs into consideration for the simple reason that the future opportunity is unknown to the accountant preparing his estimates (and they are estimates, not objective fact).

Nearly all tabulated data from any source is based on some kind of assumptions, and it is always necessary to analyze these assumptions, and to evaluate their relevance to the use to which the information is to be put.

COST ESTIMATES DEPEND

The evaluation of costs of alternatives often influences the conclusion a researcher must draw. Usually the accounting department makes these estimates, and nearly always, the estimate is the wrong one for the decision at hand. The reason is the lack of attention given to the sensitivity of any cost estimate to the purpose to which the estimate is to be put.

A case in point: the mail order firm was going through an economy wave because of slim profits, and had sent out a general request for suggestions. The accounting department suggested that if one of the two credit systems—the charge privilege--were dropped, the firm could save $500 thousand a year. Customers could still use their credit for time payment orders.

Time payment orders involved an additional time cost fee. Charge orders were treated the same as cash orders. The accounting department routinely charged half the cost of the credit operation to the charge accounts, or the already-mentioned $500 thousand. They assumed that abolishing charge would cause people to either go to time, and thus bring in more revenue, or to cash, and save the overhead.

The firm's top management was skeptical. It had long been established that the credit customer was far more profitable than the cash customer because credit customers bought more goods per season. The question was bucked to the marketing research department. What would happen if we abolished the charge privilege? Some hasty plans were made for a telephone check with some customers who had just sent in charge orders. Meanwhile, one analyst raised a single question whose answer must come from the accountants themselves: How much less would it cost to run the department if it lost the charge operation? What, in other words, was the real opportunity cost of keeping or dropping the charge operation? After some calculation, the accounting department admitted that not one penny would be saved.

On another occasion, the sales manager of a major manufacturer of simple controls, produced by automatic machinery, had an opportunity to sell a large order of several hundred thousand of one design if he could quote the right price. The current price was about 10-1/2 cents. Capacity was not fully used at the time, and the order would require no expansion of that capacity. Nevertheless the accountants came up with a price above what was already being charged.

Inspection of the items used in calculating cost revealed that over 80% of the cost estimate consisted of an overhead calculation. That overhead allocation itself contained a fairly large item for tooling, already done. But the accountant had added in new tooling, thus double counting this cost, none of which would be incurred. After paring down the costs to the only kinds that would be involved--the true variable costs--it was obvious that any price above l-1/2 cents would be clear profit!

Analysis of available information is nearly always a necessary exploratory step, needed to clarify the definition of the problem. Often it is more than that--it may yield all the information needed for a useful answer. On the other hand, very little relevant information may be available from any source. In such cases, the next step will be some exploratory research to gain an idea of what to look for.

Exploratory Research

A common form of exploration is the interviewing of persons in direct touch with similar marketing situations. The experienced merchandise buyers for retail organizations can yield dependable information on price and even on buyer motives and attitudes. Independent sales organizations, particularly manufacturer's representatives and food brokers for example, are familiar with the buying practices and motives of industrial and merchant organizations. Both merchandise buyers and sales representatives are good sources of information on price reactions as well as product performance specifications.

EXPLORATORY RESEARCH: SMALL SAMPLES CAN YIELD USEFUL RESULTS

If the respondents are really knowlegeable, not many are needed, especially in exploratory projects. In at least one case, a single respondent seemed to be enough.

A student came into the marketing professor with some hand made silver costume jewelry. "My room mate is from India," he said, and can get this stuff cheap. What would it sell for?" The professor had a personal guess, but recognizing that it was little more than that, told the student, "I'm no judge of jewelry values. I suggest you talk to the appropriate buyer at [the city's leading department store]."

A couple of weeks later, the same student came in, and told him of his reception. The buyer said it would sell for about $5 at retail, and that he would be interested.

On another occasion, a maker of large industrial valves of special design commissioned some research to find added markets. The firm sold largely through manufacturers representatives who also sold other types of valves to a much broader market. Interviews were set up with 3 of the representatives. From those interviews, the possible markets were narrowed down, and explored in a little more detail. The result was a line which added $4 million in added sales for a firm whose annual sales at the time had been about $10 million.

Another useful initial exploration is a detailed analysis of contrasting types or situations: for example, the top and bottom quartiles of the sales force, older buyers vs. younger customers, heavy users vs. light users.

At other times, the focus may be on the behavior of specific fringe segments, such as those just coming into the market, or the customers who have quit buying. When seeking information on proposed new offerings, including fashion, studies of those likely to be early adopters may be especially important. Extended observation of the behavior of a small sample of individuals may reveal the nature of the problem, or even lead directly to a useful solution.

The use of unstructured depth interviews and also of so-called focus groups have a well-established place in researching proposed new offerings and studying proposed promotional themes. In both methods, the aim is to guide the respondents into a free expression of their feelings, perceptions, and even their opinions about market situations, product usage, or product concepts. The interviewer or moderator will usually have a cue outline of items which are thought worth covering, but will not bring these up in any sequence, or even do so directly at all. The purpose is to obtain a free and thorough discussion which can uncover unsuspected reactions.

None of these methods aim at a precise tabulation of any kind. Their purpose is insight into the problem, not measurement. Nevertheless, the results may sometimes define the problem well enough that no further descriptive surveys or experimental research can be expected to add much knowledge.

Descriptive Surveys

Survey research does usually account for a major part of special project research spending. Direct question-and-answer surveys with trained interviewers are most useful when the needed information is of the type and in the form in which respondents can and will readily give accurate answers. They are the easiest to administer and analyze.

However, when the replies sought may involve feeling and attitudes, replies may not mean what they seem to. Moreover, the highly structured survey may inadvertently overlook some really crucial but unrecognized aspect of the consumer perception or reaction. Or, the answers obtained may simply reflect a conventional, generalized attitude which has no depth of feeling behind it. A really skilled interviewer could detect this in the tone of voice and body language, but not every interviewer is that perceptive, and the instructions and forms usually make no provision for recording such observations.

Less direct methods of probing are needed whenever the possible reactions involve some degree of feelings and emotions (as all attitude-related reactions do). A wide variety of psychologically oriented techniques are in use, including various forms of scaling and semantic differential tests, cartoon tests (technically labelled Thematic Apperception Tests--TAT), and other means of getting people to give expression to feelings. All have proved useful, even though two different qualified analysts can arrive at quite different interpretations of similar data. Interpretation of the data that comes out is an art which is quite personal.

Experimental Research

None of these more conventional survey or exploratory methods have proved very useful in predicting consumer behavior in situations foreign to the experience of the respondents, as in the case of proposed new designs, for example. In some such cases, experiments can be devised which force people to make choices in a manner simulating the transaction situation. The design of the experiment depends on the object of the measurement—whether product, packaging, or label design, or pricing, or promotional copy.

SIMULATING PURCHASE SITUATION PRESSURES

One area of research which is difficult to do well, and which can be critical, is finding out ahead of time what people might buy. A straight questionnaire report can yield unrealistic wishes—wishes that will later vanish when the respondents are faced with spending the money.

One method is to give them something approaching a need to make the same kind of choices under the pressure of spending. One of the methods used is to use a lottery simulation—some of the respondents are going to get their choices to keep, if they win. Opinion Research Inc. used this method in studying choices in rug patterns. Designer's sketches in kodachrome slides were shown to audiences in 120 clinics held over the country. At each clinic, respondents were told, "A rug, or its equal value in carpeting, will be given away at the end of this clinic, so in your rating of designs, remember you are choosing a rug for your own home." In one series of pretests over a 4-year period, 120 people won rugs.

The winner was taken to a distributor and allowed to pick any rug or carpeting of the same value from stock. Many of the patterns had never been produced as yet, so some had to make some kind of substitution. In 118 of the 120 instances, either the design chosen was taken, or rugs of the same dominant colors and same pattern type. One of the exceptions was a daughter whose mother had been given her win, and chose a different one than the mother had The other was a woman who decided to use the rug in her bedroom rather than the living room, as first decided, and wanted a floral design for the bedroom rather than the broadloom chosen for the living room. (Dilman M. K. Smith, **How to Avoid Mistakes When Introducing New Products**, Vantage Press, 1964, pp.79-81.)

Several forms of experiments have become part of the research kit. Respondents may be brought into actual laboratory setups, panels of respondents given enough product for extended trial or pilot test in their own homes or place of business, experiments disguised as product usage studies, advertising experiments, and even market tests for this purpose.

Market tests are seldom a useful means of testing product design or acceptance. They usually require too much commitment to production facilities for research at the development stage, or even a test of many alternative promotional approaches. Their valid use is in connection with thoroughly worked-out introductions, to discover and eliminate the "bugs" in the introductory plans before a final product launch.

However, market tests are useful in testing pricing or display alternatives within a single chain merchandise operation. The growing use of POS (point-of-sale) computer terminals in retail transactions has greatly facilitated this type of market test, and its use will probably spread with their increased coverage of outlets.

When attempting to simulate realistic choices in an experimental situation, respondents are put in a situation where they have to make a spending choice. One common method is the lottery simulation. An attractive door prize is offered, with the lucky respondents winning a substantial purchase of their own choice. Such is the common device in theater laboratory tests of proposed commercials or promotional devices. Another variation, used in packaging or display tests, is to pass out coupons in the store good for any purchase of all brands in the category studied.

Intelligence information about competitors, their positions in the market, and their capabilities and plans is just as important as information about the market itself.

Managing Marketing Intelligence Information

The opportunities open to any seller are defined by the resources, capabilities and market positions of competitors. Their reactions are a major source of the uncertainties surrounding the results of any marketing operation. Planning of strategy and tactics must make the best use possible of market intelligence. As with most intelligence of any kind, marketing intelligence simply makes use of readily available information. In marketing, especially, what any competitor does is open to full view, and much of the planning is common knowledge even before the plans reach the marketing stage. Too many outsiders are involved to keep any important move secret.

The auditing of relative market shares is routine in those offering categories in which competition is keen, as in packaged consumer goods. The awarding of a new advertising account is public news. Competitors nearly always share common suppliers of components, packaging, materials, and services of many kinds, and these become sources of information. Market tests, and even consumer panel tests, are virtually impossible to keep secret. If only a minimal lead time is needed to get into production, observable action may be enough to launch competitors into preemptive moves. The sound use of intelligence goes well beyond planning reaction. A wise system analyzes what a competitor can and might be able to do, and prepares plans that take account of such capabilities in choosing a market niche and in the use of tactics.

Evaluating the Capabilities of Competition

The primary goal of good market intelligence is the evaluation of the **capabilities and intentions** of each actual competitor, and of potential competitors. The capabilities are summed up in the **functional profile** of the seller, usually easily developed from matters of public knowledge, and even published. This profile uses information on a competitor's major investments in production facilities and in marketing effort, the financial resources available, and the seller's demonstrated objectives. It covers such points as:

- The nature and importance of the competitor's investment in production facilities
- The nature of its investment in R&D facilities and manpower
- Its developed resources and strengths in sales, and distribution facilities and organization
- Its strengths in the organization and use of marketing research and in the communications skills of advertising and sales promotions
- Its financial strength relative to other members of the industry
- Its known sales, marketing, profit and market share objectives
- Its cost structure
- Any parent-subsidiary relationships, as well as any alliances with other organizations.

The weight and focus of these various investments will inevitably shape the nature of the competitor's profit opportunities and thus limit the choice of marketing strategy. An evaluation based on this analysis will be modified by what is known about the past performance of the chief executives. When new personnel come into these positions, the evaluation may be modified by the nature of the recorded experience of the new leaders.

Organizations who have a major investment in the bricks and mortar of production facilities will tend to add offerings in which profits lay in production and cost management, and full utilization of production capacity of the type of production with which they are familiar. Thus the paper manufacturers like Scott and Kimberly-Clark, with a hefty investment in paper-making machinery, have shaped their product policy around paper-based products, Con-Agra around agricultural commodity processing (taking over Banquet Foods on which RCA was losing heavily, and making it a profit source through skilful control of production costs). White Consolidated continues to grow by adding appliance brand losers of other types of firms in the same way.

Organizations with a heavy investment in developing expertise in sales, advertising and mass distribution tend to add offerings in which the source of profit lies in these areas, such as packaged consumer goods. When the cigarette manufacturers decided to diversify, it was into beverages and personal care products (Philip Morris) and packaged foods (R.J. Reynolds)—items in which distribution strength and promotional skills are more decisive than production skills.

Substantial investment in technical research and development leads to a preference toward introduction of offerings which have some kind of

physical differentiation.   Thus Procter and Gamble, with long experience in
the sale and distribution of packaged consumer items based on some aspect
of physical difference, seeks to acquire or create brands which have some
such difference, however superficial.   ("It floats" created the market for its
first major brand--Ivory Soap.)

Developing a strong distribution system requires a major investment in
both time and money--well-organized sales training and development of
established distributor contacts.   The kinds of channels developed, and their
role in sales will determine what a seller can introduce readily.   Some types
of channels, such as those going through mass merchandisers, are best
adapted to a pull strategy, in which the role of the retailer is simply that
of stocking and display.   The producer depends on well-targetted
advertising and sales promotions to develop strong patronage loyalty, and
retailers often must stock the item in self-protection.   Such is the case
with most toiletries--soap, shampoos, hair conditioners, etc.--sold by firms
like Gillette, Colgate-Palmolive, Procter and Gamble and Lever. Such run
into difficulties when they try to use their expertise in the sale of items
requiring a "push strategy", in which the influence of the sales person at
the final point of sale can be influential.   The Toni Division of Gillette
failed at a try to enter the premium cosmetics market with a lipstick
because high end cosmetics require such a push strategy and did not then
respond to the pull strategy in which it was expert.

No cloak and dagger methods are needed to discover all that needs to be
known about any major seller's production investment patterns and cost
structures, nor about their investment in sales, advertising and promotional
strengths.   Most major producers and distributors are publicly owned, and
the details of their financial structure are a matter of published record.
Even the information on the few large privately held firms tend to be a
matter of public knowledge, within the limits necessary for an assessment,
because their hiring and purchasing efforts, as well as the character of
their personnel organization and production facilities are easily observed by
interested outsiders.   Advertising, sales, distribution channels and other
evidences of marketing expertise take place in the daylight of the market.
Production costs can be estimated from the age, size and flexibility of plant
and equipment, and from the pricing policies followed.

Divining the Intentions of Competition

The "intentions" of any seller are telegraphed by its marketing tactics and
strategy.   One useful guide to such intentions and strategy is the
classifying of its offerings, according to the kinds of efforts put behind
their promotion and sale, into three pigeonholes:

- **Developing Products:** a growing brand share, aggressive marketing
  effort support, and persistent revitalizations.   Commonly, these will be
  offerings in a general growth market, but some may be recent

introductions in a mature volume market with changing tastes.

- **Sustaining Offerings:** offerings in slow-growth of no-growth market and similar market share trends. Market support moderate, with revitalization avoiding pricing moves, if one of the firms's more important brands. If the market share is not leading, may be price repositioned. If a leading brand, the seller will sacrifice market share to maintain profit. If a non-leader, it will attempt to hold market share, but not actively seek to expand it.
- **Milking offerings:** easily identified through the lack of any competitive effort put behind their promotion and sale: little or no promotion, no reaction to competitor's tactics, no absorption of cost increases, etc.

When a seller's strategy, (and thus its priorities) changes, the treatment of its products will show up immediately, under this system of classification. Thus Liggett and Myers shifted from attempting to promote its lagging Chesterfield brand of cigarettes to a production orientation: vigorously seeking the generic market instead in the early 1980s, and carving out a respectable 2+% of market. It even ran full page ads advising people to buy store and generic brands. Brown noted that Colgate signalled a switch from its traditional soap, cosmetics and toothpaste markets in Australia after the mid-1950's, dropping the cosmetics, following a preemptive defense of its toothpaste position, and using the profits from the other lines to launch an aggressive expansion of its market position in laundry and dishwashing products.

Acquisitions are an obvious indicator of strategy direction.

When most of a seller's offerings are in the mature stage, sellers must begin to extend market intelligence beyond a mere watching of obvious close competitors. Attention needs to be directed to outside competition: competitors producing variants of their offerings which were previously unavailable, and in which significant numbers of buyers are beginning to show an interest. They also need to maintain what is best labelled as technological intelligence: careful attention and analysis of what developing technologies could offer to buyers. Thus the growing capacity of microprocessor chips in the late 1970s made possible the development of what came to be called "personal computers"--small, relatively inexpensive machines with capacities for carrying out operations available previously on far more expensive "mini-computers". Their flexibility and capacities began to invade laboratories and offices, not only expanding the market, but threatening to crowd out the mini-computers entirely.

These new small computers also were threatening those electric typewriter makers who did not modify their machines to adapt to usage as computer printers to be used in "word processing."

In fact, as the mid 1983's approaches, the typewriter seems to be on the decline. Newspapers are beginning to ask their writers and reporters to compose their material directly on word processors, to be fed directly to the computer which now carried out the typesetting functions.

The content of the needed marketing research and marketing intelligence obviously shifts as the market life cycle passes through its various stages.

Requirements for Marketing Research and Intelligence Over the Life Cycle

The type of marketing research and market intelligence information needed to support sound planning of strategy and tactics changes with the shifts in the stages of the offering life cycle. Both are needed from the first consideration of any specific introductory concept: marketing research to search out the tastes, desires, and needs of final users and the distributors in between, and marketing intelligence to assess the capabilities and intentions of actual and potential competitors.

Marketing Research and Intelligence at The Concept and Gestation Stages

Systematic marketing research can be one useful source of ideas for new offerings, especially offerings of new designs and models of established product forms, by uncovering newly developing trends in consumer tastes not well satisfied by current designs, or simply revealing the important negative aspects of designs presently on the market. What should be sought is an indication of the needed product performance specifications, not a testing of specific designs. (The latter is seldom feasible. Customers tend to express preferences in terms of their knowledge of designs currently available on the market. Rarely are they capable of designing in terms of their future desires.)

At this stage, technological analysis can be very useful, also, if accompanied by an imaginative analysis of what emerging technologies can do to establish or broaden markets. The main market intelligence needed is essentially that of competitor watching, discussed earlier.

The kinds of research and intelligence needed once the offering is launched have already been discussed in Chapter 15. The basic guidelines can be summarized as follows:

Gestation Phase

Basic research problems:
- What are the salient desire sets the offering can satisfy?
- What are the most important performance desires in these desire sets?
- What use-systems do the offerings seem likely to fit?
- What learning requirements might be involved, and how could these be minimized? Who are the likely early adopters, and how big a segment or segments do they represent?
- What communications media and distribution channels seem best fitted to reach these segments, and especially the likely early adopters?

- What value levels are likely to be perceived by early buyers, and what general price levels are likely to be perceived as attractive?

Basic intelligence need:
- Who are the actual and potential competitors?
- What are their capabilities and apparent plans?
- What are their modes of operation?
- If they seem to have any new or modified offerings in development, what is the probable timing of their release, and what their probable performance characteristics?

LOCTITE FINDS THAT A LOCKSTEP BETWEEN R&D & MR PAYS OFF

Loctite Corp. is a maker of specialty chemicals for industrial use and some related consumer products with sales around $200 thousand annually. One product its laboratories developed was an adhesive material to be used as a filler on metal parts, thought to have a potential market with industrial designers. Put on the market as a runny green liquid with the mystery label of RC 601 and brochures sprinkled with technical terms, it did not sell at all well.

Then in 1979, Loctite's marketing executives decided to take a second look at RC 601. This time, it first surveyed the industrial market to find out what was needed in such a product and who might be the buyers. As in most such industrial markets, the number of possible buyers was not large, but the answers needed took time to get. Interviews with 20 equipment designers and industrial engineers, and 40 maintenance people took 6 weeks, but gave them the leads they needed. Industrial designers, they discovered, were not looking hard for new materials. But maintenance people were always seeking shortcuts needed to keep production lines operating. In addition, RC 601, as originally formulated, was too hard to use.

The chemists now went back to work, came up with a putty-like material, and the marketing people now called it Quick Metal, promoting it with informative slogans like "keeps machinery running until the new parts arrive."

Since using a single tube of Quick Metal could save as much as 800 hours of machine downtime, it was priced to yield a margin of 85%. And since maintenance personnel are interested in results, not technical details, the marketing plan included all the hoopla of high pressure consumer goods introductions. In the first six months, industrial retailers sold over $2 million worth of Quick Metal.

[Based on "Consumer-Product Techniques Help Loctite Sell to Industry," **The Wall Street Journal**, p. 29, Apr. 2, 1981]

Introductory Phase

Main research problems
- Who are the actual buyers, and how do they fit into the adopter categories normally?
- What are the salient values they perceive in the offering?
- What use-systems are they putting the offering into?
- How much learning is required in these use-systems?

- For the systems in which the offering is being used, is the fit good, or does the offering need any modifications? Are any offering defects being experienced?
- Through what media are buyers learning of the introduction?
- In what kinds of distribution outlets are they seeking the offering, and through what distribution channels are the sales being made?
- If there are competing offerings on the market, what differences are perceived by buyers, and how much value do they perceive in these differences?
- Does the character of the initial consumer reaction seem to forecast an early rapid growth in demand, or a slow market development period?

Market intelligence focus: are competitors entering the market, or some preparing to? What seem to be their targets?

Growth Phase

Main research problems
- What trends are developing in the purchase and use systems?
- To what extent are the desire sets expanding and diversifying?

GM: THE CRITICAL VALUE OF BEING ON TOP OF THE TRENDS

In looking back over his experiences in the 1920's Alfred Sloan attributed the gains GM made in that period to the major changes in the automobile market at that time, and the fortunate coincidence for the policies GM had adopted which fit in with these trends. He makes no claim to have foreseen the trends, and readily admitted that much of the quantitative data needed to understand the trends were missing at the time, and what was known was not clearly understood. But the result was the same.

Sloan outlined four such trends he considered critical:
- Installment selling
- The used-car trade-in
- The closed body
- The annual model

Instalment buying started "in a small way" just prior to World War I, and grew to 65% of sales by 1925. GM had established GMAC in 1919 in recognition of its value in selling upgraded cars. (Ford refused to participate, and as late as 1924, was lecturing his dealers on not tying in with the trend.)

No data was available on the trend toward trade-ins until 1925, but as a seller of higher priced cars, GM encountered the trend early and adapted to it. (Again, Ford actively opposed the taking of trade-ins by his dealers.)

General Motors invested in Fisher Body early, and were in a good position to profit from the trend to the all-weather closed body.

- What model variations are needed to cover developing market segments?
- What are the price line needs which are developing?
- Are new purchase patterns developing which indicate a need to broaden distribution channels?
- What is the offering's position in the distribution outlets?
- Is there any need to improve distribution strength, and what is needed to do it?
- What attributes of the offering now seem to be of growing salience and need to be emphasized in the promotion?
- What are the growing market segments, and what media are needed to reach them?

Market intelligence need:
- Who are the competitors?
- How are the current market shares distributed and what is our position?
- What are the developing trends in those shares?
- What are the strengths of current and apparently potential competitors?
- What seems to be the market objective of each competitor?

The annual model was not, originally, a planned move, but the consequence of trying to make the models more attractive on a regular basis, as opposed to the concept of a static model which Ford was firmly wedded to at the time.

The tone of Sloan's recounting of this period implies that GM's success was due more to a coincidently good policy than to planning. Such is often the case. But GM has had problems in more recent years because the executives have consistently ignored the rising trends in consumer tastes, especially for smaller, more roadable, and more fuel efficient cars, even before the oil shock of the 1970s. When the trend became inevitable, GM's lack of design and production experience in such designs created problems.

Nowadays, we have far more information on what is happening in the market, and well proven techniques for spotting evolving trends, than was available in the 1920s. The availability of this information makes it urgent that quicker use of it be made.

Organizations of every kind need to identify developing trends and be ready to take advantage of them. A major example now unfolding has been the varying fortunes of small colleges in recent years. Some have folded, and more are on the edge. Others have prospered, as they recognized the decline of the traditional programs, particularly programs adapted to a shrinking traditional 18-20-year old cohort in the population, and establishing strongly needed adult-oriented programs. The signs of these trends have long been apparent, and even officially publicized.

Period of Competitive Turbulence

Main research problems
- What is the nature of the desire sets now leading to buying?
- What kinds of use-systems are becoming the dominant ones?
- What offering performance improvements seem to be needed to meet current desires?
- Do our offerings cover an adequate range of price levels?
- How strong is our position with the distributors?
- What is the quality of our service to distributors, and how is it viewed by them?
- How profitable is our brand for distributors, and what may be needed to make it more profitable in any way?
- Is our promotion aimed to meet the salient desires of both the customers and the distributors?
- What is the quality of our customer service all through the distribution channel?

Market intelligence needed
- What is our market share, and what are the market shares of competitors?
- What is the current trend in each case: who is gaining and who is losing out, and why?
- What are the financial, market, and technological strengths of each competitor, and how may it limit each one's plans, or forward them?
- What is our position in the distribution channels, and that of all significant competitors?

Mature Phase

Main research problems
- What aspects of our offerings are negative and should be improved?
- What changes are taking place in customer identities and habits relative to our offerings?
- Are new market segments developing, and what do they desire?
- What are the strongest perceived attributes of our offering among the heavy users? Is our promotion geared to identify us strongly with these attributes, or has some competitor already preempted this positioning?
- What new trends in consumption patterns are developing, and what new attribute perceptions are growing, with what market segments?
- What new kinds of offerings on the market, or about to enter, seem to appeal to some of the major desire sets underlying our market position?

Market intelligence requirements.
- What are the market shares and the positioning of each current

competitor?
- What are the cost structures of each?
- What are the observable objectives of each competitor, and the strengths of each?
- What potential competitors elsewhere might invade our market? Ii some have started, precisely what unfulfilled desires in our offerings are providing them with a toehold?
- What technological developments could furnish our customers with offerings more attractive in some respects than our current types of designs?
- What offerings appearing on the market seem to be appealing to some of the core desires in our customers' desire sets?

Decline Phase
- Are we sure that the current decline in industry sales is merely a temporary condition due to an economic slump, or does it appear to be due to changing consumption patterns?
- If the latter, how fast are the consumption patterns changing, and at what point may it be wise to drop out of the market?
- What new kinds of desire sets are developing which could utilize the resources now devoted to production and sale of the current offering?
- What currently growing markets seem to be adapted to our resources and skills?
- What currently stable markets are vulnerable to invasion and potentially profitable for us?

Market intelligence needed:
- Which of the current competitors is likely to hang longest in the declining phase, and profit by it?
- What opportunities seem to be available for the redeployment of our resources and skills, and when would these take up the slack?

In short, the decline brings research and intelligence full circle: to a search for new opportunities. The customers are already leaving the offering, and so are most of the competitors, voluntarily or reluctantly. The research skills should be redeployed immediately, also.

Management of Market Operations Control Information

Control Feedback: The Difference between Daydreaming And Effective Execution

Built-in provisions for management control information make the difference between self-deluding daydreams and resultful plans. As already noted, all planning is keyed to forecasts, including a forecast of the results of executing the plans. Forecasts of any kind are accurate only by accident. So all plans must be flexible and subject to modification. We can know when and how to modify in time only when firm provisions for feedback on the results are part of the plan.

Of all the management functions, market operations are most in need of provisions for information feedback. Most of market operations and results are not directly observable by the planners, nor even by those at the lower levels supervising the operations.

The perceived character and perceived value of the offering is decided by the end user, not by those doing the selling. The flow and handling of the offering is commonly in the hands of outsiders. The execution and effects of the planned communications are seldom directly observable. The efforts of competitors and their success can usually be learned only by means of some kind of planned information flow.

The purpose of operations controls is to set standards for and measure performance of the execution of plans and their cost and profit effectiveness, and to reveal new market opportunities and threats. The tools include PERT charts, sales analysis, consumer surveys and purchased services detailing final sales and consumption patterns, market share reports, salesman and distributor reports, and a miscellany of less formal information sources, including trade publications and information from suppliers.

The need for controls starts with the decision to consider the development of a specific offering. The need ends when the offering is dropped.

The marketing research staff usually has the assignment of managing control information analysis. Although controls information looks backward, at what has already happened, its role is to guide decisions as to what to do in the future. Drawing a sharp line between controls analysis and research is impossible, because the data serves a base for estimating the future, and adapting plans to that future.

The Purposes Served by Controls Information

The basic purpose of useful control information can be stated quickly: to find out, soon enough to take any needed action, how well plans are being carried out, how the results compare with expectations, and what unforeseen problems, opportunities and threats are developing internally and out there in the market.

Success in launching any new effort, from a totally new offering to a new ad campaign, requires coordination and on-time performance of a variety of people inside and outside the seller's own organization. The required schedules need to be estimated in advance. The actual performance of each key task needs to be known at the time, and adjustments made in the resources allocated or in the other plans to compensate for any unforeseen delays. The required schedules need to estimated in advance and the on-schedule performance checked as execution of the plans moves ahead.

Once any program is in operation, the organization needs feedback on the degree of success, on costs and realized profits on each part of the plan, and on ways to improve future performance.

Information is also needed on trade reaction and cooperation, on the effects of competition, and on any counterplans by competitors.

The major sources and forms of analysis include:

- PERT or Critical Path charts for any special projects or new programs
- Continuous sales analysis
- Market share studies
- Purchased consumer report services and surveys
- Individual consumer surveys
- Miscellaneous informal sources of information on plans and events in the industry, including published trade information, reports from salesmen and distributors, and information from or about industry suppliers

---

J-CARS: THE CAR THAT WASN'T THERE

GM did well so long as it was selling big cars. But its small cars have led to a peck of problems. First came the X-cars in 1979—only they didn't come into the showroom very fast. After months of publicity and advertising, so few were delivered for general sale that customers had to wait for 2 or three months for delivery, with all sorts of complaints about broken delivery promises, favoritism and price-gouging. On top of that, there were quality problems—not the kind of publicity GM wanted.

Then in the spring of 1981, the subcompact J-car Chevrolets and Pontiacs were introduced after a several month build up of promotional activity. The promotion got interested people into the show room—to see film strips, color pictures and brochures. By early June, only 31,000 had been built (only 7500 in all of May), to be rationed among 9,000 Chevrolet and Pontiac dealers. Officials blame the mix-up on an unexpected slow production startup because of a bad batch of engines and other below par parts, and a desire to be sure of quality before delivery. They claimed that the delay had been occasioned by a desire to maintain a high standard of quality to compete with the foreign cars, were prepared to "sacrifice quantity to get quality."

Despite previous problems with Vega and the X-cars, the firm had apparently not included any contingency timing allowances in its promotion, and the advertising came out on schedule even if the cars did not.

GM was hoping that its customers would wait, but Volkswagen of America reported a 30% gain in Rabbit sales in the 10-day period the J-car was out, and attributed the gain to frustrated J-car shoppers. [Ref.: "Severe Shortage of GM's New J-cars Frustrates Dealers and Customers," **The Wall Street Journal**, June 5, 1981, p. 27]

PERT and Critical Path are two forms of a tool for coordination and timing which could clearly be used more widely than they have been in marketing. Any product launch, any planned promotion, requires as much coordination of various somewhat independent efforts as any construction project involving different crafts and subcontractors. Because of the competitive character of all marketing efforts, the coordination of all of the needed tasks can often be more crucial than the timing of the completion of a building or a new plant.

Consider only a relatively routine couponing deal, involving, perhaps, the stimulation of store displays and some special labelling. The following task sequences must be thoroughly coordinated to hit the market at a planned point in time:

- Development of the artwork for the packaging, and procurement of the packaging materials in time for production
- Planning of a production run of the packaging in time to get them to the distributors, orientation of the sales force on the promotion
- Selling the promotional pack into the distributors
- Getting the pack into distributor warehouses in time for delivery to the point of final sale ahead of the advertising
- Designing the coupon
- Getting the coupons printed, if not part of some advertisement.
- Getting the advertising printed and placed ahead of publication deadlines
- Covering the major retail outlets to gain cooperation in the placing of displays and getting them to order in the special pack

All of these tasks take time. Each of the above is a set of sequences largely under separate supervision and some require coordination of the efforts of outsiders: the ad agency, a packaging supplier, distributors and retailers. Most of these sequences are under autonomous supervision, yet must work toward a coordinated schedule. If any one fails to meet the timing requirements, the promotion is dead.

And some promotions do fail because of poor coordination. The ads appear, the coupons are delivered, and the customer who goes to the retailer finds that the latter knows nothing about the promotion and does not have it in stock.

Sales analysis seeks to classify some form of continuing flow of information on sales and sales efforts in such a way as to reveal:

- The most profitable of the customer segments being served
- The effectiveness of various communications programs and promotions
- The best opportunities for greater profit
- The problem areas in the marketing or promotional plans or execution

How much is learned depends on the quality of the analysis. If conducted as a routine clerical operation, the wrong data may be collected, and the important information in the good data not recognized. It can easily be a waste of money, or a gold mine of marketing information. It can result in a mountain of useless paper or printouts, or a few pages of carefully condensed nuggets of guidance.

Purchased reports on trade movement and stocking have proved invaluable in a number of industries. The oldest and probably best known in the United

States and a number of foreign countries are the Nielsen Food and Drug Index and the Nielsen TV rating services.

The Nielsen Food and Drug index reports on the sales of every brand in certain specific categories of drug and food items in a sample of outlets, and also on related promotions. The broadcast rating service reports on set tune-ins by programs.

Less widely known services cover other industries, such as the sale of mobile homes and new car registrations.

Essentially, such services maintain a running record of market share and competitive promotional activity, by geographical area and by type of outlet.

Most industrial trade organizations also collect sales figures by member firms to produce market share data by product and by other important categories.

For frequently purchased consumer goods, a number of suppliers maintain consumer panels which keep records of their purchases. The results are a form of sales analysis, revealing the market segments purchasing, and the heavy users. Similar diaries have been used to develop broadcast ratings.

The information furnished by such services provide a type of baseline data which can be supplemented by the seller's own studies. Unfortunately, they cover only limited classes of offerings, and limited types of outlets.

Even when available, most sellers need added specifics on users, such as:
- The specific identity of the segments being served, and the motivations for purchase
- Buyers' perceptions of the offering benefits and of the values they attach to these benefits
- The market niche of each existing competitor
- The impact of specific promotional programs

This sort of information must be collected by the seller.

Both the formal and informal reports from the seller's own sales force and distributors can be extremely valuable. Both salesmen and distributors can be in a excellent position to learn consumer identities and reactions, and also may be the earliest sources of information on the actions and policies of competitors. They can be in a good position to observe something about the impact of promotional efforts. Efforts to regularize and encourage such feedback can have a very profitable pay-off. The "lost business" reports commonly used in industrial selling are one such effort at regularization.

Finally, **informal information** is often available to various executives in the seller's organization about the effects of various efforts, and about competitor's operations and plans. Sources include:
- Published news about the trade and industry
- The advertising of competitors

- Information about competitors gleaned from suppliers of materials, operating supplies, packaging, printing, advertising and other promotional services, and corridor gossip at conferences and conventions. (The purchasing department often gets access to such information)

Much of the information obtained from any source is a valuable aid to planning as well useful as controls.

Using Control Information for Planning

Control information, similar to research information, is collected and analyzed for one main purpose: to make sound judgments about the next course of action. The information itself does not produce these judgments. They are created by the art of analysis.

The purpose of PERT charts is to maintain control over the most critical aspect of any marketing project: the correct timing. Any initial PERT chart gives us only the best estimate of project completion and the identity of those activities likely to create bottlenecks. The completion date estimate then must be compared with what we consider the timing necessary to hit the "window of opportunity" right. If it looks like the schedule will miss that timing, we must then decide what price is worth paying to insure the best timing. That price may prove to be high and yet a bargain, if a miss means coming in second in a race where there is no pay-off for coming in second. The chart can then be modified by planning to "parallel" tasks that do not have to be done in sequence, and "crashing" those for which there is no alternative solution, by assuming higher costs for extra effort.

Gross market share figures have little real meaning by themselves. They usually lump together such a wide variety of offerings that some are not in competition with others in any meaningful sense. At most, they merely signal a need to check more deeply into the specifics of shares in comparison with similar competing offerings serving similar market segments. Even then, the appearance of the signal may be sluggish and delayed.

More meaningful information will normally result from the analysis of sales trends and/or profit trends in specific models sold to specific markets, especially in relatively mature markets. The early signs of a new kind of profitable demand may be buried in the mass statistics of stable overall sales. Conversely, what seems to be a relatively secure market share may represent a dependence on sales to a stagnant or declining market segment. In either case, it is necessary to pull the overall industry totals apart and scrutinize the separate elements in the offering mix and customer trends. When so analyzed, market share information can be a very useful supplement to internal sales analysis.

Internal sales analysis can be treated as a sleepy routine clerical function, piling up tabulations or printouts that no one looks at carefully. Or it can be turned into a gold mine of information pinpointing opportunities for greater profit.

PEPSI-COLA: ROUTINE SALES ACCOUNTING VS. QUALITY SALES ANALYSIS

In recent years, Pepsi-Cola has been a competitor on which Coca-Cola has found it wise to keep a respectful watch. It was not always thus. Pepsi-Cola's product had been on the market for decades before its competition was much more than a flea bite to Coke. Not that Pepsi did not try: it made consistent use of advertising, and diligently compiled all sorts of data on sales: virtually papering the walls of the offices with charts on soft drink sales by cities and brands, according to one who was there at the time.

Finally, officials decided to take a different kind of look at its own sales figures. They first asked themselves: what makes a potential customer? The answer was not much help: anyone with a mouth! Next, they asked themselves, When do people buy a soft drink? This narrowed the problem: anytime they are doing something somewhere--shopping, driving, watching a ball game, etc. Then they asked themselves, Are we at all of those places? This led to a discovery. Pepsi was well represented at the supermarket. But it was in few vending machines at gas stations, not sold in most ball parks. Customer sales analysis showed big holes in the distribution coverage needed for a product which was sold on availability.

Pepsi started plugging those holes. Suddenly, Coca-Cola, who up to that time would sell its product in any size container so long as it was the familiar 6-oz. bottle, discovered that more than one size container was needed by the market. By this time, Pepsi had become a major competitor, and still is.

One problem is the ease with which data can be piled up (at substantial cost), and the useful information ignored or omitted. Again, the quality of analysis makes the difference between useful answers from limited data collection and a clerical pile-up of too much of the wrong kind of information.

Figures never "speak for themselves." Collection should start only when a relevant research question has been formulated, and then so shaped as to give an adequate answer to that question. Once the right questions are asked of it, sales analysis can hope to furnish guidance to optimizing the allocation of marketing efforts to the most profitable market segments, and also to optimize the offering mix.

One of the more common benefits of good sales analysis is the highlighting of those market segments yielding the greatest profit relative to the promotional effort directed to them. Consequently, most sales analyses focus on identifying such segments and management gives them preference. However, the heavy user segments may not be the most profitable if all sellers are concentrating on this one segment. A smaller group may prove to be a greater potential source of future profit and/or more open to promotion.

An example was the exclusive attention paid by American auto manufacturers in the post-WWII period to the large car buyers, and the ignoring of the growing demand for more compact, more roadable small cars requiring much less service. Even the obvious success of the VW beetle left them unmoved. Because the large car had been more profitable than the small cars after the middle 1920s, they were willing to ignore this growing demand. Then the Japanese makers attacked the mass market aggressively, at a profit, and took it over, and the prestige-conscious class market was captured by the Mercedes-Benz, the BMW, the Audi and some lesser makes. Instead of moving vigorously with design and research to head off the invasion, Detroit let it gain a secure beachhead, and then went to Uncle Sam for help in trying to drive it back.

When sales analysis is used to evaluate salesmen, the effort often goes no further than a superficial counting of total sales volume This is rarely a fair measure of either the effort or the effectiveness. Sales territories vary greatly in potential yield even with the best designed of territorial allocations. Sales volume needs to be measured against carefully researched potentials, taking into account the strength of competition in each territory, and the effect of other elements in the promotional mix. Moreover, orders are usually only part of the valuable promotional efforts of salesmen, and often due more to past efforts with a customer group, often by predecessors, especially in industrial and commercial sales.

The same analytical principles can and should be applied to the evaluation of every kind of promotional effort, to the extent possible:

1. Define, in advance, a realistic, attainable task for the effort, stated in very specific terms ("make prospects aware of the offering and its benefits", "establish a specific positioning or benefit perception of the offering," promote some specific form of investigation of the offering--such as a request for more information, salesman visits, etc.," "bring orders," "make distributors and dealers aware of the promotional effort behind the offering," "open new markets and gain new customers," etc.)

2. Devise the most effective measure of the accomplishment of the objective, preferably one which can be analyzed by market segments

3. Make measurements as concurrent as possible with the effort, with the aim of determining the point of diminishing returns.

Direct response promotion of any kind is the most susceptible to relatively accurate sales analysis, but **only when advance provision** is made to identify the sources of sales. Efforts intended to generate a direct response should always contain a built-in identification tag (a keyed address, a keyed telephone reference to a specific name, keyed order blanks, etc.)

Specific surveys of buyers are useful in developing added information sometimes required to explain the patterns revealed through sales analysis or market share analysis. They can, for instance, determine the degree to which an image aimed to be associated with the offering is the one that is registering, with the right segments of the market.

Such probes are especially important in the case of new introductions, to determine what benefits in the offering are really attracting sales, and whether those benefits are of a fad character, or one that it more durable.

Fad cycles may be the introductions which are most easily misjudged, but need not be. They are always characterized by a burst of initial popularity, but not all products so greeted are fads. If they were, the automobile and television would long since have joined the dinosaurs. The distinguishing mark is the kinds of benefits perceived and the extent to which the element of novelty dominates these perceptions of value. This can only be judged from the responses of buyers, after the launch.

As can be seen, many of the objectives of control information analysis coincide with the objectives of the research effort. The difference lies only in the primary purpose of the analysis. Controls are aimed primarily at improvement of the execution of plans, marketing research at their preparation.

SUMMARY

Strategic management requires the skilled analysis of three kinds of information flow: Marketing research, market intelligence, and controls reports.

Marketing research is necessary to develop the forecasts of market size and reaction on which strategic plans must be based.

The research process consists of 6 necessary steps: analysis of the management question, formulation of a research question, a review of pertinent available information, collection of any additional primary information, analysis and interpretation of the findings, presentation of the findings in a convincing form.

Usable information is available from a wide variety of internal and published forms.

Much of the available information needs critical analysis and some analytical recasting to fit the purposes of a given study

Additional material may be collected in relatively less structured exploratory form, in more structured descriptive surveys, or in a number of experimental forms.

Market intelligence deals primarily with the information needed to evaluate the likely competition.

Generally, such evaluation of competition uses published and other observable information on competitors. The capabilities of competitors can usually be deduced from published financial data. Their intentions can be inferred from an analysis of their offerings, plus informal information coming from a number of trade sources.

Each phase of the market life cycle of an offering has its characteristic needs for research and intelligence.

Planning is meaningless without provision for a flow of information on the execution and results once put into action.

PERT creates a set of benchmarks for coordination and timing, and forecasts those tasks which need closest continuous attention.

Sales analysis reveals the best sales opportunities, highlights the problem areas, and helps measure the effectiveness of promotional efforts.

Purchased reports are often available to measure market shares and to help in the analysis of consumption patterns.

Formal and informal reports from the sales force can contribute to knowledge of market and competitive conditions.

Nearly all of the market intelligence information can, with skilled analysis, help serve the forecast needs of research also. The extent to which it does depends on the quality of the analysis and the planning which goes into designing its collection.

Sales analysis often needs to be supplemented by specific surveys of buyers to determine its meaning.

FOOD FOR THOUGHT

WHEN USING FIGURES, BE SURE TO READ THE FINE PRINT

Even when using government statistics, it is important to understand the purpose for which they were developed, and to know what is in them and what that content means for the use to which they are to be put. Some of the national economic and political problems of the 1980s can be traced directly to uses of the U. S. Department of Labor's Consumer Price Index (CPI) for purposes for which it was never designed.

The CPI was originally developed to be just what the title says: an index. This means that it was not designed as an accurate measure, least of all of the cost of living except in a very primitive, inaccurate way. It was never designed to be an inflation measure as such, and definitely not as an indication of the inflation trend over time. The U. S. Department of Commerce official series on economic trends has never used the CPI as a measure of the changes in value of the dollar, but a special "GNP deflator" constructed in a quite different manner than the CPI.

The CPI is, specifically an index of a fixed "market basket" of about 300 specific consumer items in specific fixed amounts. The contents of that basket are based on periodic surveys of annual consumer spending in sample areas around the U. S. and weighted for the spending of a fictitious young one-wage-earner family with two young children of school age, and below the teen level. The last such survey available was made in 1972, just before the 1973 oil embargo, when gasoline, for example was only around 30 cents per gallon in many areas. (Transportation cost, mostly automobile, make up about 18% of the total value of the index). Very important items in the food part of the basket are listed specifically—such as specified cuts of pork, beef, poultry, etc.

The current problems began when GM was seeking stability in its labor relations in 1948, and offered to index wages agreed upon to the CPI, in return for a 3-year contract. Post-war inflation trends made the offer attractive, and the policy spread widely around industry. Finally, in the 1970s, Congress indexed Social Security payments to the CPI. The inaccuracies of the index were one major cause of the Social Security crisis of 1981. In the 3 previous years, the wages on which Social Security taxes rest rose only 30%, while Social Security payments rose 40%. The two industries in deepest trouble—automobile and steel—had wage rates so high as to invite foreign competition and provide a red carpet for its entrance.

1. Look up the official U. S. Dept. of Labor writeup on the construction of the CPI (should be in any government depository library).

Looking over that index, and its method of compilation, what makes it an engine of inflation when used as a tool for indexing?

How does the GNP deflator differ?

Should either be used as a measure for Social Security payments, and why or why not?

THE SAMPLE FILE: CONVINCING EXECUTIVES TO ACT ON RESULTS

Communications with management is obviously a frustrating problem with marketing research staff. During a casual conversation with the Central Offices staff of the American Marketing Association some years ago, the author was surprised to learn that the address changes were about 50% per year, indicating a job turnover of the same level among the then predominantly marketing research membership. A study conducted by a friend on turnover among chemical marketing research personnel showed an only somewhat better record: a 25% turnover. The reason seems to be the difficulty experienced in getting operating executives to accept and act on research they themselves originally requested. They thus deprive such technical personnel of the reward they most prize: recognition of the success of their labors. As a result, such staff looks longingly at what appears, from the outside, as greener pastures elsewhere, and departs.

Such a rapid turnover is not good for the quality of research. The time span from planning to useful results is nearly always more than 2 years, and usually more than a four year span.

An experience with a major research effort seeking to improve the efficiency of catalog circulation at one of the general mail order companies illustrates the problem.

All such firms long ago learned that profits depend heavily on careful selectivity of those to whom catalogs are sent. Control is exercised though the recency-frequency-amount system of customer classification. A simplified record is kept of the number of orders per season for each of the previous 3 to 4 seasons, with some indication of order value. The record is far from complete, since the customer list for any house is in 7 figures, but serves the general purpose.

Catalogs are sent directly, without request, to a predetermined top set of customer lists. In addition, catalogs are also sent to the next poorer lists, up to a planned mailing, but only after these latter customers return a catalog request card mailed to them. Only about half of the request cards are returned, and management had long felt sure that these returns were from people more likely to buy than those who did not return the cards. The belief was deeply held, even though never tested.

To get a better fix on the value of each list, a detailed record is kept for some kind of smaller sample of customers: in the case of the firm referred to this sample consisted of about 100 thousand records. Getting a valid cross-section sample is complicated by the requirement that getting the information should not interfere significantly with operations, and by the customer turnover, which averaged about one-fifth per year.

The sample in use was far from valid, the results not too useful, and most of the information was too late. For this reason, the research department had an implied assignment to find a better solution any time they could. After a number of unworkable tries by others, one analyst came up with a sample design which promised to be both workable and give accurate results. After several months of intense effort, and a 2 month check against actual order experience, his system fulfilled the promise.

But management was reluctant to change from an unsatisfactory current system to one which had tested out as workable and useful. After a 6 month delay, the system was installed. At the end of the first season of operation, the results revealed an unanticipated result: due to a quirk in the mechanical selection of customer stencils, about 3,000 catalogs had been mailed counter to the plan, to customers in the sample. Some who should have received direct catalogs were sent request cards, and others who should have received request cards were given direct handling. The error was random and without question simply reflected a situation throughout the total customer list.

The analyst saw this accidental happening as a good controlled test of the assumptions underlying the request card handling. Some other research results had long before suggested to him that the assumption was not fully valid. Separate analysis of the 3000 revealed that the average sales to those who received direct catalogs were higher than sales to those in the same lists who received request handling. The difference was not large, but was consistent across the whole of the lists involved. Despite the consistency, he attributed the difference to a probable sampling variation, in the absence of a better explanation.

On the assumption that there was no gain other than full utilization of each list, he calculated what the sales might have been the previous season had the same number of catalogs been sent entirely direct, thus eliminating mailings from some of the lower value lists. The gain estimated was on the order of 20%. This would have been extremely profitable, since those extra sales would have resulted without the cost of more catalogs. He checked his calculations carefully, prepared a careful report, and submitted it. Nothing happened. Although no one questioned either the assumptions or the calculations, none of the executives above were willing to accept the results as a basis for action. They went counter to a widely held habitual understanding of the reaction of customers.

The analyst then proposed a simple sample test of the results, a test which could be conducted within the department without top approval. The test was agreed upon, but before the season was over, the analyst had left for those greener pastures. He did learn that the test came out as predicted. But still no action.

Four years later, a colleague who had stayed with the firm ran a different kind of test: a test of the effect of a late mailing of a catalog. Among the reasons for such late mailings was the use of request cards, delaying receipt for up to 2 months. The test showed that an on-time catalog produced sales of a moderately better level--just about the difference between the direct and request handlings in the original study. In addition, dropping the request card mailings would eliminate an expense item that was substantial in relation to total profits. This time, the new analyst was able to go to the president directly with the results. And the president could accept the new findings. They did not violate any habitual beliefs. Request card handling was abolished--four years late.

1. Communications problems between research staff and operations executives are not limited to marketing research. A study once published by Opinion Research revealed a similar level of misunderstanding between R&D engineers and operating management. Some of the author's experiences with supposedly fresh R&D mailing lists indicates a high turnover of R&D personnel also.

What do you think might be done to reduce these communications problems in the training of people in marketing research?

In the training of management in general?

PART V. THE BROADER RESPONSIBILITY

The exchange relationships covered by marketing management are the bonds which bind our complex communities and society together. Accordingly, any effort which focuses solely on the net monetary gains to be harvested by those transactions is bound to lead into trouble.

Sellers of any importance in that society must ultimately satisfy a wide diversity of clientele: customers of course, but also distributive intermediaries necessary to reach those customers, employees and prospective employees, investors, voters, politicians, the community at large, and the personal conscience of their own managers.

Community reaction is likely to take the form of restrictive laws, whose legal interpretation may result in as much or more damage than correction, especially if the result of indignation. A vast gray area lies between the obviousy illegal or even unethical and the purely beneficial forms of transaction. Within these gray areas, the standards are set by the conscience of the individual manager.

CHAPTER 18. MARKETING, THE COMMUNITY, AND THE GOVERNMENT

The diverse clientele to be satisfied
Avoiding the legal and regulatory restraints on action
  When sellers chase the mirage of regulatory protection
  The empty promise of fair trade laws
  Dealer protection in exchange for strong promotional effort
  Restricting import competition
  Limiting market entrance through licensing
  Public utility regulation
Avoiding future marketing crises
The gray areas of personal conscience
  Parasitic product strategies
  Package clipping
  Questionable offerings
  Questionable promotional tactics
  Exaggerated and false claims
  Borax merchandising
  Violating the implied purchase warranty
Deliberate borderline brinkmanship
Slick market tactics vs. marketing: the vital distinction

MARKETING, THE COMMUNITY, AND THE GOVERNMENT   18

Successful marketing involves far more than the mere exchange between buyers and sellers in the face of competition. In its essence, marketing relationships constitute the fabric of modern social and economic life. Continued profitable existence requires mutually satisfactory relationships with every segment of the public touched by an organization's transactions. Executives are also citizens and members of the community. They are answerable to the pressures exerted by personal conscience, by their social contacts, by the community-at-large, and by the law.

Marketing strategy and tactics must take these forces into account.

The Diverse Clientele to Be Satisfied

Marketing operations affect non-customers as well as direct customers--affect the way they live and the way they feel about an organization, its offerings, and its operation. As noted at the beginning, the aim of marketing is a mutually beneficial relationship between sellers and buyers. The total clientele to be satisfied consists of many diverse elements in the community. Each element expects a somewhat different set of satisfactions:
- Buyers and potential buyers seek the offerings the seller was established to produce
- Employees and prospective employees seek satisfying employment
- Competitors and potential competitors limit and define the market niche a seller can hope to capture
- The community at large, including all of the above, plus many others, can be concerned with how their health and welfare are affected by the organization's physical, financial and marketing operations, and by the offerings and the production operations
- Politicians must listen to all of these others if they wish for personal success

The usual organization's goal of an indefinitely long, prosperous existence will be strongly affected by the attention it pays to all of these interests and the care taken in dealing with them. Important failures to handle them well will be reflected either in the market position or by political restrictions on the freedom to make marketing decisions and to act on them.

Moreover, marketing executives are part of the social fabric of the community. They must, in the end, live with their own consciences and with the expressed attitudes of their reference groups concerning the ultimate effect of their operations on the various clientele groups in that community. Relationships with the public are either an explicit or implicit component of all marketing strategy and tactics.

In the marketplace, customers at all levels can cut down on their buying, prospects ignore messages about offerings, employees give less than their best, or quit, capable prospective employees cross the organization off their lists, investors or contributors of any kind lose faith in the continuing vitality of the organization and allot their resources elsewhere.

THE SELLER'S NEIGHBORS MUST BE KEPT FRIENDLY, TOO

The time was the summer of 1942, the place, the Zinc & Copper Branch of the War Production Board. The United States was at war with Hitler, and industry was straining to equip and supply a new army. Ammunition production was devouring the zinc and copper needed for cartridges faster than the mines could produce the ore, especially in zinc. The economists at the WPB were looking for every possible source. One appeared to be the losses experienced when scrap brass was remelted. Some rough calculations indicated the zinc that was oxidized and sent up the reclaim furnace flues was about the equivalent of 1500 tons per year: just about the amount being lost to U-boats in shipment from Argentina.

If that zinc oxide could be recovered, it would help. The economist talked to one of the secondary metals refiners. Was such recovery feasible with a bag plant. Yes, he was told. And the refiner would be glad to install it if he could get a priority for the stainless steel used in the bag plant. "We are going to have to do something sometime, anyway, or move the plant," he commented. "The neighbors are getting awfully sick of that white snow on their doorsteps every day."

Avoiding The Legal And Regulatory Restraints on Action

As with many other aspects of life, prevention of regulation is far cheaper than adapting to it. However benign the original intent of any legal restraints, the workings of legal and administrative bureaucracies almost always go well beyond the original intent of voters and legislators, to the detriment of sellers and of the community welfare.

Prevention consists of being constantly aware of the possible effects of any part of a seller's operations on any major set of voters in the community. Whenever any significant segment of the community perceives itself as being disadvantaged by some aspect of an organization's operations they are likely make themselves heard where politicians are listening, usually seeking to restrict the marketing efforts of sellers in ways that can harm the marketing process itself. The people's representatives may then find it wise to act in accordance with the complaints, constructing legal restraints with a potential for destroying or distorting competitive decisions.

Once in being, legal restraints tend to flower into constraints on marketing strategy and tactics in ways not foreseen by either the original complainers or the legislators following their lead, often in ways detrimental to those complaining.

"The law," as any attorney will tell us, "is what the courts say it is." It is also what any regulatory bureaucracy says it is. Most such bureaucracies sooner or later come under the control of legalistic empire-building administrators, with results quite the opposite of those contemplated in the original legislation. Agencies often grow and seek wider boundaries long after the disappearance of the practices which gave rise to the public discontent and the legislation. The result can grow to be a jungle of conflicting opinions on which the law profession may grow fat, if noone else does.

Many of the restrictions in force at the time this is written are so clouded by inconsistent opinions that any review of them is pointless. By luck, also, as this is written, many of them are being swept away by a new public mood for deregulation.

As someone observed long ago, "the court follows the election returns." Eventually, the irritations of regulation may themselves lead to a new public mood, one favorable to deregulation, as happened in the early 1980s, but the mood swings take a long time to develop. When the pendulum swings to deregulation, those sellers who have thrived best under the umbrella of regulation--and there will always be some--suddenly find themselves facing the need for tighter marketing management.

As a consequence, sellers need to be highly sensitive to the side effects of every part of their operations on the various publics who can be affected. They must shape their strategies and tactics in terms of long term profit potentials, avoid a myopic concentration on short run gains. Only thus can they insure themselves a long run tenure in the market place.

Any marketing strategy whose focus is primarily short term can run into direct problems in the market place, without any help from the legal profession. Strategy considerations must be heavily concerned with future patronage patterns and future needs, not solely on current market share.

When Sellers Chase the Mirage of Regulatory Protection

Competition means uncertainty, and most people do not like to live with constant uncertainty, especially well established sellers. Despite what all of history tells us about the problems of regulation, much of the regulation on our statute books have originated from demands by sellers to be protected from the competition of other sellers. Most of the rest of it has originated in the indignation of buyers who resented the efforts of sellers to avoid competition. Both kinds of legal restraints have ended in providing an umbrella for substantial numbers of sellers. Unfortunately, the umbrella has always proved to be a leaky one.

Generally, both types of umbrellas have sought to control price movements and/or market entry by new competitors. The restrictions sought have come under five headings:
- Fair trade laws
- Local content legislation or regulations
- Design or label restrictions
- Public licensing requirements
- Public utility regulations

The Empty Promise of Fair Trade Laws

Established sellers who feel themselves threatened by new kinds of aggressive low-cost competitors tend to seek some kind of governmental price protection against what they consider as "unfair" pricing. When the new kind of competition comes from other domestic sellers, the remedy sought takes some form of legally enforceable minimum price regulation, usually labelled as "fair trade" (fair, that is to the sellers' gross margins, not to buyers' pocketbooks). Such recurrent movements are nothing new. They go back at least as far as the medieval guilds, and probably farther.

The major push for such internal price protection within the United States came in the 1930s, when mass merchandisers arose in the drug industry, offering cut prices on many standard items. Retail druggist organizations, especially, were successful in getting a number of states, and then the Federal government, to pass legislation enabling these and other retailers to set statewide minimum prices on specific brands of merchandise, by agreement with the producers. Reluctant producers were, trade gossip said, forced to agree to such arrangements by threatened dealer boycotts. "Dealer protection," became the price producers had to pay to maintain established distribution of their brands. This was no small price: enforcement was up to the producer, who had to bear the burden of prosecuting customers who violated the minimums.

Fair trade has never succeeded in protecting those who sought protection, and proved far more expensive than it was worth if conscientiously enforced.

The protection sought did not protect against new and more efficient sellers because it did nothing to hurt their profits. They could still handle the items if they did not violate the minimums, and then use the higher price as a contrast to their own private brands, which often brought an even better return. Moreover, at most it meant only a somewhat different pricing mix for the entire assortment. To the extent that sales of the restricted brands were significant, the extra-high margins simply gave these new merchants that much more elbow room for attractive prices on traffic items, making their entire assortment at least as attractively priced as before, and their customers were interested in the assortment, not individual prices.

In addition, to the extent that such new sellers became important mass outlets, their sales of any item became much more attractive to producers than the limited volume left to previous dealers.

Those seeking fair price laws of any kind are asking for the economically absurd: that the producer follow an intensive distribution policy, selling to almost any dealer desiring to carry it, and allow the dealer to collect a larger margin than necessary for the services such distributors were rendering. If the market is mature, such intensive distribution is necessary and restrictions on price minimums are suicidal for the producer. When valid marketing considerations require some form of dealer protection on price, the primary element in that protection is selectivity of distribution, and the price protection needs no legal enforcement if this is the proper policy.

Dealer protection in exchange for strong promotional effort. Selective distribution is a device for limiting the number of dealers and distributors. It promotes sales volume and serves buyers well under three sets of circumstances:

- During the market development stages of any high learning offering
- For smaller producers with a relatively narrow customer franchise, at any stage of the market life cycle
- For high-price specialties with a very thin market

Distributors are not likely to fight to carry **high-learning introductions.** The kind of intensive, personal sales effort needed to generate sales volume is costly. To get this effort, the producer must allow very substantial margins to distributors, and protect their efforts by some form of territorial guarantee. The offering will not get off the ground without such intensive attention from distributors, and the protection and margins are needed to pay for their efforts. The need to pay this price evaporates as soon as the offering catches on and dealers start asking for it.

Small, specialized producers can seldom afford spending for the kind of mass advertising and promotion that gives the major brands their market strength. Such sellers must attract more aggressive distributors with relatively larger margins, and depend on these dealers to cooperate strongly with promotional plans, doing much of their own sales and promotion. Minor brands can and do establish and maintain a consumer franchise by depending entirely on a limited selection of distributors--usually dealers that handle the line exclusively.

High-end offerings with a thin potential market have a similar need for an adequate level of sales for each distributor, and thus a limitation on the number of dealers to guarantee this adequate volume. As already noted, this is true of hand-made specialty automobiles such as Rolls-Royce and Avanti, and hand-blown quality glassware, such as Steuben glassware. Even such high-end mass produced automobiles as the Cadillac and Lincoln Continental must restrict severely the number of dealers in order to maintain the level and quality of sales service needed to develop the full sales volume. The Ford Motor Company learned this the hard way when it failed to limit the number of Mercury dealers handling the Lincoln Continental dealers when it launched the first post-war model, the Mark II. The dealers became too anxious for sales and pursued "dealing tactics" which offended the class of customers who buy such luxury models, almost killing the sales.

COSTS & COMPETITION: THE DIFFERENCE BETWEEN DOMINANCE & FAILURE

The contrast between the attitudes toward cost and progress held by Andrew Carnegie and by his steel industry successors is as great as the difference between the impregnable competitive position he forged for Carnegie Steel and the present troubled market position of his successors in the U. S. steel industry.

Carnegie ran his business according to two policies: "Cut the costs and the profits will take care of themselves," and "Cut the prices; scoop the market; run the mills full." But in counting cost, he never looked back. The "remaining working life" of equipment had no value if it could be replaced by equipment which could do the job cheaper. He gave his staff standing orders to replace obsolete machinery, and in one incident, ordered a 3-month-old rolling mill ripped out when he was convinced that a different design would do a better job.

Elbert Gary, who became head of U.S. Steel after Carnegie sold out said:

"It is not at all certain that if the management that was in force at the time would have continued, the Carnegie Company would not have driven entirely out of business every steel company in the United States."

On another occasion, after testimony before a Congressional committee, one congressman remarked: "I believe you would have captured the steel trade of the world if you had stayed in business."

By contrast, one steel executive told a meeting discussing the problems of the U. S. Steel industry in the late 1970s that its foreign competitors had been able to lower costs because the war damage had given them a chance to completely reequip themselves with new technology, while the American industry could not because it still possessed older equipment with a substantial "useful working life" remaining.

Restricting Import Competition

Too many industries relax attention to cost containment once they reach the more tranquil waters of maturity. This inevitably leaves the door open for some more aggressive and more progressive foreign competitors aiming for a substantial market share, at the expense of domestic firms and domestic labor. The age-old cry of such wounded is for protection against such "unfair" competitors. Such cries of anguish can often get attention from politicians, since foreigners obviously have little political leverage, compared with the voters in the home district, and buyers are not alert to the dangers to their own standards of living.

The common remedies sought usually take one of several forms:
- Taxing imports heavily (tariffs)
- Minimum price rules, in the form of anti-dumping provisions
- Import quotas
- Onerous inspection practices, arbitrary design or quality standards, or other delaying tactics

If any of these measures succeeds for long, they pass on the cost of the industry's incompetence to buyers through higher prices. They also stimulate a flanking form of competition: competition from producers of different offerings satisfying the same desire sets.

Historically, tariffs have never proved capable of bringing up profit levels in an unprogressive industry, however much they may favor local offerings. With or without a tariff, those profits improve only when management makes every effort to keep costs down and improve productivity of its capital. The classic case is that of the textile industry in the United States, which sought, and obtained, tariff protection many times in its history. In more recent times, textiles have also benefited from negotiated import quotas. Outstanding profits did not come until the marketing solution of improved productivity was tried, successfully.

Anti-dumping laws carry a self-limiting effect: they can be enforced only when it is proved that the alleged dumpers are subsidizing their exports at the expense of local buyers. If such cannot be proved, the low cost producer will still get the market. Even when it can be, the remedy raises the import costs only to the extent of the subsidy. Moreover, no nation has clean hands in such matters. The United States has long been a dumper of agricultural commodities on the world market, at prices subsidized by local consumers.

Quotas on imports tend to stimulate the ingenuity of those exporting. When the United States pressured Japan to "voluntarily" limit its export of automobiles to the United States, for example, in terms of units, the Japanese producers shipped a higher-priced mix, raiding the more profitable luxury market.

So-called "non-tariff" barriers to imports have become a favorite tool in recent years. The French and the Japanese have used them extensively. One of the most common is to delay the movement of imported goods in various ways, including stiff inspection standards not required of domestic offerings. The French have insisted that certain Japanese imports be channeled through small, inadequately staffed customs points, where their sale was held up for months. Japan has insisted on a level of inspection of auto imports not required of domestic vehicles which drove up cost. To the extent that these work, they are obviously anti-marketing, throwing a burden on consumer choice by limiting market entrance.

Limiting Market Entrance Through Licensing

Both businesses and individual occupations must often be licensed before they can legally enter a market. The rationale behind most licensing is protection of buyers from incompetence. Whatever its primary purpose, licensing does limit market access, and some license restrictions are directly intended to limit competition: when the number of licenses is severely restricted, as is true of tavern licenses and taxicab licenses in many localities, and of acreage allotments for the growing of tobacco in some states. When so restricted, licenses become a vehicle for price supports. When transferable, which many such licenses are in some manner, the major beneficiaries are the original licensees, and they become a capital investment for those buying them out, which obviously must be paid out of their customers' pockets.

Even licensing provisions ostensibly serving a social purpose, as in occupational licenses which have no fixed limit on number of entrants, tend to be a means of curtailing competition for the benefits of the sellers. Quite often, they come under the private jurisdiction of unions or professional societies and are openly used to enforce restrictions on marketing activities, including simple advertising.

A similar end is served by specific health and safety regulations. Building standards are often so specific as to limit the use of materials and methods and bar innovations which are fully justified. For years, the Chicago building codes protected the brick masons by requiring that all exterior walls be solid masonry, and the plasterers by insisting that all interior surfaces be "continuous" which could only be done with plastering. The ostensible reason was fire safety, but other methods of construction, not permitted, were actually as safe or safer. Similar provisions can be found in the building codes across the country. Chicago was also the site of a blatant exercise of health regulations to bar the sale in Chicago markets of milk produced in nearby Wisconsin Only dairies inspected by the Chicago Department of Health were allowed to ship milk into Chicago, and the then head of that department refused to certify out-of state dairies. Nations, including the United States, have often used such arbitrary health regulations to bar imports, especially of agricultural products.

Public Utility Regulation

The explicit purpose of state and federal public utility regulation was to limit competitive entries. In fact, both the electric and telephone utilities actively sponsored such regulation for a socially acceptable reason: that duplication of transmission lines represented a waste and drove up costs in two ways: by the duplication itself, and by forfeiting the advantages of large scale production.   There can be no question that, in this case, the end result was better service at lower cost in both of these two forms of regulated utilities.

But the extension of the same form of regulation has been applied to transportation, first of railroads, then of trucking, and finally to passenger aviation.   The results in every case has been to limit and distort marketing decisions and inhibit innovation.   The arguments for limiting competition in trucking and aviation are nowhere nearly so strong as they were for central power production and for telephone service.   And in both cases, buyers often had and took the option to own their own facilities.   In every case, the bureaucracies that administer the regulation have laid a heavy hand on the kind of innovation the market thrives on.

Avoiding Future Marketing Crises

The early 1980s seemed to bring an avalanche of troubles for sellers of all kinds and even whole industries.   The apparently sudden swing to concurrent trends toward deflation and deregulation exposed a lot of organizational dry rot, bringing seemingly unstoppable sellers, from unions to the auto industry, into stormy waters.   Like dry rot, the sudden weaknesses were long in developing, with clear symptoms in the market place for those who would look for them.

Most of those who got into trouble misled themselves by a too smug attention to the size of their current market shares.   They paid too little attention to problems to be faced down the road.   Among the symptoms foretelling future problems were erosion of those market shares by new competition, taking place at the edge of their segment demand, at erosion occurring because of changing tastes in the segments at the fringes of their niches, and changes in resource structures and cost structures likely to change consumer demand patterns.   The effects showed up suddenly when economic crises put a strain on both sellers and buyers, but the trends made some crisis inevitable.

Events tend to appear due to a crisis simply because patronage patterns are habitual, and do not change readily.   When pressures cause consumers to question those habits, the change can snowball, and is as difficult to reverse as any set of habit patterns.

Sellers who remain sensitive to future possibilities are most likely to survive best when the crises hit their industries.

Such crises, of course, usually hit only once in a generation.   In between such periods, individual sellers can get into trouble by offending major groups in the community.   In addition, every marketing executive has to live with one constant personal problem--that of individual conscience, or what substitutes for one in some cases: the attitudes and feelings of the reference groups to which any of us look for approval. The problems with which personal conscience have to deal are a constant in marketing. They deal with the gray areas which lie between tactics which are clearly short-sighted or worse, and those which fulfill the wise aim of all marketing: a patronage relationship which is mutually satisfactory for both sellers and buyers.

TODAY'S PROFITS CAN CONCEAL TOMORROW'S DISASTER

Patronage weaknesses seldom show up in major sales losses immediately. The force of consumer habit tends to support a surface appearance of "all's well" long after the real situation has begun to deteriorate. One case in point was the complete change in supermarket strength in Chicago between the late 1950's and the 1970s. A&P was the leader in food market share in 1958, with National Tea a strong second, and Jewel Tea third, but not really that close to the leaders. The author was elsewhere for the next 9 years, and returned in 1967 to find Jewel on top and both A&P slipping badly. By 1972, National Tea was closing major outlets because of insufficient business, and before another 5 years had passed, withdrew entirely from the Chicago market. A&P took over some of the closed National Tea outlets, but was in trouble itself, and not in the top three chains in share any more. New chains, unknown to Chicago in 1958 had taken up the slack.

What had happened? Nothing that was not in the trends perceivable in 1958, by those who would look and listen. A brief survey of the patronage of National Tea relative to competing stores in a number of locations had shown that National had a substantially lower number of patrons than any of the surrounding stores, and that the average receipt rung up on the cash register during the same period of observation was very much lower. The difference in total sales was apparently due to some monopoly locations in new shopping areas. Some customers were complaining of the low quality of many of the offering, especially the store brands of frozen produce, and the absence of some desired items. Cheddar cheese, for example, could be bought only in the sliced form, at a per pound cost twice that of bulk cheese of the same grade at other stores.

A&P at that time was simply not following the trek to the suburbs, and was not upgrading its produce and meat departments to the extent of competitors.

Shortly after the survey, National Tea was the first chain to adopt stamps for promotional purposes, which gave the chain a major boost in volume per store for a period. But by the late 1960s, the draw of stamps was wearing off, and the lack of quality was hurting where the trade was most important: in the middle class suburbs.

The Gray Areas of Personal Conscience

Most offerings are socially and economically beneficial from any public standpoint. Some forms of market operations are clearly harmful to the buyer and to the society at large, and usually also clearly illegal. In between the two groups are a number of market tactics and market offerings which are not clearly either black or white, but some shade of gray. Most are usually legal and often quite profitable for long periods. Many of them, however, may be low in social status and respectability, at

least among groups to which executives look for approval.   Some can create
some twinge of conscience among those involved.

Four categories of market operation clearly carry some shade of gray:
- Parasitic product strategies
- Questionable offerings
- Questionable promotional tactics
- Deliberate borderline tactics

PATENTS AND COPYRIGHTS: THEIR PROTECTION CAN BE LESS THAN COMPLETE

History records that aggressive competitors often find ways to harvest the profits
due the labors of the more inventive, despite copyrights and patents.   Patents can
only be protected by suits for damages, and the infringer is free to produce while
the suit waits the leisurely procedures of the courts.   If the product has a short
enough life cycle, a competitor may find ways to get away with mayhem, if not
something like murder.

One such case was that of the disappearing firm.   A major toy maker invented a
talking doll, whose talking talents were due to a small tape recorder in the body into
which the doll's owner could insert various strips of tape.   Soon after it hit the
market, a firm sprung up making identical recorders which it sold to various firms to
use in knock-offs.   It quickly manufactured several million, it is reported, and then
was dissolved before court papers could be prepared, or indeed its ownership
identified.

Even such a long-lived offering as Eli Whitney's cotton gin may make the inventor
no profits.   Little blacksmith shops all over the country imitated it, and the early
courts were not very sympathetic to the inventor.   Historians report that Whitney
never gained any profits from the machine that revolutionized the economy of the
South.

Likewise, McCormick, as noted earlier, was essentially robbed of his patent rights
by licensees before he got his first factory built.   Patent rights at that time expired
in 14 years unless extended—1848 in his case.   Using their considerable political clout,
prominent licensees persuaded Congress to bar extension of his patent.   Fortunately,
although he had at the time sold only 2500 machines altogether, including those made
by licensees, he had built a protection more powerful than his patent: the first
market-wide sales and service network, and a strong market position his hungry
competitors never overtook.

Copyrights have a stronger form of legal protection—they are enforced by
injunctions, prohibiting, immediately, any further sale by the alleged infringer until
the case is resolved.   They cover only the specific design or expression, however.
And recently, the development of fast, inexpensive copying machines have led to
widespread infringement that is extremely easy to do and very difficult to catch up
with.   According to recent news stories, even some members of the academic
community have had whole books copied and sold through their academic bookstores,
with no recompense to either the authors or the publishers.   Similarly, the
development of relatively inexpensive taping processes have led to a profitable piracy
of recordings and videotaped movies.

Parasitic Product Strategies

Marketing innovation is the driving force behind the dynamics of our modern civilization. The most profitable marketing operations are growth period operations, when buyer interest in the innovative offering is high and growing.

Developing attractive new offerings and getting them to market is not easy, and is risky. It seems simpler to let others do the creative work and the pioneering, test the market acceptance, then jump in with full force before the innovator can get a solid market position. So long as no patents or copyrights are infringed, there is nothing illegal in such tactics.

Copying the other fellow--the knock-off--seems to be the rule in nearly every industry in which all sellers must constantly introduce new items--in markets such as those for costume jewelry, fashion apparel, toys, and textbooks. The practice is difficult to criticize whenever the imitator actually develops an offering of somewhat different design which is a better value for some market segment not well served by the original offering.

But can we defend the seller which has a deliberate policy of **never pioneering** markets, who always waits until the market is proved, then moves in with an overwhelming promotional budget to preempt the market position developed by some weaker seller? Who but the introducer loses in such a maneuver?

The immediate customer does not seem to--may even benefit to some degree at the outset. What may suffer is the innovation process itself, by robbing the imaginative of the full gain from their efforts. In the long run, of course, this can be of concern to final customers, since it may deprive them of some as yet unborn ideas. This is, at least, the rationale behind patent and copyright laws. Copyright history seems to have confirmed the validity of this rationale.

Package Clipping

One tactic used to grab an unearned market share in mature markets resembles the "coin-clipping" practiced by some monarchs at one time to relieve malnutrition of their treasuries. They would trim a not-very noticeable shaving off each gold or silver coin coming in, before paying it out again. Soon others in the kingdom were following suit, giving rise to a phenomenon still know by the name of Queen Elizabeth's treasurer, "Gresham's Law:" bad money drives out good. Once started, all coins got clipped, and only debased coins circulated, and prices rose. [The "milled edge"] cast into the edge of all metal coins except the lowest in value is an insurance against such clipping.]

The practice today is to clip the goods themselves, taking advantage of the j.n.d. principal. Sellers of packaged consumer goods long ago discovered that a small change in each of a package's three dimensions permitted a profitable decrease in volume of the contents, without being noticed by buyers. The unit volume would be stated correctly on the label, but consumers seldom look at the volume statements, and many would be easily misled into buying what appeared, at first glance, to be reasonably priced.

Another ploy is to use something other than a smooth cylindrical shape for the container, giving it something of a wasp-waist. It would be a rare consumer whose mathematical judgment of volume would be adequate to perceive the full decrease of contents in a container whose height and largest diameter were similar to those of a familiar offering of similar height and diameter.

The end result of such package size tampering is to bring down the size of every competing package on the market. But the clipper will usually have succeeded in ripping off a substantial, unearned market share, in the meantime.

The shelves of our supermarkets hold an abundance of evidence of such size tampering over the years: the large numbers of packaged items for which the volume of the contents deviates from measurement units standard to our system: prepared cereals and canned milk in 15 oz. packages (not the full 16 oz. pound or pint), large oatmeal packages in the 2lb-10oz. size instead of 3 lbs.

Many others which could be cited: cooking oil in 1-1/2 pint bottles, for instance. Until not too many years ago, the standards sizes were pint and quart. Then one well-financed grocery products firm decided it wanted a major market share, in a product that was practically a commodity. Their research conceived the idea of giving the container a pinched waist shape to insure a better grip on a surface which could get oily. That, of course, was a real benefit for buyers. But the sales people apparently discovered that such a container that was as high as the standard quart could be made with only 3/4 of a quart. This was decided upon as the introductory size, selling at about the same price as the standard quart (but with cents-off couponing to begin with). The ploy worked, and a solid market share was soon achieved. The main standard size in now 24 oz. for all brands.

Some of the odd package sizes in such items as laundry detergents may be intended to confuse any attempts to make easy price comparisons. Some other changes may represent the results of intense competition and rising production costs. This seems to have been the case with paper towels. At one time, the standard roll was 100 sheets, and a jumbo roll was 200. Then, the jumbo roll declined to 150 sheets and the standard roll to 75. Since most people buy by the roll, not the count, there seemed to be no problem. Then in the early 1980s, the "Jumbo" roll dropped to as few as 89 sheets in some brands, with one brand giving 119 sheets. As this is written, someone is finally going to have to coin a new adjective for a really large roll. [There is precedence for this: in the standard nomenclature for canned olives , the "large size" is the smallest, and the adjectives go on up from there.] Similar trends can be read in toilet paper roll sizes.

None of this package-clipping is illegal. In fact, in at least one instance, it has received the blessing of a government agency (in the substitution of the 303 size can (3-1/2 cups rather the 4 cups). But it is not marketing--the consumer gets no benefits, and probably loses something. At best, such tactics reflect a lack of ability to create real innovations.

Questionable Offerings

Offerings as well as operations can be black, white, or gray. Most offerings are "white," in the sense that they deliver perceived benefit value--and usually some positive functional values as well--in excess of their perceived cost, and continue to be perceived as doing so, and sought out. Some are undeniably "black"--they injure the buyer and /or deplete the buyers' resources beyond their perceived value, and are usually illegal as well. Hard drugs are a good example.

But some offerings may be in the shadowland between. They may be perceived by many who buy as offering benefits, the law may condone their sale. They may be profitable to sellers, and the sellers respected, and may be definitely harmful to users, socially and/or physically. Tobacco is an example of the blurred borderline.

EMERSON FOOTE AND CIGARETTES: A MATTER OF CONSCIENCE

When the Surgeon General's report of 1963 put the official stamp on the accumulating epidemiological evidence on the connection of cigarettes with cancer, Emerson Foote had a decision to make. As a former president and major partner in the advertising agency of Foote, Cone & Belding, he had gained a personal fortune from one of the major cigarette accounts—that of the American Tobacco Company. As a strong supporter of the American Cancer Society, he was committed to aiding in campaigns to eradicate smoking, which would yield no income. Both connections went back a long ways, and involved deep personal friendships.

Foote, Cone & Belding was the successor agency when that fantastic pioneer of professionalized advertising, Albert Lasker, retired at the end of 1942 from the Lord & Thomas Agency he had built into a major force. When Lasker decided to help build the funds available to the American Cancer Society in 1944, Foote was persuaded by Mary Lasker to become an advisor to the Society and helped with the campaign, which in one stroke almost doubled the funds available for cancer research. (Ironically, Albert Lasker was to die of cancer himself in 1952, although there was no evidence of any such infection at the time of his efforts for the American Cancer Society.)

When the surgeon general's report was made public, Emerson Foote almost immediately declared his resolve to avoid anything having to do with advertising cigarettes, severing all agency ties, and setting himself up as an independent advertising consultant.

Were tobacco a proposed introduction, it could not possibly gain approval for sale, with what we now know about its effects on large segments of the population. Products with far less frequent side effects have been ordered off the market, even when restricted to prescription usage--offerings with known substantial benefits. (A widely publicized example was thalidomide, a tranquilizer that had fewer side effects than any other, except in a small proportion of pregnant women.) Tobacco smoking has only one demonstrable physical benefit: some degree of soporific effect, due mainly to the carbon monoxide produced in the burning--a poison at any level of exposure. The nicotine of the first cigarette has a stimulant effect, but this is canceled out in chain smoking. Research has demonstrated that the major perceived benefits are socially-induced psychological benefits: a perception of an association with virility, reinforced by peer pressure among the young to whom this appeal is especially strong.

Ironically, when tobacco was first introduced to Europeans, it was credited with medicinal powers, and it grew to wide usage long before there was substantial medical evidence of its dangers. As a result, production and use of tobacco products became firmly embedded in the economy and social usage. For those growers who have allotments, growing tobacco yields a greater income per acre than any currently alternative crop, and the land used for cigarette tobacco is a poor producer of most crops. The manufacture and sale of cigarettes, especially, is a very profitable business, and no social stigma attaches to either the executives or the investors who draw their incomes from it. Because off the high level of brand competition and the size of the profits, the advertising contracts are very large and extremely profitable. Both the federal and state governments draw a significant proportion of their revenues from taxes on cigarettes. The offsetting costs in sickness and deaths is not very obvious to most people. While awareness of some of the effects is widespread, it exists largely at the cognitive level, and is not given affective credibility by smokers or by those engaged in the industry.

The trade in cigarettes is also profitable, directly and indirectly. They are a strong traffic item in retail outlets ranging from the ubiquitous vending machines, to gas service stations, drug stores and supermarkets. Indeed, any of these outlets whose product assortment did not include cigarettes would sacrifice some trade and see a decline in sales of other items. Communications media (other than broadcast media, forbidden by law to participate) draw significant portions of their advertising support from cigarette advertising.

Clearly, a lot of us have a stake of some sort in continuing support in the production and sale of cigarettes. If you were the head of an advertising agency with a good chance of landing a cigarette account, would you turn it down or bid for it? If you were an account executive in such an agency, would you refuse assignment to the account if your agency landed it? If a publisher of a periodical would you refuse cigarette advertising? As a merchant, would you refuse to stock cigarettes for your customers? Even as a property-owning voter, faced with a raise in taxes if cigarettes were banned from sale, would you vote for such a ban? Obviously, the only guide is conscience. (At least two major national mass publications do refuse cigarette advertising.)

The marketing of cigarettes is an extreme case of borderline gray. Other kinds of offerings fill a wide spectrum, including categories of offerings of which some are clearly desirable, and some not, with no easily definable line between the desirable and those which are socially or otherwise undesirable.

Among these latter are books, films and other communications materials dealing with sex and sexual relationships. At one extreme are works so purely scientific that any objective observer will agree on their beneficial value. At the other extreme are items which all observers, including the vendors, recognize as pure pornography with no literary, scientific or educational value. Commerce in these latter is so highly profitable that the underworld seems to be drawn to the trade like flies to molasses. In between is a wide range of works which includes some recognized as literary masterpieces or sound educational materials by most of those familiar with them, respected for their realism and sensitive treatment. But many of the less mature of all chronological ages find these same works to be a source of titillating salacious pleasure.

No clear line can be found for the simple reason that the perceived meaning depends on the developed perceptions of sex in the minds of different individuals, and this obviously differs widely with education and social background.

Another category is that of drugs of proven wide utility, but which can lead to serious effects with abuse, either by the medical profession or by individuals. Some commonly available analgesics and sedatives may offer heaven-sent relief to those in pain, but also produce side sensations when overused and sought out for a thrill by those with no need for relief from pain. Some physicians have been accused of, in effect, selling prescriptions under circumstances in which they had evidence of abuse. But very few have had their medical licenses refused by boards controlled by their peers. The firms making these drugs are highly respected, yet the quantity produced seems to be far beyond that required for the pure medical need. They are also usually a major source of profit.

Alcoholic beverages are a widely used drug with strong social approval. If it were a new drug up for approval, it might well be hailed as a major medical break-through as a relatively harmless sedative under careful use. Its utility as a mild sedative has been clearly established. For most people using it in moderation, any side effects are minor or insignificant, and its cost, even under heavy taxation, are no greater than for drugs with much more prevalent side effects. But it is also subject to abuse, and for a significant portion of the population alcohol is an addictive drug leading to serious social and physical deterioration and fatal cirrhosis of the liver. No substantial stigma attaches to those engaged in the marketing of alcoholic beverages. The advertising, like that for cigarettes, is highly profitable, and the taxes on liquors, particularly, are an important source of governmental revenue. How would you feel about profiting from the marketing of beer, wine, or hard liquors?

In all of the gray areas, those in marketing cannot escape the necessity of making their own personal decisions about their own part in the lives of others, since any action affects others, for good or bad. Such gray areas also include promotional methods as well as promotion itself.

Questionable Promotional Tactics

Promotion, especially, advertising, of any kind, is sometimes in disrepute in otherwise highly educated circles, accused of exercising undue influence over people's lives, of "manipulating people." As noted earlier, this perception of the power of advertising lacks any support in our knowledge the psychology of demand, and is definitely counter to all experience with promotion. Customers pay attention to and respond only to offerings whose benefits they understand and are actively seeking, and do not repeat purchases of offerings which do not seem to live up to the benefits promised. Advertising, in fact, is the weakest tool in the promotional kit. Personal sales is by far the strongest, but is effective only to the extent that sales people are in a position to learn the needs of each individual prospect and show how the offering meets those desires and needs. Even the salespeople strike out more often than they get to first base.

Nevertheless, some kinds of promotional tactics can make sales that do not grant the benefits they promise, and also be profitable. Three types of communications tactics can be classified as ethically questionable even though often legal:
- Exaggerated benefit claims
- "Borax merchandising" to the fearful, the anxiety-ridden, and the misinformed or prejudiced
- Violation of the implied warranty of sale

Exaggerated and False Claims. The true confidence man, who takes the money and gives nothing significant in return, has gone the way of the rattlesnake oil vendor, and is clearly outside the law. Explicitly untrue representation of the offerings has largely disappeared also, although largely within this century, and mainly in industrial countries. Truth-in-labelling laws deserves some of the credit, but important elements would include a higher degree of education and the economics of mass merchandising and promotion, which depends heavily on the kind of repeat sales which come from honestly satisfying a felt need.

What remains are some borderline operations, except in the non-commercial areas of political, medical, religious and educational quackery.

Dictionaries define quackery as "ignorantly or falsely pretending to cure"--that is, of promising benefits which cannot be delivered. Quacks of any kind succeed because any society, especially a mobile one, contains many who are fearful and anxiety-ridden, and, in mobile societies, aspiring people. As noted earlier, all of us pass through a number of important role transition periods in our lives in which such anxieties are the norm. Of all such, the adolescent period is probably the time of role change with the highest degree of anxiety, as we move out of the role of childhood toward full adulthood. As also indicated earlier, all such transitions tend to cause those involved to seek out tangible offerings perceived as associated with completion of the role change.

Those passing through such role changes thus become attentive to any promise of delivering the sought-for status: they actively seek to purchase their way through the ordeal. Sellers need not actually claim to deliver such benefits: they need only to imply that they do, especially when a given type of offering becomes widely perceived as so delivering. The cigarette advertising need only portray virile or sophisticated stereotypes to lead the susceptible to **feel** that smoking will give them that "image." The perfume and cosmetic advertising need only hint at romance to lead the anxious to believe that their use will create a sought-for popularity. The mouth wash ad needs only imply that unpopularity is due to bad breath to gain acceptance. Outright statement is neither necessary nor as effective as letting closure work.

Furthermore, such implied claims usually lead to a perception that the desired end is achieved, so that the buyers believe they have achieved their aims through the purchase. What is wrong with that?

Quackery outside the commercial sphere is often more blatant. The downtrodden and disadvantaged are led to a specific belief that some ritualistic act or statement of belief guarantees them an infinity of carefree, happy existence after their short stay on earth--they may only need to believe (and support those making the promise) to get their reward. The political quack need only promise bread and roses for everyone to draw their votes.

Even the hallowed halls of ivy are not free from some such quackery. In recent years, the news has carried tales of talented athletes recruited with scholarships and promises of a degree the recruiters knew they were unlikely to receive. And the same campus probably housed some venerable academic departments who lured impressionable adolescents into majors which were occupational blind alleys they could not afford, simply to build departmental strength.

Closely linked with such promotion is the practice of the "borax merchandiser."

Borax Merchandising. Unlike the pure confidence man, the quack delivers something, and that something is often perceived as meeting the promise. The medical quack prescribes laetrile and some other items for the cancer, the religious quack delivers an emotional experience of some kind, the over-reaching athletic department does get the prize athlete into college even when it gives him too little time for serious study. But what is delivered is partly a sham.

In merchandising, this has been given the label of **borax merchandising**, meaning that the surface appearance of what is delivered really is fraudulent--it is much less than it appears to be, and the seller is aware of this fact. Borax selling is the reverse side of the coin of exaggerated promises. Smoking does nothing to create virility or sophistication in the smoker, or to actually purvey even the ghost of such images in the eyes of others. The cancer cure does not arrest the course of the disease in any way. The low-down-payment offer of the borax seller of watches looks low only because the total price tag is outrageously high, and the down payment almost the total cost to the seller, with any other payments pure profit.

"BORAX MERCHANDISING:" WHERE IT STARTED & WHAT IT MEANS

Borax merchandising originally referred to a practice of giving cheap furniture the initial appearance of well-finished pieces. In the pre-plastics era, fine finishes were produced by applications of several coats of varnish, each left to dry, then hand-rubbed with pumice or rottenstone before applying the next. The final coat was also hand-polished. The end result was a soft gloss, and very durable. Cheap furniture was simply given a coat of stain and quick-drying cheap shellac, which had a very high gloss initially. The gloss was then toned down by a quick rubbing with dry borax, giving the finish the temporary appearance of being hand-rubbed varnish. This finish was far from durable. The label of "borax" soon tended to cover also the quality of design, which tended to lean toward the over-accented and gaudy--including the highly overstuffed pieces--that lacked the elegance of good design.

By extension, it now covers all kinds of sales operations which seem to promise far more than they are really delivering, and prey on the poorly informed. Thus merchants use borax as a label for the highly promotional "easy credit" jewelers and other merchants who charge high prices for relatively low quality merchandise. Although they do grant credit freely, their loudly proclaimed "low payments" often cover all or most of the seller's cost of goods, and the subsequent payments determine the level of profit.

Those profits can be quite high. Just how high is illustrated by a remark of a board member of one general merchandiser who had recently acquired such a credit jewelry chain. After a few cocktails, in a private meeting of company officials, he is reported to have asked: "What's wrong with borax retailing? Take that stinking little chain we got on the West Coast last year: $10 million in sales, $1 million in net profit. Look at Marshall Field: $200 million sales, $2 million net profit. Which would you rather have?"

Among fellow professionals and merchants, the borax seller does have a somewhat suspect status, but the level of profits is quite high enough to assuage any hurt feelings, and the operation sends no one to jail. What he does, however, is to violate one foundation of the modern marketing system: the implied warranty behind the sale. This more subtle violation of the transaction relationship is sometimes practiced by the less market-minded executives of some of our largest corporations.

Violating The Implied Purchase Warranty. Modern mass merchandising rests on a premise that the seller, as well as the buyer, believes that the offering does what it is represented to do: deliver a promised satisfaction, **as the buyer perceives that promise.** This was a major element on which the foundations of modern distribution were laid by such pioneers as Cyrus McCormick, Potter Palmer and Marshall Field, and Richard Sears. The explicit or implicit guarantee of "satisfaction or your money back" is the one element that separates mere "let the buyer beware" selling and the kind of continuing patronage capable of sustaining modern marketing. All borax merchandising violates this in principal, even when most buyers fail to perceive that they have been had. Unfortunately, it is sometimes violated by others whose goods would not be classed as borax, but whose treatment of customer product problems is no better.

Among such practices are to refuse to make good on the "lemons" which sometimes come off modern assembly lines, to require customers to sue to get attention to product defects, and to fight such suits to the limit, to write insurance policies, and find excuses to cut policy holders off if they file any claims, to make promises of product performance without checking on their validity, then making restitution difficult.

Some of these practices arise easily well below the top echelons in the bureaucracies necessary in any large business. Some result from the callous disregard of good marketing principles by the top bureaucrats themselves, in the comfort of mature markets and a strong market position.

Usually, the customer has little redress unless willing and able to mount a risky and expensive suit. If the problem gets bad enough across an industry, such callousness can draw legal remedies of another sort, as the auto industry of the United States has discovered, in the forced recall of vehicles. (No government had to prod that eager marketer, Cyrus McCormick, to fix problems with his harvester. He voluntarily went to considerable expense to make good on his **unlimited** guarantee and gained an almost impregnable market position.)

Most such disregard of first principles is the result of a lack of understanding of the basics of profitable customer relationships. The practice of brinkmanship is usually deliberate.

Deliberate Borderline Brinkmanship

One major problem with decreeing marketplace virtue by law or by regulation is that all such provisions simply act as a challenge to a certain kind of personality: a challenge to find some extremely profitable way of doing what is forbidden, but doing it in such a way as to stay just within the law. The rigid nature of legalistic remedies being what it is, they will always find some such way, and to profit by it.

One of the older methods of preying upon customers is the "bait-and-switch" tactic. This consists of advertising what seems to be a fantastically attractive bargain--one far too good to be true, and it is. When a customer shows up, they are shown a sample of the advertised, and are shown it is not nearly so good as they thought. But they are then shown a more expensive item, and given a strong sales pitch. The seller counts on a form of cognitive dissonance to forward sales. Customers are led to commit themselves beforehand, in their own minds, to buying. Once started, many succumb to the lure, and buy the profitable substitute. Those who still insist on the original bargain are not permitted to buy. It is the "only sample" the seller has, and replacements will take some kind to get. No, no orders can be taken. In the words of the trade, the sample is "nailed to the floor," and is not going to be sold to anyone.

Such outright bait-and-switch advertising is pretty well outside the law, today, but similar ends are usually served by stocking a very few of a thoroughly unattractive item, and using the same general disparagement of them, and glowing sales talk for the expensive substitute. Indeed, as a competitive ploy, the automobile giants have often advertised "stripped models" so stripped that few people could be expected to order them, and producing them only on special order, with substantial delays in delivery.

Among the other tactics which are hard to prove in court is the false discount offer: a discount based on a price higher than anyone is charged.

Unfortunately regulations provide scant protection in dealing with such sellers--they usually just sharpen their ill-placed ingenuity. In time, the market tends to catch up with them, but not before they have skimmed substantial profits and have spoiled the image of all business to some degree. The one consolation is that such tactics seldom win a major market share. Most customers are too well educated by the efforts of honest sellers to fall prey. These brinkmanship sellers are the last remnants of a bygone era of "buyer beware" merchants, modern day successors of those who made the term "horse trader" an epithet. They have not learned the value of a mutually profitable patronage relationship.

Slick Market Tactics versus Marketing: The Vital Distinction

The force which holds modern social and economic organization together is the mutual attraction of mutually profitable exchange relationships. Tactics such as some of those sketched above are destructive of the trust necessary to the kind of mass production and mass merchandising society necessary to support modern populations. In the end, fortunately, they tend to be self-destructive. They are tactics practiced in the market place, but they are not marketing tactics, since they depend on a continuing supply of "suckers."

Modern organizations of nearly every kind aim at an indefinitely long life, lasting well beyond the life span of their founders. The basis of continuing vitality is a continuing patronage relationship with a specific set of self-renewing and always somewhat changing market segments. Building such a patronage relationship requires carefully planned strategy, executed with compatible tactics and constant attention to the art of innovation. Without innovation, the organization withers with age. Without well executed tactics compatible with the strategy, the strategic plan itself will suffer. Without a suitable strategic plan, based on the skills of the seller, the seller's resources, and the real opportunities open to that seller, there is no sound basis for expectation of continued vitality.

SUMMARY

Continued success of a seller requires consideration of the relationships with a numerous clientele beyond those involved in the immediate transaction.

To make sure of an indefinitely long life for the organization, the seller must maintain simultaneous relationships perceived as mutually profitable with consumers, employees and prospective employees, the community at large (including competitors and potential competitors), and politicians.

Each of these various clientele has its own set of expectations with respect to the seller's operations. If those expectations are not heeded, the seller's freedom of action may be curtailed through regulation.

Competitors, including the seller, sometimes tend to think they own their customers, and move to protect their market position through some kind of restriction on competition. Such restrictions fall sooner or later, and leave the sponsors ill-prepared to face the market.

When the restrictions sought involve price protection, they fail even in the beginning, unless they are backed up with some form of restriction on distribution.

All such regulatory restrictions eventually fall into political disfavor, leading to a crisis for those who have benefited by the protection.

While crises affecting an entire industry are relatively infrequent, individual sellers are constantly exposed to problems of personal conscience in connection with their dealings in the market. There are large gray areas in market operations between the predominantly beneficial and the clearly harmful and usually illegal.

The most common gray areas are of four types: parasitic product strategies, package clipping, the promotion of questionable offerings, and questionable promotional tactics.

Parasitic sellers avoid any attempts at innovation, seeking to preempt the successes of competitors at the competitors' expense, without offering customers any added values.

Package clipping seeks to take advantage of buyers' j.n.d. in package sizes to gain a temporary cost advantage and an unearned market niche, financed by the cost advantage.

Questionable offerings are those which are legal, but which do not truly yield the satisfaction the buyers seek, and can produce substantial harm.

Questionable promotional tactics promise substantially more satisfaction than the buyer is going to experience. They include exaggerated or even patently false claims for the offering, borax merchandising, and violation of the warranty of satisfaction implied in any true marketing transaction.

All of these violate the expectation of the continuing mutual benefit relationship which marks the difference between the modern marketing system and mere market operations which cannot hope to be continuously successful.

FOOD FOR THOUGHT AND DISCUSSION

HEALTH QUESTION: Do Publications Avoid Anti-Cigarette Stories To Protect Ad Dollars?
(Reprinted from **The Wall Street Journal**, Nov. 22, 1982 by permission. ©Dow Jones & Co., 1982. All rights reserved.)

Paul Maccabee, an aggressive young reporter at the Twin Cities Reader in Minneapolis, was always alert to off-beat angles in his stories. So, when he covered a press conference announcing Brown & Williamson Tobacco Corp.'s annual Kool Jazz Festival last spring, he inserted an unexpected twist: a list of jazz greats who had died of lung cancer. The next day he was fired.

Carol Wheeler, a free-lance writer for Savvy magazine in New York, was listed on the magazine's masthead until last May, when Savvy published a review of a book titled 'The Ladykillers: Why Smoking is a Feminist Issue.' Miss Wheeler maintains that her name was subsequently stricken from Savvy's masthead because its publisher feared offending tobacco-company advertisers.

Such incidents, while isolated, are cited by anti-smoking groups like the American Cancer Society as evidence of the tobacco industry's subtle yet powerful influence over what is—and is not—published about the hazards of smoking. Although tobacco companies are not accused of heavy-handed pressure on editors and publishers, critics contend that smaller and weaker publications especially may engage in self-censorship when it comes to the smoking issue. The sheer weight of the advertising budget, critics say, is enough to make some magazines and newspapers tread lightly when covering the negative aspects of smoking, toning down stories or ignoring the issue.
Cigarettes and Print
Ever since cigarette commercials were taken off televison in 1971, tobacco companies have bought a disproportionate amount of print-media advertising. The

tobacco industry outspends all other national advertisers in newspapers, and cigarettes constitute the second-largest category of magazine advertising, behind transportation. According to the research firm Leading National Advertisers, eight cigarette companies spent $309 million last year on magazine advertising. The same companies bought $386 million in newspaper ads, according to the Newspaper Advertising Bureau.

Were it not for such outlays, anti-smoking activists suggest, the public would read far more bad news about smoking. John H. Banzhaf, founder of the anti-smoking group Action on Smoking and Health, observes that although stories about teen-age drug use and drinking frequently appear, 'I never see an article about where kids get cigarettes and what a parent group might do about it.' He cites the fire hazard of smoking and new research on combating addiction as two areas that have been underreported in the press. The American Council on Science and Health, a nonprofit group financed by various corporations and foundations, contends that magazines like the Reader's Digest and Good Housekeeping that refuse to accept cigarette advertising are much more aggressive in their coverage of the hazards of smoking.

Cigarette makers pooh-pooh such charges. 'Baloney,' says William Kloepfer, senior vice president of the Tobacco Institute, the cigarette manufacturers' lobbying group in Washington. 'The suggestion that buying an ad buys the judgment of reportorial people is a contemptible red herring.' Adds Marty Orlowski, the director of marketing services for R. J. Reynolds Tobacco Co., a unit of R. J. Reynolds Inc.' We try very hard not to get involved in the editorial side of anything. 'We're very sensitized to the whole issue.'

The Local Advertiser

The extent of advertiser influence on news has long been debated by journalists. It isn't unheard of, for example, for a newspaper to bury or kill a story detrimental to the local car dealer or grocery chain on whose advertising it depends. 'The weaker a newspaper is, the more it's prone to influence,' says Richard Gray, the dean of the journalism school at Indiana University. But he adds that such incidents are less frequent today than in the 1920s or 1930s, 'when newspapers weren't as financially stable.'

Because of the vast sums spent to promote cigarettes, because of the sophistication of the industry's media relations, and because smoking is highly controversial, cigarette makers are singled out for more criticism than most advertisers for their unspoken influence on the news. A look at how the industry places its ads, and how editors report on the smoking and health controversy, suggest that any big advertiser can, to a degree, blunt negative publicity about its product.

The American Council on Science and Health periodically surveys magazines to compare their smoking coverage with the amount of tobacco advertising revenues they receive. The council's latest survey of 18 popular publications showed that those most heavily reliant on cigarette advertising gave short shrift to the smoking issue.

Cosmopolitan and Ms.

The survey noted that Cosmopolitan, which derived 9.20% of its annual ad revenues from tobacco companies, published 155 articles on dieting between 1971 and 1981, but only eight on smoking. Among those taken to task for completely ignoring the issue were Redbook (where nearly 16% of ad revenues come from cigarettes) and Ms. (13.7%). Of Ms., the study said: 'The complete absence of articles on smoking is particularly striking in this magazine which covers many other important issues on women's health.'

Pat Carbine, editor and publisher of MS. says that the magazine has cited the hazards of smoking for women during pregnancy or when using the Pill. But its policy, it says, is to let its largely college-educated readers decide for themselves whether or not to smoke. Louis Porterfield, Cosmopolitan's publisher, says the magazines's stories about cancer do mention smoking. "We don't have a policy that we don't write about cancer and smoking because we take cigarette advertising. One isn't connected with the other," he says. Ann Mollenger Smith, editor of Redbook, calls the council's research "sloppy" and says she sent them copies of stories from Redbook that called smoking a health hazard. She says she demanded, but didn't get, an apology from the council. "Their attitude seems to be if I wasn't campaigning against smoking, I had sold out to the tobacco industry, " Mrs. Smith says.

A few years ago, Elizabeth Whelan, The American Council's Executive director, wrote an article for Harper's Bazaar on the causes of cancer. The article led off with smoking. Jane Ogle, who was then the magazine's health and beauty editor, says that when Anthony Mazzola, the magazine's editor, saw the cancer story, he said, "Christ, Jane, I can't open this article with smoking." Mrs. Ogle said she moved the smoking segment to the end of the article, "so it wouldn't jump in the face of every cigarette advertiser."

Mr. Mazzola failed to return numerous telephone calls from this newspaper. But the magazine's current health editor, Denise Fortino, says the policy still stands. In a recent story about health hazards in the office, for example, three paragraphs devoted to smoking were condensed into one, she says. Harpers's Bazaar last year received about $1 million, or 6.8%, of its ad revenues from cigarette companies, according to Publishers Information Bureau. Such spending represents "an unspoken pressure," Miss Fortino says, adding: "We do have to consider the advertisers, but we've still managed not to quench the story."

A publication that frequently crusaded against smoking could hardly hope to attract tobacco advertising. For cigarette makers—like liquor companies—are among the most persnickety about the editorial environment in which their ads appear. Says the advertising manager at a major Texas daily: "One is a poison and the other causes cancer, so they're very sensitive about it."

Most advertisers cancel ads when a news event reflects badly on their product. Airlines, for example, routinely instruct publications to drop their ads after a major airline crash. "It's a situation when you're in a very negative environment and you better use your money later," a Delta Air Lines spokesman says.

Because cigarettes exist in a perpetually negative environment, tobacco companies take special pains to see that their ads don't call undue attention to that fact. They stipulate that cigarette ads can't run near obituaries, for example, or near news stories "antithetical" to smoking or tobacco. Should a publication fail to follow these guidelines, the tobacco company usually asks for—and gets—a "make-good," or free ad, as amends.

Until recently, Reynolds went even further: Outraging many editors. it asked to be notified in advance if a publication planned to run a negative story about smoking. Reynolds dropped its policy after it received critical scrutiny from the Columbia Journalism Review and after this newspaper inquired about it.

Informal Alerts

In practice. publishing and advertising executives say, big advertisers are often informally alerted in advance about stories that could be detrimental to their business. "Almost any publication that has a brain does it," says one adman.

Editors and publishers insist that this practice doesn't inhibit them from printing a negative story. Larry Martz, an assistant manager at Newsweek, says: "If the magazine is going to run a cover story on the newest advances in the surgeon general's attitude on cancer or alcoholism, the ad guys who have that account may call up the advertiser and say, 'Charlie, I don't think you want to run this week.'" However, Mr. Martz says, "It doesn't mean editors are under any pressure not to run articles on alcoholism and cancer. The editorial side doesn't even know that call was made.."

Smaller publications aren't so well insulated from advertiser influence. Thus, when Mark Hopp, the publisher of the 100,000 Twin Cities Reader, saw Mr. Maccabee's devastating article on the Kool Jazz Festival, he was furious. Mr. Maccabee had quoted an American Cancer Society spokesman calling the Festival "a PR ploy to give respectability to cigarettes.' The 26-year-old reporter also wrote that cigarettes are linked to such ailments as Buerger's disease, 'a degenerative nicotine-linked condition which leads doctors to amputate toes and feet one at a time, like snipping grapes off a vine. Definitely not sexy. Definitely un-Kool.'

Mr. Hopp felt the Mr. Maccabee had editorialized too much. And, he concedes, he feared losing the paper's cigarette ads. "We're not big enough to change an issue like this,' Mr. Hopp says. The paper is a local publication whose job is to cover local events. We will not cover national, international or social issues.' The paper's national sales manager wrote to all its cigarette advertisers, apologizing for the story and informing them that Mr. Maccabee had been fired.

At Savvy, Wendy Crisp, the editor, says she neglected to read Miss Wheeler's review before it appeared the May issue. When it ran, she says, the magazine worried that its tone might offend cigarette advertisers. Miss Wheeler's name was removed from the masthead.

Miss Crisp concedes that she told Miss Wheeler that her name was dropped because of the review, though she says other factors were involved—including prior disagreements between the writer and Alan Bennett, Savvy's publisher. (Mr. Bennett declines to be quoted on the matter.)

Mrs. Crisp says she worried that Savvy's competitors might show the review to cigarette companies as a way of grabbing their business. "Savvy isn't a primary buy,' she says. 'It took one guy a whole year to get the Reynolds account. We're a very young magazine, and I don't want to get hurt by one lousy review.' As in the case of the Twin Cities Reader, the publisher acted without any pressure from advertisers.

The controversy about smoking has forced the tobacco companies to become increasingly ingenious in promoting their products. Sometimes, they have enlisted the help of the nation's press. For over a year, for example, Reynolds has "sponsored' the daily sports results appearing in some 72 newspapers across the nation. Reynolds buys the space devoted to the scores—previously regarded as editorial matter—and surrounds them with a flashy border touting Camel cigarettes. These "Camel Scoreboards' contain the slogan, "Camel. Where a Man Belongs," as well as the Surgeon General's warning about smoking hazards.

The Lorillard unit of Loew's Corp. currently is running ads in this newspaper called "Kent's Sports Business,' which contain stories about the business side of sports, and also feature pictures of Kent Cigarette packages and the Surgeon General's warning.

Philip Morris Inc. has become a news source by conducting "The Merit Report,' a public opinion survey on a variety of issues. The results are distributed to newspapers and television stations in hopes of a mention. The object is to help Merit cigarettes gain greater public recognition.

Even if some editors are wary of anti-smoking stories, it's difficult to argue that the public is unaware of the hazards of cigarette smoking. A 1978 Roper poll showed that more than nine out of every ten Americans believed smoking endangers a smoker's health. Editors argue that because the smoking and health story has changed little since the Surgeon General's report on 1964, there has been a dearth of smoking news to cover. "I think you have to be pretty dense not to know there's some health risk associated with cigarette smoking," says Newsweek's Mr. Martz.

Tobacco Firms Spent $1.24 Billion on Ads in 1980, FTC Says" (From **The Wall Street Journal,** Nov. 22, 1982, p.22)

WASHINGTON -- The tobacco industry spent $1.24 billion advertising cigarettes and got the average American smoker to buy 11,633 cigarettes that year, the Federal Trade Commission said.

In its latest annual report to Congress on cigarette advertising and labelling, the FTC said the industry's advertising expenditures were the highest ever, up 13% from the $1.08 billion spent in 1979. Cigarette ads in newspapers, magazines, and on billboards continue to associate smoking with outdoor and athletic activity, the FTC noted, picturing smokers engaging "in vigorous activity in a clean, refreshing outdoor environment."

In addition, the industry is spending more than ever to sponsor music concerts and other special events under a cigarette maker's name, committing nearly $17 million to such activities in 1980. Cigarette advertising on radio and television was outlawed by Congress in 1970....

The average smoker's 1980 consumption of 11,633 cigarettes, which amounts to a pack-and-a-half a day, represents an increase from the 1979 average consumption level of 11,500...

1. If Congress can ban cigarette advertising on radio and TV, as it did, why should it not ban all advertising for cigarettes? Why didn't it?

2. According to news reports, less men are smoking, but more women are. Not only are the long term effects beginning to show up in increased female mortality of smoking-related ailments, but there is epidemiological evidence that smoking during pregnancy can be harmful to the fetus. There is also little evidence that college trained women are paying any great attention to the dangers of smoking, as the MS. editors imply concerning their readers. Should women's magazines carry cigarette ads?

3. The Tobacco Institute argues that there is no direct evidence that smoking causes any of the diseases, that statistical evidence, such as the relative incidence of cancer and heart disease is not proof. Does that mean that it was unscientific to vaccinate people for small pox before Pasteur and Koch revealed the bacterial cause of the disease? Or that it was unwise for the British navy to issue lime juice to sailors to prevent scurvy was wrong before we learned about vitamins?

4. One of the more political powerful arguments for going easier on tobacco than on other questionable drugs is that it involves the jobs of so many people. But if the news estimates are correct, the second largest crop in the North Carolina, a leading cigarette tobacco state, is marijauna, raised in the mountainous areas where jobs are really scarce. Marijuana is banned legally (and not only on paper), the Agricultural Department does not support it, and localities ban the sale of merchandise used in connection with marijuana smoking. This hardly seems consistent. Can you think of a solution?

5. What about individual conduct? There is no question at all that tobacco smoke is physically irritating to large numbers of people. Should smokers light up in any public place? Should they be allowed to?

"BUYER BEWARE" WAS BURIED 100 YEARS AGO, OR WAS IT?

Chicago has some claim to be the birthplace of the modern marketing concept. Three men who set up shop there were ardent practitioners of the dictum that "the customer is right," and were the first to give birth to major corporations through strict adherence to this principle: Cyrus McCormick, the founder of International Harvester, Potter Palmer, the merchandiser who built the business that became Marshall Field, and Richard Sears, the founder of Sears Roebuck.

As noted in the earlier sketch on McCormick, from the very start of his active promotion of his reaper, he published a completely open, unlimited satisfaction-or-your-money-back guarantee on his product, and backed it up to the hilt with a service system under direct factory supervision, at considerable immediate cost at times. Potter Palmer offered his wholesale customers the same kind of guarantee shortly after he went into business in Chicago, and quickly extended it to his retail customers. The attitude, institutionalized in the organization long after Potter Palmer has sold his interests to Marshall Field, is best characterized by an order which Marshall Field himself is said to have given an assistant manager he found arguing with a customer. As reported, Field asked him, "What are you doing here?" When the manager noted that he was "settling a complaint," Field is said to have snapped, "No you are not. Give the lady what she wants." (Lloyd Wendt and Herman Kogan, **Give the Lady What She Wants: The Story of Marshall Field & Company,** Rand McNally & Co., Chicago, Ill, 1952.)

Sears learned early that building the kind of return patronage a catalog house must have requires unswerving adherence to this dictum. Every successful mail order house has followed the same principles:

- Merchandise descriptions which are so accurate that the customer perceives the goods received to be as described. (Mail order copy departments have long been known as the best school for copy writing. In one or two inches of column, the writer must make the item sound attractive, and yet make the description so accurate the customer will be completely satisfied with the goods when they arrive.)
- A wide open returns policy, with full refunds for customers returning the goods for any reason. This policy makes no exceptions. Refunds are given even for goods which have apparently had long usage and were sold years before, and for merchandise which carries competitor's brands.

As successful as such policies have been in building strong businesses, the lessons learned seem either to have been forgotten in some executive suites, or never learned there. The auto makers have been chronic offenders. Too often, they have felt that buyers of the lemons that seem to be an inevitable consequence of mass assembly should suck on them, and make no noise doing it. At one time, cars carried sales slogans on the tire covers of the spare tires mounted on the back of the cars of the 1920s. One such slogan was "Another Nash". It was widely rumored that one dissatisfied buyer, unable to get redress from the company, changed the slogan to "Never Another Nash," and was promptly sued by the company, which collected damages.

Whether or not the incident is true, the story reflects a public perception of a truculent attitude at company headquarters that lasted well into recent decades. DeLorean reported that sometime after he took over the presidency of Chevrolet in 1971, Chevrolet had been forced to recall 6.7 million 1965-69 cars with defective motor mounts which broke apart, causing the engine to lunge out of place and lock the accelerator into an open position at about 25 miles an hour. Cars were being smashed as panicky drivers crashed them or jumped out. The problem had been noted at Pontiac as early as 1965. The Pontiac design was immediately corrected to eliminate the danger and Pontiac passed its knowledge on to Chevrolet and the other divisions. Chevrolet had done nothing, nor did it respond to field reports of the problem. Customers were charged full repair bills when the problem occurred, even after a woman was killed in such an accident in 1969. Despite wide publicity, officials refused to act even when DeLorean asked the corporation to recall the models, and acted only after strong public pressure. (J. Patrick Wright, **On a Clear Day You Can See General Motors**, Wright Enterprises, Grosse Pointe, MI, 1979, pp. 57-58.)

The results of these and many other such violations of the marketing concept has been a demand for lemon laws. By the summer of 1982, lemon laws were pending in California and Pennsylvania, and Kentucky and Connecticut had put such laws on their books.

The Connecticut law was helped along by the efforts of two imaginative owners of lemons who joined forces: Dan Brochu, a local electrical engineer, and Thomas Ziemba, owner of a small Connecticut airport. Both descended on the legislature to press for the law. Ziemba circled over the state capitol in his Cessna, trailing a red banner reading "My '82 Chevy is one reason Conn. needs a lemon law" while Brochu went inside to testify. Brochu swears his 1980 Olsmobile Omega has run up more mileage going up the repair lift than it has covered on the road— the $6500 Omega has spent 135 days in the shop. According to him, "the transmission failed four times, the electrical system malfunctioned...the paint is coming off and getting worse."

Ziemba couldn't drive his $14,182 Chevrolet Caprice wagon off the lot when he got it in December because of a "big puddle of oil under it." The engine has developed a skip since, the defroster throws steam, and the radio won't work unless he first blows the horn,

The Connecticut law allows lemon owners to sue car makers directly for a replacement or a refund during the first year of ownership or during the warranty period, whichever is less—if efforts before a mediation board fail to get results.

But while the states are starting to grant relief to new car owners, the United States Senate blocked a Federal Trade Commission rule that would have required used-car dealers to tell buyers what known defects the vehicle had. "We are in essence saying to the public, we approve of shabby dealers, we approve of cheats," said Sen. Bob Packwood, who supported the FTC ruling. ...

1. Why is a customer-is-right principle any more important in automobiles than in women's dresses, furniture, or fresh produce from the supermarket?

2. The cost of a major recall such as that of the Chevrolet can run into the millions of dollars. Why should a corporation be forced to carry it out? What kind of yardstick would you apply to justify a voluntary recall of such a magnitude?

3. Should used car dealers be forced to do as the FTC rule would have required?

Why or why not?   What do used car dealers gain if they do?

4. To what extent should sellers of any kind be held to a "customer is right" policy, by political regulation?   If you see problems with public regulation, how would you suggest getting wider recognition of this rule any other way?

5. An author needing a computer with a word processing program went shopping various dealers and makes.   He spelled out precisely what he needed in the way of performance characteristics.   One of his strongest specifications was that the computer and program be able to support proportional spacing typing with a letter quality printer.   He was sold a computer which was supposed to do this, and spent some time in getting familiar with the program and getting his writing well under way, while awaiting arrival of printing equipment needed to print out the results. (The type wheels needed were not available locally.)   When it arrived, he discovered that the typing did not work on proportional spacing.

After spending several days in a futile attempt to find the difficulty, he approached the dealer, who had several suggestions, none of which worked.   He asked the dealer to find out from the computer manufacturer, but the dealer simply told him to call the manufacturer himself.   A long distance call to the manufacturer's technical support staff elicited the reply that there was "no way" to do so with their machine, but might be some indefinite number of months later with an "update" being worked upon.

When he took this information back to the dealer, the latter refused to believe him, and stalled for more time, refusing again to contact the manufacturer.   Finally, with great reluctance, the dealer agreed to a return of the machine, less a 25% discount because of the time the machine had been in use.   The dealer refused absolutely to give any credit for a $300 editing program bought for the machine, and not usable on any other make.

Who, besides the customer, were losers in this situation?   What should each do to avoid such losses in the future?

FIGHTING TOY KNOCK-OFFS: A LOSING BATTLE?

Illegal imitations--knock-offs--have always been a problem in the toy field, but have become especially troublesome in the last couple of years because of highly popular licensed characters, such as E. T., Star Wars, and Snoopy. Since there are limits to the market, any such items get most of the business and producers or merchants that do not have them are certain to lose sales.

Take the case of the E. T. dolls. Kamar International had the exclusive license to produce a stuffed E. T. doll, and LJN Toys Ltd. a similar license to produce a smaller hard plastic line.   Demand was so heavy that by November, LJN was placing orders on a 3-month waiting list despite a production of 310 thousand a day, and Kamar, with 65 Korean factories and 9 more in Taiwan and Singapore, was also placing orders on a waiting list past Christmas. But in early November, Miss Kamar, head of Kamar International, had 3 of the Korean contractors shut down because she caught them producing illegal copies for her competitors.   Besides costing her 60 thousand dolls a month, she knew other counterfeiters would fill the void.   She estimated the move would cost her $3 million in lost sales.

In such situations, retailers, lacking stock for the Christmas season which accounts for much of the year's profit, will patronize the less legitimate channels.

Part of the problem is the haziness of the legal situation, and also the difficulty of telling the good guys from the bad guys. Unlike the designer apparel field, where the counterfeits are usually sold as originals, toy copies are usually sold under a different name, and tend to have some design variations. Toy companies must prove that the copies are "substantially similar".

Furthermore even if they eventually win, it may be too late. The life of a hot item can be 2 years or less. And winning is not easy, as Ideal Toy Company proved, when sued. Ideal spent $5 million dollars around the world to protect its own Rubik's Cube puzzle patent, suing more than 100 U. S. companies. But Ideal itself was sued in turn for exploiting the Star Wars boom with its line of Star Team action figures, for which it paid no license fees. Ideal won its case by convincing the court there was enough difference in its design while they were "getting in a quick $5 million or $10 million in sales--that we got away with it," the attorney for Ideal is quoted as admitting. "I don't like to put it that way—we were just legally correct."

Part of the problem is that the firms being sued are often the toy firm's own customers. Schaper Manufacturing Co., producer of the highly popular 3-inch long working 4-wheel drive Stompers truck spent $1 million in 1982 to combat imitators. The defendants were eight of its own wholesalers, and after two years and 2 lawsuits, only one of the defendants settled out of court, agreeing to pay cash plus royalties on future sales. And the firm which settled--LJN Toys--was in turn trying to protect its own line of E. T. toys in the 1982 season!

For most kinds of offerings, established sellers have some degree of brand loyalty, but this is clearly not true of toys or costume jewelry, and is limited to a few extemely well recognized brands of apparel, at the high end, for the most part. But although Ideal Toy has been long established, as has been Parker Brothers in the toy business, competitors can apparently get a large market share with imitations which do do not carry the brand and differ in enough significant details that the courts, at least, will recognize that they are not counterfeits. Further, the mere fact that the Ideal name is on the product gives it no better chance at a market than the name of some unknown, and the same would be true of Parker Brothers.

1. How can you explain the fact that a pair of jeans, identical to the Levi in every essential detail except the name, will not get the price that a true pair of Levis will, nor get a comparable market share, or that a previously unknown car giving all of the benefits of a Chevy, but without a Chevrolet nameplate cannot even get dealers?

2. If you are a producer in any field like this, how do you get the lion's share of the results of your luck or ingenuity in developing an attractive offering?

INDEX